AUTOCAD® 2012 AND AUTOCAD LT® 2012

NO EXPERIENCE REQUIRED

AUTOCAD® 2012 AND AUTOCAD LT® 2012

NO EXPERIENCE REQUIRED

Donnie Gladfelter

Autodesk®
Official Training Guide

WILEY

Wiley Publishing, Inc.

Senior Acquisitions Editor: Willem Knibbe
Development Editor: Thomas Cirtin
Technical Editor: Melanie Perry
Production Editor: Eric Charbonneau
Copy Editor: Sharon Wilkey
Editorial Manager: Pete Gaughan
Production Manager: Tim Tate
Vice President and Executive Group Publisher: Richard Swadley
Vice President and Publisher: Neil Edde
Book Designer: Franz Baumhackl
Compositors: James D. Kramer and Craig W. Johnson, Happenstance Type-O-Rama
Proofreader: Jen Larsen, Word One New York
Indexer: Ted Laux
Project Coordinator, Cover: Katherine Crocker
Cover Designer: Ryan Sneed
Cover Image: © Dieter Spannknebel / Getty Images

Copyright © 2011 by Wiley Publishing, Inc., Indianapolis, Indiana
Published simultaneously in Canada
ISBN 978-1-118-01677-0 (pbk.)

Library of Congress Cataloging-in-Publication Data

Gladfelter, Donnie, 1982-
  AutoCAD 2012 and AutoCAD LT 2012 : no experience required / Donnie Gladfelter. -- 1st ed.
     p. cm.
   ISBN 978-1-118-01677-0 (pbk.)
   ISBN 978-1-118-13931-8 (ebk)
   ISBN 978-1-118-13930-1 (ebk)
   ISBN 978-1-118-13929-5 (ebk)
 1. AutoCAD. 2. Computer graphics. I. Title.

 T385.G5733 2011

 620'.00420285536--dc23

                      2011019560

10 9 8 7 6 5 4 3 2 1

Dear Reader,

Thank you for choosing *AutoCAD 2012 and AutoCAD LT 2012: No Experience Required*. This book is part of a family of premium-quality Sybex books, all of which are written by outstanding authors who combine practical experience with a gift for teaching.

Sybex was founded in 1976. More than 30 years later, we're still committed to producing consistently exceptional books. With each of our titles, we're working hard to set a new standard for the industry. From the paper we print on, to the authors we work with, our goal is to bring you the best books available.

I hope you see all that reflected in these pages. I'd be very interested to hear your comments and get your feedback on how we're doing. Feel free to let me know what you think about this or any other Sybex book by sending me an email at `nedde@wiley.com`. If you think you've found a technical error in this book, please visit `http://sybex.custhelp.com`. Customer feedback is critical to our efforts at Sybex.

Best regards,

NEIL EDDE
Vice President and Publisher
Sybex, an Imprint of Wiley

To my grandmother Ethel Johnson (1936–2011),
and to all who have battled cancer

ACKNOWLEDGMENTS

In more ways than I can explain, it feels like yesterday that I was getting my start in the CAD industry as an entry-level CAD technician. But that was more than a decade ago, and since then I've had the profound privilege of giving back to the CAD community through my blog (**www.thecadgeek.com**) and through the hundreds of professionals I've trained. While there's certainly no way for me to thank each one individually, without each boss, teacher, project manager, coworker, and even each user I've supported, there's absolutely no way this book would have been possible.

It's with sincere gratitude that I thank Walter Spain and Johnnie Collie, the passionate educators who first introduced me to AutoCAD at Hermitage High School and Hermitage Technical Center in Henrico County, Virginia many years ago. Their passion and dedication to inspire the next generation of design professionals is what empowered the many achievements of my own career.

Professionally, I have to thank the esteemed team of design professionals I am proud to call my coworkers at CADD Microsystems (CMI), Autodesk's 2010 Reseller of the Year. The breadth of knowledge they selflessly share not only with our customers, but with each of their coworkers, has undoubtedly allowed me to expand my own knowledge. Additionally, special thanks to the owners of CMI, Jeff Gravatte, Matt Davoren, and Susan Thomson for their support as I took on this project.

There is likewise a small army of individuals at Wiley whose dedication to their craft is apparent as you read through this book. Senior Acquisitions Editor Willem Knibbe not only rallied support for this book within Wiley, but he also made sure we were able to hit production targets even against the greatest odds. Thomas Cirtin, my developmental editor, did an exceptional job with the challenging role of managing deadlines while also ensuring that the vision of the book was executed at the highest caliber. I'm especially humbled by Melanie Perry (aka Mistress of the Dorkness, `http://mistressofthedorkness.blogspot.com`) for lending her technical expertise to this project for a second year as my technical editor. Sharon Wilkey, my copy editor, and Eric Charbonneau, my production editor, did a wonderful job ensuring that no detail was left unattended as the book was made ready for press.

At Autodesk, Heidi Hewett, Kate Morrical, and Shaan Hurley were each invaluable resources. From providing me access to AutoCAD 2012 while it was still in production, to demonstrating its long list of new features, and most important, answering my questions along the way, they were each an invaluable wealth of information.

Finally, I want to thank the most important member of the production team, my beautiful wife, Helen. She did something much greater than editing chapters or tracking schedules; she was my cheerleader when writer's block got the best of me, the one who made me laugh daily and provided a shoulder to lean on even after some of the most demanding days in her job teaching at a local school dedicated to children with autism.

ABOUT THE AUTHOR

Donnie Gladfelter is a highly visible and respected thought leader in the CAD community. He is well-known for his blog, The CAD Geek (**www.thecadgeek.com**), has worked with hundreds of design professionals as a Business Development Manager at CADD Microsystems, and is a popular speaker at Autodesk University and other industry events. He has worked with the development team at Autodesk to help shape future versions of AutoCAD, and the company has featured him in numerous video interviews, including their popular "Ask the Expert" series. Donnie also helps empower CAD professionals by providing training and services to companies around the world as a member of the Autodesk User Group International (AUGI) Board of Directors.

A proven communicator, Donnie has reached thousands of people worldwide through many publications and various public speaking engagements. As a regular speaker at Autodesk University since 2007, Donnie has presented a long list of popular sessions and served as host for Autodesk University Virtual in 2010. Other speaking engagements have drawn audiences of up to 60,000 people.

With a professional reputation founded on both integrity and loyalty, he is a highly trusted and respected member of the CAD community who has worked with product managers and developers to help shape future releases of the software. These ideals have been achieved by subscribing to a simple, but effective personal mantra to "empower CAD professionals." With an unwavering commitment to his craft, Donnie continues to embody this mantra by empowering the next generation of architecture and engineering professionals as a Business Development Manager at Autodesk's 2010 Reseller of the Year, CADD Microsystems. In that role, he helps design teams throughout the Mid-Atlantic apply technology the way they do business through frequent seminars, workshops, and classroom-style training.

Prior to joining CADD Microsystems, he was the Design Systems Specialist (assistant CAD manager) for a multidisciplinary civil engineering firm headquartered in Richmond, Virginia. An ENR 500 firm, the company employed more than 350 people in nine offices throughout the Mid-Atlantic. During his near six-year tenure there, Donnie was jointly responsible for providing the technical support and training for each of their CAD professionals. In that role, he was also responsible for the development of a collaborative BIM workflow used for a wide range of projects within the firm.

Donnie and his beautiful wife live in Richmond, Virginia.

CONTENTS

CHAPTER 5   Developing Drawing Strategies: Part 2   175

CHAPTER 8   **Controlling Text in a Drawing**   **385**

CHAPTER 9   **Using Dynamic Blocks and Tables**   **463**

CHAPTER 14   Using Layouts to Set Up a Print   745

INTRODUCTION

This book was born of the need for a simple, yet engaging tutorial that would help beginners step into the world of AutoCAD or AutoCAD LT without feeling intimidated. That tutorial has evolved over the years into a full introduction to the ways in which architects and civil and structural engineers use AutoCAD to increase their efficiency and ability to produce state-of-the-art computerized production drawings and designs.

Because AutoCAD and AutoCAD LT are so similar, it makes sense to cover the basics of both programs in one book. For most of the book, the word *AutoCAD* stands for both AutoCAD and AutoCAD LT.

When you come to a section of a chapter that applies to AutoCAD only, the icon shown here is displayed in the margin to alert you. When appropriate, extra information for AutoCAD LT users is provided to give you a work-around or otherwise keep you in step with the tutorial.

Because AutoCAD LT doesn't have 3D commands or features, the last two chapters, which are an introduction to drawing in 3D, apply only to AutoCAD. But LT users can be assured that LT is very much the same program as AutoCAD, with only minor differences. You'll be prompted when those differences, most of which are 3D features, come along.

When you come to a section that applies to one of the many new features found inside AutoCAD 2012, the icon shown here is displayed in the margin to alert you. This book is directed toward AutoCAD and AutoCAD LT novices—users who know how to use a computer and perform basic file-managing tasks, such as creating new folders and saving and moving files, but who know nothing or little about AutoCAD or LT (as I'll call AutoCAD LT throughout the book). If you're new to the construction and design professions, this book will be an excellent companion as you learn AutoCAD. If you're already practicing in those fields, you'll immediately be able to apply the skills you'll pick up from this book to real-world projects. The exercises have been successfully used to train architects, engineers, and contractors, as well as college and high school students, in the basics of AutoCAD.

For those of you in other trades and professions, the project that runs through the book—drawing a small cabin—has been kept simple so that it doesn't require special training in architecture or construction. Also, most chapters have additional information and exercises specifically designed for non-AEC (architecture, engineering, and construction) users. Anyone wanting to learn AutoCAD will find this book helpful.

What Will You Learn from This Book?

Learning AutoCAD, like learning any complex computer program, requires a significant commitment of time and attention and, to some extent, a tolerance for repetition. You must understand new concepts to operate the program and to appreciate its potential as a drafting and design tool. However, to become proficient at AutoCAD, you must also use the commands enough times to gain an intuitive sense of how they work and how parts of a drawing are constructed.

At the end of most chapters, you'll find one or more additional exercises and a checklist of the tools you have learned (or should have learned). The steps in the tutorial have a degree of repetition built into them that allows you to work through new commands several times and build up confidence before you move on to the next chapter.

Progressing through the book, the chapters fall into five general areas of study:

▶ Chapters 1 through 3 familiarize you with the organization of the AutoCAD user interface, cover a few of the basic commands, and equip you with the tools necessary to set up a new drawing, including the use of a standard such as the National CAD Standard (NCS) to organize your files.

▶ Chapters 4 and 5 introduce the basic drawing commands and develop drawing strategies that will help you use commands efficiently.

▶ Chapters 6 through 11 work with AutoCAD's major features such as blocks, hatches, and annotation. You'll also learn about using layers to organize the various components of a drawing by applying the National CAD Standard.

▶ Chapters 12 through 15 examine intermediate and advanced AutoCAD features, including managing and creating document sets by using Sheet Set Manager.

▶ Chapters 16 and 17 cover the 3D modeling tools by exploring 3D solids and 3D surfaces. You'll also learn how to apply materials to 3D objects, allowing you to produce eye-catching 3D visualizations. In the process of exploring these elements, you'll follow the steps involved in laying out the floor plan of a small cabin. You'll then learn how to generate elevations from the floor plan, and eventually you'll learn how to set up a title block and layouts to print your drawing.

Along the way, you'll also learn how to do the following:

- Use the basic drawing and modify commands in a strategic manner
- Set up layers by using an established standard
- Assign colors to your drawing
- Define and insert blocks
- Generate elevation views
- Place hatch patterns and fills on building components
- Use text in your drawing

Chapters in the latter part of the book touch on more-advanced features of AutoCAD, including the following:

- Creating dynamic drawings by using geometric and dimensional parametric constraints
- Dimensioning the floor plan
- Drawing a site plan and managing drawings of varying units
- Efficiently organizing drawing sets by using external references
- Setting up and managing drawings for printing with layouts
- Making a print of your drawing
- Working in 3D (for AutoCAD users)

All these features are taught by using the cabin as a continuing project. As a result, you'll build a set of drawings that document your progress throughout the project. You can use these drawings later as reference material if you need to refresh your memory with material covering a specific skill.

Files on the Website

If you're already somewhat familiar with AutoCAD and you're reading only some of the chapters, or if you want to check your work on the cabin against the book at different stages, you can pull accompanying files from this book's page on Wiley's website at **www.sybex.com/go/autocad2012ner**. Click the Resources & Downloads button on that page.

To further help you learn AutoCAD, a companion website is also available at www.autocadner.com that, in addition to the dataset, offers a comprehensive library of instructional videos, additional exercises, and more. Visiting this site will also let you view this book's errata and interact with the author by posing questions you may have about its contents.

Hints for Success

Because this book is essentially a step-by-step tutorial, it has a common side effect with tutorials of this type. After you finish a chapter and see that you have progressed further through the cabin project, you may wonder exactly what you just did and whether you could do it again without the help of the step-by-step instructions.

This feeling is a natural result of this type of learning tool, and you can do a couple of things to get beyond it:

► *You can work through the chapter again.* Doing so may seem tedious, but it will help you draw faster. You'll be able to accomplish the same task in half the time it took you to do it the first time. If you do a chapter a third time, you'll halve your time again. Each time you repeat a chapter, you can skip more and more of the explicit instructions, and eventually you'll be able to execute the commands and finish the chapter by just looking at the figures and glancing at the text. In many ways, this process is like learning a musical instrument. You must go slowly at first, but over time and through practice, your pace will pick up.

► *Another suggestion for honing your skills is to follow the course of the book but apply the steps to a different project.* You might draw your own living space or design a new one. If you have a real-life design project that isn't too complex, that's even better. Your chances for success in learning AutoCAD, or any computer program, are greatly increased when you're highly motivated, and a real project of an appropriate size can be the perfect motivator.

Ready, Set...

Even with some of the most knowledgeable and passionate teachers by my side, I remember how overwhelming it was to learn AutoCAD as a student in high school. With each command I learned, it seemed there were another five I had yet to learn—and that was before AutoCAD evolved into the sophisticated, Microsoft Windows–based, modeling and design platform it is today. Ironically, the biggest challenge to AutoCAD wasn't learning the commands, but learning how to apply them in the most efficient way.

For several years, my personal mantra has been simple: to empower CAD professionals. While writing this book, I didn't want to simply introduce a bunch of commands without also putting them in context and demonstrating how to apply them to efficiently create drawings. With each exercise building on the next, you'll learn not only the individual commands, but also how everything snaps together as you produce a complete document set the same way industry professionals do. As the title says, there is "no experience required"—only an interest in the subject and a willingness to learn!

Getting to Know AutoCAD

Opening either AutoCAD or AutoCAD LT for the very first time can be an intimidating experience. Faced with such an expansive collection of tools, settings, and more, where do you start? To help you answer that question, this chapter breaks down the many components of the user interface into manageable segments and introduces you to basic operations such as opening drawings. Even if you've used earlier versions of AutoCAD, you'll still want to review this chapter to become acquainted with some of the changes from recent years.

Although the 2012 release does have some subtle user interface improvements, the AutoCAD and AutoCAD LT interfaces are almost identical. Generally speaking, both platforms offer the same 2D drafting experience. The biggest difference is that AutoCAD LT has no 3D capability. AutoCAD offers many powerful tools for modeling in 3D that are not found in AutoCAD LT. (These tools are the topic of Chapter 16, "Creating 3D Geometry," and Chapter 17, "Rendering and Materials.") With so little separating the two platforms, for most purposes in this book I'll refer to both interchangeably as AutoCAD unless otherwise specified.

▶ **Opening a new drawing**

▶ **Becoming familiar with the AutoCAD and AutoCAD LT Application windows**

▶ **Modifying the display**

▶ **Displaying and arranging AutoCAD tools**

Starting AutoCAD

If you installed AutoCAD by using the default settings for the location of the program files, start the program by choosing Start ➢ Programs ➢ Autodesk ➢ AutoCAD 2012 ➢ AutoCAD 2012 or by choosing Start ➢ Programs ➢ Autodesk ➢ AutoCAD LT 2012 ➢ AutoCAD LT 2012, depending on your program. (This command path might vary depending on the Windows operating system and scheme you are using.) Alternatively, you can find and double-click the AutoCAD 2012 icon or the AutoCAD LT 2012 icon on your desktop.

N O T E   You can also use AutoCAD-based products such as AutoCAD Architecture or AutoCAD Civil 3D to learn the topics covered in this book. To use one of these vertical products, choose Start ➢ Programs ➢ Autodesk ➢ AutoCAD Product Name 2012 ➢ AutoCAD Product Name As AutoCAD 2012.

Accessing Autodesk Exchange for AutoCAD

Autodesk Exchange for AutoCAD opens when the application is first launched, and provides integrated access to the popular AutoCAD Exchange (**http:// autocad.autodesk.com**). Similar to the Welcome screen found in earlier releases, the Autodesk Exchange window shown in Figure 1.1 leads to several resources including application downloads, help content, videos, and even community-generated content such as blogs and discussion forums.

The following elements make up the Autodesk Exchange For AutoCAD window:

Home Tab   The most prominent component of the Home tab is a feature slider highlighting the latest tips, tricks, and information related to AutoCAD. As seen in Figure 1.1, below the feature slider are several links to additional resources, including a list of productivity enhancing Featured Videos and Featured Topics.

On the right edge of the Autodesk Exchange For AutoCAD window are several links. Starting from the top, you will find direct links to the top-selling AutoCAD products from the store. Just below are several Important Links to resources such as Product Support and the Subscription Center.

Help Tab   Providing easy access to the AutoCAD help system, the Help tab brings several learning resources together in one place. Here a long list of resources including product documentation, product support, blog articles, tips and tricks, expert responses to questions, and more may be browsed and searched simultaneously (see Figure 1.2).

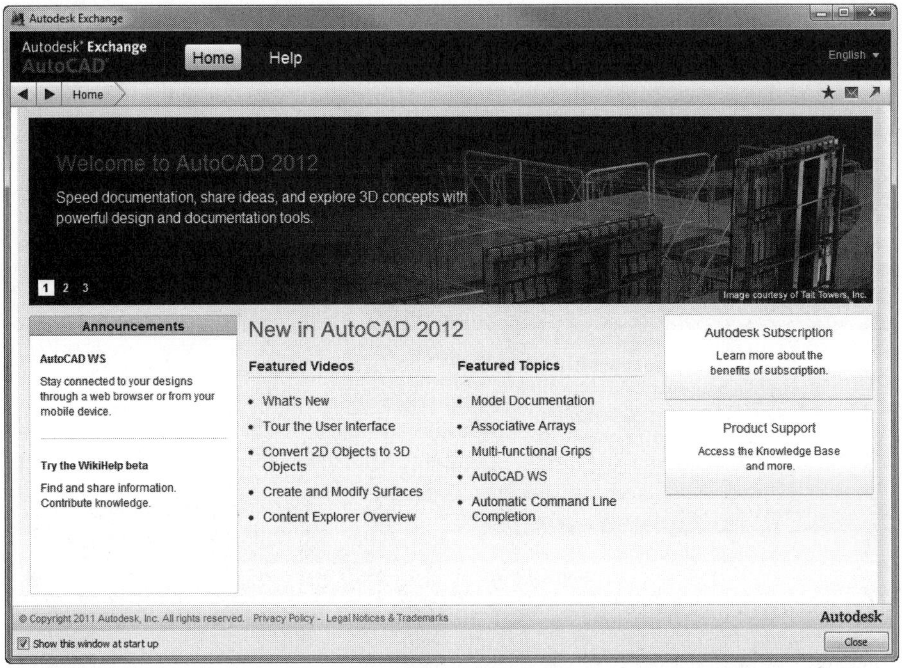

FIGURE 1.1 The Autodesk Exchange window featuring a collection of AutoCAD resources

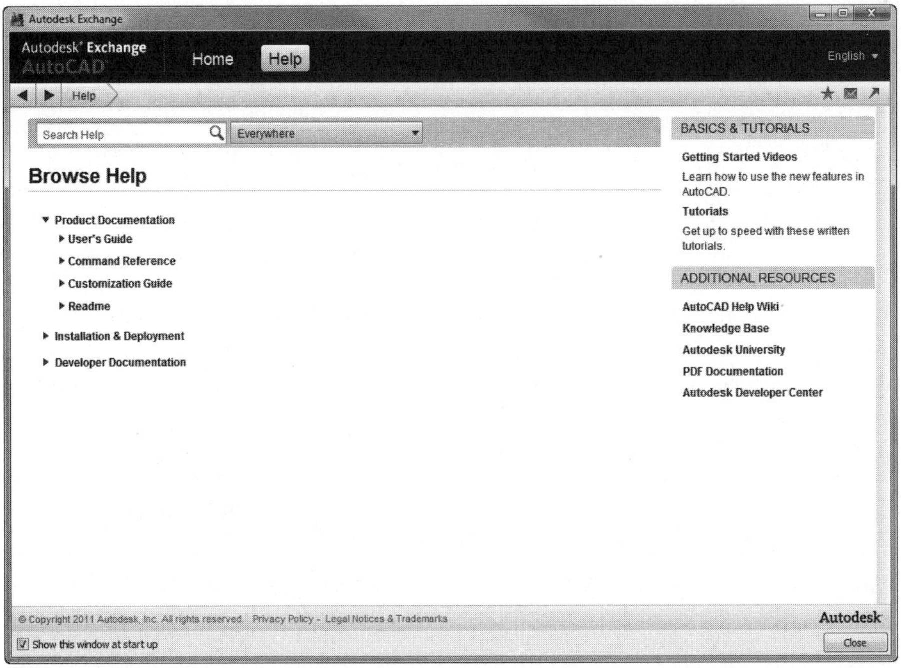

FIGURE 1.2 Accessing AutoCAD help documentation

Along the right edge of the Help tab is a list of additional resources. Among these resources is a link to a collection of Getting Started Videos. These Getting Started Videos go beyond the topic of what's new and instead dig deeper, offering a more comprehensive look at a complete process (see Figure 1.3). Here you can gain a better understanding of topics such as 3D modeling or even take a guided tour of the user interface.

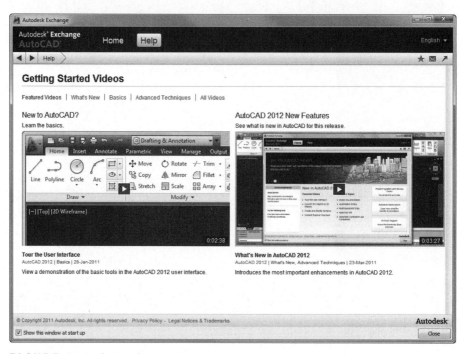

FIGURE 1.3 Getting Started Videos as found in the AutoCAD Exchange For AutoCAD window

After exploring the Autodesk Exchange For AutoCAD window, you may prefer to disable it from automatically loading each time you start the software. This can be done by deselecting the check box labeled Show This Window At Start Up in the lower-left corner of the window. Even after choosing this option, you can still quickly access the window by using the Exchange button found on the right end of the AutoCAD title bar.

Understanding the Customer Involvement Program

AutoCAD 2012 is among a large number of Autodesk products that provide the opportunity to participate in a customer involvement program (CIP). The CIP is designed to collect nonpersonal information about your Autodesk products and computer system to help the product programmers and developers design software that best meets your needs. If you haven't yet agreed or declined to participate, the Customer Involvement Program dialog box (Figure 1.4) might prompt you to join when you first start AutoCAD.

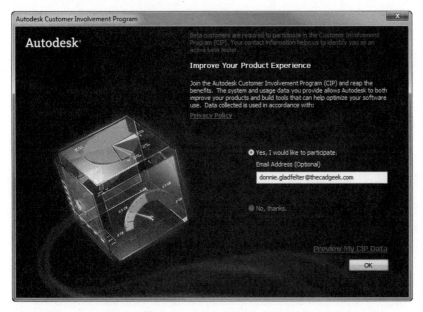

FIGURE 1.4 The Autodesk Customer Involvement Program dialog box

Participation is strictly voluntary and, if you choose to participate, AutoCAD will periodically send a small file to Autodesk containing information such as your software name and version, the commands you use, and your system configuration information. An Internet connection is required, and you must ensure that your firewall settings don't prevent the information from being transmitted.

Exploring the AutoCAD User Interface

After you dismiss all of the initial dialog boxes, AutoCAD opens to display its default user interface, or UI as it's sometimes called. Collectively known as the Application window, the user interface can be broken down into numerous parts. Many of these parts remain unchanged regardless of how the software is configured, whereas other elements may not always be viewable. I'll explain how AutoCAD chooses to configure the user interface shortly. At this point, however, your graphics window should look similar to Figure 1.5.

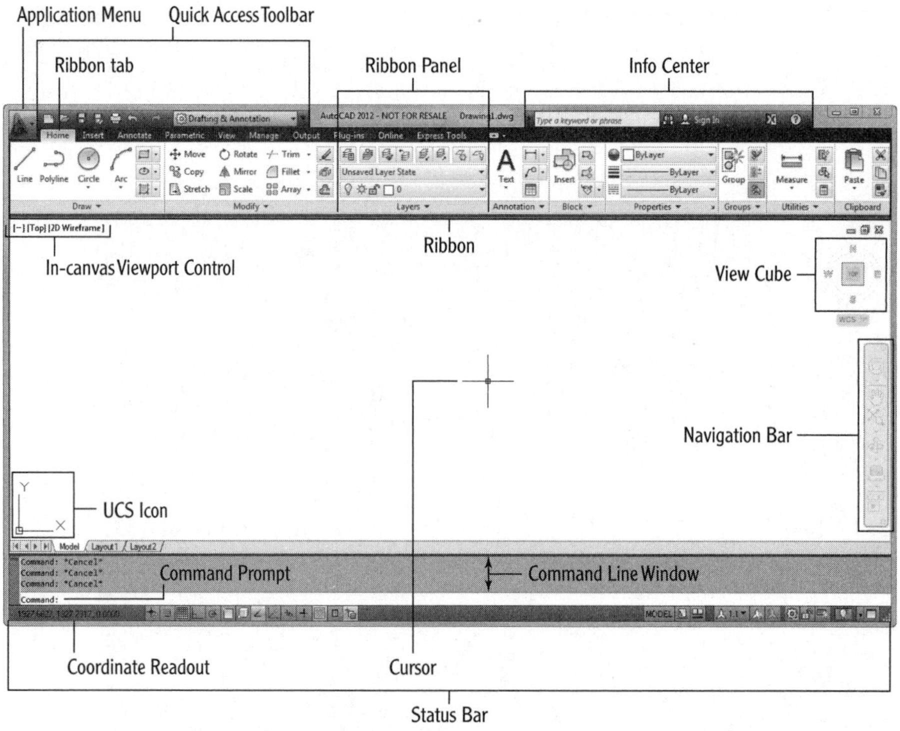

FIGURE 1.5 The AutoCAD Application window's Drafting & Annotation workspace

Using Standard AutoCAD Workspaces

AutoCAD and AutoCAD LT offer numerous dialog boxes with various combinations of buttons and text boxes. You'll learn many of their functions as you progress through the book.

AutoCAD provides the following standard workspaces:

Drafting & Annotation   Utilizing the Ribbon, this workspace (shown previously in Figure 1.5) is considered the default workspace. Unless otherwise specified, this is also the workspace used throughout this book.

AutoCAD Classic   Mimics the menu-based interface utilized prior to AutoCAD 2009.

3D Basics   Provides the core tools needed to get started with 3D modeling inside AutoCAD. (For AutoCAD users only. 3D features are not included in AutoCAD LT.)

3D Modeling   Provides the complete set of 3D modeling tools found inside AutoCAD, including materials via the Materials Browser. (For AutoCAD users only. 3D features are not included in AutoCAD LT.)

Switching the Current Workspace

Whether you choose to develop your own custom workspace or just use one that comes with the software, you may switch your current workspace at any time. As you become more comfortable with the software, you'll likely choose to build a workspace that better matches the way you use AutoCAD. You'll be using the Drafting & Annotation workspace for the first 15 chapters in this book. In the final two chapters, you'll switch to the 3D Modeling workspace (Figure 1.6). For now, however, you need to get your AutoCAD user interface to look like Figure 1.5.

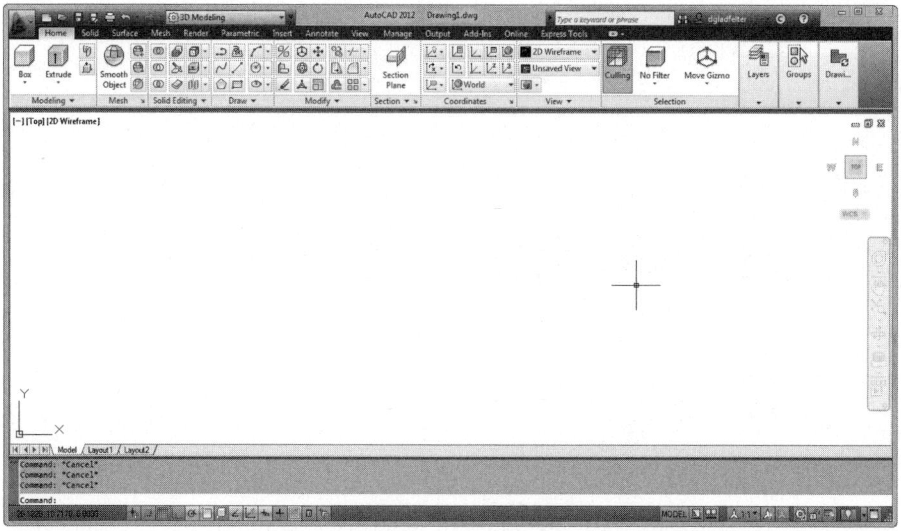

FIGURE 1.6 The AutoCAD Application window's 3D Modeling workspace

N O T E The illustrations in this book show the drawing area of the AutoCAD user interface with a white background; however, the default and preferred method is to use a dark gray or black background to reduce eyestrain. The color choice in the book is simply for readability.

If your screen looks like Figure 1.6 or isn't at all like Figure 1.7, you need to make a few changes:

1. Click the Workspace drop-down from the Quick Access toolbar, and choose Drafting & Annotation, as shown in Figure 1.7. Alternatively, Command Line users can enter the following:

   WSCURRENT⏎

   drafting & annotation⏎

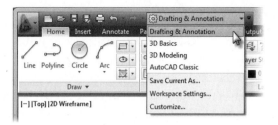
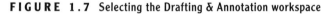

FIGURE 1.7 Selecting the Drafting & Annotation workspace

The large, dark gray area you see in the middle of the screen is called the drawing area. This infinite canvas is where you'll create your designs; however, it might need to be adjusted.

2. Using the View Control tool on the in-canvas Viewport controls, select the Top option (see Figure 1.8).

FIGURE 1.8 Selecting the Top option by using the in-canvas Viewport controls

This procedure ensures that your view is perpendicular to the drawing area. It should be as though you were looking straight down at a piece of paper on a drawing table.

3. From the in-canvas Viewport controls, click the Visual Style control to display a list of visual styles. Select the 2D Wireframe option from the list, as shown in Figure 1.9.

FIGURE 1.9 Selecting the 2D Wireframe visual style by using in-canvas Viewport controls

If the drawing area looks like a sheet of graph paper, it means the grid, a drawing aid that you'll look at later, is turned on.

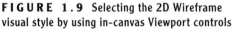 **4.** Move the cursor to the left side of the status bar at the bottom of the screen, and click the Grid Display button so it's in the Off position (unpushed with a gray, not blue, background) and the gridlines disappear. Place your cursor over any button in the status bar to reveal its name in a tooltip.

Your screen should now look similar to Figure 1.5.

Introducing the AutoCAD Application Window

At the top of the Application window (see Figure 1.10), the Ribbon and the Quick Access toolbar sit to the left, and the InfoCenter and a number of related tools sit on the right.

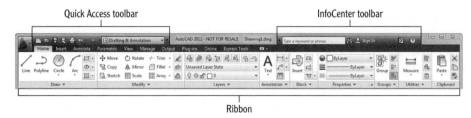

FIGURE 1.10 The Ribbon, Quick Access toolbar, and InfoCenter

The title bar and menu bar at the top of the AutoCAD LT screen are identical to those in AutoCAD, except that AutoCAD LT appears in the title bar rather than AutoCAD.

The title bar is analogous to the title bar in any Windows program. It contains the program name (AutoCAD or AutoCAD LT) and the title of the current drawing with its path, provided a drawing other than the default Drawing#.dwg is open. Below the title bar is the Ribbon, where you'll find most of the AutoCAD commands and tools needed to complete any drawing task. You'll explore the Ribbon in much more detail shortly; however, its basic concept is that related tasks are found under the different tabs, which are further segmented into panels containing similar tools.

To the far right of the title bar is the InfoCenter containing the Search, Autodesk Online Services, Exchange, and Help buttons. You can enter a question in the field to the left of the Search button to quickly access information from a number of locations, including the standard AutoCAD help system, through the drop-down panel. Autodesk Online Services allows you to sign in with your Autodesk ID, and access services that integrate with AutoCAD. The Help button is a direct link to the AutoCAD help system (also accessible by pressing the F1 key).

As noted earlier, the blank middle section of the screen is called the drawing area. Notice the movable crosshair cursor (see Figure 1.11). The crosshairs on your cursor might extend completely across the screen. Later in this chapter, you'll see how to modify the length of the crosshairs as well as make a few other changes.

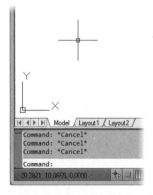

FIGURE 1.11 The crosshair cursor placed near the UCS icon

Notice the little box at the intersection of the two crosshair lines. This is one of several forms of the AutoCAD cursor, known in this form as the Aperture. When you move the cursor off the drawing area, it changes to the standard Windows pointing arrow. As you begin using commands, it will take on other forms, depending on which step of a command you're performing.

The icon composed of two lines, labeled X and Y, in the lower-left corner of the drawing area is the UCS icon (UCS stands for user coordinate system). It indicates the positive direction for the x- and y-axes.

Below the drawing area is the Command Line window, shown in Figure 1.12.

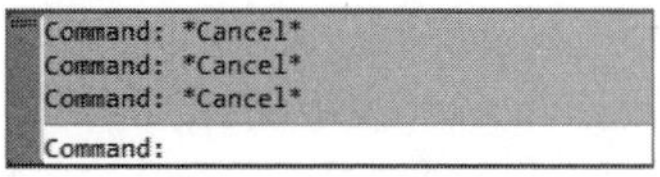

```
Command: *Cancel*
Command: *Cancel*
Command: *Cancel*
Command:
```

FIGURE 1.12 The command-line window

Most commands can be launched in a few different ways (the Command Line, Ribbon tools, and so on). Regardless of which method you choose, the Command Line window (also called the Command window) is where you will tell the program what to do and where the program tells you what's happening. It's an important feature, and you'll need to learn how it works in detail. By default, three lines of text are visible. You'll learn how to adjust the number of visible lines later in this chapter, in the "Working in the Command Line Window" section. When the Dynamic Input feature is active, much of the command window information is displayed alongside the cursor as well.

Below the command window is the status bar (see Figure 1.13).

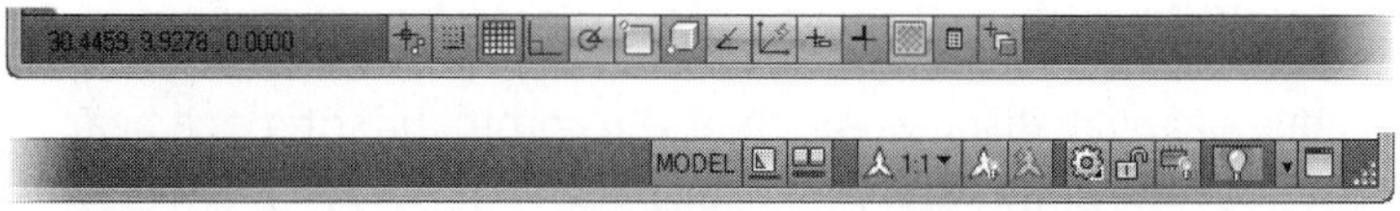

FIGURE 1.13 The left side of the status bar (top) and the right side of the status bar (bottom)

On the left end of the status bar, you'll see a coordinate readout window. In the middle are 14 buttons (LT has only 11) that activate various drawing modes. It's important to learn about the coordinate system and most of these drawing aids (Snap Mode, Grid Display, Ortho Mode, Object Snap, and so on) early as you learn to draw in AutoCAD. They will help you create neat and accurate drawings. You'll have the chance to explore each of the following drawing modes/aids throughout this book; as a preview, however, following is a complete list with a brief description of each:

Infer Constraints* When this is enabled, AutoCAD will automatically apply constraints between objects as you create or modify them.

Snap Mode Restricts movement of the cursor inside the drawing area to specified intervals.

---

* Designates drawing modes that are exclusive to AutoCAD and not available in AutoCAD LT.

Grid Display   Mimics a piece of graph paper by displaying a series of nonplotting horizontal and vertical lines displayed in the drawing's background.

Ortho Mode   Restricts movement of the cursor to 90° intervals: 0°, 90°, and 270° by default.

Polar Tracking   Frequently used in conjunction with Object Snap Tracking, Polar Tracking is an advanced drawing tool that guides cursor movement to specified increments along a polar angle. Its use is introduced in Chapter 5, "Developing Drawing Strategies: Part 2."

Object Snap   Aids you in drawing objects based on geometric reference points such as endpoint, midpoint, intersection, and so on. Mastering the use of object snaps is critical in the creation of accurate drawings.

3D Object Snap*   Similar to the standard object snaps, with more-sophisticated tools for working and interacting with 3D faces and edges.

Object Snap Tracking   An advanced drafting method introduced in Chapter 5, this allows you to draw objects with specific geometric relationships to other objects within your drawing.

Allow/Disallow Dynamic UCS*   As noted earlier, UCS stands for user coordinate system, and Dynamic UCS is used in 3D drawings.

Dynamic Input   When enabled, displays much of the command interface near the cursor (in addition to the command line itself).

Show/Hide Lineweight   Toggles the display of lineweights (discussed in Chapter 14, "Using Layouts to Set Up a Print") in the drawing area.

Show/Hide Transparency   Many objects, including layers, can be assigned a transparency value. When this toggle is on, these objects' transparency settings will take effect.

Quick Properties   Based on the type of object/objects you have selected, Quick Properties provides a contextual version of the full Properties palette near the selected object/objects. When nothing is selected, the Quick Properties will disappear from the drawing area.

Selection Cycling   Provides a contextual list of selected overlapping objects, making it easier to select the object/objects you intended to select.

---

* Designates drawing modes that are exclusive to AutoCAD and not available in AutoCAD LT.

TEXT-BASED BUTTONS OR ICONS?

Sometimes the status bar icons can be a little cryptic. If you prefer, AutoCAD can display those buttons as text instead of icons.

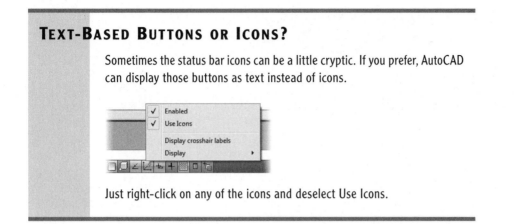

Just right-click on any of the icons and deselect Use Icons.

At the right side of the status bar are tools for navigating in the drawing area and controlling the display, tools for controlling the appearance of annotation objects in AutoCAD, and tools for controlling access to other drawings or features within the current drawing. The padlock icon controls which types of toolbars and windows are locked in their current positions on the screen. Leave it in the unlocked mode for now.

To conclude this quick introduction to the various parts of the Application window, you need to understand a couple of items that might be visible on your screen. You might have scroll bars below and to the right of the drawing area; although they can be useful, they can also take up precious space in the drawing area. They won't be of any use while working your way through this book, so you can remove them for now.

These features can be removed temporarily via the OPTIONS command. The following steps show you how:

1. To access the OPTIONS command graphically, click the Application Menu button in the upper-left corner of the AutoCAD window, and then click the Options button at the bottom of the menu (see Figure 1.14). The OPTIONS command is also accessible from the command line by typing **OPTIONS** ↵.

   The Options dialog box (shown in Figure 1.15) opens. It has ten tabs (LT has only eight) across the top that act like tabs on file folders.

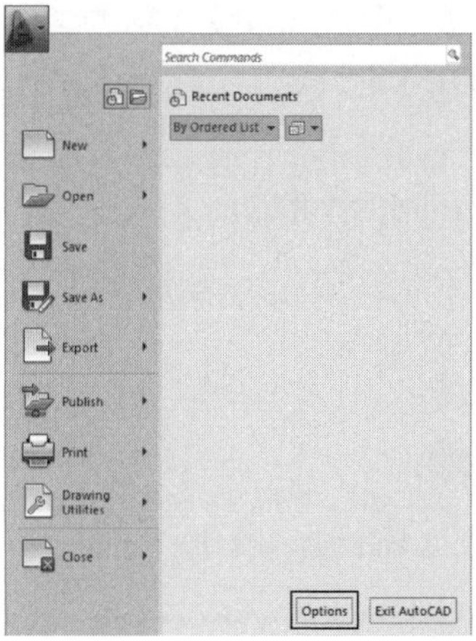

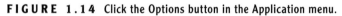

FIGURE 1.14 Click the Options button in the Application menu.

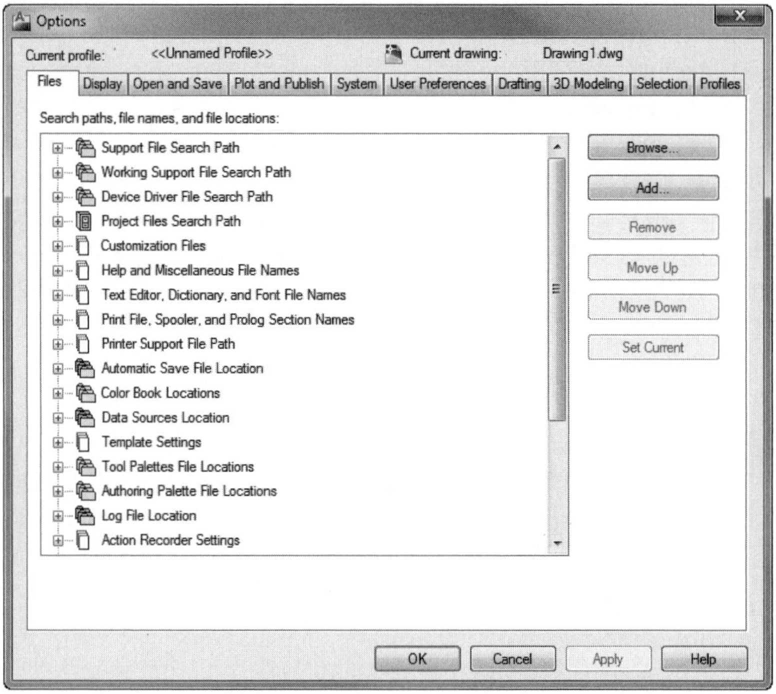

FIGURE 1.15 The Options dialog box

2. Click the Display tab, which is shown in Figure 1.16. Focus on the Window Elements group. If scroll bars are visible on the lower and right edges of the drawing area, the Display Scroll Bars In Drawing Window check box will be selected.

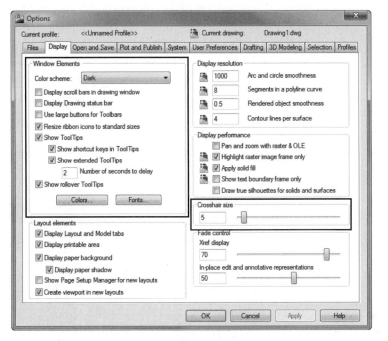

FIGURE 1.16 The Options dialog box opened at the Display tab

3. Click the check box to turn off the scroll bars. Don't click the OK button yet.

4. If you want to change the length of the lines of your crosshair cursor, go to the lower-right corner of the Display tab (the middle of the right side for LT), and move the slider to change the Crosshair Size setting, as shown previously in Figure 1.18. The crosshair length changes as a percentage of the drawing area.

5. Click OK to apply any remaining changes, and close the Options dialog box.

CHOOSING YOUR OWN DRAWING AREA BACKGROUND COLOR

By default, AutoCAD uses a dark gray color for the drawing area. Some users prefer to customize this and several other user interface elements to a color palette of their own liking. As an example, some prefer the contrast ratio of a light background color such as yellow or white over the contrast ratio offered by the darker background color. Follow these steps to change the drawing area's background color:

1. Open the Options dialog box by typing **OP**↵ at the command line, or choose Application menu ➢ Options.

2. Switch to the Display tab, and click the Colors button within the Window Elements group.

   This opens the Drawing Window Colors dialog box, where you'll customize the colors of the user interface to your liking.

3. Select 2D Model Space within the Context list, and Uniform Background within the Interface Element list of the Drawing Window Colors dialog box. The following illustration shows the changing of the colors of user interface elements within this dialog box.

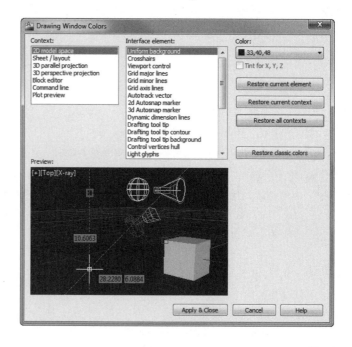

(Continues)

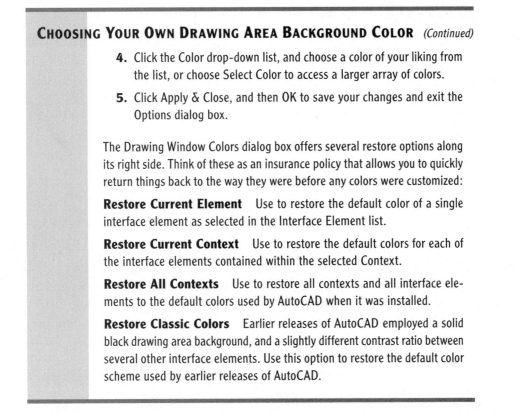

CHOOSING YOUR OWN DRAWING AREA BACKGROUND COLOR *(Continued)*

4. Click the Color drop-down list, and choose a color of your liking from the list, or choose Select Color to access a larger array of colors.

5. Click Apply & Close, and then OK to save your changes and exit the Options dialog box.

The Drawing Window Colors dialog box offers several restore options along its right side. Think of these as an insurance policy that allows you to quickly return things back to the way they were before any colors were customized:

Restore Current Element   Use to restore the default color of a single interface element as selected in the Interface Element list.

Restore Current Context   Use to restore the default colors for each of the interface elements contained within the selected Context.

Restore All Contexts   Use to restore all contexts and all interface elements to the default colors used by AutoCAD when it was installed.

Restore Classic Colors   Earlier releases of AutoCAD employed a solid black drawing area background, and a slightly different contrast ratio between several other interface elements. Use this option to restore the default color scheme used by earlier releases of AutoCAD.

Working in the Command-Line Window

Just below the drawing area is the Command-Line window. This window is separate from the drawing area and behaves like a Windows window—that is, you can drag it to a different place on the screen and resize it, although you probably shouldn't do this at first. If you currently have fewer than three lines of text in the window, you should increase the window's vertical size. To do so, move the cursor to the horizontal boundary between the drawing area and the command window until it changes to an up-and-down arrow broken by two parallel, horizontal lines.

Hold down the left mouse button, drag the cursor up by approximately the same amount that one or two lines of text would take up, and then release the mouse button (see Figure 1.17). You should see more lines of text, but you might have to try this a few times to display exactly four lines. A horizontal line will separate the top two lines of text from the bottom line of text. When you close the program, AutoCAD will save the new settings. The next time you start AutoCAD, the command window will display four lines of text.

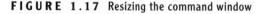

FIGURE 1.17 Resizing the command window

The command window is where you give information to AutoCAD and where AutoCAD prompts you for the next step in executing a command. It's a good practice to keep an eye on the command window as you work on your drawing. Many errors can occur when you don't check it frequently. If the Dynamic Input button on the status bar is in the On position, some of the information in the command window will appear in the drawing area next to the cursor. You'll learn about this feature when you start drawing.

Before you begin to draw in the next chapter, take a close look at the Ribbon, Application menu, toolbars, and keyboard controls.

N O T E   You can start AutoCAD commands in a number of ways: from the Ribbon, the Application menu, the command window, and the menus that appear when you right-click. When you get used to drawing with AutoCAD, you'll learn some shortcuts that start commands quickly, and you'll find the way that best suits you.

Using the Ribbon

Perhaps one of the most prominent elements of the AutoCAD interface is the Ribbon (Figure 1.20). Although the Ribbon can be positioned in various ways, its default position extends across the top of the AutoCAD window. Depending on the size of your AutoCAD window (or current screen resolution), the Ribbon may look a little different on your computer. That's because the Ribbon self-adjusts according to the size of the AutoCAD window itself. To see the Ribbon in its fully expanded state, you need to be sure to have a screen resolution wider than 1325 pixels. When the width is too narrow to display each panel fully, the panels will begin to collapse first by replacing the panels with a single button bearing the name of the panel.

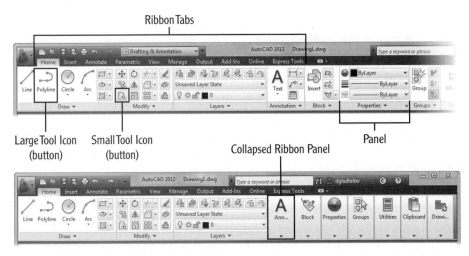

FIGURE 1.18 The Ribbon fully displaying all panels (top) and with partially and completely collapsed panels (bottom)

The Ribbon itself can be divided into three parts—tools, panels, and tabs:

Ribbon Tools   The individual icons and various drop-down lists found on the Ribbon are known as *Ribbon tools*. Clicking any of these tools launches the command associated with it.

Ribbon Panels   Similar tools are grouped together into a series of Ribbon panels. For instance, the Move, Erase, and Rotate tools modify objects. Consequently, each of these tools is found on the Modify Ribbon panel.

Ribbon Tabs   Ribbon tabs offer the highest level of organization; they group Ribbon panels by task. For instance, commands related to plotting (printing) are found on the Output tab, whereas commands related to entering text can be found on the Annotate tab.

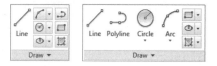

 RIBBON ENHANCEMENTS

AutoCAD 2012 introduces several interface and performance enhancements to the Ribbon. Overall Ribbon performance has been enhanced so that switching between tabs is nearly instantaneous. Beyond performance enhancements, several Ribbon tabs have been updated to make it easier to identify and access frequently used tools. These updates include the following Ribbon tabs and panels:

Home tab > Draw panel   The Draw panel from AutoCAD 2011 is on the left, and the updated Draw panel is on the right:

Home tab > Modify panel   The Modify panel from AutoCAD 2011 is on the left, and the updated Modify panel is on the right:

Insert tab > Block panel   The Block panel from AutoCAD 2011 is on the left, and the updated Block panel is on the right:

(Continues)

RIBBON ENHANCEMENTS *(Continued)*

Insert tab > Block Definition (formerly Attributes) panel The Attributes panel from AutoCAD 2011 is on the left, replaced by the new Block Definition panel on the right:

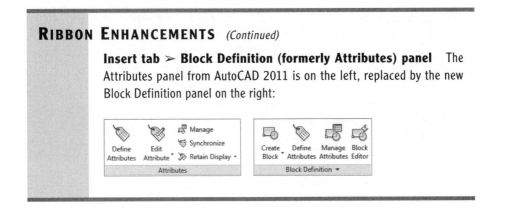

Displaying the Ribbon Tools

The Ribbon's default location is at the top of the screen, but it can be moved or docked almost anywhere on your screen. Individual panels have several display options built into them as well. In the following exercises, you will have the chance to explore many of these display options.

Collapsing, Moving, and Hiding the Ribbon

Available drawing area is always at a premium, and you can regain some of it by collapsing the Ribbon:

- ► When you click the Minimize button to the right of the Ribbon tabs once, the panels are collapsed vertically, showing only an icon for each Ribbon panel.

- ► Clicking the Minimize button a second time collapses the Ribbon further so only the tab and panel names display.

- ► Clicking it a third time collapses the Ribbon so only the tabs show. When the Ribbon is in any of these states, you can expand any panel or tab by clicking its visible panel or tab name.

- ► Clicking the Minimize button a fourth time returns the Ribbon to its default state.

Rather than cycling through each display option, you can use the small Down icon to the right of the Minimize Ribbon button to quickly switch between states. A list of available display states (Figure 1.19) will appear after clicking the Down icon. Select the desired visibility to switch directly to it, as opposed to cycling through the other options.

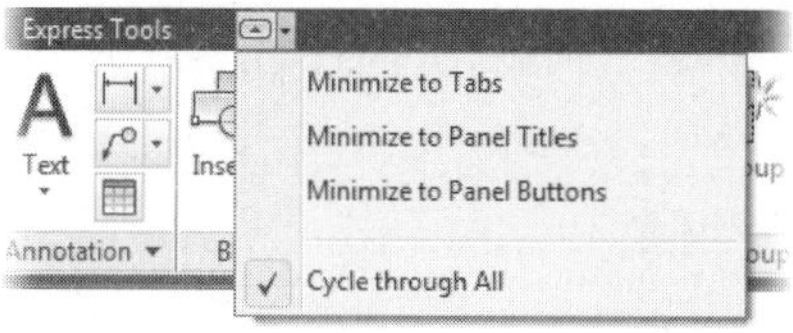

FIGURE 1.19 List of available Ribbon display states

As noted earlier, the Ribbon's default location is at the top of the screen, but it can be undocked, or floating, over the drawing area; or it can be moved to a second monitor; or docked on either side of the drawing area. To undock the Ribbon, right-click to the right of the tab names and choose Undock from the pop-up menu, as shown in Figure 1.20.

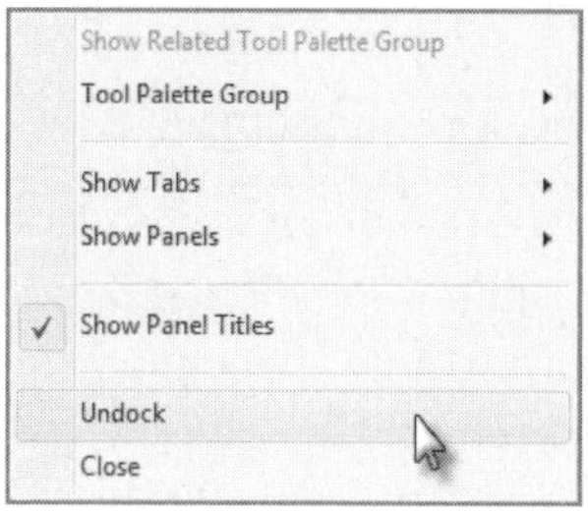

FIGURE 1.20 Undocking the Ribbon

The Ribbon detaches from the top of the drawing area and floats on the screen, as shown in Figure 1.21. To dock it, click the title bar on the side of the floating Ribbon and drag it to the side or the top of the drawing area. Experiment with detaching the Ribbon, but when you are finished, dock it back at the top so you can follow the graphics in this book more easily.

If you don't want the Ribbon at all, you can turn it off by right-clicking to the right of the Ribbon tabs and choosing Close. To turn it on, type **RIBBON**↵. You'll use the Ribbon throughout this book, so be sure to keep it on for now.

FIGURE 1.21 The Ribbon undocked
from the top of the drawing area

Using the Ribbon Tools

Each panel contains tools from a related family of functions. For example, all
the common tools for editing objects in the drawing area are consolidated in the
Modify panel. When more tools are available than will fit on the panel, an arrow
is displayed on the panel's title bar. Clicking the title bar expands the panel and
exposes the additional tools. Follow these steps to learn how the Ribbon tools
work and how they display information:

1. Click the Home tab on the Ribbon to expose the Home tab's panels
   (see the top of Figure 1.18 shown earlier).

2. Move your cursor over the Modify panel, and pause the cursor over
   the Move tool button.

   This exposes the button's tooltip, as shown at the top of Figure 1.22.
   Displaying the name of the tool, the tooltip also provides a brief

description of its function, the command line equivalent of clicking the tool, and instructions to press the F1 key to open the AutoCAD Help file to the current tool's Help page.

F I G U R E 1 . 2 2 The tooltip for the Move command

3. After a few seconds of hovering over the Move tool button, the tooltip is replaced with a cue card, as shown in Figure 1.23. Cue cards show the step-by-step implementation of the tool.

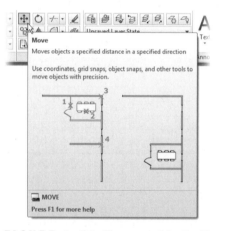

F I G U R E 1 . 2 3 The cue card for the Move command

4. Click the Modify panel's title bar to expand the panel and expose all of the Modify tools (see Figure 1.24).

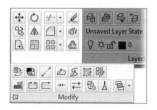

F I G U R E 1 . 2 4 The expanded Modify panel

5. Often, you may find yourself returning to the same tool on an expanded Ribbon panel. When that happens, you can pin the panel open by clicking the pushpin-shaped button in the bottom-left corner. When the panel is pinned open, it remains open even when the cursor is not hovering over it.

6. Click the button again to unpin the panel, and then move the cursor off the panel to collapse it. Regardless of whether a panel is pinned or unpinned, it will automatically collapse if you change Ribbon tabs.

7. Holding the mouse button down, click the Modify panel title, and move the cursor toward the drawing area.

   The Modify panel becomes semitransparent, allowing you to place it inside the drawing area to become a floating panel (see Figure 1.25). Floating panels display regardless of whether their host tab is current or not. This feature can be helpful when quick access to tools on separate Ribbon tabs is needed simultaneously.

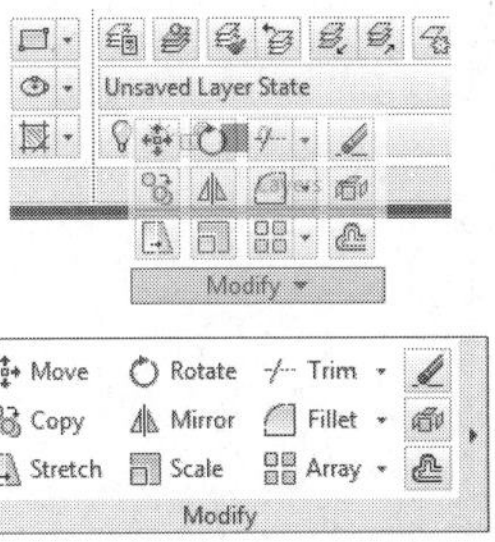

FIGURE 1.25 Dragging the Modify panel from the Ribbon (top), the Modify panel as a floating panel (bottom)

8. To return the Modify panel to the Ribbon, hover over its title and then click the Return Panels To Ribbon button shown in Figure 1.26.

Return Panels to Ribbon button

FIGURE 1.26 Using the Return Panels To Ribbon tool to restore a floating panel to its host Ribbon tab

Using the Application Menu

The Application menu contains the tools for opening, saving, and printing (plotting) your drawings, similar to the options found under the File drop-down menu in AutoCAD and many other programs. When the Application menu is open, the menus for these tools project from the upper-left corner of the AutoCAD window and cover the drawing area and any open dialog boxes.

1. Click the Application Menu button to open the Application menu.

2. The left pane of the Application menu displays the different commands. Clicking or hovering over a command displays a menu of its options in the right pane, as shown in Figure 1.27.

> **Be careful not to double-click the Application menu, because this will make AutoCAD close.**

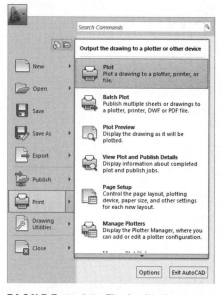

FIGURE 1.27 The Application menu showing the Print options

A bar with an up- or down-arrow at the top or bottom of the right pane indicates that additional tools are available. You can display these tools by placing your cursor over either bar.

Opening a Drawing with the Application Menu

The Application menu offers a quick method for opening drawings. You can even see a thumbnail preview of the drawings and arrange drawings that you frequently edit so they are easily accessible. Here's how:

1. To open a new AutoCAD file from the Application menu, choose New ➤ Drawing, as shown in Figure 1.28.

FIGURE 1.28 Opening a new drawing from the Application menu

This opens the Select Template dialog box, where you select a template on which to base the new drawing. Opening a file with a template is covered in Chapter 2, "Learning Basic Commands to Get Started."

2. To open an existing file from the Application menu, choose Open ➤ Drawing, as shown in Figure 1.29.

FIGURE 1.29 Opening an existing drawing from the Application menu

This opens the Select File dialog box, where you can navigate to the desired drawing file and select it.

3. To open a file that you've worked on recently, click the Recent Documents button at the top of the Application menu's left pane. This displays the most recent files opened in AutoCAD in the right pane, as shown in Figure 1.30.

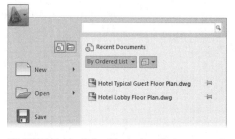

FIGURE 1.30 Displaying the recent documents in the Application menu

4. Hover over a filename in the right pane to display a thumbnail preview of the drawing and additional information, including the drawing location and AutoCAD drawing format (see Figure 1.31).

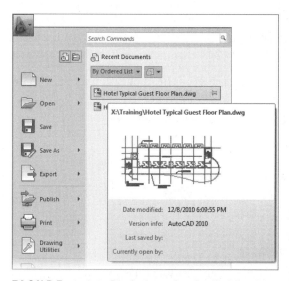

FIGURE 1.31 Displaying a thumbnail of the selected file

OPENING NEW FILES

You can open new or existing files by using the New or Open button in the Quick Access toolbar. Existing drawings can also be opened by dragging them from a Windows Explorer window to the AutoCAD title bar.

N O T E   AutoCAD 2012 uses the AutoCAD 2010 drawing (DWG) file format. This means that the files created in AutoCAD 2012 are compatible only with AutoCAD 2010, AutoCAD 2011, and AutoCAD 2012. You can share drawings with releases earlier than AutoCAD 2010 by performing a simple conversion. To convert a 2010 format drawing to a prior version, open the Application menu and then click Save As ➢ AutoCAD Drawing and choose the version you want from the Files Of Type drop-down list at the bottom of the Save Drawing As dialog box.

GETTING THE MOST OUT OF THE RECENT DOCUMENTS LIST

The Application menu offers many time-saving tips. Here are two of the best ways to use the Recent Documents list:

Access Frequently Used Drawings   For drawings you access on a regular basis, and would like to remain on the Recent Documents list, click the pushpin that displays next to its name. This will "pin" that drawing to the Recent Documents list until you unpin it.

Maximize the Number of Recent Documents   Out of the box, the Recent Document list displays only the last nine drawings you've opened. This number can be increased to fifty using the OPTIONS command, selecting the Open and Save tab, and changing the Number Of Recently-Used Files setting under the Application Menu heading.

Switching between Open Drawings

As in many programs, you can have multiple drawing files open in the same session of AutoCAD. Each drawing is stacked behind the drawings in front of it. There are several ways to switch between the open files, including using the Application menu, as shown next:

1. Start or open two or more AutoCAD files.

2. Open the Application menu, and then click the Open Documents icon at the top of the left pane. The open drawings are displayed in the right pane, as shown in Figure 1.32.

FIGURE 1.32 Displaying the open drawings by using the Application menu

3. Click on any drawing to bring it to the front of the AutoCAD window.

4. You can change the way AutoCAD displays the list of open drawings by clicking the icon near the top of the right pane and choosing one of four sizes of icons or thumbnail images to represent the open drawings.

Another option for switching between open drawings is to click the Quick View Drawings button in the status bar. This displays thumbnails for the open drawings, and you can click any thumbnail to make its drawing active. Hovering over a thumbnail displays that drawing's layouts (see Figure 1.33). Layouts are designated views of the drawing with scaled viewports looking into the drawing model. Viewports are covered in Chapter 14.

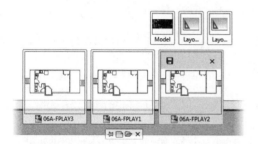

FIGURE 1.33 Displaying the open drawings with the Quick View Drawings tool

Using the Drop-Down Menus

If you prefer to use drop-down menus, they're still available in AutoCAD 2012, although they are turned off by default in the Drafting & Annotation, 3D Basics, and 3D Modeling workspaces. You can display them by switching to the AutoCAD Classic workspace, clicking the down-arrow at the right end of the Quick Access toolbar, and choosing Show Menu Bar (see Figure 1.34), or by typing **MENUBAR↵1↵**. This book focuses on the use of the Ribbon; the menus are covered here so you'll be familiar with them if you use them in the future.

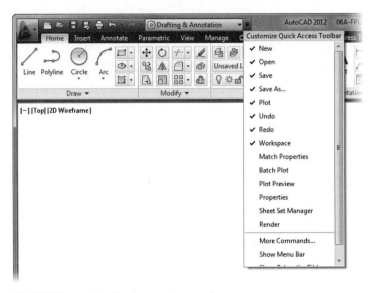

FIGURE 1.34 Turning on the menu bar

The left end of the menu bar, just below the title bar (see Figure 1.35), consists of an icon and 13 menus (11 if you don't have the Express Tools installed or are using LT). Click any of these to display a drop-down menu. The icon and the File and Edit menus are included with all Windows-compliant applications, although they are somewhat customized to work with AutoCAD. The drop-down menu associated with the icon contains commands to control the appearance and position of the drawing area.

FIGURE 1.35 The AutoCAD user interface showing the menu bar

You can turn off the menu bar by clicking the down-arrow on the right end of the Quick Access toolbar and choosing Hide Menu Bar, or by typing **MENUBAR↓0↓**.

Using the Toolbars

The AutoCAD toolbars have essentially been replaced by the Ribbon or other features, so we'll touch on them only briefly here. Toolbars, like the Ribbon panels, are collections of tools grouped by similar tasks. Like the Ribbon itself, any toolbar can be displayed or hidden without affecting the others, and they can all be docked to a side or the top of the drawing area or float freely.

Although the Ribbon has largely filled the role toolbars once played inside the software, some tools are still found only on toolbars. For this reason, some opt to build a hybrid workspace utilizing both toolbars and the Ribbon in tandem. A popular example of where this functionality may prove helpful is the Object Snap toolbar, which lacks a Ribbon equivalent.

Object Snaps are tools used to ensure accuracy as a plan is drawn, and are discussed at length in Chapter 4, "Developing Drawing Strategies: Part 1." To load the Object Snap toolbar into your current workspace, do the following:

1. On the Ribbon, click the View tab.

2. Click the Toolbars tool on the Windows panel to display a list of toolbar sets. Choose AutoCAD ➢ Object Snap from the list to open the Object Snap toolbar (see Figure 1.36).

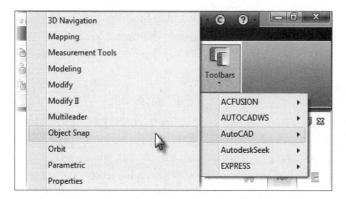

FIGURE 1.36 Loading the Object Snap toolbar

Similar to Ribbon panels, toolbars may be floating or docked. Floating toolbars are not connected to the Application window in any way, whereas docked toolbars will move with the application as it's moved between monitors, or even resized on a single monitor.

3. Drag the Object Snap toolbar to your desired location. Dragging the toolbar near any edge of the drawing area will dock the toolbar to that edge of the user interface. Figure 1.37 shows the Object Snap toolbar docked to the right edge of the drawing area.

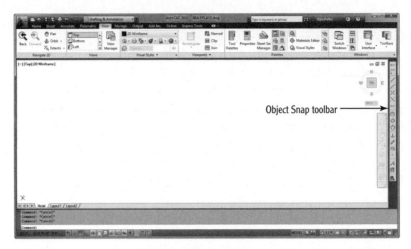

Object Snap toolbar

FIGURE 1.37 The Object Snap toolbar docked to the Application window

Take a few minutes to explore the available toolbars, and then close all but the Object Snap toolbar and hide the display of the menu bar.

Saving Workspaces

At the start of this chapter, you learned how workspaces can dramatically change the overall appearance of AutoCAD. This was illustrated in the "Exploring the AutoCAD User Interface" section of this chapter as you switched between different workspaces that ship with the software. Although many find the default workspaces more than adequate, others may prefer custom tailoring the user interface to the way they work.

From customizing the Ribbon, to loading toolbars, and beyond, AutoCAD provides a large collection of tools to personalize its layout. Regardless of the extent of your customization efforts, that configuration will be lost unless it's first saved as a workspace.

In the preceding section, you loaded the Object Snap toolbar. Follow these steps to ensure that it remains the next time you start AutoCAD:

1. Click the Workspace Switching drop-down list next to the Application menu, or on the right side of the status bar, and choose Save Current As from the menu, as shown on the left in Figure 1.38. This opens the Save Workspace dialog box, shown on the right in Figure 1.38.

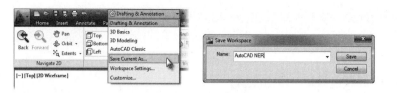

FIGURE 1.38 The Save Workspace dialog box

2. Type AutoCAD NER as the name for the workspace and click Save. The dialog box closes, and you are returned to your workspace.

Until you change it or select a different workspace, the AutoCAD NER workspace setup will remain as it is now.

When you make changes to a workspace by adding a toolbar or changing the background color of the drawing area, you can easily update the current workspace to accommodate those changes. Follow steps 1 and 2, naming the workspace again with the same name. You'll get a warning window telling you that a workspace by that name already exists and asking whether you want the new arrangement to replace the old one. Click Yes.

Using the Keyboard

The keyboard is an important tool for entering data and commands. If you're a good typist, you can gain speed in working with AutoCAD by learning how to enter commands from the keyboard. AutoCAD provides what are called alias commands—single keys or key combinations that start any of several frequently used commands. A good example of a command alias that ships with AutoCAD is the LINE command. Of course you could type LINE at the command line to launch the command, but typing the one-character alias L is much quicker and easier. You can add more aliases or change the existing ones as you become more familiar with the program.

In addition to the alias commands, you can use several of the F keys (function keys) on the top row of the keyboard as two-way or three-way toggles to turn AutoCAD functions on and off. Although buttons on the screen duplicate these functions (Snap, Grid, and so on), it's sometimes faster to use the F keys.

While working in AutoCAD, you'll need to enter a lot of data (such as dimensions and construction notes), answer questions with Yes or No, and use the arrow keys. You'll use the keyboard constantly. It might help to get into the habit of keeping your left hand on the keyboard and your right hand on the mouse if you're right-handed, or the other way around if you're left-handed.

Using the Mouse

Your mouse most likely has two buttons and a scroll wheel. So far in this chapter, you have used the left mouse button to choose menus, commands, and options, and you've held it down to drag the Ribbon. The left mouse button is the one you'll be using most often, but you'll also use the right mouse button.

While drawing, you'll use the right mouse button for the following three operations:

▶ To display a menu containing options relevant to the particular step you're in at the moment

▶ To use in combination with the Shift or Ctrl key to display a menu containing special drawing aids called object snaps

▶ To display a menu of toolbars when the pointer is on any icon of a toolbar that is currently open

The middle button with a scroll wheel serves a dual function:

▶ Pressing and holding the middle button enables you to pan throughout your drawing until you release the middle button.

▶ You can zoom in/out within your drawing: When scrolling toward the screen, you zoom into your drawing. Conversely, when scrolling away from the screen, you zoom out from your drawing.

AutoCAD makes extensive use of toolbars and the right-click menu feature. This makes your mouse an important input tool. The keyboard is necessary for inputting numeric data and text, and it has hot keys and aliases that can speed up your work; however, the mouse is the primary tool for selecting options and controlling toolbars.

The next chapter will familiarize you with a few basic commands that will enable you to draw a small diagram. If you want to take a break and close AutoCAD, choose Application menu ➤ Exit AutoCAD (lower-right corner), and choose not to save the drawing.

Are You Experienced?

Now you can...

- ☑ recognize the elements of the AutoCAD Application window
- ☑ understand how the command-line window works and why it's important
- ☑ start commands from the Ribbon
- ☑ start commands from the command line
- ☑ use the Application menu
- ☑ display the drop-down menus
- ☑ open and control the positioning of toolbars
- ☑ save a workspace of your screen setup in AutoCAD

Learning Basic Commands to Get Started

Now that you've taken a quick tour of the AutoCAD and AutoCAD LT screens, you're ready to begin drawing! This chapter introduces you to some basic commands used in drawing with AutoCAD and AutoCAD LT. To get you started, this chapter guides you through the process of drawing a simple shape.

As you create this first drawing, you'll learn to use several essential AutoCAD commands that will serve as a foundation for the rest of this book. First, you'll become familiar with the LINE command and how to draw lines at a specific length. Then I'll go over the strategy for completing the form.

▶ **Understanding coordinate systems**

▶ **Drawing your first object**

▶ **Erasing, offsetting, filleting, extending, and trimming objects in a drawing**

Using the *Line* Command

Essential to all AutoCAD drawings, LINE is the first command you'll explore as you construct the shape shown in Figure 2.1. Whenever starting a brand new drawing in AutoCAD, it's always best to take a step back and consider the object or objects you would like to construct. In this case, the shape shown in Figure 2.1 most closely resembles a square. Applying this basic strategy, you'll begin by defining each of the four sides of the square by using the LINE command, and then build upon this basic shape with several additional commands introduced later in this chapter.

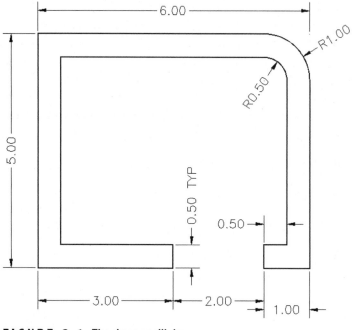

FIGURE 2.1 The shape you'll draw

In traditional architectural drafting, lines were often drawn to extend slightly past their endpoints (see Figure 2.2). Today we have entire applications that can open a CAD drawing and not only apply this effect, but make the image look hand drawn. A popular application for applying such an effect is Autodesk Impression. I won't be covering Autodesk Impression in this book; however, you can visit http://autodesk.com/impression to learn more about it.

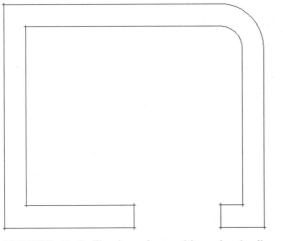

FIGURE 2.2 The shape drawn with overlapping lines

The LINE command draws a straight line segment between locations on existing objects, geometric features, or two points that you can choose anywhere within the drawing area. You can designate these points by left-clicking them on the screen, by entering the x- and y-coordinates for each point, or by entering distances and angles from an existing point. After you draw the first segment of a line, you can end the command or draw another line segment beginning from the end of the previous one. You can continue to draw adjoining line segments for as long as you like. Let's see how this works.

To be sure that you start with your drawing area set up the way it's set up for this book, expand the Application menu (the red A button in the top-left corner of the AutoCAD user interface), and then choose Close ➤ All Drawings to close any open drawings. The Application menu is shown in Figure 2.3.

Like many other Windows-based programs, AutoCAD provides many ways you can close drawings individually as well. The first and perhaps most popular way is to click the X icon in the upper-right corner of any drawing next to the Minimize and Restore icons. The Quick View Drawings feature found on the AutoCAD status bar also features a similar X icon from which drawings may be closed individually. Drawings can also be closed from the Application menu by choosing Close ➤ Current Drawing. Finally, if you're an aspiring keyboard warrior, press Ctrl+F4 (both keys at the same time) to close the current drawing.

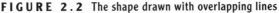

As shown in Figure 2.4, after you no longer have any drawings open, your drawing area becomes a gradient gray and blank with no crosshair cursor. The

Ribbon disappears, and only three buttons remain in the Quick Access toolbar area on the left side of the title bar (along with the three informational buttons in the Quick Access toolbar).

FIGURE 2.3 Use the Application menu to close any open drawings.

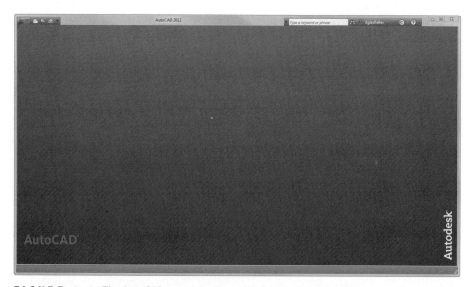

FIGURE 2.4 The AutoCAD user interface without any drawings open

Now follow these steps to begin using the LINE command:

1. Click the New button at the left end of the Quick Access toolbar. In the Select Template dialog box, select the acad.dwt file (acad1t.dwt for LT users), if it's not already selected, and click Open, as shown in Figure 2.5. The menus, crosshair cursor, and toolbars return, and you now have a blank drawing in the drawing area.

N O T E   DWT files are drawing templates with several parameters, such as dimension styles, layers, plotting settings, and more already set.

FIGURE 2.5 Choose the acad.dwt template in the Select Template dialog box.

2. On the left side, some of the tools, such as Object Snap and Dynamic Input, are turned on while others remain off. Make sure that Polar Tracking, Object Snap, Object Snap Tracking, Allow/Disallow Dynamic UCS, and Dynamic Input are turned on and all the others are turned off. You can identify the buttons by pausing over each and exposing its tooltip. Your toolbar should look similar to Figure 2.6.

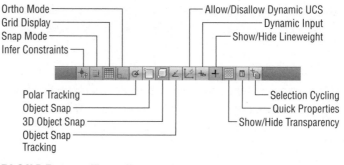

Ortho Mode
Grid Display
Snap Mode
Infer Constraints

Allow/Disallow Dynamic UCS
Dynamic Input
Show/Hide Lineweight

Polar Tracking
Object Snap
3D Object Snap
Object Snap Tracking

Selection Cycling
Quick Properties
Show/Hide Transparency

FIGURE 2.6 The toolbar as it has been set up

3. From the Ribbon, choose the Home tab ➣ Draw panel and then click the Line tool. Look at both the bottom of the command window and your cursor. Because Dynamic Input is turned on, prompts such as this one display both at the Command Line and next to the cursor (see Figure 2.7).

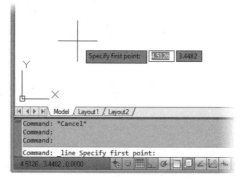

FIGURE 2.7 Both the command prompt and the cursor change to reflect the current command.

T I P You can also start the LINE command by typing LINE or L and pressing the Enter key, spacebar, or the right mouse button.

The prompt now tells you that the LINE command is started (Command: _line) and that AutoCAD is waiting for you to designate the first point of the line (Specify first point:).

4. Move the cursor onto the drawing area, and notice that the small box at the intersection of the crosshairs is not there.

When the cursor is used to select objects (the default condition), the pickbox appears in the cursor. When the cursor is used to designate a point, the pickbox is not visible. Using the left mouse button, click a random point in the drawing area to start a line.

5. Move the cursor away from the point you clicked and notice how a line segment appears that stretches like a rubber band from the point you just picked to the cursor. The line changes length and direction as you move the cursor, and these values are shown as input boxes in the drawing area.

6. Look at the command window again and notice that the prompt has changed (see Figure 2.8).

   The prompt is now telling you that AutoCAD is waiting for you to designate the next point (Specify next point or [Undo]:).

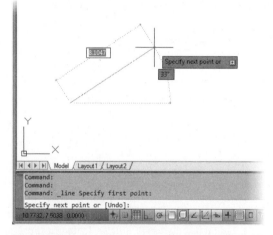

FIGURE 2.8 The command prompt changes for the next point, and the line's length and direction are shown in the drawing area.

7. Continue picking points and adding lines as you move the cursor around the screen (see Figure 2.9).

   After you draw the second segment, the command window repeats the Specify next point or [Close/Undo]: prompt each time you pick another point. The Dynamic Input fields and command prompt appear near the cursor, showing the angle and distance from the last point selected.

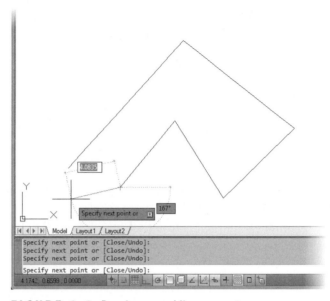

FIGURE 2.9 Drawing several line segments

8. When you've drawn six or seven line segments, press Enter (↵) to end the LINE command. The cursor separates from the last drawn line segment.

    The command prompt has returned to the bottom line. This tells you that no command is currently running.

 T I P   The Enter (↵) key exits the LINE command and several others. Another option is to right-click and choose Enter from the context menu. This may require an extra step, but it may still be faster because your eyes never leave the screen. When you're not entering data, the spacebar also acts like the Enter (↵) key and executes a command.

In this exercise, you used the left mouse button to click the Line tool on the Ribbon and also to pick several points in the drawing area to make the line segments. You then pressed Enter (↵) on the keyboard to end the LINE command.

 N O T E   In the exercises that follow, the Enter symbol (↵) is used. When I say to *type* or *enter* something, it means to type the data that follows the word *type* or *enter* and then to press the Enter key (↵). For example, rather than writing *type L and press the Enter key*, I'll write *type L↵*. Finally, although I'll capitalize the names of AutoCAD commands, be aware that commands are not case sensitive and may be entered however you wish.

Using Coordinates

A *coordinate system* consists of numbered scales that identify an initial, or base, point and the direction for measuring subsequent points on a graph. The *Cartesian Coordinate System*, named after the philosopher René Descartes, who defined the xy-coordinate system in the 1600s, consists of three numbered scales, called the x-axis, y-axis, and z-axis, that are perpendicular to each other and extend infinitely in each direction. As illustrated in Figure 2.10, each pair of axes (xy, xz, yz) forms a flat plane. Most of your time using AutoCAD will be spent drawing in the xy-plane.

The point where the scales intersect is called the *origin*. For each axis, all values on one side of the origin are positive, all values on the other side are negative, and values that fall in line with the origin have a value of 0 (zero). The divisions along the scales may be any size, but each division must be equal.

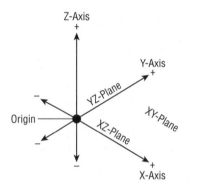

FIGURE 2.10 The x-, y-, and z-axes and the related xy-, xz-, and yz-planes

The axes divide the coordinate system into four regions called *quadrants*. Quadrant I is the region above the x-axis and to the right of the y-axis. Quadrant II is the region above the x-axis and to the left of the y-axis. Quadrant III is the region below the x-axis and to the left of the y-axis. Quadrant IV is the region below the x-axis and to the right of the y-axis. Most of your work in AutoCAD will be done in Quadrant I, and this is the area shown when you first open a drawing.

Any point on a graph can be specified by giving its coordinates relative to the origin, indicated as a combination of the X value and the Y value delineated with a comma. For example, a coordinate of 5,7 means a point on the coordinate system that is 5 units in the positive X direction and 7 units is the positive

Y direction. Figure 2.11 shows a typical Cartesian Coordinate System and the default region used as the drawing area in a new AutoCAD file.

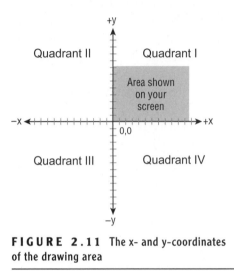

FIGURE 2.11 The x- and y-coordinates of the drawing area

N O T E   AutoCAD displays a readout for the z-coordinate as well, but you can ignore it for now because you'll be working in only two dimensions for the majority of this book. The z-coordinate always reads 0 until you work in three dimensions. (This is covered in later chapters.) AutoCAD LT doesn't have the readout for the z-coordinate because it doesn't have 3D capabilities.

In this next exercise, you'll try using the LINE command again, but instead of picking points in the drawing area with the mouse as you did before, this time enter the x- and y-coordinates for each point from the keyboard. To see how to do this, follow these steps:

1. Click the Erase button from the Home tab ➢ Modify Ribbon panel.

2. Type **ALL**↵. The objects in the drawing become dashed to indicate that they are selected.

3. Press ↵ to clear the screen.

4. Click the Dynamic Input button in the Command Line to turn off this feature. The button changes to a gray background.

Now begin drawing lines again by following these steps:

1. Start the LINE command by clicking the Line button from the Home tab ➢ Draw panel on the Ribbon.

> You can also start the ERASE command by typing E↵.

2. Type **7,2**↵ to start the first line segment at a location 7 units above and 2 units to the right of the drawing's origin point.

3. Type **11,3**↵ to determine the endpoint of the line. Then enter the following:

    9,6↵

    7,2↵

    1,4↵

    3,7↵

    9,6↵

4. Press ↵ again to end the command.

    Figure 2.12 shows the completed drawing, with coordinates and direction arrows added for clarity.

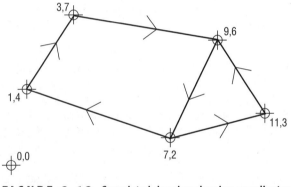

FIGURE 2.12 Completed drawing showing coordinates and direction of lines

The lines are similar to those you drew previously, but this time you know where each point is located relative to the 0,0 point. In the drawing area, every point has an absolute x- and y-coordinate. In steps 2 through 4, you entered the x- and y-coordinates for each point. For a new drawing such as this one, the origin (0,0 coordinate) is in the lower-left corner of the drawing area, and all points in the drawing area have positive x- and y-coordinates.

Let's explore how the cursor is related to the coordinates in the drawing.

1. Click the Zoom Extents button located on the navigation bar (the semitransparent vertical bar under the ViewCube), or type **ZOOM**↵ **E**↵ to adjust your view to show the extents of the drawing area.

2. Move the cursor around, and notice the left end of the status bar at the bottom of the screen. This is the coordinate readout, and it displays the coordinates of the cursor's position, as shown in Figure 2.13.

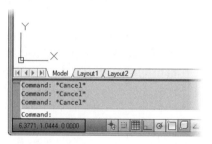

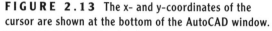

FIGURE 2.13 The x- and y-coordinates of the cursor are shown at the bottom of the AutoCAD window.

3. Move the cursor as close to the lower-left corner of the drawing area as you can without it changing into an arrow. The coordinate readout should be close to 0.0000, 0.0000, 0.0000.

4. Move the cursor to the top-left corner of the drawing area. The readout changes to something close to 0.0000, 7.0000, 0.0000, indicating that the top of the screen is 7 units from the bottom.

5. Move the cursor one more time to the upper-right corner of the drawing area. The readout still has a y-coordinate of approximately 7.0000. The x-coordinate now has a value around 10.5.

The drawing area of a new drawing is preset with the lower-left corner of the drawing at the coordinates 0,0.

N O T E   For the moment, it doesn't matter what measure of distance these units represent. I address that topic in Chapter 3, "Setting Up a Drawing." Don't worry about the four decimal places in the coordinate readout; the number of places is controlled by a setting you'll learn about soon.

Using Relative Coordinates

Once you understand the coordinate system used by AutoCAD, you can draw lines to any length and in any direction. Look at the shape shown earlier in Figure 2.1. Because you know the dimensions, you can calculate (by adding and subtracting) the absolute coordinates for each vertex—the connecting point between two line segments—and then use the LINE command to draw the shape by entering these coordinates from the keyboard. However, AutoCAD offers you several tools for drawing this box much more easily. Two of these tools are the Relative Cartesian and the Relative Polar Coordinate Systems.

When you're drawing lines, these coordinate systems use a set of new points based on the last point designated, rather than on the 0,0 point of the drawing area. They're called *relative* systems because the coordinates used are relative to the last point specified. If the first point of a line is located at the coordinate 4,6 and you want the line to extend 8 units to the right, the coordinate that is relative to the first point is 8,0 (8 units in the positive X direction and 0 units in the positive Y direction), whereas the actual—or *absolute*—coordinate of the second point is 12,6.

The Relative Cartesian Coordinate System uses relative x- and y-coordinates in the manner shown, and the Relative Polar Coordinate System relies on a distance and an angle relative to the last point specified. You'll probably favor one system over the other, but you need to know both systems because you'll sometimes find that, given the information you have at hand, one will work better than the other. A limitation of this nature is illustrated in Chapter 4, "Developing Drawing Strategies: Part 1."

When the Dynamic Input tool is turned off, you'll need to prefix the coordinate with an *at* symbol (@). In the previous example, you would enter the relative Cartesian coordinates as **@8,0**. The @ lets AutoCAD know that the numbers following it represent coordinates that are relative to the last point designated. When the Dynamic Input tool is turned on, relative coordinates are assumed, and the @ symbol is not required.

Relative Cartesian Coordinates

The Cartesian system of coordinates uses a horizontal (x) component and a vertical (y) component to locate a point relative to the 0,0 point. The relative Cartesian system uses the same components to locate the point relative to the last point picked, so it's a way of telling AutoCAD how far left or right, and up or down, to extend a line or to move an object from the last point picked (see Figure 2.14). If the direction is to the left, the x-coordinate will be negative. Similarly, if the direction is down, the y-coordinate will be negative. Use this system when you know the horizontal and vertical distances from point 1 to point 2. To enter data using this system, use this form: **@x,y**.

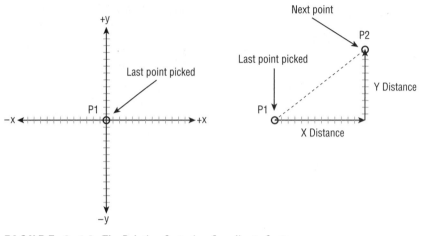

FIGURE 2.14 The Relative Cartesian Coordinate System

Relative Polar Coordinates

The Relative Polar Coordinate System requires a known distance and direction from one point to the next. Calculating the distance is straightforward: it's always positive and represents the distance away from the first point that the second point will be placed. The direction requires a convention for determining an angle. AutoCAD defines right (toward three o'clock) as the default direction of the 0° angle. All other directions are determined from a counterclockwise rotation (see Figure 2.15). On your screen, up is 90°, left is 180°, down is 270°, and a full circle is 360°. To let AutoCAD know that you're entering an angle and not a relative y-coordinate, use the less-than symbol (<) before the angle and after the distance. Therefore, in the previous example, to designate a point 8 units to the right of the first point, you would enter **@8<0** or simply **8<0** when the Dynamic Input tool is active.

 N O T E   Use the Relative Polar Coordinate System to draw a line from the first point when you know the distance and direction to its next point. Enter data using this form: *@distance<angle*.

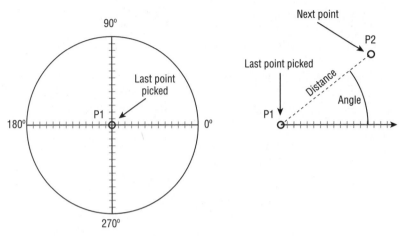

FIGURE 2.15 The Relative Polar Coordinate System

Using the Direct Distance Method

You can also draw lines by placing the cursor at any angle relative to the last point and entering a distance value at the command prompt. The line is drawn from the last point toward or through the cursor location at the length specified. The Direct Distance method is often used when either Ortho mode or Polar Tracking is turned on.

 N O T E   When in a drawing command, Ortho mode restricts the cursor to horizontal or vertical movements. Lines, for example, can be drawn only at 0°, 90°, 180°, and 270°. Ortho mode is toggled on by using the Ortho Mode button at the bottom of the user interface (UI) or by pressing the F8 key.

Drawing the Shape

Now that you have the basics, the following exercises will take you through the steps to draw the four lines that form the outline of the shape using both relative coordinate systems.

Relative Cartesian Coordinates

drawing the box, use the same drawing:

If your drawing is already blank, jump to step 2. If you still have lines on your drawing, start the ERASE command, type **ALL**↵, and then press ↵ again to delete them.

2. Start the LINE command by choosing Home tab ➤ Draw panel ➤ Line.

3. At the Specify first point: prompt in the command window, type **3,3**↵. This is an absolute Cartesian coordinate and will be the first point.

4. Type **@6,0**↵.

5. Type **@0,5**↵.

6. Turn on the Dynamic Input tool in the status bar and, if necessary, scroll the mouse wheel to zoom out to see the extents of the lines.

7. Type **-6,0**↵. Notice that because Dynamic Input is turned on, the @ symbol is no longer required to input relative coordinates.

8. Look at the command prompt. It reads Specify next point or [Close/Undo]:. Items enclosed in brackets are additional available options at that particular point of the command that can be entered at the command prompt. Only the capitalized letters are required to execute an option.

9. Type **C**↵ to execute the Close option.

Typing this letter after drawing two or more lines closes the shape by extending the next line segment from the last point specified to the first point (see Figure 2.16). It also ends the LINE command. Notice that in the command window, the prompt is Command:. This signifies that AutoCAD is ready for a new command.

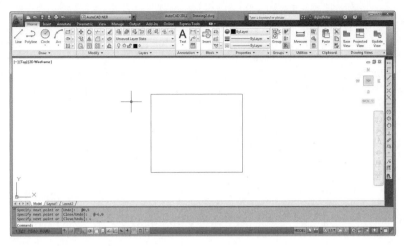

FIGURE 2.16 The first four lines of the box

Erasing Lines

To prepare to draw the box again, use the ERASE command to erase the four
lines you just drew:

 1. Start the ERASE command by choosing Home tab ➤ Modify panel ➤
Erase tool.

   Notice how the cursor changes from the crosshair to a little square.
This is called the *pickbox*. Its appearance indicates that AutoCAD is
ready for you to select objects on the screen. Also notice the command
window; it's prompting you to select objects.

2. Place the pickbox on one of the lines, and click that line when it highlights. The line changes to a dashed line to indicate that it is selected.

3. Repeat step 2 for the remaining lines.

4. Press ↵. The objects are erased, and the ERASE command ends.

N O T E   You've been introduced to two methods of selecting lines to be erased: typing ALL↵ and using the pickbox to select them. Throughout the book, you'll learn other ways to select objects. The selection process is important in AutoCAD because you need to be able to select objects quickly and precisely.

Controlling How the Selection Tools Are Displayed

When you move the cursor over an object, AutoCAD highlights the object. This is called rollover highlighting. It tells you that clicking while the object is highlighted selects that object. You have some choices as to how this highlighting appears:

1. In the Application menu, click the Options button at the bottom (Application menu ➤ Options) to open the Options dialog box.

2. Click the Selection tab.

Notice the Selection Preview group at the bottom of the left side (see Figure 2.17, left). Here you can activate or deactivate the check boxes to control whether rollover highlighting occurs when a command is running or when no command is running. If both check boxes are selected, the feature works all the time.

FIGURE 2.17 The Selection Preview group of the Selection tab in the Options dialog box (left) and the Visual Effect Settings dialog box (right)

3. Click the Visual Effect Settings button below the check boxes to open the Visual Effect Settings dialog box (see Figure 2.17, right).

There are two groups: Selection Preview Effect and Area Selection Effect. The Selection Preview Effect group controls how the rollover highlighting feature is displayed. Lines can dash, lines can thicken, and lines can both dash and thicken, depending on which radio button is selected.

4. Make any changes you want and then click OK. Back in the Options dialog box, click OK to return to your drawing.

> Feel free to experiment with these settings until you find a combination that works for you.

Using Relative Polar Coordinates

Now draw the shape again using the Relative Polar method by following these steps:

1. Start the LINE command by choosing Home tab ➢ Draw panel ➢ Line tool.

2. Type 3,3↵ to start the box at the same point.

3. Type 6<0↵. Because the Dynamic Input tool is turned on, the @ symbol is not required.

4. Type 5<90↵.

5. Type 6<180↵.

6. Type C↵ to close the box and end the LINE command. Your box once again resembles the box shown earlier in Figure 2.16.

You can see from this exercise that you can use either method to draw a simple shape. When the shapes you're drawing become more complex and the amount of available information about the shapes varies from segment to segment, one of the two relative coordinate systems will turn out to be more appropriate. As you start drawing the floor plan of the cabin in Chapters 3 and 4, you'll get more practice using these systems.

Using Direct Input

Now draw the box once more, this time using the Direct Input method by following these steps:

1. Erase the lines in your drawing as you did in a prior exercise (Home tab ➢ Modify panel ➢ Erase tool).

2. Make sure Polar Tracking is turned on; then start the LINE command.

3. Type **3,3⏎** to start the box at the same point.

4. Place the cursor so that it is directly to the right of the first point.
   When the cursor is nearly perpendicular, it will snap to a perfectly horizontal orientation. The Dynamic Input field shows a value of 0° and the distance from the first point, as shown in Figure 2.18.

FIGURE 2.18 Drawing a line by using the Direct Input method

5. Type **6⏎**. The first line is created, extending from the initial point to a point 6 units away at an angle of 0°. Notice that the @ symbol is not required when using direct input.

6. Move the cursor so that it is directly above the last point until the angle field reads 90°; then type **5⏎**. A vertical line 5 units long is drawn from the previous point.

7. Move the cursor so that it is directly to the left of the end of the last line drawn and then type **6⏎**.
   A horizontal line 6 units long is drawn from the previous point. Even though the line is drawn in the negative X direction, the minus sign (negative indicator) is not required. Because Dynamic Input was turned on, the minus sign was implied based on the location of your cursor. In other words, AutoCAD drew the line in the direction your cursor was located.

8. Type **C⏎** to close the box and end the LINE command. Your box once again resembles the box shown in Figure 2.16 earlier.

You can see from these exercises that you can use multiple methods to draw a simple shape. Showing so many methods may seem a little redundant at this point; however, as the shapes you draw become more complex and the amount of available information about the shapes varies from segment to segment, you'll likely begin choosing one method or another based on the information available to you. As you start drawing the floor plan of the cabin in Chapters 3 and 4, you'll get more practice applying these methods to more realistic scenarios, and you'll probably begin establishing the methods that work best for you.

Some additional tools make the process of drawing simple, orthogonal lines like these much easier. I introduce these tools in the following three chapters.

Using the *Offset* Command

The next task is to create the lines that represent the inside walls of the box. Because they're all equidistant from the lines you've already drawn, the OFFSET command is the appropriate command to use. You'll offset the existing lines 0.5 units to the inside.

The OFFSET command involves three steps:

1. Setting the offset distance (Specify offset distance)

2. Selecting the object to offset (Select object to offset)

3. Indicating the offset direction (Specify point on side to offset)

Here's how it works:

1. Be sure the prompt line in the command window reads Command:. If it doesn't, press the Esc key until it does. Then launch the OFFSET command by choosing the Home tab ➢ Modify panel ➢ Offset tool.

   The prompt changes to Specify offset distance or [Through/Erase/Layer] <Through>:. This is a confusing prompt, but it will become clear soon. For now, let's specify an offset distance through the keyboard.

You can also start the OFFSET command by typing O↵.

W A R N I N G   As important as it is to keep an eye on the command window, some prompts may not make sense to you until you get used to them. When using the Dynamic Input option, notice that the command prompt also appears at the cursor.

---

2. Type **0.5**↵ for a distance to offset the lines ½ unit.

   Now you move to the second stage of the command. Note that the cursor changes to a pickbox, and the prompt changes to Select object to offset or [Exit/Undo] <Exit>:.

3. Place the pickbox on one of the lines, and click the line when it highlights.

   The selected line appears dashed to indicate that it is selected (see Figure 2.19), the cursor changes back to the crosshair, and the prompt changes to Specify point on side to offset or [Exit/Multiple/Undo] <Exit>:.

   AutoCAD is telling you that to determine the direction of the offset, you must specify a point on one side of the line or the other.

You make the choice by selecting anywhere in the drawing area on the side of the line where you want the offset to occur.

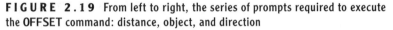

FIGURE 2.19 From left to right, the series of prompts required to execute the OFFSET command: distance, object, and direction

4. Click a point somewhere inside the box (you don't have to be precise, just so long as you select a point inside the box).

   The offset takes place, and the new line is exactly 0.5 units to the inside of the chosen line (see Figure 2.20). Notice that the pickbox comes back on. The OFFSET command is still running, and you can offset more lines by the same distance.

FIGURE 2.20 The first line is offset.

You have three more lines to offset.

5. Click another line; then click inside the box again. The second line is offset.

6. Click a third line, click inside the box; click the fourth line, and then click again inside the box (see Figure 2.21).

7. Press ↵ to end the OFFSET command.

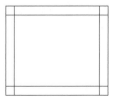

FIGURE 2.21 Four lines have been offset.

N O T E   The offset distance stays set at the last distance you specify—
0.5, in this case—until you change it.

This command is similar to the LINE command in that it keeps running until
it's stopped. With OFFSET, after the first offset, the prompts switch between Select
object to offset or [Exit/Undo] <Exit>: and Specify point on side to
offset or [Exit/Multiple/Undo] <Exit>: until you press ↵ or the spacebar
to end the command.

The inside lines are now drawn, but to complete the box, you need to clean up
the intersecting corners. To handle this task efficiently, you'll use the FILLET
command.

You can cancel a
command at any time
by pressing Esc or
by right-clicking and
choosing Cancel from
the context menu.

SPECIFYING DISTANCES FOR THE *OFFSET* COMMAND

The prompt you see in the command window after starting the OFFSET
command is:

Specify offset distance or [Through/Erase/Layer] <Through>:

This prompt describes several options for setting the offset distance:

▶ Enter a distance from the keyboard.

▶ Select two points on the screen to establish the offset distance as the
distance between those two points.

▶ Press ↵ to accept the offset distance or option that is displayed in the
prompt in the angle brackets.

▶ Type T↵ to use the Through option. When you select this option,
you're prompted to select the line to offset. You're then prompted to
pick a point. The line will be offset to that point. When you pick the
next line to offset, you then pick a new point to locate the position
of the new line. The Through option allows each line to be offset a
different distance.

▶ Type E↵, and then type Y↵ to tell AutoCAD to erase the original line
that was offset. (After doing this, however, AutoCAD continues erasing offset lines until you reset it by typing E↵ N↵ at the beginning
of the OFFSET command.)

▶ Type L↵ to use the Layer option. (I discuss this option in Chapter 6,
"Using Layers to Organize Your Drawing.")

As you become accustomed to using OFFSET, you'll find uses for each of
these options.

Using the *Fillet* Command

The FILLET command lets you round off a corner formed by two lines. You control the radius of the curve, so if you set the curve's radius to zero, the lines form a sharp corner (without a curve/arc). Thanks to this behavior of the FILLET command, it is commonly used to clean up corners such as the ones formed by the lines inside the box. You must pick points on the filleted lines to indicate portions that will remain after the fillet is implemented; otherwise, the wrong portion of the line may be retained. Figure 2.22 illustrates how to use the FILLET command to achieve the desired result.

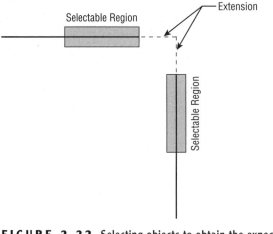

FIGURE 2.22 Selecting objects to obtain the expected result when using the FILLET command

You can also start the FILLET command by typing F↵.

🗋 Fillet **1.** When the Command Line just reads Command:, launch the FILLET command by choosing the Home tab ➢ Modify panel ➢ Fillet tool. Notice how the command window changes after you've clicked the Fillet button (see Figure 2.23).

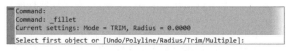
```
Command:
Command: _fillet
Current settings: Mode = TRIM, Radius = 0.0000
Select first object or [Undo/Polyline/Radius/Trim/Multiple]:
```

FIGURE 2.23 The command prompt after initiating the FILLET command

The default Fillet radius should be 0.0000 units. Like the Offset distance, the Fillet radius remains set at a constant value until you change it.

2. If your command window displays a radius of 0.0000, go on to step 3. Otherwise, type **R↵**, and then type **0↵** to change the radius to 0.

T I P   When the radius value is set higher than 0, you can temporarily override this by holding the Shift key down while picking the two objects to be filleted. They will be filleted with a radius of 0, while the value set in the FILLET command remains unchanged.

3. Move the cursor—now a pickbox—to the shape, and click two intersecting lines, as shown at the top of Figure 2.24. New in AutoCAD 2012, hovering over the second line (Figure 2.24, bottom) causes an intersection icon to appear where the fillet will occur.

The intersecting lines are both trimmed to make a sharp corner (see Figure 2.25). The FILLET command automatically ends.

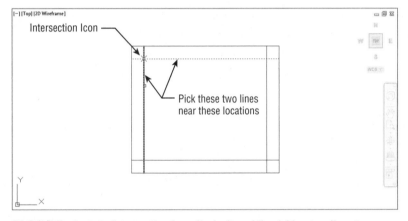

FIGURE 2.24 Intersection icon displaying while picking two lines to execute the FILLET command.

---

4. Press ↵ to restart the command, and this time type **M↵** to activate the Multiple option. Multiple repeats the FILLET command until another option is initiated at the command prompt or the command is terminated with the ↵ or Esc keys or the spacebar.

5. Fillet the lower-left and lower-right crossing lines to clean up those corners (see Figure 2.26) and press ↵.

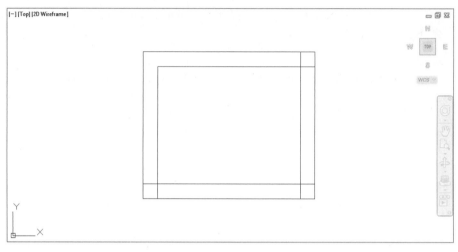

FIGURE 2.25 The first cleaned-up corner

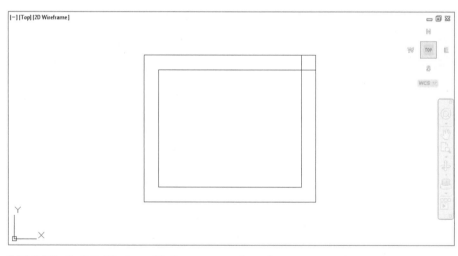

FIGURE 2.26 The box with three corners cleaned up

After a command has ended, you can restart it by pressing either ↵ or the spacebar or by right-clicking and choosing Repeat from the context menu.

T I P   In most cases, you'll get the same effect by pressing the spacebar as you get by pressing ↵. The exception is when you're entering data in a text box within a dialog box or a palette; in those cases, pressing the spacebar inserts a space.

6. Press ↵ to restart the FILLET command. This time, type **R**↵ **0.5**↵ to set the fillet radius to 0.5, and then click the two lines that make up the interior upper-right corner.

NEW

As you hover over the second line to fillet, notice the real-ti unit fillet preview that displays.

7. Restart the command, set the radius to **1.0**, and then fillet t upper-right corner. Your box should look like Figure 2.27.

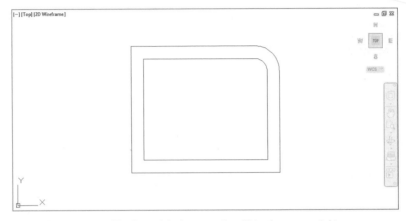

F I G U R E 2 . 2 7 The box with the curved radii in the upper-right corner

---

N O T E   If you make a mistake and pick the wrong part of a line or the wrong line, press Esc to end the command and then type U⌐. This will undo the effect of the last command.

Used together like this, the OFFSET and FILLET commands are a powerful combination of tools for laying out walls on a floor plan drawing. Because these commands are so important, let's take a closer look at them to see how they work. Both commands are in the Modify panel of the Ribbon and in the Modify menu of the menu bar, both have the option to enter a numeric value or accept the current value—for offset distance and fillet radius—and both hold that value as the default until it's changed. However, the OFFSET command keeps running until you stop it, and the FILLET command stops after each use unless the Multiple option is invoked. These commands are two of the most frequently used tools in AutoCAD. You'll learn about more of their uses in later chapters.

The FILLET command has a sister command, *CHAMFER*, which is used to bevel corners with straight lines. When the distances for the CHAMFER command are set to 0, you can use the command to clean up corners the same way that you use the FILLET command. Some users prefer to use CHAMFER rather than FILLET because they don't bevel corners, but they may at times use FILLET to round off corners. If you use CHAMFER to clean up corners, FILLET can have any radius

◄

The down-pointing arrow next to the Fillet tool opens a fly-out menu that includes the Chamfer tool.

and won't have to be overridden or reset constantly to 0. You'll develop your own preference.

Completing the Shape

The final step in completing the box (Figure 2.1 from the beginning of this chapter) is to make an opening in the bottom wall. From the diagram, you can see that the opening is 2 units wide and set off from the right inside corner by 0.5 units. To make this opening, you'll use the OFFSET command twice, changing the distance for each offset, to create marks for the opening.

Offsetting Lines to Mark an Opening

Follow these steps to establish the precise position of the opening:

1. At the command prompt, start the OFFSET command (Home tab ➢ Modify panel ➢ Offset tool).

   Notice the command window. The default distance is now set at 0.5, the offset distance you previously set to offset the outside lines of the box to make the inside lines. If the distance is different, type 0.5↵. You'll want to use this distance again. Press ↵ again to accept this preset distance.

2. Pick a point inside the vertical line on the right, and then pick a point to the left of this line. The line is offset, creating a new line 0.5 units to the left (see Figure 2.28).

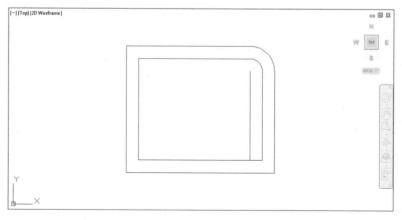

FIGURE 2.28 Offsetting the first line of the opening

3. Press ⏎ to end the OFFSET command, and then press it again to restart the command. This will allow you to reset the offset distance.

4. Enter **2** as the new offset distance and then press ⏎.

5. Click the new line and then pick a point to the left. Press ⏎ to end the OFFSET command (see Figure 2.29).

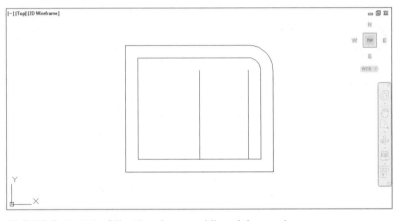

FIGURE 2.29 Offsetting the second line of the opening

You now have two new lines indicating where the opening will be. You can use these lines to form the opening when using the EXTEND and TRIM commands.

T I P   The buttons you've been clicking in this chapter are also referred to as *icons* and *tools*. When they're in dialog boxes or on the status bar, they have icons (little pictures) on them and look like buttons to push. When they're on the Ribbon or toolbars, they look like icons. But when you move the pointer arrow cursor onto one, it takes on the appearance of a button with an icon on it. I use all three terms—button, icon, and tool—interchangeably throughout this book.

Extending Lines

The EXTEND command is used to lengthen (extend) lines to meet other lines or geometric figures (called boundary edges). Executing the EXTEND command may be a little tricky at first until you see how it works. Once you understand it, however, it will become automatic. The command has two steps: First, you pick the boundary edge or edges; second, you pick the lines you want to extend to meet those boundary edges. After selecting the boundary edges, you must press ↵ before you begin selecting lines to extend. Here are the steps:

1. Launch the EXTEND command by choosing Home tab ➢ Modify panel ➢ Extend tool. If you don't see the tool, click the down-arrow next to the Trim icon and then choose Extend from the fly-out menu.

   Notice in the command window that the bottom line reads Select objects or <select all>:, but in this case you need to observe the bottom two lines of text in order to know that AutoCAD is prompting you to select boundary edges (see Figure 2.30).

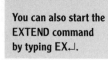

> You can also start the EXTEND command by typing EX↵.

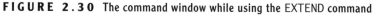

FIGURE 2.30 The command window while using the EXTEND command

2. Pick the very bottom horizontal line (see Figure 2.31) and then press ↵.

FIGURE 2.31 Selecting a line to be a boundary edge

TIP The Select Objects: prompt would be more useful if it read Select objects and press Enter when finished selecting objects:. But it doesn't. You have to train yourself to press ↵ when you finish selecting objects in order to get out of Selection mode and move on to the next step in the command.

3. Pick the two new vertical lines created by the OFFSET command. Be sure to place the pickbox somewhere on the lower halves of these lines, or AutoCAD will attempt to extend the opposite ends of the lines.

   Because there are no boundary edges that could intersect with extensions from the top end of the lines, AutoCAD will ignore your picks if you select the wrong ends. The lines are extended to the boundary edge line.

4. Press ↵ to end the EXTEND command (see Figure 2.32).

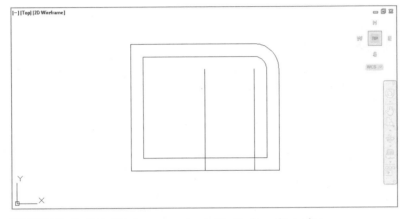

FIGURE 2.32 The lines are extended to the boundary edge.

Trimming Lines

The final step is to trim away the horizontal lines to complete the opening and the unneeded portions of the two most recent vertical lines that you offset. To do this, you use the TRIM command. Like the EXTEND command, TRIM has two steps. The first is to select reference lines. In this case, they're called cutting edges because they determine the edge or edges to which a line is trimmed. The second step is to pick the lines that are to be trimmed. Also like the EXTEND command, TRIM lets you select the objects individually or use one of the many other object selection methods found inside AutoCAD. In this lesson, you'll have a chance to try out one of these methods, known as the Fence method:

1. Choose the Home tab ➤ Modify panel, click the down-arrow next to the Extend button, and then choose Trim from the fly-out menu. This launches the TRIM command.

   Notice the command window. Similar to the EXTEND command, the bottom line prompts you to select objects or select everything in the drawing, but the second line up tells you to select cutting edges.

You can also start the TRIM command by typing TR↵.

2. Pick the two vertical offset lines that were just extended as your cutting edges, and then press ↵ (see Figure 2.33).

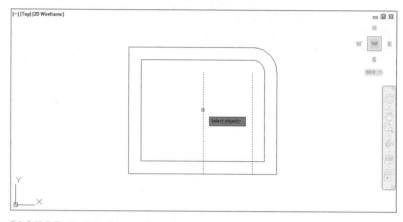

FIGURE 2.33 Lines selected to be cutting edges

3. Notice that the Command Line reads Select object to trim or shift-select to extend or [Fence/Crossing/Project/Edge/eRase/Undo]:. Type **F** to start Fence mode.

4. Your Command Line now reads Specify first fence point:. Using the Fence method, you will draw an imaginary line through the objects you want to trim. Use your cursor to draw a line that crosses the two horizontal lines across the opening, somewhere between the cutting edge lines (see Figure 2.34).

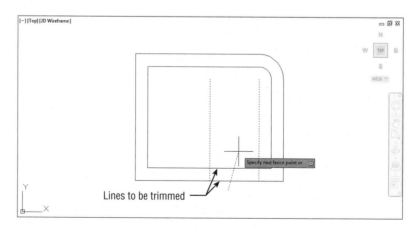

Lines to be trimmed ——

FIGURE 2.34 Lines selected to be trimmed

N O T E   Note that in these trimming procedures, the endpoints of the cutting edge lines, as well as the lines themselves, are used as cutting edges.

The opening is trimmed away (see Figure 2.35).

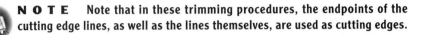
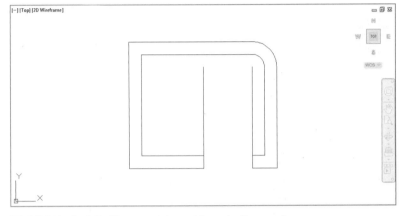

F I G U R E 2 . 3 5 Lines are trimmed to make the opening.

 N O T E   If you trim the wrong line, or the wrong part of a line, you can click the Undo button on the Quick Access toolbar, on the left side of the AutoCAD title bar. This undoes the last trim without canceling the TRIM command, and you can try again.

Now let's remove the extra part of the trimming guidelines:

1. Press ↵ twice—once to end the TRIM command and again to restart it. The Command Line asks you to Select objects or <select all>.

2. Instead of selecting your cutting edges manually, you can press ↵ once again. Doing this accepts the default <select all> option listed at the Command Line. Using this method, every object in your drawing will be treated as a cutting edge.

3. Pick the two vertical lines that extend above the new opening. Be sure to pick them above the opening (see Figure 2.36). The lines are trimmed away, and the opening is complete. Press ↵ to end the TRIM command (see Figure 2.37).

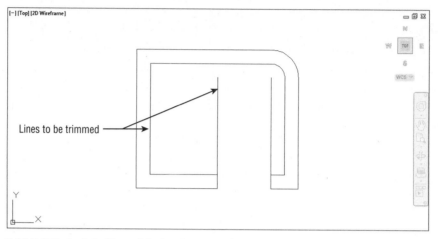

Lines to be trimmed

FIGURE 2.36 Lines picked to be trimmed

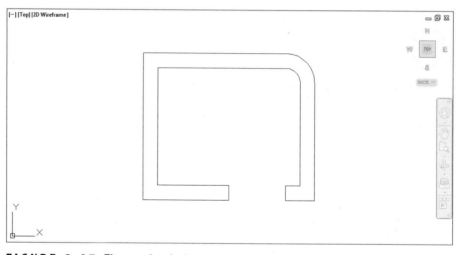

FIGURE 2.37 The completed trim

Congratulations! You've just completed the first drawing project in this book and you've covered all the tools in this chapter. These skills will be useful as you learn how to work on drawings for actual projects.

N O T E   You can check your finished shape by comparing it to Chapter02 Shape Completed.dwg, which is available from the book's website at www.sybex.com/go/autocad2012ner.

A valuable exercise at this time would be to draw this box two or three more times, until you can do it without the instructions. This will be a confidence-builder to get you ready to take on new information in the next chapter, in which you'll set up a drawing for a building.

The box you drew was 6 units by 5 units, but how big was it? You really don't know at this time because the units could represent any actual distance: inches, feet, meters, miles, and so on. Also, the box was positioned conveniently on the screen so you didn't have any problem viewing it. What if you were drawing a building that was 200 feet (60.96 meters) long and 60 feet (18.29 meters) wide or a portion of a microchip circuit that was only a few thousandths of an inch or millimeters long? In the next chapter, you'll learn how to set up a drawing for a project of a specific size.

You can save the file by clicking the Save button on the Quick Access toolbar or you can exit AutoCAD now without saving this drawing. To do the latter, expand the Application menu and then click the Exit AutoCAD button in the lower-right corner. When the dialog box asks whether you want to save changes, click No. Alternatively, you can leave AutoCAD open and go on to the following practice section or the next chapter.

If You Would Like More Practice...

Draw the object shown in Figure 2.38.

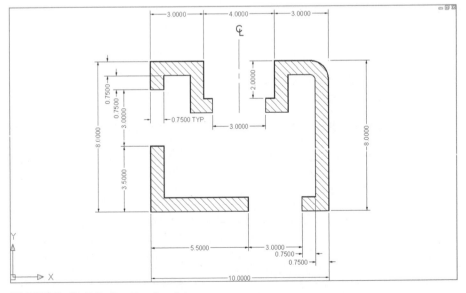

FIGURE 2.38 Practice drawing

You can use the same tools and strategy from earlier in this chapter to draw the shape. Choose New from the Application menu (Application menu ➤ New ➤ Drawing) to start a new drawing, and then use the acad.dwt template file. Here's a summary of the steps to follow:

1. Ignore the three openings at first.

2. Draw the outside edge of the shape by using one of the relative coordinate systems. To make sure the shape fits on your screen, start the outline of the box in the lower-left corner at the absolute coordinate of **1,0.5**.

3. Offset the outside lines to create the inside wall.

4. Fillet the corners to clean them up. (Lines that aren't touching can be filleted just like lines that intersect.)

5. Use the OFFSET, EXTEND, and TRIM commands to create the three openings.

Feel free to check your work against Chapter02 More Practice Completed.dwg on this book's web page. Don't worry about trying to put in the dimensions, center line, or hatch lines. You'll learn how to create those objects later in the book.

Are You Experienced?

Now you can...

- ☑ **understand the basics of coordinates**

- ☑ **distinguish between absolute and the two relative coordinate systems used by AutoCAD**

- ☑ **input coordinates by using the Direct Input method**

- ☑ **use the LINE, ERASE, OFFSET, FILLET, EXTEND, and TRIM commands to create a drawing**

Setting Up a Drawing

In Chapter 2, "Learning Basic Commands to Get Started," you explored the default drawing area that is set up when you open AutoCAD and start a new drawing. Using an assortment of common commands, you drew a box within the drawing area. If you drew the additional diagram offered as a supplemental exercise, the drawing area was set up the same way.

In this chapter, you'll learn how to set up the drawing area to lay out a floor plan for a building of a specific size. The decimal units with which you have been drawing until now will be changed to feet and inches, and the drawing area will be transformed so that it can represent an area large enough to display the floor plan of the cabin you'll be drawing.

As you learn to set up your drawing, you'll also begin exploring ways to navigate your drawing more easily, draw lines at a specified incremental distance (such as the nearest foot), and more. Finally, you'll save this drawing to a special folder on your hard drive. At the end of the chapter is a general summary of the various kinds of units that AutoCAD supports.

Whether or not you work in architecture, the tools you'll use and the skills you'll learn in this chapter will translate into nearly any discipline, enabling you to draw objects of any shape or size.

▶ **Setting up drawing units**

▶ **Using AutoCAD's grid**

▶ **Zooming in and out of a drawing**

▶ **Naming and saving a file**

Setting Up the Drawing Units

When you draw lines of a precise length in AutoCAD, you use one of five kinds of linear units. Angular units can also be any of five types. The combination you choose will largely depend on the type of drawings you plan to prepare. I present each of these linear and angular units at the end of this chapter, but for now let's focus on getting ready to begin drawing our cabin.

When you first start a new drawing, AutoCAD displays a blank drawing called Drawing#.dwg. By default, the linear and angular units inside this drawing are set to decimal numbers. The units and other basic setup parameters applied to this new drawing are based on a prototype drawing with default settings—including those for the units. This chapter covers some of the tools for changing the basic parameters of a new drawing so that you can tailor it to the cabin project or your own project. Begin by setting up new units:

N O T E   To get started with the steps in this chapter, check to be sure each of the status bar buttons except Dynamic Input are clicked to the off position—that is, they appear unpushed and with a gray background. Also make sure you are in model space by clicking the Quick View Layouts ➤ Model view found on the status bar. Later chapters introduce several additional status bar tools, and in Chapter 10, "Generating Elevations," you'll see how to use templates to set up drawings.

> If the Select Template dialog box doesn't appear after you click New from the Quick Access toolbar, choose Application menu ➤ New ➤ Drawing.

1. With AutoCAD running, close all drawings and then click the New button (on the Quick Access toolbar) to start a new drawing.

2. In the Select Template dialog box, select the acad.dwt template (see Figure 3.1), and then click Open to start a new drawing.

3. Choose Application menu ➤ Drawing Utilities ➤ Units to open the Drawing Units dialog box (UNITS command) shown in Figure 3.2. In the Length group, Decimal is currently selected. Similarly, in the Angle group, Decimal Degrees is the default.

IMPERIAL VS. METRIC MEASUREMENTS

From this point forward, I'll provide the metric equivalents in parentheses for readers who do not work in imperial units, the standard for architectural design in the United States. Throughout the majority of this book, you'll be developing drawings for a cabin with outside wall dimensions of 28'×18' (8550 mm×5490 mm).

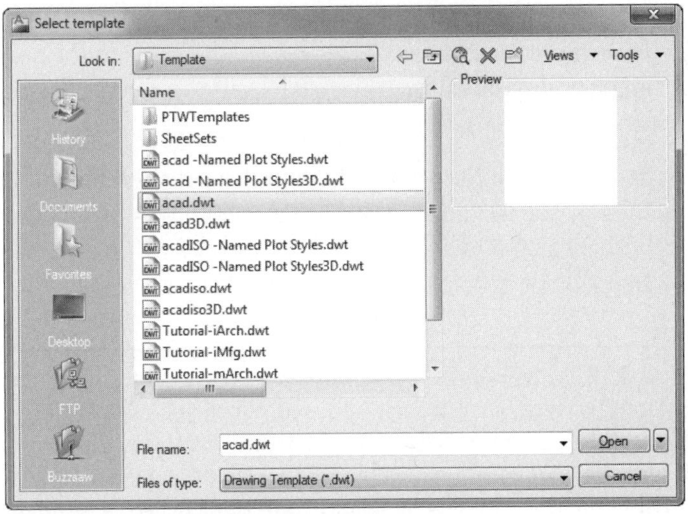

FIGURE 3.1 The Select Template dialog box

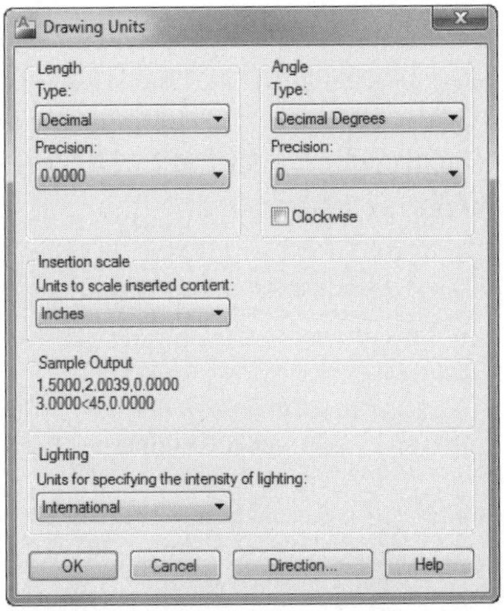

FIGURE 3.2 The Drawing Units dialog box

4. Within the Drawing Units dialog box, in the Length section, click the arrow in the Type drop-down list and select Architectural (metric users can leave this set to Decimal). These units are feet and inches, which you'll use for the cabin project.

Notice the two Precision drop-down lists at the bottom of the Length and Angle groups. When you changed the linear unit specification from Decimal to Architectural, the number in the Precision drop-down list on the left changed from 0.0000 to 0′-0¹⁄₁₆″. At this level of precision, linear distances are displayed to the nearest ¹⁄₁₆″. Metric users should set this to 0 because we won't be using units smaller than a millimeter.

5. Select some of the other Length unit types from the list, and notice the way the units appear in the Sample Output area at the bottom of the dialog box. Then select Architectural again or leave it set to Decimal for metric use.

N O T E   *Drop-down lists* are lists of options with only the selected choice displayed when the list is closed. When you click the arrow, the list opens. When you make another selection, the list closes and your new choice is displayed. When an item on the list is selected and is the focus of the program (indicated by a blue highlight), you can change the available options by using the scroll wheel on a mouse or the up- and down-arrows on the keyboard. You can choose only one item at a time from the list.

6. Click the down-arrow in the Precision drop-down list in the Length group to display the choices of precision for Architectural units (see Figure 3.3).

This setting controls the degree of precision to which AutoCAD displays a linear distance. If it's set to ¹⁄₁₆″, any line that is drawn more precisely—such as a line 6′-3¹⁄₃₂″ long—when queried, displays a length value to the nearest ¹⁄₁₆″ (which, in the example, would be 6′-3¹⁄₁₆″). However, the line is still 6′-3¹⁄₃₂″ long.

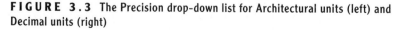

F I G U R E   3 . 3 The Precision drop-down list for Architectural units (left) and Decimal units (right)

If you change the precision setting to ⅟₃₂″ and then use the DISTANCE command to measure the distance between two features, you'll see that its length is 6′-3 ⅟₃₂″.

7. Click 0′-0 ⅟₁₆″ (0) to maintain the precision for display of linear units at ⅟₁₆″ (nearest millimeter).

If you open the Type drop-down list in the Angle group, you'll see a choice, among others, between Decimal Degrees and Deg/Min/Sec. Like so many settings in AutoCAD, the correct setting here is often dictated by the type of drawings you're preparing. Decimal angular units are the most popular choice for individuals working in architecture (or its related disciplines). On the other hand, Deg/Min/Sec are most popular in civil engineering disciplines.

Because our project is a cabin (architectural), we'll use the default Decimal Degrees throughout this book. However, the default precision setting is to the nearest degree. This may not be accurate enough, so you should change it to the nearest hundredth of a degree:

1. Click the arrow in the Precision drop-down list in the Angle group.

N O T E   When using metric units, 1 unit = 1 millimeter.

2. Select 0.00 as the precision value for angles.

The Drawing Units dialog box will now indicate that, in your drawing, you plan to use Architectural length units with a precision of ⅟₁₆″ (Decimal with a precision of 0 if using metric) and Decimal angular units with a precision of 0.00° (see Figure 3.4). This doesn't restrict the precision at which you draw, just the values that AutoCAD reports.

FIGURE 3.4 The Drawing Units dialog box for Architectural units (left), and Decimal (metric) units (right) after changes

3. Change the Insertion Scale to Inches (Millimeters for metric). This often overlooked setting allows AutoCAD to automatically scale drawings to the proper size when inserted or referenced into other drawings.

This behavior is common, as architects have to collaborate with civil engineers on projects. Architectural drawings are generally set up such that 1 unit is equal to 1 inch, whereas civil engineering drawings are set up such that 1 unit is equal to 1 foot. As an architect and engineer collaborate, their drawings must be scaled up by 12″ or down by ½₁₂, depending on whose drawing is being inserted. AutoCAD can automatically do this conversion for you, provided the Insertion Scale for your architectural drawings is set to Inches, and the civil engineering drawings to Feet.

Clicking the Direction button at the bottom of the Drawing Units dialog box opens the Direction Control dialog box, which has settings to control the direction of 0°. By default, 0° is to the right (east), and positive angular displacement goes in the counterclockwise direction. (See Figure 2.11 in Chapter 2 for an illustration of the Cartesian Coordinate System.) These are the standard settings for most users of CAD. There is no need to change them from the defaults. If you want to take a look, open the Direction Control dialog box, note the choices, and then click Cancel. You won't have occasion in the course of this book to change any of those settings.

N O T E You'll have a chance to work with the angular units in Chapter 12, "Dimensioning a Drawing," when you develop a site plan for the cabin.

4. Click OK to accept the changes and close the Drawing Units dialog box. Notice the coordinate readout in the lower-left corner of the screen: it now reads in feet and inches.

This tour of the Drawing Units dialog box has introduced you to the choices you have for the types of units and the degree of precision for linear and angular measurement. The next step in setting up a drawing is to determine its size.

N O T E If you accidentally click the mouse when the cursor is on a blank part of the drawing area, AutoCAD starts a rectangular window. I'll talk about these windows soon, but for now just press the Esc key to close the window.

Setting Up the Drawing Size

Now that you have changed the units to Architectural, the drawing area is approximately 12″ to 16″ (500 mm) wide and 9″ (300 mm) high. You can check this by moving the crosshair cursor around on the drawing area and looking at the coordinate readout, as you did in the previous chapter.

T I P When you change Decimal units to Architectural units, 1 Decimal unit translates to 1 inch. Some industries, such as civil engineering, often use Decimal units to represent feet instead of inches. If the units in their drawings are switched to Architectural, a distance that was a foot now measures as an inch. To correct this, the entire drawing must be scaled up by a factor of 12.

The drawing area is defined as the part of the screen in which you draw. You can make the distance across the drawing area larger or smaller through a process known as zooming in or out. To see how this works, you'll learn about a tool called the grid that helps you to draw and to visualize the size of your drawing.

Using the Grid

The AutoCAD grid, a pattern of horizontal and vertical gridlines that mimic the appearance of a sheet of graph paper, is used as an aid to drawing. You can set the grid to be visible or invisible. When set to visible, all but two of the horizontal and vertical gridlines display with a light gray color. One vertical gridline is colored green, whereas a single horizontal gridline is colored red. These colored gridlines reside at the 0 x (red) and 0 y (green) coordinates, and establish a boundary for Quadrant I of your drawing area, as shown in Figure 2.11 in Chapter 2.

Anything drawn above the red gridline, and to the right of the green gridline, will reside in Quadrant I, having positive x- and y-coordinate values. When working in 3D, the green and red gridlines will still graphically represent the positive x- and y-coordinates of your drawing area; however, a third z axis will also be represented in blue. Don't worry too much about the z axis quite yet, as it will be discussed in Chapter 16, "Creating 3D Geometry," and Chapter 17, "Rendering and Materials."

The area covered by the grid depends on a setting called *Drawing Limits*, explained in the section "Setting Up Drawing Limits," later in this chapter. To learn how to manipulate the grid size, you'll make the grid visible, use the Zoom

In and Zoom Out commands to vary the view of the grid, and then change the area over which the grid extends by resetting the drawing limits.

Before doing this, however, let's take a look at the icon that sits in the lower-left corner of the drawing area. This icon is known as the UCS, or user coordinate system, icon. The UCS icon provides a visual cue to how we're looking at the drawing, and will change when we're looking from a 3D perspective. You'll learn more about this in Chapter 10 when we begin our discussion on 3D. To become familiar using and interacting with the Grid in AutoCAD:

1. Move the crosshair cursor to the status bar at the bottom of the screen, and click the Grid Display button.

   The button changes from the off to the on state (with a light blue background), and a series of horizontal and vertical lines appear in the drawing area, representing a piece of graph paper.

   These lines are the grid. Preset by default to be ½″ (10 mm) apart, they extend across the entire drawing area. In the drawing area, the gridlines may measure a greater distance apart, especially if you zoom out in the drawing. This is because, in the relatively large drawing area, lines spaced ½″ (10 mm) apart would be very dense, and working with them would be difficult. AutoCAD automatically reduces the density of the displayed gridlines to maintain a reasonable appearance in the drawing area.

2. To open the Drafting Settings dialog box, right-click on the Grid Display button and then choose Settings from the context menu that appears (see Figure 3.5).

FIGURE 3.5 Displaying the Drafting Settings dialog box

 T I P   Right-clicking any of the buttons (except Ortho Mode, Allow/Disallow Dynamic UCS, and Show/Hide Transparency) on the left side of the status bar and choosing Settings opens the Drafting Settings dialog box (or other appropriate dialog box for defining the tool's parameters) to the tab with the parameters that relate to that specific button. You can also open the Drafting Settings dialog box by typing DS.↵.

3. The Snap And Grid tab of the Drafting Settings dialog box should be active (see Figure 3.6). If it's not, click the tab.

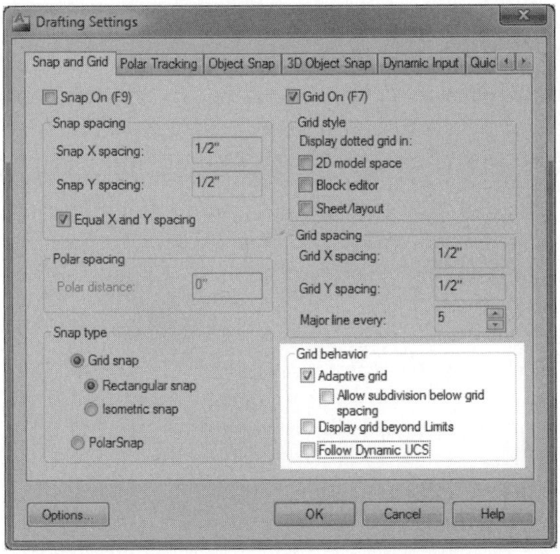

FIGURE 3.6 The Snap And Grid tab of the Drafting Settings dialog box

4. In the Grid Behavior area, be sure Adaptive Grid is checked and Display Grid Beyond Limits is unchecked. Then click OK.

   The grid now covers only the area from the origin to 12″,9″ (490 mm,290 mm), the area defined by the limits of the drawing, but extends to the extents of the drawing area. This will be evident after step 4.

   Limits are discussed in the next section. The Adaptive Grid option causes AutoCAD to reduce the number of the grid's columns and rows proportionately whenever the zoom factor would cause the grid to become too dense to be effective.

5. To display a larger area within the drawing area, scroll the mouse wheel by dragging it toward you or use the Zoom Out command by clicking the drop-down arrow next to the Zoom tool from the View tab ➢ Navigate 2D panel on the Ribbon.

   The view changes, and there are more gridlines in a denser configuration (see Figure 3.7). You may need to zoom twice to see the effect. Move the crosshair cursor to the lower-left corner of the grid, and then move it to the upper-right corner. Notice that the coordinate readout at the lower left of your screen now shows a large negative number for the lower-left corner and a larger positive number for the upper-right corner. You're displaying a greater amount of space in the drawing area. A closer inspection of the grid will reveal one vertical line colored green and a horizontal line colored red. Where these lines intersect represents the origin, or 0,0 point inside your drawing. Any point above the red line and to the right of the green line will have a positive coordinate value.

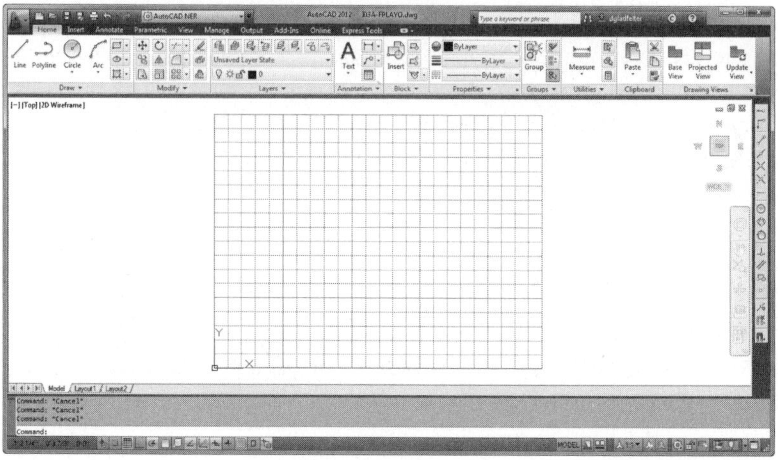

FIGURE 3.7 The grid after zooming out

6. To the left of the Grid Display button on the status bar, click the Snap Mode button. Then move the cursor back onto the grid and look at the coordinate readout again.

   The cursor stops at each grid point intersection, even those that are no longer displayed because of the zoom factor, and the readout is to the nearest half inch. The Snap tool locks the cursor onto the gridlines; even when the cursor isn't on the visible grid but somewhere outside it on the drawing area, the cursor maintains the grid spacing and jumps from one location to another.

CURSOR MOVING ERRATICALLY?

The Snap tool can be an incredibly powerful drawing aid when you intentionally turn it on. However, because the grid doesn't have to be on to use Snap, many users accidentally enable the Snap tool and then report that their cursor is moving erratically. If this happens to you at some point, remember to verify that your Snap is turned off to restore the "normal" fluid movement of the cursor.

7. Use the Zoom Out command a few more times or scroll the mouse wheel.

8. From the View tab ➤ Navigate 2D panel, choose Zoom ➤ Zoom In, or roll the scroll wheel on your mouse enough times to bring the view of the grid back to the way it appeared when it was first displayed. You aren't changing the size of the grid, just the view of it. It's like switching from a normal to a telephoto lens on a camera.

The grid is more of a guide than an actual boundary of your drawing. For most purposes, you can draw anywhere on the screen. The grid merely serves as a tool for visualizing how your drawing will be laid out.

Because it serves as a layout tool for this project, you need to increase the area covered by the grid from its present size to 60′×40′ (18 m×12 m).

Setting Up Drawing Limits

The Drawing Limits setting defines two properties in a drawing: it records the coordinates of the lower-left and upper-right corners of the grid and identifies what is displayed when the user executes a Zoom ➤ All command with only a small portion of the drawing area in use. The coordinates for the lower-left corner are 0,0 by default and are usually left at that setting. You need to change only the coordinates for the upper-right corner and change the settings so that the grid is displayed only within the limits:

1. Make sure the command window displays the Command: prompt; then type **LIMITS**↵. Notice how the command window has changed, as shown in Figure 3.8.

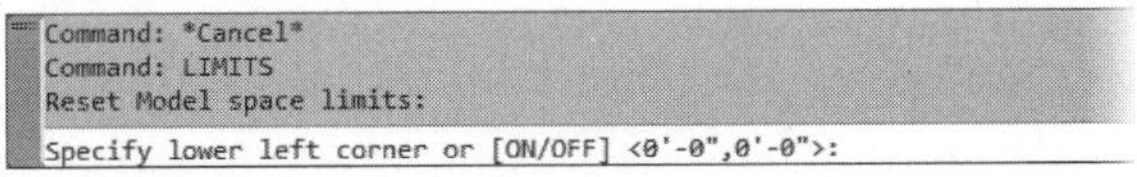

```
Command: *Cancel*
Command: LIMITS
Reset Model space limits:
Specify lower left corner or [ON/OFF] <0'-0",0'-0">:
```

FIGURE 3.8 The command window after starting the LIMITS command

The bottom command line tells you that the first step is to decide whether to change the default x- and y-coordinates for the lower-left limits, both of which are currently set at 0'-0",0'-0" (0,0). There is no need to change these.

2. Press ↵ to accept the 0'-0",0'-0" (0,0) coordinates for this corner. The bottom command line changes and now displays the coordinates for the upper-right corner of the limits. This is the setting you want to change.

3. Type **60',40'** (**18000,12000**)↵. Be sure to include the foot sign (').

> **N O T E**   AutoCAD requires that, when using Architectural units, you
> always indicate that a distance is measured in feet by using the foot sign (′).
> You don't have to use the inch sign (″) to indicate inches.

4. To bring the entire area defined by the drawing limits onto the screen,
use the ZOOM command again, but this time use the All option to bring
the drawing limits in view (see Figure 3.9).

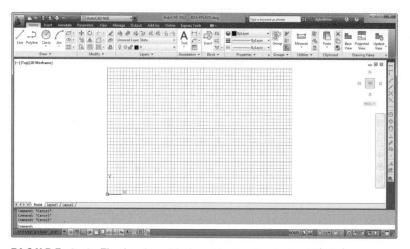

FIGURE 3.9   The drawing with the grid extending to the 60′×40′
(18,000 mm×12,000 mm) limits

From the View tab ➢ Navigate 2D panel, click the down-arrow next
to the Zoom tool and then click the All option, or type **Z↵ A↵**. The
All option zooms the view to display all the objects in the drawing or,
in a blank drawing, zooms to the limits. The drawing area expands
to display the drawing limits, and the grid changes appearance to
accommodate the new view.

5. Move the cursor from one gridline to another and watch the coordinate readout. The coordinates are still displayed to the nearest half
inch (10 mm), but the gridlines are much more than half an inch (10
mm) apart.

By default, when you zoom in or out, AutoCAD adjusts the grid spacing to
keep the gridlines from getting too close together or too far apart. In this case,
remember that you found the grid spacing to be ½″ (10 mm) by default. If the
drawing area is giving you a view of a 60′×40′ (18,000 mm×12,000 mm) grid
with gridlines at ½″ (10 mm), the grid has 1440 (1800) vertical gridlines and 960

(1200) horizontal gridlines. If the whole grid were to be shown on the screen, the gridlines would be so close together that they would be only about 1 pixel in size and would solidly fill the drawing area. So AutoCAD adjusts the spacing of the dots to keep the grid readable. You need to change that spacing to a more usable value.

For the drawing task ahead, it will be more useful to have the spacing set differently. Remember how you turned on Snap mode, and the cursor stopped at each gridline intersection? If you set the gridline spacing to 2′ (1000 mm) and the Snap Spacing to 6″ (50 mm), you can use Grid and Snap modes to help you draw the outline of the cabin, because the dimensions of the outside wall line are in whole feet (millimeters) and divisible by 2. The dimensions of the outside wall line are 28′×16′ (8550 mm×4850 mm), and the exterior walls are 6″ (150 mm) thick. Here's how:

1. Right-click the Grid Display button on the status bar, and click Settings to open the Drafting Settings dialog box one more time.

   The Drafting Settings dialog box opens, and the Snap And Grid tab is active. The settings in both the Grid and Snap areas include X and Y Spacing settings. Notice that they're all set for a spacing of ½″ (10).

2. In the Grid Spacing area, click in the Grid X Spacing text box and change ½″ (10) to 2′ (1000), as shown in Figure 3.10. Then click in the Grid Y Spacing text box. It automatically changes to match the Grid X Spacing text box.

   If you want different Grid X and Grid Y Spacing values, you must deselect the Equal X And Y Spacing option in the Snap Spacing area.

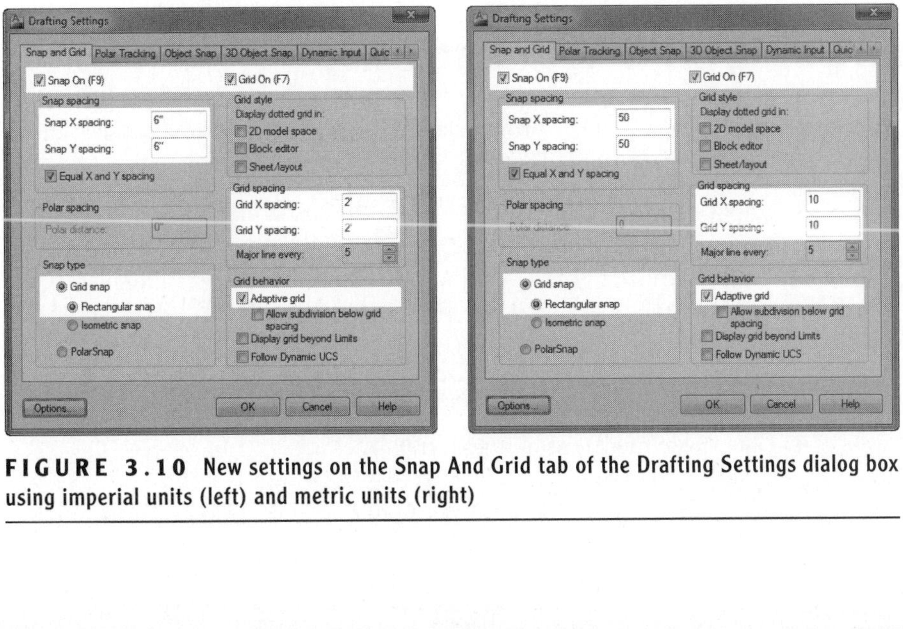

FIGURE 3.10 New settings on the Snap And Grid tab of the Drafting Settings dialog box using imperial units (left) and metric units (right)

If you set Grid Spacing to 0, the grid takes on whatever spacing you set for the Snap X Spacing and Snap Y Spacing text boxes. This is how you lock the snap and grid together.

3. In the Snap Spacing section, change the Snap X Spacing setting to 6 (50), as shown in Figure 3.10. The inch sign isn't required. Then click the Snap Y Spacing input box or press the Tab key. The Snap Y spacing automatically changes to match the Snap X Spacing setting.

4. In the Snap Type area, be sure Grid Snap and Rectangular Snap are selected (Figure 3.10).

5. In the Grid Behavior area, only Adaptive Grid should be selected. With the grid set this way, AutoCAD will adjust the number of gridlines displayed as you zoom in and out, but it won't add gridlines between the lowest grid spacing.

6. The Snap On and Grid On check boxes at the top of the dialog box should be selected. If they aren't, click them. Your Snap And Grid tab should look like Figure 3.10.

7. Click OK. The new 2′ (1000 mm) grid is now visible. Move the cursor around on the grid—be sure Snap is on. (Check the Snap Mode button on the status bar; it's pressed when Snap is on.) Notice the coordinate readout. It's displaying coordinates to the nearest 6″ (50 mm) to conform to the new 6″ (50) snap spacing. The cursor stops at several snap points between each grid dot.

8. Move the crosshair cursor to the upper-right corner of the grid and check the coordinate readout. It should display 60′-0″, 40′-0″, 0′-0″ (18000.0000, 12000.0000, 0). In AutoCAD LT, you won't have the third coordinate.

Drawing with Grid and Snap

Your drawing area now has the proper settings and is zoomed to a convenient magnification. You're ready to draw the first lines of the cabin:

1. When the command window displays the Command: prompt, start the LINE command.

2. From the Home tab ➢ Draw panel, click the Line button or type L↵.

3. Type 8',8'↵ (2500,2500↵), or move the cursor until the Dynamic Input fields indicate the cursor is over the 8′,8′ (2500,2500) point.

4. Click to define the starting point of the line.

5. Hold the crosshair cursor above and to the right of the point you just picked.

AutoCAD shows ghosted linear and angular dimensions that dynamically display the length and angle of the first line segment as the cursor moves, and a tooltip window displays the current prompt for the LINE command (see Figure 3.11).

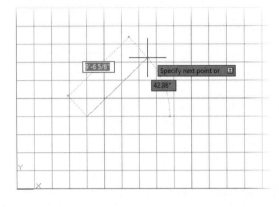

FIGURE 3.11 One point picked on the grid

6. Don't click yet. Hold the crosshair cursor directly out to the right of the first point picked and note how the linear dimension displays a distance in 6″ (50 mm) increments. The angular dimension should have an angle of 0.00°, as shown in Figure 3.12.

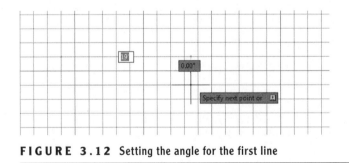

FIGURE 3.12 Setting the angle for the first line

7. Continue moving the crosshair cursor left or right until the dashed linear dimension displays 28′ (8550).

8. At this point, click the left mouse button to draw the first line of the cabin wall (see Figure 3.13).

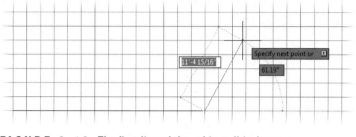

FIGURE 3.13 The first line of the cabin wall is drawn.

9. Move the crosshair cursor directly above the last point picked to a position such that the dashed linear dimension displays 18′ (5490) and the dashed angular dimension displays 90.00°, and then pick that point.

10. Move the crosshair cursor directly left of the last point picked until the dashed linear dimension displays 28′ (8550) and the dashed angular dimension displays 180.00°, and then pick that point (see Figure 3.14).

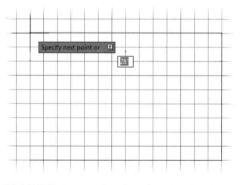

FIGURE 3.14 Drawing the second and third wall lines

11. Finally, type **C↵** to close the box.

This tells AutoCAD to draw a line from the last point picked to the first point picked and, in effect, closes the box. AutoCAD then automatically ends the LINE command (see Figure 3.15).

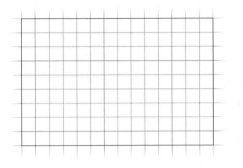

FIGURE 3.15 The completed outside wall lines

This method for laying out building lines by using Snap and Grid and Dynamic Input is useful if the dimensions all conform to a convenient rounded-off number, such as the nearest 6 inches. The key advantage to this method over just typing the relative coordinates, as you did with the box in Chapter 2, is that you avoid having to enter the numbers. You should, however, assess whether the layout you need to draw has characteristics that lend themselves to using Grid, Snap, and Dynamic Input or whether typing the relative coordinates would be more efficient. As you get more comfortable with AutoCAD, you'll see that this sort of question comes up often: which way is the most efficient? This happy dilemma is inevitable in an application with enough tools to give you many strategic choices. In Chapters 4 and 5, "Developing Drawing Strategies: Parts 1 and 2," you'll learn other techniques for drawing rectangles.

A Closer Look at Dynamic Input

The kind of information shown in dynamic display is similar to that shown in the command window, and the intent of this feature is to keep your eyes on the screen as much as possible. The specific information displayed depends, as it does on the command line, on what you're doing at the time. It's controlled by several settings that you access by right-clicking the Dynamic Input button on the status bar and selecting Settings from the context menu. This opens the Drafting Settings dialog box with the Dynamic Input tab activated (see Figure 3.16).

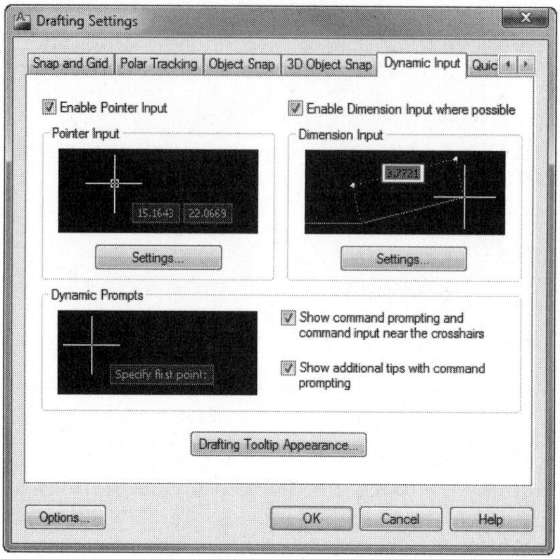

FIGURE 3.16 The Dynamic Input tab of the Drafting Settings dialog box

This tab has four check boxes (two at the top, and two near the middle on the right) and three buttons to open three feature-specific Settings dialog boxes. To make the dynamic input conform to what is shown in the book, do the following:

1. Make sure all four check boxes are selected.

2. In the Pointer Input group, click the Settings button to open the Pointer Input Settings dialog box (see Figure 3.17).

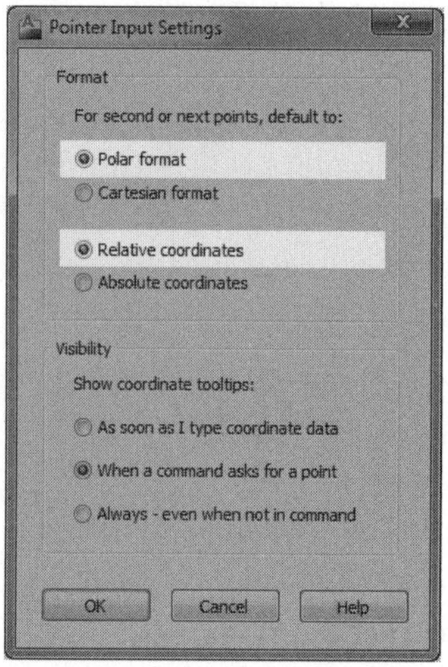

FIGURE 3.17 The Pointer Input Settings dialog box

3. In the Format group, the Polar Format and Relative Coordinates radio buttons should be selected. Click OK.

4. In the Dimension Input area of the Drafting Settings dialog box, click the Settings button to open the Dimension Input Settings dialog box (see Figure 3.18).

FIGURE 3.18 The Dimension Input Settings dialog box

5. Make sure the Show 2 Dimension Input Fields At A Time radio button is selected, and then click OK.

6. In the Dynamic Prompts group of the Drafting Settings dialog box, ensure that both Show Command Prompting And Command Input Near The Crosshairs and Show Additional Tips With Command Prompting are checked.

   AutoCAD 2012 adds the Show Additional Tips With Command Prompting option, which affords additional control when manipulating objects by using grips.

7. Below the Dynamic Prompts group of the Drafting Settings dialog box, click the Drafting Tooltip Appearance button to open the Tooltip Appearance dialog box (see Figure 3.19).

   In the Apply To group at the bottom of the box, ensure that the Override OS Settings For All Drafting Tooltips radio button is selected. Vary the Colors, Size, and Transparency settings according to your preference. (I used a setting of 0 for Size and 0% for Transparency.) Don't worry about Layout Color for now. The Model

Color you choose depends on whether your drawing area has a light or dark background. Experiment. When you're finished, click OK.

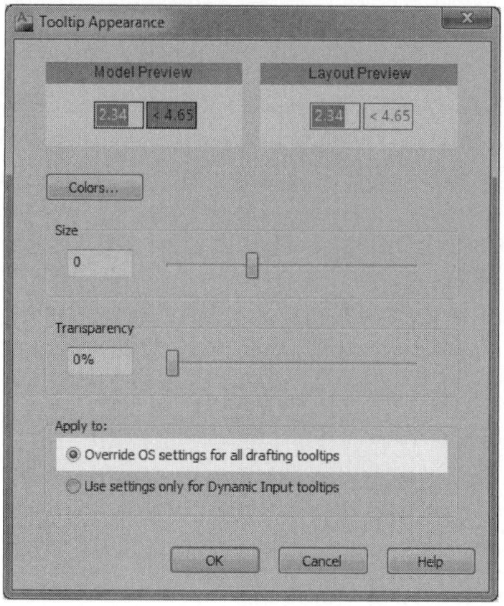

FIGURE 3.19 The Tooltip Appearance dialog box

8. Click OK again to close the Drafting Settings dialog box.

If you decide to disable Dynamic Input, you can easily do so by clicking its button in the status bar so that it's in unpushed mode (with a gray background).

Saving Your Work

As in all Windows-compliant applications, when you save an AutoCAD file for the first time by choosing Save, you can designate a name for the file and a folder in which to store it. I recommend that you create a special folder, called something like AutoCAD NER, for storing the files you'll generate as you work your way through this book. This will keep them separate from project work already on your computer, and you'll always know where to save or find a training drawing. To save your drawing, follow these steps:

1. In AutoCAD, click the Save button on the Quick Access toolbar or choose Save from the Application menu. Because you haven't named this file yet, the Save Drawing As dialog box opens, as shown in Figure 3.20.

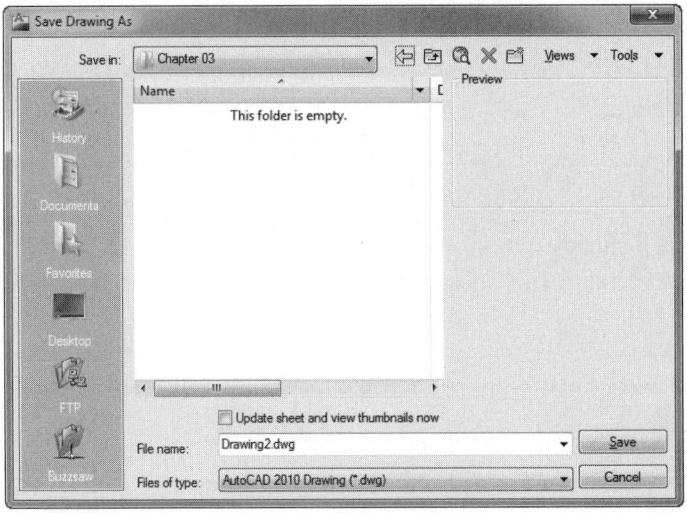

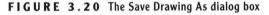

FIGURE 3.20 The Save Drawing As dialog box

The Save button in the Quick Access toolbar, the Application menu ➤ Save option, and the Ctrl+S key combination actually invoke the QSAVE (Quick Save) command in AutoCAD.

QSAVE asks for a filename only when the drawing has not yet been saved for the first time, after which it simply overwrites the existing file without prompting. Entering the SAVE command at the command line (**SAVE⏎**) always opens the Save Drawing As dialog box, where the filename and path are modified.

> **N O T E**   The actual folders and files may be different on your computer.

2. In the Save In drop-down list, designate the drive and folder where you want to save the drawing. If you're saving it on the hard drive or server, navigate to the folder in which you want to place the new AutoCAD NER folder.

3. Click the Create New Folder button near the top-right corner of the dialog box. The folder appears in the list of folders and is highlighted. It's called New Folder, and a cursor flashes just to the right of the highlighting rectangle.

4. Type AutoCAD NER⏎ (or whatever name you want to give the new folder).

5. Double-click the new folder to open it.

6. In the File Name box, change the name to **I03A-FPLAYO** (**M03A-FPLAYO**). You're not required to enter the .dwg extension.

7. Click Save. Notice that the AutoCAD title bar displays the new name of the file along with its path. It's now safe to exit AutoCAD.

8. If you want to shut down AutoCAD at this time, choose Application menu ➤ Exit AutoCAD or click the X button in the top-right corner of the AutoCAD window. Otherwise, keep your drawing up and read on.

U.S. NATIONAL CAD STANDARD (NCS)

Where applicable, this book will employ the U.S. National CAD Standard (NCS). Over the last several years, the popularity of this standard has grown immensely, and it is now in use by many of the top architectural and engineering firms. You'll learn more about the NCS when you begin learning about layers, but for now we'll stick to file naming. Per the NCS, our cabin drawing is considered a model drawing, whose standard file-naming structure is as follows:

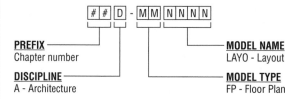

The discipline portion of an NCS filename must be one of the predefined single-letter codes listed in Chapter 6, "Using Layers to Organize Your Drawing," which explores the naming convention as applied to layer names.

The U.S. National CAD Standards have proven flexible enough to support firms both large and small. By working through this book, you'll get a good introduction to how the NCS works. If after reading this book you would like to learn more about the National CAD Standards, visit **http://nationalcadstandard.org**.

From now on, when you're directed to save the drawing, save it as *X##A-FPLAYO*, with *X* representing the unit of measure (I: imperial, M: metric), and ## indicating the two-digit number of the chapter (for example, 03 for Chapter 3). This way, you'll know where in the book to look for review, if necessary. To save the current drawing under a different name, use the Save As command (Application menu ➤ Save As, or **SAVEAS↵**).

T I P   Each time you save, check your work against the online project files. Throughout the book, you will be directed to save your cabin project in progress at major stages. Files corresponding to each stage where you save your files are available on this book's web page: www.sybex.com/go/ autocad2012ner.

You can also access a full range of additional resources including tutorials, videos, and more that are specific to the exercises in this book from www .autocadner.com.

The tools covered in this chapter are your keys to starting a new drawing from scratch and getting it ready for a specific project.

A Summary of AutoCAD's Units

The following is a brief description of each of the linear and angular unit types that AutoCAD offers and how they are used. The example distance is 2′-6½″. The example angle is 126°35′10″.

Linear Units

The linear unit types that AutoCAD uses are as follows:

Architectural   This unit type uses feet and inches with fractions. You must use the foot sign (′): for example, 2′-6½″. For this distance, enter **2'6-1/2** or **2'6.5**. For the most part, these are the units that you'll use in this book.

Decimal   This unit type uses decimal units that can represent any linear unit of measurement. You don't use the foot sign, the inch sign, or fractions. This method is especially common in the civil engineering discipline, where decimal units are used, and 1 unit is equal to 1 foot. Therefore, for the distance 2′6½″, you would need to convert the inches (6.5 inches in this case) to the decimal equivalent of a foot (6.5/12 = 0.5417). So in this case, you would enter **2.5417**.

Let's say you needed to draw a line 10′3″ long in a drawing where 1 unit was equal to 1 foot. You would need to convert the inches to the decimal equivalent of a foot. So in this case 3/12 = 0.25, and so you would enter **10.25**.

Conversely, if each unit was equal to an inch, that same 2′ 6½″ line would be entered as **30.5** because (2 × 12) + 6 = 30 and 6/12 = 0.5.

Engineering   This unit is equivalent to Architectural units except that inches are displayed as decimals rather than fractions. For a distance of 2′-6½″, enter **2′6.5** or **2.5417′**. In either method, the resulting distance is displayed as 2′-6.5″.

Fractional   These units are just like Architectural units except there is no use of feet. Everything is expressed in inches and fractions. If you enter **30-1/2** or **30.5**, the resulting distance displays as 30½.

Scientific   This unit system is similar to the Decimal unit system except for the way in which distances are displayed. If you enter **3.05E+01**, that is what is displayed. The notation always uses an expression that indicates a number from 1 to 10 that is to be multiplied by a power of 10. In this case, the power is 1, so the notation means 3.05×10, or 30.5 in Decimal units.

Angular Units

The angular unit types that AutoCAD uses are as follows:

Decimal   This type uses 360° in a circle in decimal form, with no minutes and no seconds. All angles are expressed as decimal degrees. For example, an angle of 126°35′10″ is entered as **126.586** or **126d35′10″** and displays as 126.5861. AutoCAD uses the letter *d* instead of the traditional degree symbol (°).

Deg/Min/Sec   This is the traditional system for measuring angles. In AutoCAD's notation, degrees are indicated by the lowercase *d*, the minutes use the traditional ′, and the seconds use the traditional ″. The use of this system is generally reserved for the civil engineering discipline. Most other users now use decimal angles instead and choose their preference for precision.

Grads   This unit is based on a circle being divided into 400 grads, so 90° equals 100 grads. One degree equals 1.11 grads, and 1 grad equals 0.90 degrees. AutoCAD uses *g* as the symbol for grads.

Radians   The radian is the angle from the center of a circle made by the radius of the circle being laid along the circumference of the circle.

One radian equals 57.3°, and 360° equals 6.28 radians, or 2π radians. AutoCAD uses *r* as the symbol for radians.

Surveyor   These units use bearings from the north and south directions toward the east or west direction and are expressed in degrees, minutes, and seconds. They're discussed in Chapter 12. In this example, 126°35′10″ translates to N 36d35′10″ W in bearings, or Surveyor units.

The next chapter focuses on adding to the drawing, modifying the commands you learned as part of Chapter 2, and creating strategies for solving problems that occur in the development of a floor plan.

Are You Experienced?

Now you can...

- ☑ set up linear and angular units for a new drawing

- ☑ make the grid visible and modify its coverage

- ☑ use the Zoom In and Zoom Out commands

- ☑ activate Snap mode and change the Snap and Grid spacings

- ☑ use the Zoom All function to fit the grid on the drawing area

- ☑ draw lines by using the Grid, Snap, and Dynamic Input features

- ☑ create a new folder on your hard drive from within AutoCAD

- ☑ name and save your file

Developing Drawing Strategies: Part 1

Assuming that you have worked your way through the first three chapters, you have now successfully drawn a shape (Chapter 2, "Learning Basic Commands to Get Started") as well as the outer wall lines of a cabin (Chapter 3, "Setting Up a Drawing"). From here on, you'll develop a floor plan for the cabin. In Chapter 10, "Generating Elevations," you'll work on elevations (views of the front, back, and sides of the building that show how the building will look if you're facing it). The focus in this chapter is on gaining a feel for the strategy of drawing in AutoCAD and on solving drawing problems that come up in the course of laying out a floor plan. As you work your way through this chapter, the activities will include making the walls, cutting doorway openings, and drawing the doors In Chapter 5, "Developing Drawing Strategies: Part 2," you'll add steps and two decks and you'll place fixtures and appliances in the bathroom and kitchen.

Each exercise in this chapter presents opportunities to practice using commands you already know from earlier chapters and also to learn a few new ones. Arguably more important than knowing a large number of AutoCAD commands is having the ability to take those commands and establish the best way to combine them to complete the design at hand. As you work through the exercises in this chapter and the next, I encourage you to focus less on the commands themselves and more on how they are used to get you one step closer to a finished design. Admittedly, separating the two can be hard sometimes; however, developing a strong sense of strategic thinking now will undoubtedly make you a more efficient user.

- ▶ **Making interior walls**

- ▶ **Zooming in on an area by using various zoom tools**

- ▶ **Making doors and swings**

- ▶ **Using object snaps**

- ▶ **Using the** COPY **and** MIRROR **commands**

Laying Out the Walls

For most floor plans, the walls come first. As you begin to further define the interior of your cabin by adding a closet and bathroom, certain relationships can be established with lines already in your drawing. By spending a moment to recognize these relationships, you won't need to draw as many new lines as you might expect. In this chapter, I'll show you how to build most of the new walls from the four exterior wall lines you drew in the previous chapter.

Take a moment to study the floor plan in Figure 4.1 to begin visualizing the many relationships that exist between the exterior wall boundary drawn in Chapter 3 (shown in bold), and the remaining linework that makes up the floor plan. One easily identified relationship is the lines that create the exterior wall definition. Most of the final exterior wall definition follows the outline drawn in Chapter 3. For this reason, the best strategy is to build from the existing linework in your drawing by using a series of commands found on the Modify panel on the Home tab of the Ribbon.

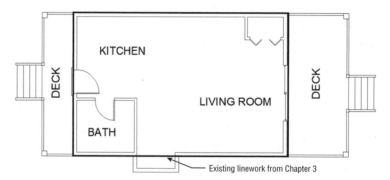

FIGURE 4.1 The exterior wall boundary drawn in Chapter 3 overlaid onto the cabin floor plan

It's possible to apply a similar strategy as both the bathroom and closet are considered. Both spaces share similar relationships with the exterior wall definitions adjacent to them. Because Modify commands allow new objects to be created from existing objects, these relationships are easily maintained as the spaces are defined.

Afterward, you'll cut four openings in these walls (interior and exterior) for the doorways.

PUTTING DYNAMIC INPUT TO USE

Because you'll be doing quite a bit of drawing in this and the next chapter, this is a good opportunity to activate the Dynamic Input feature introduced in Chapter 3 if you've turned it off. Because the purpose of this chapter is to develop drawing strategies, try turning it on and off as you work through the exercises. You'll see how the information displayed in the drawing area changes as you move from one command to another.

Commands that you enter appear only at the cursor, and not at the command line, while dynamic input is active. The feature is designed to help you avoid having to continually glance down at the command window as you work through the steps of a command. Sometimes, however, the information you need is displayed only in the command window, so you still have to glance down at it. By the time you finish Chapter 5, you'll know whether you want the feature to be active or not.

Creating Polylines from Existing Objects

Exterior walls are slightly thicker than interior walls because they are sturdier, are load bearing, and have an additional layer or two of weather protection such as siding or stucco. Accounting for these properties, the standard thickness for your exterior walls will be 6″ (150 mm). Using the tools you've already learned, you'll apply the strategy outlined at the start of this chapter to offset the four existing wall lines to the inside, creating the exterior wall definition.

This section introduces the use of polylines as an alternative to the FILLET command. Whereas a line is a single, straight object with no measurable width, polylines are composed of several straight or curved segments that can also maintain a user-defined width. When a polyline is offset, all segments are offset equally, and the corners are left sharp without the need to use the FILLET command to clean them up. Any polyline can be disassembled into its component lines and arcs by using the EXPLODE command.

NEW The JOIN command has been improved in AutoCAD 2012, and now allows objects of different types to be joined into a polyline. By using the JOIN command, you can convert any combination of lines and arcs into a single polyline, as long as the endpoints of the various segments terminate in exactly the same location. Because polylines are treated as a single object, converting the outermost perimeter into a single polyline will automate much of the cleanup as you continue creating the floor plan shown in Figure 4.2.

Most of the commands used in this exercise were presented in Chapters 2 and 3. If you need a refresher, glance back at those chapters.

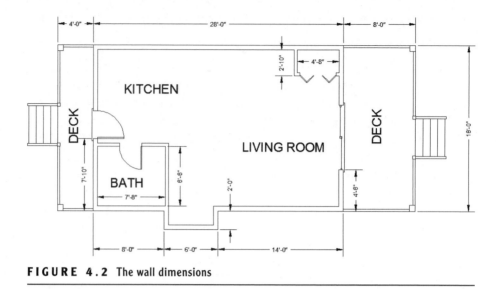

FIGURE 4.2 The wall dimensions

In this exercise you will create a polyline from the individual line segments composing the outside wall:

1. With AutoCAD running, choose Application menu ➢ Open ➢ Drawing. The Select File dialog box opens, where you can navigate to the I03A -FPLAY0.dwg (M03A-FPLAY0.dwg) you saved at the end of Chapter 3. Click Open to display the cabin drawing shown in Figure 4.3.

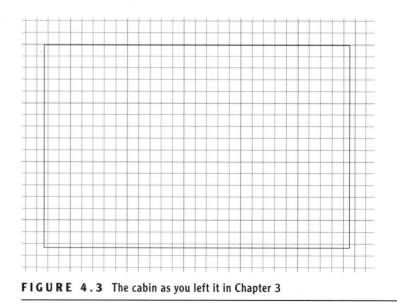

FIGURE 4.3 The cabin as you left it in Chapter 3

2. Click the Grid Display and Snap Mode icons on the status bar to turn them off (they'll change to a gray background). Alternatively, you can press F7 to turn off Grid Display and F9 to turn off Snap Mode.

3. Expand the Modify Ribbon panel found on the Home tab, and click Join, as shown in Figure 4.4. Command-line users can type J↵ to start the JOIN command.

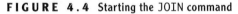

FIGURE 4.4 Starting the JOIN command

4. Select one of the exterior wall lines.

The line ghosts, and the command line prompts you to select objects to join to the line you just selected, as shown in Figure 4.5.

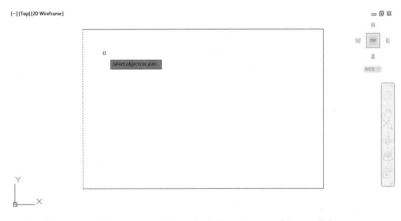

FIGURE 4.5 The command line after choosing an object to join

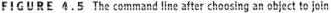

5. Select the remaining three exterior wall lines, and press the ↵ key to accept the selection set.

After accepting the selection set, the command line confirms the Join action and reads 4 objects converted to 1 polyline, as shown in Figure 4.6.

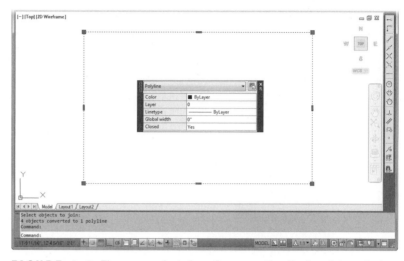

FIGURE 4.6 The command window after converting the lines into a single polyline

6. Select one segment of the polyline that forms the perimeter of the box in the drawing area.

   As shown in Figure 4.6, all four polyline segments are selected (dashed), indicating that they exist as a single object, and blue boxes appear at the corners along with blue rectangles at the midpoint of each segment. The blue boxes and rectangles, called *grips*, appear because you selected the object outside of a command. Grips are not exclusive to polylines. Grips are explained in Chapter 8, "Controlling Text in a Drawing."

7. Save your drawing as **I04-01-JoinLines.dwg** (**M04-01-JoinLines.dwg**) by using the Application menu ➢ Save As ➢ AutoCAD Drawing.

Creating and Editing Polylines

Polylines are composed of segments, which may be straight or curved lines, and vertices that terminate the segments. Each segment must have a vertex at each end, but several segments can share a single vertex. The perimeter that you drew follows the major length and width dimensions of the cabin but doesn't account for the small pop-out on the south side of the structure. In this exercise, you will add the pop-out, trim the original polyline, and then join the two polylines into a single entity:

1. If I04-01-JoinLines.dwg (M04-01-JoinLines.dwg) is not already open, click the Open button on the Quick Access toolbar.

2. Click the Polyline button in the Draw panel on the Home tab of the Ribbon to start the polyline (PLINE) command. Alternatively, you can type **PL**↵ at the command line.

3. At the Specify start point: prompt, type **16',8'** ↵ (**4850,2500**↵).

   With the Dynamic Input feature turned on, the comma not only designates the X and Y locations for the start point, but it also instructs AutoCAD to switch the current input field from the X field to the Y field.

   When Dynamic Input is turned off, the values that you type are shown in the command window.

   A rubber-banding line, similar to the one you saw when you used the LINE command, is attached to the point you designated and to the cursor.

4. Type the following:

   0,-2' ↵ (**0,-610**↵)

   6',0.↵ (**1830,0**↵)

   0,2' ↵↵ (**0,610**↵↵).

   Your screen should look like Figure 4.7.

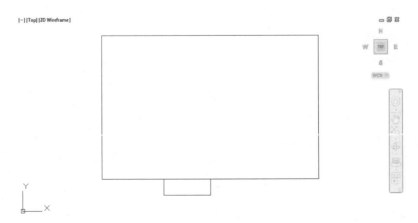

FIGURE 4.7 The pop-out added to the cabin

5. Start the TRIM command.

6. At the Select Objects or <select all>: prompt, pick the pop-out that you just drew and press ↵.

  All segments of the pop-out are ghosted to indicate that the entire polyline is designated as a cutting edge.

7. Trim the pop-out by selecting it as the cutting edge. When prompted to Select object to trim or shift-select to extend or, select the long horizontal line of the cabin between the two vertical lines that define the pop-out, as shown in Figure 4.8.

FIGURE 4.8 Selecting the polyline segment to trim away

8. Press ↵ to end the TRIM command.

9. From the expanded Modify panel on the Home tab, choose Join and then pick either of the two polylines.

10. Pick the other polyline and press ↵.

  Your drawing now consists of a single polyline made up of eight segments, as shown in Figure 4.9.

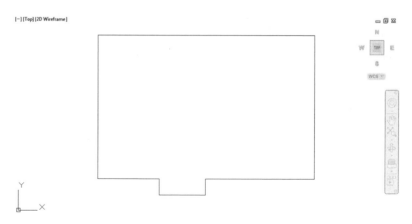

FIGURE 4.9 The polyline after trimming the original and then joining the remaining entities

11. Save your drawing as **I04-02-CreatePolylines.dwg** (**M04-02-Create**
Polylines.dwg) by choosing Application menu ➢ Save As ➢ AutoCAD
Drawing.

Creating the Exterior Wall Lines

Here you will use the OFFSET command to create all the interior lines for the
exterior walls at one time:

1. If I04-02-CreatePolylines.dwg (M04-02-CreatePolylines.dwg) is
not already open, click the Open button on the Quick Access toolbar.

2. Start the OFFSET command by clicking the Offset button on the
Modify panel. Command-line users can type **O↵** to start the OFFSET
command.

3. At the Specify offset distance or: Dynamic Input prompt, type
6↵ (**150↵**).

N O T E You don't have to enter the inch sign (″), but you're required to
enter the foot sign (′) when appropriate.

---

4. At the Select object to offset or: prompt, select the polyline.

5. Click in a blank area inside the cabin's perimeter. All segments of the
polyline are offset 6″ (150 mm) to the inside (see Figure 4.10).

6. The OFFSET command is still running; press ↵ to terminate it.

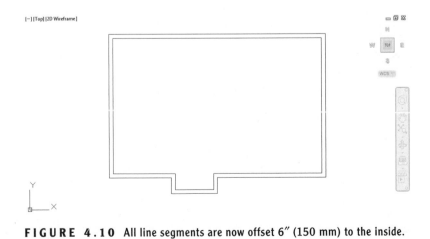

FIGURE 4.10 All line segments are now offset 6″ (150 mm) to the inside.

As you can see, there is no need to fillet the corners, and using polylines can reduce the number of steps and picks required to draw the inside lines. We'll diverge from the cabin exercise briefly to examine the capabilities of the FILLET command when used in conjunction with polylines.

7. Start the FILLET command by clicking the Fillet button from the Modify panel on the Home tab.

8. Type **R.⏎** to select the Radius option; then set the radius to **12"** (3600).

9. Select any two polyline segments that share a corner of the inner box.
   The two segments are shortened, and a curved segment with a 12" (3600 mm) radius is inserted. The polyline now has nine contiguous segments (see Figure 4.11). The FILLET command automatically ends after each fillet.

You can restart the most recently used command by pressing the spacebar or ⏎ at the command prompt or by right-clicking and choosing the Repeat option from the context menu.

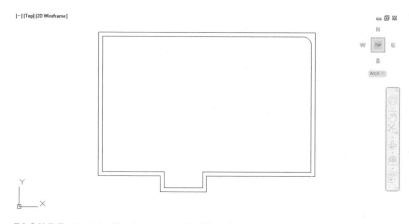

FIGURE 4.11 The first corner is filleted.

10. Press ⏎ or the spacebar to restart the FILLET command.

11. Type **P⏎** to instruct AutoCAD that the fillet is to be performed on all intersections of a polyline.

12. At the Select 2D polyline: prompt, select the inner box. All corners are now filleted (see Figure 4.12).
    You can see how the FILLET command, when used with a polyline, can save time.

13. You don't want the objects to remain as polylines for this project, so click the Undo button on the Quick Access toolbar, or type **U⏎**, until all of the filleted edges are square again.

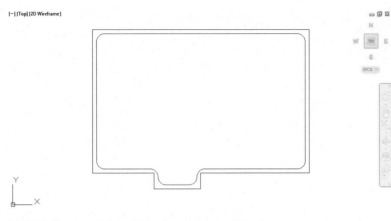

FIGURE 4.12 The polyline's corners are filleted.

TIP Selecting the down-arrow next to the Undo button on the Quick Access toolbar will display a list of recently executed commands so you can undo multiple commands at once.

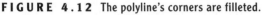

14. Click the Explode button on the Home tab ➤ Modify panel, or type X⏎ to start the EXPLODE command.

15. Select both of the polylines and then press the ⏎ key. The two polylines are now 16 separate line objects.

You will be using the OFFSET command to create the interior walls from the lines that make up the exterior walls. Exploding the polylines into individual line objects allows you to offset single, straight objects rather than the closed polylines that would require trimming to clean up.

16. Save your drawing as **I04-03-ExteriorWalls.dwg** (**M04-03-Exterior Walls.dwg**) by choosing Application menu ➤ Save As ➤ AutoCAD Drawing.

Creating the Interior Walls

Because the interior walls of your cabin are not load bearing, they can be a little thinner than the exterior walls. The standard thickness for your interior walls will be 4″ (100 mm). Using the strategy developed at the start of this chapter, you will create the cabin's interior wall lines by offsetting the exterior wall lines:

1. Make sure the drawing I04-03-ExteriorWalls.dwg (M04-03-Exterior Walls.dwg) is open; if it's not, click the Open button on the Quick Access toolbar.

2. Start the OFFSET command.

3. At the Specify Offset distance or: prompt, type 7'8.↵ (2350↵). *Leave no space between the foot sign (') and the 8.*

 N O T E AutoCAD requires that you enter a distance containing feet and inches in a particular format: no space between the foot sign (') and the inches value, and a hyphen (-) between the inches and a fraction. For example, if you're entering a distance of 6′-4¾″, you enter 6'4-3/4. The measurement is displayed in the normal way, 6′-4¾″, but you must enter it in the format that has no spaces because the spacebar acts the same as ↵ in most cases.

---

4. Click the inside line of the left exterior wall (see Figure 4.13).

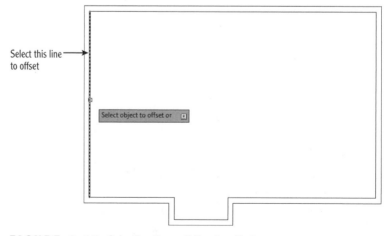

Select this line to offset

Select object to offset or

FIGURE 4.13 Selecting the wall line to offset

5. Click in a blank area to the right of the selected line. The line is offset 7'-8" (2250 mm) to the right.

6. Press ↵ twice, or press the spacebar twice.
   The OFFSET command is terminated and then restarted, and you can reset the offset distance.

 T I P In the OFFSET command, your opportunity to change the offset distance comes right after you start the command. So, if the OFFSET command is already running and you need to change the offset distance, you must stop and then restart the command. To do so, press ↵ or the spacebar twice.

---

7. Type **4**↵ (**100**↵) to reset the offset distance to 4" (100 mm).

8. Click the new line that was just offset, and then click in a blank area to the right of that line. You have created a vertical interior wall (see Figure 4.14).

9. Press ↵ twice to stop and restart the OFFSET command.

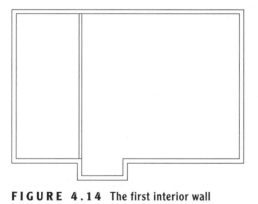

F I G U R E 4 . 1 4 The first interior wall

---

10. Type **6.5'** ↵ (**1980**↵) to set the distance for offsetting the next wall.

 N O T E With Architectural units set, you can still enter distances in decimal form for feet and inches, and AutoCAD will translate them into their appropriate form. For example, you can enter 6'-6" as 6.5', and you can enter 4½" as 4.5 without the inch sign.

11. Pick a point on the inside lower-left exterior wall line (see Figure 4.15).

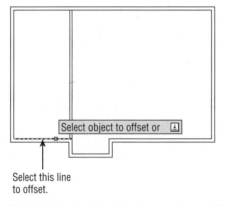

Select this line
to offset.

FIGURE 4.15 Selecting another wall line to offset

12. Click in a blank area above the line selected. The inside exterior wall line is offset to make a new interior wall line.

13. Press the spacebar twice to stop and restart the OFFSET command.

14. Type **4↵** (**100↵**). Click the new line, and click again above it. A second wall line is made, and you now have two interior walls.

15. Press the spacebar to end the **OFFSET** command.

16. Save your drawing as **I04-04-InteriorWalls.dwg** (**M04-04-Interior Walls.dwg**).

These interior wall lines form the boundary of the bathroom. You need to clean up their intersections with each other and with the exterior walls. If you take the time to do this properly, it will be easier to make changes in the future. Refer to Figure 4.2 earlier in this chapter to see where we're headed.

Cleaning Up Wall Lines

Earlier in the book, you used the FILLET command to clean up the corners of intersecting lines. You can use that command again to clean up some of the interior walls, but you'll have to use the TRIM command to do the rest of them. You'll see why as you progress through the next set of steps:

1. Make sure I04-04-InteriorWalls.dwg (M04-04-InteriorWalls.dwg) is open.

2. Assuming you have a mouse with a scroll wheel, double-click the scroll wheel to zoom to the extents of your drawing. Alternatively, you can use the Zoom Extents button found on the navigation bar or type **Z↵ E↵** at the command line.

Performing a Zoom Extents will make it easier to pick the wall lines by making the drawing larger on the screen.

3. Expand the Zoom option found on the navigation bar (Figure 4.16) and click Zoom Scale.

4. When prompted to Enter a scale factor, type **0.75x↵**. The drawing zooms out a bit.

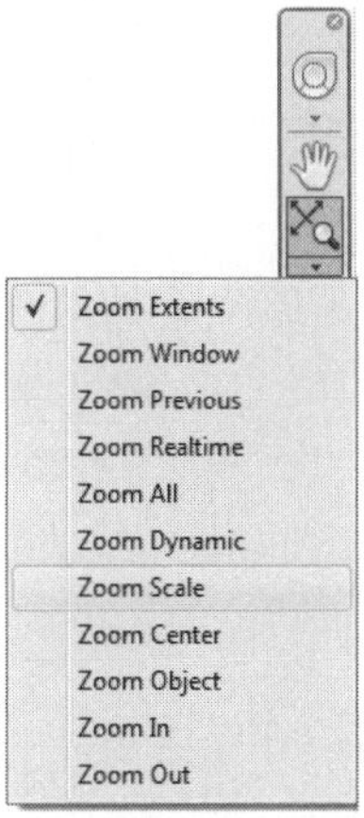

FIGURE 4.16 Selecting the Zoom Scale option from the navigation bar

You've just used two options of the ZOOM command. First, you used Zoom Extents to display all the objects in your drawing. You then zoomed to a scale (0.75′) to make the drawing 75 percent the size it was after using Zoom Extents. This is a change in magnification on the view only; the building is still 28′ (8550 mm) long and 18′ (5490 mm) wide.

5. Start the FILLET command, set the radius to **12**, and then press ↵↵ to exit the FILLET command.

6. Restart the FILLET command. Press and hold the Shift key as you click the two interior wall lines shown at the top of Figure 4.17.

The lines are filleted, and the results will look like the bottom of Figure 4.17.

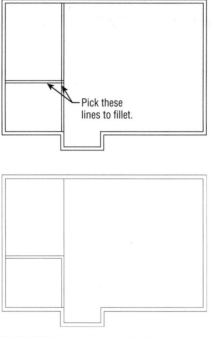

Pick these
lines to fillet.

FIGURE 4.17 Selecting the first two lines to fillet (top) and the result of the fillet (bottom)

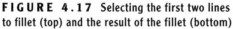

N O T E   Pressing and holding the Shift key as you select objects with the FILLET command temporarily overrides the current radius and sets it to a value of 0. In the previous example, the Fillet radius value was set to 12; however, because the Shift key was pressed, the command worked as if you had set the radius to 0.

7. Start the TRIM command, and press ↵ to skip the Select cutting edges… Select objects: prompt. This makes every edge in the drawing a cutting edge.

   Select the vertical line shown at the top of Figure 4.18. The results are shown at the bottom of Figure 4.18.

8. Save your drawing as **I04-05-WallCleanUp.dwg** (**M04-05-WallCleanUp.dwg**).

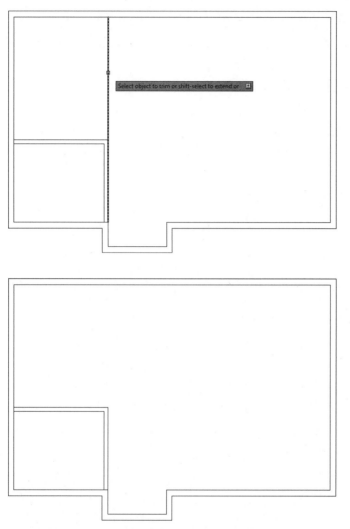

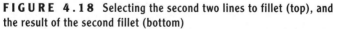

FIGURE 4.18 Selecting the second two lines to fillet (top), and the result of the second fillet (bottom)

The two new interior walls are now the correct length, but you'll have to clean up the areas where they form T-intersections with the exterior walls. The FILLET command won't work in T-intersections because too much of one of the wall lines gets deleted. You need to use the TRIM command in T-intersection cases. The FILLET command does a specific kind of trim and is easy and quick to execute, but its uses are limited (for the most part) to single intersections between two lines or multiple intersections on a polyline.

Using the *Zoom* Command

To do this trim efficiently, you need a closer view of the T-intersections. Use the ZOOM command to get a better look:

1. Make sure I04-05-WallCleanUp.dwg (M04-05-WallCleanUp.dwg) is open.

2. Type **Z**↵. Then move the crosshair cursor to a point slightly below and to the left of the upper T-intersection (see Figure 4.19), and click in a blank area outside the floor plan.

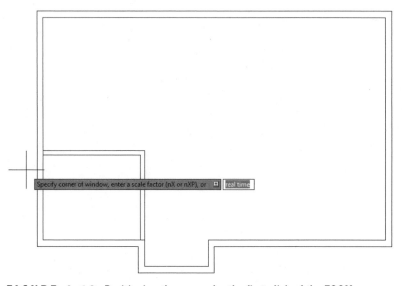

Specify corner of window, enter a scale factor (nX or nXP), or ⊞ real time

FIGURE 4.19 Positioning the cursor for the first click of the ZOOM command

3. Move the cursor up and to the right, and notice a rectangle with solid lines being drawn. Keep moving the cursor up and to the right until the rectangle encloses the upper T-intersection (see the top of Figure 4.20).

   When the rectangle fully encloses the T-intersection, click again. The view changes to a closer view of the intersection of the interior and exterior walls (see the bottom of Figure 4.20).

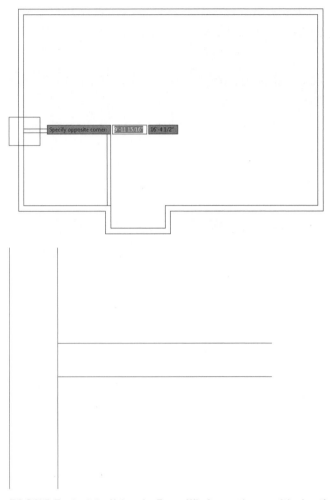

FIGURE 4.20 Using the Zoom Window option: positioning the rectangle (top), and the new view after the ZOOM command (bottom)

The rectangle you've just specified is called a *zoom window*. The area of the drawing enclosed by the zoom window becomes the view on the screen. This is one of several zoom options for changing the magnification of the view. Other zoom options are introduced later in this chapter and throughout the book.

When you start the ZOOM **command by typing Z.⌐ and then picking a point on the screen, a zoom window begins.**

4. From the Home tab ➤ Modify panel, click the Extend button.

In the command window, notice the second and third lines of text. You're being prompted to select *boundary edges* (objects to use as limits for the lines you want to extend/trim).

5. Select the two horizontal interior wall lines, and press the spacebar or ↵. The prompt changes and asks you to select the objects to be extended.

6. Press and hold the Shift key while you select the inside exterior wall line at the T-intersection that is between the two intersections with the interior wall lines that you have just picked as boundary edges (see the left of Figure 4.21).

The exterior wall line is trimmed at the T-intersection (see the right of Figure 4.21). Press the spacebar to end the TRIM command.

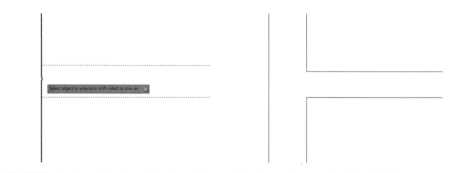

FIGURE 4.21 Selecting a line to be trimmed (left), and the result of the EXTEND command used in conjunction with the Shift key (right)

N O T E   As you've just seen with the FILLET command, pressing and holding the Shift key temporarily overrides the normal functionality of a command. For the FILLET command, the radius is temporarily set to 0. When the Shift key is used with the EXTEND command, it temporarily functions like the TRIM command. Conversely, when used with the TRIM command, it functions like the EXTEND command.

7. Return to a view of the whole drawing by typing **Z**↵ and then **P**↵.

This is the ZOOM command's Previous option, which restores the view that was active before the last use of the ZOOM command (see

Figure 4.22). This command is also available from the Zoom fly-out button on the navigation bar.

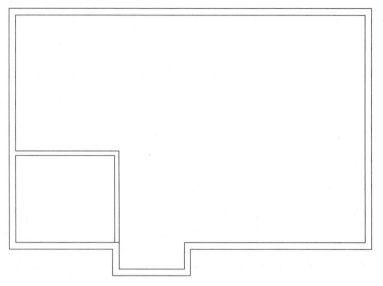

FIGURE 4.22 The result of the ZOOM Previous command

Repeat the procedure to trim the lower T-intersection. Follow these steps:

1. Type **Z↵**, and click two points to make a rectangular zoom window around the intersection.

2. Start the TRIM command, select the interior walls as cutting edges, and press the spacebar.

3. Select the inside exterior wall line between the cutting edges.

4. Press the spacebar or ↵ to end the TRIM command.

5. ZOOM Previous by typing **Z↵ P↵**. Figure 4.23 shows the results.

6. Save your drawing as **I04-06-ZoomCommand.dwg** (**M04-06-ZoomCommand.dwg**).

You need to create one more set of interior walls to represent the closet in the upper-right corner of the cabin.

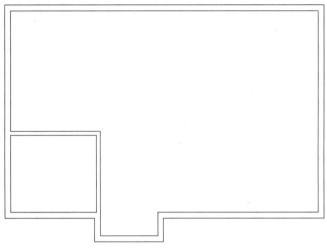

FIGURE 4.23 The second trim is completed.

Finishing the Interior Walls

You'll use the same method to create the closet walls that you used to make the first two interior walls. Briefly, this is how it's done:

1. Make sure I04-06-ZoomCommand.dwg (M04-06-ZoomCommand.dwg) is open.

2. Offset the inside line of the upper exterior wall **2'-6"** (762 mm) downward; then offset this new line **4"** (100 mm) downward (see Figure 4.24).

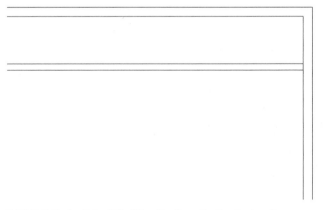

FIGURE 4.24 Offsetting the lines for the first wall

3. Offset the inside line of the right exterior wall **4'-8"** (1420 mm) to the left; then offset this new line **4"** (100 mm) to the left (see Figure 4.25).

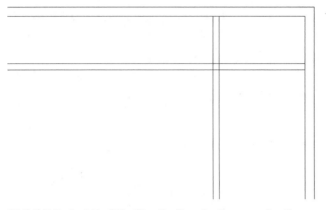

FIGURE 4.25 Offsetting the lines for the second wall

4. Use a zoom window to zoom into the closet area.

 T I P   Make a zoom window just large enough to enclose the closet. The resulting view should be large enough to allow you to fillet the corners and trim the T-intersections without zooming again.

5. Use the FILLET command to clean up the interior and exterior wall line intersections, as shown in Figure 4.26.

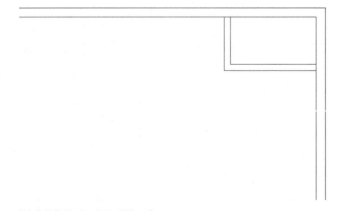

FIGURE 4.26 Fillet the two corners.

6. Use the TRIM command to trim away the short portions of the inter-secting wall lines between the two new interior walls.

   This can be accomplished with one use of the TRIM command. After you select all four of the new wall lines as cutting edges, you can trim both lines that run across the ends of the selected lines to those same cutting edges.

7. Use ZOOM Previous to restore the previous view.

   The results should look like Figure 4.27.

FIGURE 4.27 The completed interior walls

8. Save your drawing as **I04-07-FinishInteriorWalls.dwg** (**M04-07 -FinishInteriorWalls.dwg**).

You used OFFSET, FILLET, TRIM, and a couple of zooms to create the interior walls. By combining these commands, you were able to build the interior walls from the existing exterior wall definition—harnessing the relationship between both new and existing. The next task is to create four doorway openings in the interior and exterior walls. A similar strategy, employing these same commands, will be used to complete this task.

Cutting Openings in the Walls

Of the four doorway openings needed, two are on interior walls and two are on exterior walls (see Figure 4.28). Two of the openings are for swinging doors, one is for a sliding glass door, and one is for a set of bifold doors. You won't be doing the hatchings and dimensions shown in the figure—those features will be covered in future chapters.

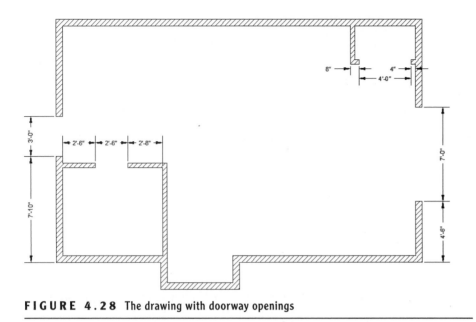

FIGURE 4.28 The drawing with doorway openings

The procedure used to make each doorway opening is the same one that you used to create the opening for the box in Chapter 2. First you establish the location of the *jambs*, or sides, of an opening. After the location of one jamb is located, the line defining that side is offset by the width of the door opening. When the jambs are established, you'll trim away the wall lines between the edges. The commands used in this exercise are OFFSET, EXTEND, and TRIM. You'll make openings for the 3'-0" (915 mm) exterior doorway first.

Creating the 3'-0" (915 mm) Exterior Opening

This opening is on the back wall of the cabin and has one side set in 7'-10" (2388 mm) from the outside corner:

1. Make sure I04-07-FinishInteriorWalls.dwg (M04-07-FinishInterior Walls.dwg) is open.

2. Start the OFFSET command, and then type 7'10⏎ (2388⏎) to set the distance to 7'-10" (2388 mm).

3. Click the lower outside line indicated in Figure 4.29, and then click in a blank area above the line you selected.

    You have to offset one line at a time because of the way the OFFSET command works.

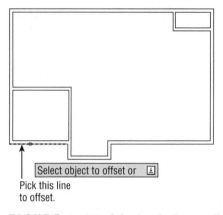

FIGURE 4.29 Selecting the line to offset

4. End and restart the OFFSET command by pressing the spacebar or ↵
twice; then type **3'**↵ (**915**↵) to set a new offset distance, and offset the
new line up (see Figure 4.30).

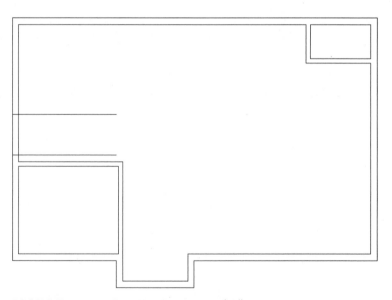

FIGURE 4.30 The offset line for the 3′-0″ (915 mm) opening

5. Start the TRIM command and press ↵ to skip the cutting edges prompt.

6. When asked to Select object to trim, enter **F**↵ for Fence at the
command line.

7. Draw a fence line as shown at the top of Figure 4.31. The result should look like the bottom of Figure 4.31.

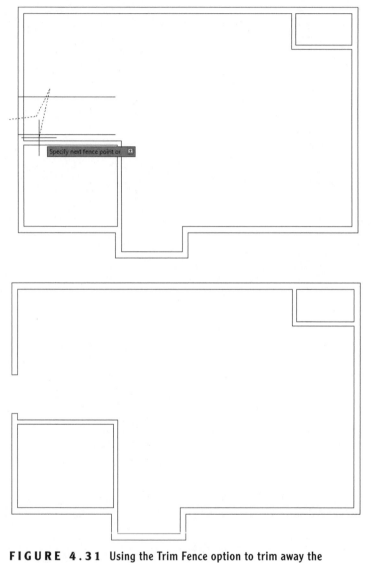

FIGURE 4.31 Using the Trim Fence option to trim away the unneeded lines

8. Save your drawing as `I04-08-3ftExterior.dwg` (`M04-08-915mm Exterior.dwg`).

Creating the 7'-0" (2134 mm) Opening

Take another look at Figure 4.28 and notice that the opening on the right side of the building has one jamb set in 4'-6" (1372 mm) from the outside corner. This opening is for the sliding glass door.

You've done this procedure before, so here's a quick summary of the steps:

1. Make sure I04-08-3ftExterior.dwg (M04-08-915mmExterior.dwg) is open.

2. Offset the lower exterior wall line 4'-6" (1372 mm).

3. Offset the new line 7'-0" (2134 mm).

4. Use the Trim Fence option used to clean up the 3'-0" opening, to complete the opening. Your cabin should look like Figure 4.32.

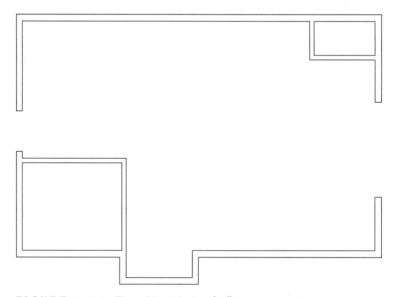

FIGURE 4.32   The cabin with the 7'-0" (2134 mm) sliding door opening

5. Save your drawing as I04-09-7ftExterior.dwg (M04-09-2134mm Exterior.dwg).

Creating the 2'-6" (762 mm) Interior Opening

The 2'-6" (762 mm) opening to the bathroom starts 30" (762 mm) from the inside of the left exterior wall. You can't simply offset the wall and trim the excess, because the offset lines would not cross both the interior wall lines. So instead you will use the EXTEND command exactly as you used it in Chapter 2:

1. Make sure I04-09-7ftExterior.dwg (M04-09-2134mmExterior.dwg) is open.

2. Start the OFFSET command and offset the interior line of the lower-left exterior wall **2′-6″** (762 mm) to the right; then offset the new line another **2′-6″** (762 mm) to the right.

3. Start the EXTEND command, and then press the spacebar or ↵ to make every edge in the drawing a boundary edge.

TIP   **If you start a new command by entering letters on the keyboard, you must first make sure that the previous command has ended by pressing the Esc key at least twice. On the other hand, if you start a new command by clicking its icon on the Ribbon, it doesn't matter whether the previous command is still running. AutoCAD will cancel it.**

---

4. Click the two jamb lines to extend them. Be sure to pick points on the lines that are near the ends that you want to extend, as shown in Figure 4.33, or the lines will be extended in the opposite direction.

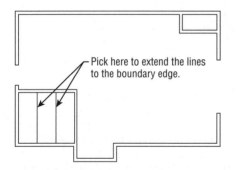

Pick here to extend the lines to the boundary edge.

FIGURE 4.33 The lines after being extended through the bathroom walls

The lines are extended through the interior walls to make the jambs (see Figure 4.33).

Keeping the EXTEND command active, you'll use the Shift key to trim away the excess lines and complete the openings. You'll do this by creating two crossing windows—first to trim the excess part of the jamb lines, and then the wall lines between the jamb lines.

5. With the EXTEND command still active, press and hold the Shift key. Keeping it pressed, select a point to the right side of the bathroom and then another to the left, as shown in Figure 4.34.

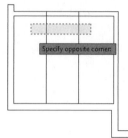
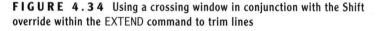

FIGURE 4.34 Using a crossing window in conjunction with the Shift override within the EXTEND command to trim lines

6. Repeat the same process you used in the previous steps. With the EXTEND command still active, press and hold the Shift key to create a crossing window through the wall, as shown in Figure 4.35. Press ⏎ to exit the EXTEND command.

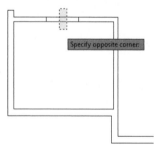
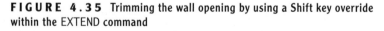

FIGURE 4.35 Trimming the wall opening by using a Shift key override within the EXTEND command

7. Save your drawing as **I04-10-30inInterior.dwg** (**M04-10-762mm Interior.dwg**).

Your cabin should appear as shown in Figure 4.36.

You can construct the closet opening by using the same procedure.

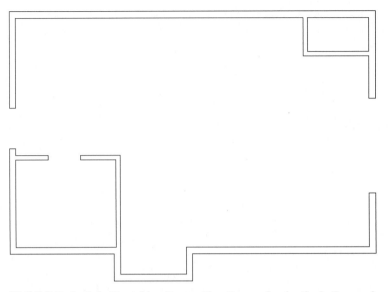

FIGURE 4.36 The cabin after creating the opening for the bathroom door

Creating the Closet Opening

This doorway is 4'-0" (1220 mm) wide and has one jamb set in 4" (100 mm) from the inside of the exterior wall. Figure 4.37 shows the three stages of fabricating this opening:

▶ The offset lines that locate the jamb lines (top left)

▶ The extended lines that form the jamb lines (top right)

▶ The completed openings after trimming (bottom)

1. Make sure I04-10-30inInterior.dwg (M04-10-762mmInterior.dwg) is open.

2. Use any combination of the OFFSET, TRIM, and EXTEND commands to create the 4'-0" (1220 mm) closet opening. Refer to the previous section on making openings for step-by-step instructions.

3. This completes the openings. Save your drawing as **I04-11-Closet Opening.dwg** (**M04-11-ClosetOpening.dwg**). The results should look like Figure 4.38.

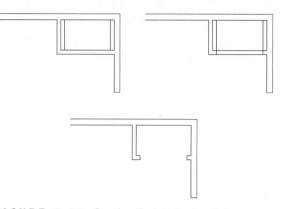

FIGURE 4.37 Creating the interior openings

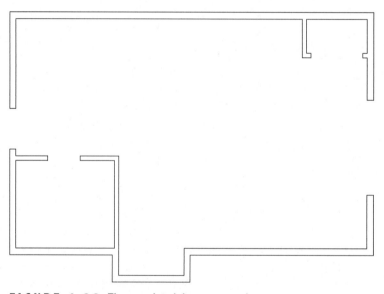

FIGURE 4.38 The completed doorway openings

As you gain more control over the commands you used here, you'll be able to anticipate how much of a task can be accomplished with each use of a command. Each opening required offsetting, extending, and trimming. It's possible to do all the openings by using each command only once. In this way, you do all the offsetting, then all the extending, and finally all the trimming. In cutting these openings, however, the arrangement of the offset lines determined how many cycles of the TRIM command were most efficient to use. If lines being trimmed and used as cutting edges cross each other, the trimming becomes complicated. For these four openings, the most efficient procedure is to use each command twice. In Chapter 8, you'll get a chance to work with more-complex, multiple trims when you draw the elevations.

WHAT TO DO WHEN YOU MAKE A MISTAKE

When you're offsetting, trimming, and extending lines, it's easy to pick the wrong line, especially in a congested drawing. Here are some tips on how to correct these errors and get back on track:

▶ You can always cancel any command by pressing the Esc key until you see the Command: prompt in the command window. Then click the Undo button on the Quick Access toolbar to undo the results of the last command. If you undo too much, click the Redo button. You can click it more than once to redo several undone commands. Redos must be performed immediately following an undo.

▶ Errors possible with the OFFSET command include setting the wrong distance, picking the wrong line to offset, and picking the wrong side to offset toward. If the distance is correct, you can continue offsetting, end the command when you have the results you want, and then erase the lines that were offset wrong. Otherwise, press Esc and undo your previous offset.

▶ Errors made with the TRIM and EXTEND commands can sometimes be corrected on the fly; you don't have to end the command because each of these commands has an Undo option. If you pick a line and it doesn't trim or extend the correct way, you can undo that last action without stopping the command and then continue trimming or extending. You can activate the Undo option used while the command is running in two ways: type U↵, or right-click and choose Undo from the context menu. Either of these actions undoes the last trim or extend, and you can try again without having to restart the command. Each time you activate the Undo option from within the command, another trim or extend is undone.

▶ The LINE command has the same Undo option as the TRIM and EXTEND commands. You can undo the last segment drawn (or the last several segments) and redraw them without stopping the command.

Now that the openings are complete, you can place doors and door swings in their appropriate doorways. In doing this, you'll be introduced to two new objects and a few new commands, and you'll have an opportunity to use the OFFSET and TRIM commands in new, strategic ways.

Creating Doors

In a floor plan, a rectangle or a line for the door and an arc showing the path of the door swing usually indicates a pivot door. The door's position varies, but it's most often shown at 90° from the closed position (see Figure 4.39). The best rule I have come across is to display the door in such a way that others working with your floor plan will be able to see how far, and in what direction, the door will swing open.

FIGURE 4.39 Possible ways to illustrate pivot doors

The cabin has four openings. Two of them need swinging doors, which open 90°. The main entry is a sliding glass door, and the closet is accessed by a pair of bifold doors. Drawing each type of door will require a different approach.

Drawing Swinging Doors

The swinging doors are of two widths: 3′ (915 mm) for exterior and 2′-6″ (762 mm) for interior (refer to Figure 4.28 earlier in this chapter). In general, doorway openings leading to the outside are wider than interior doors, with bathroom and bedroom doors usually being the narrowest. For the cabin, you'll use two sizes of swinging doors. If multiple doors of the same width existed in this design, you could draw one door of each size and then copy them to the other openings as required.

To accomplish this, we'll start with the back door (on the left side of the floor plan). The only difference between the back door and the bathroom door is size, so you'll learn how to copy and modify the back door, sizing it to fit the opening for the bathroom. It's a step that far too many AutoCAD users overlook, but taking a moment to develop a basic plan such as this one is certain to help you better understand what you're drawing while making you a more productive user.

Now that we have a plan, let's get started drawing some doors:

1. Make sure I04-11-ClosetOpening.dwg (M04-11-ClosetOpening.dwg) is open.

2. Check the status bar at the bottom of the screen and verify that Dynamic Input is enabled (a blue background).

3. Turn off the remaining drawing aids (buttons) in the status bar.

4. Right-click the Object Snap button on the status bar, and choose Settings from the context menu.

   This opens the Drafting Settings dialog box, and the Object Snap tab is activated (Figure 4.40).

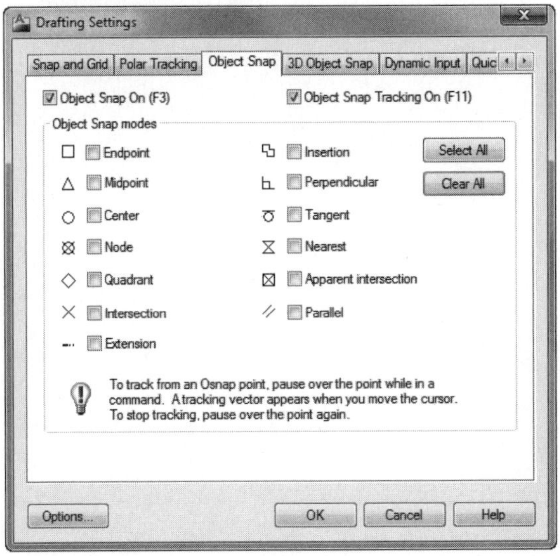

FIGURE 4.40 The Object Snap tab of the Drafting Settings dialog box

5. From the Object Snap tab within the Drafting Settings dialog box, click the Clear All button on the right and then click OK.

   This step isn't essential, as long as the Object Snap button is turned off, but it's best to be sure in this case. Object snaps are covered in depth in Chapter 5 and are used throughout the remainder of the book.

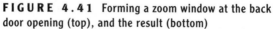

6. Launch the Zoom Window tool from the Zoom drop-down menu found on the View tab ➤ Navigate 2D panel. Alternatively, you can type **Z**↵ at the command line or use the Zoom button.

7. Pick two points to form a window around the back doorway opening, as shown in Figure 4.41 (top).

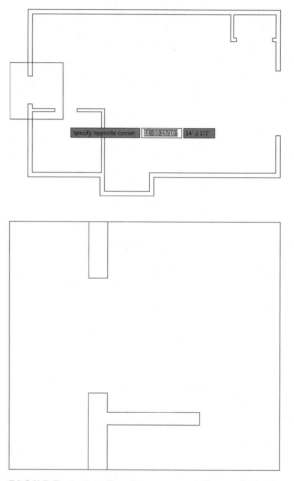

FIGURE 4.41 Forming a zoom window at the back door opening (top), and the result (bottom)

The view changes, and you now have a close-up view of the opening (see Figure 4.41, bottom). You'll draw the door in a closed position and then rotate it open.

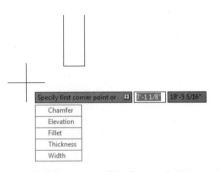

8. To begin drawing the door, use the Rectangle (RECTANG) command from the Home tab ➤ Draw panel ➤ Rectangle tool.

Notice the Command: prompt in the command window. Several options are in brackets, but the option Specify first corner point (before the brackets) is the default, and it is the one you want. You can also expose these options (see Figure 4.42) at the cursor by pressing the down-arrow on the main keyboard (not the down-arrow on the numeric keypad).

You can also start the Rectangle (RECTANG) command by typing REC.⏎ at the Command: prompt.

FIGURE 4.42 The Rectangle (RECTANG) command options exposed at the cursor

You form the rectangle in the same way that you form the zoom window—by picking two points to represent opposite corners of the rectangle. In its closed position, the door will fit exactly between the jambs, with its two right corners coinciding with the rightmost endpoints of the jambs. To make the first corner of the rectangle coincide exactly with the upper endpoint of the right jamb, you'll use an object snap to assist you.

Object snaps (or *osnaps*) allow you to pick specific points on objects such as endpoints, midpoints, the center of a circle, and so on. When the Osnap button is active, the cursor will snap to any of the options selected in the Object Snap tab of the Drafting Settings dialog box. These are called *running osnaps*, and they should be disabled from the status bar at the moment.

Osnap is short for *object snap*. The two terms are used interchangeably.

9. Type **END.**⏎ to manually specify the Endpoint osnap.

Manually specifying an osnap by entering its name at the command line will override any running osnaps that may be active. For one pick, your cursor will snap to the nearest endpoint of any line, arc, or polyline that you select and ignore any running osnaps such as Midpoint.

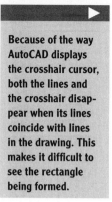

Because of the way AutoCAD displays the crosshair cursor, both the lines and the crosshair disappear when its lines coincide with lines in the drawing. This makes it difficult to see the rectangle being formed.

10. Move the cursor near the right side of the upper jamb line.

When the cursor gets very close to a line, a colored square, called a *marker*, appears at the nearest endpoint along with a tooltip that indicates which osnap is active, as shown in Figure 4.43. This shows you which endpoint in the drawing is closest to the position of the crosshair cursor at that moment.

FIGURE 4.43 The Endpoint osnap marker

11. Move the cursor until the square is positioned on the right end of the upper jamb line as shown, and then click that point.

The first corner of the rectangle now is located at that point. Move the cursor to the right and slightly down to see the rectangle being formed (see Figure 4.44, left). To locate the opposite corner, let's use the relative Cartesian coordinates discussed in Chapter 2.

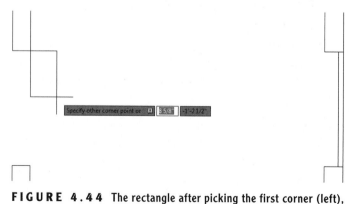

FIGURE 4.44 The rectangle after picking the first corner (left), and the completed door in a closed position (right)

12. When the command prompt shows the `Specify other corner point or [Area/Dimensions/Rotation]:` prompt, type **-1.5,-3'**↵ (**-40,-915**↵↵).

    The rectangle is drawn across the opening, creating a door in a closed position (see Figure 4.44, right). The door now needs to be rotated around its hinge point to an opened position.

    When you used the Rectangle (`RECTANG`) command to draw the swinging doors, you had to use relative Cartesian coordinates because relative polar coordinates would have required you to know the diagonal distance across the plan of the door and the angle of that distance as well.

13. Save your drawing as **I04-12-SwingingDoor.dwg** (**M04-12-Swinging Door.dwg**).

Rotating the Door

This rotation will be through an arc of 90° in the clockwise direction, making it a rotation of –90°. By default, counterclockwise rotations are positive, while clockwise rotations are negative. You'll use the `ROTATE` command to rotate the door:

1. Continue using **I04-12-SwingingDoor.dwg** (**M04-12-SwingingDoor.dwg**), or open it if it's not already open.

2. Click the Rotate button on the Home tab ➢ Modify panel or type **RO**↵. You'll see a prompt to select objects. Click the door and press ↵.

    You're prompted for a *base point*—a point around which the door will be rotated. To keep the door placed correctly, pick the hinge point for the base point. The hinge point for this opening is the right endpoint of the bottom jamb line.

3. Type **END**↵ to activate the Endpoint osnap.

4. Move the cursor near the lower-right corner of the door. When the marker is displayed at that corner, click to locate the base point.

5. Check the status bar to be sure the Ortho Mode button isn't pressed. If it is, click it to turn off Ortho (it will change to a gray background).

    When the Ortho Mode button is on (with a light blue background), the cursor is forced to move in a vertical or horizontal direction. This is useful at times, but in this instance such a restriction would keep you from being able to see the door rotate.

6. Move the cursor away from the hinge point, and see how the door rotates as the cursor moves (see the left image in Figure 4.45).

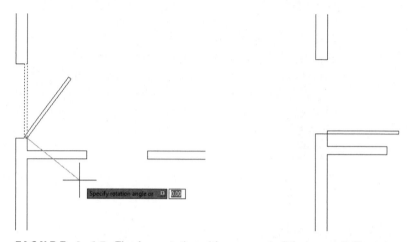

FIGURE 4.45 The door rotating with movement of the cursor (left), and the door after the 90° rotation (right)

If the door swings properly, you're reassured that you correctly selected the base point. The prompt in the command window reads `Specify rotation angle or [Copy/Reference]<0.00>:`, asking you to enter an angle.

7. Type **-90**↵. The door is rotated 90° to an open position (see the right image in Figure 4.45).

8. Save your drawing as **I04-13-RotateDoor.dwg** (**M04-13-Rotate Door.dwg**).

To finish this door, you need to add the door's swing. You'll use the ARC command for this.

Drawing the Door Swing

The swing shows the path that the outer edge of a door takes when it swings from closed to fully open. Including a swing with the door in a floor plan helps to identify the rectangle as a door and helps resolve clearance issues. You draw the swings by using the ARC command, in this case using the Endpoint osnap.

This command has many options, most of which are based on knowing three aspects of the arc, as you'll see. Here are the steps:

1. Continue using I04-13-RotateDoor.dwg (M04-13-RotateDoor.dwg), or open it if it's not already open.

2. Click the down-arrow below the Arc button from the Home tab ➤ Draw panel.

   The menu expands to show the 11 different methods for creating an arc. On the menu, 10 of the 11 options have combinations of three aspects that define an arc. The arc for this door swing needs to be drawn from the right end of the upper jamb line through a rotation of 90°. You know the start point of the arc, the center of rotation (the hinge point), and the angle through which the rotation occurs, so you can use the Start, Center, Angle option on the Arc menu.

THE OPTIONS OF THE ARC COMMAND

The position and size of an arc can be specified by a combination of its components, some of which are start point, endpoint, angle, center point, and radius. The ARC command gives you 11 options, 10 of which use three components to define the arc. With a little study of the geometric information available to you about your drawing, you can choose the option that best fits the situation.

When you start the ARC command by typing A↵, you get an abbreviated form of the command in the command prompt. You can access all 11 options of the command through this prompt, but you have to select the various components along the way.

3. From the expanded Arc menu, choose Start, Center, Angle, as shown in Figure 4.46.

   The command prompt now reads Specify start point of arc:; this is the default option. You could also start with the center point, but you would have to type C↵ before picking a point to be the center point.

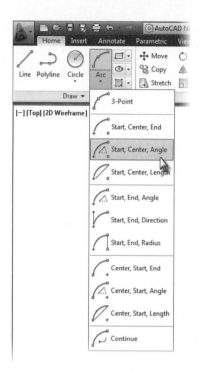

FIGURE 4.46 The expanded Arc menu

4. Activate the Endpoint osnap (type **END**↵), and pick the right endpoint of the upper jamb line, as shown in Figure 4.47.

FIGURE 4.47 Specifying the start point for the ARC command

The prompt changes to read Specify second point of arc:. Because you previously chose the Start, Center, Angle option, AutoCAD automatically chooses Center for you as the second point. That is the last part of the prompt. You'll need the Endpoint osnap again, but this time you will pick it from a menu.

5. Hold down the Shift key, and right-click in the drawing area to open a context menu containing all the available osnaps.

6. Click on the Endpoint option, as shown in Figure 4.48, to activate the Endpoint osnap.

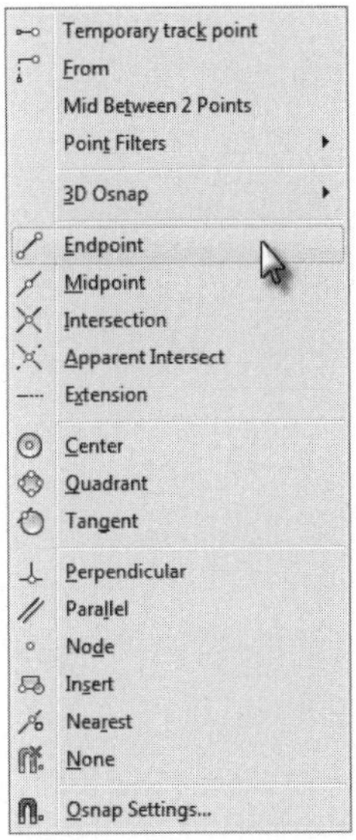

FIGURE 4.48 Select the Endpoint osnap from the Object Snap context menu.

7. Using the Endpoint osnap, select the hinge point.

The arc is now visible, and its endpoint follows the cursor's movement, but the arc is extending in the wrong direction (see the top image in Figure 4.49). The prompt displays the Specify Included Angle option.

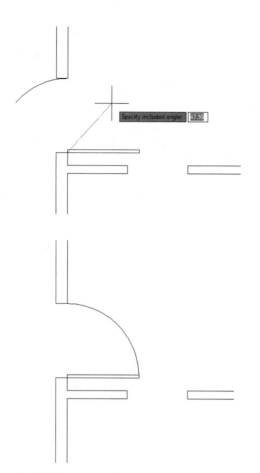

FIGURE 4.49 Drawing the arc: The ending point of the arc follows the cursor's movements (top), and the completed arc (bottom).

8. Type **-90.⌐**. The arc is completed, and the ARC command ends (see the bottom image in Figure 4.49).

9. Save your drawing as **I04-14-DoorSwing.dwg** (**M04-14-DoorSwing.dwg**).

 WARNING   In this situation, the arc must be created by selecting the jamb end first and the door end later. Arcs are made in a counterclockwise fashion, so selecting the door end first and the jamb end later would result in a 270° arc that extends behind the door and through the external wall.

The back door is completed. Next, you'll copy and then modify the back door to form the bathroom door.

Copying Objects

As you would expect, the COPY command makes a copy of the objects you select. You can locate this copy either by picking a point or by entering relative coordinates from the keyboard. For AutoCAD to position these copied objects, you must designate two points: a base point, which serves as a point of reference for where the copy move starts, and then a second point, which serves as the ending or destination point for the COPY command.

The copy is moved the same distance and direction from its original position that the second point is located from the first point. When you know the actual distance and direction to move the copy, the base point isn't critical because you specify the second point with relative polar or relative Cartesian coordinates. But in this situation, you don't know the exact distance or angle to move a copy of the back door to the bathroom door opening, so you need to choose a base point for the copy carefully.

In copying this new door and its swing to the back door opening of the cabin, you must find a point somewhere on the existing door or swing that can be located precisely on a point at the back door opening. You can choose from two points: the hinge point and the start point of the door swing. Let's use the hinge point. You usually know where the hinge point of the new door belongs, so this is easier to locate than the start point of the arc. In the following steps you'll copy the existing door so it may be used for the bathroom door opening:

1. Continue using I04-14-DoorSwing.dwg (M04-14-DoorSwing.dwg), or open it if it's not already open.

2. Click the Copy button on the Home tab ➤ Modify panel of the Ribbon or type **CO**↵ at the command line.

3. The prompt asks you to select objects to copy. Pick the door and swing and then press ↵.
   The prompt in the command window reads **Specify base point or [Displacement/mOde]<Displacement>:**.

4. Pick the hinge point by using the Endpoint osnap.
   A copy of the door and swing is attached to the crosshair cursor at the hinge point (see Figure 4.50), and the prompt changes to Specify second point or <use first point of displacement>:. You need to pick where the hinge point of the copied door will be located at the bathroom door opening.

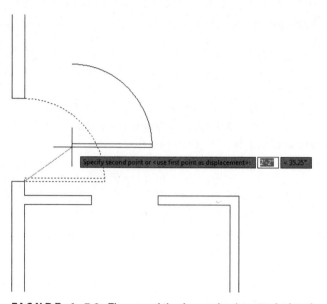

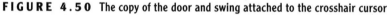

FIGURE 4.50 The copy of the door and swing attached to the crosshair cursor

5. Activate the Endpoint osnap once again. This time pick the lower end of the right jamb line on the bathroom door opening.

   The copy of the door and swing is placed in the opening (see Figure 4.51).

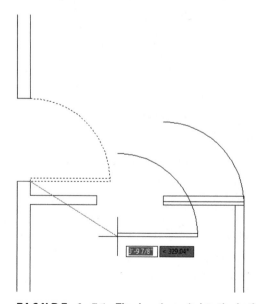

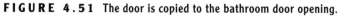

FIGURE 4.51 The door is copied to the bathroom door opening.

Looking at the command prompt, you can see that the COPY command is still running, and a copy of both the door and swing remains attached to the cursor.

6. Press ↵ to end the COPY command.

7. The door is oriented the wrong way, but you'll fix that next. Save your drawing as I04-15-CopyingObjects.dwg (M04-15-Copying Objects.dwg).

When you copy doors from one opening to another, often the orientation doesn't match. The best strategy is to use the hinge point as a point of reference and place the door where it needs to go, as you just did. Then flip or rotate the door so that it sits and swings the right way. The flipping of an object is known as *mirroring*.

Mirroring Objects

You have located the door in the opening, but it needs to be rotated 90° to be perpendicular to the wall and then flipped so that it swings to the inside of the bathroom. To do this, you'll use the ROTATE command that you used earlier, and then the MIRROR command.

The MIRROR command allows you to flip objects around an axis called the *mirror line*. You define this imaginary line by designating two points on the line. Strategic selection of the mirror line ensures the accuracy of the mirroring action, so it's critical to visualize where the proper line lies. Sometimes you'll have to draw a guideline in order to designate one or both of the endpoints.

1. Continue using I04-15-CopyingObjects.dwg (M04-15-Copying Objects.dwg), or open it if it's not already open.

2. Click the Rotate button found on the Home tab ➢ Modify panel, and select the door and swing for the bathroom door. With the door and swing selected, press ↵.

3. Activate the Endpoint osnap by typing **END**↵ and then picking the hinge point from the Specify base point: prompt.

4. At the Specify rotation angle: prompt, type **90**↵.
   The door is rotated 90°, but its orientation is incorrect, as shown in Figure 4.52.

◄

The COPY command keeps running until you end it. This allows you to make multiple copies of the same object. You'll do that in Chapter 5 when you draw the stove top.

◄

The ZOOM command is usable while the COPY command is active. Similarly, most display commands (ZOOM, PAN, and so on) share this functionality and are known as *transparent commands*.

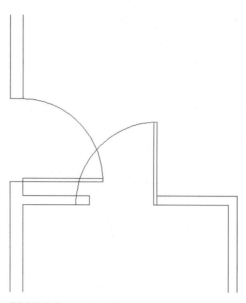

FIGURE 4.52 The door after rotating it 90°

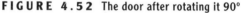

Try typing P↵ at the
Select Objects:
prompt to quickly
reselect the last
objects selected.

🔺 Mirror

5. Start the MIRROR command from the Home tab ➢ Modify panel ➢ Mirror tool button, or type **MI**↵ at the command line. Select the bathroom door and swing and then press ↵. The prompt line changes to read Specify first point of mirror line:.

6. Activate the Endpoint osnap, and then pick the hinge point of the door.
The prompt changes to read Specify second point of mirror line:, and you'll see the mirrored image of the door and the swing moving as you move the cursor around the drawing area. You're rotating the mirror line about the hinge point as you move the cursor. As the mirror line rotates, the orientation of the mirrored image changes (see Figure 4.53).

7. Press and hold the Shift key to temporarily enable Ortho mode.
A small icon displays in the upper-right quadrant of your cursor to indicate that Ortho mode is temporarily enabled, locking your cursor to increments of 90°.

8. With the Shift key pressed, select any point to the left, as shown in Figure 4.54.

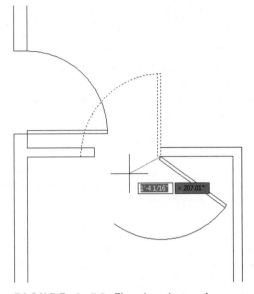
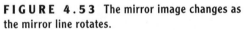

FIGURE 4.53 The mirror image changes as the mirror line rotates.

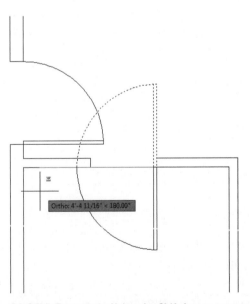
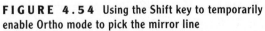

FIGURE 4.54 Using the Shift key to temporarily enable Ortho mode to pick the mirror line

Activating the temporary Ortho mode override may take a moment. You'll know the override is enabled when the small shield icon appears next to your cursor. Because Ortho mode locks your cursor to rotation increments of 90°, you don't have to be precise when selecting the second point. You can see that the point selected in Figure 4.54 is not perpendicular; however, Ortho mode ensures that the mirror line is drawn along the horizontal bathroom wall.

9. Type **Y**↵ when the command prompt reads Erase source objects? [Yes/No] <N>:.

   The flipped door is displayed, and the original one is deleted (see Figure 4.55). The MIRROR command ends.

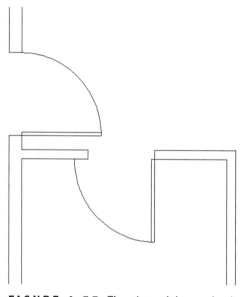

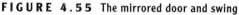

FIGURE 4.55 The mirrored door and swing

10. Save your drawing as **I04-16-MirroringObjects.dwg** (**M04-16 -MirroringObjects.dwg**).

It may take some practice to become proficient at visualizing and designating the mirror line, but once you're used to it, you'll have learned how to use a powerful tool. Because many objects—including building layouts, mechanical parts, steel beams, road cross-sections, and so on—have some symmetry to them, wise use of the MIRROR command can save you a lot of drawing time.

Now let's change the scale of the interior to match the available opening.

Scaling the Bathroom Door

You could have used the STRETCH command to make the door narrower, but that's an advanced Modify command and won't be introduced until Chapter 11, "Working with Hatches, Gradients, and Tool Palettes." Besides, the arc would have to be modified to a smaller radius. It's easier to scale the objects, and the slightly thinner door can be attributed to interior doors being thinner than exterior doors. In Chapter 9, "Using Dynamic Blocks and Tables," I'll demonstrate a dynamic block that can serve as a door block for several door sizes.

For this exercise, you will use the SCALE command to resize the bathroom door to fit the existing opening. The SCALE command changes the size of all the selected objects by an equal amount based on keyboard input or the location of the cursor. The objects scale up or down in relation to their position relative to a base point you've defined. Objects scaled up will appear to get farther away from the base point, while objects scaled down will appear to get closer.

The 30″ (762 mm) bathroom door opening is 5/6 the size of the 36″ (915 mm) back door opening; therefore, 5/6, or its decimal equivalent of 0.8333, can be used as the scale factor. Because fractions are inherently more accurate than rounded-off decimal values, we'll use the fractional scale factor:

> The scale factor 5/6 was derived by reducing 30/36. Because a 762 mm door isn't exactly 5/6 of a 915 mm door, the unreduced fraction 762/915 can be substituted to achieve an accurate scale factor.

1. Continue using I04-16-MirroringObjects.dwg (M04-16-Mirroring Objects.dwg), or open it if it's not already open.

2. Click the Zoom Window button found on the navigation bar to zoom in to the interior door opening (see Figure 4.56).

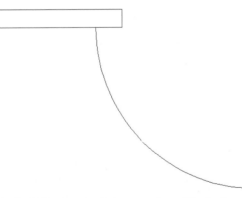

FIGURE 4.56 A close-up view of the bathroom door

3. Start the SCALE command by using the Scale button found on the Home tab ➤ Modify panel, or type **SC↵** at the command line.

4. At the Select objects: prompt, select the bathroom door and swing and then press ↵.

5. At the Specify base point: prompt, type END↵ and pick the hinge point.
   As you move the cursor, you can see the scaled version of the door change size depending on how far the cursor is located from the base point (see Figure 4.57).

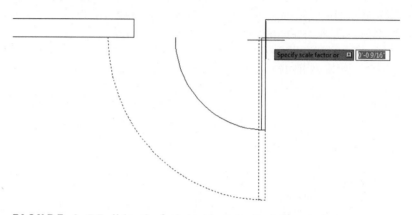

FIGURE 4.57 Using the Scale tool to resize the bathroom door

6. Type **5/6**↵ (**762/915**↵) to scale the 36″ (915 mm) door down to 30″ (762 mm).
   The rescaled door should look like Figure 4.58.

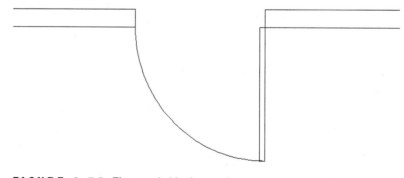

FIGURE 4.58 The rescaled bathroom door

7. Save your drawing as **I04-17-ScalingObjects.dwg** (**M04-17-Scaling Objects.dwg**).

As you can see, as long as you know the scale factor, it's easy to use the SCALE command to resize objects in your drawing. The next door to draw is the sliding glass door. This kind of door requires an entirely different strategy, but you'll use commands familiar to you by now.

Drawing a Sliding Glass Door

You will need to use the Endpoint osnap a lot while creating, copying, rotating, and mirroring objects; it's probably the most frequently used of the osnaps. Rather than activating it as needed, you will turn on Endpoint as a running osnap—an osnap that is permanently turned on:

1. Continue using I04-17-ScalingObjects.dwg (M04-17-Scaling Objects.dwg), or open it if it's not already open.

2. Right-click the Object Snap button in the status bar, and then select the Settings option in the context menu.

3. In the Object Snap tab of the Drafting Settings dialog box, check the Endpoint option.

   While the cursor is near the selection, a tooltip appears, describing the features to which the osnap moves the cursor. Take a moment to investigate what each of the osnap options does before clicking the OK button (see Figure 4.59).

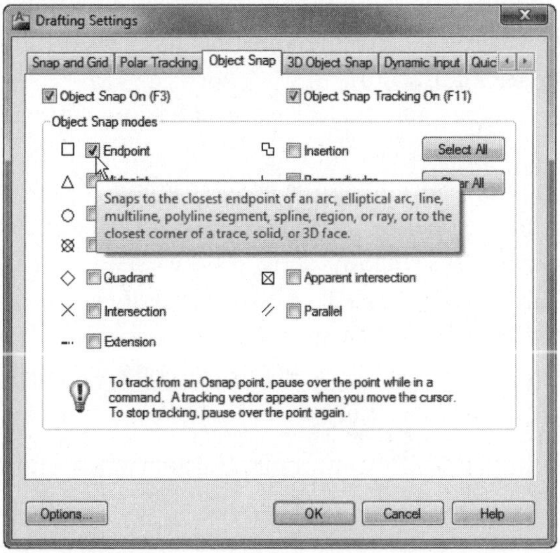

FIGURE 4.59 The Object Snap tab of the Drafting Settings dialog box

4. The osnap is active, but the running osnaps are not turned on. Click the Object Snap button to turn on (light blue background) running osnaps. Now whenever you are prompted to pick a point, a marker will appear over the nearest endpoint of the object the cursor is over.

Sliding glass doors are usually drawn to show their glass panels within the door frames, as shown in Figure 4.60.

FIGURE 4.60 A common appearance for a sliding glass door

To draw the sliding door, you'll apply the LINE, OFFSET, and TRIM commands to the 7' (2134 mm) opening you made earlier. It's a complicated exercise, but it will teach you a lot about the power of using these three commands in combination:

1. Continue using I04-17-ScalingObjects.dwg (M04-17-ScalingObjects .dwg), or open it if it's not already open.

2. Zoom out by rolling the mouse wheel toward you or by using the Zoom Extents (ZOOM) command. Zooming with the mouse wheel zooms the drawing toward or away from the location of the cursor.

3. Zoom closely around the 7' (2134 mm) opening.

    Try zooming with the scroll wheel by placing the cursor in the center of the opening and rolling the scroll wheel away from you. Make the opening as large as possible while including everything you need in the view (see Figure 4.61).

    You'll be using several osnaps for this procedure. Rather than entering each osnap, you can activate any object snap by holding down the Shift key and right-clicking in the drawing area. This opens a context menu with all the object snap options shown earlier in Figure 4.50. Selecting any of these options activates the osnap for a single pick.

    You probably noticed the list of osnaps that appeared when you right-clicked the Object Snap button in the status bar. These do not activate an osnap for a single pick; rather, they are a quick method for activating or deactivating a running osnap.

4. Offset each jamb line 2" (51 mm) into the doorway opening (see Figure 4.62).

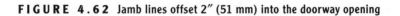

FIGURE 4.61 The view when zoomed in as closely as possible to the 7′ (2134 mm) opening

FIGURE 4.62 Jamb lines offset 2″ (51 mm) into the doorway opening

5. Start the LINE command, and choose the Midpoint osnap from the Shift+right-click context menu.

6. Place the cursor near the midpoint of the upper doorjamb line and notice that the marker, now a triangle, appears when your cursor is in the vicinity of the midpoint (see Figure 4.63).

A symbol with a distinctive shape is associated with each osnap. Click when the triangle appears at the midpoint of the jamb line.

FIGURE 4.63 Using the Midpoint osnap to select the start point of the line

7. Move the cursor over the bottom jamb line and you'll notice the Endpoint markers appear.

The Endpoint running osnap is still active, but typing in the first three letters of an osnap or clicking an osnap option from the context menu overrides it.

8. Click the Midpoint osnap option again, and move the cursor to the bottom jamb line.

9. When the triangle appears at that midpoint, click again. Press ↵ to end the LINE command.

10. Start the OFFSET command, and enter **1.5**↵ (**38**↵) to set the offset distance.

11. Pick the newly drawn line and then pick a point anywhere to the right side.

12. While the OFFSET command is still running, pick the original line again and pick another point in a blank area somewhere to the left side of the doorway opening (see Figure 4.64).

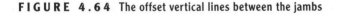

F I G U R E   4 . 6 4 The offset vertical lines between the jambs

13. Press ⏎ to end the OFFSET command.

14. In the status bar, click the Ortho Mode button to turn that mode on (light blue background). Ortho mode restricts the cursor to vertical and horizontal movements only.

15. Start the LINE command, choosing the Midpoint osnap option, and then move the cursor near the midpoint of the left vertical line.

   When the triangle marker appears at the midpoint, click to set the endpoint of the line.

16. Hold the cursor out directly to the right of the point you just selected to draw a horizontal line through the three vertical lines.

   When the cursor is about 2′ (600 mm) to the right of the three vertical lines, pick a point to set the endpoint of this guideline (see

Figure 4.65). Press ↵ to end the LINE command. Click Ortho mode off (gray background).

FIGURE 4.65 The horizontal guideline drawn through vertical lines

17. Type **0**↵ or click Offset on the Home tab ➢ Modify panel to start the OFFSET command, and then type **1**↵ (**25**↵) to set the offset distance to 1″ (25 mm).

18. Select the horizontal line you just drew, and then pick a point in a blank area anywhere above the line. Pick the first horizontal line again, and then pick anywhere below it.

   The new line has been offset 1″ (25 mm) above and below itself (see Figure 4.66). Now you have placed all the lines necessary to create the sliding glass door frames in the opening. You still need to trim back some of these lines and erase others. Press ↵ to end the OFFSET command.

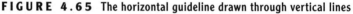

19. Start the TRIM command. When you're prompted to select cutting edges, pick the two horizontal lines that were just created with the OFFSET command and press ↵.

20. Trim the two outside vertical lines by selecting them, as shown on the left of Figure 4.67. The result is shown on the right.

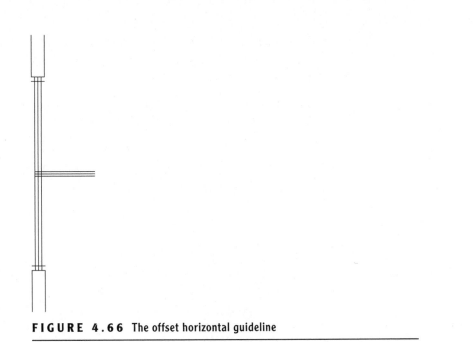

FIGURE 4.66 The offset horizontal guideline

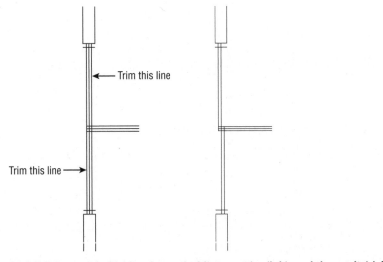

Trim this line

Trim this line →

FIGURE 4.67 Picking the vertical lines to trim (left), and the result (right)

21. Press ↵ twice to stop and restart the TRIM command.

22. When you're prompted to select cutting edges, use a special window called a *crossing window* to select all the lines visible in the drawing.

A crossing window selects everything within the window or crossing it. See the sidebar titled "Understanding Selection Windows" later in this chapter for additional information about this feature. Here's how to use a crossing window

a. Pick a point above and to the right of the opening.

b. Move the cursor to a point below and to the left of the opening, forming a semitransparent green-colored window with dashed boundary lines (see Figure 4.68).

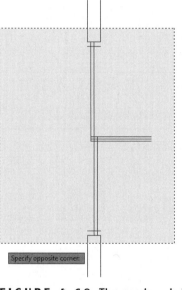

FIGURE 4.68 The crossing window for selecting cutting edges

c. Pick that point. Everything inside the rectangle or crossing an edge of it is selected.

d. Press ↵.

23. To trim the lines, pick them at the points noted on the left of Figure 4.69. When you finish trimming, the opening should look like the right side of Figure 4.69. Be sure to press ↵ to end the TRIM command.

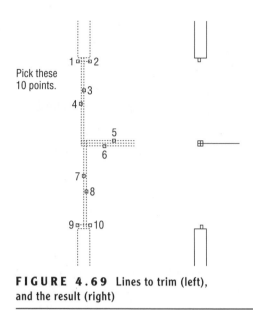

FIGURE 4.69 Lines to trim (left), and the result (right)

24. Start the ERASE command, and erase the remaining horizontal guideline.

To finish the sliding glass doors, you need to draw two lines to represent the glass panes for each door panel. Each pane of glass is centered inside its frame, so the line representing the pane will run between the midpoints of the inside edge of each frame section.

ADJUSTING TRIM WITH THE *EDGEMODE* SYSTEM VARIABLE

If all the lines don't trim as you would expect, you may have to change the setting for the EDGEMODE system variable. Cancel the trim operation and undo any trims you've made to the sliding glass door. Type **EDGEMODE**↵ and then type **0**↵. Now start the TRIM command and continue trimming.

EDGEMODE controls how the TRIM and EXTEND commands determine cutting edges. When set to its default value of 0, EDGEMODE uses the selected edge without any extensions. When set to 1, EDGEMODE extends or trims the selected object to an imaginary extension of the cutting or boundary edge.

25. Start the LINE command. Hold down the Shift key, right-click, and then select the Midpoint osnap option from the context menu.

26. For each of the two sliding door frames, draw a line from the midpoint of the inside frame (nearest the jamb) to a point perpendicular to the frame section in the middle. To do this, follow these steps:

    a. Place the cursor near the midpoint of the inside line of the frame section nearest the jamb. When the colored triangle appears there, click.

    b. Type **PER↵** or click the Perpendicular osnap from the Object Snap context menu, and move the cursor to the other frame section of that door panel.

    c. When you get near the horizontal line that represents both the inside edge of one frame section and the back edge of the frame section next to it, the colored Perpendicular osnap marker will appear on that line, as shown in Figure 4.70. When it does, select that point.

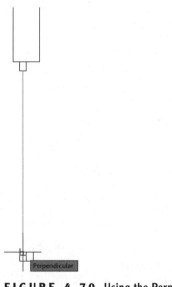

FIGURE 4.70 Using the Perpendicular osnap to set the endpoint of the line

27. Press ↵ to end the LINE command.

28. Press ↵ to restart the LINE command and repeat the procedure described in steps 25 through 27 for the other door panel, being sure to start the line at the frame section nearest the other jamb. The finished opening should look like Figure 4.71.

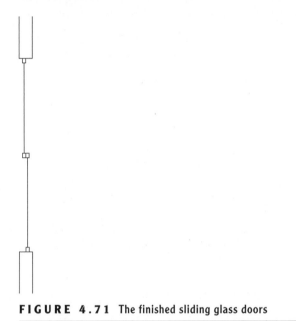

FIGURE 4.71 The finished sliding glass doors

29. Save your drawing as **I04-18-SlidingGlassDoor.dwg** (**M04-18-Sliding GlassDoor.dwg**).

Drawing the Bifold Doors

Bifold doors are generally shown with each door in a half-open position to indicate their distinctive design. Although there are four door panels on the cabin's closet door, you will need to draw only one, rotate it into place, and then create copies with the MIRROR command. To begin the exercise, you will use the PAN command to shift the view of your drawing to see the closet area without changing the zoom factor. Here is how you do it:

1. Continue using I04-18-SlidingGlassDoor.dwg (M04-18-Sliding GlassDoor.dwg), or open it if it's not already open.

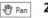 **2.** Start the PAN command from the View tab ≻ Navigate 2D panel, click the Pan button, or type **P↵** at the command line. The cursor changes appearance to look like an open hand.

3. Place the cursor near the upper jamb of the sliding glass door, and then click and drag the mouse downward until the drawing area shifts to display the closet area (see Figure 4.72).

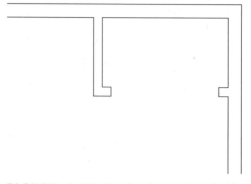

FIGURE 4.72 Pan the view to show the closet area.

4. Press the Esc key to end the PAN command, or right-click and choose Exit from the context menu.

  The closet opening is 4′ (1220 mm) wide, so you will need to make four door panels, each 1′ (305 mm) wide.

5. Start the Rectangle (RECTANG) command and specify the lower corner of the right closet jamb as the first corner point. The running Endpoint osnap ensures that the corner point is selected precisely.

6. Type **-1,-12↵** (**-25,-305↵**) to create a rectangle 1″ (25 mm) wide and 12″ (305 mm) long oriented toward the bottom of the cabin, as shown in Figure 4.73.

As an alternative to using the PAN command, you can simply hold down the scroll wheel and drag to use the pan function transparently—without exiting an active command.

 **N O T E**   It should be clear by now that when a command allows multiple picks in order to select several objects, you need to press ↵ to terminate the selection process and proceed with the command. From now on, when you are directed to select an object(s), I won't tell you to press ↵ to end the selection process.

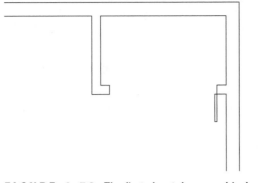

FIGURE 4.73 The first closet door panel is drawn.

7. Type **-45**↵. The door rotates 45° (see Figure 4.74), and the ROTATE command ends.

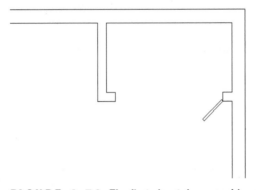

FIGURE 4.74 The first closet door panel is rotated.

8. Start the MIRROR command from the Home tab ➢ Modify panel, and then select the closet door panel.

9. Verify that Ortho mode is still turned on in the status bar. If it's not, click the Ortho Mode button or press the F8 shortcut key to turn on Ortho mode.

10. At the Specify first point of mirror line: prompt, click the far-left corner point of the selected panel.

11. Move the cursor either up or down until you see the mirror door panel directly to the left of the first panel (see Figure 4.75); then click to specify the second point of the mirror line.

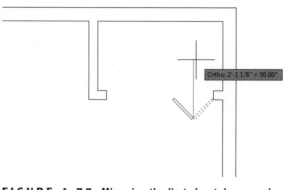

FIGURE 4.75 Mirroring the first closet door panel

12. Press ↵ to accept the default No option when prompted to erase the source object.

13. Start the MIRROR command again, and this time select both of the door panels.

14. Choose the midpoint of the back wall of the closet as the first point of the mirror line.

15. Then move the cursor downward to mirror the existing panels directly to the left, as shown in Figure 4.76.

16. Click to set the second point, and then press ↵ to retain the source objects.

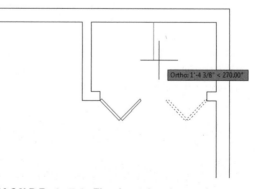

FIGURE 4.76 The closet door is complete.

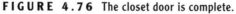

17. Click the Zoom Extents button to see the full floor plan with all doors (see Figure 4.77).

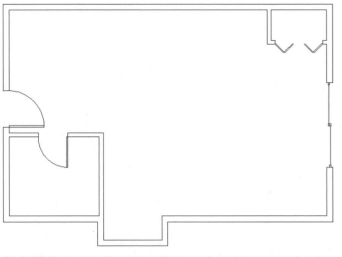

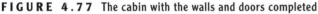

FIGURE 4.77 The cabin with the walls and doors completed

18. Save this drawing as **I04A-FPLAYO.dwg** (**M04A-FPLAYO.dwg**).

UNDERSTANDING SELECTION WINDOWS

In addition to selecting objects by using a direct pick, you can select objects by using a rectangular selection window. To use a selection window at any Select objects: prompt, pick a point at a blank spot in the drawing area to define one corner of the window and then a second point to define the opposite corner.

Selection windows come in two styles: windows and crossing windows. When you use a window selection, all objects must be entirely inside the boundary of the window to be selected. When you use a crossing window, all objects entirely within the boundary as well as any objects that cross the boundary are selected. AutoCAD distinguishes the two types of selection windows visually. Window selection areas are transparent blue and have solid boundary lines, and crossing windows are transparent green with dashed boundary lines.

By default, window selections are used when the boundary is created from left to right, and crossing selections are used when the boundary is created from right to left. By typing **W**↵ or **C**↵ at the Select objects: prompt, you can override the direction default or create a selection window even when the mouse is clicked as the cursor is over an object.

(Continues)

> ## UNDERSTANDING SELECTION WINDOWS *(Continued)*
>
> Selection windows can even be used to select objects to be trimmed or extended. For instance, visualize a horizontal line with dozens of vertical lines crossing it, and each of those lines must be trimmed back to the horizontal line. After designating the horizontal line as the cutting edge, use a crossing selection window to select all of the vertical lines on the trim side. All the lines are trimmed with two picks instead of many.

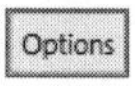

Options   To change settings that control the appearance of the crossing and regular selection windows, open the Application menu and click the Options button in the lower-right corner, or type **OP**↵ at the command line.

Click the Selection tab of the Options dialog box and then, in the Selection Preview area, click the Visual Effect Settings button, as shown in Figure 4.78.

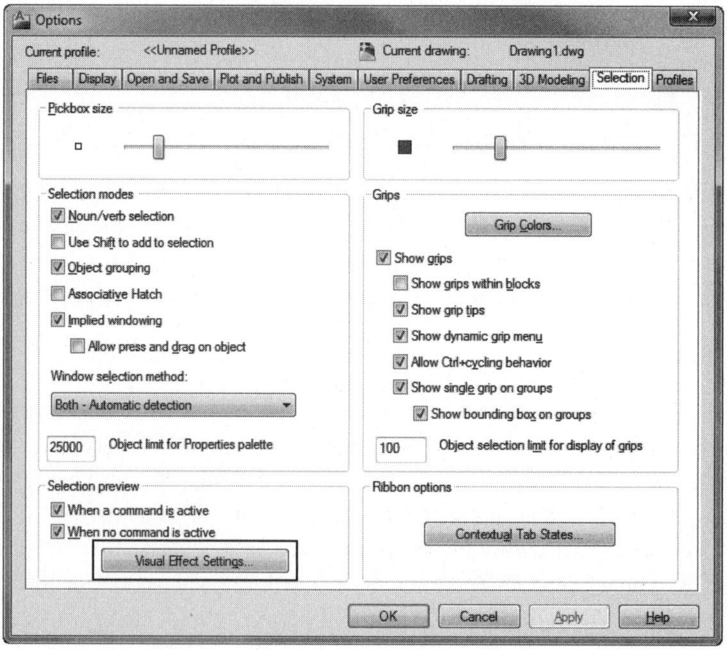

FIGURE 4.78 Click the Visual Effect Settings button.

In the Visual Effect Settings dialog box that opens (see Figure 4.79), you'll see settings in the Area Selection Effect section for controlling whether the selection windows have color in them, which color will be in each window, and the percentage of transparency of the colors. The left side of the dialog box controls the appearance of an object's highlighting when the cursor hovers over it. Experiment with different settings. Click OK twice to return to your drawing, and test the windows to see how they look.

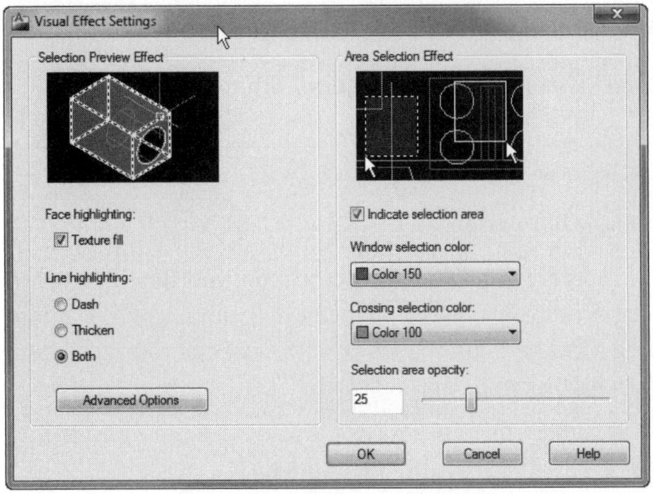

FIGURE 4.79 The Visual Effect Settings dialog box

This completes the doors for the floor plan. The focus here has been on walls and doors and the strategies for drawing them. As a result, you now have a basic floor plan for the cabin, and you'll continue to develop this plan in the next chapter.

The overall drawing strategy emphasized in this chapter uses objects already in the drawing to create new ones. You started with several lines that constituted the outside wall lines. By offsetting, filleting, extending, and trimming, you drew all the walls and openings without drawing any new lines. For the swinging doors, you made a rectangle and an arc. Then by copying, rotating, and mirroring, you formed the other swinging door. For the sliding glass door, you drew two new lines and used OFFSET, TRIM, and ERASE to finish the door. Therefore, you used four lines and created six new objects to complete the walls and doors. This is a good start in learning to use AutoCAD efficiently.

Throughout this chapter, I have indicated several instances when you can press the spacebar instead of the ↵ key. This can be handy if you keep one hand resting on the keyboard while the other hand controls the mouse. For brevity, I'll continue to instruct you to use ↵ and not mention the spacebar, but as you get better at drawing in AutoCAD, you may find the spacebar a useful substitute for ↵ in many cases. You'll determine your preference. You can substitute the spacebar for ↵ when handling the following tasks:

► Restarting the previous command

► Ending a command

► Moving from one step in a command to the next step

► Entering a new offset distance or accepting the current offset distance

► Entering relative or absolute coordinates

► Entering an angle of rotation

After working with the tools and strategies in this chapter, you should have an idea of an approach to drawing many objects. In the next chapter, you'll continue in the same vein, learning a few new commands and strategies as you add steps, a balcony, a kitchen, and a bathroom to the floor plan.

If You Would Like More Practice...

If you would like to practice the skills you have learned so far, here are some extra exercises.

An Alternative Sliding Glass Door

Here is a simplified version of the sliding glass door of the cabin, as shown in Figure 4.80. This version doesn't include any representation of the panes of glass and their frames.

FIGURE 4.80 An alternative to the sliding glass door

To draw it, use a technique similar to the one described in the previous section. Copy the jambs for the 7′ (2134 mm) opening to the right, and draw this door between them.

An Addition to the Cabin

This addition is connected to the cabin by a sidewalk and consists of a remodeled two-car garage in which one car slot has been converted into a storage area and an office (see Figure 4.81). Use the same commands and strategies you have been using up to now to draw this layout adjacent to the cabin. Save this exercise as **04A-FPGARG.dwg.**

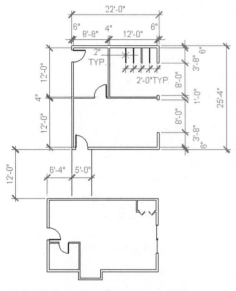

FIGURE 4.81 The garage addition

Refer to this chapter and the preceding one for specific commands. Here is the general procedure:

1. Draw the outside exterior wall lines.

2. Use OFFSET, FILLET, and TRIM to create the rest of the walls and wall lines.

3. Use OFFSET, EXTEND, and TRIM to create the openings.

4. Use RECTANGLE and ARC to create a swinging door.

5. Use COPY, ROTATE, and MIRROR to put in the rest of the doors.

6. Use OFFSET, LINE, and COPY to draw the storage partitions.

Draw Three Views of a Block

Use the tools you have learned in the last few chapters to draw the top, right side, and front views of the block shown in Figure 4.82.

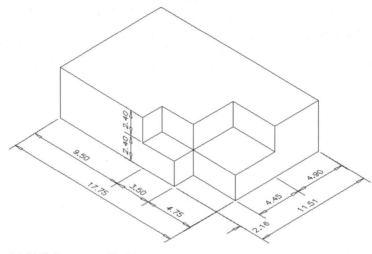

FIGURE 4.82 The block

Figure 4.83 gives you a graphic representation of the 12 steps necessary to complete the exercise.

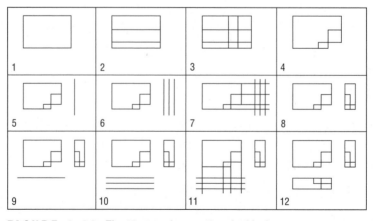

FIGURE 4.83 The 12 steps for creating the block

Here are the 12 steps in summary that correspond to the 12 drawings. Start with the top view:

1. Start a new drawing. Leave all settings at the defaults. Use relative polar or relative Cartesian coordinates and the LINE command to draw a rectangle 17.75 wide and 11.51 high. Zoom out if necessary.

2. Offset the bottom horizontal line up 2.16 and the new line up 4.45.

3. Offset the right vertical line 4.75 to the left and the new line 3.50 to the left.

4. Use the TRIM command to trim back lines and complete the view.
   Next, draw the right side view:

5. Draw a vertical line to the right of the top view. Make it longer than the top view is deep.

6. Offset the vertical line 2.4 to the right, and then offset the new line 2.4 to the right also.

7. Use the Endpoint osnap to draw lines from the corner points of the top view across the three vertical lines.

8. Trim the lines back to complete the side view.
   Finally, draw the front view:

9. Draw a horizontal line below the top view. Make it longer than the top view is wide.

10. Offset this line 2.4 down, and then offset the new line 2.4 down.

11. Use the Endpoint osnap to draw lines from the corner points of the top view, down across the three horizontal lines.

12. Trim the lines back to complete the view.

This ends the exercise. You can rotate and move each view relative to the other views in several ways. We'll look at those commands later in the book and then draw more views in Chapter 8.

Are You Experienced?

Now you can...

- ☑ create polylines

- ☑ offset exterior walls to make interior walls

- ☑ zoom in on an area with the Zoom Window (ZOOM) command and zoom back out with the Zoom Previous (ZOOM) command

- ☑ use the RECTANGLE and ARC commands to make a door

- ☑ use the Endpoint, Midpoint, and Perpendicular object snap modes

- ☑ use the Crossing Window selection tool

- ☑ use the COPY and MIRROR commands to place an existing door and swing in another opening

- ☑ use the OFFSET and TRIM commands to make a complex assembly

- ☑ begin drawing 2D representations of 3D shapes

Developing Drawing Strategies: Part 2

The preceding chapter emphasized using existing geometry (or objects) in a drawing to create new geometry. In this chapter, you'll look at new tools for forming an efficient drawing strategy. Before getting back to the cabin, I'll give you a brief overview of the tools available for starting and running commands.

▶ **Using running object snaps**

▶ **Using Polar Tracking**

▶ **Using the** STRETCH **command**

▶ **Using point filters**

▶ **Zooming and panning with the Realtime commands**

▶ **Copying and moving objects**

▶ **Using direct entry for distances**

▶ **Creating circles and ellipses**

▶ **Drawing using parametric constraints**

Starting and Running Commands

Developing a drawing strategy begins with determining the best way to start a command and when to start it. AutoCAD provides several ways to start most of the commands you'll be using. As you have seen, you can start the OFFSET, FILLET, TRIM, and EXTEND commands from either the Ribbon's Home tab ➤ Modify panel or by typing the first letter or two of the command and then pressing ↵. You can also display the menu bar and access commands from a drop-down list, or expose the Modify toolbar and choose the tools from it.

ACCESSING COMMANDS FROM THE KEYBOARD

Here's a quick recap of the methods you've used so far to run commands from the keyboard. To start the OFFSET command from the keyboard, enter **O**↵. To start the FILLET command, enter **F**↵. To start the TRIM command, enter **TR**↵; and to start the EXTEND command, enter **EX**↵. AutoCAD employs this same framework for nearly all of its commands; start commands by entering the entire name of the command (EXTEND↵), or enter the starting characters of the command (EX↵).

NEW A new autocomplete feature allows for more-efficient access to commands and, when available, the associated command alias. Pausing after entering one or more characters at the command line will display a list of commands whose prefix matches what you've typed. (The following illustration shows the autocomplete feature displaying a list of commands whose prefix matches EX.) With this list open, you can continue entering the command name or select it from the list.

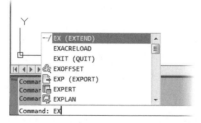

Another way to access commands from the keyboard is to press the Alt key. When you hold down the key for a second or two, AutoCAD will display a series of shortcuts across the Ribbon. Entering these one- and two-character

(Continues)

ACCESSING COMMANDS FROM THE KEYBOARD   *(Continued)*

shortcuts will allow you to navigate the Ribbon without using a mouse. For example, to start a command on the Insert Ribbon tab, press Alt and then enter **IN** followed by a second two-character code indicated by the cue cards, as shown in the following illustration. These shortened command entries can range from a single character to several characters, and are known as command-aliases.

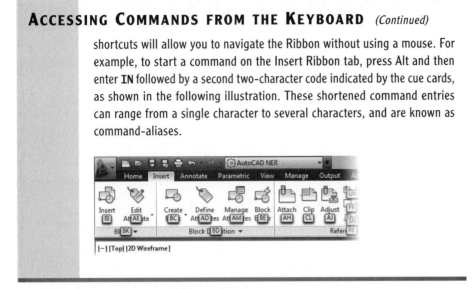

You'll determine when to use the Ribbon, menu bar, toolbars, or the keyboard based on what you're doing at the time, as well as by your personal preference. The purpose of the Ribbon is to make the most frequently used tools readily available, but keyboard entry can also be a fast method when you are using the command aliases. The menus are slower to use because they require more selections to get to a command, but they also contain more commands and options than the toolbars, as well as some commands not found on the Ribbon.

Remember that if you have just ended a command, you can restart that command by pressing ↵, by pressing the spacebar, or by right-clicking. When you right-click, a context menu appears near the cursor. The top item on this menu is Repeat Command, where *Command* is the last command used. For example, if you've just finished using the ERASE command and you right-click, the top item of the context menu is Repeat Erase. If you've used a command recently, you can select that command by pausing the cursor (hovering) over the Recent Input option and then selecting that command from the cascading menu that appears (see Figure 5.1).

N O T E   Throughout the rest of the book, I'll introduce some of the other items on the context menu. This menu is called a *context menu* because different items are displayed on it, depending on whether a command is running, which command you're using, and where you are in a command.

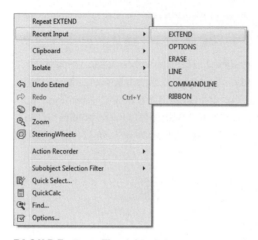

FIGURE 5.1 The right-click context menu and Recent Input cascading menu

In this chapter, I'll introduce you to several new commands and, through the step-by-step instructions, show you some alternative methods for accomplishing tasks similar to those you have already completed. You'll add front and back decks and steps, thresholds, and kitchen and bath fixtures to the cabin floor plan (see Figure 5.2). For each of these tasks, the focus will be on making your job easier by utilizing objects and geometry that are already in the drawing and on using the appropriate tools to help you accomplish tasks more quickly and efficiently.

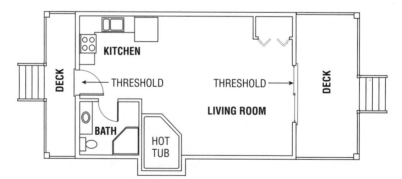

FIGURE 5.2 The cabin with front and back decks and steps, thresholds, kitchen, and bathroom

If you haven't already done so, activate the Dynamic Input button on the status bar and work with the dynamic display information shown in the drawing area as you work your way through the chapter.

Drawing the Thresholds

To get started, let's take a look at the two thresholds. Each threshold is represented with three simple lines. You could certainly manually draw these lines with the skills you've learned so far, but we want to find the most efficient way. The trick will be to see which part of the drawing you can effectively use to generate and position those lines. As illustrated in Figure 5.3, the thresholds extend 2″ (51 mm) beyond the outside wall line and run 3″ (76 mm) past either jamb line.

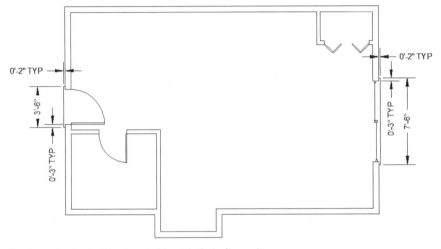

FIGURE 5.3 The thresholds with their dimensions

Drawing the Front Threshold

Thresholds generally are used on doorway openings when the level changes from one side of the opening to the other or to prevent rain and dust from entering the structure. This usually occurs at entrances that open from or to the outside. Although they are quite different in shape, each threshold for the cabin has the same geometry as the steps. The lip of each threshold is offset 2′ (51 mm) from the outside wall, and each edge runs 3″ (76 mm) past the door-jamb (see Figure 5.3). You'll use a temporary tracking point with Polar Tracking and direct entry to draw the three thresholds for the cabin.

As you can see in Figure 5.3, the front threshold is 7′-6″ (2286 mm) wide, extending 3″ (76 mm) past the doorway on each side. You can draw a line from the endpoint of one of the jamb lines down 3″ (76 mm) and then draw the perimeter of the threshold. Here's how you do it:

1. With AutoCAD running, open your cabin drawing I04A-FPLAYO.dwg (M04A-FPLAYO.dwg), and use the ZOOM command options to achieve a view similar to Figure 5.4. The file is also available from this book's web page at **www.sybex.com/go/autocad2012ner**.

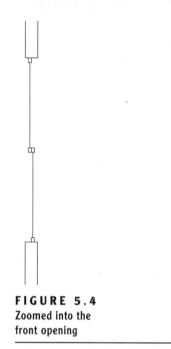

FIGURE 5.4
Zoomed into the
front opening

2. Check to make sure that all buttons on the left side of the status bar, except Ortho Mode, Object Snap, and Dynamic Input, are still in their off positions.

3. Start the LINE command.

You need to start the threshold 3″ (76 mm) below the bottom jamb, and inline with the outside wall line. Unfortunately, there is no feature to snap the cursor to at that point. The techniques that you've previously used would require offsetting the jamb line or starting the line at the jamb and drawing an overlapping line 3″ (76 mm) downward. Both of these methods would require you to erase the unnecessary line after the threshold is complete.

WAYS TO USE THE OBJECT SNAP TOOLS

You can access the Object Snap tools in several ways:

▶ The Object Snap context menu provides access to the object snaps. To open this menu, hold down the Shift key or Ctrl key and right-click.

▶ If you're using a mouse with a scroll wheel or a three-button mouse, you might be able to open the Object Snap menu by clicking the wheel or the middle mouse button. If this doesn't work, set the MBUTTONPAN variable to zero (Enter **MBUTTONPAN**↵ **0**↵). Be aware that you will no longer be able to pan by holding down the scroll wheel.

▶ When the menu bar is displayed, the Object Snap toolbar can be displayed from the Tools menu ➢ Toolbars ➢ AutoCAD ➢ Object Snap.

▶ In most cases, you can enter the first three letters of an osnap to activate it, as in **END**↵ for Endpoint.

Instead of wasting time drawing and then erasing lots of unnecessary line work, you will begin using the Object Snap Tracking tool. This tool will help eliminate the need to create unnecessary geometry. Using the Object Snap Tracking tool requires you to specify a location in the drawing area, called a *temporary tracking point*, relative to existing features or other locations.

4. Click the Object Snap Tracking button on the status bar. In this case, because the threshold starts 3″ (76 mm) below the outside corner of the lower jamb, you'll use that corner as the temporary tracking point for the start point of the line.

5. Pause the cursor over the outside corner of the lower jamb until the Endpoint osnap marker appears. A small, green cross displays inside the Endpoint osnap marker.

6. Move the cursor directly downward, and you will see an X appear at the cursor, directly below the reference point (see Figure 5.5).

The green cross indicates the temporary tracking point for the Object Snap Tracking tool, and the X indicates the point where the line will start.

7. Enter **3**↵ (**76**↵) to use the direct entry method to start the first line 3″ (76 mm) below the temporary tracking point. With the Ortho mode turned on, the point selected is directly below the corner of the jamb.

8. Hold the crosshair cursor directly to the right of the last point; when you see the alignment path and tooltip, enter **2**↵ (**51**↵), as shown in Figure 5.6.

AutoCAD draws the bottom edge of the threshold. You used direct entry with Ortho mode again, and you didn't have to enter the relative polar or the Cartesian coordinates.

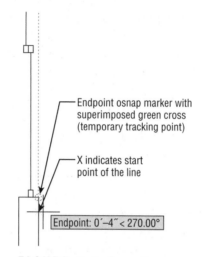
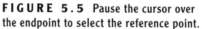

FIGURE 5.5 Pause the cursor over the endpoint to select the reference point.

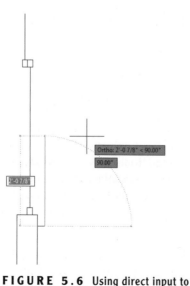
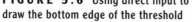

FIGURE 5.6 Using direct input to draw the bottom edge of the threshold

9. Hold the crosshair cursor directly above the last point; when you see the alignment path and tooltip, enter **7′6″**↵ (**2286**↵). AutoCAD draws the front edge of the threshold.

10. Select Perpendicular from the Object Snap context menu (Shift+right-click) and move the cursor to the outside wall line. Alternatively, you can enter **PER** at the command line to enable the Perpendicular osnap.

11. When the Perpendicular icon appears on the wall line, as shown in Figure 5.7, click to draw the top edge of the threshold.

12. Press ↵ to end the LINE command.

    The completed front threshold looks like Figure 5.8.

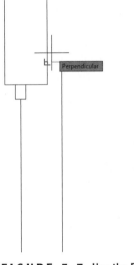

FIGURE 5.7 Use the Perpendicular osnap to draw the final line.

TIP   When using object snaps to locate points within a drawing, you do not need to select the osnap icon itself. Notice how the cursor in Figure 5.7 is located slightly above and to the right of the point AutoCAD found by using the Perpendicular object snap. Regardless of where you select, a perpendicular line will be drawn to the point highlighted by the Perpendicular osnap icon.

Admittedly, this method takes some practice to master. Still, learning how to use osnaps in this way is beneficial because you won't have to pan or zoom as often, consequently saving you time. As you continue working with object snaps, give this method a try. Remember that if you accidentally select the wrong point, you can always enter U↵ while inside many commands, such as the LINE command, to undo a single segment.

13. Use the Zoom Extents (ZOOM) command to view the completed front threshold with the whole floor plan. Remember, by default, double-clicking the middle button on a wheel mouse performs a Zoom Extents (ZOOM) command.

14. Save your drawing as **I05-01-FrontThreshold.dwg** (**M05-01-Front Threshold.dwg**) by choosing Application menu ➤ Save As ➤ AutoCAD Drawing.

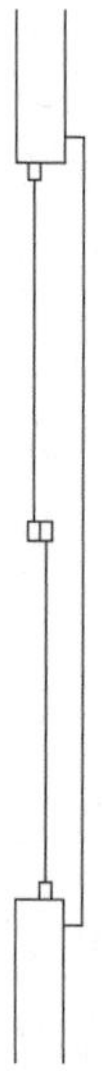

FIGURE 5.8 Completing the front threshold

Drawing the Back Threshold

The method of drawing the threshold for the back door is the same as the method used to draw the front threshold. You will use Ortho mode, direct input, and Object Snap Tracking to draw the lines. Here is how it's done:

1. Make sure I05-01-FrontThreshold.dwg (M05-01-FrontThreshold.dwg) is open.

2. Zoom and pan until the back door fills the drawing area.

3. Start the LINE command and place the cursor over the left corner of the lower jamb. Then, after the temporary tracking point cross

appears inside the endpoint marker, move the cursor directly down-ward, as shown in Figure 5.9.

4. Enter **3↵** (**76↵**) to set the start point of the line 3″ (76 mm) below the edge of the jamb.

5. Move the cursor directly to the left; then enter **2↵** (**51↵**) to draw the lower edge of the threshold.

6. Finish the threshold by moving the cursor directly upward and enter-ing **3′6″↵** (**1067↵**).

7. Use the Perpendicular object snap to draw to the edge of the threshold, perpendicular to the outside wall.

8. Press ↵ to end the LINE command. The back threshold should look like Figure 5.10.

9. Use the Zoom Extents (ZOOM) command to view the completed front and back thresholds with the whole floor plan.

10. Save your drawing as **I05-02-BackThreshold.dwg** (**M05-02-Back Threshold.dwg**).

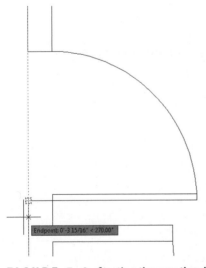

FIGURE 5.9 Starting the rear threshold

When you drew the first threshold, this exercise may have seemed complicated, but it was probably easier when you drew the second one. Like many techniques available in AutoCAD, these methods will become second nature with a little practice, and you'll use them more efficiently. In the next exercise, you will draw the cabin's front deck and stairs, and then you'll use the existing geometry to draw the back deck and stairs.

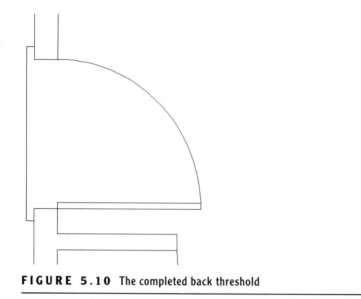

FIGURE 5.10 The completed back threshold

Drawing the Decks and Stairs

The decks consist of the platform, posts, railings, and a set of stairs. You'll begin by using the OFFSET command to draw polylines for the perimeter, to facilitate the drawing of the railing lines. Then you'll continue the construction by using lines and the OFFSET and TRIM commands. You will also begin using the Temporary Track Point osnap, an option with the Object Snap Tracking tool.

Drawing the Front Deck

Figure 5.11 shows the dimensions of the front deck you'll draw.

1. Make sure I05-02-BackThreshold.dwg (M05-02-BackThreshold.dwg) is open.

2. Right-click the Polar Tracking button on the status bar at the bottom of the screen, and then choose Settings from the context menu. The Drafting Settings dialog box opens. By default, the Polar Tracking tab is active (see Figure 5.12).

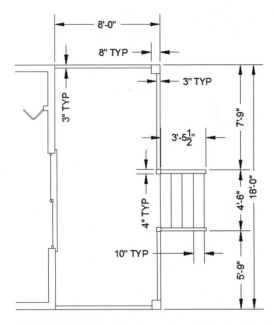

FIGURE 5.11 The dimensions of the front deck and stairs

3. Before using Polar Tracking, you need to change a few settings:

   a. Starting in the upper-left corner, click the Polar Tracking On check box.

   This has the same effect as clicking the Polar Tracking button in the status bar, or pressing F10 from the Application window.

   b. In the Polar Angle Settings area, change the Increment Angle to 45.00.

   c. In the Polar Angle Measurement area found on the right side, make sure that Absolute is selected and then click OK to exit the Drafting Settings dialog box.

   The Polar Tracking button is turned on in the status bar, and the Ortho mode is automatically turned off. Polar Tracking is similar to Ortho mode, but it provides more angular increments to which you can snap the cursor.

4. Turn off the Object Snap Tracking button in the status bar.

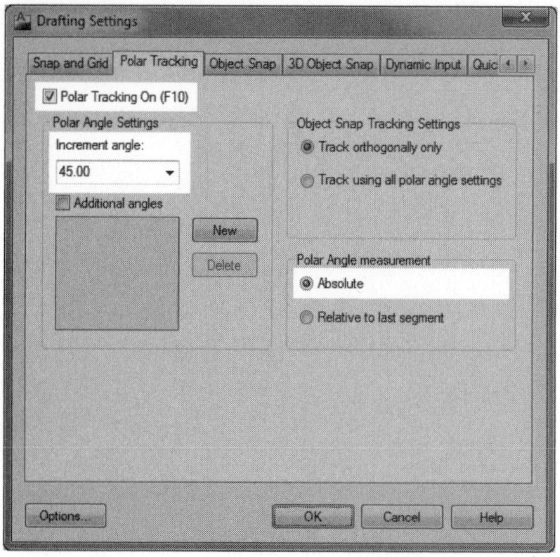

FIGURE 5.12 The Polar Tracking tab of the Drafting Settings dialog box

> Load the Object Snap toolbar from View Ribbon tab ➢ Windows panel ➢ Toolbars tool; click AutoCAD ➢ Object Snap.

The object snaps are also available from the Object Snap toolbar you loaded and saved within the AutoCAD NER workspace in Chapter 1, "Getting to Know AutoCAD." Some users prefer using the toolbar over other methods because the nonrunning osnaps can remain visible on the screen without the need to open a menu and, if necessary, the toolbars can be docked to the perimeter of the drawing area or moved to a second monitor.

5. Start the Polyline (PLINE) command and draw a polyline from the lower-right corner of the cabin to a point 8'-0" (2438 mm) to the right.

6. Click the Snap To Perpendicular button on the Object Snap toolbar. Place the cursor over the top-outside horizontal line of the cabin, and when the Snap marker appears (see Figure 5.13), click to draw the vertical line of the deck's perimeter.

7. Click the top-right corner of the cabin to complete the perimeter of the deck, and then press ↵ to end the Polyline (PLINE) command. Your drawing should look like Figure 5.14.

8. Offset the perimeter 3" (72 mm) to the inside to represent the inside and outside edges of the handrail, and then terminate the OFFSET command.

9. Save your drawing as I05-03-FrontDeck.dwg (M05-03-FrontDeck.dwg).

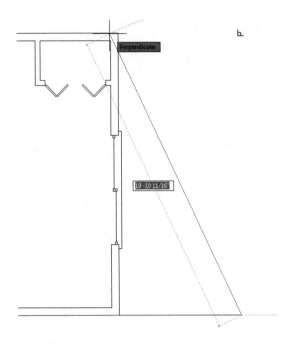

FIGURE 5.13 Drawing the vertical line perpendicular to the upper cabin wall

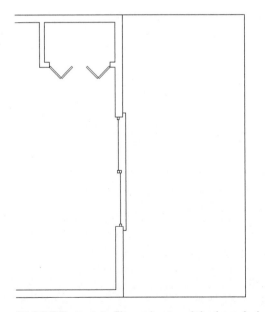

FIGURE 5.14 The perimeter of the front deck

Drawing the Deck Posts

There are four posts on the deck: two 8″ (204 mm) posts at the corners that hold up the roof, and two 4″ (102 mm) posts at the top of the stairs. You will use the Rectangle (RECTANG) command to draw the posts and the MIRROR command to copy them:

1. Make sure I05-03-FrontDeck.dwg (M05-03-FrontDeck.dwg) is open.

2. Use the Rectangle (RECTANG) command, found on the Home tab ➤ Draw panel ➤ Rectangle tool, to draw a post 8″×8″ at the lower-right corner of the desk.

   To do this, start the Rectangle (RECTANG) command. At the Specify first corner point or: prompt, click the endpoints where the lines form the lower-right corner of the deck. At the Specify other corner point or: prompt, enter -8,8↵ (-204,204) to draw the first 8″ (204 mm) post.

   The rectangle should be similar to Figure 5.15.

FIGURE 5.15 The first corner post

T I P   You can start an AutoCAD command and then select objects, or you can select the objects first and then start the command.

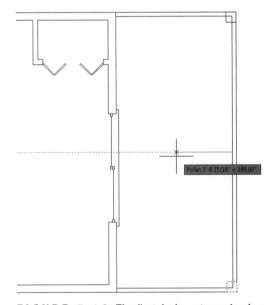

3. To create the opposite post, select the rectangle that you just drew and then start the MIRROR command (Home tab ➤ Modify panel ➤ Mirror tool).

4. At the Specify first point of mirror line: prompt, click the Snap To Midpoint button on the Object Snap toolbar. Then pause the cursor over either of the vertical handrail lines.

When a feature is symmetrical like the deck, you can use the Midpoint snap to mirror objects about the center line.

5. Move the cursor directly to the left or right, as shown in Figure 5.16, to mirror the post. Then do the following:

    a. Click to execute the mirror.

    b. Press ↵ to accept the No option for deleting the source object.

FIGURE 5.16 The first deck posts are in place.

6. Use the TRIM command to trim the short polyline segments that fall within the posts.

When you are finished, each segment should look similar to Figure 5.17.

7. Save your drawing as **I05-04-DeckPosts.dwg** (**M05-04-DeckPosts.dwg**).

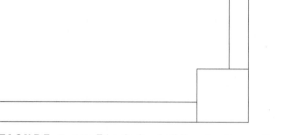
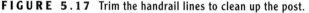

FIGURE 5.17 Trim the handrail lines to clean up the post.

The 4″ (102 mm) posts at the top of the stairs are centered on the 3″ (72 mm) handrails on the deck and on the stairs. To create the lower small post, you need to locate the bottom-right corner at a point ½″ (15 mm) to the right of the front handrail and 5′-8½ (1740 mm) from the bottom-right corner of the deck. Follow these steps:

1. Make sure I05-04-DeckPosts.dwg (M05-04-DeckPosts.dwg) is open.

2. Select the large lower post and start the COPY command from the Home tab ➣ Modify panel on the Ribbon.

3. Select the lower-right corner point as the base point and then, at the Specify second point or: prompt, enter .5,5′8.5″ (15,1740).

4. Press ↵ to end the COPY command. The copied post appears as shown in Figure 5.18.

5. Zoom in to the new post. The bottom-right corner of the post is located in the correct location, but the post is twice the size that it should be.

6. Start the SCALE command by clicking the Scale button from the Home tab ➣ Modify panel; then select the new rectangle.

7. With the SCALE command active, select the lower-right corner as the base point. Then move the cursor to see the effect when the scale is based from that corner. A copy of the selected object appears, as shown in Figure 5.19.

8. Enter **0.5**↵ to scale the rectangle to 50 percent of its current size.

9. Save your drawing as **I05-05-StairPosts.dwg** (**M05-05-Stair Posts.dwg**).

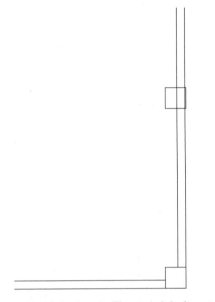

FIGURE 5.18 The copied deck post

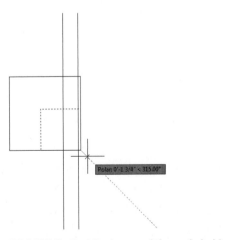

Polar: 0'-1 3/4" < 315.00"

FIGURE 5.19 A copy of the scaled object appears as you move the cursor.

Drawing the Stairs

You could mirror the 4″ (102 mm) rectangle now to create the reciprocal post, but we'll wait until the stair handrails are complete and then mirror both objects at once. The first stair handrail is 3″ (76 mm) wide and centered on the 4″ (102 mm) post, so you'll use a temporary tracking point to locate the first point of the line.

1. Make sure I05-05-StairPosts.dwg (M05-05-StairPosts.dwg) is open.

2. Start the LINE command and click the Temporary Track Point button in the Object Snap toolbar, or enter **TT↵** at the command line.

3. Using the running Endpoint osnap, click the lower-right corner of the small post to locate the temporary tracking point.

4. With the temporary tracking point located, move the cursor directly upward and enter **.5↵ (13↵)** to place the start point ½″ (13 mm) above the corner.

5. To complete the handrail, do the following:

   a. Move the cursor directly to the right and enter **3′5.5↵ (1054↵)**.

   b. Move the cursor directly upward and enter **3↵ (72↵)**.

   c. Move the cursor directly to the left and enter **3′5.5↵ (1054↵)**. Instead of entering the exact distance of the final line, you could also use the Perpendicular object snap to complete the handrail.

   Your first handrail should look like Figure 5.20.

6. Save your drawing as **I05-06-DrawStairRail.dwg (M05-06-DrawStair Rail.dwg)**.

Mirroring the Post and Railing

You can now mirror the post and railing to draw them on the opposite side of the stairway. You can't use the midpoint of the deck's perimeter line as one point of the mirror line, because the stair is centered on the front door and not on the deck. You can, however, use the midpoint of the front door's threshold.

1. Make sure I05-06-DrawStairRail.dwg (M05-06-DrawStairRail.dwg) is open.

2. Select the 4″ (102 mm) post and all three lines that make up the hand-rail. Try using a window selection (drag from left to right) to select the objects rather than picking them one at a time.

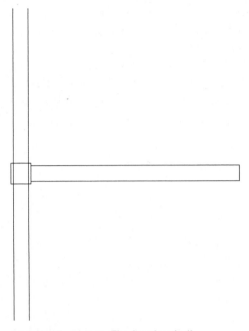

FIGURE 5.20 The first handrail

3. Start the MIRROR command.

4. Use the Midpoint osnap and then specify the midpoint of the vertical threshold line as the first point of the mirror line, as shown in Figure 5.21.

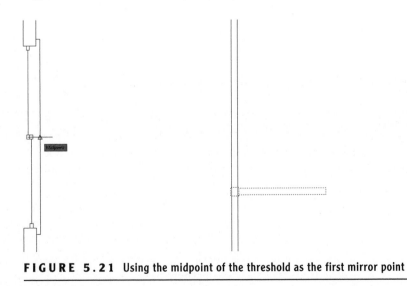

FIGURE 5.21 Using the midpoint of the threshold as the first mirror point

5. Move the cursor to the right and then click to specify the second point of the mirror line. Press ⏎ to retain the source objects.
   Your deck should look like Figure 5.22.

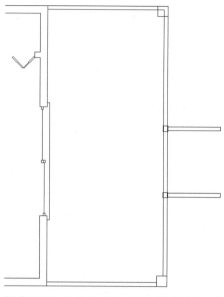

FIGURE 5.22 The deck with both handrails

6. Zoom in until you can see both stair handrails and posts.

7. Break the outside perimeter line of the deck into individual line entities by using the EXPLODE command.

8. Start the COPY command from the Home tab ➢ Modify panel. Select the outside perimeter line of the deck to begin building the stairs.

9. Pick any point near the stairs at the Specify base point: prompt.

NEW   10. Enable the Array option of the COPY command by entering A⏎ at the Specify second point: prompt.

11. Use the following values to complete the array:

   a. Enter 5⏎ at the Enter number of items to array: prompt.

   b. Move your cursor directly to the right, and enter 10⏎ (254⏎) at the Specify second point or: prompt (see Figure 5.23).

New to AutoCAD 2012, the COPY command now includes an Array option that enables you to create a linear nonassociative array.

12. Assuming the preview looks like Figure 5.24, press ⏎ to accept the array. The COPY command ends, and your stairs are drawn.

Now you will use the TRIM command to trim away the stair lines that extend into and beyond the railings and the lines that pass through the 4″ (102 mm) posts.

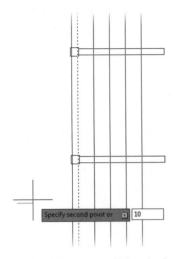

FIGURE 5.23 Using the Array function of the COPY command to create stairs for the deck

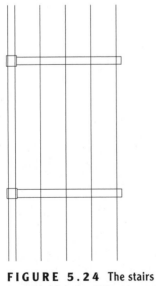

FIGURE 5.24 The stairs created using the COPY command

13. Start the TRIM command. Select both of the inside lines of the stairway handrails and the 4″ (102 mm) post polylines as the cutting edge objects.

 T I P   Make sure that you do not select the offset perimeter polylines as cutting edges. When polylines are selected as cutting edges and then as the trimmed objects, they are trimmed back to the endpoint nearest to the picked location.

14. Trim the four stair lines on both sides of the railing.

15. Of the two vertical lines that extend between the two posts, trim only the left vertical line.

16. Trim away the four short lines that pass through the two 4″ (102 mm) posts, and erase the additional line along the inside perimeter.

When complete, your front stairway should look like Figure 5.25.

17. Zoom to the drawing's extents.

18. Save your drawing as **I05-07-FrontStairs.dwg (M05-07-Front Stairs.dwg)**.

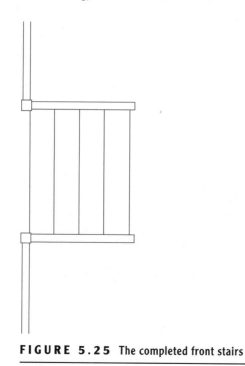

FIGURE 5.25 The completed front stairs

Drawing the Back Deck and Stairs

The deck, handrails, posts, and stairs at the rear portion of the cabin are similar to the same features at the front of the cabin. One of the most significant strengths of CAD software over traditional hand drafting is the ability to use existing geometry and linework in a drawing to create additional identical or similar objects. In this section, you will first mirror the front deck to the back of the cabin. I will then introduce you to the STRETCH command to adjust the lines to match the cabin's structure. Figure 5.26 shows the dimensions of the rear deck that are different from those on the front deck.

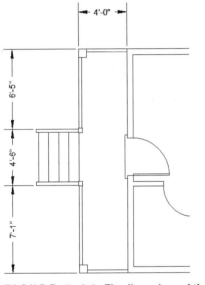

FIGURE 5.26 The dimensions of the rear deck and stairs

Mirroring the Front Deck

Several similarities exist between the front and back decks of the cabin. Using these similarities to your advantage, the following steps utilize this existing geometry by mirroring the front deck to the back of the cabin:

1. Make sure I05-07-FrontStairs.dwg (M05-07-FrontStairs.dwg) is open.

2. Verify that the following drawing modes are active:

- ► Polar Tracking
- ► Object Snap
- ► Dynamic Input

3. Start the MIRROR command.

4. Use a crossing selection window to select all the components of the front deck, but do not select the cabin wall, front door, or threshold.

   If you inadvertently select an unwanted object, hold down the Shift key and pick the object again to deselect it. The dashed, selected set should look like Figure 5.27.

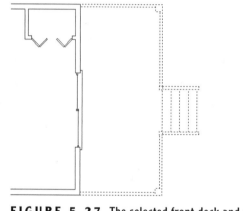

FIGURE 5.27 The selected front deck and steps

5. At the Specify first point of mirror line: prompt, activate the Midpoint osnap and click near the midpoint of the top, outside wall line.

   As discussed earlier, as long as the Midpoint snap marker displays at the correct midpoint, it is not necessary to pick the exact midpoint of the line.

6. Move the cursor downward. With Polar Tracking active, the cursor is restricted to the 270° angle, causing the deck to be mirrored perfectly to the rear of the cabin, as shown in Figure 5.28.

7. Click to define the mirror line and press ↵ to retain the source objects. The front deck is mirrored to the back of the cabin.

8. Save your drawing as **I05-08-MirrorDeck.dwg** (**M05-08-Mirror Deck.dwg**).

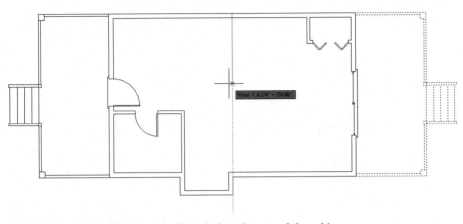
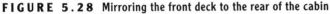

FIGURE 5.28 Mirroring the front deck to the rear of the cabin

Using the *Stretch* Command to Size the Deck

The STRETCH command is used to lengthen or shorten objects in the drawing area. The major restriction when using it is that the objects must be selected with a crossing window or crossing polygon, so be sure to define your selection window from right to left or to enter **CR↵** at the Select objects: prompt.

When part of an object resides inside the crossing window borders, the portion inside the window is moved, the portion crossing the border is stretched, and the portion outside the border is unaffected. When an object is completely inside the crossing window, it is affected as if the MOVE command were used.

Figure 5.29 shows the result when the top portion of the objects in a drawing are selected and stretched. The far-left image shows a crossing selection window encompassing the entire top portion of the objects, and the middle-left image shows the result of stretching the objects upward. The middle-right image shows a crossing selection window encompassing only the right half of the top portion of the objects, and the far-right image shows the result of stretching the objects upward. Some objects, such as circles, ellipses, and blocks, cannot be stretched.

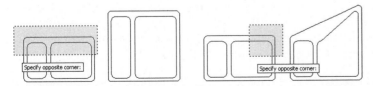
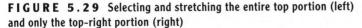

FIGURE 5.29 Selecting and stretching the entire top portion (left) and only the top-right portion (right)

Take the following steps to fix the rear deck and stairs by using the STRETCH command:

1. Make sure I05-08-MirrorDeck.dwg (M05-08-MirrorDeck.dwg) is open.

2. Zoom in to the rear deck and stairs.

3. Start the STRETCH command from the Home tab ➢ Modify panel ➢ Stretch tool, or enter **S**↵ at the command line.

4. At the Select objects: prompt, place the cursor above the deck and to the right of the stairs, but be sure the point is to the left of the threshold (see Figure 5.30).

5. At the Specify opposite corner: prompt, click a point outside and to the left of the deck, as shown in Figure 5.30. The deck objects ghost to indicate that they are selected. Press ↵ to discontinue selecting objects.

   Like the MOVE command, STRETCH requires you to specify a base point and a second point to define the result of the stretch. The selected objects are stretched to the same distance and angle as the relationship between those two points. For example, after selecting objects to stretch on the right side of the drawing area, you can select a base point on the left side of the drawing area and a second point 2″ above the base point. The selected objects on the left are stretched upward 2″.

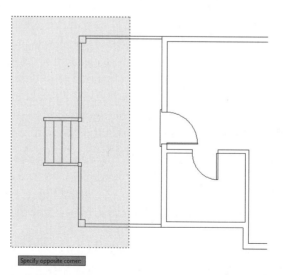

FIGURE 5.30 Selecting the deck components for the STRETCH command

You can reference objects or features in the drawing area or select a random point for the base and specify the angle and distance for the second point.

6. The open end of the deck needs to be stretched 4'-0" (1220 mm) to the right. Pick a point anywhere in the drawing area and then move the cursor to the right. You will see the deck stretching to the right, while a ghosted version remains in place (see Figure 5.31).

7. Enter 4↵ (1220↵). The deck is stretched 4'-0" (1220 mm) to the right.

8. Save your drawing as I05-09-StretchDeck.dwg (M05-09-Stretch Deck.dwg).

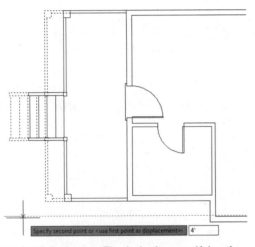

FIGURE 5.31 The deck after specifying the base point for the STRETCH command

Using Point Filters to Finish the Deck

To complete the back deck, you need to align the center of the stair with the center of the door. To do this, we'll combine what you already know about object snaps with the STRETCH command and a feature named point filters. *Point filters*, also called *coordinate filters*, are tools you can utilize to use only the X, Y, or Z value of a selected point in the drawing area.

For example, suppose you want to stretch an object to the center of a rectangle but you don't know where that center is located. You could draw a bunch of construction lines, only to erase them in a few minutes, or you could forgo all of that with point filters. In this scenario, you would use the X point filter and pick the midpoint of a horizontal line from the rectangle; then you'd use the Y point filter and pick the midpoint of a vertical line from the rectangle.

The resulting location is at the intersection of the midpoint of the two sides of the rectangle at the center point. More important, you didn't spend any unnecessary time drawing and then erasing construction lines. Let's take a look at how you can employ this same method to finish the back deck. Follow these steps:

1. Make sure I05-09-StretchDeck.dwg (M05-09-StretchDeck.dwg) is open.

2. Verify that Polar Tracking, Object Snap, and Dynamic Input are still enabled and then turn on the Midpoint and Endpoint object snaps from the Drafting Settings dialog box, as shown in Figure 5.32.

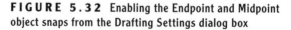

FIGURE 5.32 Enabling the Endpoint and Midpoint object snaps from the Drafting Settings dialog box

3. Create a crossing selection window around the stairs, stair handrails, and stair posts, as shown in Figure 5.33.

4. At the Specify base point or: prompt, use the Midpoint osnap and pick the midpoint of the top step.

5. At the Specify second point or: prompt, hold the Shift key down and right-click to open the Osnap context menu. Choose Point Filters ➤ .X (Figure 5.34).

This allows you to pick a point that is horizontally (X) equal to the same location as the point you selected in step 2 and vertically (Y) equal to the midpoint of the threshold.

The prompt in the command window has .X appended to indicate that AutoCAD will use only the X component of the next location picked.

6. Click either endpoint of the top step. This point is in line with the midpoint you picked in step 2, so the stretch will move the stairs vertically, not horizontally.

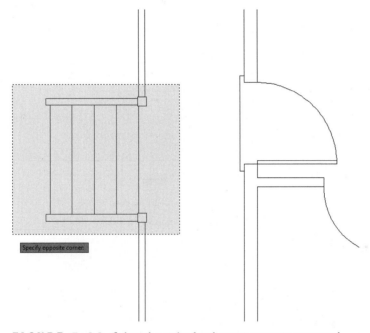

FIGURE 5.33 Select the stairs for the next STRETCH command.

FIGURE 5.34 Select the .X point filter from the Object Snap context menu.

Move the cursor around in the drawing area and you'll see that the movement of the stairs is now restricted to the y-axis. In the command window, the notation (need YZ) is appended to the prompt, indicating that AutoCAD will use only the Y and Z components of the next location picked. (Only the y-axis is referenced if you are using AutoCAD LT.)

7. Click the Snap To Midpoint button in the Object Snap toolbar, and then click the midpoint of the threshold (see Figure 5.35).

8. The stairs are moved vertically and centered on the back door. Zoom to the drawing's extents. Your drawing should look like Figure 5.36.

9. Save your file as **I05-10-PointFilter.dwg** (**M05-10-PointFilter.dwg**).

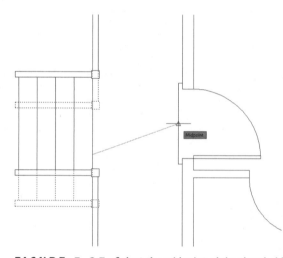

FIGURE 5.35 Select the midpoint of the threshold as the Y and Z components of the second point.

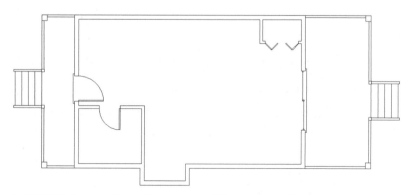

FIGURE 5.36 The cabin after completing the back deck

Laying Out the Kitchen

The kitchen for the cabin will have a stove, a refrigerator, and a counter with a sink. The refrigerator is set 2" (51 mm) from the back wall. Approaching this drawing task, your goal is to think about the easiest and fastest way to complete it. The first step in deciding on an efficient approach is to ascertain what information you have about the various parts and what existing elements in the drawing will be available to assist you. Figure 5.37 gives you the basic dimensions, and you'll get more-detailed information about the sink and stove as you progress through the exercise.

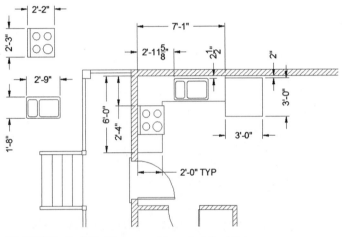

FIGURE 5.37 The general layout of the kitchen

Drawing the Counter

Although the counter is in two pieces, you'll draw it as one piece and then cut out a section for the stove. Try two ways to draw the counter to see which method is more efficient.

Method 1: Using Object Snap Tracking and Direct Entry

The first drawing method uses Object Snap Tracking and direct entry:

1. Continue with the drawing from the previous exercise or open I05-10-PointFilter.dwg (M05-10-PointFilter.dwg) from the book's web page.

2. Use a zoom window to zoom your view so that it is about the same magnification as Figure 5.38.

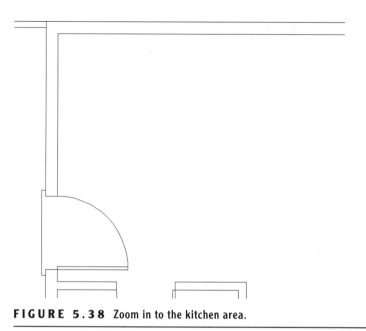

FIGURE 5.38 Zoom in to the kitchen area.

3. From the status bar, turn on Object Snap Tracking. Verify that Polar Tracking, Object Snap, and Dynamic Input are still on. The rest of the buttons should be off.

4. Start the LINE command to begin drawing the counter.

5. Place the cursor near the lower end of the right-rear doorjamb line, where the door swing meets the wall. A small cross is superimposed over the Endpoint osnap icon, indicating the reference location for Object Snap Tracking.

6. Move the cursor upward. Then enter **8.┘** (**204.┘**) to start the counter line 8″ (204 mm) from the corner of the jamb (see Figure 5.39).

7. Hold the crosshair cursor directly to the right of the first point of the line, and enter **2′.┘** (**610.┘**).

8. Hold the crosshair cursor upward, and enter **4′.┘** (**1220.┘**).
   At this point, you have drawn two line segments defining the counter on the back wall of the cabin. You can see the dimensions in Figure 5.37, shown earlier.

9. Hold the cursor to the right again, and enter **5′1″.┘** (**1550.┘**) to draw the long counter line that runs in front of the sink.

10. Select the Perpendicular osnap and then pick the inside wall line, as shown in Figure 5.40, to complete the counter.

11. Press ↵ to end the LINE command.

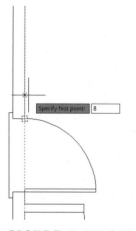

FIGURE 5.39 Setting the location for the first counter line

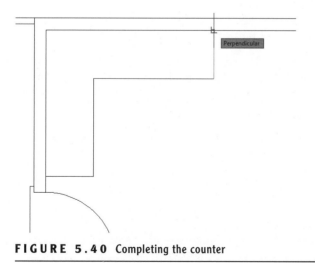

FIGURE 5.40 Completing the counter

Method 2: Using *Offset* and *Fillet*

As with launching commands, most tasks in AutoCAD give you options galore for completing them. Although some methods are viewed as being more efficient than others, the "best" method is often a matter of personal preference. In this exercise, you're going to draw the same counter you drew in the previous exercise, except this time you will use the OFFSET and FILLET commands.

To complete this exercise, you'll need to erase the countertop you just drew. You could use the ERASE command to do this, but because all four of the line segments were drawn in one cycle of the LINE command, you can also use the UNDO command.

1. Click the Undo button on the Quick Access toolbar, enter U↲ at the command line, or use the standard Windows keyboard shortcut Ctrl+Z.

   Alternatively, you can open I05-10-PointFilter.dwg (M05-10-Point Filter.dwg) from the book's web page.

   The counter you just drew should disappear. If you ended the LINE command while drawing the counter and had to restart it before you finished, you might have to click the Undo button more than once.

   If you undo too much, click the Redo button, which is just to the right of Undo.

   Now you'll draw the counter again, this time using the OFFSET and FILLET commands.

2. Offset both the left inside wall line and the top inside wall line 2′ (610 mm) to the inside of the cabin.

3. Stop and then restart the OFFSET command. This time, offset the inside left wall line 7′-1″ (2159 mm) to the right.

4. Next, offset the inside top wall line 6′-0″ (1829 mm) downward—the sum of the two counter dimensions and the stove dimension (see Figure 5.41).

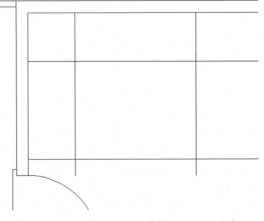

FIGURE 5.41 Offsetting wall lines to create the counter

T I P   As discussed earlier, if the FILLET command has a nonzero radius setting that you want to keep, hold down the Shift key to set the radius to zero for one use of the command. After the command ends, the radius returns to its nonzero setting.

5. Use the FILLET command with a radius of zero to clean up the three corners. Be sure to click on the portions of the lines that you want to retain.

6. Save your file as **I05-11-KitchenCounter.dwg** (**M05-11-Kitchen Counter.dwg**).

Now that you have tried both ways, you can decide which of the two methods is more practical for you. Both are powerful techniques for laying out orthogonal patterns of lines for walls, counters, and other objects.

UNDOING AND REDOING IN AUTOCAD

AutoCAD has various Undo options, and they operate quite differently:

▶ When you click the Undo button on the Quick Access toolbar, you're using the AutoCAD U command. You can also start it by entering **U↵**. The U command works like the Undo command for Windows-compliant applications by undoing the results of the previous commands one step at a time. Using the Ctrl+Z hot-key combination also executes the U command.

▶ The UNDO command in AutoCAD has many options, and you start it by entering **UNDO↵**. You use this approach when you want to undo everything you've done since you last saved your drawing or to undo back to a point in your drawing session that you specified earlier by using the Mark option. Be careful when you use the UNDO command; you can easily lose a lot of your work.

▶ The OOPS command is a special Undo tool that restores the last objects erased, even if the ERASE command wasn't the last command executed.

▶ The REDO command will undo the effect of several undo operations. So, if you undo a few steps too many, you can still get them back. The Redo tool must be used immediately after using the Undo tool.

▶ Both the Undo and Redo buttons on the Quick Access toolbar have small down-arrows to their right. Clicking these arrows displays a drop-down menu showing a list of the recent commands used (Undo) or undone (Redo). When there are several commands to be undone or redone, selecting the command to be undone may be faster than clicking the Undo or Redo button repeatedly.

Drawing the Stove and Refrigerator

The stove and refrigerator are simple rectangles. Here you will use the Temporary
Tracking Point osnap to locate the first corner of each shape:

1. Make sure I05-11-KitchenCounter.dwg (M05-11-KitchenCounter.dwg)
   is open.

2. To begin drawing the refrigerator, click the Rectangle button on the
   Home tab ➤ Draw panel, or enter **REC**↵ at the command line.

3. Verify that Object Snap, Object Snap Tracking, and Dynamic Input are
   still enabled on the status bar.

4. Place your cursor near the upper end of the right side of the counter,
   letting the running Endpoint osnap establish an object snap tracking
   point.

5. Move your cursor down and enter **2**↵ (**51**↵), as shown in Figure 5.42.

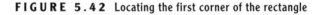

FIGURE 5.42 Locating the first corner of the rectangle

This starts the rectangle 2″ (51 mm) from the back wall, along the
side of the counter.

6. To specify the opposite corner of the rectangle, enter **36,-36**↵ **914,
   -914**↵.

   The Rectangle (RECTANG) command ends, and the refrigerator is
   drawn at the end of the counter that is running along the back wall.
   Next, you'll use a similar process to draw a basic outline of the stove.

7. Right-click and choose Repeat RECTANG from the context menu that
   opens.

8. Use the technique from step 4, but pick the lower end of the left side
   of the counter as the tracking point.

9. Hold the cursor directly above that point, and enter **1′5″**↵ or **17**↵ (**432**↵),
   and then enter **26,27**↵ (**660,686**↵) to complete the rectangle.

10. Use the TRIM command to trim away the front edge of the counter that passes through the stove.

Your kitchen should look like Figure 5.43.

11. Save your file as I05-12-Refrigerator.dwg (M05-12-Refrigerator.dwg).

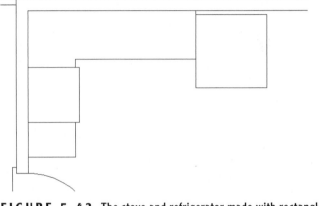

FIGURE 5.43 The stove and refrigerator made with rectangles

N O T E   Because the stove rectangle is drawn as a polyline, you need to select only one segment of it for all sides of the rectangle to be selected and, in this case, for them to become cutting edges.

Completing the Stove with Parametrics

At this point, the cabin is really starting to take shape with the numerous lines, arcs, and polylines you have drawn so far. There is, however, a significant disconnect between what you see and what AutoCAD sees while viewing the cabin. To you, it's a cabin; you see how the stairs are spaced equally, how the wall intersections form perpendicular angles, and in general how objects relate to other objects within your drawing.

AutoCAD, on the other hand, sees nothing more than a collection of lines, arcs, and polylines. It doesn't know that walls should form 90° angles where they intersect, or that the two lines representing door openings should be parallel and spaced a certain distance apart. Currently, every object inside your drawing is independent from the other objects in your drawing.

Parametric drawing offers a solution to this disconnect; it allows you to define both geometric and dimensional constraints to the objects inside your drawing. Whereas dimensional constraints must be applied manually, geometric constraints may be applied manually, automatically, or inferred while drawing. Using the dimensions shown in Figure 5.44, you'll have the chance to explore each of these methods as you use parametrics to complete the stove.

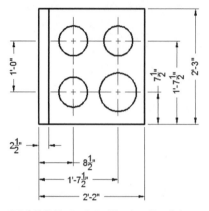

FIGURE 5.44 The details of the stove

AUTOCAD LT USERS

The AutoCAD LT Ribbon does not include tools for creating geometric or dimensional constraints because parametric drawing is one of the features found only in the full version of AutoCAD. Because AutoCAD LT users will not be able to complete the next several exercises on parametric drawing, please substitute the following exercise to complete the stove:

1. Make sure I05-12-Refrigerator.dwg (M05-12 -Refrigerator.dwg) is open.

2. Start the INSERT command by using the Insert button found on the Insert tab ➢ Block panel. The Insert dialog box appears.

3. Click the Browse button to browse to the file I05-StoveInsert.dwg (M05-StoveInsert.dwg) found inside the Chapter 5 data directory.

   If you haven't already, you can download this file from this book's web page at **www.sybex.com/go/autocad2012ner** or **www .autocadner.com**.

4. You are taken back to the Insert dialog box. Before clicking OK, select the Specify On-Screen check box under Insertion Point, and the Explode check box in the lower-left corner.

(Continues)

AutoCAD LT Users *(Continued)*

These should be the only two check boxes selected inside the Insert dialog box, as shown in the following illustration.

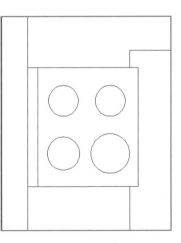

5. Use the Endpoint osnap to select the lower-back corner of the stove.

The stove is completed as the remaining geometry is inserted into the drawing.

6. Save your file as **I05-16-CompleteStove.dwg** (**M05-16 -CompleteStove.dwg**).

Proceed to the "Drawing the Kitchen Sink" exercise later in this chapter.

Getting Started with Geometric Constraints

The first step to using parametric drawing is to define how objects should interact geometrically. This is done by assigning geometric constraints to your model. These constraints will reinforce the use of tools such as object snaps to define the intersection of two lines as coincident, or two lines forming a right angle as perpendicular. Because you're not yet dealing with size, the primary focus in this exercise is to ensure that objects that should intersect do, objects that should form right angles are indeed perpendicular, and parallel lines are truly parallel.

Assuming you were diligent in creating your linework, the Auto Constrain tool will automatically determine and assign the necessary geometric constraints. Follow these steps to autoconstrain your stove:

1. Make sure I05-12-Refrigerator.dwg (M05-12-Refrigerator.dwg) is open, and zoom in to a closer view of the stove.

2. Select the current outline of the stove, and click the Auto Constrain tool, found on the Parametric tab ≻ Geometric panel.

   After you invoke Auto Constrain, a series of icons appear along the perimeter of the stove, as shown in Figure 5.45. These icons illustrate the geometric relationships AutoCAD established between the four lines that define the outline of your stove.

> **If no icons appear after you invoke Auto Constrain, use the Show All tool found on the Parametric tab ≻ Geometric panel.**

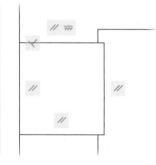

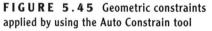

FIGURE 5.45 Geometric constraints applied by using the Auto Constrain tool

The positioning of these icons may be slightly different than shown in Figure 5.45; it's more important to verify that you have the same geometric constraints as shown.

3. Hover the cursor over the Geometric Constraint icons that are shown around the perimeter of the stove.

The geometric relationship displays as you hover over each Geometric Constraint icon. For instance, the parallel geometric constraint highlights both the adjacent Geometric Constraint icon and the line to which the two lines are parallel. This inquiry method is an especially helpful way of visualizing which objects relate to other objects inside your drawing.

 4. Turn on Infer Constraints from the status bar. In addition, Object Snap, Object Snap Tracking, and Dynamic Input should still be on.

5. Use the LINE command and the Nearest and Perpendicular object snaps to draw a vertical line, as shown in Figure 5.46.

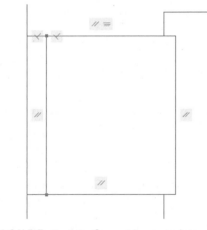

FIGURE 5.46 Geometric constraints inferred after drawing a line

6. Save your file as **I05-13-AutoConstrain.dwg** (**M05-13-Auto Constrain.dwg**).

Don't worry about being terribly accurate at this point. You'll apply dimensional constraints in a moment. Right now you're interested in only the geometric relationships between objects.

Drawing the Stove Burners

ACAD
ONLY

The next step is to draw the circles that represent the burners. As with the last exercise, we're not overly concerned about size at this point.

Instead, the focus is on getting the geometry correct first, and then you'll come back to further constrain the stove with dimensional constraints.

1. Make sure I05-13-AutoConstrain.dwg (M05-13-AutoConstrain.dwg) is open.

Circle

2. Click the down-arrow next to the Circle tool, found on the Home tab ➤ Draw panel, and look at the fly-out menu, as shown in Figure 5.47.

Center, Radius
Center, Diameter
2-Point
3-Point
Tan, Tan, Radius
Tan, Tan, Tan

FIGURE 5.47 The CIRCLE command's fly-out menu

You have six options for constructing a circle:

▶ The first two (Center, Radius; and Center, Diameter) require you to specify a point as the center of the circle and to enter a radius or a diameter.

▶ You use the next two (2-Point and 3-Point) when you know two or three points that the circle must intersect.

▶ The last two options (Tan, Tan, Radius; and Tan, Tan, Tan) use tangents and a radius, or just tangents, respectively, to form a circle.

Notice that each circle construction method has a unique icon on the left side of the fly-out menu. Whichever method was used last becomes the default method when you click the Circle button, and its icon appears on the button.

3. Choose the Center, Radius option from the fly-out menu.

4. The command prompt changes from Specify center point for circle or: to Base point:. Draw four circles as shown in Figure 5.48.

5. Save your file as **I05-14-StoveBurners.dwg** (**M05-14-StoveBurners.dwg**).

   Once again, your intent at this point is to develop a solid geometric representation of the stove. Before applying dimensional constraints, I'll show you how to add some additional geometric constraints.

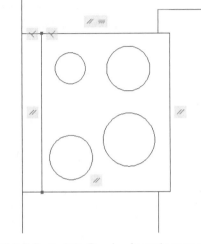

FIGURE 5.48 Rough schematic representation of the stove

Applying Additional Geometric Constraints

ACAD ONLY
You've seen how the Auto Constrain and Infer Constraints features make it easy to add geometric constraints to your drawing. Although both are incredibly powerful features, sometimes you need an extra degree of control over how geometric constraints are added to your drawing. For this reason, you have the option of manually adding geometric constraints to objects inside your drawing.

Even if you had been more deliberate in drawing the burners with the proper alignment and size, the Auto Constrain feature would still have a difficult time establishing how the four burners truly interact with one another. Consequently, to ensure that the constraints are correctly applied, the best approach in this case is to manually define the necessary geometric constraints. To do this, you'll use many of the individual constraint icons found on the Parametric tab ➤ Geometric panel.

1. Make sure I05-14-StoveBurners.dwg (M05-14-StoveBurners.dwg) is open.

2. Confirm that Infer Constraints, Object Snap, Object Snap Tracking, and Dynamic Input are still enabled on the status bar.

3. Click the Horizontal constraint tool from the Parametric tab ➤ Geometric panel.

4. From the `Select an object or [2Points]:` prompt, press the down-arrow to select 2Points, as shown in Figure 5.49.

5. Hover over the top-left burner, and select it when a small red circle with an X appears in the center, as shown on the left in Figure 5.50.

6. From the `Select second point:` prompt, use the same method to select the center point of the top-right burner, as shown on the right in Figure 5.50.

The two right burners (as if you were working at the stove and facing the rear deck) are now constrained horizontally; this means that although the two burners may be located anywhere along the y-axis, they will always be aligned along the x-axis. You can try this out by using the MOVE command to move either one of the burners. Notice how the second burner also moves even though it was not selected.

FIGURE 5.49 Selecting the 2Point option when using Dynamic Input

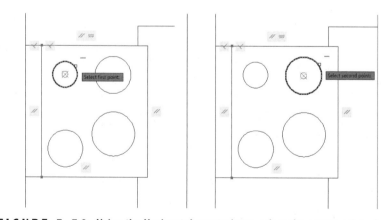

FIGURE 5.50 Using the Horizontal constraint to select the center point of the circle

7. Use the Horizontal constraint once again, repeating steps 5 and 6 to constrain the two burners on the left side of the stove.

   All of the burners are now constrained horizontally; however, there is no relationship between the left and right burners. To fix this, you will continue constraining the burners, this time applying Vertical constraints between the right and left burners.

8. Click the Vertical constraint tool from the Parametric tab ➤ Geometric panel.

9. At the Select an object or [2Points]: prompt, click the down-arrow to select 2Points using Dynamic Input.

10. Use the Vertical 2Point constraint tool to select the center points of the two front burners.

11. Repeat the Vertical constraint tool once again, this time selecting the center points of the two rear burners.

    Each of the burners is now fully constrained horizontally and vertically. Notice how moving a single burner also moves the two adjacent burners. Note the Constraint icons under each of the burners; your stove should look like Figure 5.51.

    Because three of the burners are the same size, you can use the Equal geometric constraint to build a relationship between the two right burners and the back-left burner. It's important to remember that the focus here is to get the geometry correct. You'll apply dimensional constraints shortly to correctly size each of the burners.

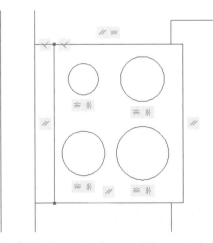

FIGURE 5.51 Burners fully constrained horizontally and vertically

= **12.** Click the Equal constraint tool from the Parametric tab ➤ Geometric panel.

13. Select the back-right burner and then the front-right burner to set the radius of each equal to the back-right burner.

14. Repeat the process once again, this time selecting the back-right burner and the back-left burner.

    Your stove should look like Figure 5.52.

15. Save your file as **I05-15-GeometricConstraints.dwg** (**M05-15 -GeometricConstraints.dwg**).

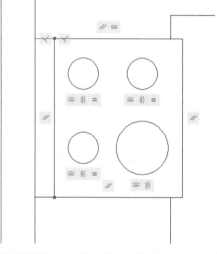

FIGURE 5.52 Stove with Equal constraints applied to three burners

Applying Dimensional Constraints

ACAD ONLY The previous several exercises gave you the opportunity to focus on geometry, not dimensions. Although the stove is geometrically correct, it's currently drawn with a series of arbitrary dimensions. *Dimensional constraints* let you assign real values to the geometry in your drawing. Thanks to the geometric constraints you have already applied to the stove, you'll need to apply dimensional constraints to only a few key points. The geometric constraints will handle the rest for you automatically, ensuring that the integrity of the relationships is retained.

Dimensional constraints function similarly to regular dimensions in AutoCAD. You'll have the chance to take a closer look at dimensions in Chapter 12,

"Dimensioning a Drawing," but your experience with parametrics will certainly provide a great foundation from which to build. One core difference between regular dimensions and parametric dimensions is that parametric dimensions require you to select both an object and a point. In contrast, regular dimensions require you to specify only a point. You'll use the dimensions shown earlier in Figure 5.44 to apply the necessary dimensional constraints.

1. Make sure I05-15-GeometricConstraints.dwg (M05-15-Geometric Constraints.dwg) is open.

2. Add a Linear dimensional constraint to the stove's rear control panel, as follows:

   a. Choose the Linear dimensional constraint from the Parametric tab ➤ Dimensional panel.

   b. Hover over the bottom-right corner of the stove and then click to accept the endpoint.

   c. Hover over the lower endpoint for the line representing the stove's control panel, and click to accept the point.

   d. Specify a location for the dimensional constraint, and then enter **2.5"** (64 mm) as the value for d1 (see Figure 5.53).

3. Using the Linear tool found on the Parametric tab ➤ Dimensional panel once again, add an 8 ½ (216 mm) constraint between the back-lower corner and the center point of the left-rear burner.

4. Continue using the Linear tool to add the following dimensional constraints:

   a. Add a 1' 7½" (495 mm) constraint between the back-lower corner and the center point of the left-front burner.

   b. Add a 7½" (190 mm) constraint between the lower-front corner of the stove and the left-front burner.

   c. Add a 1' 7½" (495 mm) constraint between the lower-front corner of the stove and the right-front burner.

   Figure 5.54 shows the result. You have created a total of five Linear constraints. These constraints have correctly positioned the rear control panel and each of the four burners for the stove. The only thing left to do is correctly size each of the four burners.

Because you used the Equal geometric constraint on three of the burners, properly sizing the burners will require only two Radius constraints.

5. Choose the Radius tool from the Parametric tab ➤ Dimensional panel.

6. From the `Select arc or circle:` prompt, select the front-right burner and choose a position for the dimensional constraint.

7. Enter a value of **3½"(89mm)** for the rad1 constraint.

The Equal geometric constraint updates the radius of the back-right and back-left burners to match the **3½"(89mm)** radius you specified for the front-right burner.

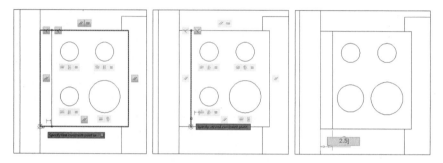

FIGURE 5.53 Applying a Linear dimensional constraint to the stove's control panel

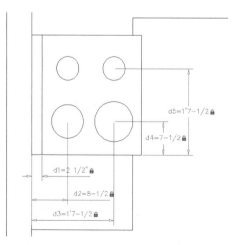

FIGURE 5.54 Linear constraints applied to the stove

8. Repeat steps 5 through 7 to apply a Radius constraint on the front-left burner. When prompted for the radius, enter **rad1+1↵** (**rad1+25**). Figure 5.55 shows the result.

Much as formulas can reference the value of other cells in Microsoft Excel, dimensional constraints can reference other dimensional constraints. In this example, you referenced a constraint applied to the front-right burner by entering its name (rad1). The expression rad1+1 is actually a mathematical expression telling AutoCAD to gather the value of rad1 (3½″), and add 1″ to it for a total radius of 4½″ (114 mm).

9. Save your file as **I05-16-CompleteStove.dwg** (**M05-16-Complete Stove.dwg**).

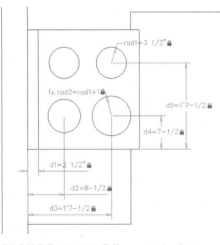

FIGURE 5.55 Fully constrained stove

Drawing the Kitchen Sink

In this section, you'll draw a double sink with one basin larger than the other (see Figure 5.56). You'll use OFFSET, FILLET, and TRIM to create the sink from the counter and wall lines.

1. Make sure I05-16-CompleteStove.dwg (M05-16-CompleteStove.dwg) is open. Zoom in to the sink area, keeping the edges of the refrigerator and stove in view.

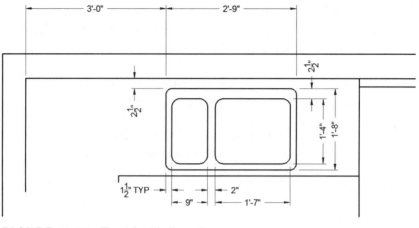

FIGURE 5.56 The sink with dimensions

2. Create the top and bottom edges by using the OFFSET command:

   a. Offset the inside wall line 2 ½″ (64 mm) down.

   b. Restart the OFFSET command, and offset the inside wall line 1′8″ (508 mm) down.

   This forms the top and bottom edges of the sink. Next, you will draw the left and right edges of the sink.

 3. From the status bar, turn on Selection Cycling.

4. Restart the OFFSET command, and set the offset distance to **16″** (406 mm).
   You're going to offset the right side of the counter 1′-4″ (406 mm) to the left, but it coincides with the left side of the refrigerator. You'll use Selection Cycling to ensure that you select the correct line.

5. At the Select object to offset: prompt, select the right edge of the counter. Because you enabled Selection Cycling in step 3, and both the right edge of the counter and left edge of the refrigerator coincide with one another, the Selection dialog box displays (see Figure 5.57).

6. Select the Line option from the Selection dialog box, and complete the OFFSET command by picking a point to the left of the selected line. Notice how the object highlighted in the Selection dialog box also highlights (dashes) inside the drawing (see Figure 5.57).

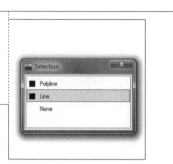

FIGURE 5.57 Using Selection Cycling to select the right edge of the counter

7. Offset this new line 2′9″ (838 mm) to the left. This forms the outside edge of the sink (see the top of Figure 5.58).

8. Fillet the corners of this rectangle to clean them up, using a radius of zero.

9. Perform the following offsets to draw the sink basins, as follows:

   a. Offset the left side, bottom, and right side of the sink 1.5″ (38 mm) to the inside.

   b. Offset the top side 2.5″ (64 mm) to the inside.

   c. Offset the left basin edge to the right 9″ (229 mm).

   d. Offset the right basin edge to the left 1′7″ (483 mm).This forms the basis of the inside sink lines (see the middle of Figure 5.58).

10. Trim away the horizontal top and bottom inside sink lines between the two middle vertical sink lines.

11. Fillet the four corners of each basin with a 2″ (51mm) radius to clean them up. Use the Multiple option of the FILLET command so that you won't need to restart the command continually.

12. Fillet all four outside sink corners with a 1.5″ (38mm) radius. This finishes the sink (see the bottom of Figure 5.58). Use Zoom Previous to view the whole kitchen with the completed sink.

13. Save your file as **I05-17-KitchenSink.dwg** (**M05-17-KitchenSink.dwg**).

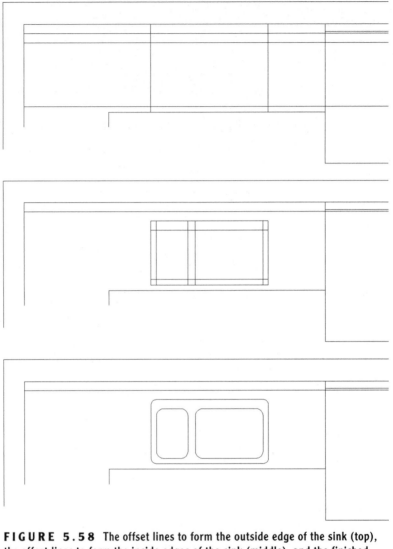

FIGURE 5.58 The offset lines to form the outside edge of the sink (top), the offset lines to form the inside edges of the sink (middle), and the finished sink (bottom)

This completes the kitchen area. You drew no new lines to complete this task because you created most of them by offsetting existing lines and then trimming or filleting them. Keep this in mind as you move on to the bathroom.

Constructing the Bathroom

The bathroom has three fixtures—a sink, a shower, and a toilet—as well as a mirror and a shelving unit. While you are drawing the bathroom, you'll draw the hot tub in the main room as well (see Figure 5.59). When drawing these fixtures, you'll use a few object snaps over and over again. You can set one or more of the osnap choices to run continually until you turn them off. That way, you won't have to select them each time.

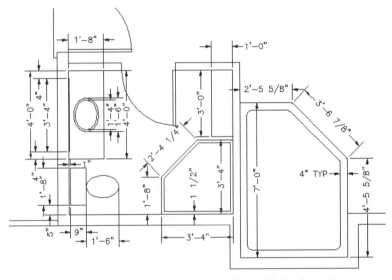

FIGURE 5.59 The bathroom fixtures and hot tub with dimensions

Setting Running Object Snaps

You'll set three osnaps to run continually for now, until you get used to how they work:

1. Make sure I05-17-KitchenSink.dwg (M05-17-KitchenSink.dwg) is open.

2. Right-click the Object Snap button on the status bar and then choose Settings from the context menu to open the Drafting Settings dialog box.

   By default, the Object Snap tab is current (see Figure 5.60).

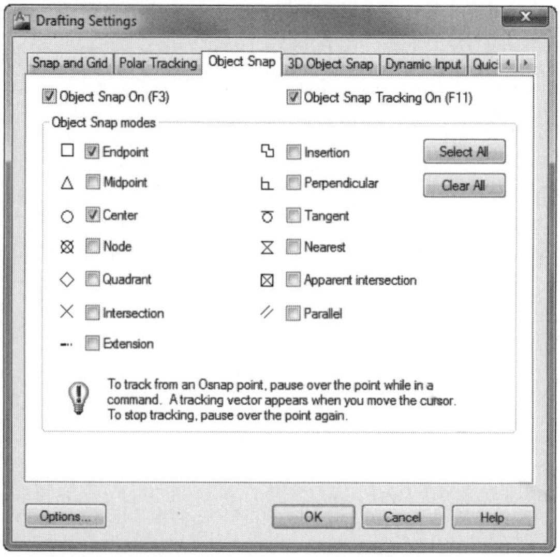

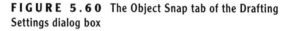

FIGURE 5.60 The Object Snap tab of the Drafting Settings dialog box

Each of the 13 osnap options has a check box and a symbol next to it. The symbol appears as a marker in the drawing when you select a particular osnap, and the cursor is near a point where you can use that osnap. You can select any number of osnaps to be running at a time.

N O T E   You can choose a different color for the markers if you want. If you're using a dark background in the drawing area, use a bright color, such as yellow. For a white background, try blue. To change colors, start the OPTIONS command and then choose the Colors button from the Drafting tab.

3. From the Object Snap tab of the Drafting Settings dialog box, click the check boxes next to Endpoint, Midpoint, and Intersection. Also ensure that the check box next to Object Snap On is selected in the upper-left corner of the dialog box.

4. Click OK to close the dialog box.

The Endpoint, Midpoint, and Intersection osnaps will now be active anytime you're prompted to select a point on the drawing. You can deactivate them by turning off the Object Snap button in the status bar or by pressing F3.

Now you're ready to begin drawing the bathroom. The shower determines the placement of the other two items, so let's start there.

Drawing a Shower Unit

You'll start the shower unit with a rectangle and then trim away one corner. As you start this exercise, check the status bar. The Polar Tracking, Object Snap, Object Snap Tracking, and Dynamic Input buttons should be in their on positions. The rest of the buttons should be off. Follow these steps:

1. Make sure I05-17-KitchenSink.dwg (M05-17-KitchenSink.dwg) is open.

2. Verify that Polar Tracking, Object Snap, Object Snap Tracking, and Dynamic Input are turned on. The remaining drawing modes should be turned off.

3. Enter Z↵ E↵ or click the Zoom Extents button to zoom to the drawing's extents. Then use the zoom window or the scroll wheel to view the bathroom close up.

4. Start the Rectangle (RECTANG) command and use the following settings:

   a. For the first point, move the cursor to the lower-right inside corner of the room. As soon as the Endpoint osnap marker appears on the endpoint that you want to snap to, click. This places the first corner of the rectangle at the endpoint.

   b. For the second point, enter **-40,40**↵ (**-1016,1016**↵).

T I P Remember, if you are not using Dynamic Input, you need to enter the @ symbol before entering relative coordinates.

If you are not using Dynamic Input and don't get the rectangle you want after entering the relative coordinates for the second corner, click the Options button at the bottom of the Application menu to open the Options dialog box. Click the User Preferences tab.

In the upper-right corner in the Priority For Coordinate Data Entry area, be sure that the button next to Keyboard Entry Except Scripts is active, and then click OK. Try the rectangle again.

5. Start the CHAMFER command from the Home tab ➤ Modify panel. If the Chamfer tool isn't visible on the Ribbon, click the down-arrow next to the Fillet tool, as shown in Figure 5.61.

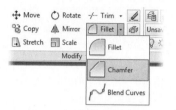

FIGURE 5.61 Starting the CHAMFER command from the Modify Ribbon panel

6. From the Select first line or [Undo/Polyline/Distance/Angle/Trim/mEthod/Multiple]: prompt, enter **D**↵ to set a chamfer distance.

7. Enter 1'-8" (508 mm) for the first and second chamfer distances.

8. Select the vertical shower edge as the first chamfer line, and the horizontal shower edge as the second chamfer edge (see Figure 5.62).

   (NEW) As you hover over the second line, a preview of the resulting chamfer displays, similar to the display for the FILLET command. This allows you to confirm the chamfer distance values before completing the command.

9. Offset the shower polyline inward 1-½" (38 mm), as shown in Figure 5.63.

10. Save your file as **I05-18-Shower.dwg** (**M05-18-Shower.dwg**).

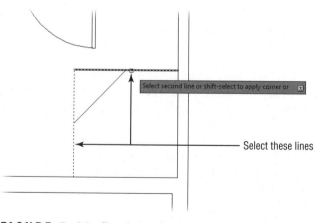

FIGURE 5.62 Chamfering the shower edges

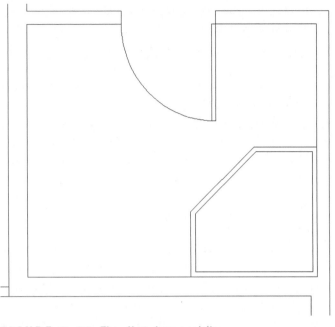

FIGURE 5.63 The offset shower polyline

Next, you'll draw the sink to the right of the shower.

Drawing the Bathroom Sink and Mirror

You'll offset a line and draw an ellipse for this fixture while you practice using the Temporary Tracking Point osnap option in the process. The Endpoint and Midpoint osnaps are still running.

1. Make sure I05-18-Shower.dwg (M05-18-Shower.dwg) is open, and zoom in to the sink area with a zoom window.

2. Complete the following offsets to draw the vertical limits of the sink counter and the mirror:

   a. Offset the top-inside wall line down 4′ (1219mm).

   b. Offset the new line up 4″ (102mm).

   c. Offset the top-inside wall down 4″ (102mm).

3. Complete the following offsets to draw the horizontal limits of the sink counter and the mirror:

   a. Offset the left inside wall 1′-8″ (508mm) to the right.

   b. Offset the same inside wall line ½″ (13mm) to frame the counter and the mirror.

   Your sink area should look like Figure 5.64.

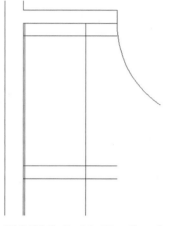

FIGURE 5.64   The offset shower polyline

4. Use the FILLET command to clean up the lines to form the sink counter and mirror. You will have to zoom in to each end of the mirror to select the correct end of the mirror's sides and fillet the lines properly. Figure 5.65 shows the partially completed sink and mirror.

5. Click the down-arrow next to the Ellipse button on the Home tab ➤ Draw panel and choose the Center option. Alternatively, you can enter EL↵ C↵ to start the command from the command line.

6. Place the cursor near the midpoint of the bottom counter line. When the small cross appears in the osnap marker, the first tracking point is established.

7. Establish the center point of the sink counter by using Object Snap Tracking:

   a. Move the crosshair cursor to the midpoint of the vertical line that defines the front of the counter.

b. Move the cursor to the left when the cross appears in the Midpoint osnap marker. A small, dark X appears at the intersection to indicate the point that AutoCAD will use for the center point of the ellipse (see Figure 5.66).

c. Click to define the center point.

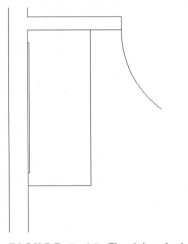

FIGURE 5.65 The sink and mirror

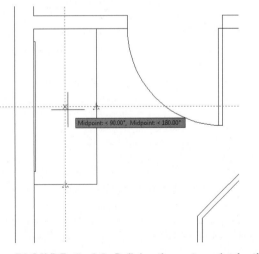

FIGURE 5.66 Defining the center point for the ellipse

Instead of using the direct entry method to define a point with the Object Snap Tracking tool, you just used two different object snaps to define one point.

8. The ELLIPSE command requires you to specify a distance for each of the major and minor axes:

    a. Hold the crosshair cursor directly to the right of the center point. Enter 5↵ (127↵).

    b. Hold the crosshair cursor directly above the center and enter 7↵ (178↵).

The ellipse is constructed, and the sink fixture is nearly complete.

9. Use the Offset tool to offset the ellipse 1″ (25mm) to the outside (see Figure 5.67).

Leave the view on your screen as it is for a moment.

10. Save your file as **I05-19-BathroomSink.dwg** (**M05-19-Bathroom Sink.dwg**).

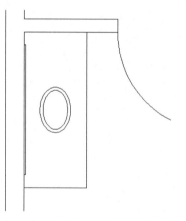

FIGURE 5.67 The completed sink fixture

 **WARNING**   Be aware that offsetting an ellipse does not create a new ellipse, but instead creates a polyline with several small segments.

The toilet and the shelves are the final fixtures necessary in the bathroom. You'll use the ELLIPSE command again, along with the RECTANGLE command, to draw them. You'll also learn about a couple of new display options.

Positioning the Toilet and Shelves

The shelves are a simple rectangle measuring 3′×1′ (914 mm×305 mm). The toilet consists of a rectangle and an ellipse centered between the sink and the wall. The tank is offset 1″ (25 mm) from the back wall and is 9″×20″ (229 mm×508 mm). The ellipse representing the seat measures 18″ (457 mm) in one direction and 12″ (304 mm) in the other.

1. Make sure I05-19-BathroomSink.dwg (M05-19-BathroomSink.dwg) is open.

2. On the navigation bar, click the Pan button. The cursor changes to a small hand to indicate that you are in Pan Realtime mode. Position the cursor in the lower part of the drawing area, with the view still zoomed in on the sink.

3. Drag the cursor up and to the right until the toilet area comes into view. The drawing slides along with the movement of the cursor. If necessary, zoom in and then pan again until you have the toilet area centered in the drawing area.

> **T I P** You can also perform a pan, a lateral change in the viewing area with no change in zoom factor, by holding down the middle mouse button or scroll wheel. The MBUTTONPAN variable must be set to 1 (enter MBUTTONPAN↵1↵) for this functionality to be available. Now that most people use a wheel mouse, this manner of panning is becoming the preferred method. Rolling the wheel to zoom is also common.

4. Right-click and choose Zoom from the context menu that opens. Alternatively, you can enter Z↵↵ at the command line to execute the Zoom Realtime operation. Back in the drawing, the cursor changes to a magnifying glass with plus and minus signs.

5. Position the Zoom Realtime cursor near the top of the drawing and hold down the left mouse button. Drag the cursor down, and watch the view being zoomed out in real time. Move the cursor up, still holding down the mouse button.

   Position the cursor in such a way that you have a good view of the toilet area and then release the mouse button. Right-click again, and choose Exit from the context menu to end Zoom Realtime.

   With Zoom Realtime, moving the cursor to the left or right has no effect on the view. The magnification is controlled solely by the up-and-down motion.

These zooming options are convenient tools for adjusting the view of your drawing. Let's move on to the toilet first. You need to find a way to position the toilet accurately, centering it between the wall and shower. The midpoint of the left wall line isn't useful because the wall line runs behind the shower. You'll have to use a reference point to locate the starting point for the toilet tank. The lower-left corner of the tank is 5″ (127 mm) from the bottom wall and 1″ (25 mm) from the left wall. Because there is no osnap feature to define the location on the left wall, you will use the From osnap to locate the corner.

1. Make sure I05-19-BathroomSink.dwg (M05-19-BathroomSink.dwg) is open.

2. Start the Rectangle (RECTANG) command and click the Snap From button in the Object Snap toolbar.

   At the Base point: prompt, click the lower-left inside corner of the bathroom.

3. Enter @1,5↵ (@25,127↵) to place the first corner of the rectangle and then 9,20↵ (229,508↵).

   The 9″×20″ (229 mm×508 mm) toilet tank is drawn centered on the left wall (see the left of Figure 5.68).

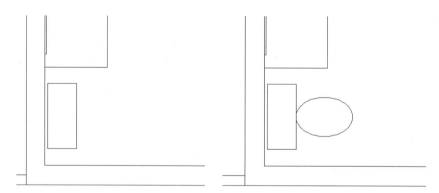

FIGURE 5.68 The toilet tank in place (left) and the completed toilet (right)

4. Start the ELLIPSE command. If you start it from the Ribbon, be sure to select the Axis, End Ellipse tool from the Home tab ➢ Draw panel. The command window displays a default prompt of Specify axis endpoint of ellipse or:.

   Using the Specify Axis Endpoint option and the running Midpoint osnap, you can easily define the ellipse's location and first axis from one end of the ellipse to the other.

5. Move the cursor near the midpoint of the right side of the tank, and when the triangle shows up there, click. This starts the ellipse.

6. Hold the crosshair cursor out to the right of the rectangle, and enter 1′6↵ (457↵). This sets the first axis.

   Now, as you move the crosshair cursor, you'll see that a line starts at the center of the ellipse, and the cursor's movement controls the size of the other axis.

   To designate the second axis, you need to enter the distance from the center of the axis to the end of it, or half the overall length of the axis.

7. Hold the crosshair cursor directly above or below the center point, and enter 6↵ (152↵).

   The ellipse is complete, so you've finished the toilet (see the right of Figure 5.68).

8. To complete the fixtures, construct the shelves by drawing a 3′-0″× 1′-0″ (914 mm×305 mm) rectangle from the upper-right corner of the bathroom.

   Figure 5.59 earlier in the chapter shows the proper orientation. Zoom out, and your completed bathroom should look like Figure 5.69.

9. Save your file as **I05-20-BathroomToilet.dwg** (**M05-20-Bathroom Toilet.dwg**).

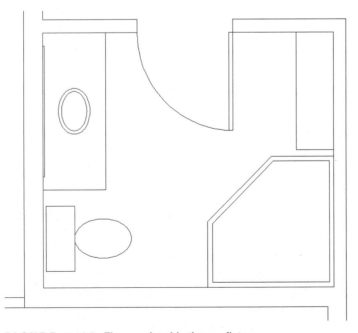

FIGURE 5.69 The completed bathroom fixtures

T I P You can snap the features of an ellipse or a circle by using the Center or Quadrant object snaps. If an ellipse is rotated, the Quadrant points will be located at the two points where the curves are sharpest and the two points where the curves are flattest. The Quadrant snaps will always remain at the four points of a circle or arc that project vertically or horizontally from the center point regardless of the object's orientation.

Drawing the Hot Tub

What is a cabin without a hot tub to relax in? You'll complete the cabin fixtures by using a polyline to draw the outside perimeter of the hot tub, offsetting this polyline to the inside and then filleting the appropriate corners. Here's how it's done:

1. Make sure I05-20-BathroomToilet.dwg (M05-20-BathroomToilet.dwg) is open, and verify that the Polar Tracking button is still turned on in the status bar.

2. Start the Polyline (PLINE) command and click the bottom-left inside corner of the pop-out to the right of the bathroom, as shown in Figure 5.70.

FIGURE 5.70 Starting the hot tub polyline

3. Click the endpoint to the right, on the opposite end of the pop-out.

4. Move the cursor directly above the last point and enter **4′5-5/8″⏎** (**1362⏎**) to draw the first vertical line. Refer to Figure 5.59 for the dimensions of the hot tub.

Earlier in this chapter, you set the Polar Tracking Increment Angle value to 45.00 in the Drafting Settings dialog box. This setting lets you easily place the cursor at 45° increments from a set point rather than at the 90° increments provided by using Ortho mode.

5. Place the cursor above and to the left of the current last point, until the Polar Snap tooltip reads 135°. Then enter **3′6-7/8″⏎ (1089⏎)** to draw the diagonal line (see Figure 5.71).

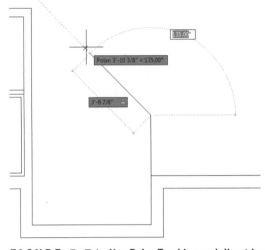

Polar: 3′-10 3/8″ < 135.00°

3′-6 7/8″

135.00°

FIGURE 5.71 Use Polar Tracking and direct input to draw the diagonal line.

6. Use the Perpendicular osnap to draw the top horizontal line from the last point to the outside of the bathroom wall.

7. Finally, enter **C⏎** at the command line to close the polyline and end the Polyline (PLINE) command.

8. Use the OFFSET command to offset the polyline 4″ (102 mm) to the inside.

9. Start the FILLET command and set the Radius value to 3″ (76).

10. Then fillet the two outside corners that project into the cabin (see Figure 5.72).

11. Stop and then restart the FILLET command, but this time choose the Polyline option.

12. Click the inside polyline to fillet all the corners at one time.

13. Zoom to the drawing's extents. Your cabin should look like Figure 5.73.

14. Save your drawing as **I05A-FPLAYO.dwg** (**M05A-FPLAYO.dwg**).

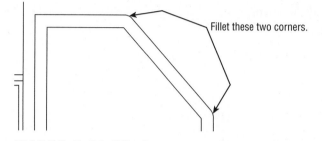

Fillet these two corners.

FIGURE 5.72 Fillet the two corners that extend into the cabin.

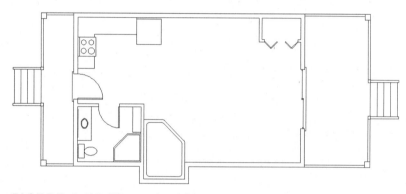

FIGURE 5.73 The completed floor plan zoomed to fill the screen

Using Pan Realtime and Zoom Realtime

The Pan and Zoom buttons are next to each other on the navigation bar. In addition to using the panel buttons, you can start Pan by entering **P↵** and can start Zoom Realtime by entering **Z↵↵**.

You can also start Pan or Zoom by right-clicking at the Command: prompt and then choosing Pan or Zoom from the context menu, or by clicking the Pan or Zoom button in the middle of the status bar. If you try this, you'll find that it's easier than clicking the Pan or Zoom button.

(Continues)

Using Pan Realtime and Zoom Realtime *(Continued)*

Like most AutoCAD commands, the Zoom and Pan Realtime commands offer several options, including the following:

Exit Ends the Zoom Realtime or Pan Realtime command.

Pan Switches to Pan Realtime from Zoom Realtime.

Zoom Switches to Zoom Realtime from Pan Realtime.

3D Orbit Is a special viewing tool for 3D that is covered in later chapters.

Zoom Window Allows you to make a zoom window without first ending Pan Realtime or Zoom Realtime. You pick a point, hold down the left mouse button, and then drag open a window in your drawing. When you release the button, you're zoomed in to the window you made, and Pan Realtime or Zoom Realtime resumes.

Zoom Original Restores the view of your drawing that you had when you began Pan Realtime or Zoom Realtime.

Zoom Extents Zooms to the drawing extents.

To end Pan Realtime or Zoom Realtime, press the Esc key, press ↵, or right-click and choose Exit from the context menu.

When Pan Realtime or Zoom Realtime is running, AutoCAD is in a special mode that makes the status bar invisible and, therefore, unusable.

If You Would Like More Practice...

The following are several additional exercises that will give you the opportunity to practice the skills and techniques you have learned.

Drawing the Cabin Again

As is true for almost any skill, the key to mastery is practice. Redrawing the entire cabin might seem daunting at this point, when you think of how long it took you to get here. But if you try it all again, starting from Chapter 3, "Setting Up a Drawing," you'll find that it will take about half the time it did the first time. If you do it a third time, it'll take half that time. Once you understand the techniques and how the commands work, feel free to experiment with alternative techniques to accomplish tasks and with other options for the commands.

Drawing Something Else

If you have a specific project in mind that you would like to draw in AutoCAD, so much the better. Try drawing the floor plan of your home or a classroom.

Drawing Some Furniture for the Cabin

Once you put some furniture in the cabin, you'll quickly see how small it is! But it can still accept some basic furniture without seeming too cramped. You should be able to add the following:

- ▶ Kitchen—a table and chairs
- ▶ Living room—a short couch or love seat, coffee table, easy chair, and a fireplace
- ▶ Bedroom—a double bed, chest, and nightstand

Use a tape measure and go around your office or home to determine the approximate dimensions of each piece. The goal here is not so much to ensure accuracy of scale but to practice drawing in AutoCAD. Figure 5.74 shows the floor plan with these pieces of furniture. If you draw the bed shown here, try using the Spline tool for the curved, turned-down sheets. It's on the expanded Draw panel. You'll see how it works after a little experimentation.

Drawing a Gasket

Figure 5.75 shows a gasket that is symmetrical around its vertical and horizontal axes. This symmetry will allow you to use the MIRROR command to create much of the drawing.

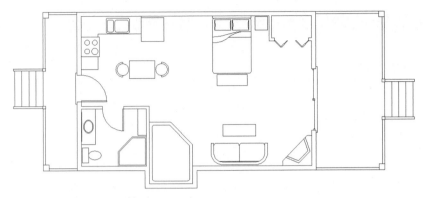

FIGURE 5.74 The floor plan with furniture

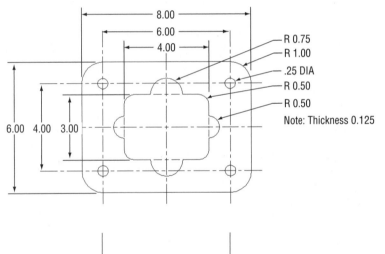

R 0.75
R 1.00
.25 DIA
R 0.50
R 0.50
Note: Thickness 0.125

8.00
6.00
4.00

6.00   4.00   3.00

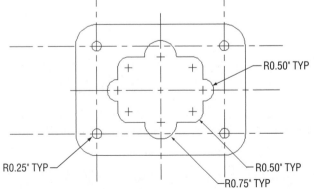

R0.50" TYP
R0.50" TYP
R0.75" TYP
R0.25" TYP

FIGURE 5.75 A gasket

The diagram in Figure 5.76 summarizes the steps.

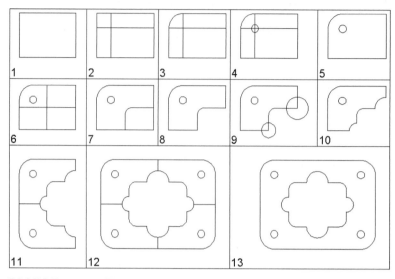

FIGURE 5.76 The 13 steps to creating the gasket

To draw the gasket, set Linear Units to Engineering with a precision of 0'-0.00". Set Angular Units to Decimal with a precision of 0.00. Now, follow these steps:

1. Use the LINE command to draw a rectangle 4" wide and 3" high.

2. Offset the upper horizontal line and the left vertical line 1" to the inside of the rectangle.

3. Use FILLET with a radius set to 1" on the upper-left corner of the original rectangle.

4. Draw the circle with the 0.25" radius, using the intersection of the two offset lines as the center.

5. Erase the offset lines.

6. Offset the right vertical line 2" to the left and the bottom horizontal line 1.5" up.

7. Use FILLET with a radius of 0.50" on the intersection of these two lines, retaining the right and lower segments.

8. Trim back the lower-right corner of the original rectangle.

9. Draw circles with 0.50" and 0.75" radii on the bottom and right sides of the shape.

10. Use TRIM to remove unneeded lines.

11. Use MIRROR to flip the shape down.

12. Use MIRROR again to flip the shape to the right.

13. Erase unneeded lines. (Each line to be erased is really two lines.)

14. If you are using AutoCAD, and not LT, add the Equal constraint so that all four circles remain the same size.

15. Save this drawing, naming it **05-Gasket.dwg**.

Drawing a Parking Lot

Figure 5.77 shows a parking lot partially bordered by sidewalks and streets.

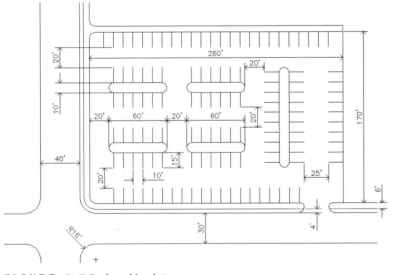

FIGURE 5.77 A parking lot

You'll get a lot of practice using the OFFSET and FILLET commands while completing this drawing. Guidelines will help you, so don't be afraid to use them. Note the tip at the end of this section. Here's a summary of the steps:

1. Set Linear and Angular units to Decimal, each with a precision of 0.0.

2. Set the Insertion Scale to Feet. Assume that 1 linear decimal unit equals 1″.

3. Set Polar Tracking to 90°, and turn it on.

4. Set the Endpoint and Midpoint osnaps to be running.

5. Set Snap to 10, Grid to 0, and Drawing Limits to 400, 250.

6. Zoom All.

7. Use Grid and Snap to draw the large 260′×170′ rectangle by using the LINE command and relative Cartesian coordinates, as you did in Chapter 3.

8. Turn off the Grid and Snap.

9. Offset three of the lines 6′ to the outside to make the sidewalk.

10. On two sides, offset the outer sidewalk line 4′ to the outside to make the curb.

11. Then, offset the curb lines 30′ and 40′ to make the street.

12. Draw extra lines to make the street intersection.

13. Fillet and trim lines to create the curved corners of the intersection and sidewalks.

14. Offset the lines of the inner rectangle to the inside to make guidelines for the parking strips and islands.

15. Use FILLET and TRIM to finish the drawing.

16. If you choose to save this drawing, name it I05-ParkingLot.dwg (M05-ParkingLot.dwg).

> When using decimal units as feet, you don't need to use the foot sign (′) when you enter distances.

 T I P   Using the FILLET command on two parallel lines creates a semi-circle to connect them. Try it on the islands in the parking area.

Are You Experienced?

Now you can...

- ☑ use the Temporary Tracking Point and Snap From object snaps to create and use tracking points

- ☑ use the Perpendicular and Intersection osnaps

- ☑ set up and use running osnaps

☑ **use the** STRETCH **command**

☑ **use the Properties palette and the Quick Properties dialog box**

☑ **move around the drawing area with Zoom Realtime and Pan Realtime**

☑ **use point filters**

☑ **use the** CIRCLE **and** ELLIPSE **commands**

☑ **move and duplicate objects with the** MOVE **and** COPY **commands**

☑ **use parametric drawing with geometric and dimensional constraints**

Using Layers to Organize Your Drawing

Before the age of computers, drafters used sets of transparent overlays on their drafting tables. These overlays were sheets that stacked one on top of the other, and the drafters could see through several at a time. Specific kinds of information were drawn on each overlay. All of them related spatially so that several overlays might be drawn for the same floor plan. Drawings for each discipline, such as plumbing, electrical, or HVAC, as well as charts and tables, were drawn on separate overlays so that the floor plans did not have to be replicated for every type of drawing produced. Each overlay had small holes punched near the corners so the drafter could position the overlay onto buttons, called *registration points*, that were taped to the drawing board. Because all overlays had holes punched at the same locations with respect to the drawing, information on the set of overlays was kept in alignment.

To help you organize your drawing, AutoCAD provides you with an amazing tool called *layers*, which can be thought of as a computerized form of the transparent overlays, only much more powerful and flexible. In manual drafting, you could use only four or five overlays at a time before the information on the bottom overlay became unreadable. (Copying the drawing meant sending all the layers through the blueprint machine together.) In AutoCAD, you aren't limited in the number of layers you can use. You can have hundreds of layers, and complex CAD drawings often do.

▶ **Creating new layers**

▶ **Assigning a color and a linetype to layers**

▶ **Moving existing objects onto a new layer**

▶ **Controlling the visibility of layers**

▶ **Working with linetypes**

▶ **Isolating objects by layer**

▶ **Using the Action Recorder**

▶ **Creating layer states**

Using Layers as an Organizing Tool

To understand what layers are and why they are so useful, think again about the transparent overlay sheets used in hand drafting. Each overlay is designed to be printed. The bottom sheet might be a basic floor plan. To create an overlay sheet for a structural drawing, the drafter traces over only the lines of the floor plan that the overlay needs and then adds new information pertinent to that sheet. For the next overlay, the drafter performs the same task again. Each sheet, then, contains some information in common as well as data unique to that sheet.

In AutoCAD, using layers allows you to generate all the sheets for a set of overlays from a single file (see Figure 6.1). Nothing needs to be drawn twice or traced. The wall layout is on one layer, and the rooflines are on another. Doors are on a third. You can control the visibility of layers so that you can make all objects residing on a layer temporarily invisible. This feature lets you put all information keyed to a particular floor plan in one DWG file. From that drawing, you can produce a series of derived drawings—such as the foundation plan, the second-floor plan, the reflected ceiling plan, and the roof plan—by making a different combination of layers visible for each drawing or drawing layout (layouts are covered in Chapter 14, "Using Layouts to Set Up a Print"). When you make a print, you decide which layers will be visible. Consequently, in a set of drawings, each sheet based on the floor plan displays a unique combination of layers, all of which are in one file.

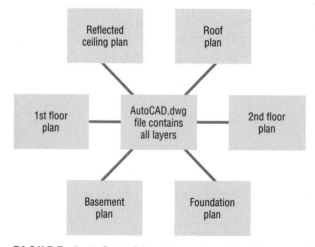

FIGURE 6.1 Several drawings can be created from one file.

N O T E   A typical project such as a building can easily amass more than 100 layers. Managing so many layers from a single DWG file can prove tricky at times, and so layers are but one of several organizational methods AutoCAD provides. Another method, using external references (*xrefs*), is a little more advanced but provides an extra level of flexibility needed for many real-world projects. You'll have the chance to explore xrefs in detail in Chapter 13, "Managing External References."

As an organizing tool, layers allow you to classify the various objects in a computerized drawing—lines, arcs, circles, and so on—according to the component of the building they represent, such as doors, walls, windows, dimensions, and notes. Each layer is assigned a color, and all objects placed on the layer take on that assigned default color unless you specify a different color for the objects. This lets you easily distinguish between objects that represent separate components of the building (see Figure 6.2). You can quickly tell which layer a given object or group of objects is on.

First, you'll look at the procedure for achieving this level of organization, which is to set up the new layers and then move existing objects onto them. Following that, you'll learn how to create new objects on a specific layer and find out which objects reside on which layers.

Setting Up Layers

All AutoCAD drawings have one layer in common: layer 0. *Layer 0* is the default layer in all new drawings. If you don't add any new layers to a drawing, everything you create in that drawing is on layer 0. In fact, everything so far in the cabin drawing has been drawn on layer 0.

All objects in AutoCAD are assigned a layer. In this book, I'll refer to objects assigned to a particular layer as *being on* that layer. You can place objects on a layer in two ways: you can move or copy them to the layer, or you can create them on the layer in the first place. You'll learn how to do both in this chapter. However, first you need to learn how to set up layers. To see how you do this, you'll create seven new layers for your cabin drawing, and then move the existing objects in your drawing onto the first five of these layers. After that, you'll create new objects on the Headers and Roof layers.

In much the same way that you used the U.S. National CAD Standard (NCS) to name your DWG file in Chapter 3, "Setting Up a Drawing," you'll also follow the NCS in naming your layers. Although filenames and layer names are each unique in many ways, the NCS naming convention is much the same for both. Before creating any layers, let's have a quick look at the basic structure we'll use to name the layers, illustrated in Figure 6.3.

A best practice is to let layer properties (color, linetype, and so on) dictate the properties of individual objects. Avoid manually changing (overriding) properties of objects, such as lines and arcs, in an AutoCAD drawing.

◀

◀

Objects and layers are analogous to people and countries; just as all people must reside in some country, so too must all objects be on some layer.

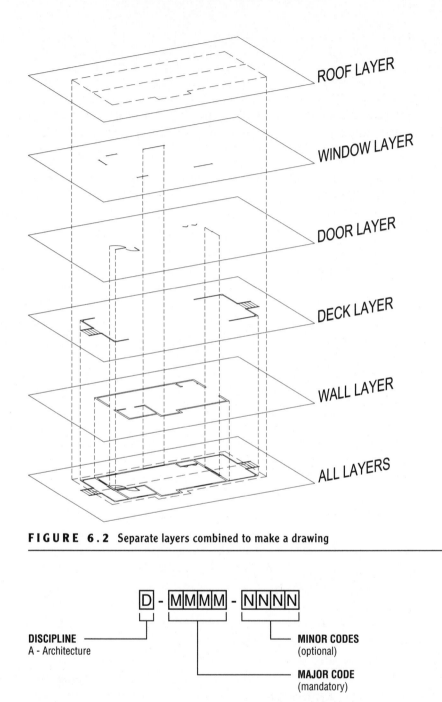

FIGURE 6.2 Separate layers combined to make a drawing

FIGURE 6.3 National CAD Standard layer-naming framework

Discipline [D]   The discipline designator specifies the trade to which a layer belongs. In larger projects, it also helps establish ownership of a specific portion of a design. For instance, the only people on the design team who would use A layers would be the members of the architectural design team. E layers would be reserved for the electrical design team, and so on. The standard discipline designators in NCS are the same for filenames and layers and are listed in Table 6.1.

T A B L E   6 . 1 NCS Discipline Designator Codes

Code	Discipline
G	General
H	Hazardous Materials
V	Survey/Mapping
B	Geotechnical
W	Civil Works
C	Civil
L	Landscape
S	Structural
A	Architectural
I	Interiors
Q	Equipment
F	Fire Protection
P	Plumbing
D	Process
M	Mechanical
E	Electrical
T	Telecommunications
R	Resource

(Continues)

TABLE 6.1 *(Continued)*

Code	Discipline
X	Other Disciplines
Z	Contractor/Shop Drawings
O	Operations

Major Discipline Designator [*MMMM*] At a minimum, each layer must contain both a discipline [*D*] code and a Major Discipline Designator [*MMMM*]. The Major Discipline Designator is always four characters in length, and it helps to group like objects together in the layer list. For instance, you may have multiple types of walls, but regardless of type, each wall layer would begin with A-WALL.

Minor Discipline Designator [*NNNN*] Sometimes you may need to classify your layers further. In the case of walls, you may have a layer for the centerline of your wall (A-WALL-CNTR), another for fire-rated walls (A-WALL-FIRE), and yet another for partial or half-walls (A-WALL-PRHT). Like the major designators, all Minor Discipline Designators should be four characters. Minor codes, unlike major designators, can be stacked together to achieve the necessary level of granularity. For instance, you might name the partial wall centerline layer A-WALL-PRHT-CNTR.

With the U.S. National CAD Standard growing in popularity, chances are you'll have to work with drawings using its prescribed framework at some point once you begin working on your own designs. You now have a good understanding of what the U.S. National CAD Standards are and, more important, how to "decode" NCS layer names when you encounter them. More information on the U.S. National CAD Standard can be found at **`www.nationalcadstandard.org`**.

Knowing every detail about NCS is not necessary to complete the exercises in this book. As in the example you're about to complete for working with layers, I'll provide all the information you need to create layers inside the framework. To begin creating new layers, take the following steps:

1. Open AutoCAD and then open `I05A-FPLAYO.dwg` (`M05A-FPLAYO.dwg`)—both imperial and metric versions are included in the Chapter 6 data folder. Make sure the Home tab is active and the Layers panel is in the Ribbon, centered just above the drawing area on your screen.

2. Expand the panel and you will see, as shown in Figure 6.4, that it contains several buttons, two drop-down lists, and a slider bar for controlling layers.

FIGURE 6.4 The expanded Layers panel

Several panels to the right is the Properties panel (see Figure 6.5), with four drop-down lists for controlling colors, lineweights, linetypes, and plot styles, and a slider for transparency. Once again, best practices discourage changing the properties of individual objects to anything other than ByLayer/ByBlock unless absolutely necessary.

A *linetype* is the appearance style of a line, such as Continuous, Dashed, or Dash-Dot.

FIGURE 6.5 The expanded Properties panel

3. Click the Layer Properties button on the left end of the Layers panel to open the Layer Properties Manager palette (see Figure 6.6).

Notice the large open area in the middle right of the dialog box with layer 0 listed at the top of the Name column. This is the Layer List box. All the layers in a drawing are listed here, along with their current states and properties. I05A-FPLAYO.dwg (M05A-FPLAYO.dwg) has only one layer so far.

FIGURE 6.6 The Layer Properties Manager palette

To the left of the Layer List box is the Layer Filters tree view box, where you can define which layers to display in the Layer List box. The Layer Properties Manager palette has nine buttons along the top to perform layer and filter management tasks. You'll see an Invert Filter check box at the bottom of the palette.

Before setting up new layers, look for a moment at the Layer List box. The Layer Properties Manager palette is considered *modeless* because you can leave it open while you continue to work on your drawing. This means you can leave the palette open and move it away from your drawing area, where it can remain constantly open, waiting for you to input changes without having to stop to open the palette each time. Being modeless also means that your changes are instantly reflected in the drawing area, and you don't need to close the palette to see the effects of your actions.

Using the Layer List Box

Each layer has five properties—Color, Linetype, Lineweight, Transparency, and Plot Style—that determine the appearance of the objects on that layer. You may need to resize the columns to see the complete column name. You do this by placing the cursor between the columns and dragging left or right. Look at the layer 0 row in the list and notice the square and the word *white* in the Color column. The square is black (or white if you have a black background for your drawing area), but the name of the color is White whether the square is black or white. Continuous is in the Linetype column. This tells you that layer 0 has been assigned the color White (meaning black or white) and the Continuous linetype by default.

 N O T E   If you set up your drawing area so that the background is white, AutoCAD automatically changes the color assigned to white in the Layer List box to black, so lines that would ordinarily appear as white on a black background will appear as black on the white background. When you then switch to a black background, the black lines change to white lines. This allows the lines to be visible regardless of the background color, and AutoCAD doesn't have to assign a new color to a layer that has been assigned the White setting when you switch background colors.

The five columns to the left of the Color column are Status, Name, On, Freeze, and Lock. They each have icons or text in the layer 0 row. These columns represent some of the status modes, or *states*, of the layer, and they control whether objects on a layer are visible, whether they can be changed, or on which layer new objects are created. I'll discuss the visibility and status of layers later in this chapter, and I'll discuss the columns to the right of the Linetype column—Lineweight, Transparency, Plot Style, Plot, New VP Freeze, and Description—in Chapter 15, "Printing an AutoCAD Drawing." Don't worry about them right now.

Creating New Layers and Assigning Colors

Let's create a few new layers, name them, and assign them colors:

1. Continue using I05A-FPLAYO.dwg (M05A-FPLAYO.dwg), or open it if it's not already open.

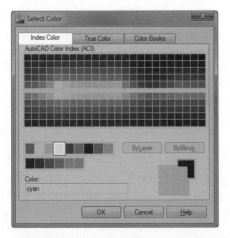

2. In the toolbar at the top of the Layer Properties Manager, click the New Layer icon. A new layer named Layer1 appears in the list. The layer's name is highlighted, which means you can rename it by entering another name now.

3. Enter A-WALL↵. Layer1 changes to A-WALL. The row for the A-WALL layer should still be highlighted (see Figure 6.7).

FIGURE 6.7 The Layer Properties Manager with a new layer named A-WALL

4. To open the Select Color dialog box, click the word *white* in the Color column for the A-WALL row (see Figure 6.8).

Notice the three tabs at the top: Index Color, True Color, and Color Books. Each has a different selection of colors available to AutoCAD.

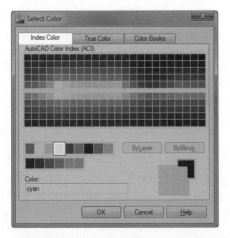

FIGURE 6.8 The Index Color tab in the Select Color dialog box

5. Make sure the Index Color tab is selected, and click the Cyan (Index Color: 4) color swatch.

The Select Color dialog box is composed of three sets of color swatches. Color swatches for Index Colors 10 through 249 are found in the upper portion of the dialog, and colors 1–9 and colors 250–255 are found in the lower portion of the dialog.

Each color swatch has an index number associated with it. This number provides the flexibility of graphically selecting the desired color swatch, or entering the numerical value associated with it. Index Colors 1–7 represent primary colors including Red, Yellow, Green, Cyan, Blue, Magenta, and White/Black. They may be specified by number or textual name.

 T I P   As you move the cursor over the available color swatches, the index color number, from 1 through 255, and the RGB (True Color) values appear beneath the large field of 240 choices.

6. Click OK to close the Select Color dialog box. In the Layer List box of the Layer Properties Manager palette, you can see that the color square for the A-WALL layer has changed to cyan.

COLOR MODES

The Index Color tab provides the option to choose from the 255 distinct colors in the AutoCAD Color Index (ACI). Using the True Color tab, you can set each of the color parameters of the Red, Green, and Blue (RGB) or Hue, Saturation, and Value (HSV) components of the final color to any value between 0 and of 255, resulting in over 16 million combinations. The Color Books tab lets you access thousands of color definitions that are provided by several color standards, such as Pantone and Digital Image Correlation (DIC). These definitions are used to match the colors used on your system to physical swatches that are used by designers.

As you create your new list of layers and assign colors to them, notice how each color looks in your drawing. Some are easier to see on a screen with a light background, and others do better against a dark background. In this book, I'll assign colors that work well with a black background. If your system has a white background, you might want to use darker colors, which you can find in the array of 240 color swatches in the upper half of the Index Color tab.

You'll continue creating new layers and assigning colors to them. You'll master this procedure as you add a new layer or two in each chapter throughout the rest of the book:

1. In the Layer Properties Manager palette, click the New Layer button, or right-click in the Layer List box and choose New Layer from the list of commands in the context menu.

2. Enter A-DOOR↵ to change the name of the layer.

3. Pick the color square in the A-DOOR row.

4. When the Select Color dialog box opens, click the color 40 square in the uppermost collection of color swatches within the Select Color dialog box. Click OK.

5. Repeat these steps, creating the layers shown in Table 6.2 with their assigned colors.

   Pick the colors from the collection of color swatches within the Select Color dialog box, or manually enter the index color number in the Color text box at the bottom of the dialog. In the row of nine colors, the ninth swatch might not be clearly visible when it is close to the background color of the dialog box.

   Notice that when a new layer appears in the Layer List box, it initially takes on the properties of the layer that was previously selected.

6. Save your drawing as **I06-01-CreateLayers.dwg** (**M06-01-Create Layers.dwg**) by choosing Application menu ➢ Save As ➢ AutoCAD Drawing.

TABLE 6.2 Layers and Colors for the Cabin Drawing

Layer Name	Color
A-DECK-STRS	81
A-DECK	84
A-FLOR-FIXT	1
A-WALL-HEAD	11
A-ROOF	Green (3)

(Continues)

TABLE 6.2 *(Continued)*

Layer Name	Color
Created in earlier exercises:	
A-WALL	Cyan (4)
A-DOOR	40

N O T E   Blue might or might not read well on a black background. If you don't like the way it looks, try picking a lighter shade of blue from the array of 240 colors on the Index Color tab. Likewise, yellow might not read well on a lighter background; try picking a darker shade of yellow from the Index Color tab.

When finished, the layer list should have eight layers with their assigned colors in the color squares of each row (see Figure 6.9). All layers are assigned the Continuous linetype by default. This is convenient because most building components are represented in the floor plan by continuous lines, but the roof—because of its position above the walls—needs to be represented by a dashed line. Later you'll assign the Dashed linetype to the A-ROOF layer.

FIGURE 6.9 The Layer List box, in the Layer Properties Manager palette, with the seven new layers and layer 0

NAMING LAYERS

You can name layers in a variety of ways. With their different color assignments, layers make it possible for you to easily distinguish which objects in your drawing represent walls or other parts of your building. Most offices follow a standard for organizing layers by name and color. You've already had a chance to begin using the U.S. National CAD Standard. The International Organization for Standardization (ISO) also publishes a layering standard.

(Continues)

NAMING LAYERS *(Continued)*

Both are often adopted by architecture and engineering firms and customized to fit their specific needs.

With the cabin drawing, you'll start developing a basic set of layers. Once you learn how to manage the set you're using here, tackling more-complex layering systems will come naturally. In more-complex drawings, you might need several layers for variations of the same building component, landscape element, or machine part. You might replace the A-WALL layer, for example, with several layers, such as Existing Walls to Remain (A-WALL-E), Walls to Be Demolished (A-WALL-D), and New Walls (A-WALL-N).

When you name layers, you can use uppercase and lowercase letters, and AutoCAD will preserve them. But AutoCAD doesn't distinguish between them and treats Walls, WALLS, and walls as the same layer.

Looking at the Other Tabs in the Select Color Dialog Box

AutoCAD also supports a True Color palette and various Pantone, DIC, and RAL color groups. Although I won't cover these features in any depth in this book, let's take a quick look at them before moving on. Feel free to follow along as you explore these additional tabs by making a copy of your 06A-FPLAY1.dwg file; you won't save any changes you make in this section.

The True Color Tab   With the Layer Properties Manager palette open, click one of the color swatches in the Layer List box to open the Select Color dialog box again. Then click the True Color tab. In the upper-right corner, the Color Model drop-down list displays either RGB or HSL. The display for the Red, Green, Blue (RGB) color model looks like the left side of Figure 6.10, and the Hue, Saturation, Luminance (HSL) model looks like the right side of Figure 6.10.

The RGB option shows three horizontal color bands, one for each of the three primary colors (red, green, and blue). Move the sliders on each band to set a number from 0 to 255, or enter a number in the input box for each color. The three primary color values that combine to make up the final color appear at the bottom and on the right side, and the rectangles in the lower-right corner show the currently selected and previously selected color.

The HSL screen displays a rectangle of colors and a vertical band with a slider. Drag the crosshairs around on the rectangle. The color in the front rectangle in the lower-right corner changes as you move the crosshairs. Moving the crosshairs left or right takes the Hue value through a range of 361 values. Moving it up or down changes the percentage of saturation, or *intensity*, with the top of the rectangle representing 100 percent.

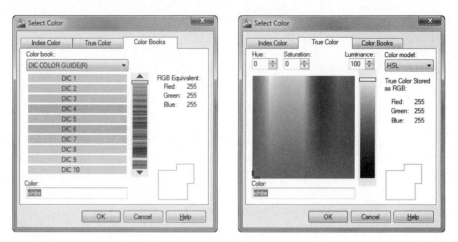

FIGURE 6.10 The True Color tab with the RGB color model (left) and the HSL color model (right)

USING AUTOCAD'S TRADITIONAL COLORS

The traditional set of 255 colors for AutoCAD is set up in such a way that the first seven colors are named (Red, Blue, and so on) and numbered (1 through 7), whereas the other 248 colors have only numbers.

As you saw on the Index Color tab of the Select Color dialog box, AutoCAD has three groupings of colors: a large array of swatches in the top half and two rows of swatches below. Moving the cursor over a swatch displays its AutoCAD number below the array as well as its Red, Green, Blue (RGB) values. The RGB values indicate the amount of each color, a number from 0 (none) to 255 (all), that is mixed with the other two base colors to make the selected color. Click a swatch to assign it to the layer that has been selected in the Layer Properties Manager palette.

You should avoid using colors that resemble the background color, such as colors 250 or 18 with a black background. The objects with these colors could become visually lost in the drawing area. Be aware of this if your drawings might be sent to someone who doesn't use your color standards so that they can work efficiently with the drawings.

The Array of 240 Colors   In the top half of the dialog box are colors numbered 10 through 249, arranged in 24 columns, each having 10 swatches.

The Row of Nine Standard Color Swatches   This group includes colors 1 through 9. The first seven colors in this group also have names: Red (1),

(Continues)

USING AUTOCAD'S TRADITIONAL COLORS *(Continued)*

Yellow (2), Green (3), Cyan (4), Blue (5), Magenta (6), and White/Black (7). Colors 8 and 9 have numbers only. Color 7 is named White, but it will be black if you're using a white background color.

The Row of Six Gray Shades   These colors are often assigned screening values (such as 50 percent, 75 percent, and so on), numbering 250 through 255. As pure color assignments, they range from almost black to almost white.

These 255 colors, plus the background color, make up the traditional AutoCAD 256-color palette. Two additional colors are in a group by themselves, Logical Colors, and are represented by buttons on the Index Color tab.

The two buttons in this grouping—ByLayer and ByBlock—represent two ways you can assign a color to objects (such as lines, circles, text, and so on) via the layer they are on or via the block they are part of, rather than to the objects themselves. (Blocks are covered in the next chapter.) When you assign cyan to the A-WALL layer and place all objects representing walls on that layer, all wall objects are automatically assigned the color ByLayer and take on the color of their layer—in this case, cyan.

You can change the color of an object to one other than the assigned layer color by selecting the object and choosing a color from the Color Control drop-down list in the Properties panel. Setting an object's color directly is not always the best practice, however, and you should try to maintain color assignments by layer whenever practical.

The slider to the right of the rectangle controls the luminance, which, like saturation, varies from 0 percent (representing black) to 100 percent (or white). A luminance of 100 percent maximizes a color's brightness but washes out all of the hue.

The Color text box displays the currently selected color's three RGB numbers. You can also specify a color by entering numbers in the individual input boxes for Hue, Saturation, and Luminance—or the boxes for Red, Green, and Blue in the RGB screen. You can use the up- and down-arrows in these boxes to scroll through the possible settings.

If you select a color by using the RGB or HSL screen, that color appears in the Layer List box of the Layer Properties Manager palette by its three RGB numbers (see Figure 6.11).

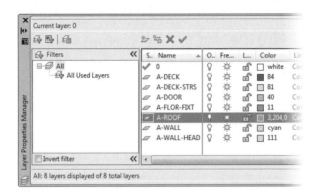

FIGURE 6.11 The Layer Properties Manager with the Roof layer assigned a color that is not part of the standard AutoCAD 255-color list

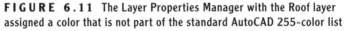

The Color column might be compressed in such a way that the names of colors in the list are abbreviated. You can widen the column by dragging the divider at the right of the title farther to the right.

With the combination of 256 values for each of the three primary colors, you now have more than 16 million colors to choose from in AutoCAD.

The Color Books Tab   The Color Books tab displays the colors of the selected color book (see the image on the left side of Figure 6.12). AutoCAD has 20 color books. Each book appears in the Color Book drop-down list at the top of the tab; the current book appears in the box. Below that, a set of colors that corresponds to the position of the slider is displayed in bars. Moving the slider to a new position displays another set of colors. Click a displayed color bar to select it, and then click OK. The color appears in the Layer Properties Manager Layer List box by its identifying name and number (see the image on the right side of Figure 6.12).

Later in the book, you'll create new layers and assign them colors of your choice. Use this opportunity to explore the True Color and Color Books tabs of the Select Color dialog box, and try using some of these colors in your drawing. Keep the Layer Properties Manager palette open. You'll use it to assign linetypes in the next section.

You can delete selected layers by using the Delete Layer button, shaped like a red X, in the Layer Properties Manager palette. You can delete only empty layers—those containing no objects. You can identify empty layers in the Layer Properties Manager by the grayed-out icon in the Status column.

Assigning Linetypes to Layers

When you assign a color to a layer, you can choose any color supported by your system. This is not so with linetypes. Each new drawing has only one linetype loaded into it by default (the Continuous linetype). You must load any other line-types you need from an outside file:

1. If it's not open already, open I06-01-CreateLayers.dwg (M06-01-Create Layers.dwg) by clicking the Open button located on the Quick Access toolbar.

2. In the Layer Properties Manager palette, click Continuous in the column for the A-ROOF layer to open the Select Linetype dialog box (see Figure 6.13). In the Loaded Linetypes list, only Continuous appears. No other linetypes have been loaded into this drawing.

3. Click Load to open the Load Or Reload Linetypes dialog box.

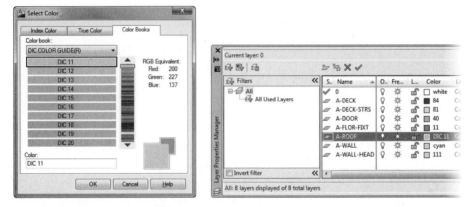

FIGURE 6.12 The Color Books tab in the Select Color dialog box (left) and the layer list with an assigned DIC number (right)

FIGURE 6.13 The Select Linetype dialog box

4. Scroll down the list to the Dashed, Dashed2, and DashedX2 linetypes (see Figure 6.14). Notice how, in this family, the dashed lines are different sizes.

5. Click DASHED in the left column and then click OK. You're returned to the Select Linetype dialog box. The Dashed linetype has been added to the Linetype list under Continuous (see Figure 6.15).

6. Click Dashed to highlight it and then click OK. In the Layer Properties Manager palette, the A-ROOF layer has been assigned the Dashed linetype (see Figure 6.16).

7. Save your drawing as **I06-02-AssigningLinetypes.dwg** (**M06-02 -AssigningLinetypes.dwg**) by choosing Application menu ➤ Save As ➤ AutoCAD Drawing.

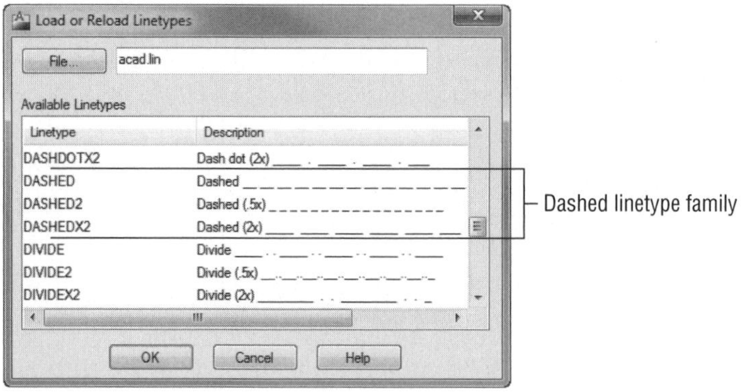

FIGURE 6.14 The list of available linetypes scrolled to the three Dashed linetypes

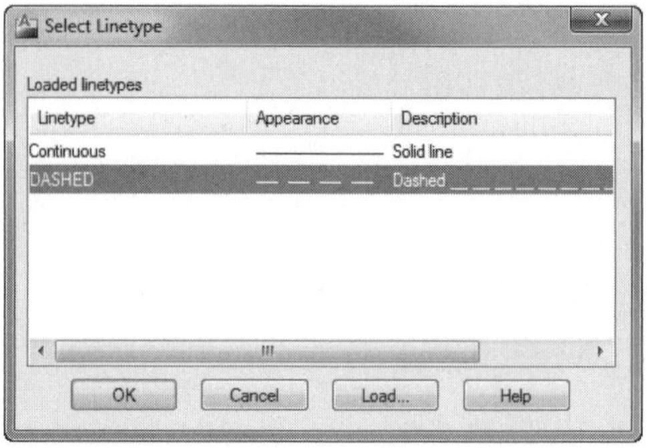

FIGURE 6.15 The Select Linetype dialog box with the Dashed linetype loaded

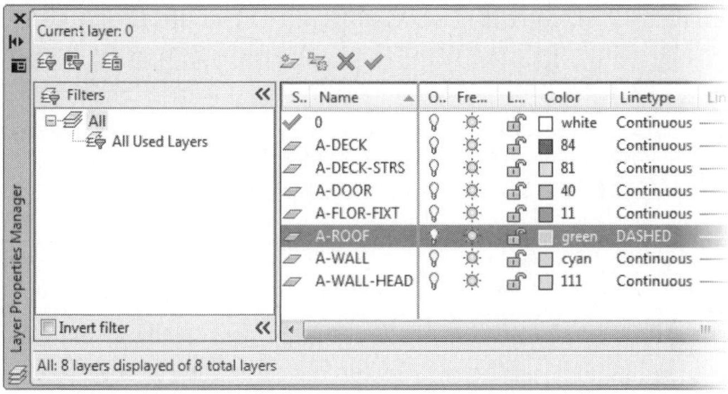

FIGURE 6.16 The Layer Properties Manager with the A-ROOF layer assigned the Dashed linetype

TIP   You can select or deselect all the available linetypes in the Load Or Reload Linetypes dialog box by right-clicking and choosing Select All or Clear All from the context menu. You can also select multiple linetypes by holding down the Ctrl or Shift key and clicking.

Learning More about Lineweight

In the Layer Properties Manager palette is a column for the Lineweight property. When you first create a layer, it is assigned the default lineweight. Just as you assigned a color and a linetype for each new layer in the cabin drawing, you can also assign a lineweight. Once assigned, lineweights can be displayed so you can see how your drawing will look when printed.

NOTE   The Lineweight layer property is just one of three ways the plotted thickness of lines is commonly controlled. The oldest and generally most common method is to instruct AutoCAD to plot objects of different colors with different thicknesses. This is done by setting up a CTB file. Similarly, by using Plot Styles, you can configure an STB file to work in much the same way as CTB files. Each method has its own advantages and disadvantages, which are discussed in Chapter 15.

Using the Current Layer as a Drawing Tool

Now is a good time to look at what it means for a layer to be *current*. Notice the green check mark above the Layer List box in the Layer Properties Manager palette. The same green check mark appears in the Status column in the layer 0 row. The name of the current layer, in this case, 0, appears in the upper-left corner of the dialog box.

AUTOCAD'S LINETYPES

The Available Linetypes list in the Load Or Reload Linetypes dialog box contains 45 linetypes. They fall into three groups:

Acad_ISO The first 14 linetypes are in the Acad_ISO family (as noted earlier, ISO is the International Organization for Standardization). They are set up to be used in metric drawings and have lineweight, or pen-width, settings.

Standard Below the ISO linetypes are eight families of three linetypes each, mixed with seven special linetypes that contain graphic symbols. Each family has one basic linetype and two that are multiples of it: one has dashes twice the size (called, for example, DashedX2), and one has dashes half the size (called Dashed2), as you saw earlier in Figure 6.14. Having an assortment of different sizes of one style of linetype is helpful for distinguishing between building components, such as foundation walls and beams, which, in addition to rooflines, might also need dashed lines.

Complex Mixed in with the Standard linetypes are seven linetypes that contain symbols, letters, or words. You can use these linetypes to indicate specific elements in the drawing, such as fences, hot-water lines, railroad tracks, and others.

It isn't difficult to create or acquire your own custom linetypes. You can do so in four ways:

Using Notepad

Start the Windows Notepad program and navigate to the Support folder for AutoCAD 2012. The folder is usually found at this location: C:\Documents and Settings*Your Name*\Application Data\Autodesk\AutoCAD 2012\R18.2\enu\Support (Windows XP), or C:\Users*Your Name*\ appdata\roaming\autodesk\AutoCAD 2012\r18.2\enu\support (Windows Vista/Windows 7). LT users will see *AutoCAD LT* instead of *AutoCAD 2012*.

Open the file named acad.lin. Its type is listed as AutoCAD Linetype Definition when you pause the cursor over the filename. It contains the definition codes for all the linetypes; they are easy to figure out. Copy an existing pattern and modify it to create your own. I recommend that you back up the acad.lin file before making any modifications to it.

(Continues)

AUTOCAD'S LINETYPES *(Continued)*

```
acad.lin - Notepad                                              □ ▢ ✕
File   Edit   Format   View   Help
;;    AutoCAD Linetype Definition file
;;    Version 3.0
;;    Copyright (C) 1991-2010 by Autodesk, Inc.   All Rights Reserved.
;;
;;    Note: in order to ease migration of this file when upgrading
;;    to a future version of AutoCAD, it is recommended that you add
;;    your customizations to the User Defined Linetypes section at the
;;    end of this file.
;;
*BORDER,Border __ __ . __ __ . __ __ . __ __ . __ __ .
A,.5,-.25,.5,-.25,0,-.25
*BORDER2,Border (.5x) __.__.__.__.__.__.__.__.__.
A,.25,-.125,.25,-.125,0,-.125
*BORDERX2,Border (2x) ___  ___   .   ___  ___   .   ___
A,1.0,-.5,1.0,-.5,0,-.5

*CENTER,Center ___ _ ___ _ ___ _ ___ _ ___ _ ___
A,1.25,-.25,.25,-.25
*CENTER2,Center (.5x) __ _ __ _ __ _ __ _ __ _ __
A,.75,-.125,.125,-.125
*CENTERX2,Center (2x) _____ __ _____ __ _____
A,2.5,-.5,.5,-.5

*DASHDOT,Dash dot __ . __ . __ . __ . __ . __ .
A,.5,-.25,0,-.25
*DASHDOT2,Dash dot (.5x) _._._._._._._._._._._._.
A,.25,-.125,0,-.125
*DASHDOTX2,Dash dot (2x) ___   .   ___   .   ___   .   ___
A,1.0,-.5,0,-.5

*DASHED,Dashed __ __ __ __ __ __ __ __ __ __
```

Using the Linetype **Command**

Enter **-LINETYPE**↵, (the hyphen (-) command prefix executes a command-line version of the command rather than a dialog-based version) and then enter **C**↵ for the Create option. You'll be guided through the steps to create your own LIN file or add to an existing file. To use the LINETYPE command, you need to know the definition codes. Use Notepad until you get a feel for the codes.

Using Existing Linetypes

You can often find an acceptable linetype, created by other AutoCAD users, on the Internet or in various industry publications. Many are free, and some are available at a reasonable cost. The line code is simply appended to the acad.lin file on your system.

Using Express Tools

The MKLTYPE command, found on the Express Tools tab ➢ expanded Tools panel ➢ Make Linetype tool, automates much of the creation of custom linetypes. You can use it to draw a sample line segment with dashes, text, symbols, or the like placed over the line, and quickly define a new linetype. A tip for using this tool is to draw your line at its plotted length (not scaled length). For instance, if a line segment measures 0.1″ in length when plotted, then draw the line 0.1″ in length.

At any time, one, and only one, layer is set as the current layer. When a layer is current, all objects you draw will be on that layer and will take on the properties assigned to that layer unless directed otherwise. Because layer 0 is current—and has been current so far in this book—all objects that you have drawn so far are on layer 0 and have the linetype and color that are specified by default for layer 0: Continuous and White (or Black), respectively. If you make the A-WALL layer current, any new lines you draw will be Continuous and Cyan. If the A-ROOF layer is current, any new lines will be Dashed and Blue. Here's how to make the A-WALL layer the current layer:

1. If it's not open already, open I06-02-AssigningLinetypes.dwg (M06-02-AssigningLinetypes.dwg) by clicking the Open button on the Quick Access toolbar.

2. Click the A-WALL layer in the Layer List box to highlight it, and then click the Set Current green check mark above the Layer List box.

   Alternatively, you can double-click the A-WALL layer, or highlight it and press Alt+C. The A-WALL layer replaces layer 0 as the current layer, and the name appears in the text field at the top of the dialog box. The green check mark also appears next to the A-WALL layer in the Layer List box.

T I P   When the Status column is displayed, AutoCAD must evaluate the objects and layers several times during the drawing process. This can cause a lag when the drawing is large and the list of layers is extensive. You can hide the Status, or any other column, by right-clicking the column name and then clicking any selected option in the context menu that appears.

---

3. Click the Auto-Hide button near the top-left corner of the Layer Properties Manager palette.

   Auto-Hide causes the palette to collapse down to the title bar. You can expand it by doing one of the following:

   ▶ To expand the dialog box temporarily, pause the cursor over the title bar.

   ▶ To permanently expand it, click Auto-Hide again.

4. Look at the Layer drop-down list on the Ribbon's Layers panel. Most of the symbols you saw in the Layer List box, in the Layer Properties Manager palette, are on this drop-down list. The A-WALL layer is the visible entry on the list and has a cyan square (the color you assigned

to the A-WALL layer earlier). The layer is visible in this list when it's collapsed and no objects are selected in the current layer.

5. Now look at your drawing. Nothing has changed because the objects in the drawing are still on layer 0.

You need to move the objects in the drawing onto their proper layers. To do this, you'll use the Layer drop-down list on the Layers panel to assign each object to one of the new layers.

Assigning Objects to Layers

When assigning existing objects in the drawing to new layers, your strategy will be to begin by selecting several of the objects that belong on the same layer and that are easiest to select. You'll reassign them to their new layer by using the Layer drop-down list. You'll then move to a set of objects that belong on a different layer or that belong on the same layer as the previously selected object but are slightly more difficult to select, and so on.

1. If it's not already, open I06-02-AssigningLinetypes.dwg (M06-02 -AssigningLinetypes.dwg) by clicking the Open button located on the Quick Access toolbar. Verify that the A-WALL layer is set as current as outlined in the "Using the Current Layer as a Drawing Tool" exercise earlier.

2. In the drawing, click and drag a selection window down and to the left to use a crossing selection window (green box with dashed lines) to select the front deck, as shown at the top of Figure 6.17.

   Grips appear and the lines *ghost* (become dashed), signaling that the objects have been selected.

N O T E   See the next section, "Selecting Objects with Selection Windows," for a complete description of the window selection process.

---

3. Hold the Shift key down and select the front stairs with a crossing selection, as shown in the middle image in Figure 6.17. The stair lines appear solid again.

Selecting objects with the Shift key pressed causes objects that are already selected to become unselected (removed from the selection set), while there is no effect on unselected objects.

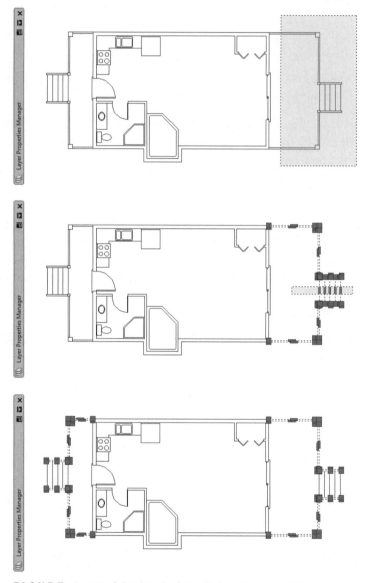

FIGURE 6.17 Selecting the front deck (top), deselecting the front stairs (middle), and the completed selection (bottom)

4. Repeat the process on the rear deck so that the deck is selected but the back stairs are not. The selected components should look like the bottom image in Figure 6.17.

Notice also that in the Layer drop-down list, the layer being displayed now is layer 0 rather than A-WALL, the current layer. When objects are selected with no command running, the Layer drop-down list displays the layer to which the selected objects are currently assigned. If selected objects are on more than one layer, the Layer drop-down list is blank.

5. Click the Layer drop-down list to open it (see Figure 6.18).

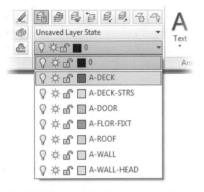

FIGURE 6.18 The expanded Layer drop-down list

6. Click the A-DECK layer. The list closes. The A-DECK layer appears in the Layer drop-down list. The deck lines have been moved to the A-DECK layer and are now green.

7. Press Esc to deselect the lines and remove the grips. The current layer, A-WALL, returns to the Layer drop-down list.

8. Save your drawing as `I06-03-AssigningLayers.dwg` (`M06-03 -AssigningLayers.dwg`) using the Application menu ➤ Save As ➤ AutoCAD Drawing.

This is the process you need to go through for each object so it will be placed on the proper layer. In the next section, you'll move the thresholds and steps to the A-DECK-STRS layer. You'll select the threshold and steps by using a selection window.

Selecting Objects with Selection Windows

AutoCAD has two types of selection windows: the regular selection window and the crossing window. The crossing window is represented by dashed lines, and its interior is, by default, a semitransparent light green color. The regular window is represented by solid lines, and its interior is a semitransparent lavender color when using a white background and blue when using a black background.

By default, AutoCAD is set up so that whenever no command is running and the prompt in the command window is Command:, you can pick objects one at a time or start a regular or crossing window. If you pick an object, it is selected and its grips appear. If you select a blank area of the drawing, this starts a selection window. If you then move the cursor to the right of the point just picked, you create a regular window. If you move the cursor to the left, you create a crossing window. You'll use both crossing and regular selection windows to select the thresholds and steps:

1. Make sure I06-03-AssigningLayers.dwg (M06-03-Assigning Layers.dwg) is open.

2. Zoom in to the sliding glass door area. Click the Object Snap button on the status bar (or press F3) to turn it off, if it isn't already off.

3. Select the threshold for the sliding glass door by using a crossing window selection. To do that, follow these steps:

   a. Hold the crosshair cursor above and to the right of the upper-right corner of the sliding glass door's threshold—still inside the perimeter of the deck—as shown on the left side of Figure 6.19.

   b. Click that point.

   c. Move the cursor down and to the left until you have made a tall, thin crossing window that completely encloses the right edge of the threshold and is crossed on its left edge by the short, horizontal connecting lines, as shown on the right side of Figure 6.19.

   d. Click again.

   The three lines that make up the threshold are selected.

4. Click the Layer drop-down list to open it, and then click the A-DECK -STRS layer. The front threshold is now on the A-DECK-STRS layer.

5. Using the Zoom Previous tool, from the Zoom fly-out menu in the navigation bar (ViewCube on the right-hand side of the drawing area), enter **Z↵ P↵** or simply use the scroll wheel to return to a view of the entire drawing.

When you zoom or pan with the Zoom or Pan tool, the grips are deselected. When you zoom or pan using the scroll wheel, they are not.

6. Zoom in to the threshold at the back door. You will use a regular selection window to select this threshold.

7. Start a selection window slightly above and to the left of the threshold and drag down and to the right, as shown in Figure 6.20. Be sure to enclose the horizontal threshold lines completely.

8. Move the selected lines to the A-DECK-STRS layer the same way you did in step 3.

9. Save your drawing as **I06-04-SelectingObjects.dwg** (**M06-04 -SelectingObjects.dwg**) using the Application menu ➤ Save As ➤ AutoCAD Drawing.

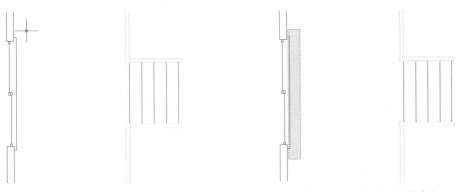

FIGURE 6.19 Starting the crossing selection window (left) and completing it (right)

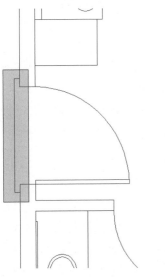

FIGURE 6.20 Selecting the threshold with a regular selection window

Using the Quick Properties Panel

The Quick Properties panel provides access to several of the most commonly changed parameters of the selected objects. You can quickly change the selected object's layer, color, and linetype, as well as several parameters specific to the type of object selected. For example, the Radius parameter is available when a circle is selected, and the Closed option is available when a polyline is selected. When multiple objects are selected, only the parameters common to all are displayed. You will use the Quick Properties panel to change the layer of the front and back stairs:

1. Make sure I06-04-SelectingObjects.dwg (M06-04-Selecting Objects.dwg) is open.

2. Use crossing selection windows to select each of the lines illustrating the front and back stairs.

   The grips appear, indicating the objects are selected. For lines, grips appear at each endpoint and at the midpoint of each segment; for polylines, they appear at each endpoint, and a stretch grip appears at the midpoint of each linear segment. When endpoints of lines coincide, their grips overlap. When lines are very short, their grips might appear to overlap, but that is just the result of the zoom factor.

3. Click the Quick Properties button in the status bar. The Quick Properties panel opens in the drawing, as shown in Figure 6.21.

4. Click in the Layer field. Then click to expand the Layer drop-down list and choose the A-DECK-STRS layer, as shown in Figure 6.22.

   All ten polylines representing the stairs are now on the Steps layer.

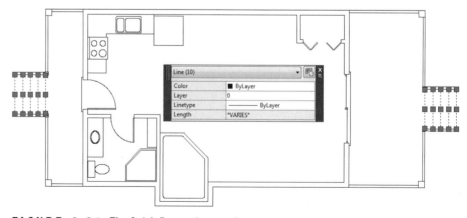

FIGURE 6.21 The Quick Properties panel

5. Press the Esc key to deselect the objects and remove the grips. Even when it is turned on, the Quick Properties panel disappears when no objects are selected.

6. Save your drawing as **I06-05-QuickProperties.dwg** (**M06-05 -QuickProperties.dwg**) using the Application menu ➢ Save As ➢ AutoCAD Drawing.

Grips have other uses besides signaling that an object has been selected. You'll learn about some of these as you progress through the chapters.

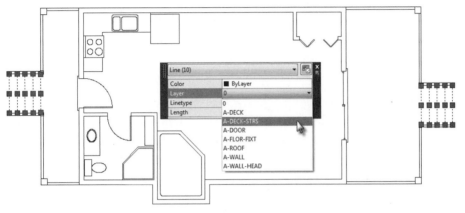

FIGURE 6.22 Assigning the objects to the Steps layer

Selecting the Doors and Swings

To select the doors and swings, you can use crossing windows. Let's examine this task closely to learn more valuable skills for selecting objects:

1. Make sure I06-05-QuickProperties.dwg (M06-05-Quick Properties.dwg) is open.

2. Without any objects selected, use a crossing window to select the back door, as shown in Figure 6.23. To do this, follow these steps:

   a. To begin a new selection window, use the cursor to select a point in the clear space to the right of the back door.

   b. Move your cursor to the left (the selection window box should be green with a dashed border).

   c. Pick a point to the left that crosses the back door and swing, but doesn't cross the wall line, as shown at the top of Figure 6.23.

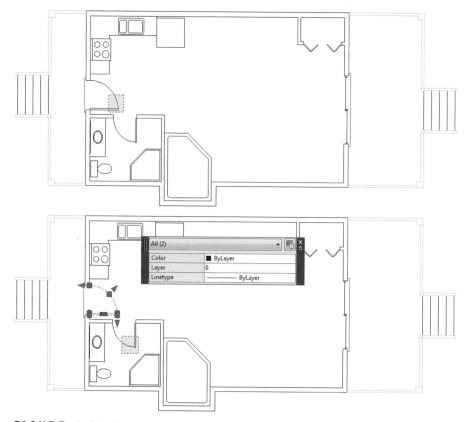

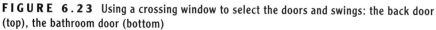

FIGURE 6.23 Using a crossing window to select the doors and swings: the back door (top), the bathroom door (bottom)

After you complete your selection by using a crossing window, the back door and its swing highlight (dash) to indicate that they are selected. Additionally, the Quick Properties panel reappears to display the number of objects selected.

Because you selected more than one type of object (a polyline and an arc), the Quick Properties panel reads All (2) as opposed to listing the specific type of object selected. AutoCAD will list the specific type of object selected only if everything selected is of the same object type (a set of polylines, arcs, lines, and so on).

3. Move to the bathroom and select its door by using another crossing window (with the back door still selected), as shown at the bottom of Figure 6.23. To do this, follow these steps:

   a. Use the crosshair cursor to click in the clear space below the door, starting a new crossing window.

b. With your crossing window (green with a dashed border) started, proceed to move your cursor up to select a point that crosses the bathroom door and swing without crossing any wall lines or any of the fixtures (see the bottom of Figure 6.23).

The bathroom door and swing are selected, and the quantity listed in the Quick View Properties palette updates.

4. Select the four rectangles that make up the closet doors; then open the Layer drop-down list from either the Layers panel or the Quick Properties panel and select the A-DOOR layer, as shown in Figure 6.24.

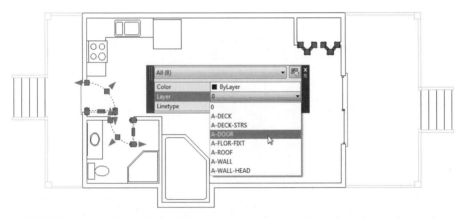

FIGURE 6.24 Using the Quick Properties panel's Layer drop-down list to change the layer of the door objects

All of the doors you selected have been moved from layer 0 to the A-DOOR layer, and now display in orange (the color assigned to the A-DOOR layer).

5. Press Esc to deselect the objects and remove the grips.

6. Save your drawing as **I06-06-DoorSwings.dwg (M06-06-Door Swings.dwg)** using the Application menu ➢ Save As ➢ AutoCAD Drawing.

For the sliding glass door, it's awkward to create a crossing window from left to right because positioning the pickbox between the threshold lines and the sliding door can be difficult. In this situation, use a regular window to select the objects:

1. Make sure I06-06-DoorSwings.dwg (M06-06-DoorSwings.dwg) is open.

2. Zoom in to the area of the sliding glass door.

3. Use a regular selection window to select the sliding glass door at the front of the cabin. To do this, follow these steps:

   a. Select a point to the left of the balcony opening. By selecting a point, a new selection window is started.

   b. Move your cursor and pick a point to the right of the sliding glass window until the right edge of the window (blue background with solid boundary line) is just inside the wall, but just to the right of the sliding glass door itself (as shown in Figure 6.25).

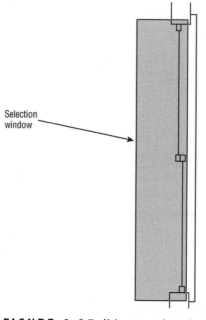

Selection window

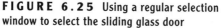

FIGURE 6.25 Using a regular selection window to select the sliding glass door

The entire sliding glass door assembly is selected, but not the jambs, walls, threshold, or balcony. Many grips appear, as 13 lines make up the sliding glass door, and each has three grips: a grip at each endpoint and a grip at each midpoint. Many of the grips overlap.

4. Open the Layer drop-down list and select the A-DOOR layer.

5. Press Esc to deselect the objects and remove the grips.

6. Then use the Zoom Extents tool found by selecting the View tab ➤ Navigate panel ➤ Zoom Extents tool from the zoom fly-out menu, or you can double-click the middle-button/scroll wheel on your mouse.

      You have a full view of the floor plan, where each of the doors are red and are found on the A-DOOR layer.

7. Save your drawing as `I06-07-SlidingDoor.dwg` (`M06-07-Sliding Door.dwg`) using the Application menu ➤ Save As ➤ AutoCAD Drawing.

The next task is to move the kitchen and bathroom counters and fixtures and the hot tub onto the A-FLOR-FIXT layer. In doing this, you'll learn how to deselect some objects from a group of selected objects.

Selecting the Kitchen and Bathroom Fixtures

Sometimes it's more efficient to select more objects than you want and then deselect those you don't want. You'll see how this is done when you select the kitchen and bathroom fixtures:

1. Make sure `I06-07-SlidingDoor.dwg` (`M06-07-SlidingDoor.dwg`) is open.

2. To start a crossing window, pick a point in the kitchen area just below and to the right of the refrigerator but above the back door.

3. Move the cursor to the top left and up, until the upper-left corner of the crossing window is to the left of the left edge of the counter and inside the back wall, as shown at the top of Figure 6.26.

4. When you have your cursor placement correct, click that point. The entire kitchen counter area and fixtures are selected.

5. Move down to the bathroom, and pick a point inside the shower near the bottom-right corner, being careful not to touch any lines with the crosshair cursor.

6. Move the crosshair cursor up and to the left, until the lower-left corner of the crossing window is in the middle of the sink (see the middle of Figure 6.26). When you have the selection window positioned this way, click that point. All the bathroom fixtures, except the mirror, are selected.

7. From left to right, drag a regular window that encompasses the mirror, as shown at the bottom of Figure 6.26. It doesn't matter whether the selection window surrounds objects that are already selected.

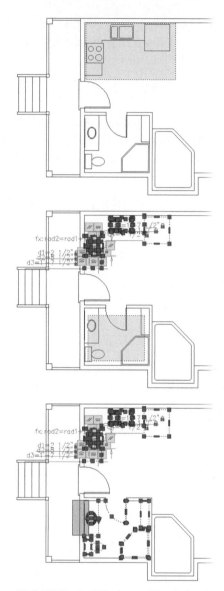

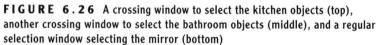

FIGURE 6.26 A crossing window to select the kitchen objects (top), another crossing window to select the bathroom objects (middle), and a regular selection window selecting the mirror (bottom)

8. To complete the selection set, drag a crossing selection window that crosses both of the hot tub polylines that encroach into the living room.

9. Hold down the Shift key, and then pick the selected door and swing in the bathroom.

   Be careful to not pick a grip. As you pick the objects, their lines become solid again and their grips disappear, letting you know they have been deselected, or removed from the selection set (see Figure 6.27). Be sure to pick the inside wall lines in the kitchen at locations where they don't coincide with the stove or counter.

10. Release the Shift key.

11. Open the Layer drop-down list, and select the A-FLOR-FIXT layer. The fixtures are now on the A-FLOR-FIXT layer and are color 11.

12. Press the Esc key to deselect the objects.

13. Save your drawing as **I06-08-SelectingFixtures.dwg** (**M06-08 -SelectingFixtures.dwg**) using the Application menu ➤ Save As ➤ AutoCAD Drawing.

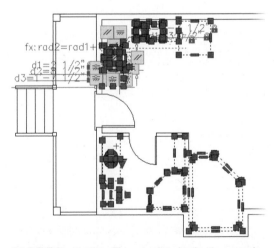

FIGURE 6.27 The completed selection set after removing the door swing and back wall line

The last objects to move onto a new layer are the wall lines. It won't be easy to select the wall lines by using conventional methods because so many other objects in the drawing are in the way. However, because the only objects remaining on layer 0 are the walls for your cabin, you can use the Select Similar command.

Selecting Walls by Using the Select Similar Command

In the last several exercises, you learned how to select objects by using both a regular window and a crossing window. Although there are several ways to make regular and crossing selections (such as when you used the Fence option to trim lines in Chapter 2, "Learning Basic Commands to Get Started"), these remain the two fundamental ways to select multiple objects at once inside AutoCAD. The Select Similar option introduced in this release expands on that concept and adds a way to select multiple objects that have some similarity all at once.

To try out this selection method, you'll select objects whose similarity is that they are lines on layer 0. That is, all lines currently drawn on layer 0 will be selected. Although only lines are drawn on layer 0, if you had both arcs and lines on layer 0, and used the Select Similar command on a line, only the lines would be selected. Again, because lines are the only objects on layer 0, the Select Similar command is perfect for this particular application.

1. Make sure I06-08-SelectingFixtures.dwg (M06-08-Selecting Fixtures.dwg) is open.

2. Select any line currently drawn on layer 0 that represents a wall within your cabin (see Figure 6.28).

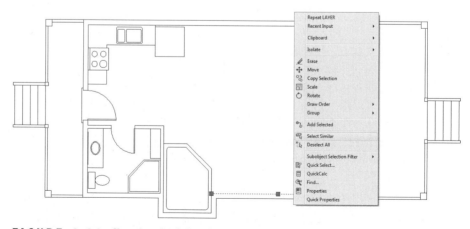

FIGURE 6.28 Choosing the Select Similar right-click menu option after selecting a single wall line

3. Being careful not to deselect the line on layer 0, right-click and select the Select Similar option, as shown in Figure 6.28. The Select Similar command selects all of the lines on layer 0.

4. Use the Quick Properties panel to select the A-WALL layer (see Figure 6.29).

5. Save the current drawing as **I06-09-SelectSimilar.dwg** (**M06-09-SelectSimilar.dwg**) by using the Save icon on the Quick Access toolbar.

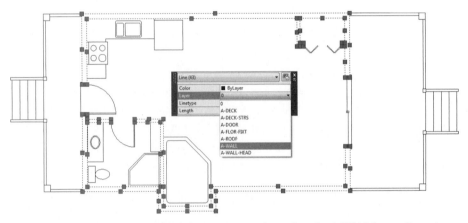

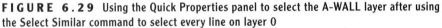

FIGURE 6.29 Using the Quick Properties panel to select the A-WALL layer after using the Select Similar command to select every line on layer 0

SELECTING OBJECTS IN YOUR DRAWING

As you select objects in the cabin drawing to move them onto their prescribed layers, you use various selection tools. Mastering these important tools will greatly enhance your performance as an AutoCAD user. As you select objects by picking them and windowing them, you're building a selection set. You might want to remove objects from that selection set later. Here is a summary of the basic selection tools that you have used so far, with a couple of additions:

Picking

This is the basic, bottom-line selection tool. Click the line, circle, or other object to select it. If no command is running, grips appear on the selected

(Continues)

SELECTING OBJECTS IN YOUR DRAWING *(Continued)*

object, and the object becomes dashed. If a command is running and you're being prompted with Select objects:, grips don't appear, but the object is selected and ghosts (changes to a dashed appearance).

In AutoCAD, you can select objects and then issue a command, or you can issue the command first and then select the objects as directed. For instance, whether you selected an object and then entered **E**↵, or entered **E**↵ and then selected an object, the object would be erased regardless.

Selecting a Window Automatically

To start a window, click a location that is in an empty portion of the screen, where there are no objects. To form a regular window, move your cursor to the right. To form a crossing window, move your cursor to the left. This feature is called *implied windowing*, and it works this way if no command is running or if one is running and the prompt reads Select objects:.

If the geometry of your drawing makes forming a crossing or regular selection window difficult because of the need to move from right to left (crossing) or from left to right (regular), you can force one or the other by entering **C**↵ or **W**↵, respectively, but only if a command is running.

Removing Objects from a Selection Set

At some point, you'll find it more efficient to select more objects than you want and then remove the unwanted ones. You can do this in three ways:

▶ To remove a couple of objects, hold down the Shift key and pick the objects.

▶ To remove objects from the selection set, hold down the Shift key and use one of the selection window types.

▶ If a command is running, enter **R**↵, and then use the selection tools (picking, windows, and so on) without the Shift key to remove objects from the selection set.

If you are in a command and need to add objects back to the selection set after removing some, enter **A**↵. This puts you back into selection mode, and you can continue adding objects to the set.

Turning Off and Freezing Layers

You can make layers invisible either by turning them off or by freezing them. When a layer is turned off or frozen, the objects on that layer are invisible. These two procedures operate in almost the same way and perform about the same function, with one significant difference: objects on frozen layers cannot be selected with the All option, while objects on layers that are off can be selected. For example, if you enter E⏎ A⏎⏎ to erase all objects, all the visible and invisible objects on the layers turned off are deleted, while the objects on frozen layers remain in the drawing but are still invisible. Here is a good rule to follow: If you want a layer to be invisible for only a short time, turn it off; if you prefer that it be invisible semipermanently, freeze it.

For the task at hand, you'll turn off all layers except for the A-WALL and A-DOOR layers to reveal a more simplified look of your floor plan. Afterward, you'll learn how to restore the visibility of all layers in your drawing at once.

1. Make sure I06-09-SelectSimilar.dwg (M06-09-SelectSimilar.dwg) is open.

2. Click the Layer Properties button on the Layers panel to open the Layer Properties Manager palette, or expand the palette if it is still collapsed on your screen.

3. Click the Settings button in the upper-right corner of the Layer Properties Manager palette. The Layer Settings dialog box opens.

4. In the Dialog Settings group near the bottom, enable the Indicate Layers In Use option (see Figure 6.30), and click OK.
   Notice that layer 0 is still first in the list and that the other layers have been reorganized alphabetically (see the top of Figure 6.31). Also, notice the icons in the Status column:

   ▶ A green check mark signifies that the A-WALL layer is current.

   ▶ The light blue layer icons signify that those layers (0, A-DECK, A-DECK-STRS, A-DOOR, and A-FLOR-FIXT) now have objects on them.

   ▶ The light gray layer icons tell you that those layers (A-ROOF and A-WALL-HEAD) don't have any objects on them.

   Because the A-WALL layer is current and has a green check mark in the Status column, you can't tell whether the layer has any objects on it.

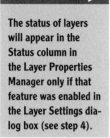

The status of layers will appear in the Status column in the Layer Properties Manager only if that feature was enabled in the Layer Settings dialog box (see step 4).

You have to make a different layer current and then check whether the Walls icon is blue or gray.

5. Click the A-DECK layer to highlight it.

6. Then hold down the Shift key and click the A-DECK-STRS layer. Both the A-DECK and A-DECK-STRS layers should be highlighted within the Layer Properties Manager.

7. Move the arrow cursor over to the On column, which has a lit light-bulb as a symbol for each layer row.

8. Click one of the lightbulbs of the selected layers (see the bottom of Figure 6.31).

The lit lightbulb symbols all change to unlit bulbs for the A-DECK and A-DECK-STRS layers.

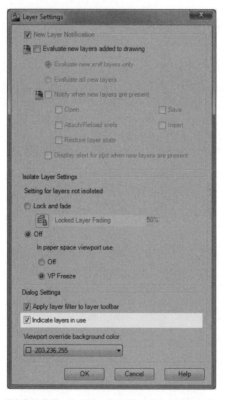

FIGURE 6.30 Enabling the Indicate Layers In Use option from the Layer Settings dialog box

9. Collapse or close the Layer Properties Manager or simply move it out of the way. Both the deck (A-DECK) and the stairs leading up to the deck (A-DECK-STRS) are invisible (see Figure 6.32).

10. From the Home tab ➤ Layers panel, select the Off tool and then click any object on the A-FLOR-FIXT (color 11) layer. By selecting an object on the A-FLOR-FIXT layer, you have graphically turned that layer off, making the objects on it invisible (see the top of Figure 6.33).

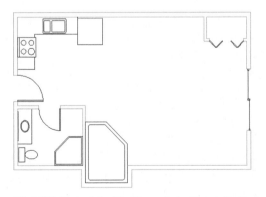

FIGURE 6.31 The layers, now listed alphabetically (top), and after turning off the selected layers (bottom)

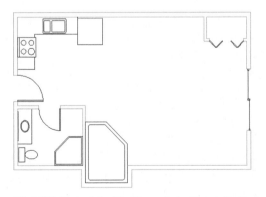

FIGURE 6.32 The floor plan without the deck shown

11. Press Esc to end the Off command.

 12. To restore the visibility of all layers at once by turning them on, expand the Home tab ➢ Layers panel and select the Turn All Layers On tool. The bottom of Figure 6.33 shows the result.

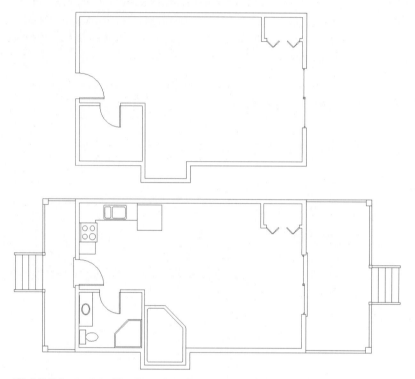

FIGURE 6.33 The floor plan after turning off the A-FLOR-FIXT layer (top), and with the visibility of all layers restored (bottom)

Two of your layers, A-ROOF and A-WALL-HEAD, still have no objects on them because these components haven't been drawn yet. You'll draw the headers now.

Drawing the Headers

Most door and window openings don't extend to the ceiling. The portion of the wall above the opening and below the ceiling is the *header*. The term comes from the name of the beam inside the wall that spans the opening. In a floor plan, wall lines usually stop at the door and window openings, but you need lines across the gap between jamb lines to show that an opening doesn't extend to the ceiling; hence, you'll create the header.

To draw headers directly onto the correct layer, you need to make the A-WALL-HEAD layer current. As you've seen, you can use the Layer Properties Manager palette. But you can also use a shortcut, the Layer drop-down list in the Layers panel, which you have just been using to move objects from one layer to another:

1. Make sure I06-09-SelectSimilar.dwg (M06-09-SelectSimilar.dwg) is open.

2. From the Home tab ➢ Layers panel, click the Layer drop-down list to display a list of layers, or click the down-arrow button on the right end.

   The drop-down list opens, displaying a list of the layers in your drawing. If you have more than 10 layers, a scroll bar becomes operational, giving you access to all the layers.

3. Click the A-WALL-HEAD layer. The drop-down list closes.

   A-WALL-HEAD appears in the list box (see Figure 6.34), telling you that the Headers layer has replaced Walls as the current layer.

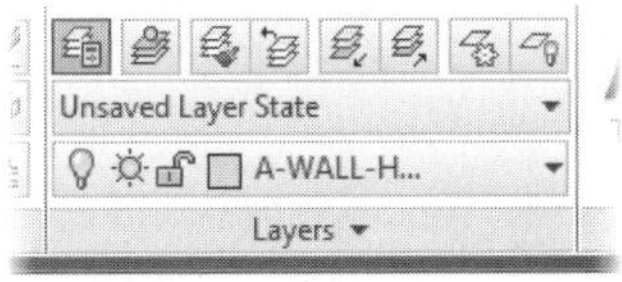

FIGURE 6.34 The A-WALL-HEAD layer is now shown as current in the Layers panel.

> If the list of layers in the layer drop-down is not sorted alphabetically, try increasing the value of the MAXSORT system variable.

4. Make sure object snaps (osnaps) are enabled by clicking the Object Snap button on the status bar or by pressing F3. The Endpoint, Midpoint, and Intersection osnaps are now active. If they aren't, right-click the Object Snap button and, in the context menu, click the osnaps that you want active.

5. From the Home tab ➢ Layers panel, click the Freeze tool. As you begin to draw the headers, other objects such as the doors and thresholds may get in the way. You'll use the Freeze tool to graphically select the layers instead of opening the Layer Properties Manager to freeze the respective layers.

6. At the Select an object on the layer to be frozen or: prompt, click one door or door swing (A-DOOR) and one threshold (A-DECK-STRS). All the objects on the Doors and Steps layers temporarily disappear.

7. Press Esc to end the Freeze command.

   You need to draw two parallel lines across each of the three openings, from the endpoint of one jamb line to the corresponding endpoint of the jamb on the opposite side of the opening.

8. To start the LINE command, enter L↵ or click the Line button from the Home tab ➤ Draw panel.

9. Move the cursor near the upper end of the left jamb for the back door, until the colored snap marker appears at the upper-left endpoint of the jamb line, and then click.

10. Move the cursor to the left end of the lower jamb, and click to complete the line.

11. Right-click once to open a context menu near your cursor (see Figure 6.35).

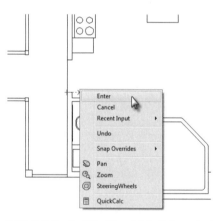

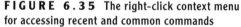

FIGURE 6.35 The right-click context menu for accessing recent and common commands

12. Choose Enter from the menu, and then right-click again to open another context menu at the cursor, as shown in Figure 6.36.

13. Choose Repeat LINE.

14. Move to the right endpoint of the upper jamb line for the back door.

15. With the same technique used in steps 6 through 12, draw the lower header line across the opening. You can see the results in the left image of Figure 6.37.

16. Keep using the same procedure to draw the rest of the header lines for the remaining three doorway openings. The floor plan will look like the right image of Figure 6.37.

17. Save this drawing as **I06-10-Headers.dwg** (**M06-10-Headers.dwg**).

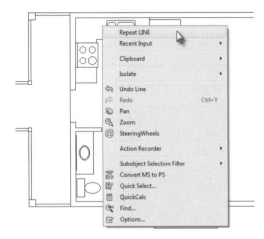

FIGURE 6.36 A second right-click context menu with additional commands available

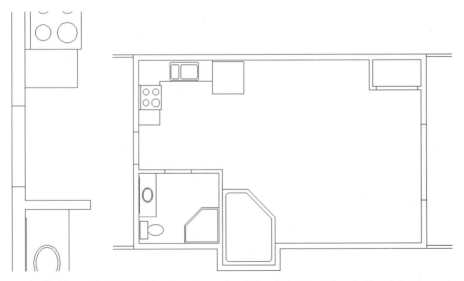

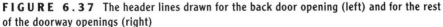

FIGURE 6.37 The header lines drawn for the back door opening (left) and for the rest of the doorway openings (right)

Drawing the Roof

You've seen that the Layer drop-down list is a shortcut that allows you to pick a different layer quickly as the current layer and to turn off or turn on individual layers. You've also learned how to use the Layer Properties Manager palette to create new layers or to turn off many layers at a time. You'll learn about another tool for changing the current layer as you draw the rooflines.

Before you start to draw the rooflines, refer to Figure 6.38 and note the lines representing different parts of the roof:

▶ Eight *eaves lines* around the perimeter of the building, representing the lowest edge of the roof

▶ One *ridgeline*, representing the peak of the roof

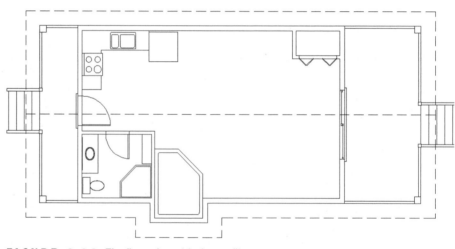

FIGURE 6.38 The floor plan with the rooflines

The roof for the cabin is called a *double-pitched roof* because the panels slope down to the eaves on only two sides. You'll start by drawing the eaves.

Creating the Eaves

Because the roof extends beyond the exterior walls the same distance on all sides of the building, you can generate the eaves lines by offsetting the outside wall lines:

1. Make sure I06-10-Headers.dwg (M06-10-Headers.dwg) is open.

2. Open the Layer drop-down list, and select the A-ROOF layer to make it current.

3. Start the OFFSET command from the Home tab ➤ Modify panel ➤ Offset tool, or enter **O**↵ from the command line. Then follow these steps:

    a. At the Specify offset distance or prompt, press the down-arrow and select the Layer option (see the left image of Figure 6.39).

FIGURE 6.39 Choosing the Layer option (left) and the current option (right)

    b. The second prompt reads Enter layer option for offset objects. Press the down-arrow and select the Current option, or enter **C**↵ to instruct AutoCAD to create offsets on the current layer (A-ROOF), as shown in the right image of Figure 6.39.

4. Enter **1´6**↵ (**457**↵) when prompted to specify the offset distance.

5. Pick the upper-left, vertical, outside handrail polyline, and then pick a point to the left of that polyline to offset it to the outside. The L-shaped offset line is on the Roof layer.

6. Move to another side of the cabin, pick the lower-right, outside handrail polyline, and offset it to the outside.

7. Repeat this process for the three outside wall lines that define the pop-out on the bottom of the cabin and the short, horizontal, outside wall line to the left of the pop-out.

    You have one offset element on each side of the cabin (see Figure 6.40).

8. Press ↵ to end the OFFSET command.

9. Start the FILLET command from the Home tab ➤ Modify panel ➤ Offset tool.

10. Verify that the fillet radius is set to zero by entering **R**↵ and then **0**↵ (or use the Shift key to override the radius value).

11. Starting with the horizontal portion of the upper-left, L-shaped polyline, click two of these newly offset lines that are on adjacent sides of the building.

12. Work around the building in a clockwise manner, being sure to click the half of the line nearest the corner where the two selected lines will meet (see the top of Figure 6.41).

The lines extend to meet each other and form a corner (see the bottom of Figure 6.41). The FILLET command ends.

13. Press ↵ to restart the FILLET command, and then enter **M**↵ to select the Multiple option.

Pick the remaining pairs of adjacent lines that will meet at the corners. When you try to fillet the final section, you'll get a warning at the command prompt that reads Lines belonging to polylines must be consecutive or separated by one segment, and the command prompt returns to Select first object or:.

Although it looks as though the polyline has a single gap between two adjacent segments, in actuality the gap is between the first (vertical) segment and the eighth (horizontal) segment. You can't use the PEDIT command's Close option yet because it would add an additional, diagonal segment from the polylines' existing endpoints. You could explode the polyline into individual lines, execute the fillet, and then use PEDIT to join them, but in this case you'll use the polylines' grips to close the gap.

14. Press the Esc key to terminate the FILLET command.

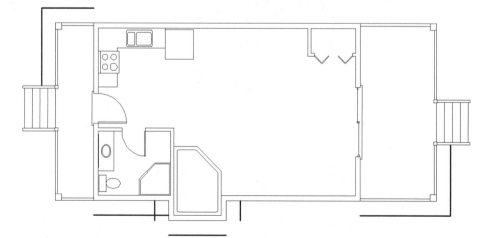

FIGURE 6.40 One outside wall line is offset to each side of the building.

15. Click the polyline to select it and display its grips.

You can temporarily turn off the Quick Properties panel by clicking the X in the upper-right corner, or you can turn it off completely by clicking the Object Properties button in the status bar.

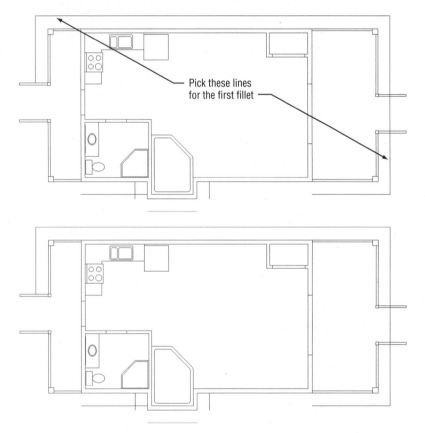

Pick these lines
for the first fillet

FIGURE 6.41 Picking lines to fillet one of the eaves' corners (top), and the result (bottom)

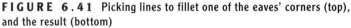

STARTING OBJECT SNAPS

By now, you know that you can activate a nonrunning osnap by using the Ctrl+right-click menu or the Object Snap toolbar, or by typing the shortcut keys. From now on, I'll simply instruct you to activate a specific object snap, and you can use the method you prefer.

16. Click the grip at the open left endpoint of the horizontal segment (see the top of Figure 6.42).

    The grip turns red to signify that it is *hot* (active) and can be manipulated.

17. Start the Perpendicular osnap, place the cursor over the open, vertical segment, and then click when the marker appears. The horizontal line is extended to the location perpendicular to the vertical line.

18. Select the grip at the open end of the vertical segment to make it hot.

19. Then click the open end of the horizontal line to move the first endpoint there (see the bottom of Figure 6.42).

20. Finally, use the JOIN command on the Home tab ≻ expanded Modify panel to select each of the rooflines and create a closed polyline.

    Visually, there is no difference in the perimeter of the roof, but AutoCAD no longer sees an open polyline. Closed polylines are almost always preferable in case you need to extrude a 2D object into a 3D object, and using closed polylines is generally a cleaner drafting practice. Your completed roof perimeter should look like Figure 6.43.

21. Save this drawing as **I06-11-DrawingRoof.dwg** (**M06-11-Drawing Roof.dwg**).

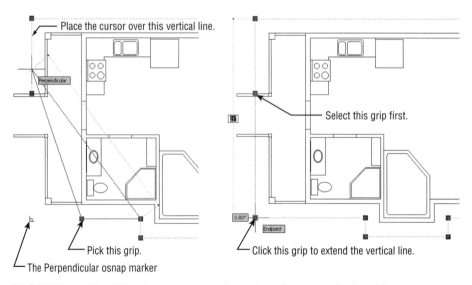

FIGURE 6.42 Using the grip to move the horizontal endpoint (top) and the vertical endpoint (bottom)

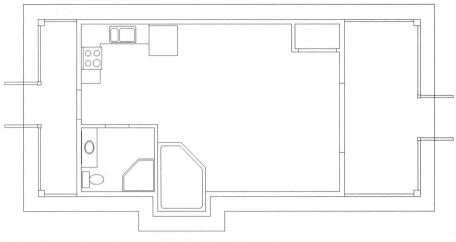

FIGURE 6.43 The completed eaves lines after filleting

Setting a Linetype Scale Factor

Currently it's hard to see that the lines drawn on the A-ROOF layer are indeed dashed, as specified in the Layer Properties Manager. Unless you zoom in to a line on the A-ROOF layer, the lines look continuous, like the objects on the other layers in your drawing. This is because the dashes inside the DASHED linetype are set up to be ½″ (13 mm) long with ¼″ (6 mm) spaces. Using the linetype scale, or LTSCALE as many call it, you will tell AutoCAD how to scale your linetypes.

Interestingly enough, a drawing's linetype scale is actually controlled by three separate LTSCALE variables:

> LTSCALE (Linetype Scale)
>
> PSLTSCALE (Paper Space Linetype Scale)
>
> MSLTSCALE (Model Space Linetype Scale)

With three variables to choose from, it's probably easy to see how one of the most debated topics among AutoCAD users is what setting should be used for these variables. I'll show you two of the more popular ways people choose to set these variables. The first is more of a manual approach, and the second is what I like to call LTSCALE Auto Pilot.

In comparison to the LTSCALE variable itself, both PSLTSCALE and MSLTSCALE are relative newcomers. Consequently, many users still prefer to calculate their LTSCALE value manually. A common architectural scale is ½″ = 1′-0″. To make the dashes plot (print) ½ long (as desired) divide 12″ (1 foot) into ½″ (12″ ÷ ½″ = 24).

If you set LTSCALE to 24, PSLTSCALE to 0, and MSLTSCALE to 0, the dashes for the DASHED linetype assigned to the A-ROOF layer will plot ½″ long. A big drawback to this method is that your dashes will be ½″ long only if you plot your drawing at a scale of ½″ = 1′-0″. Plotting your drawing at a scale of ¼″ = 1′-0″ would translate to the dashes in your drawing plotting ¼″ long.

If you're confused by this method of calculating and setting the various LTSCALE variables, you're not alone. The method I'm going to show you next is both a little easier and more modern than the first way I showed you. The following steps will demonstrate how to put LTSCALE on Auto Pilot:

 N O T E   **The imperial to metric conversion is approximated.**

1. Make sure I06-11-DrawingRoof.dwg (M06-11-DrawingRoof.dwg) is open.

2. Enter **LTSCALE↵** or **LTS↵**. The prompt in the command window reads Enter new linetype scale factor <1.0000>:.

3. Enter **1↵** to set the linetype scale factor to 1. Nothing changes quite yet, as the default value for LTSCALE is 1.

4. Enter **PSLTSCALE↵**.

5. When prompted to Enter new value for PSLTSCALE:, enter **1↵**.

6. Enter **MSLTSCALE↵**.

7. When prompted to Enter new value for MSLTSCALE:, enter **1↵**.

8. Change the Annotation Scale of your drawing by clicking the Scale drop-down on the status bar.

9. Select ½″ = 1′-0″ from the list of scales, as shown in Figure 6.44.

   If you aren't satisfied with the dash size, as illustrated in Figure 6.45, change the Annotation Scale as you did in steps 8 and 9. An advantage to this method is you can preview any scale (by changing the Annotation Scale) without affecting any drawing sheets in your project. Layout viewports have an Annotation Scale much like the Annotation Scale property you just changed for model space. With LTSCALE, PSLTSCALE, and

MSLTSCALE each set to 1, AutoCAD will automatically calculate the correct linetype scale based on the properties of each individual view.

10. Save this drawing as **I06-12-LinetypeScale.dwg** (**M06-12-Linetype Scale.dwg**).

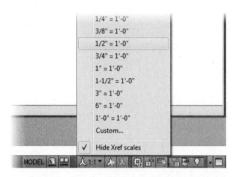

If your linetypes do not dash after you've changed the Annotation Scale, enter REA↵ at the command line to perform a REGENALL.

FIGURE 6.44 The Annotation Scale list

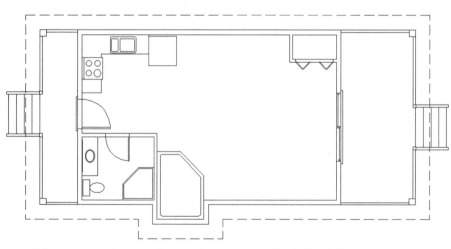

FIGURE 6.45 The eaves lines on the Roof layer with visible dashes

Drawing the Ridgeline

To finish the roof, you'll draw a single line to represent the peak of the roof that extends from the front of the cabin to the back. Because of the pop-out, the roof is not symmetrical, so the ridgeline will be centered on the two longest vertical sections.

Look at the Linetype drop-down list on the Properties panel (see Figure 6.46). A dashed line with the name ByLayer appears there. ByLayer tells you that the current linetype will be whatever linetype has been assigned to the current layer. In the case of the A-ROOF layer, the assigned linetype is Dashed. (You'll read more about ByLayer later in this chapter.)

FIGURE 6.46 The Linetype drop-down list

To draw the ridgeline, follow these steps:

1. Continue using I06-12-LinetypeScale.dwg (M06-12-Linetype Scale.dwg) or open it if it's not already open.

2. Start the LINE command and activate the Midpoint object snap.

3. Start the line from the midpoint of the right vertical roofline.

4. Start the Perpendicular osnap, and then click the vertical roofline on the opposite side of the cabin.

5. Terminate the LINE command.
   Your cabin should look like Figure 6.47.

6. Save this drawing as **I06-13-Ridgeline.dwg** (**M06-13-Ridgeline.dwg**).

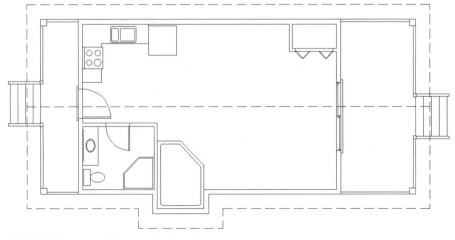

FIGURE 6.47 The completed roof

Using the Layer Walk Tool

Before saving the next drawing, you will use the Make Object's Layer Current button (Home tab ➤ Layers palette) to make the A-DOOR layer current. You will then use the Layer Walk tool to verify the contents of each layer by isolating them one at a time:

1. Make sure I06-13-Ridgeline.dwg (M06-13-Ridgeline.dwg) is open.

2. Expand the Layers panel, and click the Pin button in the lower-right corner. This causes the panel to stay open after the cursor moves off it, instead of autocollapsing.

3. Verify that all layers are in a Thaw state by using the Thaw All Layers tool found on the Home tab ➤ Layers panel.

4. Click the Make Object's Layer Current button in the top row of buttons in the Layers panel. You'll get the Select object whose layer will become current: prompt.

5. Pick one of the door or swing lines. The A-DOOR layer replaces A-ROOF in the Layer drop-down list, telling you the A-DOOR layer is now the current layer.

T I P   The Make Object's Layer Current button works two ways. You can click the button and then select the object whose layer will become current, or you can select an object that's on the target layer and then click the button. If you use the latter method to select multiple objects, they must all reside on the current layer, or the tool will prompt you to select an object.

---

6. Click the LayerWalk button in the extended Layers panel to open the LayerWalk dialog box, shown in Figure 6.48.

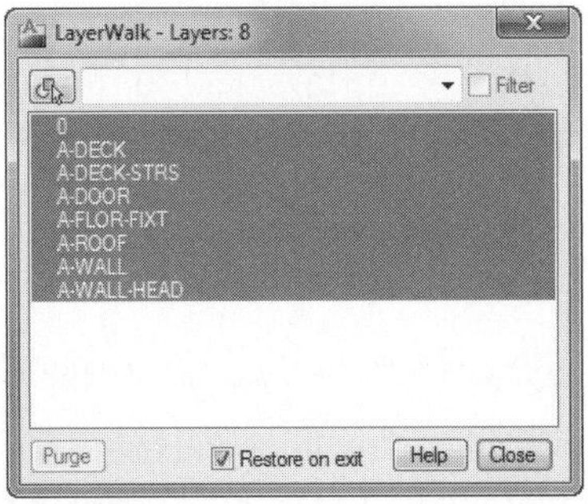

FIGURE 6.48 The LayerWalk dialog box

7. Select a layer other than layer 0, and the drawing area shows only the objects on that layer.

8. Use the up- and down-arrows to "walk" through the drawing's layers, verifying that the objects reside on the correct layers. The top of Figure 6.49 shows the cabin drawing with the A-FLOR-FIXT layer selected.

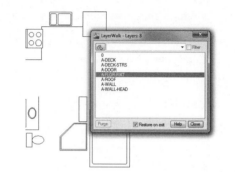
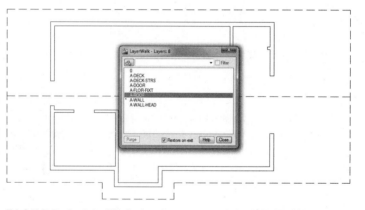
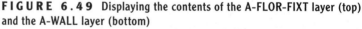

FIGURE 6.49 Displaying the contents of the A-FLOR-FIXT layer (top) and the A-WALL layer (bottom)

If you double-click a layer name, that layer stays displayed even when it isn't highlighted, and an asterisk appears next to the layer name. Figure 6.49 (bottom) shows the cabin drawing with the A-ROOF layer selected and the A-WALL layer locked on.

9. Close the LayerWalk dialog box.

10. Click the Unpin button to unpin the expanded Layers panel.

By drawing the rooflines, you have completed most of the exercises for this chapter. The cabin floor plan is almost complete. In the next chapter, you'll complete the floor plan by using a grouping tool called a *block* to place windows in the external walls. The rest of this chapter contains a short discussion about color, linetypes, and lineweights and how they work with layers and objects. You'll also look at the Action Recorder feature to record and play back repetitive tasks.

Setting Properties of Layers and Objects

This section covers a few concepts you should consider when assigning properties to layers and objects.

Selecting Colors for Layers and Objects

First, you must decide whether you prefer a light or dark background color for the drawing area. This is generally a personal preference, but the lighting in your work area can be a contributing factor. Bright work areas usually make it difficult to read monitors easily, and with a dark background color on your screen in a brightly lit room, you'll often get distracting reflections on the screen. Eyestrain can result. Darkening your work area will usually minimize these effects. If that's not possible, you might have to live with a lighter background.

   Next, look at the colors in your drawing. If the background of your drawing area is white, notice which colors are the easiest to read. For most monitors, yellow, light gray, and cyan are somewhat faded, while blue, green, red, and magenta are easily read. If your drawing area background is black, the blue is sometimes too dark to read easily, but the rest of the colors that you have used so far usually read well. This is one reason that most users prefer the black or at least a dark background color.

Assigning a Color or a Linetype to an Object Instead of a Layer

You can also assign properties of layers, such as color, linetype, and lineweight, to objects. For example, think about the A-ROOF layer. It's assigned the Dashed linetype. A line on the A-ROOF layer can be assigned the Continuous linetype, even though all other lines on the Roof layer are dashed. The same is true for color and lineweight. Occasionally, this makes sense, especially for linetypes, but that is the exception rather than the rule. To make such a change, follow these steps:

1. Select the line.

2. Open the Properties palette.

3. Change the linetype from ByLayer to the linetype of your choice.

You can also use the Properties toolbar to make quick changes to an object's appearance.

T I P   It's a generally accepted best practice that an object's color, linetype, lineweight, and transparency should all be ByLayer. However, it's not uncommon to receive a drawing with lots of object overrides (usually from a third party, and usually irrelevant to anyone else). Use the SETBYLAYER command to clean this up quickly.

In this chapter, you have seen how to assign colors and linetypes to layers in order to control the way objects on those layers appear. That is the rule to follow. When objects are assigned properties that vary from those of their layer, the result can be confusing to someone working with your drawing file, because the objects don't appear to be on their assigned layer. If the object's properties match those of another layer, you can mistakenly think the object is on that layer.

Making a Color or a Linetype Current

If you look at the Properties panel for a moment, you'll see lists to the right of the Layer drop-down list. The first three of these lists are the Color, Linetype, and Lineweight controls. You use these tools to set a color, linetype, or lineweight to be current. When this is done, each object subsequently created will be assigned the current linetype, lineweight, and/or color, regardless of which linetype, lineweight, and color have been assigned to the current layer. If, for example, the A-DOOR layer is set as the current layer, and the Dashed linetype and green color are assigned as current, any lines drawn are dashed and green but still on the A-DOOR layer. This isn't a good way to set up the system of layers, linetypes, and colors because of the obvious confusion it will create in your drawing, but beginners often accidentally do this.

The best way to maintain maximum control of your drawing is to keep the current linetype, lineweight, and color set to ByLayer, as they are by default. When you do this, colors and linetypes are controlled by the layers, and an object takes on the color and linetype of the layer it is on. If this configuration is accidentally disturbed, and objects are created with the wrong color or linetype, you can correct the situation without too much trouble:

1. Reset the current color, lineweight, and linetype to ByLayer by using the drop-down lists on the Properties panel.

2. Select all problem objects.

3. Use the Properties palette or Quick Properties panel to change the linetype, lineweight, or color to ByLayer.

The objects will take on the color, lineweight, and linetype of the layer to which they have been assigned, and you can quickly tell whether they are on their proper layers.

Using the Action Recorder

 One of the most useful tools in AutoCAD 2012 is the Action Recorder. With this feature, you can perform repetitive tasks and save the steps to a file, called a *macro*, which can be played back any time you need to repeat those steps in any drawing. For example, if you need to draw several countersunk holes in a plate at a specified distance, you can prompt the user for a start point, angle, diameter, and spacing, and then let AutoCAD do the work. The Action Recorder creates the macros for you without the need for you to learn macro programming.

For this example, you will add two new layers to your drawing and then make one of them the current layer. The practice of adding your standards to a drawing from someone else (a client, contractor, and so on) is common. Follow these steps to create the action:

1. Click the Manage tab from the Ribbon to display a series of panels that contain tools for managing a drawing's interface and standards.

2. Click the Record button (Manage tab ➤ Action Recorder panel). The Record button changes to a Stop button, and the panel pins itself open, as shown in Figure 6.50. A large red dot appears at the cursor to remind you that the actions are being recorded.
   You'll use the command line to start the LAYER command. The - prefix starts the command without opening the Layer Properties Manager palette.

3. Enter **-LAYER**↵.

4. Enter **N**↵ or pick New from the list that appears at the cursor.

5. Enter **L-PLNT**↵ to name the new layer. Both methods for selecting an option work equally well.

6. Select the New option again, and enter **E-POWR**↵ to create and name the new layer.

7. Choose the Set option.

8. Enter **E-POWR**↵ to make the E-POWR layer current and end the LAYER command.

9. Click the Stop button to discontinue recording the actions. Your Action Recorder panel should look like Figure 6.51.

10. In the Action Macro dialog box that opens (see Figure 6.52), enter **New_Layers.⏎** in the Action Macro Command Name field, and add a description if you like.

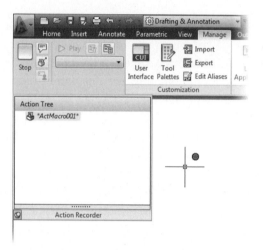

FIGURE 6.50 The Action Recorder panel as it appears when the actions are being recorded

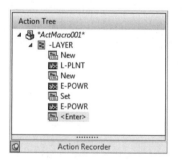

FIGURE 6.51 The Action Recorder after creating the new layers and setting the current layer

WARNING   Special characters, such as spaces or slashes, are not permitted in action filenames.

Action Macro

Action Macro Command Name:

New_Layers

File Name:

New_Layers.actm

Folder Path:

C:\Users\GladD\appdata\roaming\autodesk\autocad ironman beta 2\r1

Description:

Add the L-PLNT and E-POWR layers to a drawing ans makes E-POWR current

Restore pre-playback view

☑ When pausing for user input

☐ Once playback finishes

☑ Check for inconsistencies when playback begins

OK   Cancel   Help

FIGURE 6.52 The Action Macro dialog box

11. Click OK, and the macro is saved as `New_Layers.actm` in the `C:\ Users\username\appdata\roaming\autodesk\autocad 2012\ r18.2\enu\support\actions` folder (a copy is also available on this book's web page).

T I P **Those using Windows XP can find the macro in** `C:\Documents and Settings\Your Name\Application Data\Autodesk\AutoCAD 2012\R18.2\enu\Support\Actions`.

12. Unpin the Action Recorder panel so that it can collapse.

13. Open a new drawing file.

14. Make sure the New_Layers macro name appears in the Available Action Macro field, and click the Play button, as shown in Figure 6.53.

15. Click Close when the Action Macro dialog box indicates that the macro has run through completion (see Figure 6.54).

16. Switch to the Home tab, and then open the Layer drop-down list in the Layers panel. You will see the new layers the macro created.

17. Save your cabin drawing as `I06-14-ActionMacro.dwg` (`M06-14-Action Macro.dwg`).

F I G U R E 6 . 5 3 Playing the New_Layers macro in the Action Recorder panel

Action Macro – Playback Complete	
The playback of the action macro is complete.	
☐ Do not show me this message again	Close

F I G U R E 6 . 5 4 The Action Macro dialog box

As you can see, action macros are easy to record and can save you time when repetitive tasks are required. You could have easily set layers' colors, linetypes, or on/off statuses, or performed other layer-related tasks. The Action Recorder is quite powerful and can save a great amount of time when you use it to create macros specific to your needs. In the next section, you will look at a method of saving and recalling all the settings for the layers in your drawings. You can close the blank drawing without saving the changes.

Creating Layer States

Even a drawing that reads well when printed may get cluttered in the viewports, and it can become difficult to execute a command properly. Often, you will find yourself freezing or turning off the same layers to execute a specific task and then making them visible again. In the course of your workday, you might issue the same sequence of layer commands dozens of times. To make this task more efficient, layer states are available. *Layer states* are named settings in which you can save the conditions of the layers, such as On, Frozen, or Current, and restore them through the Layer States Manager dialog box. The following exercise demonstrates how to create a layer state that shows only the floor plan and not the roof or fixtures:

1. Continue using the drawing you used to complete the previous Action Recorder exercise, or open I06-15-ActionMacro.dwg (M06-15-Action Macro.dwg).

2. In the Cabin drawing, make layer 0 the current layer.

3. From the Layer drop-down list or the Layer Properties Manager palette, freeze the A-ROOF and A-FLOR-FIXT layers.

4. On the Layers panel, click the Layer States drop-down list, which currently shows Unsaved Layer State, and click Manage Layer States, as shown in Figure 6.55.

FIGURE 6.55 Accessing the Layer States Manager

The Layer States Manager dialog box opens (see Figure 6.56).

5. Click the New button to create a new saved layer state.

6. In the New Layer State To Save dialog box, enter **Floor Plan** in the New Layer State Name field. If you like, enter a description for the layer state as well (see Figure 6.57).

7. Click the OK button when you are finished.

8. The new layer state appears in the Layer States Manager dialog box, as shown in Figure 6.58. Click the Close button to close the Layer States Manager dialog box.

9. Thaw the Roof and Fixtures layers. The objects on those layers become visible again.

10. Open the Layer States Manager dialog box again.

11. Click the More Restore Options button—the right-facing arrow at the bottom-right corner—to display additional options.

The items shown in the Layer Properties To Restore section are, when checked, the features of the layer state that are affected when it is restored. It is important to note that if you make changes to a layer's color or lineweight, those changes are lost when the layer state is restored if those features are checked here.

12. Uncheck the Color, Linetype, and Lineweight options (see Figure 6.59), and then click the Restore button.

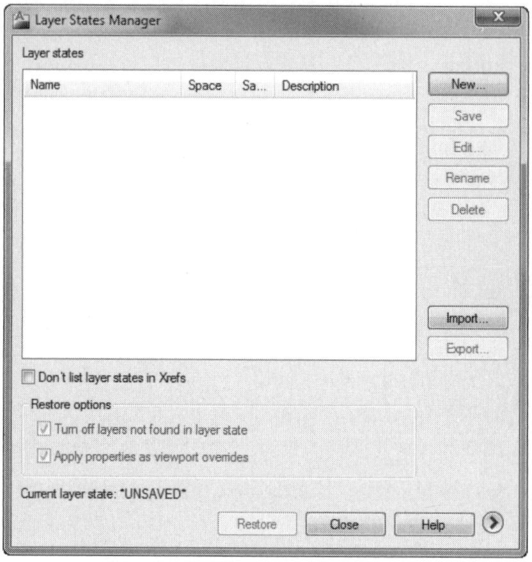

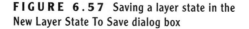

FIGURE 6.56 The Layer States Manager dialog box

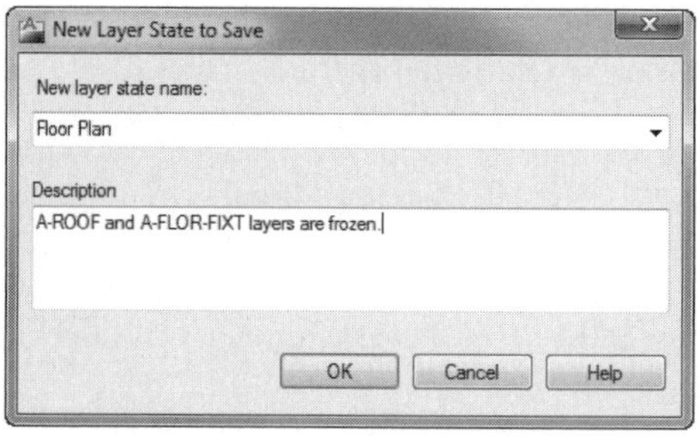

FIGURE 6.57 Saving a layer state in the New Layer State To Save dialog box

The Roof and Fixtures layers are frozen again (see Figure 6.60), and Floor Plan appears in the Layer State drop-down list.

13. Save this drawing as **I06A-FPLAY0.dwg** (**M06A-FPLAY0.dwg**).

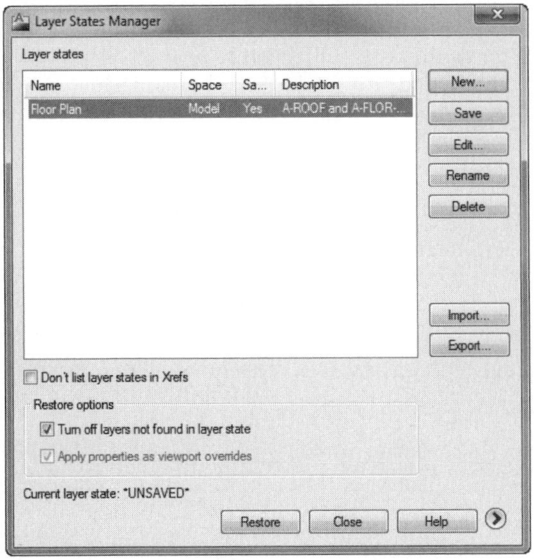

FIGURE 6.58 The Layer States Manager dialog box showing the new layer state

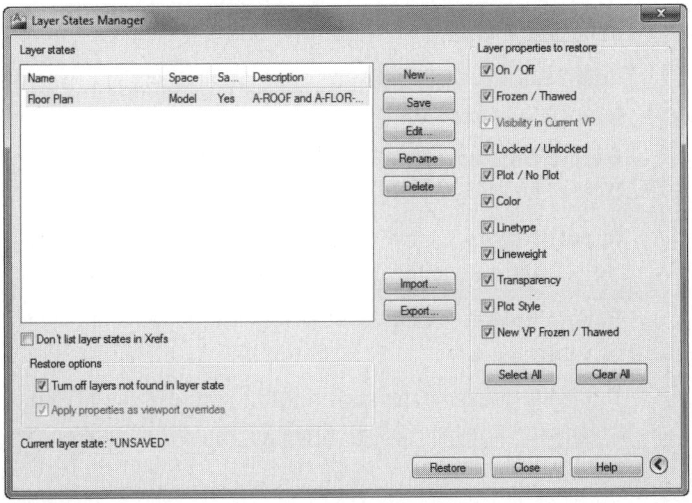

FIGURE 6.59 The Layer States Manager dialog box with the restore options selected

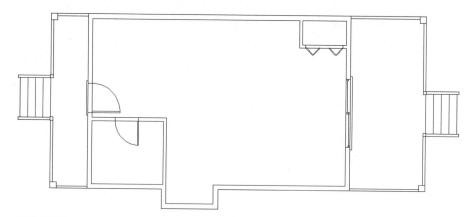

FIGURE 6.60 The cabin with the Roof and Fixtures layers frozen

As you can see, saving layer states can reduce the number of steps it takes to restore a specific set of layer properties. In a complex drawing, it isn't uncommon to have a dozen or more saved layer states.

USING THE LAYER STATES MANAGER

You also use the Layer States Manager dialog box to manage existing layer states. Here are its primary features:

Layer States List Box   Displays a list of previously saved layer states.

Restore Button   Restores the layer state that is highlighted in the Layer States list box.

Edit Button   Opens the Edit Layer State dialog box, where the current layer state's properties are edited.

Delete Button   Deletes a layer state. This doesn't affect the current layer setup.

Import Button   Imports an LAS file, from a DWG, DWS, or DWT file, as a new layer state in the current drawing.

Export Button   Exports the chosen saved layer state to be saved as an LAS file.

To modify a layer state, restore it to be the current layer state and then change it. To rename a layer state, highlight it, click its name, and enter the new name.

If You Would Like More Practice...

All trades and professions that use AutoCAD have their own standards for naming and organizing layers. The following suggestions urge you to apply this chapter's concepts to your individual use of the program.

Experimenting with Linetypes and Linetype Scales

Choose Save As to save I06A-FPLAY0.dwg (M06A-FPLAY0.dwg) to a new file called **I06A-FPLAY9_Linetype.dwg** (M06A-FPLAY9_Linetype.dwg). Then experiment with the linetypes and linetype scales (Global and Object) to get a feel for how the linetypes look and how the scales work. You won't be using this practice file again, so feel free to draw new objects that will make it convenient for you to work with linetypes. Here are some suggestions for linetypes to experiment with:

- ▶ Dashed2 or Dashed (0.5×)
- ▶ DashedX2 or Dashed (2×)
- ▶ Hidden (as compared to Dashed)
- ▶ Phantom
- ▶ DASHDOT
- ▶ Fenceline2
- ▶ Hot_Water_Supply

Here is a summary of the steps to get a new linetype into your drawing:

1. Create a new layer or highlight an existing layer.

2. In the Layer Properties Manager, click the linetype name in the Linetype column for the chosen layer.

3. Click the Load button.

4. Highlight a linetype in the list and click OK.

5. Highlight the new linetype in the Linetype Manager dialog box and click OK.

6. Make the layer with the new linetype the current layer, and then click OK to close the Layer Properties Manager.

7. Draw objects.

Once you have a few linetypes represented in the drawing, open the Linetype Manager dialog box and experiment with the Global and Object linetype scale factors.

Setting Up Layers for Your Own Trade or Profession

Open a new drawing, and set up approximately 10 layers that you might use in your own profession. Assign colors and linetypes to them. Most activities that use CAD have some layers in common, such as Centerline, Border or Titleblock, Drawing Symbols, Dimensions, and Text or Lettering.

Are You Experienced?

Now you can...

- ☑ create new layers and assign them a color and a linetype
- ☑ load a new linetype into your current drawing file
- ☑ move existing objects onto a new layer
- ☑ turn layers off and on
- ☑ freeze and thaw layers
- ☑ make a layer current and create objects on the current layer
- ☑ use the Layer Walk tool to verify that objects are on the proper layers
- ☑ reset the linetype scale factor globally or for a selected object
- ☑ record action macros
- ☑ create layer states

Combining Objects into Blocks

Computer drafting derives much of its efficiency from a feature that makes it possible to combine a collection of objects into an entity that behaves as a single object. AutoCAD calls these grouped objects a *block*. The AutoCAD tools that work specifically with blocks make it possible to do the following:

- ▶ Create a block in your current drawing
- ▶ Repeatedly place copies of a block in precise locations in your drawing
- ▶ Share blocks between drawings
- ▶ Create DWG files either from blocks or from portions of your current drawing
- ▶ Store blocks on a palette for easy reuse in any drawing

In general, objects best suited to becoming part of a block are the components that are repeatedly used in your drawings. In architecture and construction, examples of these components are doors, windows, and fixtures; or drawing symbols, such as a North arrow; or labels for a section cut line (which is shown in Figure 7.1 in the first section of this chapter). In mechanical drawings, these can be countersunk and counterbored holes, screws, bolts, fasteners, switches, or any other objects that you find yourself repeatedly drawing. In your cabin drawing, you'll convert the doors with swings into blocks. You'll then create a new block that you'll use to place the windows in the cabin drawing. To accomplish these tasks, you need to learn two new commands: BLOCK and INSERT.

- ▶ **Creating and inserting blocks**
- ▶ **Using the WBLOCK command**
- ▶ **Detecting blocks in a drawing**
- ▶ **Working with AutoCAD's DesignCenter**
- ▶ **Controlling the appearance of palettes on your screen**

Making a Block for a Door

When making a block, you create a *block definition*. This is an entity that is stored in the drawing file and consists of the following components:

► The block name

► An insertion point to help you place the block in the drawing

► The objects to be grouped into the block

You specify each of these in the course of using the BLOCK command. When the command is completed, the objects are designated as a single block, and the block definition is stored with the drawing file. You then insert additional copies of the block into the drawing by using the INSERT command.

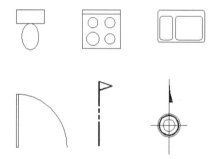

FIGURE 7.1   Examples of blocks often used in architectural drawings

ABOUT COMMANDS AND TOOLS

In earlier chapters, I told you exactly what to click or enter to launch a command. Now that you're familiar with AutoCAD's interface, I'll simply instruct you to start a command or tool. In general, I'll refer to a command by the tooltip that appears when you place the cursor on the command's icon on the Ribbon or the command as it is entered at the Command: prompt.

I'll refer to tools and commands that do not have an icon on the Ribbon by their name on the associated menu, toolbar, or other interface element such as the status bar. In the rare case that the command doesn't appear in either place, I'll tell you what to enter in the command window. Any command can be started by entering its name or an alias at the Command: prompt, while others have keyboard shortcuts. Where applicable, I'll mention the command aliases and keyboard shortcuts.

Before you create a block, you must consider the layers on which the objects to be blocked reside. When objects on layer 0 are grouped into a block, they take on the color and linetype of the layer that is current when the block is inserted or the layer to which you move the block. Objects on other layers retain the properties of their original layers, regardless of which color or linetype has been assigned to the current layer. This is one characteristic that distinguishes layer 0 from all other layers.

While it's technically possible to create blocks on any layer of your choice, the generally accepted best practice is to always define blocks that are to be used as symbols in a drawing on layer 0. It is also recommended that the color, linetype, and lineweight each be set to ByLayer or ByBlock. Drawing your blocks with these properties in mind does a number of things.

First and foremost, it helps ensure that when you insert a block on a given layer, the block functions as if it were drawn on that layer. By using the ByLayer or ByBlock settings, you help avoid the confusion often experienced with colors and linetypes in blocks. This allows the display of blocks to be determined in the same context as the other linework in your drawing, in the Layer Properties Manager. Consequently, changes within the Layer Properties Manager apply to blocks the same as they would to other linework in your drawing. In the coming exercises, I'll show you how to follow these best practices while converting some of the objects already in your drawing into blocks and creating some new blocks of your own.

To get started, you'll see how to create blocks from objects already in your drawing. You'll create a block for the back exterior door, and call it A-DOOR-36IN to match the NCS naming convention used throughout this book. For the insertion point, you need to assign a point on or near the door that will facilitate its placement as a block in your drawing. The hinge point makes the best insertion point.

For this chapter, the Endpoint osnap should be running most of the time, and Polar Tracking should be off. Follow these steps to set up your drawing:

1. Continue using the I06A-FPLAY0.dwg (M06A-FPLAY0.dwg) drawing you created in Chapter 6, "Using Layers to Organize Your Drawing." If you're starting a new session, you can download this file from the book's website at **www.sybex.com/go/autocad2012ner** or from **www.autocadner.com**.

2. Click the Layer drop-down list, and click the sun icon for the A-WALL -HEAD layer to freeze it.

3. Then click the A-DOOR layer to close the list.
   The A-DOOR layer is now current, and the sun next to the A-WALL -HEAD layer turns into a snowflake. In addition to the A-WALL-HEAD layer, the A-FLOR-FIXT and A-ROOF layers should still be frozen from Chapter 6 (see Figure 7.2).

The objects that compose blocks can reside on more than one layer.

You're using the Freeze option for layers this time because you won't need to see the lines on the A-ROOF, A-FLOR-FIXT, and A-WALL-HEAD layers for a while. This might be a good time to consider creating another layer state.

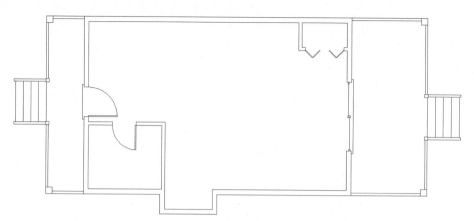

FIGURE 7.2 The floor plan with the A-FLOR-FIXTA-ROOF and A-WALL-HEAD layers frozen

4. Check the status bar, and make sure the Object Snap button is in the On position.

5. Right-click the Object Snap button to display the Object Snap tab inside the Drafting Settings dialog box.

6. Make sure that, at a minimum, the Endpoint osnap is running. If it isn't, select the Endpoint Object Snap check box on the Drafting Settings dialog box.

7. In the status bar, turn Polar Tracking off if it's on.

 TIP   The features in the status bar and their particular options are general AutoCAD settings and are not saved as properties of any particular drawing. Changes made on the status bar in one drawing are in effect when any subsequent drawings are opened or accessed.

8. Turn off Quick Properties to prevent the Quick Properties panel from opening whenever an object is selected.

Now you're ready to make blocks:

You can also start the BLOCK **command by entering B↵.**

1. Click the Create Block button found on the Insert tab ➤ Block Definition panel.

    The Block Definition dialog box opens, where you can specify some basic parameters about your block.

2. Notice the flashing cursor in the Name text box. Type **A-DOOR-36IN** (**A-DOOR-0915**), but don't press ↵ (see Figure 7.3).

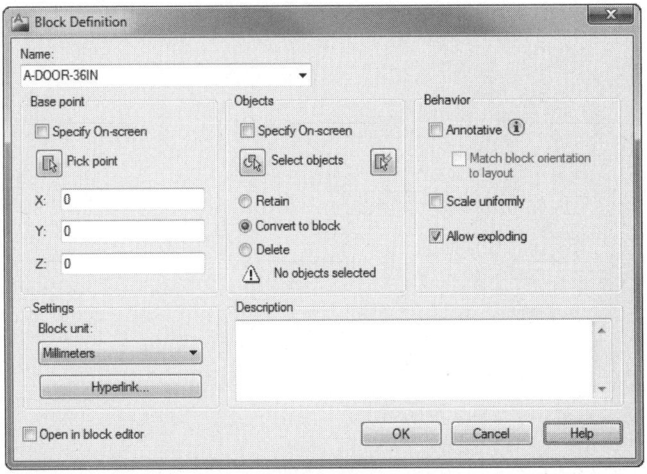

FIGURE 7.3 The Block Definition dialog box

3. Click the Pick Point button in the Base Point area of the Block Definition dialog box.

The dialog box temporarily closes, and you're returned to your drawing.

4. Use the scroll wheel on the mouse to zoom in to the back door area in your drawing.

5. Move the cursor to the back door area, and position it near the hinge point of the door. When the Endpoint marker appears on the hinge point (see Figure 7.4), click.

This selects the insertion point for the door, and the Block Definition dialog box returns. The insertion point is the location, relative to the cursor, that the block references when it is inserted.

6. Click the Select Objects button in the Objects area of the Block Definition dialog box.

You're returned to the drawing again. The cursor changes to a pickbox, and the command window displays the Select objects: prompt.

7. Select the door and swing, and then press ↵.

You're returned to the Block Definition dialog box.

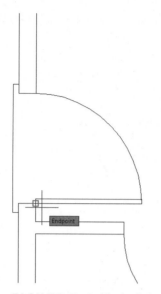

F I G U R E 7 . 4 The back door opening when
the hinge point is picked as the insertion point

8. At the bottom of the Objects area, the count of selected objects appears.
Just above that are three radio buttons. Click the Delete radio button if
it's not already selected.

   The Delete option erases the selected objects after the block definition is created, requiring you to insert the block into the drawing.

   The Convert To Block option replaces objects with a block definition
as soon as the block is created. In this situation, the Convert To Block
option would be a better choice, but it's a good idea to get some practice using the INSERT command, so click Delete.

9. Enter a description of the block in the Description field and make sure
Inches or Millimeters is specified in the Block Unit drop-down list,
depending on the units you are using.

   The Block Definition dialog box should look similar to Figure 7.5.

10. At the bottom of the dialog box, be sure the Open In Block Editor check
box is selected, and then click OK to close the dialog box.

   The Block Editor loads, displaying the A-DOOR-36IN (A-DOOR-0915)
block you just created (see Figure 7.6).

   Because the objects, in this case the door and swing, used to create
the A-DOOR-36IN (A-DOOR-0915) block were drawn on the A-DOOR

layer, the objects within the block are also on that layer. As discussed earlier, the preferred practice is to define blocks such as this one on layer 0 so they're easier to manage.

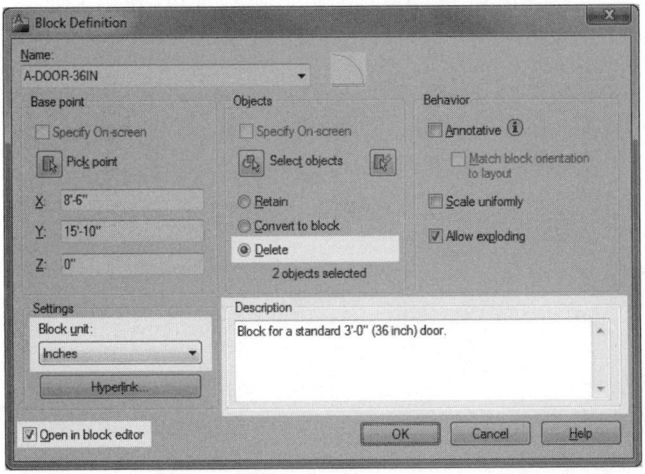

FIGURE 7.5 Defining the A-DOOR-36IN (A-DOOR-0915) settings within the Block Definition dialog box

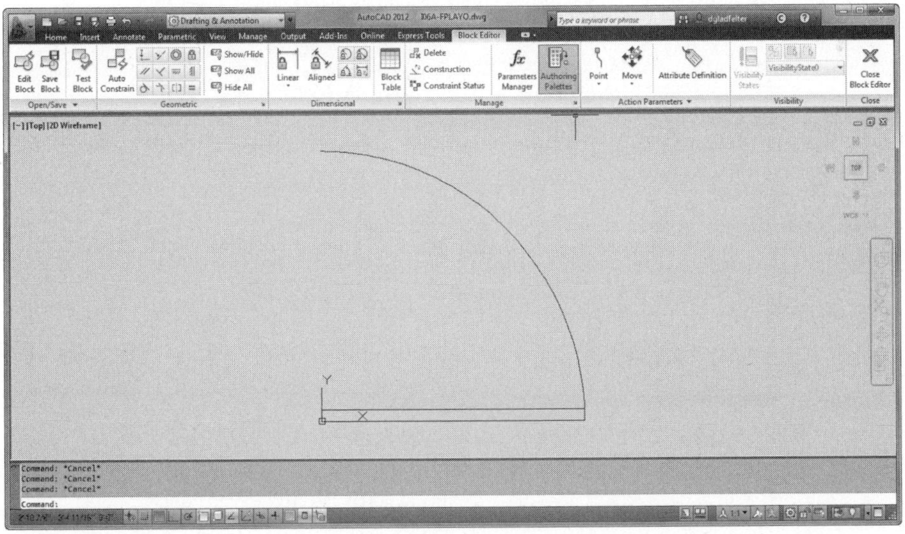

FIGURE 7.6 The Block Editor displaying the A-DOOR-36IN (A-DOOR-0915) block

11. Select the door and swing inside the Block Editor, and change its layer to layer 0 by using the Layer drop-down on the Home tab ➢ Layers panel (see Figure 7.7).

12. Click the Close Block Editor button found on the contextual Close panel appended to the end of any Ribbon tab.

13. If prompted, choose Save The Changes To A-DOOR-36IN (A-DOOR-0915) from the Block – Changes Not Saved dialog box, as shown in Figure 7.8.

14. Save your drawing as `I07-01-DoorBlock.dwg` (`M07-01-DoorBlock.dwg`) by choosing Application menu ➢ Save As ➢ AutoCAD Drawing.

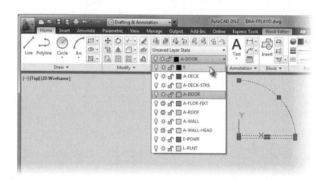

FIGURE 7.7 Changing the door's layer inside the Block Editor

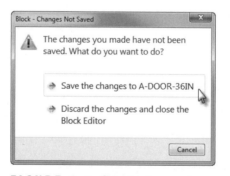

FIGURE 7.8 Choosing to save changes
from the Block – Changes Not Saved dialog box

You have now created a block definition called A-DOOR-36IN (A-DOOR-0915). Block definitions are stored electronically with the drawing file. You need to insert the A-DOOR-36IN (A-DOOR-0915) block (known formally as a *block reference*) into the back door opening to replace the door and swing that were just deleted when the block was created.

Inserting the Door Block

You'll use the INSERT command to place the A-DOOR-36IN (A-DOOR-0915) block back into the drawing.

1. Make sure I07-01-DoorBlock.dwg (M07-01-DoorBlock.dwg) is open, and set the A-DOOR layer as the current layer.

2. Click the Insert button found on the Insert tab ➢ Block panel.
   This opens the Insert dialog box, where you will choose the block you would like to insert into your drawing.

3. From the Insert dialog box, choose the A-DOOR-36IN (A-DOOR-0915) block by using the Name drop-down list found at the top of the dialog box.
   A preview of the block appears in the upper-right corner (see Figure 7.9). Below the Name list are three groups with the Specify On-Screen option. These are used for the insertion procedure.

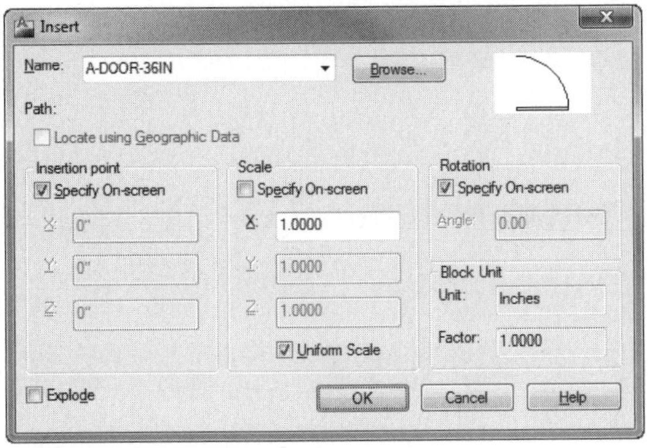

FIGURE 7.9 The Insert dialog box

4. With the A-DOOR-36IN (A-DOOR-0915) block specified, choose the following settings within the Insert dialog box:

   a. Under the Insertion Point group, check the Specify On-Screen option.

   b. Under the Scale group, uncheck the Specify On-Screen option.

   c. Under the Rotation group, check the Specify On-Screen option.

   d. Make sure the Explode check box in the lower-left corner is unchecked. Explode disassembles the block into its component parts upon insertion into the drawing.

5. Click OK to return to your drawing. The A-DOOR-36IN (A-DOOR-0915) block is now attached to the cursor, with the hinge point coinciding with the intersection of the crosshairs (see Figure 7.10).

   The command window reads Specify insertion point or [Basepoint/Scale/X/Y/Z/Rotate]:.

6. With the Endpoint osnap running, move the cursor toward the right end of the lower jamb line in the back door opening.

7. When the Endpoint marker appears at the jamb line's lower-right endpoint, click.

   The A-DOOR-036IN (A-DOOR-0915) block is no longer attached to the cursor, and its insertion point has been placed at the right end of the lower jamb line. The block now rotates as you move the cursor (see the left of Figure 7.11).

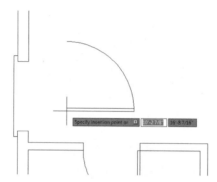

FIGURE 7.10 The A-DOOR-36IN (A-DOOR-0915) block attached to the cursor

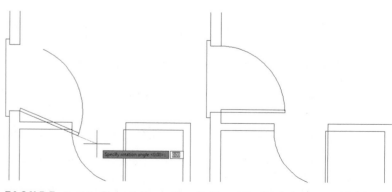

FIGURE 7.11 The rotation option (left) and the final placement (right)

8. At the `Specify rotation angle <0.00>:` prompt, press ↵ again to accept the default angle of 0°.

   The A-DOOR-36IN (A-DOOR-0915) block properly appears in the drawing (see the right of Figure 7.11).

9. Save your drawing as **I07-02-BlockInsert.dwg** (**M07-02-Block Insert.dwg**) by choosing Application menu ➤ Save As ➤ AutoCAD Drawing.

Each time a block is inserted, you can specify the following on the screen or in the Insert dialog box:

▶ The location of the insertion point of the block

▶ The X and Y scale factors

▶ The Z scale factor in the dialog box (used for 3D drawings, in AutoCAD only)

▶ The rotation angle

As you insert blocks, you can stretch or flip them horizontally by specifying a negative X scale factor, or vertically by specifying a negative Y scale factor—or you can rotate them from their original orientations. Because you created the A-DOOR-36IN (A-DOOR-0915) block from the door and swing that occupied the back door opening, and the size was the same, inserting this block back into the back door opening required no rotation, so you followed the defaults. You can insert the same block into the back door opening and flip the door horizontally by flipping the Y scale factor. This technique has been largely superseded by the use of dynamic blocks, discussed later in this chapter and in Chapter 9, "Using Dynamic Blocks and Tables," so I don't demonstrate it in this book.

> ◀
>
> Nothing has changed about the geometry of the door, but it's now a different kind of object. It was a rectangle and an arc; now it's a *block reference* comprising a rectangle and an arc.

Doors are traditionally sorted into four categories, depending on which side the hinges and doorknob are on and which way the door swings open. To be able to use one door block for all openings of the same size, you need to know the following:

▶ How the door and swing in the block are oriented

▶ Where the hinge point is to be in the next opening

▶ How the block has to be flipped and/or rotated during the insertion process to fit properly in the next doorway opening

Blocking and Inserting the Interior Door

Because the interior door is smaller, you need to make a new block for it. You could insert the A-DOOR-36IN (A-DOOR-0915) block with a 5/6 (762/915) scale factor, but this would also reduce the door thickness by the same factor, and you don't want that.

On the other hand, for consistency, it's a good idea to orient all door blocks the same way, and the bathroom door is turned relative to the A-DOOR-36IN (A-DOOR-0915) block. You'll move and rotate the bathroom door and its swing to orient it like the back door:

1. Make sure I07-02-BlockInsert.dwg (M07-02-BlockInsert.dwg) is open.

> After you finish the swinging doors, I'll go into some detail about AutoCAD's dynamic block, which you can use for all swinging doors.

2. Use Zoom Window to define a window that encloses the bathroom door. The view changes to a close-up of the area enclosed in your window (see Figure 7.12).

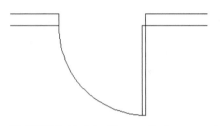

FIGURE 7.12 The result of a zoom window

3. Repeat a procedure similar to the one you used to make a block out of the back door and swing to make a block out of the bathroom door and swing. Here is a summary of the steps:

   a. Start the BLOCK command. (Click the Create Block button on the Home tab ➤ Block Definition panel.)

   b. In the dialog box, type **A-DOOR-30IN (A-DOOR-0762)** to name the new block. Don't press ↵.

   c. Click the Pick Point button, and pick the hinge point of the bathroom door.

   d. Click the Select Objects button, and pick the door and swing. Then press ↵.

   e. In the Objects area, make sure the Delete radio button is selected.

   f. Make sure the Block Unit option is correct and add a description.

   g. Select the Open In Block Editor check box, and then click OK. The door and swing disappear, and the Block Editor will open to display the block you just created.

4. Use the Layer drop-down on the Home tab ➢ Layers panel to change the layer of the door and swing to layer 0 from within the Block Editor. After changing the layer, click Close Block Editor, being sure to save changes.

5. Insert the A-DOOR-30IN (A-DOOR-0762) block in the bathroom doorway opening. Follow the steps carefully. Here's a summary:

   a. Start the INSERT command.

   b. Open the Name drop-down list, select A-DOOR-30IN (A-DOOR-0762), and then click OK.

   c. Pick the bottom end of the right jamb line.

   d. Accept the scale factors of 1 and the default 0 for the rotation.

N O T E   If all your doors are at 90° angles, you can turn on Ortho mode to speed up the rotation process. With Ortho active, wherever you move the cursor at the `Specify rotation angle <0.00>:` prompt, the rotations are restricted to 90° increments.

6. Use the Zoom Extents tool to show all of the cabin in the drawing area (see Figure 7.13).

7. Save your drawing as `I07-03-InteriorDoor.dwg` (`M07-03-Interior Door.dwg`).

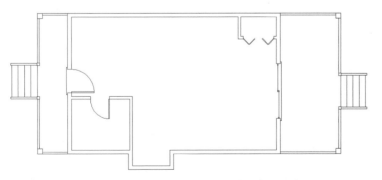

FIGURE 7.13 The floor plan with all swinging doors converted into blocks

T I P   If you have trouble anticipating how a block such as the door block needs to be flipped or rotated during insertion, don't worry about it; just be sure to locate the insertion point accurately in the drawing. Then, after the block is inserted, you can flip or turn it by using the MIRROR and ROTATE commands.

This view looks the same as the view you started with at the beginning of this chapter (see Figure 7.2). Blocks look the same as other objects, and you can't detect them by sight. They're useful because you can use them over and over again in a drawing or in many drawings, and because the block is a combination of two or more (and sometimes many more) objects represented as a single object. Your next task is to learn how to detect a block, but first, I'll discuss AutoCAD's dynamic block feature.

Using Dynamic Blocks

Dynamic blocks are blocks whose appearance can be changed in a variety of ways, depending on how they are set up. Any block can be transformed into a dynamic block, and AutoCAD offers several sample dynamic blocks that have already been set up. Take a door block, for example. By adding extra parameters and controls to the block, you could use a single dynamic block for openings in a variety of preset sizes. The arc size would change, but the thickness of the door would remain the same. After you insert a dynamic block, click it. As shown in Figure 7.14, light blue arrows (grips) appear at opposite sides of the opening to indicate that these are adjustable parameters. This is just an example and not steps for you to follow at this time. You will have a chance to work with dynamic blocks in Chapter 9.

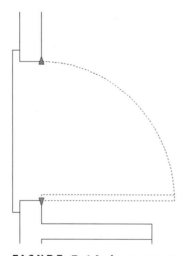

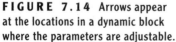

FIGURE 7.14 Arrows appear at the locations in a dynamic block where the parameters are adjustable.

THE FATE OF OBJECTS USED TO MAKE A BLOCK

The three radio buttons in the Objects group of the Block Definition dialog box represent the options you have for objects transformed into a block:

Retain   The objects remain unblocked. Click this if you want to make several similar blocks from the same set of objects.

Convert To Block   The objects become the block reference. Click this if the first use of the block has geometry identical to that of the set of objects it's replacing.

Delete   The objects are automatically erased after the block has been defined. Click this if the first use of the block will be at a different scale, orientation, or location from the set of objects it's replacing.

When you click the arrow at the end of the door swing arc, the dynamics begin and markers appear below the opening (see Figure 7.15), indicating the preset sizes to which the door and swing can be changed. In this example, you can use the door for openings from 2'-0" to 3'-6", at 6" intervals. (The tooltip shows where the cursor is, not the door size.)

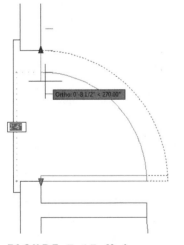

FIGURE 7.15 Markers appear at the increments where the door's swing can be adjusted.

Once you set a new size, the door and swing take on that size, as shown in Figure 7.16, whereas the door thickness remains the same. Now you can move this door to a smaller opening.

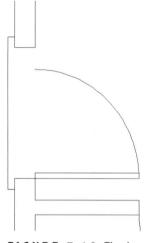

FIGURE 7.16 The dynamic door block with a smaller door and swing

Later in this chapter, when I introduce *palettes*, I'll show you where to find AutoCAD's sample dynamic blocks. For instructions on creating and using dynamic blocks, see Chapter 9.

Understanding and Using Groups

NEW   Another way you can make several objects act as one is to use the GROUP command. *Groups* differ from *blocks* in that they do not replace separate objects with a single definition but instead associate several objects by name so they react as if they were a single object. This feature has been enhanced in AutoCAD 2012.

Selecting one member object from the group selects all the members. Unlike objects in a block, members of a group can be added or removed, and you can toggle the group to allow the individual members to be selected. Use groups when you know the association between the objects is not permanent, and use blocks when it might be. The procedure for creating a group is as follows:

> **Some similar programs use the term *named selection set* to represent what AutoCAD calls a group.**

1. Make sure I07-03-InteriorDoor.dwg (M07-03-InteriorDoor.dwg) is open.

2. Start the **GROUP** command by clicking the Group button on the Home tab ➤ Groups panel.

3. Select the four rectangles that compose the closet door, as shown in Figure 7.17. Do not press ↵ yet.

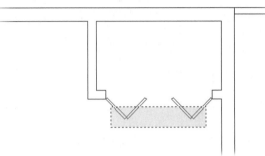

FIGURE 7.17 Selecting the closet door

4. With the closet door selected, enter **N**↵ at the command line to specify a name for your group.

5. At the Enter a group name: prompt, name your group **CLOSETDOOR**. Press ↵ to define the group name.

The command line confirms the group creation, and reads Group "CLOSETDOOR" has been created.

6. Select any one of the four rectangles that define the closet door.

Although you selected only one door panel, all four door panels highlight, and a bounding box defining the extents of your CLOSETDOOR group displays along with a single grip at the group's *centroid* (see Figure 7.18).

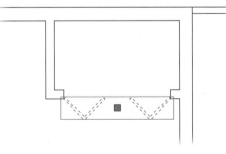

FIGURE 7.18 The CLOSETDOOR group in a selected state with bounding box and centroid grip

7. Click the Group Selection On/Off button on the Home tab ➤ Groups panel to temporarily turn off group selection.

8. Select any one of the four door panels that define the closet door.
Because Group Selection is currently disabled, only the panel you selected is highlighted (see Figure 7.19). In this state, you could modify the polyline defining the door panel you selected as if it were an ungrouped entity.

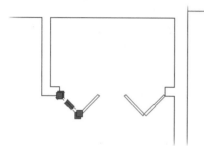

FIGURE 7.19 Single object within the CLOSETDOOR group selected with Group Selection turned Off

Groups are oftentimes utilized as a temporary drafting tool. As such, to ensure that your AutoCAD drawings remain uncluttered and performing at their best, you'll want to dispose of unneeded groups when you're finished with them.

9. Click the Group Selection On/Off button once again, this time to re-enable Group Selection. The Group Selection On/Off icon should display with a blue background.

10. Select any one of the four door panels to select the CLOSETDOOR group.

11. Click the Ungroup button on the Home tab ➤ Groups panel.
The CLOSETDOOR group is discarded, and the command window reads Group CLOSETDOOR exploded.

While limited in the number of creation, editing, and management tools, AutoCAD has included a Groups feature for many releases. Despite these limitations, the Group object itself is the same in AutoCAD 2012 as it was in earlier versions, making it possible to freely exchange drawings with groups between all recent AutoCAD versions.

Finding Blocks in a Drawing

You can detect blocks in a drawing in at least three ways: by using grips, by using the LIST command, and by looking at the Properties palette.

Using Grips to Detect a Block

Grips appear on objects that are selected when no command is started. When an object that isn't a block is selected, grips appear at strategic places, such as endpoints, midpoints, and center points. But if you select a block, by default only one grip appears, and it's always located at the block's insertion point. Because of this, clicking an object when no command is started is a quick way to see whether the object is a block:

1. Make sure I07-03-InteriorDoor.dwg (M07-03-InteriorDoor.dwg) is open.

2. Click one of the door swings.
   The door and swing turn into dashed lines, and a square blue grip appears at the hinge point, as shown in Figure 7.20.

3. Press Esc to clear the grip.

4. Expand the Application menu.

5. Click the Options button at the bottom of the menu to open the Options dialog box, and then click the Selection tab.

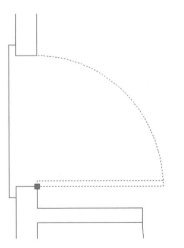

FIGURE 7.20 Blocks have only one grip, which is at the insertion point.

The Grips group is on the right side, and Show Grips Within Blocks is unchecked by default (see Figure 7.21). If this option is checked, grips appear on all objects in the block as if they weren't blocked when you click a block with no command running. Leave this setting unchecked.

You can also change the size of the grip and any of the three color states. By default, unselected grips are blue, grips that you click to select are red, and grips over which you pause the cursor are green.

6. Click OK or Cancel to close the Options dialog box.

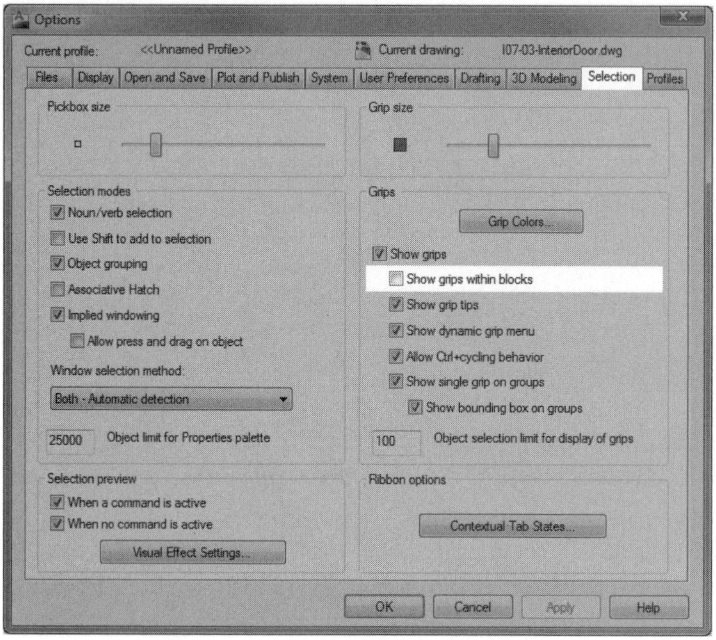

FIGURE 7.21 The Show Grips Within Blocks option

You'll look at grips in more detail in Chapter 12, "Dimensioning a Drawing." You might need to know more about a block than just whether something *is* one. If that is the case, you'll need to use the LIST command.

Using the List Command to Detect a Block

Much like the Properties palette, the LIST command can be used to gather information about a selected object. Although both are effective tools for reporting information about objects in a drawing, the LIST command only displays information. Unlike in the Properties palette, you cannot make changes to properties such as the layer. Despite this limitation, many users like the lightweight and concise nature of the LIST command, and prefer it to the Properties palette. The following exercise demonstrates how to use the LIST command to learn more about a block:

1. Continue using I07-03-InteriorDoor.dwg (M07-03-InteriorDoor.dwg), or open it if it's not already open.

2. Click the List button from the Home tab ➤ expanded Properties panel, or enter **LI**↵ at the Command: prompt.

3. Click the back door block, and then press ↵.

   The AutoCAD text window temporarily covers the drawing area (see Figure 7.22). In the text window, you can see the words BLOCK REFERENCE Layer: "A-DOOR", followed by 12 lines of text. These 13 lines describe the block you selected.

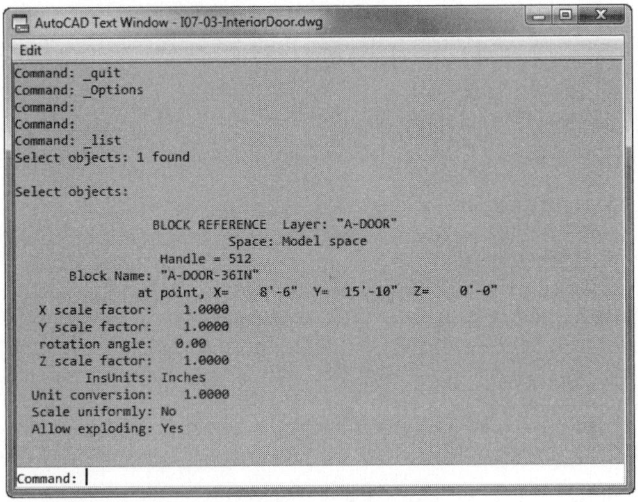

FIGURE 7.22 The AutoCAD text window

The information stored in the text window includes the following:

▶ What the object is (block reference)

▶ The layer the object is on (A-DOOR layer)

▶ The name of the block (A-DOOR-36IN)

▶ The coordinates of the insertion point in the drawing

▶ The X, Y, and Z scale factors

▶ The rotation angle

4. Press F2 to close the AutoCAD text window.

5. Right-click, and choose Repeat LIST from the context menu.

6. At the Select objects: prompt, select each of the lines that make up the back staircase.

7. Click one of the wall lines and then press ↵.

T I P   The AutoCAD text window isn't exclusively for use with the LIST command. Instead, it is a constantly scrolling history of the command prompt. The F2 key acts as a toggle to turn the window on and off. You can even copy information from all but the bottom line for use inside or outside AutoCAD. The text window displays only one page of information at a time and then pauses while the Press ENTER to continue: prompt appears at the command line. Press ↵ to continue. If you need to see information that has scrolled off the window, use the scroll bar on the right side or roll the mouse wheel to bring the information back into view.

The text window appears again, and you can see information about the stair lines that you selected.

If the last line reads Press ENTER to continue:, the amount of information is too large for the text window.

8. Press ↵ to display the remaining information.

9. Press F2 several times to switch back and forth between the text window and the drawing, or move the text window so that you can see the command line.

Notice that the last two or three lines in the text window appear in the command window at the bottom of the drawing (see Figure 7.23), depending on the size of your command window.

10. Press F2 to close the text window.

Using the Properties Palette to Examine a Block

In Chapter 6, you used the Properties palette to change the individual linetype scale for the roof objects. It can also be a tool for investigating objects in your drawing. When the Properties palette is open and only one object is selected, the palette displays data specific to the selected object. If multiple objects are selected, it shows only the data shared by those objects.

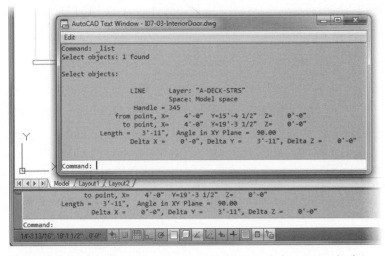

FIGURE 7.23 The bottom few lines of the text window appear in the command window as well.

Given the contextual nature of the Properties palette, it's important to note this behavior. As an example, information such as the name of a block will display only when one or more of that same block is selected. By contrast, selecting both a block and a line will display only the properties both objects share (such as layer), omitting differences (such as block name).

1. Continue using I07-03-InteriorDoor.dwg (M07-03-InteriorDoor .dwg), or open it if it's not already open.

2. Select one of the door blocks.

3. Click the Properties button on the View tab ➢ Palettes panel of the Ribbon. Alternatively, you can right-click and choose Properties from the context menu, or press Ctrl+1.

   The Properties palette opens.

   The data displayed on the palette is similar to that displayed when you used the LIST command, but it's in a slightly different form (see Figure 7.24). At the top of the dialog box, a drop-down list displays the type of object selected—in this case, a block reference. The fields that are white signify items that you can change directly in the palette, and items that are grayed out cannot be changed. You can't change any values in the AutoCAD text window.

4. Close the Properties palette by clicking the X in the upper-left or upper-right corner. Then press Esc to deselect the door block.

Block insertion means the same thing as block reference, and both are casually called blocks.

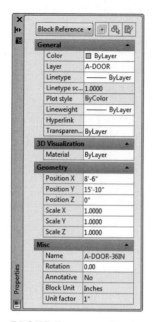

FIGURE 7.24 The Properties palette with a door block selected

 T I P   The X you click to close the Properties palette is in the upper-left or upper-right corner of the palette if it's floating and in the upper-right corner if it's docked.

If you're ever working on a drawing that someone else created, these tools for finding out about objects will be invaluable. The next exercise on working with blocks involves placing windows in the walls of the cabin.

Creating a Window Block

You can create all the windows in the cabin floor plan from one block, even though the windows are four different sizes (see Figure 7.25). You'll create a window block and then go from room to room to insert the block into the walls:

1. Continue using I07-03-InteriorDoor.dwg (M07-03-InteriorDoor .dwg), or open it if it's not already open.

2. Make layer 0 the current layer.

3. Right-click the Object Snap button on the status bar and click the Midpoint and Perpendicular osnaps, if necessary, to set them as running osnaps, and then deselect Intersection.

The Osnap menu should look similar to Figure 7.26. Turn on the Object Snap option in the status bar.

4. Using a zoom window, zoom in to a horizontal section of wall where there are no jamb lines or intersections with other walls (see Figure 7.27).

Because the widths of the windows in the cabin are multiples of 12" (305 mm), you can insert a block made from a 12" (305 mm) wide window for each window, and you can apply an X scale factor to the block to make it the right width. The first step is to draw a 12" (305 mm) wide window inside the wall lines.

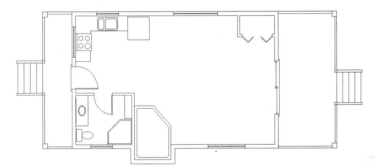

FIGURE 7.25 The cabin windows in the floor plan

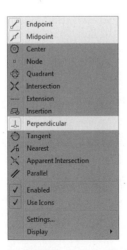

FIGURE 7.26 The Osnap menu

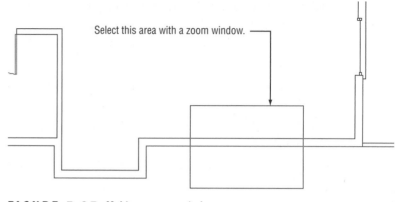

Select this area with a zoom window.

FIGURE 7.27 Making a zoom window

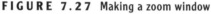

5. Start the LINE command, and then click the Nearest Osnap button on the Shift+right-click menu or enter **NEA↵**.

The Nearest osnap will allow you to start a line on one of the wall lines; it snaps the cursor to any part of any object under the cursor and guarantees that the objects form an intersection but do not cross.

> Use the Nearest Osnap button when you want to locate a point somewhere on an object but aren't concerned exactly where on the object the point is located.

6. Move the cursor to the upper wall line, a little to the left of the center of the screen and, with the hourglass-shaped marker displayed as shown in Figure 7.28, click.

A line begins on the upper wall line.

Nearest

FIGURE 7.28 Starting the line by using the Nearest osnap

7. Move the cursor to the lower wall line. The Perpendicular marker appears directly below the point you previously picked. When it's displayed, click.

The line is drawn between the wall lines, as shown in Figure 7.29. Press ↵ to end the LINE command.

8. Start the OFFSET command, and set the offset distance to **12 (305)**.

9. Pick the line you just drew, and then pick a point to the right of that line. The line is offset 12″ (305 mm) to the right. Press ↵ to end the OFFSET command.

10. Start the LINE command again to draw a line between the midpoint of the line you first drew and the midpoint, or, perpendicular to the line that was just offset.

    After pressing ↵ to end the LINE command, your drawing should look like Figure 7.30.

11. Save your drawing as **I07-04-WindowBlock.dwg** (**M07-04-WindowBlock .dwg**) by choosing Application menu ➢ Save As ➢ AutoCAD Drawing.

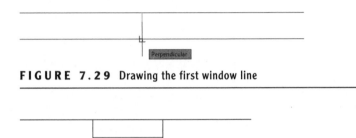

FIGURE 7.29 Drawing the first window line

FIGURE 7.30 Completed lines for the window block

The three lines you've drawn will make up a window block. They represent the two jamb lines and the glass (usually called *glazing*). By varying the X scale factor from 2 to 6, you can create windows 2′ (610 mm), 3′ (915 mm), 4′ (1220 mm), 5′ (1525 mm), and 6′ (1830 mm) wide. This is a single-line representation, with no double lines to indicate the frames, so for scaling the blocks, there is no thickness issue as there was with the doors.

Before you create the block, you need to decide the best place for the insertion point. For the doors, you chose the hinge point because you always know where it will be in the drawing. Locating a similar strategic point for the window is a little more difficult but certainly possible.

You know the insertion point shouldn't be on the horizontal line representing the glazing, because the insertion point will always rest in the middle of the wall. There is no guideline in the drawing for the middle of wall, and doing so would require a temporary tracking point every time a window is inserted. Windows are usually dimensioned to the midpoint of the glazing line rather than to either jamb line, so you don't want the insertion point to be at the endpoint of a jamb line. The insertion point needs to be positioned on a wall line but also lined up with the midpoint of the glazing line.

To locate this point, you'll use an object snap called Mid Between 2 Points. As the name suggests, the *M2P osnap*, as it's commonly called, snaps to a point midway between two other points you select. Follow these steps to set the base point for the window block along the outside wall line and midway between the window's edges:

1. Make sure I07-04-WindowBlock.dwg (M07-04-WindowBlock.dwg) is open.

2. Start the BLOCK command by clicking the Create Block button on the Home tab ➤ Block panel.

3. In the Block Definition dialog box, enter **A-GLAZ** for the block name, and then click the Pick Point button.

4. Back in the drawing, activate the Mid Between 2 Points option found on the Shift+right-click context menu. Alternatively you can enter M2P↵ at the command line.

   The Mid Between 2 Points object snap is rather unique in that it is generally used in conjunction with other osnaps, and is not found on the Object Snap toolbar. In this case, you want to find the midpoint between two endpoints.

5. With the Endpoint osnap running, move the cursor to the lower end of the left window jamb (see Figure 7.31) and click when the Endpoint marker appears.

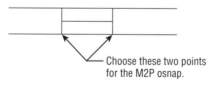

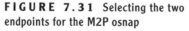

Choose these two points for the M2P osnap.

FIGURE 7.31 Selecting the two endpoints for the M2P osnap

6. Click the lower end of the right jamb to define the insertion point midway between the two endpoints that you picked.

As mentioned earlier, in the architectural discipline, windows are often referred to as *glazing*. The U.S. National CAD Standard also uses the term, making the NCS code for windows GLAZ.

7. In the Block Definition dialog box, click the Select Objects button.

8. Back in the drawing, select the two jamb lines and the glazing line, and then press ↵.

9. Back in the dialog box, make sure of the following:

   ▶ The Open In Block Editor check box at the bottom is unchecked.

   ▶ The Delete radio button is selected.

   ▶ Units is set to Inches (Millimeters).

10. Click OK.

   The A-GLAZ block has been defined, and the 12″ (305 mm) window has been erased.

11. Use Zoom Previous to zoom out to a view of the whole floor plan.

12. Save your drawing as `I07-05-WindowDefinition.dwg` (`M07-05 -WindowDefinition.dwg`).

This completes the definition of the block that will represent the windows. The next task is to insert the A-GLAZ block where the windows will be located and scale them properly.

Inserting the Window Block

Several factors come into play when you're deciding where to locate windows in a floor plan:

   ▶ The structure of the building

   ▶ The appearance of windows from outside the building

   ▶ The appearance of windows from inside a room

   ▶ The location of fixtures that might interfere with placement

   ▶ The sun angle and climate considerations

For this exercise, you'll work on the windows for each room, starting with the kitchen, and make a total of five windows at either 3′-0″, 4′-0″, 5′-0″, or 6′-0″ wide (see Figure 7.32).

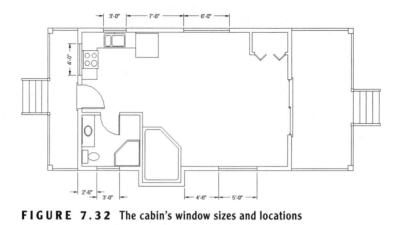

FIGURE 7.32 The cabin's window sizes and locations

Rotating a Block during Insertion

As you can see in Figure 7.32, the kitchen has windows on two walls: one 4'-0" (1220 mm) window centered over the stove in the back wall and one 3'-0" (915 mm) window centered over the sink in the top wall. You'll make the 4' (1220 mm) window first:

1. Make sure I07-05-WindowDefinition.dwg (M07-05-Window Definition.dwg) is open.

2. Thaw the A-FLOR-FIXT layer; you'll need to see the sink and stove to place the windows properly.

3. Zoom in to a view of the kitchen so you can see both walls, as shown in Figure 7.33.

4. Click the Polar Tracking button on the status bar to turn on Polar Tracking.

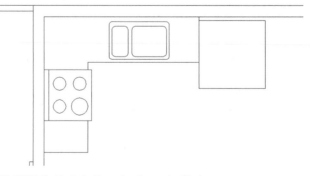

FIGURE 7.33 Zooming in to the kitchen

Polar Tracking, Object Snap, Object Snap Tracking, and Dynamic Input should now be in their On positions.

5. Create a new layer by clicking the Layer Properties button and then clicking the New Layer button in the Layer Properties Manager dialog box.

   The new Layer1 layer appears and is highlighted. Enter **A-GLAZ**⏎ to rename the layer.

6. Click the Color swatch in the A-GLAZ row to open the Select Color dialog box, with the white swatch highlighted and *white* listed in the Color text box.

7. Enter 31⏎ to change the color to a bright orange. The Select Color dialog box closes.

8. With A-GLAZ still highlighted in the Layer Properties Manager dialog box, click the Set Current button, or double-click the name of the layer, to make the A-GLAZ layer current.

9. Close or autohide the Layer Properties Manager.

10. Start the INSERT command (click the Insert button in the Block panel).

11. Open the Name drop-down list in the Insert dialog box.

12. In the list of blocks, click A-GLAZ. Be sure all three Specify On-Screen check boxes are selected, and then click OK.

    In your drawing, the 12″ (305 mm) window block is attached to the cursor at the insertion point (see Figure 7.34).

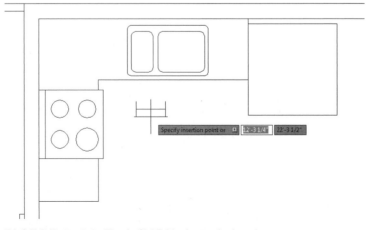

FIGURE 7.34 The A-GLAZ block attached to the cursor

Note that it's still in the same horizontal orientation that it was in when you defined the block. To fit it into the left wall, you'll need to rotate it as you insert it.

13. Move the cursor along the inside wall line near the midpoint of the stove.

The stove line overlaps the wall line, and the midpoints of each are close together.

14. Make sure the cursor is over the stove's midpoint (the lower of the two, as shown at the left of Figure 7.35), and then click.

15. You're prompted for an X scale factor. This is a 4′-0″ (1220 mm) window, so enter **4.⌐**.

16. For the Y scale factor, enter **1.⌐**.

The window block is now 4′-0″ (1220 mm), and you are prompted for the rotation angle.

17. From the Specify rotation angle prompt, move the cursor so that it's directly above the insertion point.

The Polar Tracking lines and tooltip appear (see the middle image of Figure 7.35). They show you how the window will be positioned if the rotation stays at 90°. The window fits nicely into the wall here.

> The Y scale factor will be 1 for all the A-GLAZ blocks because all walls that have windows are 6″ wide—the same width as the A-GLAZ block.

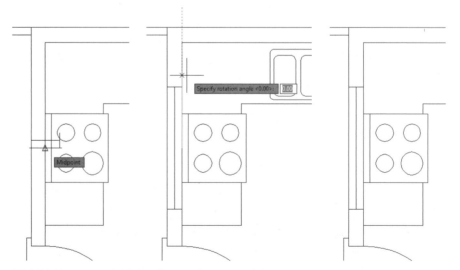

FIGURE 7.35 Selecting the stove's midpoint as the insertion point (left), rotating the A-GLAZ block 90° (middle), and the final position (right)

18. With the tracking line and tooltip visible, click.

    The A-GLAZ block appears in the left wall. The INSERT block command ends (see the right of Figure 7.36).

19. Save this drawing as **I07-06-BlockRotate.dwg** (**M07-06-Block Rotate.dwg**).

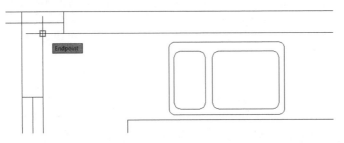

FIGURE 7.36 Setting the first tracking point to locate the window block

Using Snap Tracking to Set the Insertion Point

The window over the sink is centered on the sink, but the sink line doesn't overlap the wall as did the stove line. You'll use the same snap tracking procedure that you used in Chapter 5, "Developing Drawing Strategies: Part 2," to set the window block's insertion point without the need to draw extraneous geometry. Refer to Figure 7.32, shown earlier, as a reference as you follow the procedure here:

1. Make sure I07-06-BlockRotate.dwg (M07-06-BlockRotate.dwg) is open.

2. Use the Pan and Zoom tools to get a better view of the top wall of the cabin.

    You want to create one 3′-0″ (915 mm) window, centered over the sink. Be sure the Endpoint and Midpoint osnaps are running, and turn off the Perpendicular osnap.

3. Start the INSERT command.

4. Ensure that A-GLAZ is in the Name drop-down list, and check that all Specify On-Screen check boxes are marked. Click OK.

5. At the Specify insertion point: prompt, position the crosshair cursor over the intersection of the inside wall lines in the top-left corner of the cabin, as shown in Figure 7.36 in the previous section.

6. When the temporary track point appears inside the Endpoint marker, move the cursor, without clicking, over the Midpoint marker for the topmost line of the sink.

7. When the temporary track point appears inside the Midpoint marker, move the cursor directly above that point to the intersection of the two track points. You have set, or *acquired*, two temporary tracking points without using the Temporary Tracking Point osnap.

T I P   When Object Snap Tracking is turned on and the plus sign (+) appears at the Object Snap marker, a tracking point has been acquired. It remains acquired until you place the cursor directly on the object snap symbol a second time or until that part of the command is done.

When the crosshair reaches a point directly above the first tracking point, a vertical tracking line appears, and the tooltip identifies the intersection of the two tracking lines as Endpoint: <0.00°, Midpoint: <90.00° (see Figure 7.37).

8. When you see this tooltip, click. This places the insertion point on the inside wall line, centered over the sink.

9. At the X scale factor prompt, enter 3⏎.

10. Then, at the Y scale factor prompt, enter 1⏎. Press ⏎ again to accept the default rotation angle of 0°.

   The 3'-0" (915 mm) window is inserted into the wall behind the sink. Your kitchen with the second window block inserted should look like Figure 7.38.

11. Save this drawing as I07-07-OsnapTracking.dwg (M07-07-Osnap Tracking.dwg).

As you can see, by using the Object Snap Tracking tool, you can quickly and precisely locate an insertion point even when a snappable feature doesn't exist.

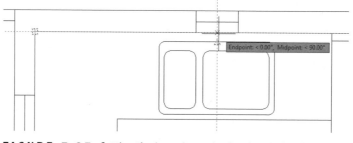

F I G U R E 7.37 Setting the insertion point for the window block

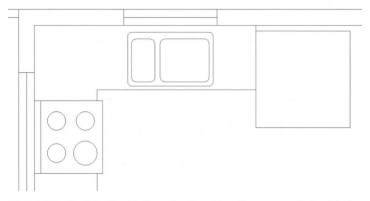

FIGURE 7.38 The kitchen after inserting the second window block

 T I P   When using Object Snap Tracking, you'll inevitably acquire a tracking point that you don't need or want. To remove it, place the crosshair cursor on it momentarily. The tracking point will disappear.

Changing a Block's Scale Factor by Using Object Properties

You've inserted two different-sized window blocks at two different rotations. Just three remain to be inserted: one in the bathroom and two in the living room. You'll copy the horizontal kitchen window into the living room and then use the Properties palette to change the block's scale, resulting in a 6′-0″ (1830 mm) window.

1. Make sure I07-07-OsnapTracking.dwg (M07-07-OsnapTracking.dwg) is open.

2. Pan and zoom to get a good view of the kitchen and the top of the living room.

    Referring back to Figure 7.32, you see that the windows are 7′-6″ (2286 mm) apart. Because the insertion points are centered horizontally in the blocks, the insertion points of the two windows are 12′-0″ (3659 mm) apart. You need to copy the 3′-0″ (915 mm) kitchen window 12′-0″ (3659 mm) to the right.

3. Select the 3′-0″ (915 mm) kitchen window and click the Copy tool from the Home tab ➤ Modify panel.

4. At the Specify base point: prompt, click anywhere in the drawing area.
    Clicking near the block that you are moving will keep everything visually compact.

5. Move the cursor directly to the right.

6. At the `Specify second point or <use first point as displacement>:` prompt, enter **12'⏎** (**3659⏎**), as shown in Figure 7.39, and press ⏎ again to terminate the COPY command.
The window is copied 12'-0" (3659 mm) to the right.

7. Select the new window block, right-click, and then choose Properties from the context menu to open the Properties palette.

8. In the Geometry rollout, locate the Scale X parameter and change its value to **6**, as shown in Figure 7.40.

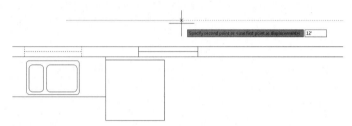

FIGURE 7.39 Copying the kitchen window 12' to the right

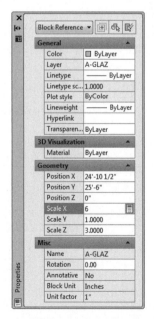

FIGURE 7.40 Change the block's X scale factor in the Properties palette.

9. The window in the living room is now 6′-0″ (1830 mm) wide. Close the Properties palette, and press Esc to deselect the new window.

10. Save this drawing as `I07-08-ObjectProperties.dwg` (`M07-08-Object Properties.dwg`).

As you've seen, you can change many of an object's parameters, including the scale factors for a block definition, by using the Properties palette.

Finishing the Windows

The last two windows to insert are both in the bottom wall, one in the living room and one in the bathroom. You'll use skills you've already developed to place them:

1. Make sure `I07-08-ObjectProperties.dwg` (`M07-08-ObjectProperties.dwg`) is open.

2. Use the Zoom and Pan tools to adjust your view of the drawing down to the bottom wall between the front wall and the hot tub.

This window is 5′-0″ (1525 mm) wide, and its insertion point is 7′-0″ (2134 mm) from the pop-out for the hot tub (4′-6″ + 2′-6″, or 1372 mm + 762 mm).

3. Place the cursor over the intersection of the outside wall lines on the upper-right side of the pop-out, as shown in Figure 7.41.

4. Start the INSERT command, verify that A-GLAZ appears in the Name field, and click OK.

5. Move the cursor directly to the right and enter 7'↵ (2134↵).

The window is inserted 7′-0″ (2134 mm) to the right of the corner.

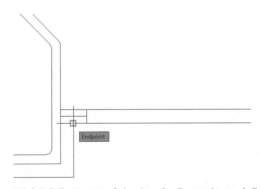

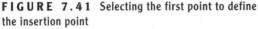

FIGURE 7.41 Selecting the first point to define the insertion point

6. Give the new block an X scale factor of **5**, a Y scale factor of **1**, and a rotation of 0″. The new window appears as shown in Figure 7.42.

   The final window to draw is the 3′-0″ (915 mm) window in the bathroom. The insertion point is located 4′-0″ (1220 mm) from the bottom-left outside corner of the cabin. To create this window, you'll copy the living room window that you just drew and then change the X scale factor by using the Properties palette.

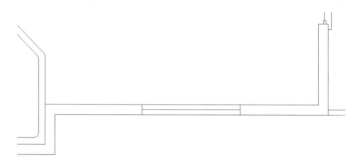

FIGURE 7.42 The new 5′-0″ (1525 mm) window in the living room

---

T I P   If you can't recall a typed-in command, you can enter the first letter or two of the command and then use the Tab key to cycle through all the AutoCAD commands that begin with the letters you entered. When the correct command appears at the command prompt, press Enter to activate it.

7. Select the 5′-0″ (1525 mm) window in the living room and start the COPY command.

8. At the Specify base point: prompt, hold down the Shift key and press the right mouse button to open the Object Snap context menu.

9. Click the Insert icon to activate the Insertion Point object snap and temporarily disable the running osnaps.

10. Place the cursor over the window block until the Insert marker appears (see Figure 7.43); then click to define the base point for the COPY command as the insertion point of the block.

11. At the Specify second point or <use first point as displacement>: prompt, pause the cursor over the bottom-left outside corner of the cabin to acquire a temporary track point.

12. Move the cursor directly to the right, and enter **4'␛** (**1220␛**), as shown in Figure 7.44.

   The window is copied to its new location 4'-0" (1220 mm) from the corner.

13. Press ␛ again to end the COPY command.

14. Select the new window and open the Properties palette.

15. Change the Scale X parameter to 3.

   The window resizes to 3'-0" (915 mm) wide, as shown in Figure 7.45.

16. Close the Properties palette and press Esc to end the COPY command.

T I P   In a cluttered area, you can enter NON␛ at any Select Point: or Select Objects: prompt to disable all running osnaps for the duration of a single pick.

---

17. Perform a Zoom Extents either by using the navigation bar or by double-clicking the middle button of your scroll wheel mouse.

   This changes the view to include all the visible lines, and the view fills the drawing area.

FIGURE 7.43 Snapping to the insertion point of the block

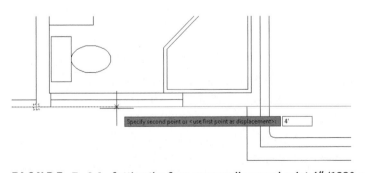
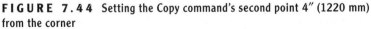

FIGURE 7.44 Setting the Copy command's second point 4" (1220 mm) from the corner

18. Use the scroll wheel to zoom out a little from the Extents view so that all objects are set in slightly from the edge of the drawing area.

Your drawing, with all the windows in place, should look like Figure 7.46.

19. Save this drawing as `I07-09-FinishingWindows.dwg` (`M07-09 -FinishingWindows.dwg`).

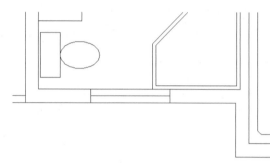

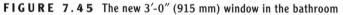

FIGURE 7.45 The new 3'-0" (915 mm) window in the bathroom

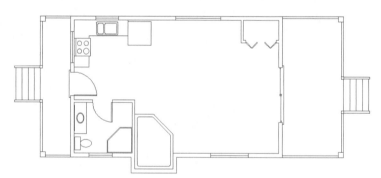

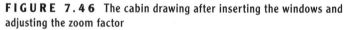

FIGURE 7.46 The cabin drawing after inserting the windows and adjusting the zoom factor

You have inserted five windows into the floor plan, each generated from the A-GLAZ block. You created the A-GLAZ block on layer 0 and then made the A-GLAZ layer current, so each window block reference took on the characteristics of the A-GLAZ layer when it was inserted.

You can disassociate the components of blocks by using the EXPLODE command. The tool is found in the Home tab ➤ Modify panel or on the bottom item on the Modify menu. Exploding a block has the effect of reducing the block to the objects that make it up. Exploding the A-GLAZ block reduces it to three lines, all on layer 0.

TIP All your windows are in walls 6″ (150 mm) thick, so the windows are all 6″ (150 mm) deep. But what if you want to put a window block in a 4″ (100 mm) wall between two interior rooms? You can still use the A-GLAZ block. During insertion, you change the Y scale factor to 2/3 to reflect the change in thickness of the wall.

Typically, when you choose to EXPLODE a block, you want the linework to retain the layer displayed in your drawing. Users of AutoCAD (not AutoCAD LT) have another command named BURST that does just that. You can find the BURST command and the Explode Attributes button on the Express Tools tab ➤ Blocks panel. Like the EXPLODE command, BURST reduces the A-GLAZ block into three lines, but they will retain the correct A-GLAZ layer.

Revising a Block

◄

You can also start the EXPLODE command by entering EXPLODE↵.

One of the biggest advantages to using blocks over manually drawing items such as doors and windows in your drawing is the ease with which blocks can be modified. Earlier you used the Block Editor as you were defining blocks. In this section, you'll use the Block Editor again, this time not to define a new block but to modify an existing one. More specifically, you'll modify the A-GLAZ (window) block and see how the changes you make are reflected throughout your drawing.

Let's say that the client who's building the cabin finds out that double glazing is required in all windows. You'll want the windows to show two lines for the glass. If you revise the A-GLAZ block definition, the changes you make in one block reference will be made in all six windows.

1. Make sure I07-09-FinishingWindows.dwg (M07-09-FinishingWindows.dwg) is open.

NOTE Using standard commands, you can MOVE, ROTATE, COPY, ERASE, SCALE, and EXPLODE blocks. All objects in a block are associated and behave as if they were one object.

2. Select the A-GLAZ block inserted over the stove, right-click to display the context menu, and select Block Editor, as shown in Figure 7.47.

    Alternatively, you can access the Block Editor from the Insert tab ➤ Block Definition panel ➤ Block Editor tool, or by entering **BEDIT**↵ at the command line.

    In the drawing area, the rest of the drawing disappears, the background turns gray, and the Block Editor tab and panels appear in the Ribbon.

Only the A-GLAZ block and the Block Authoring Palettes remain (see Figure 7.48). You are now in the Block Editor mode.

3. Use the OFFSET command to offset the glazing line 0.5″ (13 mm) up and down. Then erase the original horizontal line (see Figure 7.49). This window block now has double glazing.

4. On the Open/Save panel, click the Save Block button.

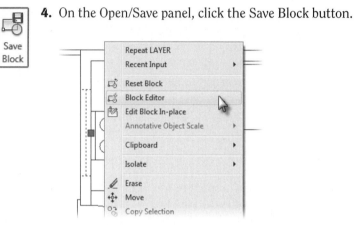

FIGURE 7.47 Accessing the Block Editor from the context menu

FIGURE 7.48 The drawing area and Ribbon in the Block Editor mode

5. In the Close panel, at the far-right end of the Ribbon, click the Close button.

> The Block Editor closes, and you are returned to the cabin drawing.

6. Use the Zoom Previous tool to view the entire drawing. All windows in the cabin now have double glazing.

7. Zoom in to a closer look at the kitchen in order to view some of the modified window block references (see Figure 7.50).

8. Use Zoom Previous to see a view of the entire floor plan.

9. Save this drawing as **I07A-FPLAYO.dwg** (**M07A-FPLAYO.dwg**).

If you click the Close button without saving the changes to the block, an AutoCAD warning window appears, allowing you to save the changes or exit the Block Editor without saving the changes.

FIGURE 7.49 The result of the modifications to the A-GLAZ block

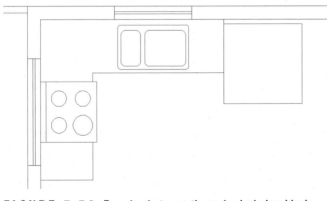

FIGURE 7.50 Zooming in to see the revised window blocks with double glazing

Sharing Information between Drawings

You can transfer most of the information in a drawing to another drawing. You can do so in several ways, depending on the kind of information that you need to transfer. You can drag blocks and lines from one open drawing to another when both drawings are visible on the screen. You can copy layers, blocks, and other named objects from a closed drawing into an open one by using the DesignCenter. I'll demonstrate these two features—and touch on a few others—as I finish this chapter. Note that these features don't contribute to our cabin project, so the drawing changes you make in the following sections are only temporary and won't be saved.

Dragging and Dropping between Two Open Drawings

In AutoCAD 2012, several drawings can be open at the same time, just like documents in a word processing program. You can control which one is visible, or you can tile two or more to be visible simultaneously. When more than one drawing is visible, you can drag objects from one drawing to another.

> *Named objects are, quite simply, AutoCAD objects with names, such as blocks and layers. Lines, circles, and arcs don't have individual names, so they aren't named objects.*

> *When you open the Application menu and then click the Open Drawings button, a list of the open drawings is displayed. To bring the file you want in front of the others, click it.*

> *The new drawing might be called* Drawing2.dwg *or* Drawing3.dwg. *This doesn't affect how the exercise works.*

1. With I07A-FPLAYO.dwg (M07A-FPLAYO.dwg) as the current drawing, click the New button on the Quick Access toolbar.

2. In the Select Template dialog box, click the arrow next to the Open button and then click the Open With No Template—Imperial (Metric) option. These actions open a blank drawing.

3. Click the Tile Vertically button from the View tab ➤ Windows panel.
   The new blank drawing (called Drawing#.dwg) appears alongside I07A-FPLAYO.dwg (M07A-FPLAYO.dwg), as shown in Figure 7.51.
   Each drawing has a title bar, but only one drawing can be active at a time. At this time, the blank drawing (probably named Drawing1) should be active. If it is, its title bar is dark blue or some other color, and the I07A-FPLAYO.dwg (M07A-FPLAYO.dwg) title bar is grayed out. If your I07A-FPLAYO.dwg (M07A-FPLAYO.dwg) drawing is active instead, click once in the blank drawing.

4. Open the Application menu, and then click Drawing Utilities ➤ Units. The Drawing Units dialog box opens.

5. Change the type of units in the Length group to Architectural (or Decimal if you are working in metric), and then click OK.

6. Click the I07A-FPLAYO.dwg (M07A-FPLAYO.dwg) drawing to make it active.

7. Perform a Zoom Extents, and then use the scroll wheel to zoom out a little.

8. Use the Layer drop-down list to make the A-WALL layer current, and then turn off the A-DECK-STRS, A-DOOR, A-FLOR-FIXT, and A-GLAZ layers.

    The walls (A-WALL) and decks (A-DECK) should be the only lines visible.

9. Use a selection window to select the cabin with its decks. Grips appear on all lines.

10. Place the cursor on one of the wall lines at a point where there are no grips, and then click and hold down the left mouse button and move the mouse.

    A copy of the selected cabin lines is attached to the mouse as if you had used the MOVE command (see Figure 7.52).

11. Drag the cursor across the drawing to the center of the blank drawing, and then release the mouse button.

    The blank drawing is now active and contains the lines for the walls and decks (see Figure 7.53).

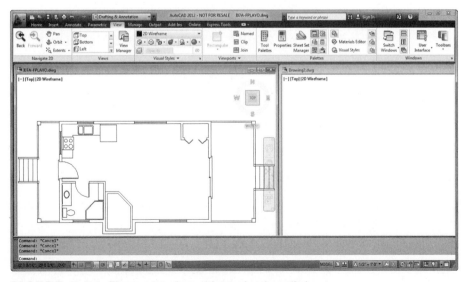

FIGURE 7.51 The user interface with two drawings tiled

12. Zoom out so that you can see the entire drawing.

13. Open the Layer drop-down list, and note that the new drawing (Drawing# .dwg in the example) now has the A-DECK and A-WALL layers.

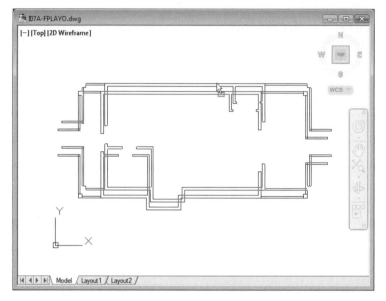

FIGURE 7.52 Dragging a selection of objects

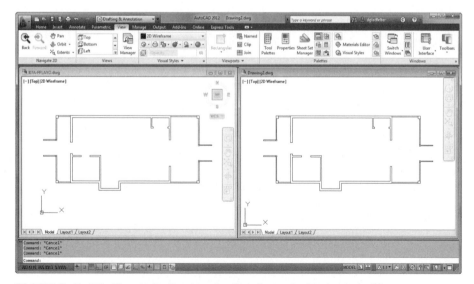

FIGURE 7.53 The result after dragging lines from one drawing to another

In this fashion, you can drag any visible objects from one drawing into another, including blocks. If you drag and drop a block, its definition is copied to the new drawing, along with all layers used by objects in the block. A shortcoming of this method is that you're simply inserting the objects into the other at an arbitrary coordinate. Since most plan sets are assembled so that the lower-left corner is at a certain coordinate (4′,8′ in our case), the usefulness of this procedure is limited.

There is a way around this limitation. If you drag with the right mouse button instead of the left, a context menu will appear, providing a few options for placing the objects in the receiving drawing. Among the options available from the context menu is Paste To Orig Coords. This option will still insert the selected objects into the new drawing, but instead of inserting them at an arbitrary point, will insert them in the same place they were located in the original drawing.

Copying Objects between Drawings

If you don't choose to have both open drawings visible at the same time, you can always use the Copy and Paste tools available in most Windows-based programs. Here's the general procedure:

1. Click the Maximize icon in the upper-right corner of the new drawing. The new drawing fills the screen.

2. Click the Switch Windows button from the View tab ➤ Windows panel. When the menu opens, notice at the bottom that the open drawings are displayed and the active one is checked (see Figure 7.54).

3. Click the I07A-FPLAYO.dwg (M07A-FPLAYO.dwg) drawing. It replaces the new drawing as the active drawing and fills the screen.

4. Turn on the layers you turned off previously. Leave the A-WALL-HEAD and A-ROOF layers frozen.

T I P Because the A-WALL-HEAD and A-ROOF layers are frozen, and the other layers that aren't visible at the moment are turned off, you can use the LAYON command. As its name implies, the LAYON command turns on every layer in a drawing. You can find the LAYON command on the Home tab ➤ expanded Layers panel ➤ Turn All Layers On tool.

---

5. Select the fixtures in the kitchen and bath from this drawing by using the selection tools you have learned, and then right-click and choose Clipboard ➤ Copy With Base Point from the context menu.
   You're prompted to specify a base point in the I07A-FPLAYO.dwg (M07A-FPLAYO.dwg) drawing.

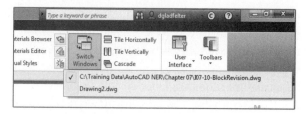

FIGURE 7.54 The Open Drawing menu with
`Drawing2.dwg` active

6. Click the upper-left corner of the building by using the Endpoint osnap, and press Esc to deselect the objects.

7. In the Window panel, click the Switch Windows button and then click `Drawing#.dwg` to make it active.

 T I P   You can also cycle through the open drawings by holding down the Ctrl key and then pressing the Tab key.

8. Right-click and choose Clipboard ➤ Paste from the context menu or press Ctrl+V.

9. Pick the upper-left corner of the building by using the Endpoint osnap. The fixtures are accurately positioned in the new drawing.

If you check the layers, you'll see that the new drawing now has an A-FLOR -FIXT layer, in addition to the A-WALL and A-DECK layers.

Using AutoCAD's DesignCenter

The DesignCenter is a tool for copying named objects (blocks, layers, text styles, and so on) to an opened drawing from an unopened one. You can't copy lines, circles, and other unnamed objects unless they are part of a block. You'll see how this works by bringing some layers and a block into your new drawing from `I07A-FPLAYO.dwg` (`M07A-FPLAYO.dwg`):

1. Make `I07A-FPLAYO.dwg` (`M07A-FPLAYO.dwg`) current, and then close it. Don't save changes.

2. Maximize the window for your new drawing if it isn't already maximized.

3. Open the DesignCenter from the Insert tab ➤ Content panel ➤ Design Center tool. Alternatively, you can also open the DesignCenter by pressing Ctrl+2, or entering **DC**⏎ at the command line.

The DesignCenter palette appears on the drawing area. It can be docked, floating, or if floating, hidden (see Figure 7.55). Your screen might not look exactly like the samples shown here. The tree diagram of file folders on the left might or might not be visible. Also, your DesignCenter might be wider or narrower.

4. Click the Tree View toggle button at the top of the DesignCenter (the fourth button from the right) a few times to close and open the file folder tree diagram.

You can resize the DesignCenter horizontally (and vertically as well, if it's floating), and you can resize the subpanels inside. If Auto-Hide is on, the DesignCenter hides behind the title bar until you put your cursor on it. Leave the tree view open.

5. Click the Load button in the upper-left corner of the DesignCenter palette to open the Load dialog box. Navigate to your `Training Data` folder and open it.

6. Highlight `I07A-FPLAYO.dwg` (`M07A-FPLAYO.dwg`), and click Open. The Load dialog box closes, and you are returned to your drawing.

Now the left side of the DesignCenter lists your drawings in the `Training Data` folder and `I07A-FPLAYO.dwg` (`M07A-FPLAYO.dwg`) is highlighted; the right side of the DesignCenter shows the types of objects in `I07A-FPLAYO.dwg` that are available to be copied into the current drawing—in this case, `Drawing3.dwg` (see the top of Figure 7.56).

7. On the left side once again, click the plus symbol (+) to the left of `I07A-FPLAYO.dwg` (`M07A-FPLAYO.dwg`).

The list of named objects in the right panel now appears below `I07A-FPLAYO.dwg` (`M07A-FPLAYO.dwg`) in the tree view on the left.

8. Click the Layers icon on the left side. The list of layers in `I07A-FPLAYO.dwg` (`M07A-FPLAYO.dwg`) appears in the panel on the right (see the bottom of Figure 7.56).

9. Click the Views button above the right window of the DesignCenter (the button on the far right), and choose List in the menu that opens.

This changes the view of layers displayed from icons into a list.

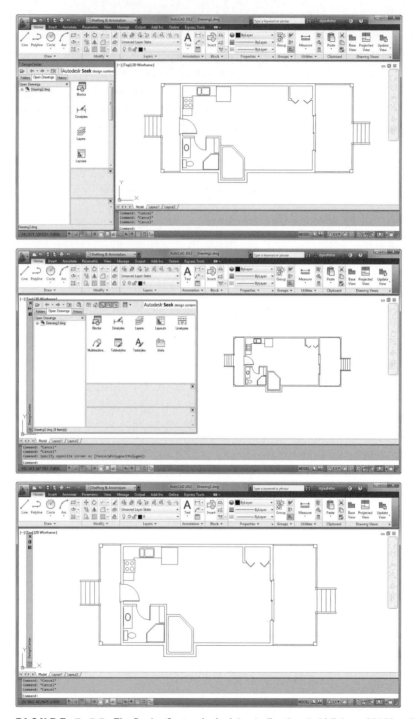

FIGURE 7.55 The DesignCenter docked (top), floating (middle), and hidden (bottom)

10. Use the Shift and Ctrl keys to help you select all the layers except 0, A-DECK, A-FLOR-FIXT, and A-WALL (see Figure 7.57).

11. Right-click one of the highlighted layers in the right window, and choose Add Layer(s) from the context menu that opens.

12. Open the Layer drop-down list on the Layers panel. It now displays all the layers of the I07A-FPLAYO.dwg (M07A-FPLAYO.dwg) drawing, including those you just transferred to the Drawing#.dwg drawing.

If you prefer dragging and dropping, click and hold the left mouse button, drag the cursor onto the drawing, and then release the mouse button.

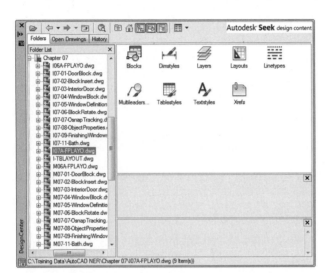

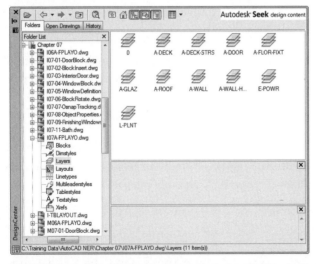

FIGURE 7.56 The DesignCenter displaying the files in the Training Data folder on the left and accessible objects on the right (top) and types of accessible objects on the left (bottom)

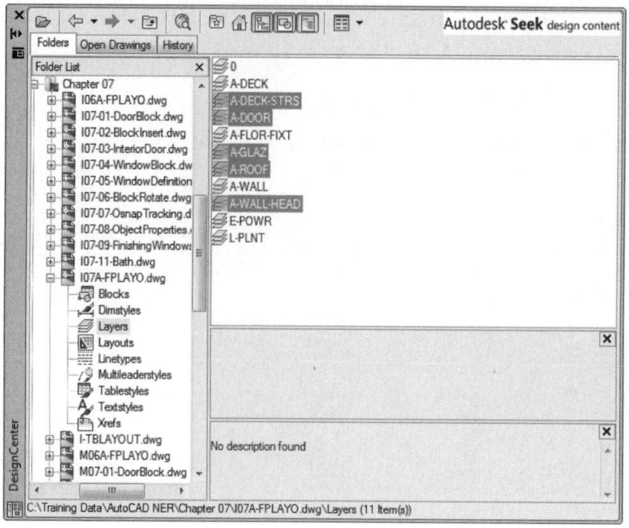

FIGURE 7.57 The DesignCenter with the layers to grab highlighted

Now let's see how this process works when you want to get a block from another drawing:

1. On the left side of the DesignCenter, click Blocks in the list under the I07A-FPLAYO.dwg (M07A-FPLAYO.dwg) drawing.

    On the right side, the list of blocks in that drawing appears (see the top of Figure 7.58).

2. Click A-DOOR-36IN (A-DOOR-0915) in the right panel, and then, if necessary, click the Preview button at the top of the DesignCenter.

    A picture of the block appears in the lower-right corner of the DesignCenter (see the bottom of Figure 7.58). You can resize the preview pane vertically.

3. Open the Layer list, and make A-DOOR the current layer.

4. Dock the DesignCenter on the left side of the drawing area if it's not already there, and then zoom in to the back door area of the drawing (see Figure 7.59). The Endpoint osnap should be running.

5. In the DesignCenter, click and drag A-DOOR-36IN from the list to the drawing, and continue to hold the left mouse button down after the block appears at the cursor.

    As the cursor comes onto the drawing, the A-DOOR-36IN block appears. Use the Endpoint osnap to locate the block at the opening, as you did earlier in this chapter (see Figure 7.60).

6. Click the Close icon in the upper-right corner of the DesignCenter to close it.

7. Keep your new drawing open in case you want to use it in the first few practice exercises at the end of this chapter. Otherwise, close it without saving it.

You can also right-click and drag a block from the DesignCenter into the current drawing. If you do this, a context menu appears; click Insert Block. This opens the Insert dialog box, and you can complete the insertion procedure.

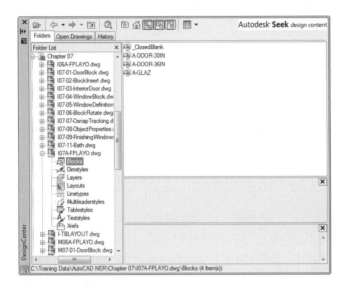

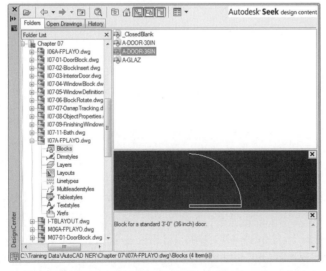

FIGURE 7.58 The DesignCenter with Blocks selected (top) and with the A-DOOR-036IN (A-DOOR-0915) block selected and Preview turned on (bottom)

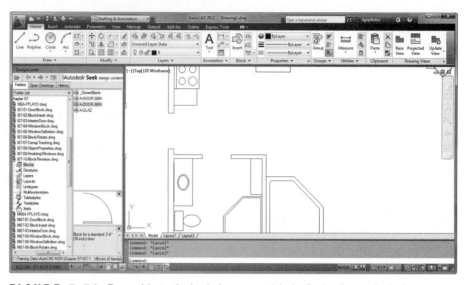

FIGURE 7.59 Zoomed in to the back door area with the DesignCenter docked

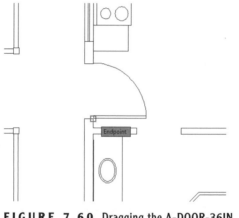

FIGURE 7.60 Dragging the A-DOOR-36IN
block into Drawing# from the DesignCenter

By doing this insertion, you've made the A-DOOR-36IN (A-DOOR-0915) block a part of your new drawing, and you can reinsert it in that drawing without the DesignCenter.

At the top of the DesignCenter window, the buttons on the left are tools for navigating through drives and folders to find the files you need to access; the buttons on the right give you options for viewing the named objects in the window.

Other Ways to Share Information between Drawings

You can transfer information between drawings in several other ways. This section looks at three of them:

▶ Use the WBLOCK command to take a portion of a drawing and create a new drawing file from the selected objects.

▶ Insert any DWG drawing file into any other drawing file.

▶ Create palettes of blocks that can be accessed for any drawing.

Using the *Wblock Command*

To perform a Write Block, or WBLOCK, operation, you create a new file by telling AutoCAD which elements of the current drawing you want in the new file. Let's say you want to create a new DWG file for the bathroom of the cabin. Here are the steps:

1. Open I07A-FPLAYO.dwg (M07A-FPLAYO.dwg), and then pan and zoom to see the bathroom.

2. Click the Create Block ➢ Write Block tool on the Insert tab ➢ Block Definition panel to start the WBLOCK command, as shown in Figure 7.61.

3. At the top, under the Source group, click the Objects radio button (see Figure 7.62).

    In the middle portion, the Base Point and Objects groups are similar to those for creating a block.

    As mentioned earlier, most project teams will establish a common location for their project. Assuming each of the drawings in your project are located in the same place, you can use 0,0,0 as the base point for the blocks you create with the WBLOCK command. You can accept the default Base Point of 0,0,0 to retain this common point in your cabin project.

4. In the Objects group, click the Select Objects button.

5. Use a window as well as individual picks to select everything you want to include, and press ↵.

6. Click the Retain radio button in this group, if necessary, so that the selected objects aren't deleted from the current drawing.

If you select with a crossing window here, you'll get more than you need, but you can clean up the new drawing later.

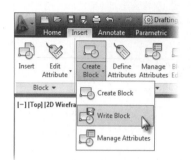

FIGURE 7.61 Starting the Write Block (WBLOCK) command from the Ribbon

FIGURE 7.62 The Write Block dialog box

DesignCenter Options

Here's a brief description of the functions of the DesignCenter buttons, from left to right:

Load   Opens the Load dialog box, which you use to navigate to the drive, folder, or file from which you want to borrow named AutoCAD objects.

Back   Moves you one step back in your navigation procedure.

(Continues)

DESIGNCENTER OPTIONS *(Continued)*

Forward   Moves you one step forward in your navigation procedure.

Up   Moves up one level in the folder/file/named objects tree.

Search   Opens a Search dialog box in which you can search for a file.

Favorites   Displays a list of files and folders that you have previously set up.

Home   Navigates to the DesignCenter folder in the AutoCAD program. This folder has subfolders of sample files that contain libraries of blocks and other named objects to import through the DesignCenter. You can designate a different Home folder by selecting the folder, right-clicking, and then choosing Set As Home from the context menu.

Tree View Toggle   Opens or shuts the left panel that displays the logical tree of folders, files, and unnamed objects.

Preview   Opens or shuts a preview window at the bottom of the right palette window. When you highlight a drawing or block in the palette window, a preview appears. You can resize the preview pane.

Description   Displays or hides a previously written description of a block or drawing. You can resize the Description pane.

Views   Controls how the items in the palette window are displayed. There are four choices: Large Icons, Small Icons, List, and Details.

7. In the Destination area, enter a filename—say, **I07-11-Bath.dwg** (**M07-11-Bath.dwg**)—for the new drawing, and choose a folder in which to save it.

8. In the Insert Units drop-down list, select Inches or Millimeters, in case the new drawing is used in a drawing that has units other than Architectural or Decimal.

9. Click OK. A preview window briefly appears, the command ends, and the selected material is now a new drawing file located in the folder that you specified.

10. Close the I07A-FPLAYO.dwg (M07A-FPLAYO.dwg) drawing without saving any changes.

You can use the WBLOCK command in three ways, which are available via radio buttons at the top of the Write Block dialog box in the Source group. Here's a brief description of each:

Block   To make a drawing file out of a block that's defined in the current drawing, select the name of the block from the drop-down list at the top and then follow the procedure in steps 4 through 8 in the preceding exercise. When you follow this procedure, the objects in the new drawing are no longer a block. Wblocking a block has the effect of exploding it.

Entire Drawing   Click this button to *purge* a drawing of unwanted objects such as layers that have no objects on them and block definitions that have no references in the drawing. You aren't prompted to select anything except the information called for in the preceding steps 4 through 8. You can keep the same drawing name or enter a new one. A preferable way to accomplish the same task is to use the PURGE command:

1. Open the Application menu.

2. Click Drawing Utilities ➤ Purge or enter **PURGE**↵ to open the Purge dialog box.

3. Select which features you want to purge.

Objects   You select which objects to use to create a new file, as in the preceding steps 1 through 8.

Inserting One Drawing into Another

When you insert a drawing into another drawing, it comes in as a block. You use the same Insert tool that you use to insert blocks, but in a slightly different way. For example, in the previous section, you Wblocked a portion of I07A-FPLAYO.dwg (M07A-FPLAYO.dwg) and made a new file called I07-11-Bath.dwg. Now suppose you want to insert I07-11-Bath.dwg into a new drawing. Take the following steps:

1. Start a new drawing, Drawing#.dwg, and set it as current.

2. Start the INSERT command.

3. In the Insert dialog box, click the Browse button, and then navigate to the folder containing I07-11-Bath.dwg (M07-11-Bath.dwg).

4. Open that folder, highlight I07-11-Bath.dwg, and then click Open to return to the Insert dialog box.

   The drawing file that you selected is now displayed in the Name drop-down list. At this point, a copy of I07-11-Bath.dwg has been converted to a block definition in Drawing#.dwg.

5. Set the insertion parameters and then click OK.

   You can uncheck Specify On-Screen and accept the defaults for each parameter.

6. Finish the insertion procedure as if you were inserting a block.

   The contents of I07-11-Bath.dwg are displayed in your new drawing at the same location they were found in I07A-FPLAY0.dwg (M07A -FPLAY0.dwg).

You transfer blocks between drawings by dragging and dropping or by using the DesignCenter. You can also convert them into DWG files by using the WBLOCK command, and you can insert them back into other DWG files as blocks by using the INSERT command. These blocks become disassociated when they leave the drawing and can be inserted as a block when they enter another drawing.

Exploring AutoCAD's Palettes

AutoCAD provides a tool called *palettes* to make blocks and other features or tools easily accessible for any drawing. You'll now take a brief look at the sample palettes that come with AutoCAD and see how to manage them on the screen:

1. Open I07A-FPLAY0.dwg (M07A-FPLAY0.dwg), and zoom to the drawing's extents.

2. Use the scroll wheel to zoom out a little.

3. If palettes aren't already visible in the drawing area, click the Tool Palettes button, found on the View tab ➤ Palettes panel, to display the palettes (see Figure 7.63).

4. Click the Architectural tab to display its content on the palette. Its tab might be abbreviated to read *Archit*, but pausing the cursor over the tab displays a tooltip showing the entire tab name.

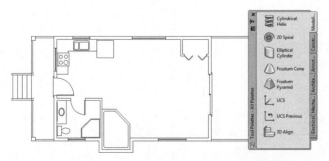

FIGURE 7.63 The tool palettes displayed on the screen

Notice the scroll bar next to the title bar (see Figure 7.64). This appears when there is more content than the palette can show. Blocks that are shown with a lightning bolt symbol as part of the icon are dynamic blocks.

5. Move the cursor to the title bar.

6. Right-click and choose Transparency from the context menu to open the Transparency dialog box (see Figure 7.65).

FIGURE 7.64 The tool palettes with the Architectural tab active

FIGURE 7.65 The Transparency dialog box

A Few Words about Tool Palettes

You can also open the tool palettes from the menu bar by clicking Tools ➢ Palettes ➢ Tool Palettes, or by using the Ctrl+3 shortcut keys. Like the DesignCenter palette, tool palettes can be floating or docked on either side of the drawing area, and the navigation bar can be on the left or right side.

Your palettes might appear different from those shown in a couple of ways. The ones shown here are positioned on the right side but aren't docked there. Yours might be transparent, showing your drawing beneath them, or your palettes might be hidden and show only the title bar. In Figure 7.63, several tabs are on the right side of the palette area, indicating the available palettes. On its left side is the palette title bar with control icons at the top and bottom.

On each palette is its content. The Hatches sample palette has hatch patterns and fills (discussed in Chapter 11, "Working with Hatches, Gradients, and Tool Palettes"), and the Draw and Modify palettes contain commands from the Draw and Modify toolbars, respectively.

Here you can toggle transparency on and off and adjust the degree of transparency for the tool palettes and many other palettes in the software.

 W A R N I N G   AutoCAD might display a notification dialog box, rather than the Transparency dialog box, if your video driver and operating system combination is unable to display palette transparency.

7. Configure the Transparency dialog box as follows:

   a. Ensure that the Disable All Window Transparency (Global) check box is not selected.

   b. In the General section, move the Opacity slider to its mid-position or a bit on the Solid side.

   c. Set the Rollover to 100% Opacity so the palette is solid whenever the cursor is over it.

   d. Click OK.

   Now the drawing is visible through the palettes (see Figure 7.66).

8. Right-click the palettes' title bar, and choose Auto-Hide from the context menu.

9. When the menu closes, move the cursor off the palettes.

The palettes disappear except for the title bar (see Figure 7.67). When you move the cursor back onto the title bar, the palettes reappear— a handy feature.

10. Close I07A-FPLAY0.dwg (M07A-FPLAY0.dwg) without saving any changes.

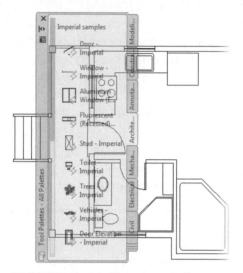

FIGURE 7.66 The palettes in Transparent mode

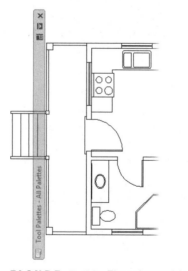

FIGURE 7.67 The palettes title bar with Auto-Hide on

With both Transparency and Auto-Hide active, the palettes are less intrusive and take up less screen area, but they remain easily accessible. In Chapter 11, you'll learn more about the Tool Palette feature, palette properties, and how to set up new palettes and change existing ones.

When they are in floating mode, the Properties palette and DesignCenter also have the Auto-Hide option.

If You Would Like More Practice...

This chapter has outlined the procedures for setting up and using blocks, the WBLOCK command, and AutoCAD's DesignCenter. Blocks follow a set of complex rules, some of which are beyond the scope of this book.

Here are some suggestions that will give you some practice in working with blocks, drag-and-drop procedures, and the DesignCenter:

► Make blocks out of any of the fixtures in the bathroom or kitchen. Try to decide on the best location to use for the insertion point of each fixture. Then insert them back into the I07A-FPLAYO.dwg (M07A-FPLAYO.dwg) drawing in their original locations. Create them on layer 0, and then insert them on the A-FLOR-FIXT layer. Here's a list of the fixtures:

  ► Shower

  ► Bathroom sink and counter

  ► Toilet

  ► Stove

  ► Kitchen sink

  ► Refrigerator

  ► Hot tub

► At the end of Chapter 5, I suggested creating pieces of furniture for the kitchen, living room, and bedroom of the cabin. If you did that, it will be good practice to make blocks out of those pieces and insert them into the cabin floor plan. If you didn't do that exercise, you can do so now and then convert the pieces of furniture into blocks.

► Drag some of the dynamic blocks from the Civil, Structural, Electrical, Mechanical, Architectural, and Annotation sample palettes into the I07A-FPLAYO.dwg (M07A-FPLAYO.dwg) drawing, and experiment with them to see how they work. Figure 7.68 shows the cabin with a few trees and a car added from the Architectural palette.

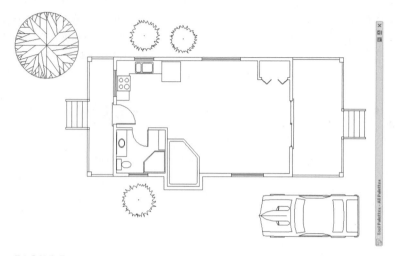

FIGURE 7.68 Trees and a car added from the Architectural palette

▶ If you work in a profession or trade not directly concerned with architecture or construction, develop a few blocks that you can use in your own work:

   ▶ Electrical diagrams consist of many simple symbols, each of which can be a block.

   ▶ Cams and gears—or gear teeth—and other engine parts that have been made into blocks can be assembled into a mechanical drawing.

   ▶ Plumbing diagrams, like electrical ones, use a variety of symbols repetitively—valves, meters, pumps, and joints. You can easily make them into blocks and then reassemble them into the diagram.

   In each of these examples, choosing the most useful location for the insertion point will determine whether the block that you create will be a handy tool or a big frustration.

Are You Experienced?

Now you can...

- ☑ create blocks out of existing objects in your drawing

- ☑ insert blocks into your drawing

- ☑ vary the size and rotation of blocks as they are inserted

- ☑ detect blocks in a drawing

- ☑ use point filters to locate an insertion point

- ☑ revise a block

- ☑ drag and drop objects from one drawing to another

- ☑ use AutoCAD's DesignCenter

- ☑ use the WBLOCK command

- ☑ open palettes and control their appearance

Controlling Text in a Drawing

You have many uses for text in your drawings, including titles of views, notes, and dimensions. It's not uncommon for the majority of a page to be covered with text outlining pertinent information such as titles, design requirements, and other project details. Each of these might require a different height, orientation, justification, and style of lettering. To control text, you'll need to learn how to do the following:

- ▶ Set up text styles to determine how the text will look
- ▶ Specify where the text will be and enter it in the drawing
- ▶ Modify the text already in your drawing

AutoCAD offers several tools for annotating your designs including, single and multiline text, dimensions, and multileaders. Similar to the way you combined the use of several drawing tools to establish the geometry of your cabin; each of these annotation tools are typically combined to help tell the story of your design. For example, you may choose to apply *single-line* text for titles, whereas *multiline* text is likely better suited for the large blocks of text typical of longer notes.

You'll progress through this chapter by first looking at the process of setting up text styles. You'll then start placing and modifying single-line text in the cabin drawing. Finally, you'll look at the methods for creating and controlling multiline text as it's used for notes and tables. If you work in a non-AEC (Architecture, Engineering, and Construction) profession or trade, be assured that the features presented in this chapter will apply directly to your work. The basic principles of working with text in AutoCAD and LT apply universally.

- ▶ **Setting up text styles**
- ▶ **Placing new text in a drawing**
- ▶ **Modifying text in a drawing**
- ▶ **Working with gridlines**
- ▶ **Managing single-line and multiline text**
- ▶ **Adding hyperlinks**
- ▶ **Using Spell Check**

Setting Up Text Styles

In AutoCAD, a *text style* consists of a combination of a style name, a text font, a height, a width factor, an oblique angle, and a few other mostly static settings. You specify these text style properties with the help of a dialog box that opens when you start the STYLE command. You'll begin by setting up two text styles— one for labeling the rooms in the floor plan and the other for putting titles on the two views. You'll need a new layer for text:

1. Open the I07A-FPLAYO.dwg (M07A-FPLAYO.dwg) drawing.

2. Zoom out so that you can see the entire drawing.

3. Create a new layer named **A-ANNO-TEXT.** Assign it a color YELLOW (2), and make it current.

4. Thaw all the other layers.

5. Click the Annotate tab to display the panels relevant to text and dimensioning and save the file as **I08-01-TextLayer.dwg** (**M08-01 -TextLayer.dwg**).

   Your drawing should look like Figure 8.1.

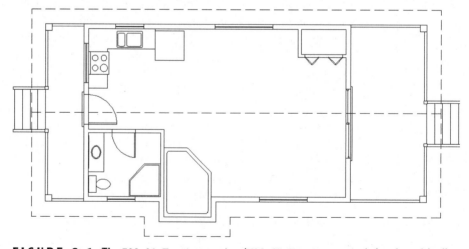

FIGURE 8.1 The I08-01-TextLayer.dwg (M08-01-TextLayer.dwg) **drawing with all layers displayed**

Determining Text and Drawing Scale

When you set up text styles for a drawing, you have to determine the height of the text letters. To make this determination, you first need to decide the scale at which the final drawing will be printed.

In traditional drafting, you can ignore the drawing scale and set the actual height of each kind of text. This is possible because, although the drawing is to a scale, the text doesn't have to conform to that scale and is drawn full size.

In AutoCAD, a feature called *layouts* makes it possible to set the height of text in the same way—that is, at the height at which it will be printed. You'll learn about using layouts in Chapter 14, "Using Layouts to Set Up a Print." In that chapter, you'll place text on layouts; in this chapter, I'll demonstrate how you use text without layouts. You'll place text in the cabin drawing. The drawing is actual size, but the text has to be much larger than actual size because both the drawing and its text will be scaled down by the same factor in the process of printing the drawing.

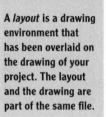

A *layout* is a drawing environment that has been overlaid on the drawing of your project. The layout and the drawing are part of the same file.

In this drawing, you'll use a final scale of 1/4″ = 1′-0″ ? (1:50). This scale has a true ratio of 1:48 (1:50) and a scale factor of 48 (50). Table 8.1 lists AutoCAD's standard scales and corresponding ratios. If you want text to be 1/8″ (3.5 mm) high when you print the drawing at 1/4″ (1:50) scale, multiply 1/8″ (3.5 mm) by the scale factor of 48 (50) to get 6″ (175 mm) for the text height. You calculate the imperial scale factor by inverting the scale fraction (1/4 = 4/1) and multiplying it by 12. You can check that calculated text height by studying the floor plan for a moment and noting the sizes of the building components represented in the drawing. The stair tread depth is 10″, and the text will be slightly smaller.

TABLE 8.1 Standard scales and their corresponding ratios

True Scale	Scale Factor
1″ = 1′-0″	12
½″ = 1′-0″	24
¼″ = 1′-0″	48
3/16″ = 1′-0″	64
1/8″ = 1′-0″	96
1/16″ = 1′-0″	192

Similarly, when using decimal units, the scale factor is derived by dividing the second number in the ratio by the first—for example, 1:50 has a scale factor of 50, and 1:60 has a scale factor of 60.

Defining a Text Style for View Titles

Now that you have a good idea of the required text height, it's time to define a new text style. Each new AutoCAD DWG file comes with two predefined text styles: Standard and Annotative. They reflect the two types of text styles you can create inside AutoCAD. You'll learn more about Annotative text styles in the next exercise, so for now we'll focus only on Standard text styles, or *static text styles* as they're sometimes called.

To create Standard text styles, you must calculate the correct Model Space Text Height setting so that your text will plot at the correct height when your drawing is plotted at scale. For this exercise, you'll create a text style for text that will be plotted at a scale of 1/4″ = 1′. To get started with your first text style, follow these steps:

1. Make sure I08-01-TextLayer.dwg (M08-01-TextLayer.dwg) is open.

You can also start the STYLE command by opening the menu bar and choosing Format ➢ Text Style.

2. On the Home tab ➢ expanded Annotation panel, click the Text Style button (see Figure 8.2), or enter **ST↵** to start the STYLE command.

FIGURE 8.2 Starting the STYLE command

After you start the STYLE command, the Text Style dialog box shown in Figure 8.3 opens.

In the Styles area of the Text Styles dialog box, you'll see the default Standard text style as well as the Annotative text style.

3. With the Standard text style highlighted, click New to open the New Text Style dialog box.

   You'll see a highlighted Style Name text box set to *style1*. When you enter a new style name, it will replace style1.

4. Enter A-Title↵ in the Style Name text box, as shown in Figure 8.4.

   The New Text Style dialog box closes, and in the Text Style dialog box, A-Title appears highlighted in the Styles list.

   You've created a new text style named A-Title. It has settings identical to those of the Standard text style, and it's now the current text style. Next, you'll change some of the settings for this new style.

5. Move down to the Font group, and click the Font Name drop-down list to open it.

   A list of fonts appears; the number of choices depends on what software is installed on your computer. AutoCAD can use both its native SHX (Compiled Shape) font files and Windows TTF (TrueType font) files.

6. Scroll through the list until you find Arial, and then click it.

   Notice the TT icon to the left of the font name. This icon tells you that Arial font is a TrueType (.ttf) font.

◄

By default, all new DWG files have the Standard text style as the current text style.

◄

A *font* is a collection of text characters and symbols that all share a characteristic style of design and proportion.

FIGURE 8.3 The Text Style dialog box, where you'll begin setting up text styles

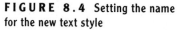

FIGURE 8.4 Setting the name for the new text style

The list closes, and in the Font Name text box, the Arial font replaces the txt.shx font that was previously there. In the Preview area in the lower-left corner, a sample of the Arial font replaces that of the txt .shx font.

7. Because view labels are generally emphasized, change the Font Style from Regular to Bold.

    The preview in the lower-left corner updates to reflect the Font Style change.

8. Press the Tab key a few times to move to the next text box. The Height setting is highlighted at the default of 0'-0" (0).

9. Enter 12 (350) and then press Tab again. A height of 1'-0" replaces the initial imperial measurement of 12".

    Since the A-Title text style will be used for headings and titles, it will use a plotted height of 1/4" (7 mm). Once again, the model space height for this text was derived by multiplying the plotted height 1/4" (7 mm) by the drawing scale factor 48 (50). Your Text Style dialog box should look like Figure 8.5.

    You won't need to change any of the other parameters that define the new text style. They can all stay at their default settings.

10. Click the Apply button at the bottom of the dialog box.

    The A-Title text style is saved with the current drawing and becomes the current text style. The current text style appears in the Text Style drop-down list in the Text panel, as shown in Figure 8.6.

11. Click Close to exit the Text Style dialog box.

12. Save your drawing as **I08-02-TitleStyle.dwg (M08-02-Title Style.dwg)**.

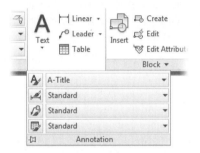

FIGURE 8.5 The Text Style dialog box after setting up the Title style

FIGURE 8.6 The Text Style drop-down
list after setting A-Title as the current style

When you define a new text style, you first name the new style. This has the effect of making a copy of the current text style settings, giving them the new name, and making the new text style current. You then change the settings for this new style and save the changes by clicking Apply.

Of the many fonts available in AutoCAD, you'll use only a few for your drawings. Some are set up for foreign languages or mapping symbols. Others would appear out of place on architectural or technical drawings but might be just right for an advertising brochure or a flyer. Later in this chapter, you'll have a chance to experiment with the available fonts.

The current text style is similar to the current layer. All text created while a text style is current will follow the parameters or settings of that text style.

SHX AND TTF FONTS

AutoCAD text styles can use either the AutoCAD SHX (Compiled Shape) font files or the Windows TTF (TrueType font) files on your system. The SHX fonts are older files that were originally designed for use with pen plotters, which required the pen tip to follow a precise vector. When you zoom in to an AutoCAD SHX font or print it large on a drawing, the straight line segments that compose it become apparent. Two more fonts in the Roman font family—romant (triplex) and romanc (complex)—have multiple, closely set lines and allow for larger text to be created while minimizing this straight-line effect.

TrueType fonts are mathematical representations of vector formats and are common in most Windows applications. Many fonts are available, and you can use them with no loss of crispness, regardless of the size of the font or the zoom factor in the drawing.

Until recently, the use of TTF fonts over the AutoCAD-specific SHX fonts would dramatically affect system performance. With performance the paramount concern, SHX fonts became the de facto standard. Recent advancements have made the performance differences between the two negligible. In fact, the default acad.dwt drawing template from Autodesk has used the TTF font Arial over the former SHX font for the last several releases of AutoCAD. The use of TTF fonts is also preferred over SHX fonts for the purposes of electronic archiving; SHX fonts cannot be searched or indexed by Windows. To follow this trend and ensure compatibility, this book also utilizes the TTF Arial font over the older SHX fonts for annotating your cabin.

Refer to Figure 8.3 for a moment, and note that the Standard text style has a height of 0′-0″ (0). When the current text style has a height set to 0, you're prompted to enter a height each time you begin to place single-line text in the drawing. The default height for the A-Title text style will scale to 1/4″ (or 0.25 for decimal units and 7 for metric) when plotted. Multiline text will use the default height of 1/4″ (7 mm) unless you change it.

Placing Titles of Views in the Drawing

After creating a text style, you're ready to begin adding text to your drawing. Before you can do that, you must first choose which type of text you would like to use: single-line or multiline text. The differences between them were discussed at the start of this chapter, but to summarize: single-line text is limited to one line, and multiline text can support multiple lines of text for things like paragraphs.

Because the view title needs only a single line of text, you'll use the Single Line Text tool in this exercise. So you can experience the differences for yourself, a later exercise will utilize multiline text instead of the single-line text you'll use here.

1. Make sure I08-02-TitleStyle.dwg (M08-02-TitleStyle.dwg) is open.

2. Use the Zoom and Pan tools to make your view similar to the one shown in Figure 8.7.

3. Set up your osnaps and status bar options so that Polar Tracking and Object Snap are on and the Endpoint and Midpoint osnaps are running.

4. Drop a line from the midpoint of the ridgeline in the floor plan straight down to a point near the bottom of the screen.

5. Offset the horizontal, outside wall line to the right of the pop-out in the floor plan down 6′ (1830 mm), as shown in Figure 8.8.

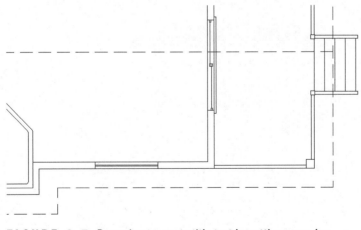

FIGURE 8.7 Preparing to create title text by setting your view

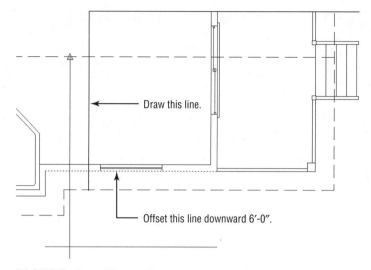

Draw this line.

Offset this line downward 6′-0″.

FIGURE 8.8   The new lines created after offsetting the ridge line and the pop-out

6. Verify that the Text Style drop-down menu found on the Annotate tab ➢ Text panel matches Figure 8.9 and has the A-Title text style set as current.

  The current text style, A-Title in this example, determines the text style used by any new text objects you create.

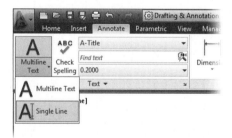

FIGURE 8.9   Verifying the current text style (A-Title), and starting the Single Line Text (TEXT) command

| A | Single Line | **7.** Click the down-arrow below the Multiline text button in the Text panel and click the Single Line Text button in the fly-out menu, or enter **DT**↵ to start the TEXT command—the command used for single-line text.

The command window reports information about the current text style: Current text style: "A-Title" Text height: 1'-0" (350) Annotative: No. The window then prompts you: Specify start point of text or [Justify/Style]:.

You will use the Justify option to change the justification to Middle.

8. Enter **J**↵ or press the down-arrow on the keyboard until Justify is selected at the cursor prompt, and then press ↵.

All the possible justification points appear in the prompt, as shown in Figure 8.10.

9. Enter **C**↵ to choose Center as the justification.

10. Use the Shift+right-click menu to choose the Intersection osnap, and pick the intersection of the guideline and the offset line.

11. At the Specify rotation angle of text: prompt, press ↵ to accept the default angle of 0°, or enter **0**↵ if 0° is not the default.

A flashing I-shaped cursor superimposed over a narrow box appears at the intersection (see Figure 8.11).

12. With Caps Lock on, enter **FLOOR PLAN**↵.

The text is centered at the intersection as you enter it, and the cursor moves down to allow you to enter another line (see the left image in Figure 8.12).

13. Press ↵ again to end the TEXT command.

The text is centered relative to the vertical guideline and sits on the offset line (see the right image of Figure 8.11).

14. Erase the offset line and the vertical guideline. Your drawing will look like Figure 8.13.

15. Save your drawing as **I08-03-ViewTitle.dwg** (**M08-03-ViewTitle.dwg**).

> ▶
>
> The justification point for the text functions like the insertion point for blocks.

You specified a location for the text in two steps: first, you set the justification point of each line of text to be centered horizontally; second, you used the Intersection osnap to position the justification point at the intersection of the two guidelines. I'll discuss justification in more depth a little later in this chapter.

Next, you'll use a similar procedure to begin adding room labels to the interior of your cabin.

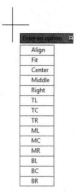

FIGURE 8.10 The single-line text justification options

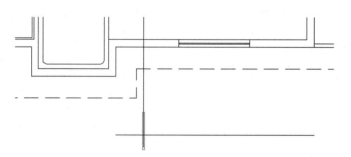

FIGURE 8.11 The text cursor sits on the guidelines.

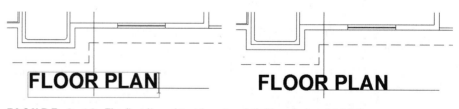
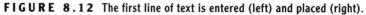

FIGURE 8.12 The first line of text is entered (left) and placed (right).

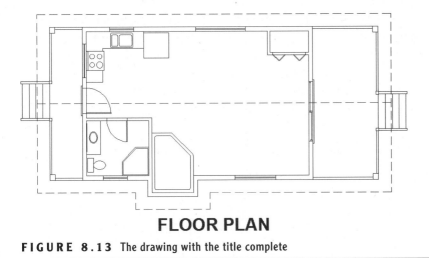

FLOOR PLAN

FIGURE 8.13 The drawing with the title complete

Using Annotative Text

You just finished using the Single Line Text tool in conjunction with the Standard text style A-Title to label your floor plan. Before you could create the A-Title text style, you had to use Table 8.1 to calculate the correct model space text height manually. Standard text styles, which require you to calculate the Height parameter manually, work great if you need to display your drawing at only a single scale.

Most plan sets include a combination of overall plan sheets, layout plan sheets, enlarged view sheets, and so on, so you'll probably need to establish a way to address annotation for each scale. Users who annotate their drawings in model space have traditionally solved this dilemma by creating separate text layers for each scale. Although this method works, it increases the possibility of errors because you're copying text and must remember to update each copy as revisions happen.

Another way to approach the dilemma of multiple scales, which also simplifies calculating the correct height for model space text, is the use of *annotative text*. Rather than calculating the correct model space height, by using annotative text you'll simply specify at what height you would like the text to plot. Using the Annotative Scaling features, AutoCAD will use the annotation scale to determine the correct height for your text.

Likewise, because annotative text objects can have multiple annotation scales assigned to them, annotative text also helps solve the dilemma of managing annotation at multiple scales. Assigning multiple annotation scales to a single piece of text allows you to display and position that one text entity at multiple scales. In other words, annotative text helps you reduce potential annotation errors by allowing you to manage one text entity, not one text entity for each scale.

Defining an Annotative Text Style

To get started with annotative text, you must first create an Annotative text style. Creating Annotative text styles is incredibly similar to creating Standard text styles. The biggest difference is that you will specify a Paper Space Height setting instead of the more generic Height parameter used with Standard text styles.

1. Make sure I08-03-ViewTitle.dwg (M08-03-ViewTitle.dwg) is open.

2. Start the STYLE command by entering **ST**↵ at the command line, or by choosing Manage Text Styles from the Text Style drop-down list found on the Annotate tab ➢ Text panel.

   The Text Style dialog box opens, where you will begin defining a new Annotative text style.

3. Select the A-Title style from the list on the left side of the Text Style dialog box, and click the New button.

   The New Text Style dialog box opens, prompting you for a name of your new text style.

4. Enter **A-Label** as the name, and click OK to return to the Text Style dialog box (see Figure 8.14).

   A new text style called A-Label is created and is now the current text style. Its font, height, and other settings are copied from the A-Title text style. Now you'll make changes to these settings to define the A-Label text style.

5. Leave Arial as the Font Name, and change Font Style from Bold to Regular.

   The list closes, and Regular appears as the chosen Font Style.

6. Under the Size group within the Text Style dialog box, click the Annotative check box, as shown in Figure 8.15, but leave the Match Text Orientation To Layout box unchecked.

Notice how the Height parameter changes from Height to Paper Space Height.

7. Enter 1/8″ (3.5) for the Paper Text Height.

The Text Style dialog box should look like Figure 8.16. Notice the small icon next to the A-Label text style you just created. This icon distinguishes Annotative text styles from non-Annotative, or Standard, text styles in the Text Style dialog box, and it is used throughout the software to refer to the annotative tools inside AutoCAD.

8. Click Apply, and then click Close.

9. Save your drawing as **I08-04-AnnotativeStyle.dwg** (**M08-04 -AnnotativeStyle.dwg**).

If you press ⏎ after entering the height, the new style is automatically applied, meaning that it is saved and made the current text style. Don't do this if you need to change other settings for the style.

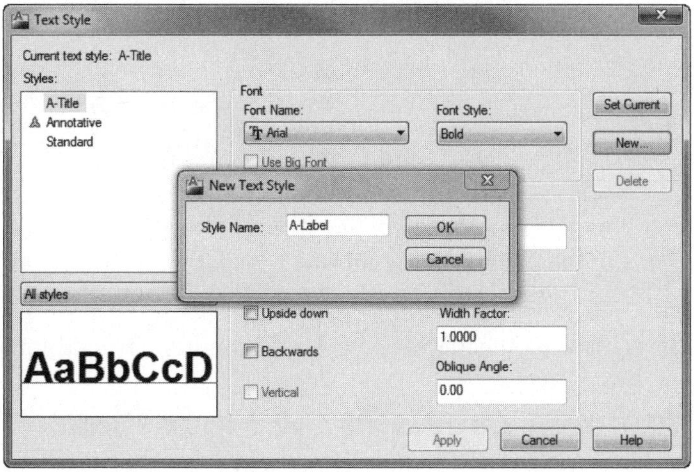

FIGURE 8.14 Setting the name for the new text style

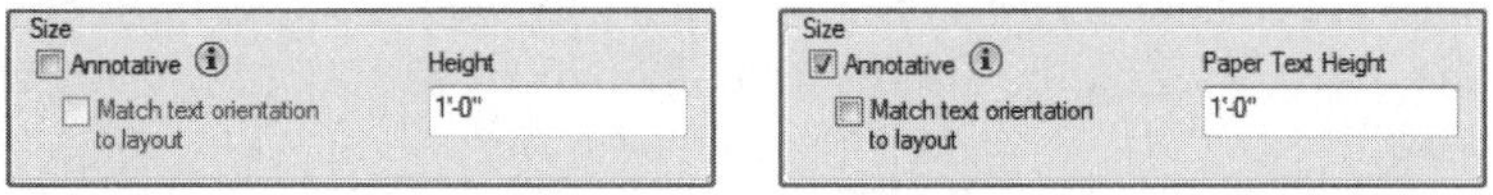

FIGURE 8.15 The Size group inside the Text Style dialog box with the Annotative option unchecked (left) and checked (right)

WARNING Depending on the drawing's precision, the Paper Text Height may round to 4 mm after you enter 3.5 mm. Despite rounding to 4 mm, AutoCAD will still create text with a height of 3.5 mm as entered in the Text Style dialog box. To verify, use the UNITS command to change the Length Precision property to 0.0.

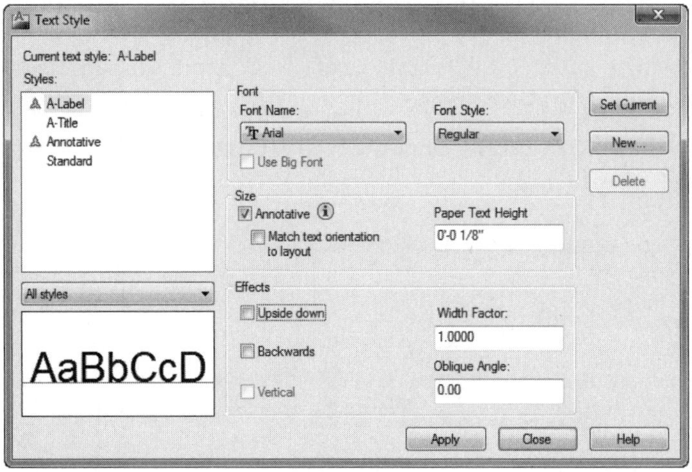

FIGURE 8.16 The Text Style dialog box after setting up the A-Label style

Now that you have an Annotative text style, you can start creating annotative text.

Placing Room Labels in the Floor Plan

To label the rooms inside your cabin, you'll use the Annotative A-Label text style you just created. Using Annotative text styles is very similar to using Standard text styles to create text, although you will need to ensure that the Annotative settings are correctly set so the text you create will be scaled correctly. The following exercise will walk you through how to create annotative single-line text entities:

1. Make sure I08-04-AnnotativeStyle.dwg (M08-04-Annotative Style.dwg) is open.

2. Click the Ortho Mode, Polar Tracking, and Object Snap buttons on the status bar to turn off these features.

3. Click the Annotation Scale button found on the status bar, and change the scale to 1/4″ = 1′-0″ ⏎, as shown in Figure 8.17.

T I P   It's important to set the annotation scale before you create any annotative text objects, because AutoCAD will use this as the default scale for the text objects you create. The current annotation scale is always displayed next to the Annotation Scale icon on the status bar. With this in mind, it's a good idea to get in the habit of glancing at the status bar to check this setting before creating annotative objects such as text.

4. Verify that the A-Label text style is current by expanding the Text Style drop-down list on the Annotate tab ➤ Text panel to display a list of all the text styles in the drawing.

   If necessary, click A-Label, as shown in Figure 8.18, to make Label the current style.

FIGURE 8.17 Changing the annotation scale from the status bar

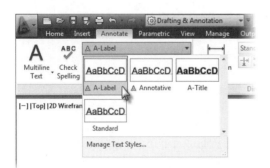

FIGURE 8.18 Selecting a new, current text style in the Text panel

VIEW TITLES HIGHLIGHTING AFTER STARTING THE TEXT COMMAND?

The FLOOR PLAN view title text may become highlighted after starting the TEXT command. This happens whenever you start the TEXT command for the second time within any single drawing session—that is, when you haven't closed or otherwise reopened the current drawing since you last created text.

Starting the TEXT command for the second time will highlight the last text string you created. Pressing ↵ with this text highlighted at the Specify start point of text or [Justify/Style]: prompt will continue that string by creating a second string directly below it. This same behavior is seen later in this exercise as each room name is stacked on individual lines of text.

5. Start the TEXT command to begin creating the room labels.

6. Pick a point in the living room between the refrigerator and the closet.

7. Press ↵ at the rotation prompt. The text cursor appears at the point you picked.

8. With Caps Lock on, enter **KITCHEN↵ LIVING ROOM↵ BATH↵↵**.
The TEXT command ends. You have three lines of text in the kitchen and living room area (see Figure 8.19).

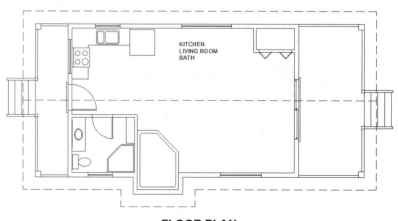

FLOOR PLAN

FIGURE 8.19 The three room labels placed in the cabin

9. Move your cursor over one of the text objects you just created.

Notice that the same Annotative icon used in the Text Style dialog box appears in the upper-right quadrant of the cursor to quickly identify that the object (a piece of text in this case) is Annotative.

10. Save your drawing as `I08-05-RoomLabels.dwg` (`M08-05-Room Labels.dwg`).

For this text, you used the default Left justification, and each line of text was positioned directly below the previous line at a spacing set by AutoCAD. In many cases, it's more efficient to enter a list of words or phrases first and then move the text to its appropriate location. That's what you're doing for this text. When you know the location of the insertion point for the next line, you can click that point, instead of pressing ↵ at the end of the current line. This starts the next line of text at the selected location.

Moving Text and Working with Annotation Scales

Like most objects in AutoCAD, text can be moved by using the MOVE command or by using the grips associated with a given object. In most cases, there is no difference between using the MOVE command and using the grips to do what is known as a *grip edit*. Annotative text objects are an exception to this rule.

Using the grips associated with a piece of annotative text moves that piece of text only for the current Annotation Scale. At other scales, that same piece of text will remain in its previous location. You'll get to explore the difference between the two as you begin positioning the room labels in your cabin. Figure 8.20 shows how the text will look after it is moved into position.

1. Make sure `I08-05-RoomLabels.dwg` (`M08-05-RoomLabels.dwg`) is open.

2. Next to the annotation scale in the status bar, make sure the Annotation Visibility (left) and Automatically Add Scales (right) buttons are in the on position.

In the case of Annotation Visibility, the on position is represented by a yellow lightbulb, and for Automatically Add Scales, a yellow lightning bolt is used.

3. Change the annotation scale to 1/2″ = 1′-0″↵↵.

The KITCHEN, LIVING ROOM, and BATH text size changes to reflect the newly selected annotation scale.

4. Select the BATH text, and start the MOVE command found on the Home tab ➤ Modify panel.

5. Move the BATH text between the bathroom cabinet and shower, as shown in Figure 8.20.

6. Repeat the MOVE command by pressing ↵, moving the KITCHEN text to the position shown in Figure 8.20.

7. Click the LIVING ROOM text. One grip appears at the justification point.

8. Click the grip to activate it. The LIVING ROOM text is attached to the cursor and moves with it (see the top of Figure 8.21).

   The STRETCH command automatically starts. Because text can't be stretched, the STRETCH command functions like the MOVE command.

9. Move the cursor just above the roof centerline near the middle of the living room, and then click to place text at its new location.

10. Press Esc to deselect the text and remove the grip.

11. From the status bar, change the annotation scale back to 1/4″ = 1′-0″↵↵.

    The text size for each of the room labels gets larger, and the location for the LIVING ROOM text reverts to its original location, as shown at the bottom of Figure 8.21.

12. Save your drawing as **I08-06-MovingText.dwg** (**M08-06-Moving Text.dwg**).

FLOOR PLAN

FIGURE 8.20 The LIVING ROOM, KITCHEN, and BATH text moved to their proper positions

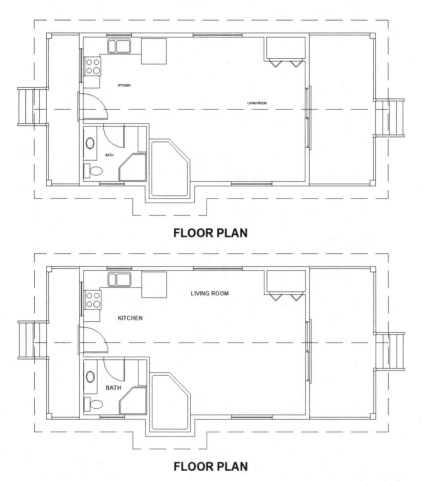

FLOOR PLAN

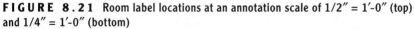

FLOOR PLAN

FIGURE 8.21 Room label locations at an annotation scale of 1/2″ = 1′-0″ (top) and 1/4″ = 1′-0″ (bottom)

An *annotative object* displays at the scale assigned to it. When you created the room labels, the annotation scale was set to 1/4″ = 1′-0″↵↵, and so it was the scale AutoCAD used to correctly size room labels. At that point, your room labels were set up to display only at a scale of 1/4″ = 1′-0″↵↵.

At the start of this exercise, you verified that the Add Annotation Scales button was turned on and then changed the annotation scale from 1/4″ = 1′-0″↵↵ to 1/2″ = 1′-0″↵↵. In doing that, you added the 1/2″ = 1′-0″↵↵ scale to each of the three annotative objects in your drawing. Your room labels were then set up to display at both scales.

When plans are being prepared at different scales, it's often necessary to place annotation objects such as text in different locations for some or all of the scales. This is done to avoid conflicts with other objects in the drawing and to make plans as readable as possible. This is the reason annotative objects allow you to specify multiple insertion points for each annotation scale assigned to an object. Likewise, this is where moving annotative objects by using grips differs from using the MOVE command.

As you saw with the KITCHEN and BATH text, the MOVE command changes the location for the entire text object, including its multiple annotation scales. On the other hand, using grips to move an annotative object moves only the object for the current annotation scale. As illustrated with the LIVING ROOM text, you used grips to move its location for the 1/2″ = 1′-0″⌐⌐ scale, but the original location was retained for the 1/4″ = 1′-0″⌐⌐ scale.

Synchronizing Annotative Text Scale Positions

Use the following procedure to move the 1/4″ = 1′-0″⌐⌐ LIVING ROOM text to the same location as the 1/2″ = 1′-0″⌐⌐ LIVING ROOM text:

1. Make sure I08-06-MovingText.dwg (M08-06-MovingText.dwg) is open.

2. Change the annotation scale back to 1/2″ = 1′-0″⌐⌐ by using the Annotation Scale menu on the status bar.
   The LIVING ROOM text moves to its correct location on the screen.

3. Select the LIVING ROOM text.
   A blue grip appears at the insertion point of the 1/2″ = 1′-0″⌐⌐ text, and the location of the 1/4″= 1′-0″⌐⌐ text is shown ghosted (see Figure 8.22).

4. With the LIVING ROOM text still selected, right-click and choose Annotative Object Scale ➤ Synchronize Multiple-Scale Positions from the contextual menu shown in Figure 8.23.

5. Change the annotation scale to 1/4″ = 1′-0″⌐⌐ by using the Annotation Scale menu on the status bar.

6. Using the Synchronize Multiple-Scale Positions tool, move the 1/4″ = 1′-0″⌐⌐ LIVING ROOM text so that it and the 1/2″ = 1′-0″⌐⌐ text share the same insertion point (see Figure 8.24).

7. Save your drawing as **I08-07-SyncPosition.dwg** (**M08-07-Sync Position.dwg**).

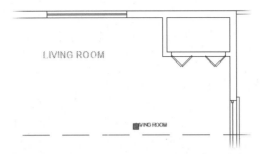

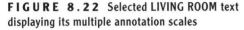

FIGURE 8.22 Selected LIVING ROOM text displaying its multiple annotation scales

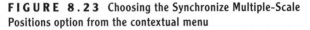

FIGURE 8.23 Choosing the Synchronize Multiple-Scale Positions option from the contextual menu

As you've seen, you have a couple of options when positioning text in a drawing. Annotative text is easier to size than standard text; however, using the grip at the insertion point will place the text at different locations for each scale, which may be an undesired result. When working with annotative text, the better choice is the MOVE command, although the Synchronize Multiple-Scale Positions option will help correct text placement if you erroneously use the insertion-point grip.

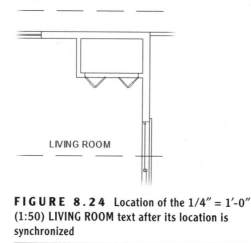

FIGURE 8.24 Location of the 1/4″ = 1′-0″ (1:50) LIVING ROOM text after its location is synchronized

Even with the versatility that annotative text provides in the placement of text, occasionally the free space in a drawing will be so limited that a line and a piece of text will coincide. A common solution is to break the line where the text overlaps. To demonstrate how you might solve this type of issue in your own drawings, in the next section you'll need to erase part of a line where text intersects.

Breaking Lines with the *Break* Command

The BREAK command chops a line into two lines. When you're working with text that intersects a line, you'll usually want a gap between the lines after the break. The BREAK command provides this option as well as others. Follow these steps:

1. Make sure I08-07-SyncPosition.dwg (M08-07-SyncPosition.dwg) is open.

2. Enter **UNDO↵ M↵** to set the undo mark so you can return your drawing to the state it is in now.

3. Select the LIVING ROOM text and use the MOVE command to move it so that it rests on the ridgeline, as shown in Figure 8.25.

4. Turn off Object Snap, and start the BREAK command by selecting the Break button found inside the extended Modify panel on the Home tab.

5. Place the pickbox on the ridgeline just to the right of the text and click. The line ghosts, and the cursor changes to the crosshair cursor. You just selected the line to break and picked one of the break points.

> You can also start the BREAK **command** by entering **BR↵**.

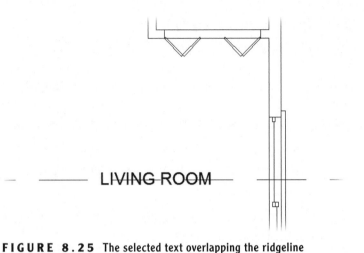

FIGURE 8.25 The selected text overlapping the ridgeline

6. Put the crosshair cursor on the ridgeline just to the left of the text, and pick that point.

   The line is broken around the text, and the BREAK command ends. As you can see in Figure 8.26, the text is easier to read now than it was when the line was running through it.

7. You don't want to retain your drawing in its current state, so enter **UNDO↵ B↵** to revert to the undo point that you set with the Mark option.

8. Continue to the next exercise without saving changes.

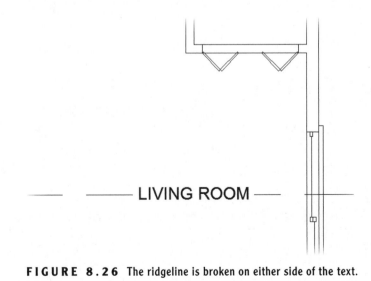

FIGURE 8.26 The ridgeline is broken on either side of the text.

Breaking Lines with the *Trim* Command

When selecting cutting edges to be used by the TRIM command, you almost
always select a linear object, line, arc, or polyline. A less-known feature of the
TRIM command is that text objects may also be used as cutting edges. The end
result is much the same as when you used the BREAK command, but the TRIM
command ensures that the gap between the line and text is equal on both sides.

1. Continue using I08-07-SyncPosition.dwg (M08-07-SyncPosition.dwg).

2. Enter **UNDO.**↵ **M.**↵ to set the undo mark so you can return your drawing
   to the state it is in now.

3. Start the TRIM command from the Home tab ➤ Modify panel, or enter
   TR.↵ at the command line.

4. When prompted to Select Cutting Edges, select the LIVING ROOM
   text and press ↵.

5. At the Select Object To Trim Or Shift-Select To Extend prompt,
   select a point along the ridgeline where the LIVING ROOM text overlaps it, as shown in Figure 8.27.

6. Press ↵ to end the TRIM command.

   The ridgeline is trimmed along the LIVING ROOM text object, as
   shown in Figure 8.28.

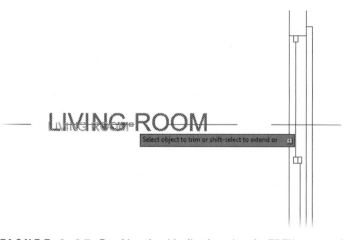

FIGURE 8.27 Breaking the ridgeline by using the TRIM command

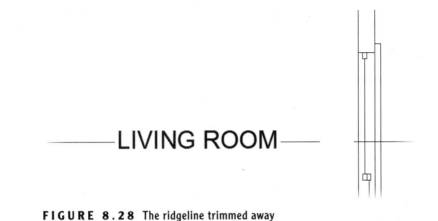

FIGURE 8.28 The ridgeline trimmed away

7. To reset the position of the LIVING ROOM text and undo trimming the ridgeline, enter **UNDO.↵ B.↵**.

8. Continue to the next exercise without saving changes.

TIP   The multiline text objects have a mask feature that creates an envelope over and around the text, hiding the objects behind it. Unlike the breaking-lines approach, the masked objects reappear when you move the text. Masking is not supported for single-line text, but the Text Mask utility is available in the Express Tools. Express Tools are not included with AutoCAD LT.

Using Text in a Grid

AutoCAD provides a grid, which you worked with in Chapter 3, "Setting Up a Drawing." The grid is a tool for visualizing the size of the drawing area and for drawing lines whose geometry conforms to the spacing of the dots or lines. Many floor plans have a separate *structural grid*, created specifically for the project and made up of lines running vertically and horizontally through key structural components of the building. At one end of each gridline, a circle or a hexagon is placed, and a letter or number is centered in the shape to identify it. This kind of grid is usually reserved for large, complex drawings, but you'll put a small grid on the cabin floor plan to learn the basic method for laying one out:

1. Make sure I08-07-SyncPosition.dwg (M08-07-SyncPosition.dwg) is open.

2. Create a new layer called **A-GRID**. Assign it color Red (1) and make it current.

3. Offset the roofline polyline 10′ (3050 mm).

4. Pan and zoom as necessary so that the cabin is centered onscreen and takes up only about 75 percent of the drawing area.

5. Turn Object Snap on if it's off; set the Endpoint, Midpoint, and Perpendicular osnaps to be running; and then start the LINE command.

6. Draw lines from the upper-left and upper-right inside corners of the walls up to the offset roofline.

7. Draw lines from the upper-left and lower-left inside corners of the exterior walls to the vertical offset line on the left (see Figure 8.29).

   The gridlines need to be centered on the structural member they are identifying, in this case an 8×8 (204×204) column.

A CLOSER LOOK AT THE *BREAK* COMMAND

Use your own judgment to determine how far from the text a line must be broken back. You have to strike a balance between making the text easy to read and keeping what the broken line represents clear.

Here are some options for the BREAK command:

▶ Ordinarily, when you select a line to be broken, the point where you pick the line becomes the beginning of the break. If the point where the break needs to start is at the intersection of two lines, you must select the line to be broken somewhere other than at a break point. Otherwise, AutoCAD won't know which line you want to break. In that case, after selecting the line to break, enter F↵. You'll be prompted to pick the first point of the break, and the command continues. Now that AutoCAD knows which line you want to break, you can use the Intersection osnap to pick the intersection of two lines.

▶ To break a line into two segments without leaving a gap, do the following:

  1. Click the Break At Point button, which is on the expanded Modify panel. You might want to do this to place one part of a line on a different layer from the rest of the line.

(Continues)

A CLOSER LOOK AT THE BREAK COMMAND *(Continued)*

2. Start the command.

3. Select the line to break.

4. Pick the point on the line where the break is to occur, using an osnap if necessary.

AutoCAD makes the break and ends the command.

---

8. Start the OFFSET command, enter **E↵ Y↵** to set the Erase parameter, and then set the offset distance to 4″ (102 mm). Now, when an object is offset, the original is erased.

9. Offset each of the gridlines 4″ (102 mm) toward the inside of the cabin.
You may notice that the toilet will interfere with the new column in the lower-left corner of the cabin.

10. Move the toilet up 4″ (102 mm) to add clearance and then adjust the size of the sink counter and mirror as well.
Now you need to draw gridlines for the posts at the corners of the decks.

11. From the horizontal midpoint of the top-right and top-left deck posts, draw lines vertically to the offset roofline.

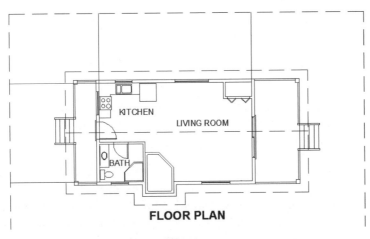

FIGURE 8.29 The first gridlines

12. Next, draw lines from the upper-left and lower-left deck posts horizontally to the offset roofline.

13. This time add a jog to each column line so that their endpoints are not too close to the endpoints of the existing horizontal column lines (see Figure 8.30). You need to leave space for the column tag and don't want them to overlap.

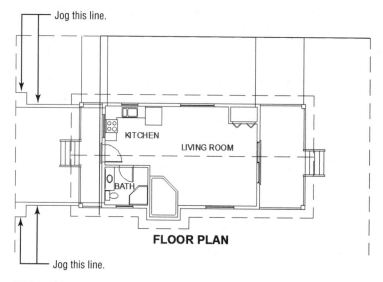

FIGURE 8.30 The column lines for the deck posts

The column lines should not extend all the way to the cabin; there should be a gap to keep the drawing from getting congested and confusing.

14. Use the TRIM command to trim each of the column lines back to the roofline, as shown in Figure 8.31.

15. Start the LENGTHEN command by clicking the Lengthen tool found on the extended Modify panel of the Home tab. Alternatively, you can enter LEN↵ at the command line.

> Use the F8 key to toggle Ortho Mode on and off, to keep the jogged lines straight.

16. Enter DE↵ to choose the Delta option at the Select an object or [DElta/Percent/Total/DYnamic] prompt.

The Delta option will let you change the length of a line, arc, or polyline by a specified distance. In this case, you want to subtract 6″ (150 mm) from the total length of each gridline.

17. To subtract 6″ (150 mm) from each gridline, enter **-6**↵ (**-150**↵) at the `Enter delta length or [Angle] <0'-0">:` prompt.

18. Select each of the eight column lines near where it intersects with the offset roofline.

   Upon selecting each column line, its length will be shortened by 6″ (150 mm).

19. Erase the roofline offset you created in step 3, and then zoom out to a view that includes the floor plan and the gridlines (see Figure 8.32).

20. Save your drawing as **I08-08-GridLine.dwg** (**M08-08-GridLine.dwg**).

When several osnaps are running, the marker for only one (and not necessarily the correct one) appears at a time. By pressing the Tab key, you can cycle through all the running osnaps for every object your cursor is over or near.

FIGURE 8.31 The column lines are trimmed back to the newly offset rooflines.

FIGURE 8.32 The cabin with the completed gridlines drawn and the offset roofline deleted

This completes the gridlines. To finish the grid, you need to add a circle with a letter or a number in it to the left or upper end of the lines. You'll use letters across the top and numbers running down the side:

1. Make sure `I08-08-GridLine.dwg` (`M08-08-GridLine.dwg`) is open.

2. From the Home tab ➢ Draw panel, expand the Circle fly-out menu and click 2-Point.

   The 2-Point option draws a circle defined by selecting two opposite points of the circle's diameter.

3. At the `Specify first end point of circle's diameter:` prompt, pick the upper end of the leftmost vertical gridline.

4. Turn Ortho mode on, and then move the cursor directly above the last point and enter **12″** (**305**) at the `Specify second end point of circle's diameter:` prompt.

   This places a circle 12″ (305 mm) in diameter at the top of the gridline (see the left image of Figure 8.33). Note that you can enable drawing modes with a command active.

5. Turn Ortho Mode off, and click the KITCHEN text. A grip appears.

6. Click the grip. Type **C** for *copy* and then press ↵.

7. Activate the Center osnap, and click the circle on the grid.

   The KITCHEN text appears on the circle, with the lower-left corner of the text at the center of the circle (see the right image of Figure 8.33).

8. Press Esc twice, once to end the Stretch function and again to clear the grip.

9. Click the copy of the KITCHEN text that is now on the grid, right-click to bring up the context menu, and then click Properties to open the Properties palette.

   Text appears on the drop-down list at the top, telling you that you've selected a text object.

10. Use the Properties palette to make the following changes to the KITCHEN text:

    a. Under General, change Layer to A-GRID (see Figure 8.34).

    b. Under Text, change Contents from KITCHEN to A.

    c. Change the Justify setting from Left to Middle Center.

T I P   This exercise might seem like a roundabout way to generate letters for the grid symbols, but it is meant to show you how easy it is to use text from one part of the drawing for a completely different text purpose. It's a handy technique, as long as you want to use a font that has been chosen for a previously defined text style. A faster way to do this is to use the Single Line Text tool. With the Justify setting set to Middle, use the Center osnap to place the text cursor at the center of the circle, and then enter A↵↵.

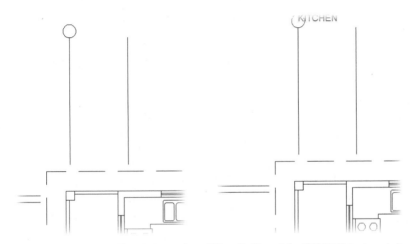

F I G U R E   8 . 3 3   The circle on the gridline (left) and the KITCHEN text copied to the circle (right)

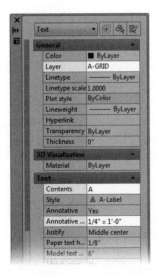

F I G U R E   8 . 3 4   Modifying the KITCHEN text by using the Properties palette

For each change, follow these steps in the Properties palette:

1. Click the category in the left column that needs to change. If the setting is on a drop-down list, an arrow appears in the right column.

2. Click the down-arrow to open the list. In the case of the KITCHEN text, just highlight it because there is no drop-down list.

3. Click the new setting or enter it.

4. When you've finished, close the Properties palette and press Esc to deselect the text.

5. Save your drawing as `I08-09-GridBubble.dwg` (`M08-09-Grid Bubble.dwg`).

The KITCHEN text changes to the letter A, is centered in the grid circle, and moves to the Grid layer (see Figure 8.35).

You used the Center osnap on the KITCHEN text to position its justification point at the center of the circle. You then modified the justification point from the Left position (which is short for *Base Left*) to the Middle Center position. The Middle Center position is the middle of the line of text, horizontally and vertically. So what you did had the effect of centering the text in the circle. You'll now look briefly at text justification.

FLOOR PLAN

FIGURE 8.35 The grid circle with the letter A

Justifying Text

Each line of single-line text is an object. It has a justification point, which is similar to the insertion points on blocks. When drawing, you can use the Insert osnap to precisely locate the justification point of text (or the insertion point of blocks) and thereby control the text's position on the drawing. When you use the Single Line Text or TEXT command, the default justification point is the lower-left corner of the line of text. At the TEXT prompt (Specify start point of text or [Justify/Style]:), if you enter J↵, you get the prompt Enter an option [Align/Fit/Center/Middle/Right/TL/TC/TR/ML/MC/MR/BL/BC/BR]:. These are your justification options.

Figure 8.36 shows most of these options. The dots are in three columns—left, center, and right—and in four rows—top, middle, lower, and base. The names of the justification locations are based on these columns and rows. For example, you have TL for Top Left, MR for Middle Right, and so on. The third row down doesn't use the name Lower; it simply goes by Left, Center, and Right. Left is the default justification position, so it's not in the list of options. The Middle position sometimes coincides with the Middle Center position, but not always. For example, if a line of text has *descenders*—portions of lowercase letters that drop below the baseline, such as *j* and *p*—the Middle position drops below the Middle Center position. Finally, the lowest row, the *Base row*, sits just below the letters at the lowest point of any descenders.

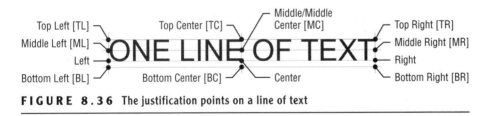

FIGURE 8.36 The justification points on a line of text

Finishing the Grid

To finish the grid, you need to copy the grid circle and its text to each gridline and then change the text:

1. Make sure I08-09-GridBubble.dwg (M08-09-GridBubble.dwg) is open.

2. Make sure Object Snap is turned on, and enable the Endpoint and Quadrant osnaps.

3. At the command prompt, select both the letter *A* and the circle.

    Grips appear: two for the text, one at the original justification point, and one at the new justification point; one at the center of the circle; and one at each of the circle's quadrant points.

4. Right-click and choose Copy Selection from the context menu. Pick the upper endpoint of the grid with the *A* as the base point.

5. Pick the top end of each vertical gridline.

6. Right-click and choose Enter to terminate the command (see Figure 8.37).

7. Move back to the original grid circle and select the grip on the right side of the circle to activate it.

8. Right-click, choose Copy Selection from the context menu, and pick the right Quadrant of the circle as the base point.

9. Copy the circle to the left endpoint for each of the horizontal gridlines.

10. Press Esc to deselect the objects and remove the grips. Then, if necessary, use the STRETCH command to adjust the jogged lines and eliminate any overlap.

    Now you'll use the DDEDIT command to change the text in each circle.

11. Be sure Caps Lock is on, and then double-click the letter *A* in the second grid circle from the left in the top row.

    The text now has a blue background to indicate that it is being edited.

12. Enter B↵. The *A* changes to *B*.

13. Click the *A* in the next circle to the right, and then enter C↵. The *A* changes to a *C*.

14. Repeat this process for the remaining five grid circle letters, changing them to D, 1, 2, 3, and 4.

15. Press ↵ to end the Edit Text command.

    The letters and numbers are all in place, and the grid is complete (see Figure 8.38).

16. Save this drawing as **I08-10-CompleteGrid.dwg (M08-10-Complete Grid.dwg)**.

> You can also start the DDEDIT command by opening the menu bar and choosing Modify ➢ Object ➢ Text ➢ Edit, or by entering TEDIT↵. These methods display additional command-line options.

> Editing text is one of the situations in which pressing the spacebar does not have the same effect as pressing ↵.

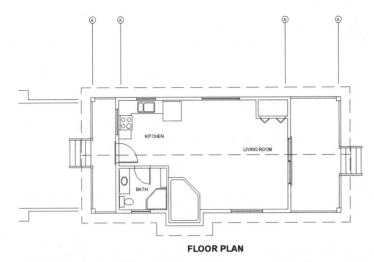

FIGURE 8.37 The grid circle and letter are copied to the top of all three vertical lines.

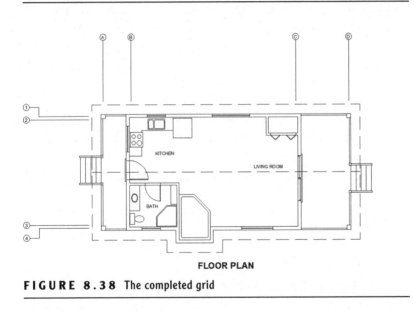

FIGURE 8.38 The completed grid

Often, it's easier to copy existing text and modify it than to create new text, and grips are a handy way to copy text. Using the command (technically called TEDIT) is a quick way to modify the wording of short lines of text, meaning those that consist of a word or a few letters. The Properties palette is useful for changing all aspects of a line of text.

For the next exercise with text, you'll get a chance to set up some more new text styles, place text precisely, and use the DDEDIT command again to modify text content. You'll do all this while you develop a title block for your drawing.

Creating a Title Block and Border

The first step in creating a title block and border for the cabin drawing is deciding on a sheet size for printing the final drawing. Because many people have access to 11″×17″ (297×420) format printers, you'll use that sheet size. So if you print the drawing at a scale of 1/4″ = 1′-0″ (1: 50), will the drawing fit on the sheet?

To answer that question, you have to ask how big an area will fit on an 11″×17″ (A3 -297 mm×420 mm) sheet at 1/4″ = 1′-0″ (1:50) scale. The answer is quite simple. Every inch (millimeter) on the sheet represents 48″ (50 mm) in the drawing (because 12″ divided by 1/4 is 48″, and 50 mm divided by 1 is 50 mm). Therefore, you multiply each dimension of the sheet in inches (millimeters) by 48 (50). For this sheet, you multiply 11″×48 (297 mm×50) to get 528″ (14,850 mm), or 45′-4″ (see Figure 8.39). You multiply 17″×48 (420 mm×50) to get 816″ (21,000 mm), or 68′ (21 meters), as shown in Figure 8.39. So, the 11″×17″ (297 mm×420 mm) sheet represents a rectangle with dimensions of approximately 528″×816″ (14,850 mm×21,000 mm) at a scale of 1/4″ = 1′-0″ (1:50), which is usually called quarter-inch scale.

Because most printers and plotters are not full-bleed devices, you'll need to factor in room for a margin around the outer edge of your sheet. Although the floor plan fits without any problems, you may need to adjust the column lines for them to fit into the printable area. Chapter 14 discusses layouts, and you will learn how to display the content of a single drawing at different scales—likely solving this issue. Even when you account for the unprintable area around the perimeter of the sheet, there should be plenty of room for your cabin drawing. This is the information you need to start creating the title block.

Drawing the Border

The border of the drawing will be set in from the edge of the sheet. Here are the steps:

1. Make sure I08-10-CompleteGrid.dwg (M08-10-CompleteGrid.dwg) is open.

2. Create a new layer called **A-ANNO-TTLB**. Assign the color Green (3) and make this layer current.

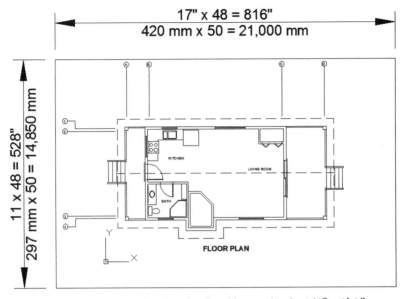

17" x 48 = 816"
420 mm x 50 = 21,000 mm

11 x 48 = 528"
297 mm x 50 = 14,850 mm

KITCHEN

LIVING ROOM

BATH

FLOOR PLAN

FIGURE 8.39 Approximating the viewable area for the 1/4″ = 1′-0″ (1:50) scale

3. Start the Rectangle (RECTANG) command (used in Chapter 4, "Developing Drawing Strategies: Part 1," to make the doors).

4. At the prompt, enter **0,0**↵. Then enter **68′, 48′**↵ (**21000,14850**↵). This draws a rectangle that may extend off the top of the screen.

5. Use Zoom Extents to zoom out until the entire rectangle is visible in the drawing area (see Figure 8.40).

    You need to fit the drawing into the rectangle as if you were fitting it on a sheet of paper. The easiest and safest way to do this is to move the rectangle over to enclose the drawing. You'll leave plenty of room for the elevations that you will draw in a later chapter.

6. At the command prompt, click the rectangle to select it. Grips appear at the corners of the rectangle.

7. Click the lower-left grip.

8. Press the spacebar once to switch from Stretch mode to Move mode.

9. Move the rectangle over the drawing (see the top of Figure 8.41).

Once you activate a grip and the Stretch function begins, pressing the space-bar toggles through the other four commands in this order: Move, Rotate, Scale, Mirror.

10. When the rectangle is approximately in the position shown at the bottom of Figure 8.41, click.

11. Press Esc to deselect the rectangle. The rectangle is positioned around the drawing and represents the edge of the sheet.

12. You need a border set in from the edge. Offset the rectangle 2′ (650 mm) to the inside.

    With a scale of 1/4″ = 1′-0″ (1: 50), each 1′-0″ (50 mm) on the drawing will be represented by 1/4″ (1 mm) on the sheet. So, a 2′ (500 mm) off-set distance will create an offset of 1/2″ (13 mm) on the printed sheet.

13. Double-click the inside rectangle to start the PEDIT command.

14. Enter W↵ 2↵↵ (50↵↵).

    This command sets the width of the inside rectangle's segments to 2′ (50 mm).

15. Move both rectangles to center the cabin.

16. Use Zoom Extents, and then zoom out a little to create a view in which the drawing with its border nearly fills the screen (see Figure 8.42).

17. Save this drawing as **I08-11-BorderFrame.dwg** (**M08-11-Border Frame.dwg**).

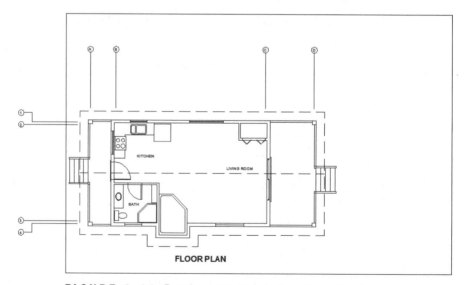

FIGURE 8.40 Zooming out to include the entire rectangle

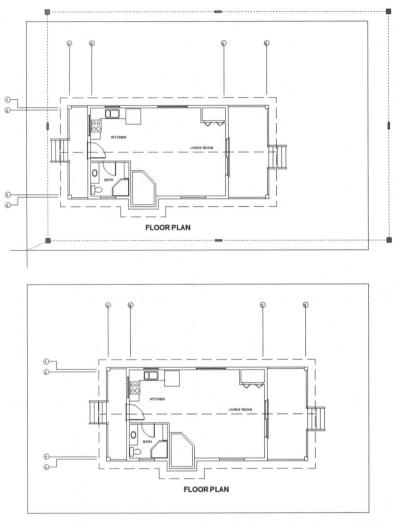

FIGURE 8.41 Moving the rectangle with grips (top) and the results (bottom)

The outer rectangle represents the edge of the sheet of paper, and the thicker, inner rectangle is the drawing's border.

Constructing a Title Block

The *title block* is a box that contains general information about a drawing, such as the name of the project, the design company, and the date of the drawing. It will be set up along the right edge of the border and will use the same special line, the *polyline*, which is created when the Rectangle (RECTANG) command is executed.

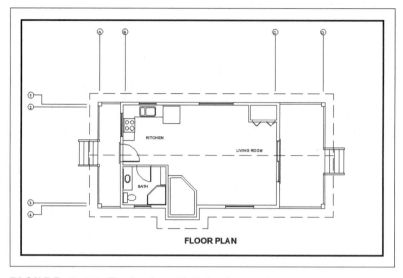

FIGURE 8.42 The drawing with its border

You first used the Rectangle (RECTANG) command in Chapter 4 for drawing the doors. At that time, I mentioned that rectangles created with this command consist of a polyline whose four segments are grouped as one object. In step 14 of the previous section, you saw that these segments could have varying widths.

These same principles will be applied as you construct the title block for your cabin project. You'll draw a series of rectangles that will eventually contain information about your project and drawing such as project name, drawing title, and drawing scale. The ability of a polyline, what the RECTANG command creates, to have a width makes it useful in constructing title blocks. You'll use the RECTANG and PLINE commands to draw the various lines that make up the title block, and then you'll fill in the text:

1. Make sure I08-11-BorderFrame.dwg (M08-11-BorderFrame.dwg) is open.

2. With the entire title block frame in view, start the STRETCH command found on the Home tab ➤ Modify panel.

3. At the Select objects: prompt, create a crossing window selection around the inner-right edge, as shown at the top of Figure 8.43, and press ↵.

4. Pick any point in the drawing at the Specify base point prompt.

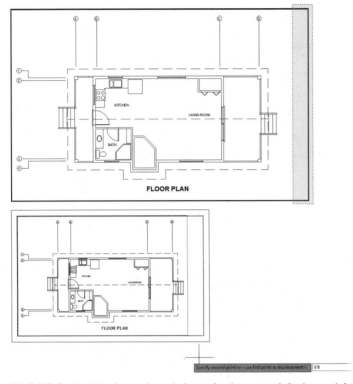

FIGURE 8.43 A crossing window selection around the inner-right title block edge (top), and specifying the displacement distance (bottom)

5. With Ortho Mode turned on, move your cursor to the left, and use direct distance entry to specify a displacement of 6'-6" (2050 mm) as shown at the bottom of Figure 8.43.

   By reducing the inner frame's width, you now have enough room to include both project and drawing information along the right edge of your plan sheet. The rectangles and polylines you'll draw next will help provide structure to this data.

6. Ensure that Object Snap and Object Snap Tracking are both enabled with Endpoint chosen as a running object snap.

7. Zoom in to the upper-right corner of your title block, bringing both the inner and outer title block frames into view.

8. Start the Rectangle (RECTANG) command, and use Object Snap Tracking to begin drawing a rectangle 6" (150 mm) to the right of the inner title block frame, as shown in Figure 8.44.

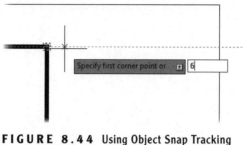

FIGURE 8.44 Using Object Snap Tracking to acquire the rectangle starting point

9. Enter **72,-72** (**1900,-1900**) at the Specify other corner point prompt to complete the rectangle. The top rectangle shown in Figure 8.45 is drawn.

10. Using the same process, acquire a point 6″ (150 mm) below the rectangle; create another 72″×72″ (1900 mm×1900 mm) rectangle, shown as the bottom rectangle in Figure 8.45.

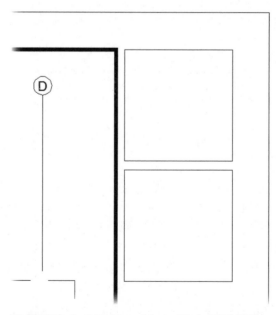

FIGURE 8.45 Accurately positioned 72″×72″ (1900 mm×1900 mm) title block components

11. Repeat steps 8 and 9 to create a 72″×96″ (1900 mm×2440 mm) rect-angle 6″ (150 mm) to the right of the lower-right title block frame.

12. Use Object Snap Tracking to compose the final rectangle 6″ (150 mm) below the top series of rectangles, and 6″ (150 mm) above the bottom rectangle, as shown in Figure 8.46).

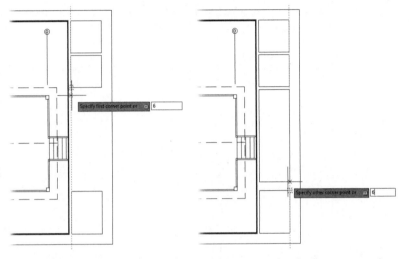

FIGURE 8.46 Using Object Snap Tracking to acquire the first corner point (left) and second corner point (right)

13. Use the Match Properties (MATCHPROP) command found on the Home tab ➢ Clipboard panel to assign the correct polyline width to each of the newly created rectangles.

    a. At the Select source object prompt, select the inner title block frame that's currently bolder (thicker) than the other lines in your drawing.

    b. At the Select destination object(s) prompt, select each of the rectangles drawn during this exercise along the right edge of the title block by using the selection method of your choice. Press ↵ to exit the command.

Each of the object properties such as layer, lineweight, and width are synchronized between the source and destination objects (see Figure 8.47).

14. Use the LINE command to subdivide the lower two rectangles along the right edge of your title block (see Figure 8.48).

    a. Create three horizontal lines each spaced 2′ (610 mm) apart inside the lower rectangle.

    b. Use the Midpoint osnap to vertically subdivide the largest rectangle.

15. Save this drawing as **I08-12-CompleteFrame.dwg** (**M08-12-Complete Frame.dwg**).

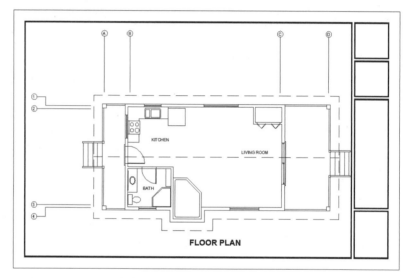

FIGURE 8.47 The completed rectangle stack along the right title block edge

MATCHING PROPERTIES WITH THE MATCH PROPERTIES COMMAND

The Match Properties (MATCHPROP) command is an excellent way to easily synchronize the properties between any two AutoCAD objects. Although the source and destination objects do not need to be of the same object type (text to text, lines to lines, and so forth), it is important to recognize that only shared properties will be matched. For example, it's possible to match the inner title block (polyline) frame with a piece of text; however, Global Width, a property exclusive to polylines, would not be applied to any text entities.

(Continues)

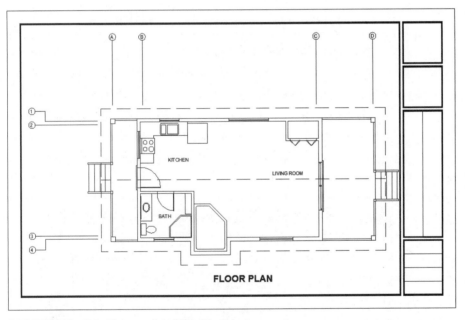

FIGURE 8.48 The completed title block frame

Putting Text in the Title Block

The title block has several boxes that will each contain distinct pieces of information. The two uppermost boxes will contain information related to your company, including its logo and contact information. Below these two uppermost boxes, the largest box will contain the name of the project and the current drawing's title. Finally, the lowermost box will contain information specific to this drawing:

drawing scale, submittal date, creator's initials (yours), and drawing or sheet number. Most title block layouts contain this information and more, depending on the complexity of the job.

You need to put labels in some of the boxes to identify what information will appear there. For this, you need to set up a new text style:

1. Make sure I08-12-CompleteFrame.dwg (M08-12-CompleteFrame.dwg) is open.

2. Create a new layer named **A-ANNO-TTLB-TEXT**. Assign it a color Cyan (4) and make it current.

3. On the Text panel under the Ribbon's Annotate tab, expand the Text Style drop-down list and click Manage Text Styles.

4. The A-Label text style should still be current. If not, then select it.

5. Click New, enter **A-Ttlb**, and then click OK.

6. Leave the font set to Arial, but deselect the Annotative check box and change the height to 6″ (175).

7. Assuming the Text Style dialog box looks like Figure 8.49, click Apply and then Close. A-Ttlb is the current text style.

8. Be sure Caps Lock is on, and start the Single Line Text or TEXT command.

> **If you press ↵ after changing the height, the Apply button turns gray and unselectable. Pressing ↵ at this point has the same effect as clicking the Apply button.**

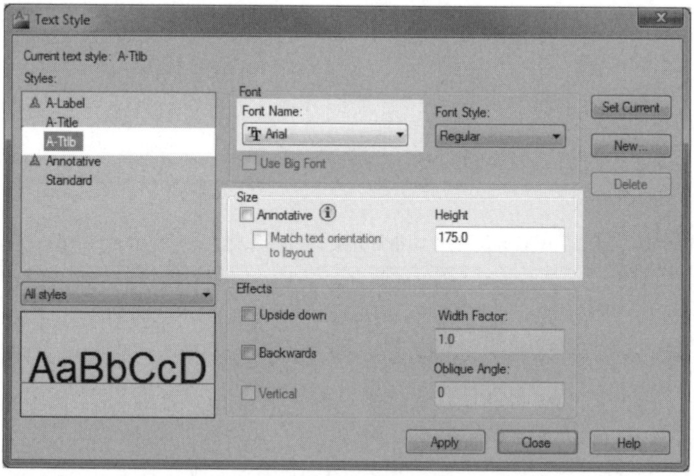

FIGURE 8.49 Using the A-Label text style as a template for the A-Ttlb text style

9. Enter **J⏎** at the command line to open the text justification options, and then **TL⏎** to specify a Top Left justification.

10. Use the Endpoint osnap to pick the upper-left corner of the lowermost box.

11. Press ⏎ at the rotation prompt. Enter SCALE:⏎⏎.

    The word *SCALE:* appears in the lowermost box (see the top of Figure 8.50). Don't worry about the box's boundary overlapping the SCALE text, as you'll fix this in a moment.

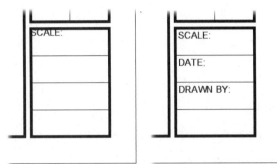

FIGURE 8.50 One line of text placed (top), and the completed title block labels (bottom)

12. Use the COPY command to copy this text to the two boxes below it, using the endpoint of the horizontal lines above each of the boxes as the base and displacement points.

13. Double-click the topmost copied text to start the TEDIT command.

14. Enter DATE: and press ⏎. Pick the lower copy of text. The blue editing background returns.

15. Enter DRAWN BY: and press ⏎. Press ⏎ to end the DDEDIT command.

16. Position each of the labels by using the MOVE command.

17. Pick any point in the drawing as a base point, and enter **@3,-3⏎** (**@75, -75⏎**) for the second point to move the labels into place (see the right of Figure 8.50).

18. Save this drawing as **I08-13-DrawingLabels.dwg** (**M08-13-Drawing Labels.dwg**).

> The closer you zoom in, the more precisely you'll be able to fine-tune the location of the text. You'll need to zoom out to check how it looks.

Using the DDEDIT command is a quick way to change the wording of text and to correct spelling. You have to change one line at a time, but the command keeps running until you stop it. You can also change the Contents text box in the Properties palette.

The final area to work on in this lowermost box is where the sheet number appears. This sheet number will serve as the unique identifier distinguishing it from all other drawing sheets in your plan set. For many of the same reasons page numbers in this and many other books are found in the corners of each page, sheet numbers are typically placed in a similar fashion. To aid in making the sheet number of each drawing in your plan set easy to read and identify, you'll place it in the lower-right corner and create a new text style.

1. Make sure I08-13-DrawingLabels.dwg (M08-13-DrawingLabels.dwg) is open.

2. Open the Text Style dialog box and click New.

3. Turn off Caps Lock, then enter **A-Snbr** and click OK.

4. Leave Arial as the font, and change the height to **12″** (350).

5. Click Apply and then click Close. A-Snbr is now the current text style.

6. Start the TEXT command and enter **J**↵.

7. Enter **MC**↵ to set the justification to the top center of the text.

8. Right-click to select the Mid Between 2 Points osnap, and use the Endpoint osnap to pick the two endpoints along the top of the bottom-right box, as shown in Figure 8.51.

9. Press ↵ at the rotation prompt.

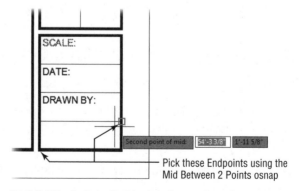
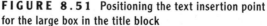

FIGURE 8.51 Positioning the text insertion point for the large box in the title block

10. Turn Caps Lock back on, and then enter **A-101**⏎⏎.

    The sheet number text is correctly positioned within its designated block (see Figure 8.52).

11. With Polar Tracking on, use the MOVE command to move the text down and center it vertically in the box (see Figure 8.52).

12. Save this drawing as **I08-14-SheetNumber.dwg** (**M08-14-Sheet Number.dwg**).

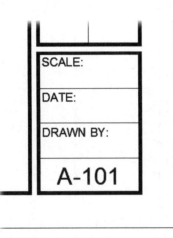

FIGURE 8.52 The sheet number text after being inserted

Remember, when you select the text to move it, you have to pick each line because they are two separate objects.

Now it's time for you to experiment, using the techniques you just learned to fill in the text for the other boxes.

The tallest of the four boxes composing your title block will be used to designate both the project name and sheet title. Like the other boxes, you'll designate each of these respective areas with a label.

1. Make sure I08-14-SheetNumber.dwg (M08-14-SheetNumber.dwg) is open.

2. Use the ZOOM command to bring the lower edge of the tallest box composing your title block into view.

3. Set the A-Ttlb text style as current, and start the Single Line Text (TEXT) command.

4. Set the justification to Top Left (**TL**), and choose the bottom-left endpoint as the start point.

5. At the Specify rotation angle of text prompt, enter **90**⏎.

6. Turn Caps Lock on if it's not already, and then enter **PROJECT:**⮠⮠.

7. Repeat the procedure outlined in steps 3–5 to create the SHEET TITLE: label in the area to the right of your PROJECT: label. Your drawing should look like the left of Figure 8.53.

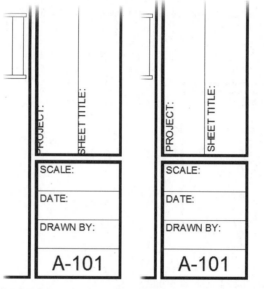

FIGURE 8.53 Defining the PROJECT and SHEET TITLE areas (left), and positioning the labels (right)

8. Position the PROJECT: and SHEET TITLE: labels by using the MOVE command.

9. Choose any point in your drawing as a base point, and then specify a displacement of **@3,3**⮠ (**@75,75**⮠).

   Your drawing should match the right of Figure 8.53.

10. Using the A-Ttlb text style and a text justification of Bottom Right, fill in the following information:

    ▶ SCALE: 1/4″= 1′-0″ (1:50)

    ▶ DATE: *Enter any date*

    ▶ DRAWN BY: *Enter your initials*

11. Use the MOVE command to position each of the title block entries **@-3,3**⮠ (**@-75,75**⮠) to the left.

12. Use the A-Snbr text style to fill in the project name, **SUMMER CABIN**, and sheet title, **FIRST FLOOR PLAN**, using the following parameters:

   a. Apply the Bottom Center (BC) text justification, and snap to the midpoint of the bottom line for each area.

   b. Specify a text rotation angle of 90°.

   Your drawing should match Figure 8.54.

FIGURE 8.54 The completed lower title block boxes

13. Use the collection of Draw and Modify commands you've learned so far to create your own logo in the uppermost title block box, or insert I08-Logo.dwg (M08-Logo.dwg) with these steps:

   a. Click Insert on the Insert tab ➢ Block panel to start the INSERT command.

   b. From the Insert dialog box, click Browse to locate the I08-Logo .dwg (M08-Logo.dwg) file. You can find this file in the Chapter 8 download found at **www.sybex.com/go/autocad2012ner**.

    c. If it's not already, check Specify On-Screen for Insertion Point, and uncheck Specify On-Screen for both Scale and Rotation. Click OK.

    d. Using the Endpoint osnap, pick the lower-left corner of the uppermost title block box (see Figure 8.55).

14. Save this drawing as **I08-15-TtlbLogo.dwg** (**M08-15-TtlbLogo.dwg**).

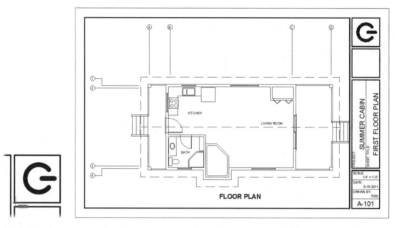

FIGURE 8.55 Inserting the title block logo (left), and the completed title block (right)

> Use the EXPLODE command to turn multiline text into single-line text, to unblock objects in a block reference, and to convert a polyline into regular lines. Click the Explode button on the Modify panel to start the command.
>
> ▶

Using Multiline Text

Multiline text (often referred to as *Mtext*) is more complex than single-line text. You can use it in the same way you used single-line text in this chapter, but it can do more. When you have several lines of text or when you need certain words within a line of text to appear different from the adjacent words, multiline text is the best feature to use.

A paragraph of multiline text is a single entity. The text wraps around, and you can easily modify the length of a line after you place the text in the drawing. Within the multiline text entity, all text can be edited and behaves as if it were in a word processor. You can give a special word or letter of the text its own text style or color. Everything you learned about defining a new text style applies to multiline text, because both kinds of text use the same text styles. Just as polylines become lines when exploded, multiline text is reduced to single-line text when exploded.

Dimensions use multiline text, and any text that is imported into an AutoCAD drawing from a word processing document or text editor becomes multiline text in the drawing. In this section, you'll learn how to place a paragraph of multiline text in the cabin drawing and then modify it. In Chapter 12, you'll work with dimension text and text with leader lines, both of which use multiline text.

T I P   **If you are using AutoCAD and have the Express Tools installed, the TXT2MTXT command (on the menu bar, click Express ➢ Text ➢ Convert Text To Mtext) changes the selected Text objects into Mtext objects. When multiple lines of text are selected, they are converted into a single Mtext object. LT does not have the Express Tools available.**

Finishing the Title Block

In addition to the logo you inserted a moment ago, most title blocks will also contain basic company contact information. Since contact information usually spans several lines, multiline text is a perfect candidate to put the final touch on the composition of your title block.

1. Make sure I08-15-TtlbLogo.dwg (M08-15-TtlbLogo.dwg) is open, and verify that the A-ANNO-TTLB-TEXT layer is set as current.

2. Start the MTEXT command by clicking the Multiline Text button found on the Annotate tab ➢ Text panel. If the Multiline Text button isn't visible, click the down-arrow beneath the Single Line text button, and choose it from the list.

3. Use the Endpoint osnap to choose the upper-left and lower-right corners of the title block box directly below the logo box (see Figure 8.56).

4. Enter the following information (see Figure 8.57):

   ▶ Company Name

   ▶ Street Address

   ▶ City, State, and Postal Code

   ▶ Telephone Number

   ▶ Website

5. Click anywhere outside the text box, or click the Close Text Editor button on the contextual Text Editor tab ➢ Close panel. This closes the Multiline Text Editor and inserts your text into the drawing (see Figure 8.57).

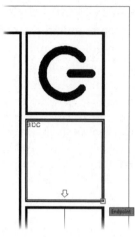

FIGURE 8.56 Defining the multiline text box within the title block

FIGURE 8.57 The company contact information placed within the title block before modifying formatting

   Although the title block box now includes the necessary contact information, it's likely not very legible. You may choose to do any number of things to make this text more legible: place greater emphasis on the company name or fix text-wrapping issues such as the City, State, Zip text seen in Figure 8.57. Thanks to the additional formatting options that multiline text provides, each of these modifications are easily applied:

1. With your cursor placed over any character within your text box, double-click to open the contextual Text Editor Ribbon tab.

2. Click the Justification button found on the contextual Text Editor tab ➢ Paragraph panel to apply a Middle Center text justification. The text is centered both vertically and horizontally within the text box.

3. Use your cursor to highlight the Company Name text.

4. Click the Bold button on the contextual Text Editor tab ➢ Formatting panel.

5. Still inside the Multiline Text Editor, highlight the Street Address, City, State, and Postal Code, Telephone Number, and Website text.

6. Reduce the text height for each of the selected components by entering 5 (125) within the Ribbon Combo Box - Text Height area of the Style panel on the contextual Text Editor tab.

7. Ensure that your text is correctly positioned both horizontally and vertically by using the Middle Center justification option.

8. On the contextual Text Editor tab ➢ Paragraph panel, expand the Justification button and choose Middle Center.

9. Click anywhere outside the text box, or click the Close Text Editor button on the contextual Text Editor tab ➢ Close panel.

10. Your title block should now resemble Figure 8.58. Save this drawing as `I08-15-TtlbLogo.dwg` (`M08-15-TtlbLogo.dwg`).

Using tools familiar to anyone who has used a word processor such as Microsoft Word, you were able to quickly increase the legibility of the text within the company contact title block box. This is just one example of how multiline text can prove itself invaluable when working with several lines of text at once.

Beyond the formatting tools explored in this first exercise involving multiline text, it's also important to note how text within a block of multiline text interacts with the other text within the same block. Changing the size of all but the company name from 6″ (175 mm) to 5″ (125 mm) also changed the spacing between each line of text. Had this been several strings of single-line text, the vertical relationship between each line of text would not have been retained.

FIGURE 8.58 The completed title block

Using Mtext for General Notes

The preceding exercise introduced you to several of the multiline text formatting options available. This expansive list of formatting options is especially helpful when managing large blocks of text such as the general notes typically found on many plan sheets. Expanding on this concept, the next several exercises will introduce you to many of these formatting options as you add general notes to your drawing.

Adding Columns to Mtext

To fit large blocks of text (like General Notes) onto a plan sheet, it's oftentimes necessary to divide the text into a series of columns. Complete the following steps to format the General Notes for your cabin drawing into multiple columns:

1. Make sure I08-15-TtlbLogo.dwg (M08-15-TtlbLogo.dwg) is open.

2. Click the Make Object's Layer Current button on the Layers panel.

3. Click the FLOOR PLAN text to make the A-ANNO -TEXT layer current.

4. If it isn't already, change the current text style to A-Label from the Annotate tab ➤ Text panel.

5. Zoom in to the blank area to the left of the title block, in the lower-left corner of the cabin drawing.

6. Start the MTEXT command by clicking the Multiline Text button found on the Annotate tab ➤ Text panel, and press F3 to turn Object Snap off temporarily.

The command window displays the name of the current text style and height and prompts you to specify a first corner.

7. Select a point near the left border, vertically in line with the roofline.

The prompt now reads Specify opposite corner or [Height/ Justify/Line spacing/Rotation/Style/Width/Columns]:. These are all the options for the Multiline Text (MTEXT) command.

Unlike single-line text, Mtext uses a window to define the width of the text, rather than a point for the justification point.

8. Drag open a window that fills the space between the left border and the left side of the pop-out.

This defines the line width for the multiline text (see Figure 8.59). Click to finish the window.

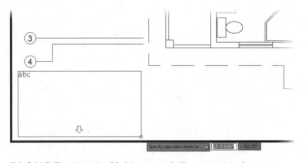

FIGURE 8.59 Making a multiline text window

Once you've defined the Multiline Text window, the Text Editor contextual Ribbon opens, providing options to configure and edit your Mtext entities. The Text Editor contextual Ribbon tab and its associated panels appear in the Ribbon.

The Style and Formatting panels allow you to see the current text style and its font and height, as shown in Figure 8.60. Just above the rectangle you defined, the Multiline Text Editor opens. This is where you'll enter the text.

FIGURE 8.60 The Style and Formatting panels on the Text Editor tab

9. Enter the following text, using single spacing and pressing ↵ only at the end of the first line and at the end of each note. Lines that are longer than the window that you dragged out will wrap automatically:

GENERAL NOTES:

All work shall be in accordance with the 2000 Ed. Uniform Building Code and all local ordinances.

Roof can be built steeper for climates with heavy snowfall.

All windows to be double-paned.

10. When you've finished, click a blank spot in the drawing area.

The text appears in the drawing (see the top of Figure 8.61). The window you specified was used only to define the line length. Its height doesn't control how far down the text extends; that is determined by how much text you enter.

Before you adjust the text to fit the area, you will have AutoCAD add numbering to the notes.

11. Double-click anywhere on the new text to display the Multiline Text Editor and the Mtext panels.

12. Move the cursor to the upper-left corner of the window containing the text and in front of the *A* in the first word (*All*) of the first note.

13. Hold down the left mouse button, and drag to the right and down until all the remaining text is highlighted. Release the mouse button.

14. Expand the Bullets And Numbering drop-down list in the contextual Text Editor tab ➤ Paragraph panel and then choose Numbered from the cascading menu that pops up (see the middle of Figure 8.61).

15. The note numbers appear. Click the Close Text Editor button on the Close panel.

16. Select the text object and open the Properties palette.

17. Select the GENERAL NOTES: text, and in the Text rollout, highlight the Annotation Text Height input field and change the value from 1/8″ (5) to 3/16″ (4.5), and press ↵.

AutoCAD redraws the GENERAL NOTES: text larger.

GENERAL NOTES:
All work shall be in accordance with the 2000 Ed.
Uniform Building Code and all local ordinances.
Roof can be built steeper for climates with higher
snowfall.
All windows to be double-paned.

GENERAL NOTES:
1. All work shall be in accordance with the 2000 Ed.
   Uniform Building Code and all local
   ordinances.

2. Roof can be built steeper for climates with higher
   snowfall.
3. All windows to be double-paned.

FIGURE 8.61 Mtext in the drawing (top), adding the
note numbers (middle), and the modified text (bottom)

18. Use the grip at the upper-right corner of the text to stretch the text box farther to the right.

The text reconfigures to fit the new constraints (see the bottom of Figure 8.61).

19. Double-click the Mtext again. The Text Editor tab opens.

20. Place your cursor after the *ordinances* text. Expand the Columns tool on the contextual Text Editor tab ➤ Insert panel, and choose Insert Column Break, as shown at the top of Figure 8.62. Your Mtext entity should look like the bottom of Figure 8.62 after inserting the column break.

> Inserting a column break may insert an additional number in the GENERAL NOTES numbered list. If this happens, use the backspace key to remove the additional line.

21. Use the double-arrow to the far right of the Multiline Text Editor to position the new column closer to the first column on the left, as shown in Figure 8.63.

22. Use the diamond grip between the two columns to adjust the width for both columns so they will fit along the lower edge of your drawing (see the top of Figure 8.64).

Your GENERAL NOTES text block should look like the bottom image in Figure 8.64.

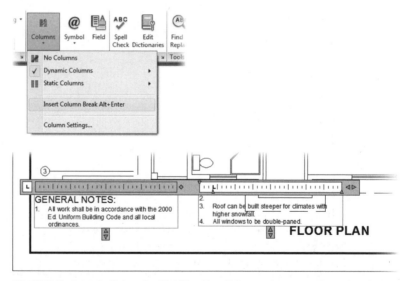

FIGURE 8.62 Using the Multiline Text Editor to insert a column break (top) and a new column (bottom)

23. Complete the composition of your drawing sheet by using the MOVE and STRETCH commands.

   a. Move the GENERAL NOTES text to the lower-left corner of the title block drawing area.

   b. After positioning the GENERAL NOTES text, move the title block down until the cabin fits neatly within the upper-border area and the notes are unobstructed.

   c. Use the STRETCH command to bring the vertical column grid-lines within the title block drawing area.

   Once complete, your drawing should resemble Figure 8.65.

Use this slider to adjust column spacing

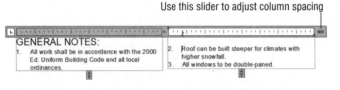

FIGURE 8.63 Using the column slider to adjust column spacing

Use this slider to adjust column width

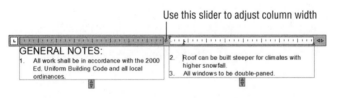

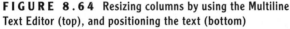

FIGURE 8.64 Resizing columns by using the Multiline Text Editor (top), and positioning the text (bottom)

Formatting Individual Words within Mtext Entities

When TrueType fonts are used in AutoCAD drawings, any combination of formatting options may be applied. For example, you may choose to apply bold or italicized formatting to some portion of a Mtext entity. To see how to change individual words within the text, you'll underline and bold the Uniform Building Code text:

1. Zoom into and double-click the Mtext again.

2. Use the same technique as you did earlier to highlight only the Uniform Building Code text.

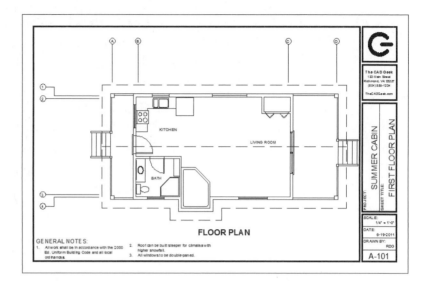

FIGURE 8.65 The results of text and title block adjustments

3. Click the Bold and Underline buttons on the Formatting panel. This underlines the selected text and displays the bold feature.

4. Click in the drawing area.
AutoCAD redraws the text with the changes (see Figure 8.66).

5. Save this drawing as **I08-16-GeneralNotes.dwg** (**M08-16-General Notes.dwg**).

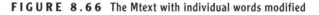

GENERAL NOTES:
1.   All work shall be in accordance with the 2000
     Ed. **Uniform Building Code** and all local
     ordinances.

FIGURE 8.66 The Mtext with individual words modified

You just created an Mtext entity and organized your GENERAL NOTES into columns. Organizing large blocks of text is commonly done in many plan sets. While you could create multiple Mtext entities to organize your text into columns, the column feature provides a much more comprehensive approach. By keeping everything contained inside a single Mtext entity, you'll ensure that features such as numbered lists work in a more predictable manner.

In addition to columns, you also learned how to format individual words within an Mtext entity. You can italicize individual words and give them a different color or height from the rest of the Mtext by using the other tools on the Multiline Text panel. I encourage you to experiment with all these tools to become familiar with them. Another feature of Mtext is the ability to insert hyperlinks.

Adding a Hyperlink

You have the ability to add *hyperlinks*, links to web pages or files, to the body of an Mtext object. When a hyperlink to a URL exists, anyone with the drawing open can hold down the Ctrl button and click the link to open the associated page in their web browser. Hyperlinks can also point to local or network files, causing the file's associated application to open when they are clicked. Here is the procedure for adding a hyperlink:

1. Make sure I08-16-GeneralNotes.dwg (M08-16-GeneralNotes.dwg) is open.

2. Double-click the Mtext object.

3. Highlight the Uniform Building Code text to indicate where you want the hyperlink to appear.

4. On the contextual Text Editor tab ➢ Insert panel, click Field, or right-click and choose Insert Field from the context menu.

5. In the Field Category section of the Field dialog box that opens, select Linked.

6. Next, select Hyperlink from the Field Names section directly below the Field Category section.

7. In the Text To Display field, enter **Uniform Building Code**.
   This is the text that will appear in the tooltip when the cursor hovers over the hyperlink (see Figure 8.67).

8. Click the Hyperlink button; then, in the Edit Hyperlink dialog box (see Figure 8.68), you can do any of the following:

   ▶ Enter the web page or filename and path in the Type The File Or Web Page Name box.

   ▶ Click the File button under Browse For to select a file that you will link to the text.

   ▶ Click the Web Page button under Browse For to navigate to the web page that you will link to the text.

9. Ensure that Existing File Or Web Page is selected on the right side of the dialog box, and then enter http://www.iccsafe.org into the Type The File Or Web Page Name text box.

10. Click OK twice to close both the Edit Hyperlink and Field dialog boxes.

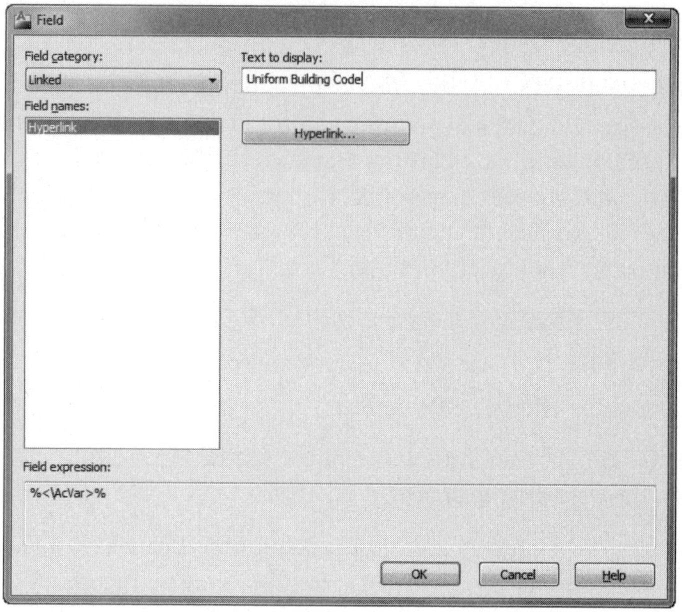

FIGURE 8.67 The Field dialog box

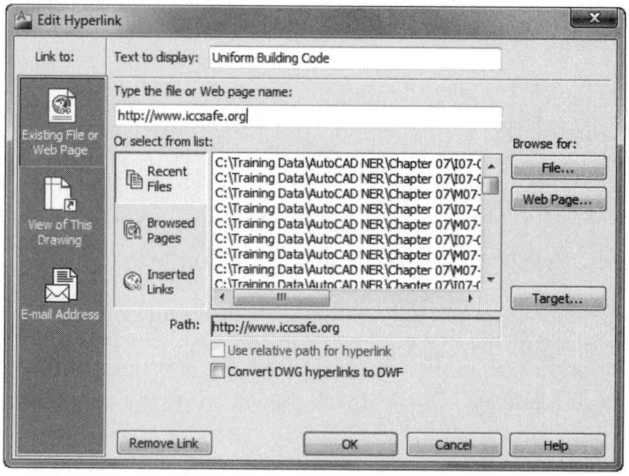

FIGURE 8.68 The Edit Hyperlink dialog box

11. Click a blank area to deselect the Mtext.

    The link appears as text with a gray background; the background doesn't appear in a printed drawing.

12. Hover the cursor over the gray background (see Figure 8.69).

    The cursor changes to the hyperlink cursor.

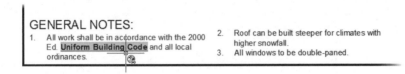
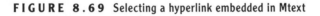

GENERAL NOTES:

1. All work shall be in accordance with the 2000 Ed. Uniform Building Code and all local ordinances.

2. Roof can be built steeper for climates with higher snowfall.

3. All windows to be double-paned.

FIGURE 8.69 Selecting a hyperlink embedded in Mtext

13. Hold the Ctrl key down and click the background.

    This opens your browser and navigates to the selected web page.

14. Perform a Zoom Extents, and then save this drawing as **I08-17-Hyperlink.dwg** (**M08-17-Hyperlink.dwg**).

Your drawing should look like Figure 8.70.

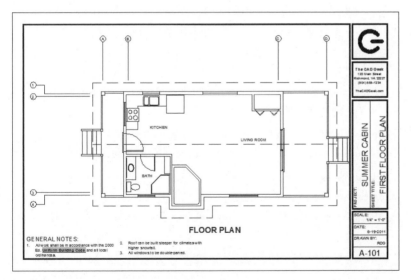

FIGURE 8.70 The cabin with the text added

Using the Spell-Check Feature

Like most programs with word processing capability, AutoCAD includes a spell-check feature to identify potential spelling errors. The spell check can be run to look for errors in a selected single-line or multiline text object. There is also a real-time spell-check feature to spot misspellings as you type and to suggest alternative words.

Realtime Spell-Checking

Follow these steps to see the spell-check feature in action:

1. Make sure I08-17-Hyperlink.dwg (M08-17-Hyperlink.dwg) is open.

2. Zoom in to the notes at the bottom of the drawing area and move them up enough to allow space for one more line of text.

3. Expand the Mtext window down to accommodate the next line of text.

4. Double-click the notes, place the cursor just past the period at the end of the third note, and type ↵Soler panels, by SolCorp, are available.↵↵. (You are intentionally misspelling *solar*.)

   The fourth numbered note is appended to the others.

5. From the contextual Text Editor tab, click the Spell Check button, found on the Spell Check panel, to enable spell check.

6. Notice how the words *Soler* and *SolCorp* are underlined with a dashed line (see Figure 8.71).

   This is how the real-time spell-check tool identifies the words the AutoCAD dictionary doesn't recognize.

7. Position the cursor in the word Soler, and right-click to open a context menu. At the top of the menu are spelling suggestions.

8. Click or pause the cursor over the More Suggestions options; then click Solar, as shown in Figure 8.72.

   Soler is replaced with *Solar* in the selected Mtext.

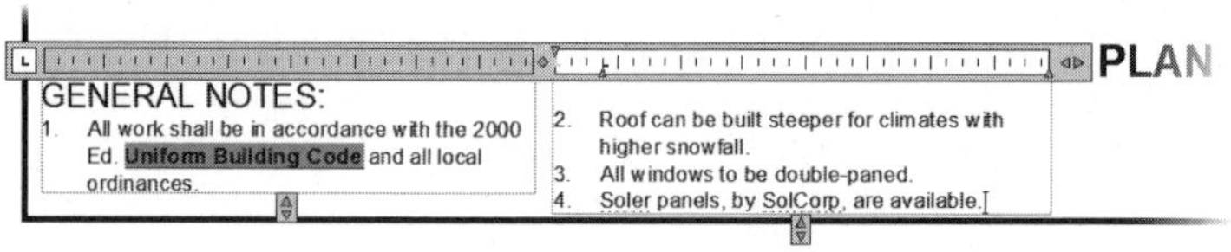

FIGURE 8.71 The new line of text with the misspelled words

Many words that you frequently use, such as company, city, or individual names, may not exist in the AutoCAD dictionary and will be flagged as misspelled words. You can easily add words to the dictionary to keep these words from being flagged repeatedly.

9. Put the cursor in the word SolCorp, and right-click to open the context menu.

10. Near the top of the menu, click Add To Dictionary (see Figure 8.73). SolCorp is added to the AutoCAD dictionary and is no longer underlined.

11. Save this drawing as **I08-18-SpellCheck.dwg** (**M08-18-SpellCheck.dwg**).

Solder	
Solver	
Sole	
More Suggestions ▶	Spooler
	Solar
Add to Dictionary	Scolder
Ignore All	Seller
	Smolder
Select All Ctrl+A	Solders
Cut Ctrl+X	Solvers
Copy Ctrl+C	Spoiler
Paste Ctrl+V	Older
Paste Special ▶	Slier
Insert Field... Ctrl+F	

FIGURE 8.72 Using the context menu to replace a misspelled word

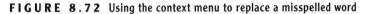

Sloop
Solo
Selector
More Suggestions   ▶
Add to Dictionary
Ignore All
Select All   Ctrl+A
Cut   Ctrl+X
Copy   Ctrl+C
Paste   Ctrl+V
Paste Special   ▶

FIGURE 8.73 Adding a word to the AutoCAD dictionary

Spell-Checking an Entire Drawing

Often, drawings can have many separate text elements in the form of single-line text, multiline text, and dimensions. Although you can select each object individually, you can also run the Spell Check tool on the entire drawing. Here's how:

1. Make sure I08-18-SpellCheck.dwg (M08-18-SpellCheck.dwg) is open.

2. Make sure nothing is selected in the drawing. Then, under the Annotate tab, click the Check Spelling button in the Annotate tab ➤ Text panel.

3. In the Check Spelling dialog box that opens, choose Entire Drawing in the Where To Check drop-down list and then click Start.

   AutoCAD checks the entire drawing for words that do not exist in the dictionary, highlights them, and offers suggestions for apparently misspelled words, such as the initials RDG in Figure 8.74.

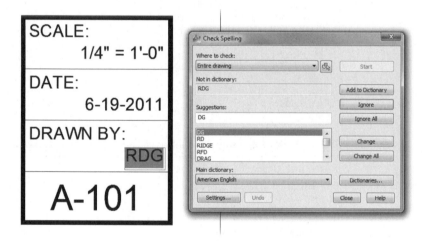

FIGURE 8.74 The Check Spelling dialog box and an unknown word

4. When an unknown word is identified, you can do any of the following:

   ▶ Click Add To Dictionary to add the word to the AutoCAD dictionary.

   ▶ Click Ignore to take no action and continue searching the drawing for misspelled words.

   ▶ Click Ignore All to take no action and continue searching the drawing for misspelled words, ignoring all occurrences of the flagged word.

▶ Select a word in the Suggestions list and then click Change to replace the flagged word with the suggested word.

▶ Select a word in the Suggestions list and then click Change All to replace the flagged word with the suggested word and automatically substitute all occurrences of the flagged word for the suggested word.

5. When the spell-checking task is finished, do the following:

   a. Click OK in the Spell Check Complete dialog box.

   b. Click Close in the Check Spelling dialog box.

6. Perform a Zoom Extents, and then save this drawing as **I08A-FPLAY0.dwg** (**M08A-FPLAY0.dwg**).

Exploring Other Aspects of Multiline Text

Multiline text has several other features that I can only touch on in this book. I encourage you to experiment with any features that you might find useful to your work.

Using Justification Points

Mtext has justification points similar to those of single-line text, and they behave the same way. The default justification point for Mtext, however, is the upper-left corner of the body of text, and the available options are for nine points distributed around the perimeter of the body of text and at the center (see Figure 8.75).

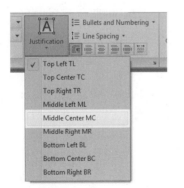

FIGURE 8.75 Justification points for Mtext

When you need to modify the justification of Mtext, double-click the text to open the Multiline Text Editor and display the Text Editor tab and panels. In the Paragraph panel, click the Justification button and then click the justification preference from the fly-out menu, as shown in Figure 8.76. I'll describe the other items on this menu in the following "Tools for Modifying Multiline Text" sidebar.

FIGURE 8.76 Modifying the justification of Mtext

Tools for Modifying Multiline Text

Here's a brief summary of the various features of the contextual Text Editor tab's panels that are available whenever Mtext is selected with a double-click:

The Style Panel

Style List   Lists all existing text styles in the drawing file.

Annotative Button   Toggles the Annotative property for text and dimensions. This property can cause the text to scale automatically as necessary. Chapter 12 covers annotation.

Text Height Drop-Down Text Box   Sets the height for selected text or sets the height for subsequently entered text.

The Formatting Panel

Bold, Italic, Underline, and Overline Buttons   Changes selected text or sets up for subsequently entered text.

Make Uppercase and Make Lowercase Buttons   Changes the case of the selected text to all uppercase or all lowercase.

(Continues)

TOOLS FOR MODIFYING MULTILINE TEXT *(Continued)*

Font Drop-Down List   Sets the font for the selected text or sets the font for subsequently entered text.

Color Drop-Down List   Changes the color of a selected portion of text or sets a color for subsequently entered text.

Background Mask Button   Sets the parameters for using a background mask to hide objects behind the text.

Oblique Angle Spinner Buttons   Sets the selected text to an oblique angle off the vertical, from −85° to the left to 85° to the right.

Tracking Spinner Buttons   Adjusts the spacing between selected letters from a minimum of 75 percent of the default spacing to a maximum of four times the default spacing.

Width Factor Spinner Buttons   Adjusts the width of selected letters and the spacing between them from a minimum of 10 percent of the default width and spacing to a maximum of 10 times the default.

Stack   Creates fractions and tolerance forms by stacking text objects and *mleaders*.

The Paragraph Panel

Justification Button   Displays a menu with the nine Mtext justification choices.

Bullets and Numbering Button   Opens a fly-out menu for controlling numbering and bullets.

Line Spacing Button   Opens a fly-out menu for controlling spacing between lines of text.

Combine Paragraphs Button   Removes the line break between two or more paragraphs, and combines them into a single paragraph.

Paragraph Button   Clicking the arrow on the right opens the Paragraph dialog box where you can set tab and paragraph spacing, indents, and other paragraph-related parameters.

Left, Center, Right, Justify, and Distribute Buttons   Justifies the selected text accordingly.

The Insert Panel

Columns Button   Opens a menu for controlling the column options.

(Continues)

TOOLS FOR MODIFYING MULTILINE TEXT *(Continued)*

Symbol Button   Opens a menu of symbols to insert into the Mtext where the cursor rests.

Field Button   Begins the process of inserting a field in the Mtext in place of selected text or where the cursor rests in the text.

The Spell Check Panel

Spell Check Button   Runs the Spell Check utility.

Edit Dictionaries   Opens the Dictionaries dialog box, where custom dictionaries can be selected and edited.

The Tools Panel

Find & Replace Button   Opens the Find and Replace dialog box, where you can specify a text string to search for and the text string that will replace it.

Import Text   Imports a word processing or text file into an AutoCAD drawing. The maximum size allowed is 32 KB, so the smallest document possible in some versions of Microsoft Word is too large. You can, however, use files in text-only or RTF formats. Clicking the Import Text button opens the Select File dialog box that displays only files with the `.txt` and `.rtf` extensions. You can bring in text files with other extensions if you enter the full filename with its extension and if they aren't larger than 32 KB. Text comes in as Mtext and uses the current text style, height setting, and layer. The imported file might not retain complex code fields for such elements as tabs, multiple margin indents, and so on.

AutoCAPS   When checked, capitalizes all text.

The Options Panel

More   Displays a menu with several options for adjusting the parameters for text, Mtext, and the Multiline Text Editor.

Ruler Button   Toggles the ruler above the Mtext to be visible or invisible.

Undo Button   Undoes the last editing action.

Redo Button   Redoes the last undo.

The Close Panel

Close Button   Deselects the Mtext and closes the Multiline Text tab.

(Continues)

TOOLS FOR MODIFYING MULTILINE TEXT *(Continued)*

The Mtext Context Menu

The features of the Mtext context menu, the menu that appears when you place your cursor in the text or highlight text and right-click, are as follows:

Spelling Suggestions If the highlighted text is not in the dictionary, a set of suggested words is displayed along with a cascading menu with additional word options.

Add to Dictionary and Ignore All Two more actions available when misspelled words are highlighted.

Select All Selects and highlights all the text in the selected Mtext object.

Cut Copies the selected text to the Windows Clipboard and deletes it from the Mtext object.

Copy Copies the selected text to the Windows Clipboard.

Paste Pastes text from the Windows Clipboard to the cursor location in the Mtext objects.

Paste Special Displays a submenu containing additional methods for pasting content into an Mtext object.

Insert Field Opens the Field dialog box, which you use to insert a field into the selected text. If you select text containing a field, this menu item changes to three menu items: Edit Field, Update Field, and Convert Field To Text.

Symbol Imports symbols (such as diameter, degree, and so on) that aren't available in the font you're using.

Import Text Imports a word processing or text file into an AutoCAD drawing, as described under "The Tools Panel" earlier in this sidebar.

Paragraph Alignment Sets the justification for the selected Mtext.

Paragraph Opens the Paragraph dialog box. It has settings for indenting the first line and subsequent paragraphs of Mtext (similar to what the sliders do on the ruler above the Multiline Text Editor window) and tab stop positions.

Bullets and Lists Opens a fly-out menu that offers various options for using the listing features.

Columns Provides access to the column parameters.

(Continues)

TOOLS FOR MODIFYING MULTILINE TEXT *(Continued)*

Find and Replace   Opens the Replace dialog box, in which you search for a word or a series of words (text string) and replace them with text that you specify.

Change Case   Changes the case of all highlighted text to uppercase or lowercase.

AutoCAPS   When checked, capitalizes all text.

Character Set   Opens a menu of several languages. When applicable, the codes of the selected language are applied to selected text.

Combine Paragraphs   Joins highlighted individual paragraphs into one paragraph.

Remove Formatting   Removes formatting, such as bold, underline, and so on, from highlighted text.

Background Mask   Opens the Background Mask dialog box in which you specify color for and activate a background mask to go behind the selected Mtext object.

Editor Settings   Opens a menu where you can select whether certain features appear, such as the ruler or toolbar.

Help   Opens the AutoCAD Help file at the entry regarding Mtext.

Cancel   Closes the menu.

Adding Special Characters

With Mtext, you can add special characters—the degree symbol, the diameter symbol, and so on—that aren't included in most font character packages. You'll have a chance to do this in Chapter 12.

If you want to experiment with the Mtext in the cabin drawing, make a copy of it and place it outside the title block. Double-click it and see what you can learn about the Multiline Text Editor, the tools found in the panels located under the Multiline Text tab, and the Mtext shortcut menu. The preceding "Tools for Modifying Multiline Text" sidebar summarizes the features of the latter two.

If You Would Like More Practice...

Trades and professions other than architecture and construction use text with AutoCAD and LT in the same way as demonstrated in this chapter.

For more practice using single-line text, follow these steps:

1. Close all drawings, and then open 08A-FPGARG.dwg.

2. Using the DesignCenter, bring in the A-Title and A-Label text styles from the 08A-FPLAY0 drawing while it's closed.

3. Place labels on the features that were added:

   ▶ Use the A-Title text style to identify the addition as **GARAGE**.

   ▶ Use the A-Label text style to give the features the following names: **WALKWAY, STORAGE, OFFICE,** and **CAR.**

For more practice using Mtext, follow these steps:

1. Open 08A-FPLAY0, and zoom into the blank space between the notes and the title block.

2. Create a new text style called A-Desc that uses the Times New Roman font and a height of 8″ (204 mm).

3. Start Mtext, and specify a rectangle for the text that covers the area between the notes and the title bar.

4. Enter the following text exactly as shown here, spelling errors and all:

   This is a design for a small vaction cabin. It contains approximately 380 square feet of living space and includes one bedroom and one bath. It can be adopted to provide shelter in all climates and can be modified to allow constuction that uses local building materials. Please sund all inquiries to the manufacturer.

5. Double-click the new text and make these changes:

   a. Correct all spelling errors by using the Spell Check tool or real-time spell checking.

   b. Change *square feet* to **sq. ft.**

   c. Bold the following: *one bedroom, one bath, all climates,* and *local building materials.*

   d. Italicize the last sentence.

Are You Experienced?

Now you can...

- ☑ set up text styles
- ☑ place single-line text in a drawing for titles and room labels
- ☑ create a structural grid for a drawing
- ☑ modify single-line text
- ☑ construct a title block and place text in it
- ☑ open AutoCAD template files
- ☑ place Mtext in a drawing
- ☑ modify Mtext in several ways
- ☑ add a hyperlink to an Mtext object
- ☑ check the spelling in a drawing

Using Dynamic Blocks and Tables

In Chapter 7, "Combining Objects into Blocks," you explored creating and using blocks to combine separate objects into a single, complex object to aid in selecting objects and editing properties. Chapter 8, "Controlling Text in a Drawing," covered the addition of text into drawings. In this chapter, you will expand your knowledge of blocks and use text inside blocks and tables to display information about specific features of the drawing.

The blocks you've worked with have been static collections of objects that you have inserted throughout your drawing as doors or windows. Each instance of the same block was visually identical to the others, and you were able to scale the window blocks along one axis and without distortion to fit the walls. Blocks can also contain textual information, called *attributes*, which are specific to an individual block instance. Blocks do not have to remain static and unchanging. In this chapter, you will learn how to define your blocks so that they can change as required, without needing to explode the blocks and modify the component objects.

After exploring blocks further, you'll learn how to create a table to act as a door schedule, displaying the door type, unit price, and total cost. A *schedule* is a chart in a drawing that contains logically organized information about a particular component of a project, such as a steel base plate, valve, bolt, screw, door, window, or room finish. Each of these components has its own schedule. Information in a door schedule, for example, might include size, material, finish, location, and type of jamb.

- ▶ **Adding block attributes**
- ▶ **Calculating area**
- ▶ **Adding fields as attributes**
- ▶ **Creating dynamic blocks**
- ▶ **Creating tables**
- ▶ **Extracting data from attributes into tables**

Using Attributes for a Grid

In Chapter 8, you added a series of gridlines to your cabin. These gridlines were placed at the centerlines of structural components such as walls or columns. Especially in larger plans, these gridlines often provide critical points of reference for collaborating with contractors and other consultants over the phone. What makes the structural gridlines so useful is the way they're labeled. Gridlines are most often labeled using a circle or hexagon with numbers running in one direction (horizontally or vertically), and letters running in the other. Because more-elaborate floor plans will likely have multiple closets, it's rather ambiguous to ask someone to look at the closet in a plan. Instead you might say, "Have a look at the closet near gridline intersection C2."

Just as the gridlines help make your printed plans more useful, blocks can do the same inside your drawings by combining multiple related objects into a single AutoCAD entity. Because each grid needs to have a unique letter or number, creating a static block as you did in Chapter 7 won't work for this application. Instead, you need a block that can display a unique number or letter for each block insertion. You can achieve this level of interaction with any block by adding attributes to its definition.

A simple but handy use of attributes is to make the letter or number in the circle an attribute and then make a block out of the attribute and circle. By redoing the grid symbols in the cabin drawing, you'll learn how to set up attributes and create a new block that can be used in any other drawing. Because you'll define the block as an *annotative block*, the grid label blocks you create will not be scale dependent.

1. Open I08-A-FPLAYO.dwg (M08-A-FPLAYO.dwg).

    The drawing consists of the floor plan with a structural grid, notes, and a title block.

2. Make sure the A-GRID layer is current, and then freeze the A-ANNO -TTLB and A-ANNO-TTLB-TEXT layers.

 T I P   You've already seen how the –LAYER command can be used to create new layers, but it can also be useful in layer management. Instead of freezing the two A-ANNO-TTLB layers individually, try entering –LAYER↵ F↵ *TTLB*↵↵. This command sequence tells AutoCAD to freeze all TTLB layers at once. The asterisk (*) is a wildcard character that tells AutoCAD to look for any layers with TTLB in their names—and in this case freeze them.

3. Zoom in to the floor plan, keeping the grid visible.

In this case, the letters run horizontally across the top, and the numbers run vertically along the side.

4. Erase all the circles, letters, and numbers in the grid except for A and 1. Leave the gridlines intact (see Figure 9.1).

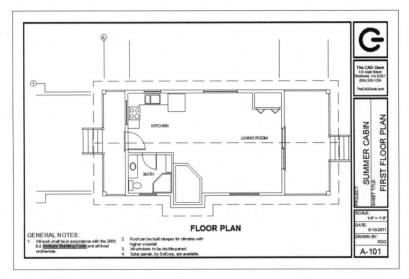

FIGURE 9.1 The floor plan of I08-A-FPLAYO (M08-A-FPLAYO) with all but two grid symbols erased

5. Turn off the Automatically Add Annotative Scales mode from the status bar (the icon dims, and the lightbulb turns gray).

6. Change your current annotation scale to 1:1, as shown in Figure 9.2.

7. Start the SCALE command.

8. Select the top-left circle and press ↵.

9. At the Specify base point: prompt, use the Endpoint osnap, and pick the endpoint of the gridline where it meets the circle.

10. Enter 1/48↵ (1/50↵).

This reduces the circle to its actual plot height.

11. Repeat steps 7–9 for the circle on the left side.

12. Start the ATTDEF command by clicking the Define Attributes button on the Insert tab ➤ Block Definition panel. The Attribute Definition dialog box opens (see Figure 9.3).

In the Attribute group are three text boxes: Tag, Prompt, and Default. The cursor is flashing in the Tag text box. Think of the letter in the grid circle. It's a grid letter, which is a tag that provides the visual textual information.

13. Enter **GRID-LETTER.** *Don't* press ↵.

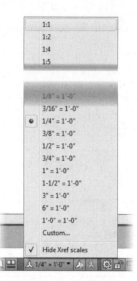

FIGURE 9.2 Changing the current annotation scale to 1:1

FIGURE 9.3 The Attribute Definition dialog box

14. Press the Tab key to move to the Prompt text box.

Here you enter a prompt that will display for a future user. When a user inserts a block containing the attribute, the prompt will ask the user to input text for the tag.

15. Key in **Enter grid letter**, again *without* pressing ↵.

16. Press Tab to move to the Default text box.

Here you enter a default or sample value that will be used if the future user presses ↵ instead of entering a new value. You want the letter capitalized in this case, so enter **A**.

This sets up the attribute so that the user setting up the grid will be prompted to enter the grid letter and will be given a default of A. The capital A lets the user know that the letter should be uppercase.

The lower portion of the dialog box is where you set up parameters for the attribute text: location in the drawing, justification, text style, height, and rotation.

17. Click the Justification drop-down list, and select Middle Center.

18. Choose A-Label in the Text Style list box.

Because the A-Label text style is annotative, the Annotative check box is automatically selected. Likewise, because a text height other than 0′-0″ (0) is associated with the A-Label text style, the Text Height text box is grayed out.

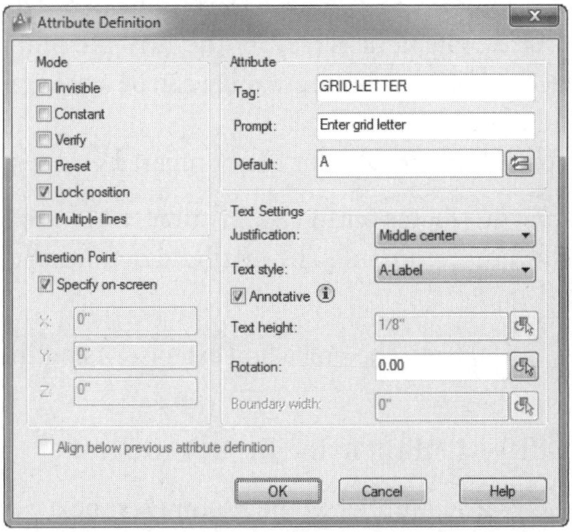

FIGURE 9.4 The Attribute Definition dialog box showing the appropriate values

19. Make sure the only check box selected in the Mode group is Lock Position. The Attribute Definition dialog box should look like Figure 9.4.

20. Click OK. Doing so returns you to the drawing to pick an insertion point.

21. Back in the drawing, use the Center osnap, and click the circle at the top of the grid.

GRID-LETTER is centered over the circle (see Figure 9.5), and the ATTDEF command ends.

FIGURE 9.5 The first attribute definition placed in the grid circle

The text over the circle is called the *attribute definition*. Its function in AutoCAD is similar to that of a block definition. When you made the A-GLAZ block for the windows, the definition was a 12″ (305 mm) long window with an insertion point. When the A-GLAZ block is inserted, you can use the original block definition to make windows of various sizes. The same is true for the attribute definition. When it becomes part of a block that's inserted, the attribute can be any letter you want. You'll see that happen in a minute.

First make a similar attribute definition for the numbered grid symbol:

1. Click the Define Attributes button again or enter **ATT**↵ to start the Attribute Definition command. The Attribute Definition dialog box opens again.

2. Repeat steps 7 to 20 from the preceding exercise, using the following guidelines:

   a. Enter **GRID-NUMBER** in the Tag text box.

   b. Enter **Enter grid number** in the Prompt text box.

   c. Enter 1 in the Default text box.

    d. Select Middle Center from the Justification drop-down list.

    e. Click OK, use the Center osnap, and click the grid circle on the left.

The second attribute definition is centered over the circle (see Figure 9.6).

3. Save your drawing as `I09-01-DefineAttribute.dwg` (`M09-01-Define Attribute.dwg`).

GRID-NUMBER

FIGURE 9.6 The second attribute definition is placed.

You now have two attribute definitions and are ready to make each of them part of a block that includes the circle over which they're currently centered.

Defining Blocks with Attributes

You have to define two blocks for the grid symbols and their attributes. The insertion point for the block used for the top of the grid should be at the lowest point of the circle. The insertion point for the block used for the left side should be at the point on the circle farthest to the right. Follow these steps:

1. Make sure `I09-01-DefineAttribute.dwg` (`M09-01-DefineAttribute .dwg`) is open.

2. Click the Create Block button on the Block Definition panel to start the `BLOCK` command, and open the Block Definition dialog box.

3. In the Name drop-down list, enter GRID-V (for vertical) and then click the Pick Point button in the Base Point group.

4. In the drawing, use the Endpoint osnap and select the gridline that ends at the circle on top.

5. In the Block Definition dialog box that reopens, click the Select Objects button in the Objects group.

6. In the drawing, select the circle and attribute definition on the top. Press ↵.

The Block Definition dialog box reopens once again.

7. Click the Annotative check box in the Behavior group.

8. Be sure the Delete button is selected in the Objects group.

9. Verify that the Block Definition dialog box looks like Figure 9.7 and click OK.

The block is defined and includes the attribute definition. In the drawing, the top circle and attribute definition have been deleted.

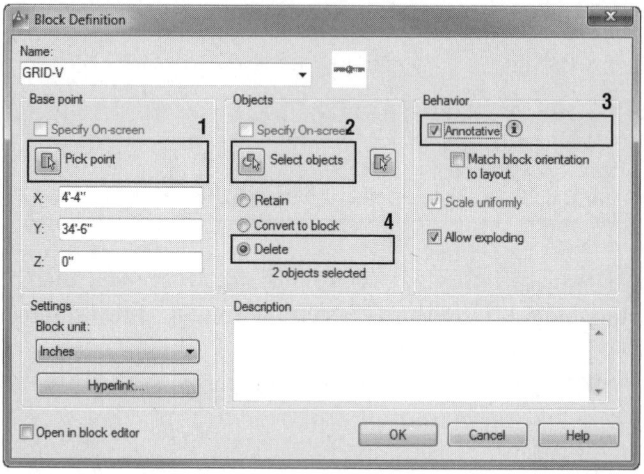

FIGURE 9.7 The Block Definition dialog box for the GRID-V attribute block

10. Click the Create button again.

11. Repeat steps 2 through 8 to define a second block for the circle and attribute definition on the left side. Use the following guidelines:

    a. Enter GRID-H from the Name drop-down list.

    b. Click Pick Point. Use the Endpoint osnap, and pick the horizontal gridline that ends at the rightmost point of the grid circle on the left of the floor plan.

    c. When selecting objects, select the circle on the left and its attribute definition.

When you complete the command, you have a second block definition that includes an attribute definition and no grid circles in the drawing.

12. Save your drawing as **I09-02-BlockDefinition.dwg** (**M09-02-Block Definition.dwg**).

Inserting Blocks with Attributes

Let's insert these blocks (which are now grid symbols) at the endpoints of the grid-lines. As you insert them, you'll assign them the appropriate letter or number, but first you'll make sure that AutoCAD uses a dialog box to prompt for the user input:

1. Make sure I09-02-BlockDefinition.dwg (M09-02-BlockDefinition.dwg) is open.

2. From the status bar, change the annotation scale to 1/4″ = 1′-0″ ↵↵.

3. Be sure the Endpoint osnap is running, and then enter **ATTDIA**↵.

4. If the value in the angle brackets is set to 0, press ↵. Otherwise, enter **0**↵.

5. Click the Insert button in the Block panel or enter **I**↵.

6. In the Insert dialog box, open the Name drop-down list, and select GRID-V.

7. Be sure the Specify On-Screen box is checked for Insertion Point but not for Scale and Rotation, so that those values remain constant among the blocks and you're not prompted to change them. Click OK.

8. Click the leftmost vertical gridline in the drawing.
   Now look at the bottom line in the command window or the command prompt at the cursor, as shown in Figure 9.8. This is the text you entered in the Attribute Definition dialog box for the prompt. *A* is the text you entered as the default value. The last line also appears at the command prompt attached to the cursor.

9. To accept the default value for this gridline, press ↵.

10. Pressing ↵ inserts the grid symbol at the endpoint of the leftmost vertical gridline (see Figure 9.9).

11. Press ↵ to restart the INSERT command.

12. Click OK to accept GRID-V as the current block to be inserted.

13. Click the gridline to the right of the one you just selected.

14. At the Enter grid letter <A>: prompt, enter **B**↵.
    The second grid symbol is inserted on a gridline, and the letter B is located in the circle. Be sure to use a capital B here; the tag will not prevent you from using a lowercase letter, but drawing standards require consistency.

The ATTDIA variable defines whether the INSERT command opens a dialog box or prompts the user at the command prompt for attribute information. When the variable is set to 0, no dialog box is used.

Although you defined the GRID-V block at a much smaller scale, notice how it inserts at the correct scale. Just as text does, an annotative block sizes itself based on the current annotation scale when you insert it.

15. Repeat steps 12 through 14 to insert the other two grid symbols across the top of the floor plan, incrementing the values for each.

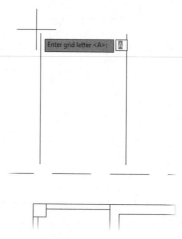

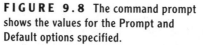

FIGURE 9.8 The command prompt shows the values for the Prompt and Default options specified.

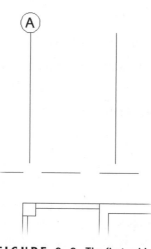

FIGURE 9.9 The first grid symbol block is inserted.

16. Continue repeating steps 12 through 14, but select the GRID-H block for the four grid symbols that run down the left side of the floor plan. The result should look like Figure 9.10.

17. Save your drawing as I09-03-InsertAttribute.dwg (M09-03-Insert Attribute.dwg).

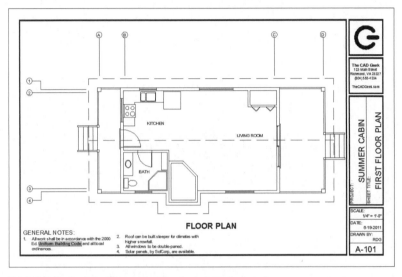

FIGURE 9.10 The grid with all symbols inserted

Editing Attribute Text

To illustrate how you can edit attribute text, let's assume you decide to change the C grid symbol to B1. You must then change the D symbol to C. Here are the steps:

1. Make sure I09-03-InsertAttribute.dwg (M09-03-InsertAttribute .dwg) is open.

2. Double-click the C grid symbol.

    Doing so opens the Enhanced Attribute Editor dialog box shown in Figure 9.11. You can change several items here, but you want to change only the Value parameter.

3. Be sure the Attribute tab is selected. Highlight C in the Value text box, enter B1, and then click the Apply button.

    B1 replaces C in the larger window where the tag, prompt, and value appear together.

4. Click OK to close the dialog box.

 N O T E   Because you set the justification point for the attribute text to Middle Center and located the text at the center of the grid circle, the B1 text is centered in the circle just like the single letters.

5. Double-click the D grid symbol.

6. In the Enhanced Attribute Editor dialog box, repeat step 3 to change D to C. The attributes are updated (see Figure 9.12).

7. Save your drawing as **I09-04-EditAttributes.dwg** (**M09-04-Edit Attributes.dwg**).

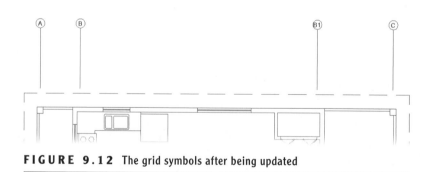

FIGURE 9.11   The Enhanced Attribute Editor dialog box

FIGURE 9.12   The grid symbols after being updated

The exercises in this chapter so far have illustrated the basic procedures for defining, inserting, and changing attributes. You can apply these same procedures to the process of setting up a title block in which attributes are used for text that changes from one sheet to the next. You can now move to a more complex application of the attribute feature to see its full power.

Setting Up Multiple Attributes in a Block

The cabin has three rooms and two decks, with the kitchen and living room sharing the same space. Each room has a different area and floor covering. You can store this information, along with the room name, in the drawing as attributes. You'll set up a block that consists of three attributes (name, area, and covering). You'll then insert the block back into the floor plan. As you may remember, the text style for the room labels is A-Label. You'll use that for the attributes.

You have to erase the room labels for now, but it will be handy to mark their justification points. That way, you can insert the attribute exactly where the label text is now. Follow these steps:

1. Make sure I09-04-EditAttributes.dwg (M09-04-EditAttributes .dwg) is open.

 2. Thaw the A-ANNO-TTLB-TEXT layer.

3. With layer 0 current, from the menu bar, expand the Utilities panel on the Home tab and choose Point Style, or enter **DDPTYPE**↵ to open the Point Style dialog box (see Figure 9.13).

FIGURE 9.13 The Point Style dialog box

N O T E   A *point* is a single location in space, defined by an X, Y, and Z position, with no area or volume. The Point Style dialog box determines how the marker at the point location appears. By default, the point appears as a single pixel, which can be visually lost in the drawing.

4. Click the fourth point style example in the second row (the one with a circle and an X). Then click OK to close the dialog box.

5. Set the Insertion osnap to be running, and then click the Multiple Points button on the expanded Draw panel on the Home tab to start the POINT command.

6. Place the cursor on the LIVING ROOM text.

7. When the Insertion symbol appears at the lower-left corner, click to place the point object. *Don't end the command yet.*

8. Repeat step 6 for the KITCHEN and BATH labels.
   The decks don't have any associated text in this drawing, so you can place the attribute anywhere you want.

9. Press Esc to end the POINT command.

10. Erase the LIVING ROOM, KITCHEN, and BATH labels.
    The drawing should look like Figure 9.14.

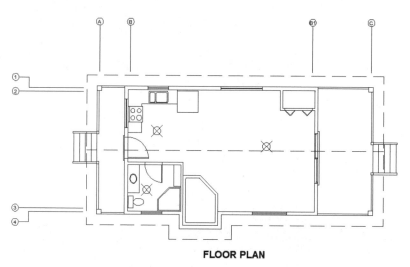

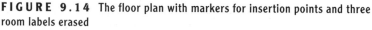

FLOOR PLAN

FIGURE 9.14 The floor plan with markers for insertion points and three room labels erased

11. Change the current annotation scale to 1:1 from the status bar.

12. Make layer 0 current.

13. Click the Define Attributes button on the Insert tab ➢ Block Definition panel to open the Attribute Definition dialog box.

14. Enter the following:

> ▶ For Tag, enter **RM_NAME**.

> ▶ For Prompt, enter **Room name**.

> ▶ For Default, enter **LIVING ROOM**. This default value will remind the user to use all uppercase letters.

15. In the bottom half of the dialog box, the settings for the text stay the same. Click OK.

16. In the drawing, click above the cabin and between the B and B1 gridlines. This places the first attribute definition in the drawing (see Figure 9.15).

Because you're going to make a block out of it and reinsert it into the rooms, you don't have to place the attribute definition where the room labels are; any open area in the drawing is fine.

T I P   Because you're drawing at a scale of 1:1, the attribute definition will be very small in relation to the rest of your drawing. Instead of using Zoom Window, try selecting the attribute definition and then choosing the Zoom Object option from the navigation bar. This will zoom in on the selected attribute definition.

FIGURE 9.15 The room name attribute definition placed in the drawing

17. Press ↵ to restart the ATTDEF command. For this attribute, enter the following:

   ▶ For Tag, enter **RM_AREA**.

   ▶ For Prompt, enter **Area of room**.

   ▶ For Default, enter **10.00 Sq. Ft. (10.00 M2)**. This will show the user the proper format for the area.

18. In the Mode group, click to activate Invisible.

   The Invisible mode makes the attribute values invisible in the drawing, but they're still stored there and can be accessed when required.

19. In the lower-left corner of the dialog box, click the Align Below Previous Attribute Definition check box.

   All the text options fade out (see Figure 9.16). The style is the same as that of the first attribute, and this attribute definition will appear right below the first one.

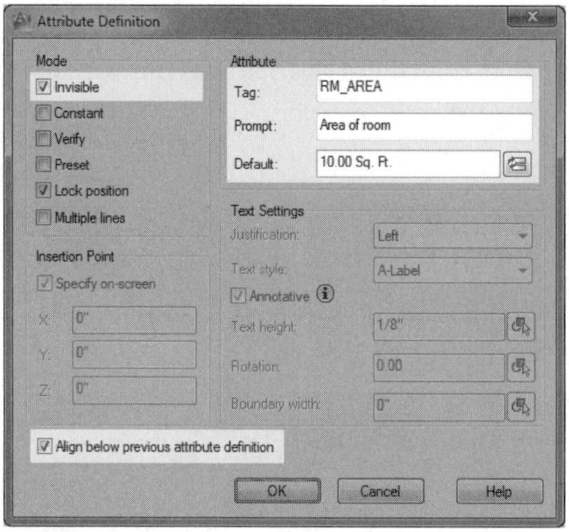

FIGURE 9.16 Setting the proper values in the Attribute Definition dialog box

20. Click OK. The second attribute definition appears in the drawing below the first one.

21. Repeat steps 17 to 19 to define the third attribute:

   ▶ For Tag, enter **RM_FLOOR**.

▸ For Prompt, enter **Floor Material**.

▸ For Default, enter **Wood Parquet**.

22. Click OK. All three attribute definitions are now in the drawing (see Figure 9.17).

23. Save your drawing as `I09-05-MultipleAttributes.dwg` (`M09-05-MultipleAttributes.dwg`).

FIGURE 9.17 The floor plan with all three attribute definitions

Now you'll make a block out of the three attributes.

Defining a Block with Multiple Attributes

A block with attributes usually includes lines or other geometric objects along with the attribute definitions, but it doesn't have to do so. In this case, the three attribute definitions are the sole content of the block, and the block's insertion point is the justification point for the first attribute: the room label text. Follow these steps to define the block:

1. Make sure `I09-05-MultipleAttributes.dwg` (`M09-05-Multiple Attributes.dwg`) is open.

2. Click the Create button found on the Insert tab ▸ Block Definition panel to start the BLOCK command.

3. In the Block Definition dialog box, enter **A-ROOM-IDEN** for the name.

4. Click the Pick Point button.

5. In the drawing, use the Insert osnap and choose the top attribute definition.

Doing so aligns the justification point of this attribute with the insertion point of the block.

6. Back in the Block Definition dialog box, click the Select Objects button.

7. In the drawing, pick each attribute definition individually in the order you created them.

Selecting them in this order causes them to be listed in the Enter Attributes dialog box in the same order.

8. Press ↵ after selecting the last attribute definition.

9. After being sure Delete is still selected, check the Annotative check box to enable it, making the A-ROOM-IDEN block Annotative.

10. Assuming the Block Definition dialog box looks like Figure 9.18, click OK to dismiss the dialog box.

The A-ROOM-IDEN block is defined, and the attribute definitions are deleted from the drawing.

11. Save your drawing as `I09-06-MultiAttBlock.dwg` (`M09-06-Multi AttBlock.dwg`).

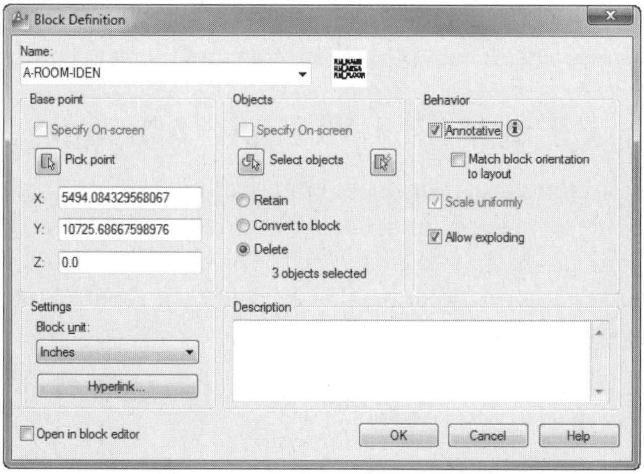

FIGURE 9.18 The Block Definition dialog box for the A-ROOM-IDEN block

You're almost ready to insert the A-ROOM-IDEN block in each of the three rooms and the decks. But first you need to calculate the area of each room.

Calculating Areas

You can calculate areas in a drawing by using the HATCH command in conjunction with the Properties palette or by using the Area tool. Because area calculations are made over and over again in design, construction, and manufacturing, the AREA and MEASUREGEOM commands are important tools. You can calculate an overall area and then subtract subareas from it, or you can add subareas together to make a total. Chapter 11, "Working with Hatches, Gradients, and Tool Palettes," covers hatches.

For this exercise, you'll use the Area tool to calculate the areas of the five floor spaces in the floor plan. You need to write down the areas after you make the calculations. Follow these steps:

1. Make sure I09-06-MultiAttBlock.dwg (M09-06-MultiAttBlock.dwg) is open.

2. Create a new layer named **A-AREA-NPLT**, and make it the current layer.

3. Freeze all the other layers except A-DECK, A-GLAZ, and A-WALL. Your drawing should look like Figure 9.19.

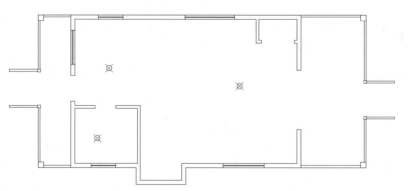

FIGURE 9.19 The floor plan with all layers turned off except A-AREA-NPLT, A-DECK, A-WALL, and A-GLAZ

The lines you'll draw on the A-AREA-NPLT layer will be used for reference and not plotted in your final plans. This is why we're using the NCS code NPLT, which stands for *No Plot*.

T I P   When you want to select all the layers in a drawing except a few, select those few layers in the Layer Properties Manager, right-click, and choose Invert Selection from the context menu. The unselected layers become selected, and the selected layers are deselected.

4. Make sure that the Endpoint osnap is running.

5. Draw a closed polyline around the inside of each room. To delineate the kitchen from the living room, use the left edge of the large window near the closet as the right edge of the kitchen, and use the bathroom wall as the lower limit.

6. Draw a polyline around each of the decks by using the Perpendicular object snap to draw the segments through the posts on the decks' outside corners.
   Your cabin should be divided as shown in Figure 9.20.

7. Save your drawing as **I09-07-AreaBoundary.dwg (M09-07-Area Boundary.dwg)**.

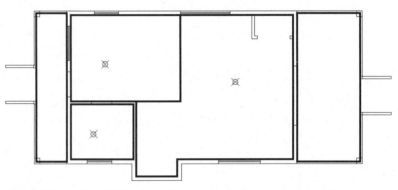

FIGURE 9.20 Divide the cabin into five distinct sections by using closed polylines.

Now that the perimeter lines are drawn, you need to calculate the area bound by them:

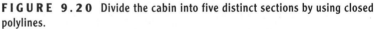

1. Make sure I09-07-AreaBoundary.dwg (M09-07-AreaBoundary.dwg) is open.

2. Turn on Selection Cycling from the status bar.
   This will help you select the polylines you just drew when they overlap other lines in the drawing.

3. From the Home tab ➤ Utilities panel, click the down-arrow under the Measure button, and then select the Area option, as shown in Figure 9.21.

4. At the Specify first corner point or [Object/Add area/Subtract area/eXit]: prompt, enter **O**↵ to switch to Object mode and then select the bathroom polyline.

    If the Selection dialog box opens after you've made your selection, hover over each of the objects displayed in the list until you find the polyline along the perimeter of the bathroom highlights (see Figure 9.22).

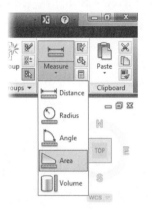

FIGURE 9.21 Starting the
Measure Area command

FIGURE 9.22 Using Selection Cycling to select
the polyline along the bathroom's perimeter

5. The area of the polyline turns green in the drawing area. Press the F2 key to open the AutoCAD text window.

    The text window displays the results of your calculation: Area = 7176.00 square in. (49.8333 square ft.), Perimeter = 28'-4". (Area = 4455000, Perimeter = 8460). You'll also notice that you're not actually in the AREA command; you're in the Area option of the MEASUREGEOM (Measure Geometry) command. This command combines many of the older inquiry commands such as AREA and DISTANCE into a single command.

6. Write down the area in square feet (square millimeters) to check against the number calculated in the next section.

7. Press ⏎ to restart the Area option.

8. Enter 0⏎, and then click the kitchen polyline.

    The area should be 135.9792 square feet (12660810). Write down this number. (You can round it to two decimal places; you just want to be able to verify the numbers that AutoCAD will calculate.)

9. Repeat this process for the living room, where the area should be 278.3542 square feet (26201990).

10. Write down 278.35 (26201990).

11. Repeat this process one last time for the front and back decks. The areas should be 135.63 square feet (12648636) and 65.63 square feet (6126516), respectively.

12. Thaw all the layers except A-ANNO-TTLB and A-ANNO-TTLB-TEXT, and make the A-ANNO -TEXT layer current.

 N O T E   The Add and Subtract options in the Area prompt allow you to add together areas you have calculated and to subtract areas from each other. If you're going to add or subtract areas, enter A⏎ after you start the AREA command. Then, after each calculation, you'll be given the Add and Subtract options. If you don't enter A at the beginning, you can make only one calculation at a time.

To use the Properties palette to calculate an area, select the polyline to be measured, open the Properties palette, and then scroll down to the Area readout in the Geometry rollout. The area appears in square inches and square feet. This also works for hatch patterns, which are covered in Chapter 11.

Inserting the Room Information Block

You have five areas calculated and recorded, and you are ready to insert the A-ROOM-IDEN block. When you inserted the grid symbols as blocks with attributes earlier in this chapter, the prompts for the attribute text appeared in the command window. With multiple attributes in a block, it's more convenient to display all the prompts in a dialog box. Let's change the setting that makes the dialog box replace the command prompts:

1. Continue using I09-07-AreaBoundary.dwg (M09-07-AreaBoundary.dwg), or open it if it's not already open.

2. Enter **ATTDIA**↵.

3. At the prompt, enter **1**↵.
   This allows the dialog box containing the prompts to open during the insertion process.

4. Set the Node osnap to be the only one running, and make sure the Object Snap button is turned on. The Node osnap snaps the cursor to a point object.

5. If it's not already set, change your annotation scale to 1/4″ = 1′-0″ (1:50) from the status bar.

6. Click the Insert button from the Insert tab ➤ Block panel.

7. In the Insert dialog box, select A-ROOM-IDEN from the Name drop-down list and then click OK.

8. Select the point object that marks the justification point for the LIVING ROOM label text to open the Edit Attributes dialog box (see Figure 9.23).

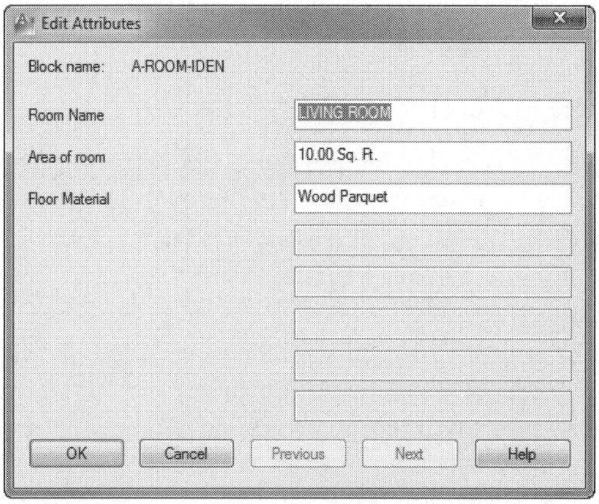

FIGURE 9.23 The Edit Attributes dialog box

9. The only change you need to make is the value for Area Of Room. The defaults are correct for the other two items.

   Rather than inputting text, you'll instruct the attribute to read the Area parameter from the polyline.

10. Press the Tab key to highlight the Area Of Room box, right-click, and choose Insert Field from the context menu, as shown in Figure 9.24.

11. The Field dialog box opens. In the Field Names column, choose Object, and click the Select Object button (see Figure 9.25).

    The dialog box closes so that you can pick the object that the field will reference.

12. Select the polyline that follows the perimeter of the living room.

    The Field dialog box reopens with additional content in its list boxes.

13. Select Area in the Property column, Architectural (Decimal) in the Format column, and 0.00 in the Precision drop-down list.

    The correct area measurement appears in the top-right corner of the dialog box (see Figure 9.26).

    If you're working in Architectural units, you can skip to step 19. If you're working in metric units, continue with the next step.

    Notice the value in the Preview window in the top-right corner of the dialog box. The number is much too large to be defining the area of the living room in square meters; instead, it's showing the area in square millimeters. Therefore, you need to multiply the value calculated by a conversion factor to display the correct value.

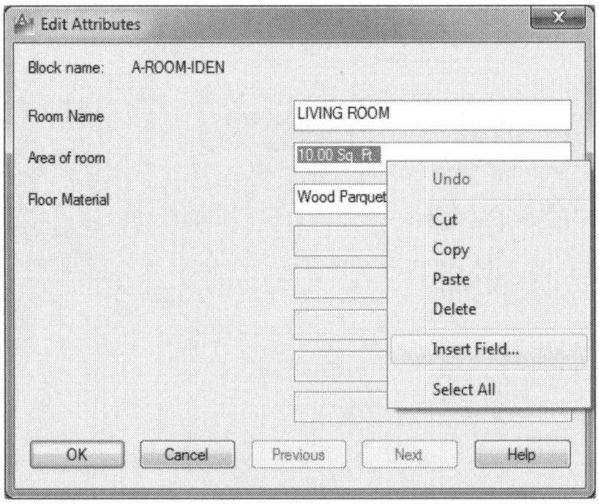

FIGURE 9.24 Inserting a field as an attribute

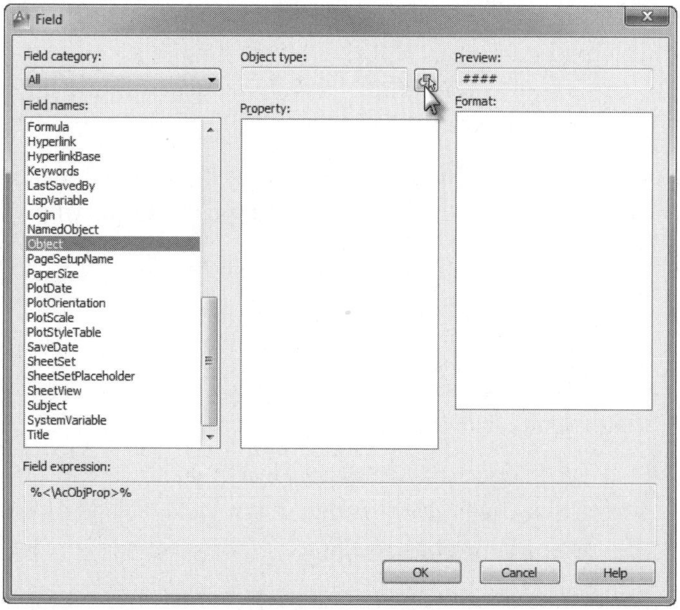

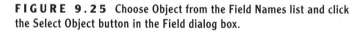

FIGURE 9.25 Choose Object from the Field Names list and click the Select Object button in the Field dialog box.

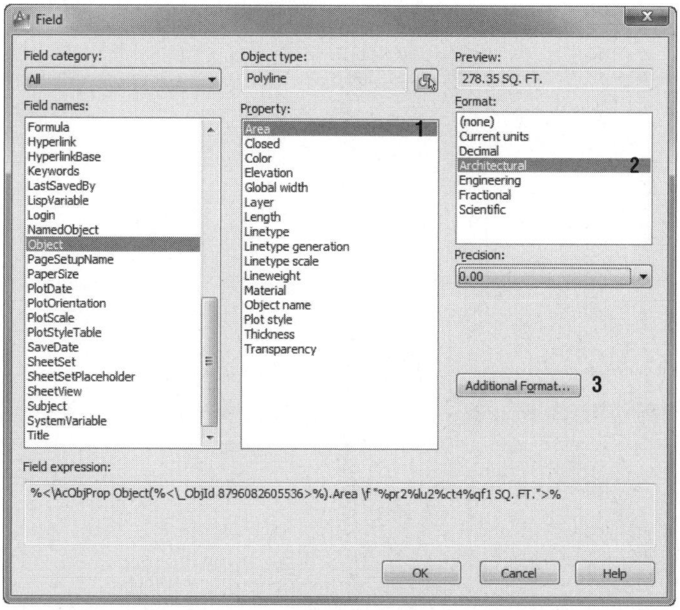

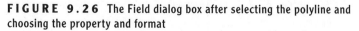

FIGURE 9.26 The Field dialog box after selecting the polyline and choosing the property and format

14. Click the Additional Format button to open the Additional Format dialog box.

    One square meter equals 1,000,000 square millimeters (1000×1000), so each square millimeter is 1/1,000,000 of a square meter.

15. To figure out the conversion factor needed to convert square inches into square feet, divide 1 by 1,000,000 and you'll come up with 0.000001.

16. Enter **0.000001** in the Conversion Factor field.

17. To identify the units, enter **M2** in the Suffix field.

    Be sure to place a space prior to the *M* to ensure a gap between the suffix and the calculated area. Your Additional Format dialog box should look like Figure 9.27.

18. Click OK to close the Additional Format dialog box.

    Note that the Preview section in the Field dialog box now shows the correct value of 26.18 M2, as you can see in Figure 9.28.

19. Click OK to close the Field dialog box and return to the Edit Attributes dialog box.

    The Area Of Room value is now shown with a gray background, as you can see in Figure 9.29, to identify it as a field rather than a text element.

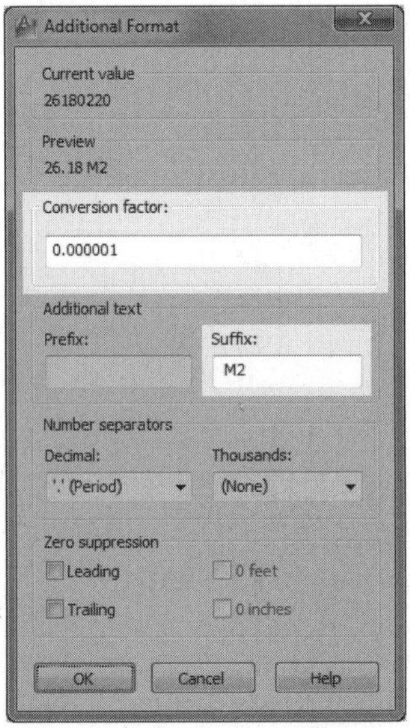

FIGURE 9.27 The Additional Format dialog box

20. Click OK to insert the A-ROOM-IDEN block into the drawing in the living room.

    The room label is the only visible attribute (see Figure 9.30). You set the other two attributes to be invisible.

21. Save your drawing as **I09-08-InsertInfoBlock.dwg** (**M09-08-Insert InfoBlock.dwg**).

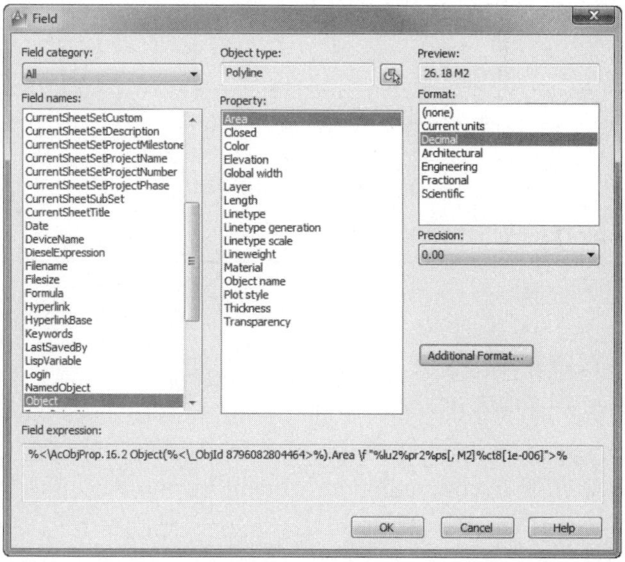

FIGURE 9.28 The Field dialog box after changing the values in the Additional Format dialog box

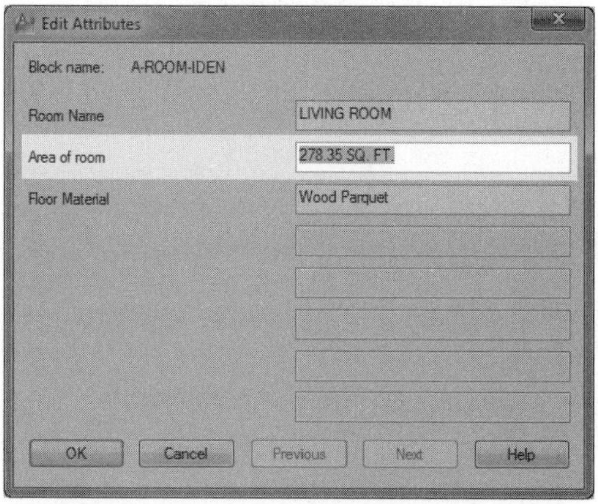

FIGURE 9.29 The Edit Attributes dialog box with a field for the Area Of Room value

FLOOR PLAN

FIGURE 9.30 The first A-ROOM-INFO block is inserted.

Editing Attributes

The remaining four block insertions are almost identical to the first one, with just a few specific changes: changing the room name and referencing a different polyline. Follow these steps to copy and modify the block and attributes that you've created:

1. Make sure I09-08-InsertInfoBlock.dwg (M09-08-InsertInfoBlock .dwg) is open.

2. Select the LIVING ROOM attribute and, using the Node osnap, copy it to the node at the insertion point for the BATH text.

3. Double-click the new attribute to open the Enhanced Attribute Editor dialog box and select the RM_AREA row, as shown in Figure 9.31.

4. Double-click the 278.35 SF (26.18 M2) value with the gray background at the bottom of the dialog box to open the Field dialog box, where you can edit the preferences and references.

5. Inside the Field dialog box, click the Select Object button near the Object Type field.
   Both dialog boxes disappear, and the cursor turns into a pickbox.

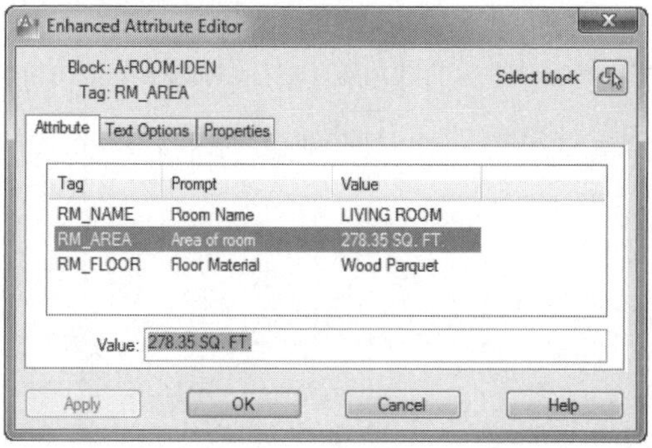

FIGURE 9.31 Select the RM_AREA row in the Enhanced Attribute Editor.

6. Select the polyline that follows the perimeter of the bathroom. If you're using metric units, do the following:

    a. Click the Additional Format button when the Field dialog box reappears.

    b. Repeat steps 14 to 16 from the previous exercise.

7. Click OK to close the Field dialog box and return to the Enhanced Attribute Editor dialog box.

8. Select the RM_NAME row.

9. At the bottom of the dialog box, highlight LIVING ROOM and enter BATH to replace the text.

10. Change the floor material to **Tile**.

11. Click OK to close the dialog box.
    The revised BATH attribute is now properly placed in the drawing.

12. Repeat steps 2 through 11, substituting **KITCHEN**, **FRONT DECK**, and **BACK DECK** for the room name attribute and selecting the appropriate polyline as a reference for each block.
    There are no node point objects for the deck text, so you can just rotate and place the attribute a little left of center on the appropriate deck. For the decks, change the floor material to **Cedar Planks**. Metric users will need to open the Additional Format dialog box for

each block and add the conversion factor and suffix for each block. When you are finished, your cabin should look like Figure 9.32.

13. Save your drawing as **I09-09-EditRoomAttributes.dwg** (**M09-09-Edit RoomAttributes.dwg**).

FLOOR PLAN

FIGURE 9.32 All A-ROOM-IDEN blocks inserted

EDITING TOOLS FOR ATTRIBUTES

The attribute-editing tools seem complicated at first because their names are similar, but they are easily distinguishable once you get used to them and know how to use them. Here are descriptions of five attribute-editing tools:

The Edit Attributes Dialog Box

This is the same dialog box displayed in the process of inserting a block that has attributes, if the ATTDIA setting is set to 1. This dialog box is used to change attribute values only. Enter **ATTEDIT↵** to use it to edit values of attributes already in your drawing. You will be prompted to select a block reference in your drawing. When you do that, the Edit Attributes dialog box appears.

The Enhanced Attribute Editor Dialog Box

With this dialog box, you can edit values and the properties of the attribute text—such as color, layer, text style, and so on. When you enter **EATTEDIT↵**, or click Modify ➢ Object ➢ Attribute ➢ Single, or click the Edit Attribute (Single) button in the Block panel on the Insert tab, and then pick a block

(Continues)

EDITING TOOLS FOR ATTRIBUTES *(Continued)*

that has attributes, the dialog box opens. Double-clicking the block has the same effect.

The Properties Palette

Use the Properties palette to edit most properties of attribute definitions. Select the attribute definition, and then right-click and choose Properties to open the Properties palette. Then scroll down to the Attributes rollout.

The Block Attribute Manager

Click the Manage Attributes button in the expanded Block panel on the Home tab, or enter **BATTMAN** at the command line to open the Block Attribute Manager dialog box. There you can select a block and edit the various parts of each attribute definition that the block contains, such as the tag, prompt, and value.

The –ATTEDIT Command

You can also edit more than one attribute at a time by clicking the Edit Attributes (Multiple) from the Attributes panel of the Insert tab, or by choosing Modify ➢ Object ➢ Attribute ➢ Global, or by entering **–ATTEDIT**↵. The prompt reads Edit attributes one at a time? [Yes/No] <Y>. If you accept the default of Yes, you're taken through a series of options for selecting attributes to edit. Select the attributes to edit, and then press ↵ to end the selection process. A large **X** appears at the insertion point of one of the selected attributes. At this point, you get the following prompt: Enter an option [Value/Position/Height/Angle/Style/Layer/Color/Next] <N>:, allowing you to modify any of the characteristics listed in the prompt for the attribute with the **X**. Press ↵ to move to the next selected attribute.

If you respond to the first prompt with No, you're taken through a similar set of selection options. You're then asked to enter a current value to be changed and to enter the new value after the change. You can change the values of attributes globally by using the ATTEDIT command this way.

Controlling the Visibility of Attributes

The floor plan looks the same as it did at the beginning of this exercise, except for the addition of the deck labels. But it includes more than meets the eye.

What was regular text is now an attribute, and your drawing is "smarter" than it was before. The next few steps illustrate the display controls for the visible and invisible attributes:

1. Make sure I09-09-EditRoomAttributes.dwg (M09-09-EditRoom Attributes.dwg) is open.

2. On the Insert tab ➢ Expanded Block panel, click the down-arrow next to the Retain Attribute Display button, and click Display All Attributes, as shown in Figure 9.33.

   All the attributes, including those designated as invisible, appear with the room labels (see Figure 9.34).

FIGURE 9.33 Selecting the Display All Attributes option

FLOOR PLAN

FIGURE 9.34 The floor plan with all attributes displayed

N O T E   Like the hyperlink you added to the notes in Chapter 8, the fields are shown with a gray background, but this background does not appear in the printed drawings. As you can see, one of the benefits of using attributes over simple text is the ability to control their visibility. However, their true strength is the ability to output attribute values to spreadsheets or databases. When you use fields and formulas (covered in the "Creating a Table" section later in this chapter), the attribute can adjust its values as the circumstances change, as shown in Figure 9.34.

3. Start the STRETCH command and drag a crossing window to enclose part of the front deck, as shown in Figure 9.35.

4. Pick any location in the drawing area as the base point, move the cursor to the right, and then click to stretch the deck, as shown in Figure 9.36. Use Ortho mode or Polar Tracking to stretch the objects directly to the right.

    The deck is now larger, but the attribute showing the area remains at its previous value. Attributes need to be instructed to reevaluate or regenerate themselves. This can happen whenever a drawing is opened or when the REGEN or REGENALL commands are issued.

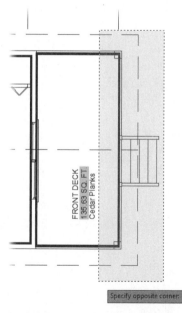

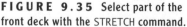

F I G U R E 9 . 3 5 Select part of the front deck with the STRETCH command.

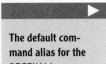

The default command alias for the REGENALL command is REA. For the REGEN command, the default alias is RE.

5. From the menu bar, choose View ≻ Regen All or enter **REA**↵.

The area updates to show the true value for the associated polyline (see Figure 9.37).

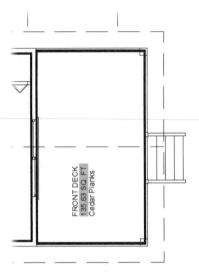

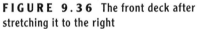

FIGURE 9.36 The front deck after stretching it to the right

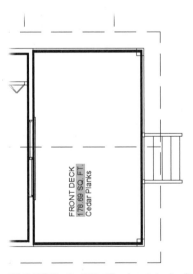

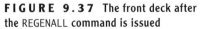

FIGURE 9.37 The front deck after the REGENALL command is issued

6. You don't want the deck at this larger size, so click the Undo button in the Quick Access toolbar, or press **U**↵ until your drawing is in the state it was just before the STRETCH command was executed.

    The visibility of the attributes, as you defined them in the Attribute Definition dialog box, is called their *normal* state.

7. To return them to this state, click the down-arrow next to the Display All Attributes button on the expanded Block panel within the Insert tab, and then click Retain Attribute Display (see Figure 9.38).

    All the attributes return to their normal state (see Figure 9.39).

FIGURE 9.38 Returning the attribute display to normal

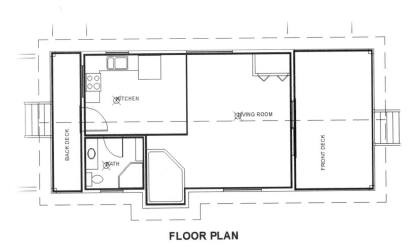

FLOOR PLAN

FIGURE 9.39 All the attributes in their normal state

The Display All Attributes and Hide All Attributes options make all attributes in a drawing visible or invisible, regardless of how you set the Visible/Invisible mode in the attribute definition. The Normal setting allows an attribute to be displayed only if the Visible/Invisible mode was set to Visible in the definition.

Exploring Other Uses for Attributes

Along with grid symbols and room, window, and door schedules, another common use for attributes is in standardized title blocks, particularly in facilities management and interior design. You can specify every piece of equipment such as pumps, electrical panels, HVAC air handling units, and even office furniture in a building with attributes. You can then extract the data and generate a schedule that is used to build a database in which ordering and maintenance information can be referenced. Many equipment manufacturers have developed their own proprietary software that works with AutoCAD and automatically sets up attributes when you insert their blocks of the equipment, which they have predrawn and included in the software package.

Attributes are also being used more and more in maps drawn in AutoCAD, which are then imported into geographical information system (GIS) software (a powerful analysis and presentation tool). When map symbols, such as building numbers, are blocks containing an attribute, they're transformed in the GIS program in such a way that you can set up links between the map features (buildings) and database tables that contain information about the map features. In this way, you can perform analyses on the database tables, and the results automatically appear graphically on the map. (For example, you could quickly locate all buildings that have a total usable area greater than a specified square footage.)

In the next section, you'll go through an exercise that demonstrates how you can create dynamic blocks that vary their appearance based on user input.

Creating a Dynamic Block

In Chapter 7, you created blocks for the windows and doors. However, because of the door block's schematic appearance, you were not able to scale it as you did with the window block. Scaling the door and swing would have allowed one door block to fit into any size opening, but it would have also scaled the thickness of the door differently for each door width. *Dynamic blocks* are standard blocks with additional functionality to allow certain features to change without affecting all objects in the block. The door blocks are an excellent opportunity to explore the abilities of AutoCAD's dynamic blocks.

The basic procedure for setting up a dynamic block has the following stages:

1. Create the block by using the BLOCK command.

2. Right-click the block and choose Block Editor.

3. Click a parameter, and follow the command window prompts to create the parameter.

4. Click the Actions tab, and click an action to associate with the parameter.

5. Follow the command window prompts to set up the action.

6. Use the Properties palette to rename and specify settings for the parameter and any actions associated with it.

7. Save your work back to the block definition and close the Block Editor.

You'll work through this process by converting the A-DOOR-36IN (A-DOOR-0915) block from your cabin drawing into a dynamic block in a new drawing:

1. With I09-09-EditRoomAttributes.dwg (M09-09-EditRoom Attributes.dwg) as the current drawing, zoom in to the floor plan at the back of the cabin.

2. Right-click in a blank area of your drawing and select Clipboard ➤ Copy With Basepoint from the context menu that appears.
   The command prompt changes to Specify base point:.

3. Use the Insert osnap to select the insertion point of the back door block as the base point.

4. Select the back door block and press ↵.
   This copies the door block to the Windows Clipboard.

5. Start a new drawing. Change the Length units to Architectural (Decimal), verifying that Insertion Scale is set to Inches (Millimeters).

6. From the Home tab ➤ Clipboard panel, choose the Paste tool, and when prompted to specify the base point, enter **0,0**↵.
   The A-DOOR-36IN (A-DOOR-0915) block is inserted into your new drawing. Perform a Zoom Extents to bring the entire block in view.

7. Save your new drawing containing the A-DOOR-36IN (A-DOOR-0915) block as **I09-10-DynamicBlock.dwg** (**M09-10-DynamicBlock.dwg**).

8. Select the door block, right-click, and choose Block Editor from the context menu.

   The drawing area turns gray, and the Block Authoring palettes open along with the Block Editor contextual tab to indicate that you are in the Block Editor.

9. Pan the view, and adjust the Block Authoring palettes so that your screen looks similar to Figure 9.40.

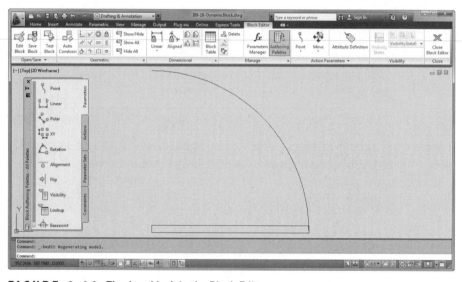

FIGURE 9.40 The door block in the Block Editor

You want to be able to use this door block for openings of the following widths: 2′-0″, 2′-6″, 3′-0″, and 3′-6″ (609 mm, 762 mm, 915 mm, and 1068 mm).

Setting Up Parameters and Actions

You'll use the Linear parameter to set up the 6″ (153 mm) increments for the door width. Then you'll associate a Stretch action with that parameter to allow the door width to change, and you'll associate a Scale action to allow the door swing to change. Follow these steps:

1. Make sure I09-10-DynamicBlock.dwg (M09-10-DynamicBlock.dwg) is open.

2. Make sure Parameters is the active palette in the Block Authoring Palettes panel, and then click the Linear Parameter icon (see Figure 9.41).

3. Make sure the Endpoint osnap is running.

4. Click the lower-left corner of the door, and then click the open endpoint of the door swing.

5. Move the cursor to position the dimension symbol a little to the left of the door block, and then click to place it (see Figure 9.42).

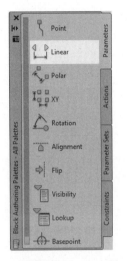

FIGURE 9.41 The Linear parameter in the Block Authoring palettes

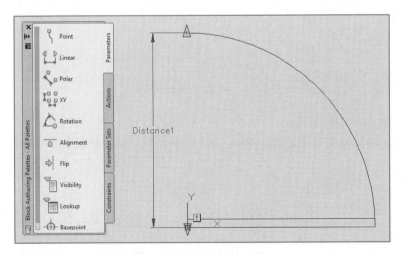

FIGURE 9.42 The Linear parameter is placed.

For the Distance parameter to work, it must be paired with a Dynamic Block action. Note the small exclamation symbol on a square yellow background. This reminds you that no action has been associated with this parameter. You'll set up the Stretch action first:

1. Click the Actions tab on the Block Authoring Palettes palette set, and then click the Stretch icon.

2. Select the Distance parameter (Distance1) to the left of the door, and then click the up-pointing arrow at the end of the door swing (see Figure 9.43).

3. At the Specify opposite corner of stretch frame or [CPolygon]: prompt (see the top of Figure 9.44), form a crossing polygon around the right half of the door, clicking each of the opposing corners rather than clicking and dragging, as shown at the bottom of Figure 9.44.

4. At the Select objects: prompt, select the door and then press ↵. The Stretch Action icon appears near the end of the door swing (see Figure 9.45).

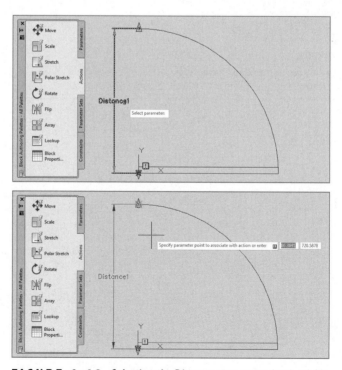

FIGURE 9.43 Selecting the Distance parameter (top), picking the linear grip (bottom)

5. Click the Scale Action icon on the Actions palette.

The Scale Action icon appears next to the Stretch Action icon, as shown in Figure 9.45.

6. Select the Distance (`Distance1`) parameter again, select the arc, and then press ↵.

7. Minimize the Block Authoring palettes.

8. Save your drawing as **I09-11-ParametersActions.dwg** (**M09-11-ParametersActions.dwg**).

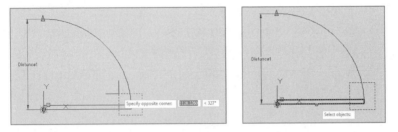

FIGURE 9.44 Defining the stretch frame (left), and selecting the door objects (right)

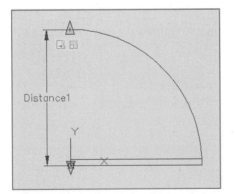

FIGURE 9.45 The A-DOOR-36IN block with the Stretch and Scale actions assigned to the Distance parameter

This completes your work with the Block Authoring palettes. You'll accomplish the rest of the tasks with the Properties palette.

Fine-Tuning the Dynamic Block with the Properties Palette

The Distance Linear parameter shows the width of the opening and is perpendicular to the door's width. You need to set up an offset angle so the door width changes as the opening width changes. Then you need to set up the incremental widths and rename the parameter and actions. You'll set up the increments first:

1. Make sure I09-11-ParametersActions.dwg (M09-11-Parameters Actions.dwg) is open.

2. Select the Distance parameter and then open the Properties palette.

3. In the Property Labels section on the palette, change Distance Name from Distance1 to **Door Opening**.

4. Scroll down to the Value Set section, and click the Dist Type text box, which reads None.

5. Open the drop-down list and select Increment.

6. Moving down, line by line, set the following values:

   ▶ Dist Increment to 6″ (**153**)

   ▶ Dist Minimum to 2′ (**609**)

   ▶ Dist Maximum to 3′-6″ (**1068**)

   See Figure 9.46.

7. Deselect the Distance parameter.
   The block now has the increment markers for the door opening widths (see Figure 9.47).

Now, the final task is to fine-tune the Stretch and Scale actions that control the door size and swing:

1. Click the Stretch Action symbol near the end of the door swing.
   The symbol, the Distance parameter, and the window you drew earlier ghost.

2. In the Properties palette, scroll down to the Overrides section; for Angle Offset, enter 270↵.
   This is the direction the door will stretch relative to movement of the open end of the door swing arc. The Distance multiplier stays at 1.0000 because you don't want the width of the door to change in the same proportion as the width of the opening.

3. In the Misc section, change Action Name from Stretch to **Door Size**.

4. Deselect this action, and select the Scale action.

5. In the Misc section of the Properties palette, change Action Name from Scale to **Door Swing Size**.

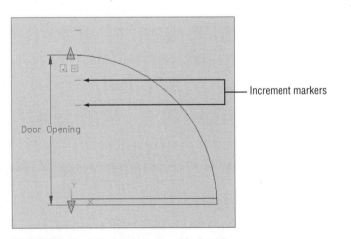

FIGURE 9.46 Change the parameters in the Properties dialog box.

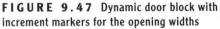

FIGURE 9.47 Dynamic door block with increment markers for the opening widths

6. Click the Test Block button found on the Block Editor contextual tab ➢ Open/Save panel:

A new window opens with the block displayed in the drawing area; the Block Editor contextual tab disappears; and the contextual Close panel (green background) opens on the far right side of the Ribbon.

7. Select the block, and then use the light blue arrow to test the Distance parameter you added to the A-DOOR-36IN (A-DOOR-0915) block, as shown in Figure 9.48.

8. After testing the block, click the Close Test Block Window button on the contextual Close panel found to the right of any Ribbon tab.

9. Close the Properties palette, and click the Save Block button in the Open/Save panel under the Block Editor contextual tab.

10. Click the Close Block Editor button at the right end of the Ribbon to return to the drawing.

    Because the A-DOOR-36IN (A-DOOR-0915) block is now dynamic and able to illustrate doors ranging in size, let's give the block a more appropriate name.

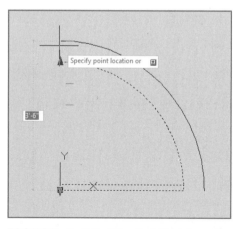

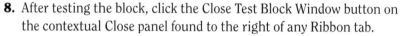

FIGURE 9.48 Using Test Block to verify the functionality of the Distance parameter

11. Enter **RENAME** at the command line to open the Rename dialog box shown in Figure 9.49.

12. Select Blocks under the Named Objects group within the Rename dialog box.

13. Select the A-DOOR-36IN (A-DOOR-0915) block in the Items list, and enter **A-DOOR** in the Rename To text box, as shown in Figure 9.49.

14. Click OK after entering the new A-DOOR name.

15. Save the drawing as **I09-DynDoor.dwg** (**M09-DynDoor.dwg**) in the same folder as your other Chapter 9 drawings, and then close the drawing.

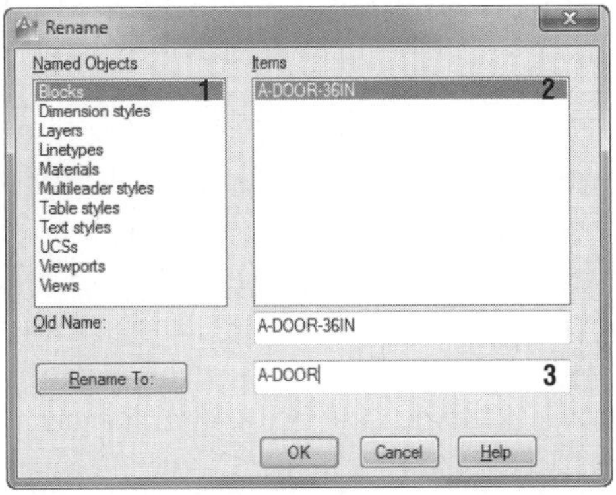

FIGURE 9.49 Renaming the A-DOOR-36IN (A-DOOR-0915) block to A-DOOR by using the RENAME command

Inserting a Dynamic Block

When you use this block in your floor plans, insert it just as you would a regular door block. Then copy it to the various doorway openings in the plan, orient it, and adjust its size to fit the openings. You can easily edit dynamic blocks, which are a versatile feature to have at your disposal.

You'll use the dynamic door block that you just created to replace the doors in your cabin:

1. In the I09-09-EditRoomAttributes.dwg (M09-09-EditRoom Attributes.dwg) drawing, delete the two existing swing doors.

2. Make the A-DOOR layer current, and then freeze the A-ANNO-TEXT, A-AREA-NPLT, A-GRID, A-ROOF, A-WALL-HEAD, and A-FLOR-FIXT layers.

Your drawing should look like Figure 9.50.

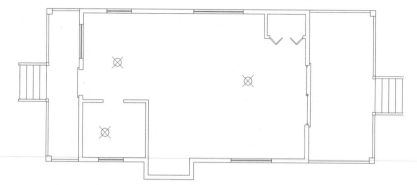

FIGURE 9.50 The cabin drawing with most of the layers frozen and the doors deleted

You will use the A-DOOR block you defined in the I09-DynDoor (M09-DynDoor) drawing. Because it will take the place of both the A-DOOR-36IN (A-DOOR-0915) and A-DOOR-30IN (A-DOOR-0762) blocks, it's best to remove both from the I09-09-EditRoomAttributes (M09-09-EditRoomAttributes) drawing. Spending a moment to perform some drawing maintenance and clean out unneeded objects will help achieve the best drawing performance. You will delete the block definition by using the Purge dialog box.

3. On the Application menu, select Drawing Utilities ➤ Purge or enter **PURGE**↵ to open the Purge dialog box.

4. Click the plus sign (+) to expand the Blocks entry to see the two door blocks (see Figure 9.51).

5. Select the Blocks entry, check the Purge Nested Items option, and make sure Confirm Each Object To Be Purged is unchecked.

6. Click the Purge button and then close the dialog box.

T I P   You can purge only those objects and features that do not exist in the drawing, such as deleted blocks, empty layers, or linetypes that are not used. Some items, including layer 0 and the Standard text style, can't be purged. AutoCAD can also accumulate registered applications (regapps), usually from third-party applications or features no longer used in the current drawing, and geometry lines with a length of 0. To eliminate them, you must enter -PURGE↵ to start the PURGE command without the dialog box and then enter R↵. The All option (A↵) will not purge these types of objects. Run PURGE often to eliminate accumulated junk in your drawing that contributes to larger file sizes and slower performance.

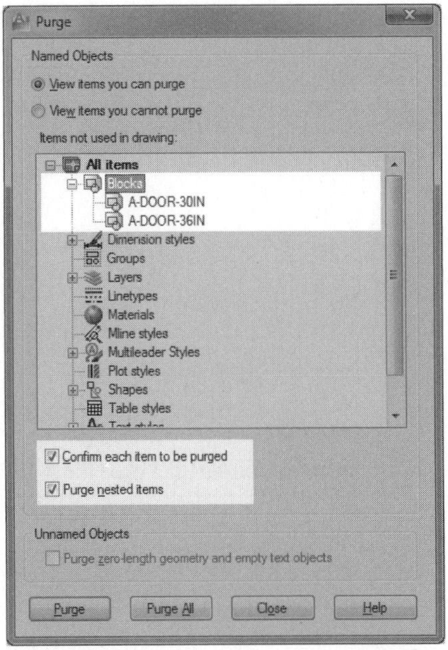

FIGURE 9.51 Deleting the block references with the Purge dialog box

7. With the Endpoint osnap and Polar Tracking running, click the Design Center button on the View tab ➢ Palettes panel.

8. Click the Folders tab in the DesignCenter palette that opens.

9. Use the folder tree to browse to the I09-DynDoor.dwg (M09-DynDoor .dwg) drawing you just saved in your dataset directory.

   The I09-DynDoor.dwg (M09-DynDoor.dwg) file can also be found in the Chapter 9 download on the book's website at **http://sybex.com/go/ autocad2012ner** or the companion website at **http://autocadner.com**.

10. Expand the I09-DynDoor (M09-DynDoor) drawing inside the Design Center palette to select the Blocks option.

11. Right-click the A-DOOR block and select Insert Block (see Figure 9.52).

    The Insert dialog box opens, where you can specify how you would like the A-DOOR block inserted into your drawing.

12. Verify that the only check box selected within the Insert dialog box is the Specify On-Screen check box under the Insertion Point group, and click OK.

    The A-DOOR dynamic door block appears attached to the cursor.

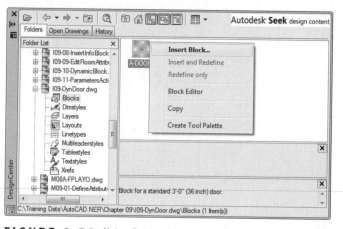

FIGURE 9.52 Using DesignCenter to insert the dynamic A-DOOR block

13. Click the lower-right corner of the back door opening to insert the block.
    This is a 3′-0″ (915 mm) door opening, so you don't need to modify the block.

14. Press ↵ to restart the INSERT command.

15. In the Insert dialog box, check the Specify On-Screen options under Rotation.

    a. Enter -1 for the X scale.

    b. Enter 1 for the Y and Z scales.

16. Click the lower-right corner of the bathroom opening to place the door.

17. Using Polar Tracking, move your cursor to rotate the door as shown in Figure 9.53.
    The door is placed properly, but as shown in Figure 9.53, the default size is too large for the opening.

18. Close DesignCenter if it's still open, and select the bathroom door block to reveal the blue dynamic arrows (see Figure 9.54).

19. Select the left arrow and drag it up to the corner of the opening.
    Notice how the length of the door changes as well (see Figure 9.55).

20. Click to set the door size, and then press Esc to deselect the door.
    The door block is scaled properly with no distortion to the width of the door itself (see Figure 9.56).

21. Save your drawing as **I09-12-InsertDynBlock.dwg** (**M09-12-Insert DynBlock.dwg**).

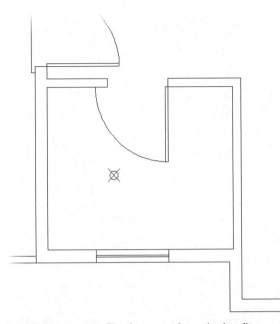

FIGURE 9.53 The door must be resized to fit.

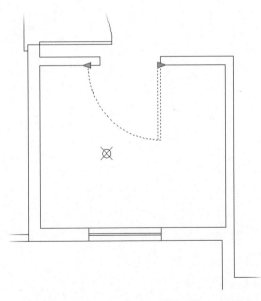

FIGURE 9.54 The dynamic block's resizing arrows

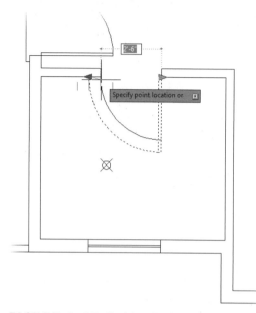

FIGURE 9.55 Resizing the dynamic block

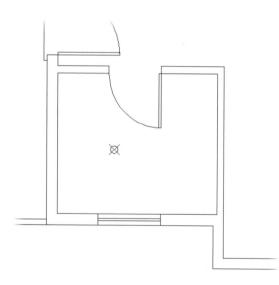

FIGURE 9.56 The dynamic door block scaled to fit the 2′ 6″ (762 mm) door opening

This completes the section on dynamic blocks. If you want to experiment with the dynamic block feature, examine the sample dynamic blocks to see how they work and are set up, and try to create one of your own. The next section covers the methods for creating a table.

Creating a Table

Most professions that use AutoCAD use tables to consolidate and display data in organized formats. Architectural construction documents usually include at least three basic tables: door, window, and room finish schedules. These are usually drawn in table form, and they display the various construction and material specifications for each door or window type or for each room. In mechanical drawings, the bill of materials and other specifications can be found in tables. To illustrate the AutoCAD tools for creating tables, you'll construct a simple door schedule for the cabin.

You create tables in AutoCAD by first creating a table style and then creating a table using that style. It's a process similar to that of defining a text style and then inserting text in a drawing using that style.

Defining a Table Style

Table styles are more complex than text styles. They include parameters for the width and height of rows and columns and, among other elements, at least one text style.

1. Make I09-12-InsertDynBlock.dwg (M09-12-InsertDynBlock.dwg) the current drawing if it isn't already.

2. Create a new layer called **A-ANNO-TABL**, assign it color number 62, and make it the current layer.

3. Click the Annotate tab. Then click the small arrow in the Tables panel's title bar to open the Table Style dialog box (see Figure 9.57).

   On the left is the Styles list box. It displays all the defined table styles. To the right of that is a Preview Of window that displays the current table style—in this case, the Standard style because it's the only one defined so far. Below the Styles list box is a drop-down list called List that gives you options for which table styles to display. To the right of the preview window are four buttons.

4. Click the New button to open the Create New Table Style dialog box.

5. In the New Style Name text box, enter **Schedule**, as shown in Figure 9.58, to create a new table style name, and click Continue.

The New Table Style dialog box opens with Schedule in the title bar (see Figure 9.59). The new style you're defining will be like the Standard style with the changes you make here. The drop-down list in the Cell Styles section contains the three parts of the sample table at the bottom-right corner of the dialog box: Data, Header, and Title.

You can specify text and line characteristics for each of the three parts. Be sure the Data option is active in the Cell Styles group.

T I P   Not only can each table have its own style, but each cell can have a distinct style as well. By using the Launches The Create A New Cell Style Dialog Box and Launches The Manage Cell Styles Dialog Box buttons in the top-right corner of the New Table Style dialog box, you can design and apply any number of cell styles within a table.

 6. Click the Text tab, and then click the Text Style ellipsis button to the right of the Text Style drop-down list to open the Text Style dialog box. You want a new text style for the door schedule.

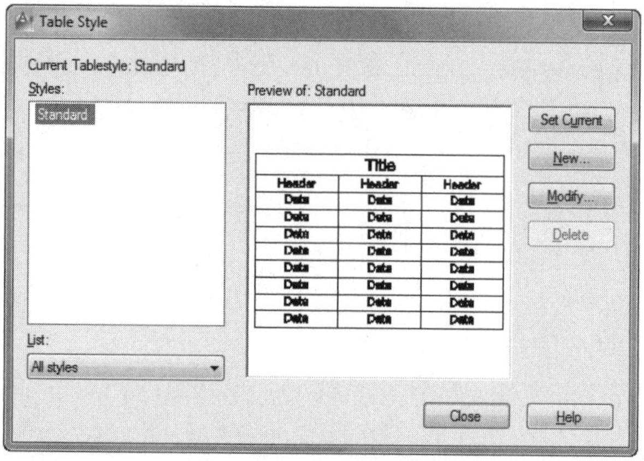

FIGURE 9.57 The Table Style dialog box

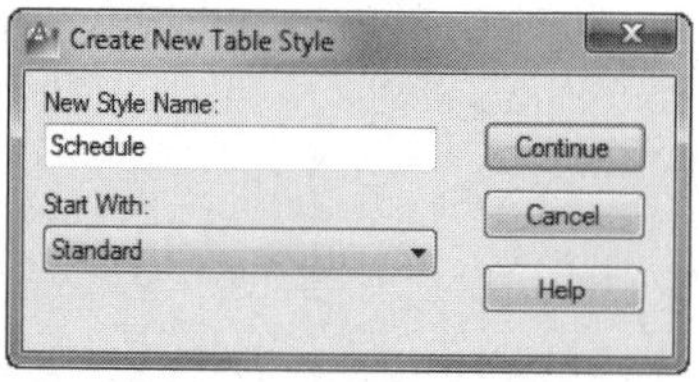

FIGURE 9.58 Naming the new table style

7. Define a new style called **A-Tabl**, and use the Arial font and a 0′-0″ (0) height.

   A Height value here allows you to control the height in the New Table Style dialog box.

8. Click Apply and then click Close.

   The table style now appears in the Text Style drop-down list, and the data cells in the two preview windows now show the Arial font.

9. Set Text Height to 6″ (152). Leave Text Color and Text Angle at their default settings.

10. Switch to the General tab and click the ellipsis button at the end of the Format row. In the Table Cell Format dialog box, change Data Type to Text and change Format to (None), as shown in Figure 9.60. Then click OK.

    The selected data type prevents numeric data from justifying to the right, rather than following the specified Middle Center option.

11. Change Alignment to Middle Center. The General tab should look like Figure 9.61.

12. In the Cell Styles drop-down list at the top of the dialog box, choose Header to expose its parameters.

13. In the Text tab, choose the same text style (A-Tabl) and set the height to 9″ (229).

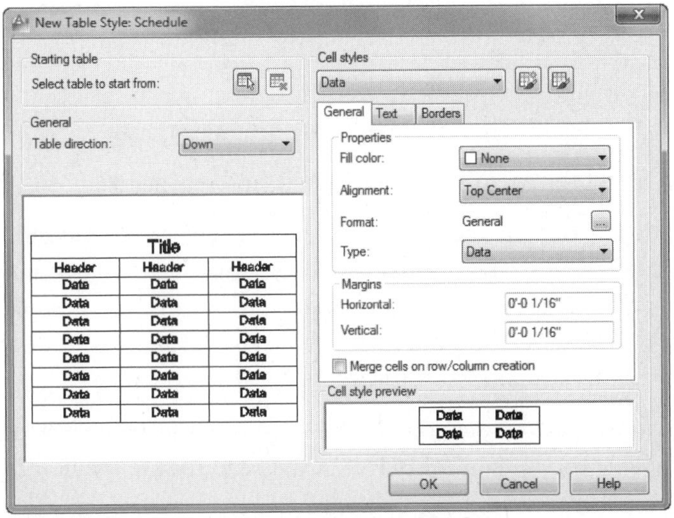

FIGURE 9.59 The New Table Style dialog box

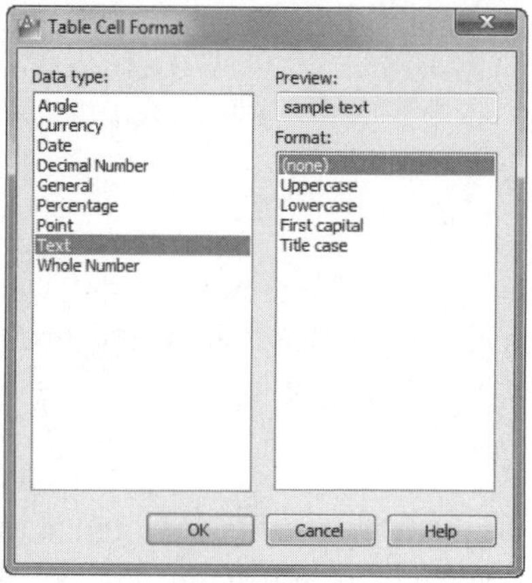

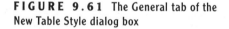

FIGURE 9.60 Changing the data format in the Table Cell Format dialog box

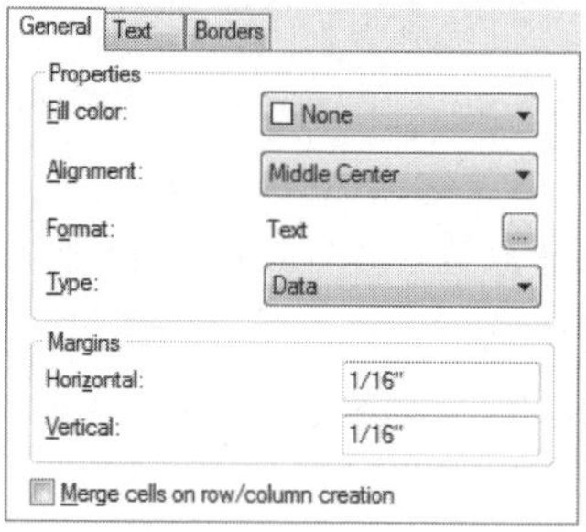

FIGURE 9.61 The General tab of the New Table Style dialog box

14. Choose Title from the Cell Styles drop-down list.

15. Select the A-TABL text style again, and set the height to 12″ (305).

16. In the General tab, set the Horizontal and Vertical Margins to 4″ (102). You'll leave the Border properties at their default settings. These control the visibility of the horizontal and vertical lines of the table, their lineweights, and their colors. Your profession or discipline might have its own standard for these parameters.

17. In the General section, on the left side of the dialog box, make sure Table Direction is set to Down. Click OK to save the new table style.

18. Back in the Table Style dialog box, in the Styles list, click Schedule to highlight it, and then click the Set Current button to make it the current table style (see Figure 9.62). Click Close.

19. Save your drawing as `I09-13-TableStyle.dwg` (`M09-13-Table Style.dwg`).

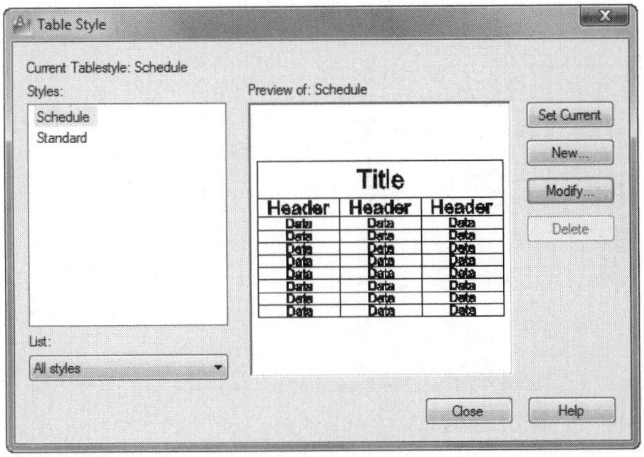

FIGURE 9.62 The Table Style dialog box with Door Schedule as the current table style

Now, let's look at the geometry of the new table.

Designing a Table

The parameters in the Schedule table style have set the height of the rows. You now need to determine the width of the columns and figure out how many columns and rows you need for the door schedule. You do this as you insert a new table. Remember that Schedule is the current table style. Follow these steps:

1. Make sure `I09-13-TableStyle.dwg` (`M09-13-TableStyle.dwg`) is open.

2. Zoom and pan so that you can see the area below the cabin.

3. In the Annotate tab's Tables panel, click the Table button to open the Insert Table dialog box (see Figure 9.63).

In the Table Style group, Schedule appears in the Table Style drop-down list because it's now the current table style. An abstract version of the table appears below in the preview area.

4. On the right side, click the Specify Window radio button if necessary. You'll make a window to define the extents of the table.

The table won't fit inside the title block perimeter, but I'll show you how to give it its own title block in Chapter 14, "Using Layouts to Set Up a Print."

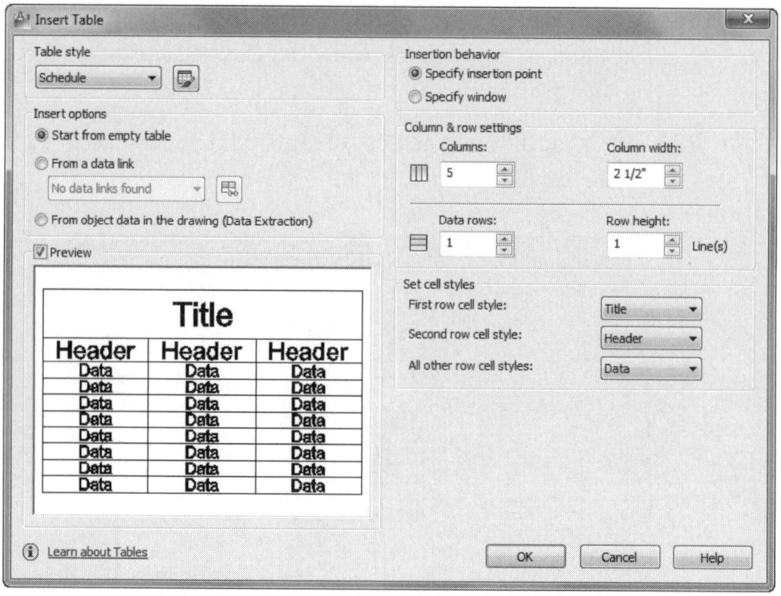

FIGURE 9.63 The Insert Table dialog box

5. Below, in the Column & Row Settings group, click the Columns and Row Height textboxes.

   You need to define only the number of columns in the table. You won't worry about the row height for now; it's determined by the number of lines of text, and you're using only one line of text.

6. You'll have six categories to describe the doors, so set the Columns box to 6.

   Each column is initially set to the same width. You can adjust it later.

7. Click OK.

8. Back in the drawing, turn off Object Snap and Polar Tracking on the status bar.

9. Click a point that is left of center and below the cabin.

   This establishes the upper-left corner of the new table, so make sure it's below the extents of the title block border.

10. Drag the cursor across the drawing and down until the screen displays a table that has eight rows (six data rows, a header row, and title row) and then release the mouse button (see Figure 9.64).

    The new table appears; its title bar has a flashing cursor and a light gray background. The background above and to the left of the table is dark gray. The table's columns are indicated by letters, and the rows are numbered. The Text Editor contextual tab and panels appear in the Ribbon.

11. With Caps Lock on, enter **DOOR SCHEDULE**↵.

   The cursor moves to the upper-left cell on the table. This is the row for the column headers.

12. With Caps Lock on, enter **SYM**, and press the Tab key to highlight the next column header to the right.

13. Moving across the header row, do the following:

   a. Enter (in caps) **NAME** and press the Tab key.

   b. Enter **H&W** and press the Tab key.

   c. Enter **TYPE** and press the Tab key.

   d. Enter **MAT'L** and press the Tab key.

   e. Enter **COST**↵.

   This completes the row of column heads (see the top of Figure 9.65).

14. Partially fill in the data for the door schedule that's shown at the bottom of Figure 9.65 in the same manner.

N O T E   Pressing the Tab key instead of ↵ moves the activated cell left to right across each row and then down to the next row. Pressing ↵ moves the activated cell down each column and then ends the command. For the Glass and Aluminum material, don't press ↵ to move to the next line; simply keep typing. The text wraps automatically, and the cell height changes to accommodate the additional lines of text.

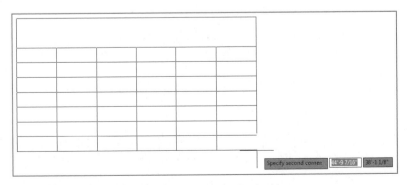

Specify second corner: 44'-9 7/16"   38'-1 1/8"

FIGURE 9.64 The new table inserted in the drawing

DOOR SCHEDULE					
SYM	NAME	H&W	TYPE	MAT'L	COST

DOOR SCHEDULE					
SYM	NAME	H&W	TYPE	MAT'L	COST
1	Front	7' x 7'	Sliding	Glass and Aluminum	
2	Back	3' x 7'			
3	Bath	2'6" x 7'			
4	Closet	4' x 7'			

FIGURE 9.65 The table with its title and column heads (left), and the table partially filled in (right)

15. You don't have to enter everything from scratch; it's easy to copy the contents of one cell into other cells:

   a. Enter Swinging in cell D4 and then highlight the text.

   b. Press Ctrl+C to copy the highlighted text to the Windows Clipboard.

   c. Deselect the current cell, and then select the cell below it by clicking in cell D5.

   d. Press Ctrl+V to paste the word *Swinging* into the selected cell.

16. Complete the Type and Material columns, as shown in Figure 9.66.

17. Save your drawing as **I09-14-CreateTable.dwg** (**M09-14-Create Table.dwg**).

	A	B	C	D	E	F
1	DOOR SCHEDULE					
2	SYM	NAME	H&W	TYPE	MAT'L	COST
3	1	Front	7' x 7'	Sliding	Glass and Aluminum	
4	2	Back	3' x 7'	Swinging	Wood SC	
5	3	Bath	2'6" x 7'	Swinging	Wood HC	
6	4	Closet	4' x 7'	Bi-Fold	Wood HC	
7						
8						

FIGURE 9.66 The table with its text-based cells filled in

SETTING THE CELL STYLE

If a cell justification doesn't appear correctly, or you want to change the style of a cell or range of cells, select the cells you want to change. In the Cell Styles

(Continues)

SETTING THE CELL STYLE *(Continued)*

panel under the Table Cell tab, expand the Cell Justification fly-out button and choose the appropriate style.

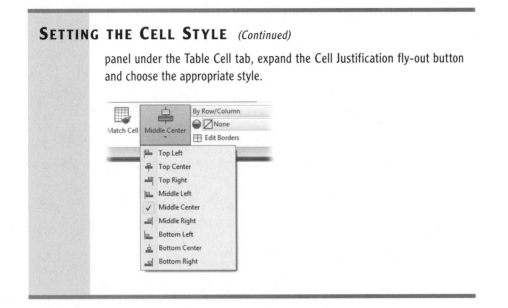

Adding Formulas to a Table

Currently, all the data cells are configured to hold text information and not numbers. You will now change the Cost column to read the information as numbers and then sum the values in the bottom cell with a formula:

1. Make sure I09-14-CreateTable.dwg (M09-14-CreateTable.dwg) is open.

2. Select all the cells below the Cost header in column F by clicking in cell F3, holding down the Shift key, and then clicking in cell F8.

3. Right-click and choose Data Format from the context menu.

4. In the Table Cell Format dialog box that opens, choose Currency for Data Type.

5. Choose 0.00 from the Precision drop-down list (see Figure 9.67).

6. If necessary, change the Symbol value to the symbol of your local currency.

7. Click OK to close the dialog box.

8. In the Cost column, enter the following:

   ▶ 350 for the front door

- ▶ 105 for the back door

- ▶ 85 for the bathroom door

- ▶ 65 for the closet door

AutoCAD automatically formats the numbers to two decimal places and adds a dollar sign to each, as shown in Figure 9.68.

9. Click in the empty cell at the bottom of the Cost column to select it.

10. In the Insert panel, click the Formula button and then choose Sum, as shown in Figure 9.69.

   As in a spreadsheet, a Sum formula adds the values of all the cells in a selected region.

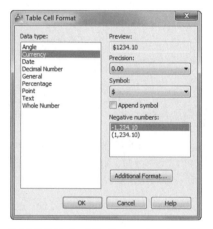

FIGURE 9.67   Formatting the table cells

DOOR SCHEDULE					
SYM	NAME	H&W	TYPE	MAT'L	COST
1	Front	7' x 7'	Sliding	Glass and Aluminum	$350.00
2	Back	3' x 7'	Swinging	Wood SC	$105.00
3	Bath	2'6" x 7'	Swinging	Wood HC	$85.00
4	Closet	4' x 7'	Bi-Fold	Wood HC	$65.00

FIGURE 9.68   The Cost column filled in

11. At the `Select first corner of table cell range:` prompt, click in cell F3, the first door cost cell.

12. At the `Select second corner of table cell range:` prompt, click in cell F6, the bottom door cost cell.

13. The formula "=SUM(F3:F6)" appears in cell F8. Click anywhere outside the table to deselect the cell and display its calculated value of $605.00, as shown in Figure 9.70.

14. Save your drawing as `I09-15-TableFormula.dwg` (`M09-15-TableFormula.dwg`).

 TIP   You would expect that the formatting assigned to the cell previously would carry through to the formula, but it doesn't always. You might need to reformat individual cells as required.

FIGURE 9.69 Adding a formula to the cell

DOOR SCHEDULE

SYM	NAME	H&W	TYPE	MAT'L	COST
1	Front	7' x 7'	Sliding	Glass and Aluminum	$350.00
2	Back	3' x 7'	Swinging	Wood SC	$105.00
3	Bath	2'6" x 7'	Swinging	Wood HC	$85.00
4	Closet	4' x 7'	Bi-Fold	Wood HC	$65.00
					$605.00

FIGURE 9.70 The completed table

The table is finished, and now you just need to do a little cleanup in your drawing to avoid any problems in the future and to tie elements in the drawing back to the table:

1. Make sure I09-15-TableFormula.dwg (M09-15-TableFormula.dwg) is open.

2. Thaw the A-ANNO-TEXT, A-ANNO-TTLB-TEXT, and A-ANNO-TTLB layers.

3. Move your table as required, so that it doesn't overlap the notes or title block.

4. Select one of the point objects you used to place the room name blocks, right-click, and choose Select Similar to select each of the points.

5. Press the Delete key to remove the points from your drawing.
   You need a symbol for each door that corresponds with each number in the SYM column.

6. With the A-ANNO-TABL layer current, draw a circle with a radius of 6″ (175).

7. Press the Single Line Text button in the Annotation panel under the Home tab.

8. Right-click and choose the Justify option from the context menu.

9. Choose the Middle option so the text will be centered around the insertion point.

10. Activate the Center osnap and then click the circle.

11. Set the height to 6″ (175) and the rotation angle to 0.

12. When the blinking cursor appears at the center of the circle, enter 1↵↵. The number 1 is centered in the circle.

13. Move the symbol near the front door, as shown in Figure 9.71, and then copy it to locations near the other three doors.

14. Edit each of the symbol's numbers so they correspond with their entry in the SYM column.
    Your drawing should look like Figure 9.72.

15. Thaw the A-GRID layer, and save this drawing as **I09-16-DoorTags .dwg** (**M09-16-DoorTags.dwg**).

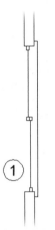

FIGURE 9.71 The first door symbol placed by the front door

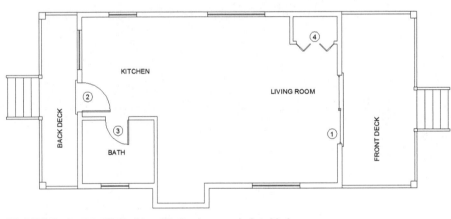

FIGURE 9.72 The cabin with the door symbols added

Creating Tables from Attributes

Early in this chapter, you replaced your static room labels with more-versatile attribute blocks. The A-ROOM-IDEN attribute block you defined for your room labels contains three attributes; one set to a visible state and two set to an invisible view state. As you may recall, the two invisible attributes allowed you to enter the area (RM_AREA) and floor material (RM_FLOOR) for each room.

Even though you cannot see either of these attributes in the drawing area, both are still accessible by other parts of the software. You can pull the values from all three attributes contained within the A-ROOM-IDEN block into a table by using the Data Extraction feature of the TABLE command. Using a data extraction table, AutoCAD will scan your drawing for every insertion of the A-ROOM -IDEN block and compile its data (attributes) into a table that will serve as your Room Schedule. Let me show you how:

1. Continue using I09-16-DoorTags.dwg (M09-16-DoorTags.dwg), or open it if it isn't already open.

2. Start the TABLE command from the Annotate tab ➢ Tables panel to open the Insert Table dialog box.

3. Select the From Object Data In the Drawing (Data Extraction) option found within the Insert Options group of the Insert Table dialog box, as shown in Figure 9.73, and then click OK.

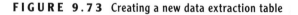

FIGURE 9.73 Creating a new data extraction table

The Data Extraction Wizard opens. This eight-part wizard will walk you through the creation of a data extraction table.

4. From the Data Extraction - Begin (Page 1 of 8) dialog box, select the Create A New Data Extraction option and then click Next.
   The Save Data Extraction As dialog box opens.

5. Browse to your Chapter 9 Training Dataset folder within the Save Data Extraction As dialog box, enter **I-RoomArea (M-RoomArea)** in the File Name text box, and click Save.

   The Save Data Extraction As dialog box closes, and you're taken to the second step within the Data Extraction Wizard.

6. Choose the Drawings/Sheet Set option.

7. Check the Include Current Drawing check box within the Data Extraction - Define Data Source dialog box, and click Next.

T I P   Although in this case you're extracting data only from the current drawing, data extraction tables can pull information from multiple drawings all at once. This feature is useful when using data extraction tables for quantity takeoffs when each floor of a multilevel building is stored in a separate drawing.

Next, the Data Extraction Wizard asks you to specify the objects from which to extract data. In this case, you're interested only in the data contained within the A-ROOM-IDEN block.

8. Uncheck the Display All Object Types check box and choose the Display Blocks Only option.

9. Right-click one of the objects listed within the Objects group of the dialog box and choose Uncheck All.

10. Select the check box next to the A-ROOM-IDEN object.

    The Data Extraction - Select Objects (Page 3 of 8) dialog box should look like Figure 9.74. After selecting the A-ROOM-IDEN block, click Next to move on to the next step of the wizard.

    Next, you need to specify the attributes (properties) you want the data extraction table to include. In this case, you're interested in only the three block attributes contained within the A-ROOM-IDEN block.

11. Click the Category header to sort the properties by category type.

    This brings the Attributes category to the top of the list.

12. Uncheck the check boxes next to the RM-NAME, RM_AREA, and RM_FLOOR properties.

13. Right-click in the list area and select Invert Selection.

    This deselects all but the three block attributes contained within your room identification block.

14. Double-click in the Display Name cell for the RM_NAME attribute, and enter **ROOM**.

15. Repeat by entering **AREA** for the RM_AREA attribute and **MATL** for the RM_FLOOR attribute.

The Display Names will be used as the column headings in your table.

Verify that the Data Extraction - Select Properties (Page 4 of 8) dialog box looks like Figure 9.75, and click Next to continue.

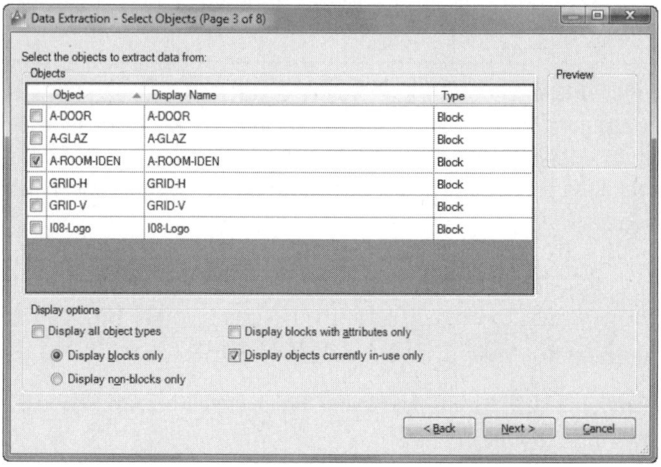

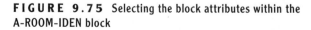

FIGURE 9.74 Selecting the A-ROOM-IDEN block within the Data Extraction Wizard

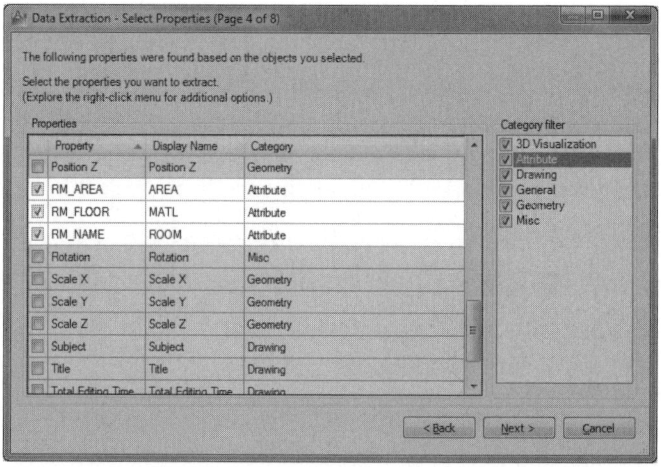

FIGURE 9.75 Selecting the block attributes within the A-ROOM-IDEN block

You have now selected the data you want included in your data extraction table. The Refine Data portion of the Data Extraction Wizard will allow you to order the columns, and to choose whether to include or exclude the block name and count.

16. Uncheck the Show Count Column and Show Name Column check boxes, as shown in Figure 9.76, and click Next to continue.

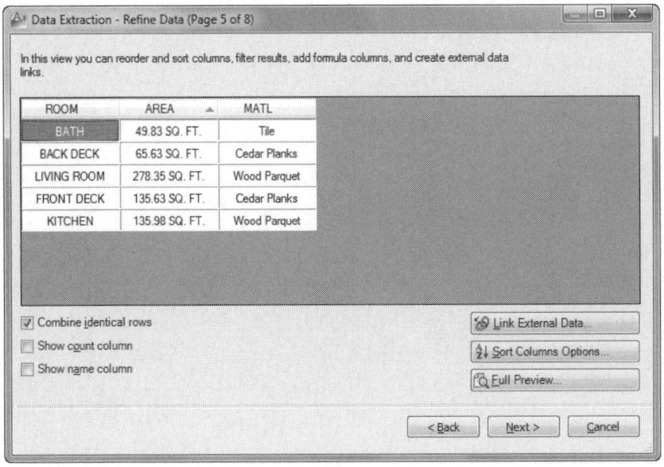

FIGURE 9.76 Choosing the display and order of your data extraction columns

If you were further analyzing your data in a program such as Microsoft Excel, you could send the data extracted from your drawing to an external XLS file.

17. Since our goal is to create a Room schedule, choose the Insert Data Extraction Table Into Drawing check box, and click Next.

After you've chosen to insert the data extraction table into your drawing, the Data Extraction Wizard will prompt you to select which table style you would like to use along with a title for your table.

18. Verify that the Schedule table style is selected inside the Table Style group of the dialog box, and then enter **ROOM SCHEDULE** in the Enter A Title For Your Table text box (see Figure 9.77). Click Next to continue.

19. You've finished the Data Extraction Wizard; click Finish.

20. Use the cursor to choose a location for your ROOM SCHEDULE near the DOOR SCHEDULE you created earlier (see the top of Figure 9.78).

Your ROOM SCHEDULE inserts to display the block attribute values from the A-ROOM-IDEN block in table form (see the bottom of Figure 9.78).

21. Save your drawing as **I09-17-DataExtraction.dwg** (**M09-7-Data Extraction.dwg**).

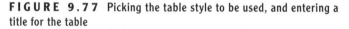

FIGURE 9.77 Picking the table style to be used, and entering a title for the table

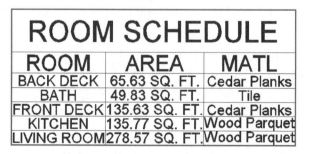

FIGURE 9.78 Placing the ROOM SCHEDULE table (top), and the results of the data extraction (bottom)

Modifying the Table Display

The ROOM SCHEDULE data extraction is now inserted into your drawing as an AutoCAD Table object. Although the correct table style is in use, its display needs to be tweaked.

1. Make sure I09-17-DataExtraction.dwg (M09-17-DataExtraction.dwg) is open.

2. Open the Properties palette from the View tab ➢ Palettes palette, and select the ROOM SCHEDULE table.

3. Change the Table Width property within the Table group to 20′ (6 m), as shown in Figure 9.79.

4. Select the ROOM cell (A2), press and hold the Shift key, and select the lower right cell C7, as shown in Figure 9.80.

5. Under the Cell heading within the Properties panel, change the Vertical Cell Margin property to 2″ (50 mm), as shown in see Figure 9.81.

6. Press Esc to deselect the ROOM SCHEDULE table.

7. Save your drawing as **I09A-FPLAYO.dwg** (**M09A-FPLAYO.dwg**).

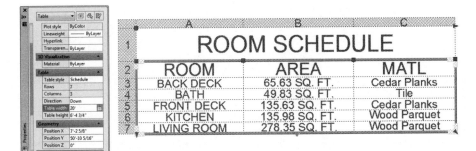

FIGURE 9.79 Adjusting the width of the ROOM SCHEDULE table

	A	B	C
1	ROOM SCHEDULE		
2	ROOM	AREA	MATL
3	BACK DECK	65.63 SQ. FT.	Cedar Planks
4	BATH	49.83 SQ. FT.	Tile
5	FRONT DECK	135.63 SQ. FT.	Cedar Planks
6	KITCHEN	135.98 SQ. FT.	Wood Parquet
7	LIVING ROOM	278.35 SQ. FT.	Wood Parquet

FIGURE 9.80 Selecting multiple table cells

Your final table should look like the one shown in Figure 9.82.

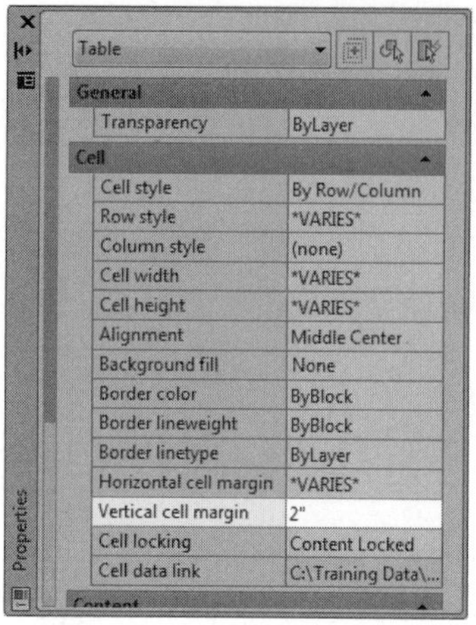

FIGURE 9.81 Modifying the
Vertical Cell Margin

ROOM SCHEDULE		
ROOM	AREA	MATL
BACK DECK	65.63 SQ. FT.	Cedar Planks
BATH	49.83 SQ. FT.	Tile
FRONT DECK	135.63 SQ. FT.	Cedar Planks
KITCHEN	135.98 SQ. FT.	Wood Parquet
LIVING ROOM	278.35 SQ. FT.	Wood Parquet

FIGURE 9.82 The completed ROOM SCHEDULE table

This concludes the chapter on dynamic blocks and tables. In the next chapter, you'll look at adding the elevations to the drawings.

This has been a quick tour of the features of attributes and the commands used to set them up and modify the data they contain. In the process, you saw several ways you can use them in an AutoCAD drawing. If you continue to work with attributes, you'll find them to be a powerful tool and a way to link information in your AutoCAD drawing to other applications. You also explored the methods for creating dynamic blocks that change as required to match your drawing's needs. Finally, you created a table to display the door schedule information and added a formula to calculate the total cost.

If You Would Like More Practice...

Blocks and attributes are commonly used in title blocks. For more practice using attributes, you can try the following:

► Replace the title block text with attributes.

► Add attributes to the window blocks.

► Experiment with the dynamic block functionality by creating window blocks that can be dragged to the appropriate width without resorting to scaling the blocks.

► Add a window schedule to calculate the cost of the cabin's windows.

Are You Experienced?

Now you can...

☑ **set up blocks with attributes**

☑ **control the visibility of the attributes**

☑ **calculate the area of an enclosed space**

☑ **create dynamic blocks**

☑ **define a table style**

☑ **create a table complete with formulas**

☑ **create a table by extracting data from objects in the drawing**

Generating Elevations

Now that you have created all the building components that will be in the floor plan, it's a good time to draw the exterior elevations. *Elevations* are horizontal views of the building, seen as if you were standing facing the building instead of looking down at it, as you do with a floor plan. An elevation view shows you how windows and doors fit into the walls and gives you an idea of how the building will look from the outside. In most architectural design projects, the drawings include at least four exterior elevations: front, back, and one for each side.

I'll go over how to create the south elevation first. Then I'll discuss some of the considerations necessary to complete the other elevations, and you'll have an opportunity to draw them on your own.

In mechanical drawing, the item being drawn is often a machine part or a fixture. The drafter uses *orthographic projection*—a method for illustrating an object in views set at right angles to each other: front, top, side, back, and so on—instead of elevations and plans. An exercise later in this chapter will give you practice with orthographic projection, but the procedure will be the same, whether you're drawing buildings or mechanical objects.

▶ **Drawing an exterior elevation from a floor plan**

▶ **Using grips to copy objects**

▶ **Setting up, naming, and saving user coordinate systems and views**

▶ **Transferring lines from one elevation to another**

▶ **Moving and rotating elevations**

Drawing the South Elevation

The first elevation view you'll create is the south view. This will reflect the appearance of the cabin as if you were looking at it from the side with the bath and living room windows. Before starting on these elevation views, however, you'll need to create some additional layers. These layers will mimic many of the layers already in your drawing, but will use the major ELEV code to distinguish them from the layers used for your floor plan.

1. Open I09A-FPLAYO.dwg (M09A-FPLAYO.dwg).

2. Open the Layer Properties Manager palette from the Home tab ➤ Layers panel.

3. Using the New Layer button, create the layers with the properties shown in the following table.

Layer	Color	Linetype
A-ELEV-DECK	3 (Green)	Continuous
A-ELEV-DECK-STRS	82	Continuous
A-ELEV-DOOR	1 (Red)	Continuous
A-ELEV-FNDN	11	Continuous
A-ELEV-GLAZ	31	Continuous
A-ELEV-ROOF	4 (Cyan)	Continuous
A-ELEV-TEXT	2 (Yellow)	Continuous
A-ELEV-WALL	84	Continuous

4. Save this drawing as I10-01-ElevLayers.dwg (M10-01-Elev Layers.dwg).

Creating the South Elevation

You draw the elevation by using techniques similar to those used on a traditional drafting board. You'll draw the south elevation view of the cabin directly below the floor plan by dropping lines down from key points on the floor plan and intersecting them with horizontal lines representing the heights of the corresponding components in the elevation. Figure 10.1 shows those heights. For this project, we'll consider the top of the screen to be north.

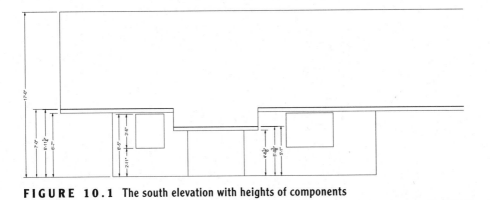

FIGURE 10.1 The south elevation with heights of components

Follow these steps:

1. Continue using I10-01-ElevLayers.dwg (M10-01-ElevLayers.dwg), or open it if it's not already open.

2. Freeze the A-ANNO-TABL, A-ANNO-TEXT, A-ANNO-TTLB, A-ANNO -TTLB-TEXT, and A-GRID layers. The A-AREA-NPLT layer should already be frozen, but check it and freeze it if it is still thawed. Thaw the A-ROOF layer.

3. Offset the bottom horizontal wall line that is to the right of the pop-out 30′ (9144 mm) down. The offset line may be off the screen.

4. Perform a Zoom Extents; then zoom out just enough to bring the off-set wall line up off the bottom edge of the drawing area.

5. Select the object and, when the grips are visible, click the left grip.

6. Use the Perpendicular osnap to stretch the line to the left extent of the building, as shown in Figure 10.2.

7. Deselect the offset line. When done, your drawing should look like Figure 10.3.

8. Save this drawing as **I10-02-SouthElevPlacement.dwg** (**M10-02-South ElevPlacement.dwg**).

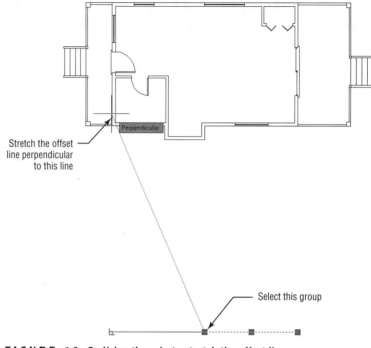

Stretch the offset
line perpendicular
to this line

Perpendicular

Select this group

FIGURE 10.2 Using the grip to stretch the offset line

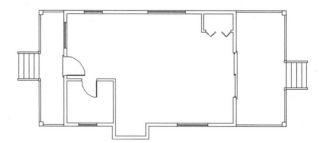

FIGURE 10.3 The floor plan with space below it for the south elevation

Setting Up Lines for the Heights

The line you offset establishes a baseline to represent the ground or the bottom of the cabin. You can now offset the other height lines from the baseline or from other height lines:

1. Continue using I10-02-SouthElevPlacement.dwg (M10-02-SouthElev Placement.dwg), or open it if it's not already open.

2. Check the status bar to make sure that Polar Tracking, Object Snap, and Dynamic Input are in their on positions while the other buttons are off. The Endpoint osnap should be running.

3. Change the layer of the offset line from A-WALL to A-ELEV-WALL, and perform the following offsets:

   ▶ Offset the base line 6′-7″ (2007 mm) up to mark the lowest edge of the roof supports and the bottom edge of the soffit.

   ▶ Offset the same line 6′-11¼″ (2115 mm) and again 7′-0″ (2134 mm) to establish the lower and upper heights of the roof covering, respectively.

   ▶ Finally, offset the base line up 17′-0″ (5182 mm) to mark the ridgeline of the roof.

   The lines should look like those shown in Figure 10.4.

4. Offset the base line 2′-11″ (889 mm) to represent the bottom of the windows.

> ◀
>
> A *soffit* is the underside of the roof overhang that extends from the outside edge of the roof back to the wall.

FIGURE 10.4 Lines representing different heights in the elevation

5. Offset the offset line 3′-6″ (1069 mm) to mark the top.

6. To complete the lines representing different heights in the elevation, copy the three horizontal rooflines down 1′-11″ (584 mm).

   These will be the lines at the edge of the roof, where it covers the pop-out (see Figure 10.5). Note that two of the lines appear to be at the same height). Use a crossing selection window to select the lines; be sure not to select the line representing the tops of the windows.

7. Save this drawing as **I10-03-SouthElevOffsets.dwg** (**M10-03-South ElevOffsets.dwg**).

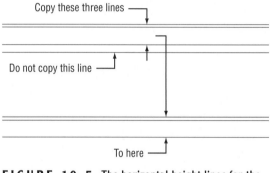

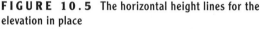

FIGURE 10.5 The horizontal height lines for the elevation in place

Each of these lines represents the height of one or more components of the cabin. Now you'll drop lines down from the points in the floor plan that coincide with components that will be visible in the elevation. The south elevation will consist of the exterior walls, two windows, the pop-out, and the roof.

Using Construction Lines to Project Elevation Points

As you know, to create a standard line, you must define both a starting and ending point for the line. But in addition to the standard LINE command, AutoCAD offers two additional types of lines: rays and construction lines.

Rays   Rays are a mix between standard and construction lines. Rays have a starting point but no end point.

Construction Lines   Construction lines have neither a starting nor an ending point, and extend to infinity in both directions.

Both rays and construction lines can be trimmed in much the same way as standard lines. Since by definition a construction line is a line of infinite length, trimming it will force it to extend to infinity in one direction. Consequently, using the TRIM command on a construction line will, at a minimum, turn it into a ray. Similarly, using the TRIM command on a ray will define an endpoint, consequently reducing it into a standard AutoCAD *line*.

You'll use construction lines to project key points from your floor plan to the area within the drawing where you will draw your south elevation. As you do this, pay attention to the way construction lines are reduced into rays, and rays into standard lines.

1. Continue using I10-03-SouthElevOffsets.dwg (M10-03-SouthElev Offsets.dwg), or open it if it's not already open.

2. Zoom in to the floor plan, and make sure Object Snap is turned on with the Endpoint osnap enabled.

3. Start the XLINE (Construction Line) command from the expanded Draw panel on the Home tab.

4. Enter **V↵** at the Specify a point or [Hor/Ver/Ang/Bisect/Offset]: prompt to choose the Ver, or Vertical, option.

    With the Vertical option, the XLINE command will create a vertical line extending to your south elevation and beyond at each point you select.

5. Using the Endpoint osnap, choose the lower-left outside wall by the bathroom, as shown in Figure 10.6. Keep this drawing open as you continue to the next exercise.

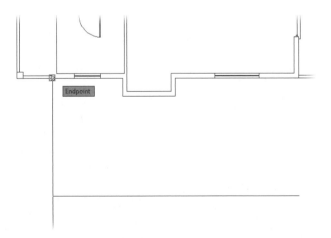

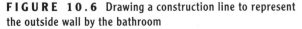

FIGURE 10.6 Drawing a construction line to represent the outside wall by the bathroom

Copying Objects by Using Grips

Construction lines, like most other objects in AutoCAD, have a number of *grips*. Selecting the construction line you just drew will make three grips (blue boxes) appear. Grips can be used to modify objects in your drawing quickly and easily. Among the possible operations using grips is the Copy function. You'll create the remaining projection points by using this method:

1. Select the construction line you just drew.

   Three grips appear along the construction line: one at the insertion point, and two more above and below it (see Figure 10.7).

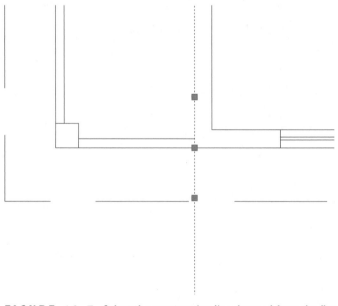

FIGURE 10.7 Select the construction line dropped from the floor plan.

The STRETCH command is a modifying tool that you use to lengthen or shorten lines and other objects. You'll have another chance to use it in Chapter 11, "Working with Hatches, Gradients, and Tool Palettes."

2. Click the middle grip on the construction line (this is the same point you used to insert the construction line).

   The grip changes color from blue to red, and the prompt changes to Specify stretch point or [Base point/Copy/Undo/eXit]:. This is the STRETCH command. Any time you activate a grip, the STRETCH command automatically starts.

3. Right-click and choose Copy from the context menu.

    This starts the COPY command, using the selected grip as the first point.

4. With the Endpoint osnap running, select each of the 11 endpoints shown in Figure 10.8.

    The construction line is copied to each of these corners, and extends down to where you'll draw the south elevation.

Every command that works with grips has a Copy option, which keeps the original object "as is" while you modify the copy. You can copy with grips in ways not possible with the COPY command.

 W A R N I N G   You may need to restart the Copy tool if each of the 11 destination endpoints is not viewable when the command is started.

5. Press Esc twice to end the command and deselect the line. Your drawing resembles Figure 10.9.

6. Save this drawing as **I10-04-ProjectionLines.dwg** (**M10-04 -ProjectionLines.dwg**).

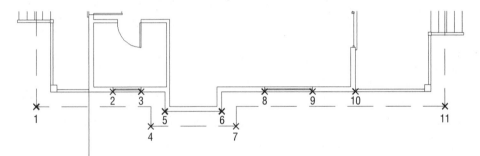

FIGURE 10.8 Copy the construction line to the 11 points shown here.

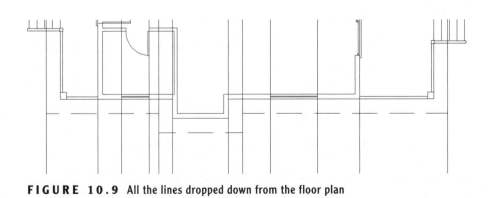

FIGURE 10.9 All the lines dropped down from the floor plan

In the next section, you'll trim the lines as necessary to continue the elevation drawing.

Getting a Grip on Grips

In Chapter 7, "Combining Objects into Blocks," you saw how to use grips to detect whether an object is a block. Grips actually serve a larger function. The STRETCH command will automatically start when you select a single grip. With a single grip selected, the right-click menu offers a list of additional tools for editing objects quickly by using one or more of the following five commands: STRETCH, MOVE, ROTATE, SCALE, and MIRROR. These commands operate a little differently when using grips than when using them otherwise.

The commands can also perform a few more tasks with the help of grips. Each command has a Copy option. So, for example, if you rotate an object with grips, you can keep the original object unchanged while you make multiple copies of the object in various angles of rotation. You can't do this by using the ROTATE command in the regular way or by using the regular COPY command.

To use grips, follow these steps:

1. When no commands have been started, click an object that you want to modify.

2. Click the grip that will be the base point for the command's execution.

3. Right-click at this point, and choose any of the five commands just described from the context menu that opens on the drawing area.

   You can also cycle through these commands by pressing the spacebar and watching the command prompt.

4. When you see the command you need, execute the necessary option.

5. Enter X↵ when you're finished.

6. Press Esc to deselect the object.

The key to being able to use grips efficiently is knowing which grip to select to start the process. This requires a good understanding of the five commands that work with grips.

This book doesn't cover grips in depth, but it introduces you to the basics. You'll get a chance to use the MOVE command with grips in this chapter, and you'll use grips again when you get to Chapter 12, "Dimensioning a Drawing."

(Continues)

GETTING A GRIP ON GRIPS *(Continued)*

Keep the following in mind when working with grips:

▶ Each of the five commands available for use with grips requires a base point. For MIRROR, for example, the base point is the first point of the mirror line. By default, the *base point* is the grip that you select to activate the process. But you can change base points, as follows:

1. Select a grip, and enter **B**↵.

2. Pick a different point to serve as a base point.

3. Continue the command.

▶ When you use the Copy option with the MOVE command, you're essentially using the regular COPY command.

Trimming Lines in the Elevation

The next task is to extend and trim the appropriate lines in the elevation. You'll start by extending the rooflines:

1. Continue using I10-04-ProjectionLines.dwg (M10-04-Projection Lines.dwg), or open it if it's not already open.

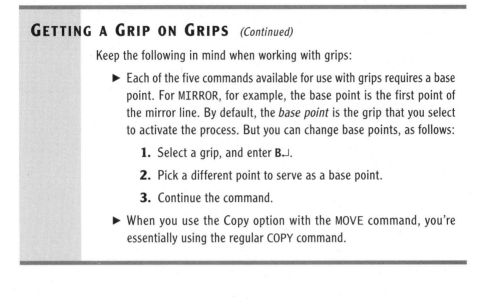

2. Click the Extend button in the Modify panel of the Home tab, and then select the two outermost construction lines extending from the roofline in plan view and press ↵. These are the boundary edges.

3. Click once on each end of the top four horizontal lines: the ridgeline, the top and bottom of the roof covering, and the bottom of the soffit (see Figure 10.10).

4. Start the TRIM command, and press ↵ when prompted to select cutting edges.

   By not selecting any cutting edges, every edge in the drawing is used as a cutting edge.

5. Enter **F**↵ to choose the Fence option.

6. Draw a fence line along the bottom of your elevation, as shown in Figure 10.11.

7. Press ↵ ↵ to apply the fence line and end the TRIM command.

8. Select one of the vertical lines extending down from the floor plan, and open the Properties palette (Ctrl+1).

   The roof extends a little farther than the rest of the roof where the hot tub is located.

9. Start the TRIM command, and select the two lines shown at the top of Figure 10.12.

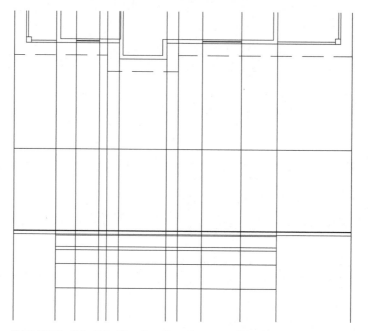

FIGURE 10.10 The elevation after extending the rooflines

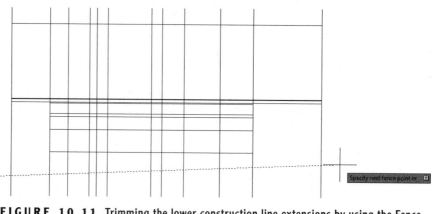
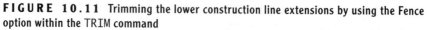

FIGURE 10.11 Trimming the lower construction line extensions by using the Fence option within the TRIM command

N O T E   Notice that the extension lines are no longer construction lines. By using the TRIM command, you defined a start point for each construction line where it intersected a cutting edge. Since construction lines extend to infinity in both directions, our line is reduced to a ray. As you may recall, a ray has a start point but no endpoint.

10. After choosing the cutting edges, pick above and below the cutting edges, as shown at the bottom of Figure 10.12, to trim the construction lines.

11. Start the TRIM command again, and select the two roof extension lines you just created along with the bottom roofline as cutting edges (see Figure 10.13).

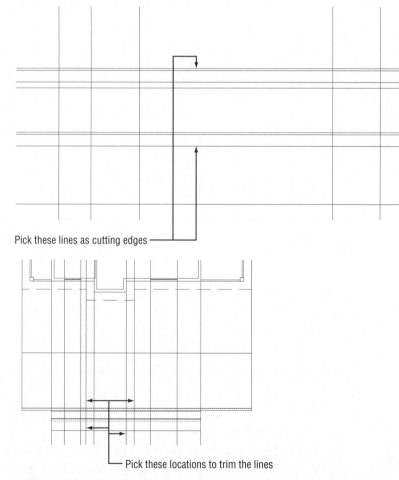

Pick these lines as cutting edges

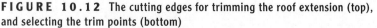

Pick these locations to trim the lines

F I G U R E 1 0 . 1 2 The cutting edges for trimming the roof extension (top), and selecting the trim points (bottom)

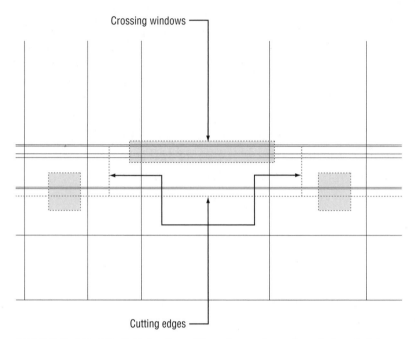

Crossing windows

Cutting edges

FIGURE 10.13 Defining the cutting edges and crossing windows to trim the roof extension

12. Use a total of three crossing windows to complete the TRIM command, as shown in Figure 10.13.

 13. Start the FILLET command from the Home tab ➢ Modify panel.

14. Using a 0 radius, pick the left side of the top roofline and the rear (left-side) vertical roof extension line.

15. Repeat the FILLET command, this time selecting the right side of the top roofline and the front (left-side) vertical roof extension line.
   This completes the roof outline in your elevation view. The only thing left to do is clean up the lines defining the two windows.

16. From the extended Modify panel within the Home tab, choose the Break At Point tool.

17. Select the lower window line at the Select object: prompt, and use the Midpoint osnap to specify the break point.
   Visually the line will appear unchanged; however, selecting it will reveal that the line has been divided into two separate line segments.

18. Zoom in to the bathroom window, and start the FILLET command.

19. Enter M↵ to select the Multiple option at the Select first object prompt.

20. Using a Fillet radius of 0, fillet each of the four corners of the bathroom window, as shown in Figure 10.14.

21. Repeat steps 16 and 17 to complete the living room window toward the front of your cabin.

22. Complete the elevation view by using the TRIM command to trim the two vertical lines representing the front and rear outside walls to the roof soffit line. When finished, the elevation should resemble Figure 10.15.

23. Save the current drawing as I10-05-TrimElevation.dwg (M10-05-TrimElevation.dwg).

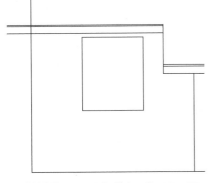

FIGURE 10.14 Using the FILLET command to complete the bathroom window

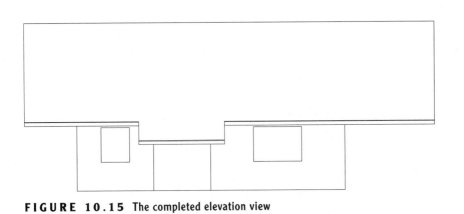

FIGURE 10.15 The completed elevation view

This is the basic process for generating an elevation: drop lines down from the floor plan, and trim the lines that need to be trimmed. The trick is to learn to see the picture you want somewhere among all the crossed lines and then to be able to use the TRIM command accurately to cut away the appropriate lines.

TIPS FOR USING THE *TRIM* AND *EXTEND* COMMANDS

TRIM and EXTEND are sister commands. Here are a few tips on how they work:

Basic Operation

Both commands involve two steps: selecting cutting edges (TRIM) or boundary edges (EXTEND) and then selecting the lines to be trimmed or extended:

1. Select the cutting or boundary edges, and then press ↵.

2. Pick lines to trim or extend.

3. Press ↵ to end the commands.

You can use the Fence option or a selection window to select several lines to trim or extend at one time.

Trimming and Extending in the Same Command

If you find that a cutting edge for trimming can also serve as a boundary edge for extending, hold down the Shift key and click a line to extend it to the cutting edge. The opposite is true for the EXTEND command.

Correcting Errors

It's easy to make a mistake in selecting cutting or boundary edges or in trimming and extending. You can correct a mistake in two ways:

▶ If you select the wrong cutting or boundary edge, do the following:

    1. Enter **R**↵ and then choose the lines again that were picked in error. They will lose their highlighting.

    2. If you need to keep selecting cutting or boundary edges, enter **A**↵ and select new lines.

    3. When finished, press ↵ to move to the second part of the command.

(Continues)

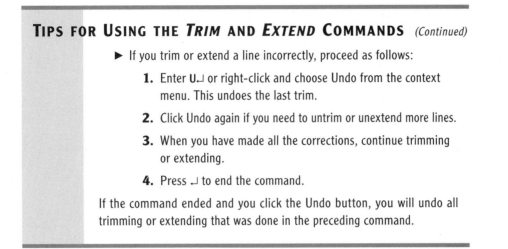

TIPS FOR USING THE *TRIM* AND *EXTEND* COMMANDS *(Continued)*

▶ If you trim or extend a line incorrectly, proceed as follows:

1. Enter **U**↵ or right-click and choose Undo from the context menu. This undoes the last trim.

2. Click Undo again if you need to untrim or unextend more lines.

3. When you have made all the corrections, continue trimming or extending.

4. Press ↵ to end the command.

If the command ended and you click the Undo button, you will undo all trimming or extending that was done in the preceding command.

Assigning Elevation Layers

You set the A-ELEV-WALL layer as current as you began drawing your elevation view. At that point, you were mostly interested in getting the elevation's geometry in place, and not as interested in layers. With the geometry in place, now is a good time to pause for a moment and place everything on the correct layers. Currently, the exterior walls, roof, and windows are drawn. Follow these steps to assign the A-ELEV-WALL, A-ELEV-ROOF, and A-ELEV-GLAZ, respectively, to those objects:

1. Continue using I10-05-TrimElevation.dwg (M10-05-Trim Elevation.dwg), or open it if it's not already open.

2. Select the lines shown in Figure 10.16, and use the layer pull-down found on the Layers panel of the Home tab to assign the A-ELEV-ROOF layer.

3. Repeat step 2, this time selecting the bathroom and living room windows and assigning the A-ELEV-GLAZ layer.

4. Select the four vertical lines and the horizontal line running along the bottom of your elevation view, and using the process shown in step 2, assign the A-ELEV-WALL layer.

5. Save the current drawing as **I10-06-AssignLayers.dwg** (**M10-06 -AssignLayers.dwg**).

With each component of your elevation view on the proper layer, you can begin to refine the view further. Currently, the elevation view does not illustrate your deck, stairs, or foundation. Let's begin adding these components, starting with the front and rear decks.

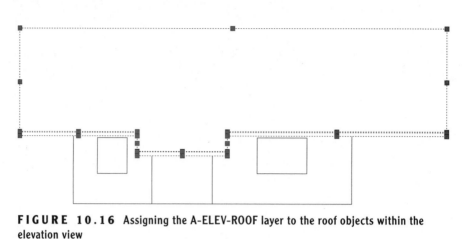

FIGURE 10.16 Assigning the A-ELEV-ROOF layer to the roof objects within the elevation view

Drawing the Decks in Elevation

The cabin sits on an 18″ (457 mm) foundation (which you'll add in the "Drawing the Supports and Foundation" section later in this chapter), with the surrounding land falling away from it at a slight angle. On the front and back sides are decks with stairways to step up to the door levels. In this section, you'll draw the front deck first, mirror it to the other end, and then adjust the second deck to match the conditions at the back of the cabin.

Drawing the Front Deck

Figure 10.17 shows the dimensions required to draw the horizontal elements of the stairway, while most vertical lines are dropped from the floor plan.

Follow these steps to draw the front deck:

1. Continue using I10-06-AssignLayers.dwg (M10-06-AssignLayers.dwg), or open it if it's not already open.

2. Make the A-ELEV-DECK layer current.

3. Draw a horizontal line from the elevation's bottom-right corner of the wall directly to the right.

   Make sure the line extends beyond the limits of the stairway in the floor plan.

4. Start the XLINE (Construction Line) command.

5. Choose the Vertical option, and draw lines from the corner post, the stairs, and the end of the railing in the floor plan, as shown in Figure 10.18.

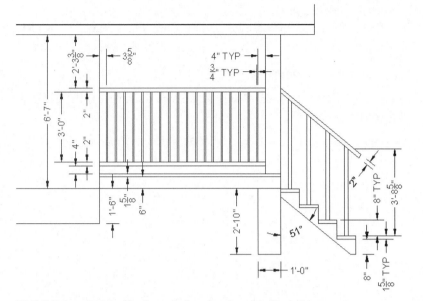

FIGURE 10.17 The front deck and stairs with dimensions

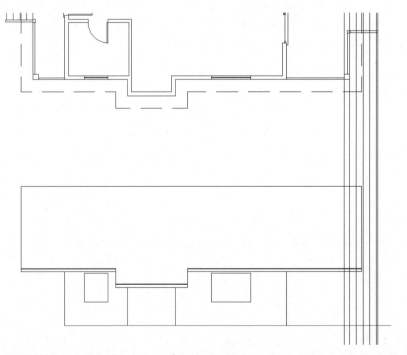

FIGURE 10.18 Vertical construction lines drawn from deck post, stairs, and railings

6. Zoom in to the right end of the cabin elevation.

   Here you're going to first offset the horizontal line several times and then trim the resulting lines back to the lines that represent the post.

7. Start the OFFSET command.

8. Offset the horizontal line upward 6″ (152 mm), and press the Esc key to exit the command.

9. Repeat steps 7 and 8 five times, offsetting the original line up by these distances:

   7 5/8″ (194 mm)

   11 5/8″ (295 mm)

   1′-1 5/8″ (346 mm)

   4′-1 5/8″ (1260 mm)

   4′-3 5/8″ (1312 mm)

   The right end of your elevation should look like Figure 10.19.

10. Start the TRIM command and select the two post lines, the soffit line, and the third horizontal deck line (deck surface) from the bottom as the cutting edges (see Figure 10.20).

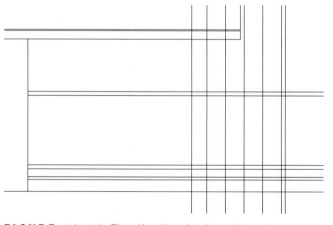

FIGURE 10.19 The offset lines for the stairs

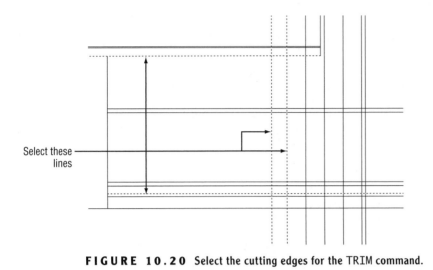

Select these
lines

FIGURE 10.20 Select the cutting edges for the TRIM command.

11. Continue using the TRIM command to clean up the construction lines you drew by doing the following:

    a. Trim all the deck horizontal lines to the right post line, and then trim the top four deck lines again, this time to the left post line.

    b. Trim the vertical post lines back to the soffit line on top and the third horizontal deck line below.

    c. Next, draw a short vertical line from the bottom of the right post line to the lowest horizontal line, as shown in Figure 10.21.

12. Save the current drawing as **I10-06-FrontDeck.dwg (M10-06-FrontDeck.dwg)**.

Drawing the Railing Posts with a Path Array

The railing posts are ¾″ (20 mm) square components that are 3′-0″ (915 mm) long and spaced with a 4″ (102 mm) gap between each one. Once the first object is drawn, you could apply strategies learned in earlier chapters to manually copy the remaining posts. AutoCAD 2012 introduces several new options for arraying objects.

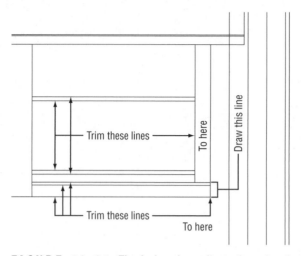

FIGURE 10.21 The deck and post lines after trimming
them back to their proper lengths

As you will see in a moment, the ARRAY command provides an efficient way to copy objects as an associative group. This associative group can be created in any one of three distinct ways: rectangular, polar, or what you'll use in this exercise—path. Using the Path Array (ARRAYPATH) command, each of the vertical railing posts will be created using only a single instance of one command. Here's how:

1. Continue using I10-06-FrontDeck.dwg (M10-06-FrontDeck.dwg), or open it if it's not already open.

2. Offset the left post line 4" (102 mm) to the left, and then offset this line another ¾" (20 mm).

3. Trim these two lines back to the lower edge of the upper rail and to the upper edge of the lower rail (see Figure 10.22).

4. On the Home tab ➢ Modify panel, expand the Array button and select Path Array, as shown in Figure 10.23.

5. At the Select objects: prompt, select the two lines composing the vertical railing post, as shown earlier in Figure 10.22. Press ↵.

6. Define the direction you would like to copy the vertical railing by selecting the lower horizontal railing line at the Select path curve: prompt (also shown earlier in Figure 10.22).

7. Since the total number of posts is currently unknown, enter an arbitrary number, such as **5**, at the Enter number of items along path or [Orientation/Expression] <Orientation>: prompt.

8. Enter **4⏎** (**102⏎**) at the Specify the distance between items along path or [Divide/Total/Expression] <Divide evenly along path>: prompt to complete the array shown in Figure 10.24.

9. Using the Endpoint object snap, start the Measure Distance (MEASUREGEOM) command on the Home tab ➢ Utilities panel to measure between the railing posts.

   Notice the actual distance between railing posts is 3′-¾″ (82 mm), not 4″ (102 mm) as you may have expected. Similar to using the COPY command, you must take into account the entire object, in this case a 4″ (102 mm) space, plus the railing width of ¾″ (20 mm) for a total array distance of 4-¾″ (122 mm).

   Since the path array is an associative object, correcting this distance is easily done from a contextual Array Ribbon tab.

10. Select any one of the five railing posts to open the contextual Array Ribbon tab.

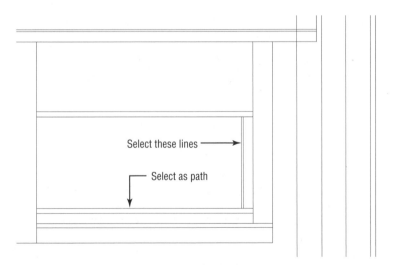

Select these lines ⟶

⌐ Select as path

FIGURE 10.22 Draw the first railing post.

11. On the Items panel of the contextual Array tab, change the Item Spacing value to 4¾″ (122 mm), as shown in Figure 10.25.

The distance between each railing post updates to the intended 4″ (102 mm) spacing. Next you'll modify the array to fill the entire deck railing area.

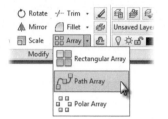

FIGURE 10.23 Starting the Path Array (ARRAYPATH) command from the Ribbon

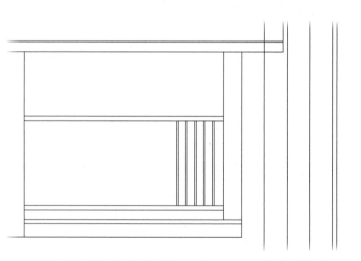

FIGURE 10.24 Vertical railing posts created with the Path Array (ARRAYPATH) command

FIGURE 10.25 Modifying the Item Spacing value from the contextual Array Ribbon tab

12. With the railing posts still selected, click the arrow grip on the far left of the array.

  This is the Item Count grip, which will allow you to make additional copies of the railing posts by moving your cursor (see the top of Figure 10.26).

13. Move your cursor to the left, until the entire deck railing area is filled, as shown at the bottom of Figure 10.26.

14. Save the current drawing as **I10-07-RailingArray.dwg** (**M10-07 -RailingArray.dwg**). The completed railing array should match Figure 10.27.

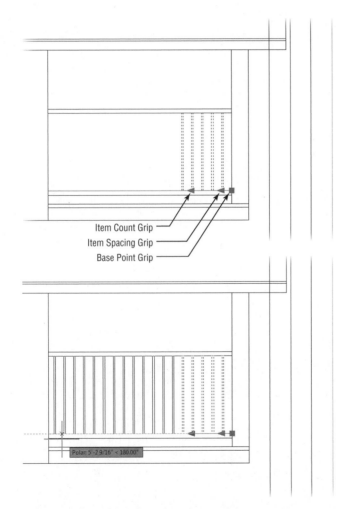

FIGURE 10.26 Identification of Path Array grips (top), and using grips to change the item count (bottom)

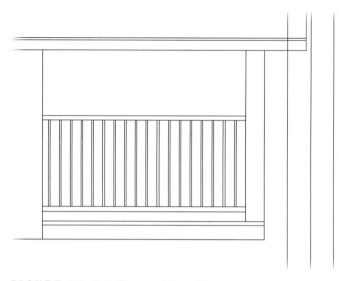

FIGURE 10.27 The completed railings

Drawing the Stairs

There are four steps leading up to the cabin, each with an 8″ (204 mm) *rise* and a 1⅝″(41 mm) thick tread. The 10″ (254 mm) length of the steps, also called the *run*, is based on the lines dropped from the steps in the floor plan.

1. Continue using I10-07-RailingArray.dwg (M10-07-RailingArray .dwg), or open it if it's not already open.

2. Using Object Snap Tracking and direct input, draw a line from a point 8″ (204 mm) below the top of the deck directly to the right, well beyond the last vertical step line, as shown in Figure 10.28.

3. Using the OFFSET command, make three copies of this line, each one 8″ (204 mm) below the previous.

   These lines are the tops of the stair treads.

4. Offset each of the stair tread lines downward 1⅝″ (41 mm), as shown in Figure 10.29.

5. Using the vertical step lines as cutting edges, trim each of the steps to its proper 10″ (254 mm) length.

   Try using a crossing window to select multiple lines to trim at one time.

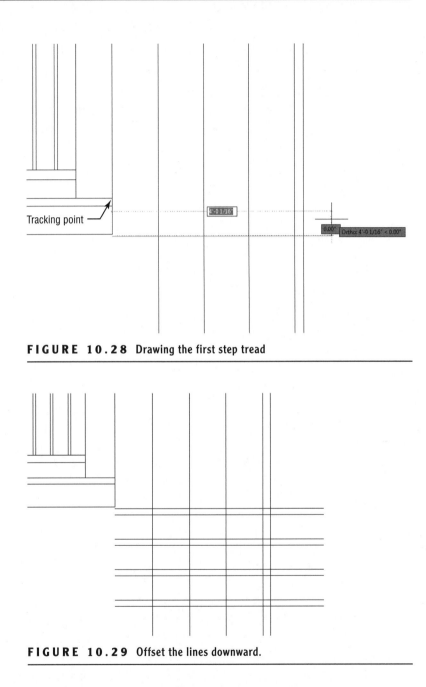

FIGURE 10.28 Drawing the first step tread

FIGURE 10.29 Offset the lines downward.

6. Next, use the horizontal step lines as cutting edges to trim back the vertical lines, leaving the short, vertical line between each step intact. Your stairway should look like Figure 10.30.

For the *stringer* (the support for the steps), you need a line that matches the angle between each step.

7. Draw a line from the top-right corner of the first step to the top-right corner of the last step, and then offset this line 10″ (254 mm) so the copy appears below the stairs, as shown in Figure 10.31.

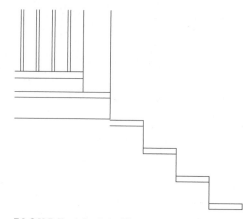

FIGURE 10.30 The steps after trimming away the extraneous lines

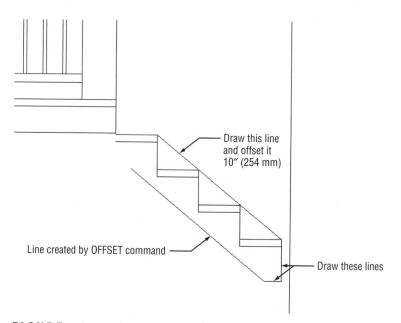

Draw this line and offset it 10″ (254 mm)

Line created by OFFSET command

Draw these lines

FIGURE 10.31 Drawing the stringer

8. Draw a line from the bottom of the lowest step tread 8″ (204 mm) downward and then a few feet directly to the left.

9. Fillet the bottom-left corner of the stringer with a radius of 0, as shown in Figure 10.31.

    The last parts of the stairway to draw are the 2″ (51 mm) railing posts and the handrail.

10. Move the angled line at the top of the stairs up 3′-6″ (1067 mm) and then offset it upward 2″ (51 mm).

11. Extend the upper line until it intersects the post on the left and the last remaining vertical line dropped from the floor plan.

12. Extend the lower line only to the post on the left, as shown in Figure 10.32.

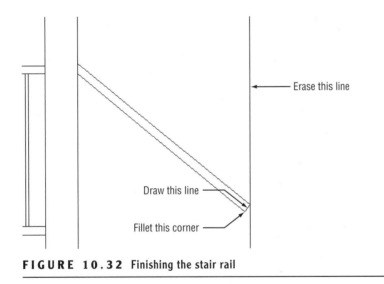

FIGURE 10.32 Finishing the stair rail

13. Draw a line from the right endpoint of the upper railing line, perpendicular to the lower line, and then fillet the corner.

14. Erase the vertical line that extends from the floor plan (see Figure 10.32 shown previously).

15. To create the posts, draw a line from the midpoint of a stair tread upward and then offset it 1″ (25.5 mm) to the left and right.

16. Erase the original line and then trim or extend the other two lines until they intersect with the lower railing line.

17. Using the top-right corner of each step as a reference point, copy the post to the other three steps.

   When you're finished, your deck should look like Figure 10.33.

18. Save the current drawing as **I10-08-StairElevation.dwg (M10-08 -StairElevation.dwg)**.

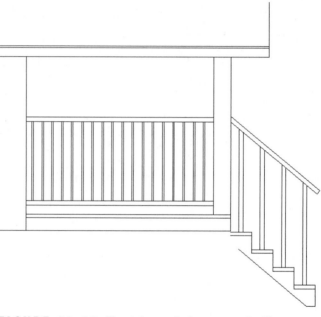

FIGURE 10.33 The stairway, deck, posts, and railings

Drawing the Supports and Foundation

The cabin rests on a foundation, and the decks are supported by concrete posts. You can quickly draw these by using the Rectangle (RECTANG) command with object snaps and the Object Snap Tracking tool.

1. Continue using I10-08-StairElevation.dwg (M10-08-Stair Elevation.dwg), or open it if it's not already open.

2. Using the Layer drop-down, change the current layer to A-ELEV -FNDN from the Home tab ➤ Layers panel.

3. Start the Rectangle (RECTANG) command, and draw a rectangle with its first point at the right end of the lowest horizontal deck line and the second point 1' (305 mm) to the left and 2'-10" (864 mm) below that point (in other words, at –1',–2'-10" or at–305,–864 mm).

4. Extend the lower stringer line until it intersects the support post, as shown in Figure 10.34.

5. Zoom out so that you can see the entire cabin, and start the Rectangle (RECTANG) command again.

6. At the Specify first corner point or: prompt, click the lower-right corner of the cabin's exterior wall.

7. At the Specify other corner point or: prompt, pause the cursor over the lower-left corner of the cabin's exterior wall until the temporary track point appears. Then move the cursor directly downward and enter 18↵ (457↵).

    The foundation rectangle is shown in Figure 10.35.

8. Save the current drawing as **I10-09-SupportFoundation.dwg** (**M10-09-SupportFoundation.dwg**).

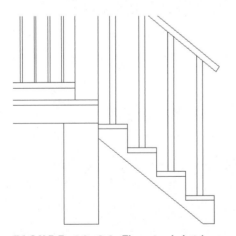

FIGURE 10.34 The extended stringer and the first deck support post

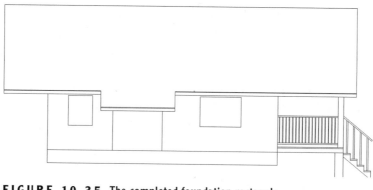

FIGURE 10.35 The completed foundation rectangle

Mirroring the Deck

From this view, the decks, stairways, post, and supports are nearly symmetrical, making the Mirror tool an excellent choice for creating most of the objects on the back deck. The front deck is wider than the back deck, but an efficient use of the ERASE and TRIM commands can quickly fix that.

1. Continue using I10-09-SupportFoundation.dwg (M10-09-Support Foundation.dwg), or open it if it's not already open.

2. Start the MIRROR command, and then select all the components of the deck, stairs, railings, posts, and the concrete support.

3. At the Specify first point of mirror line: prompt, use the Midpoint osnap to select the midpoint of the roof.

4. At the Specify second point of mirror line: prompt, pick a point directly below the first point.

   The components on the right remain ghosted, while the new components on the left appear solid, as shown in Figure 10.36.

5. When prompted whether to erase source objects, press ⏎ to accept the default No option to retain the selected objects on the right.

6. Zoom in to the back deck to clean up the mirrored linework by doing the following:

   a. Select any one of the vertical railing posts, and use the Item Count grip to adjust the number of railings so that they fill only the area to the left of the exterior wall.

   b. Trim the horizontal deck lines back to that wall line, including the line that overlaps the top of the foundation.

Try enabling Selection Cycling on the status bar to help you select the line that overlaps the top of the foundation.

Your back deck should look like Figure 10.37.

7. Save the current drawing as **I10-10-DeckMirror.dwg** (**M10-10-Deck Mirror.dwg**).

WARNING   Trimming the horizontal deck lines prior to adjusting the Path Array will open an Associative Path Array error dialog box. This dialog box is simply warning that your array extends beyond the length of the path (or in this case, line) that was selected when the array was created.

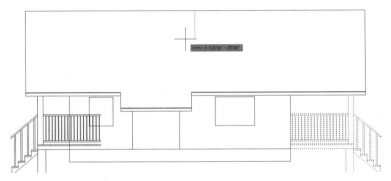

FIGURE 10.36 The front deck mirrored to the back of the cabin

---

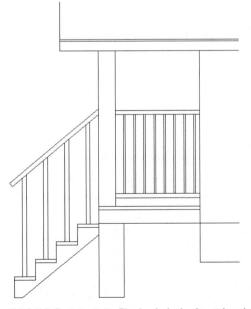

FIGURE 10.37 The back deck after trimming and erasing unneeded lines

---

Generating the Other Elevations

The full set of drawings that contractors use to construct a building includes an elevation for each side of the building. In traditional drafting, the elevations were usually drawn on separate sheets. This required transferring measurements from one drawing to another by taping drawings next to each other, turning the floor plan around to orient it to each elevation, and using several other cumbersome techniques. You do it about the same way on the computer, but it's much easier to move the drawing around. You'll be more accurate, and you can quickly borrow parts from one elevation to use in another.

Making the Opposite Elevation

Because the north elevation shares components and sizes with the south elevation, you can mirror the front elevation to the rear of the building and then make the necessary changes:

1. Open I10-10-DeckMirror.dwg (M10-10-DeckMirror.dwg), if it's not already open.

2. Change the view to include space above the floor plan for the elevation on the opposite side of the building.

3. Use the Pan tool, or hold down the scroll wheel, to move the view of the floor plan to the middle of the screen.

4. Then zoom out the view enough to include the front elevation.

5. Start the MIRROR command.

6. Use a window to select the south elevation and then press ↵.

7. For the mirror line, select the Midpoint osnap and pick the left edge line of the ridgeline in the floor plan.

8. With Polar Tracking on, hold the crosshair cursor directly to the right of the point you just picked (see the top of Figure 10.38) and pick another point. At the Erase source objects?[Yes/No]<N>: prompt, press ↵ to accept the default of No.

   The first side elevation is mirrored to the opposite side of the cabin (see the right of Figure 10.38). You can now make the necessary changes to the new elevation so that it correctly describes the south elevation of the cabin. However, you might find it easier to work if the view is right side up.

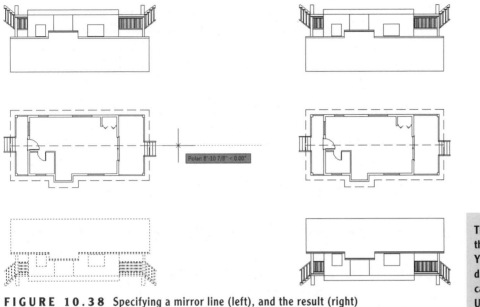

FIGURE 10.38 Specifying a mirror line (left), and the result (right)

> The UCS defines the positive X and Y directions in your drawing. A drawing can have several UCSs, but can use only one at a time.

> The WCS is the default UCS for all new drawings and remains available in all drawings.

Take a look at the icon, currently located at the origin, for a moment. The two lines in the icon show the positive X and Y directions of the current user coordinate system (UCS). That is the world coordinate system (WCS), which is the default system for all AutoCAD drawings. You'll change the orientation of the icon to the drawing and then change the orientation of the drawing to the screen.

9. Using the ViewCube found in the upper-right corner of the drawing area, click the UCS drop-down menu and select New UCS, as shown in Figure 10.39.

10. To rotate the current UCS 180° about the z-axis, type **Z↵ 180↵** at the Specify origin of UCS or [Face/NAmed/OBject/Previous/View/World/X/Y/Z/ZAxis] <World>: prompt.

    This rotates the UCS icon 180° around the z-axis, to an upside-down position. The square box at the intersection of the x- and y-axes disappears, showing that you're no longer using the default WCS (see Figure 10.40).

11. Start the PLAN command by entering **PLAN↵** at the command line and then **C↵** to select the Current UCS option.

The entire drawing is rotated 180°, and the mirrored elevation is now right side up. Note that the UCS icon is now oriented the way it used to be, but the square in the icon is still missing. This signals that the current UCS is not the WCS.

N O T E   You used the UCS command to reorient the UCS icon relative to the drawing. You then used the Current option of the PLAN command to reorient the drawing on the screen so that the positive X and Y directions of the current UCS are directed to the right and upward, respectively. This process is a little bit like turning your monitor upside down to get the correct orientation—but easier.

12. Zoom in to the lower edge of the floor plan and the mirrored elevation (see Figure 10.41). Now you can work on the rear elevation.

13. Save the current drawing as I10-11-OppositeElevation.dwg (M10-11-OppositeElevation.dwg).

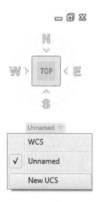

FIGURE 10.39 Creating a new UCS by using the ViewCube

FIGURE 10.40 The UCS icon showing the UCS rotated 180°

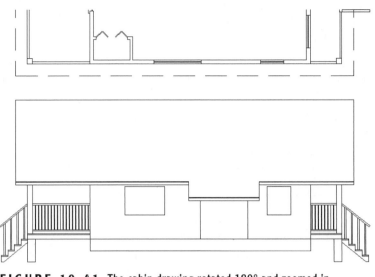

FIGURE 10.41 The cabin drawing rotated 180° and zoomed in

Revising the New South Elevation

A brief inspection will tell you that the decks and stairs don't need any changes. The windows and roof need revisions, however, and the pop-out doesn't exist on this side of the cabin:

▶ The two remaining windows need to be resized and repositioned.

▶ The roof needs to be a series of straight, unbroken lines.

▶ The vertical pop-out lines and the pop-out roof extension need to be deleted.

You can accomplish these tasks quickly by using commands with which you're now familiar:

1. Continue using I10-11-OppositeElevation.dwg (M10-11-Opposite Elevation.dwg), or open it if it's not already open.

2. Use the ERASE command to remove the following:

   ▶ The roof offset

   ▶ The walls for the roof offset

   ▶ The vertical lines from the remaining windows

After removing these lines, your elevation view should look like Figure 10.42.

3. Zoom in to the area where the roof extension was previously located. The gap left after erasing the pop-out needs to be reconstructed.

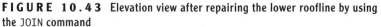

4. Start the JOIN command by choosing the Home tab ➤ extended Modify panel ➤ Join tool.

5. Pick the top roofline at the Select source object: prompt, and then choose the adjacent top roofline.

6. Press ↵ to end the command, and join the two segments into a single line segment.

7. Repeat step 6 for the two remaining rooflines.

After you've joined each of the rooflines into three individual segments, your view should look like Figure 10.43.

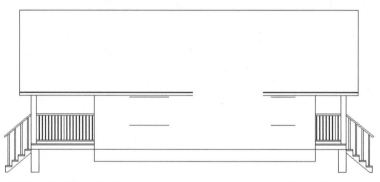

FIGURE 10.42 Erasing the unneeded elements copied from the original south elevation

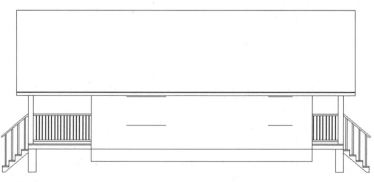

FIGURE 10.43 Elevation view after repairing the lower roofline by using the JOIN command

8. Change the current layer to A-ELEV-GLAZ by using either the Ribbon or the LAYER command.

9. Using the Construction Line tool found on the Draw panel of the Home tab, create extension lines from the jambs of the two windows in the floor plan.

    Once these are drawn, your elevation will look like Figure 10.44.

10. Use the FILLET command to construct the new windows. If necessary, use Selection Cycling to aid in selecting the correct line when filleting the top of your windows.

    Your elevation should look like Figure 10.45.

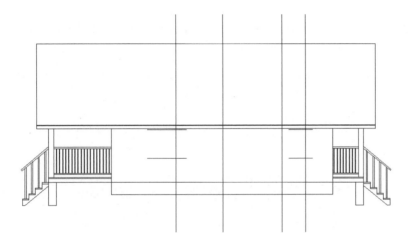

FIGURE 10.44 Construction lines drawn from the floor plan windows to the elevation view

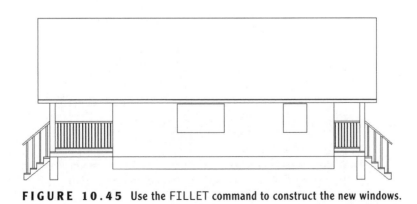

FIGURE 10.45 Use the FILLET command to construct the new windows.

You need to save the UCS you used to work on this elevation so that you can quickly return to it in the future, from the WCS or from any other UCS you might be in. The default AutoCAD workspace does not include access to UCS commands. To access these UCS commands, you'll load an additional Ribbon panel to the View Ribbon tab.

11. Switch to the View Ribbon tab.

12. Right-click the Navigate 2D panel title, and select Show Panels ➤ Coordinates (see the top of Figure 10.46).

    The Coordinates Ribbon panel is now included within the View Ribbon tab (see bottom of Figure 10.46).

13. Click the UCS, Named UCS button on the Coordinates panel of the View tab to open the UCS dialog box. Alternatively, you can enter **UCSMAN** at the command line.

14. From the UCS dialog box, click the Named UCSs tab, and then click the current UCS name (currently named Unnamed) once to highlight the text. Then select **North_Elev (Figure 10.47)**.

    This will allow you to recall the UCS if you need to work on this elevation again.

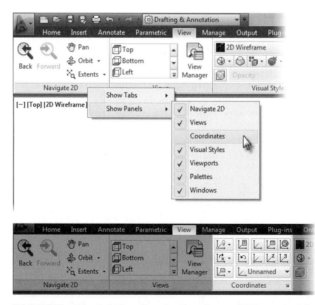

FIGURE 10.46 Loading the Coordinates Ribbon panel (top), and the Coordinates panel loaded onto the View Ribbon tab (bottom)

15. Click OK to exit the dialog box.

T I P **You can save any UCS in this way. The WCS is a permanent part of all drawings, so you never need to save it.**

You can also save the view to be able to recall it quickly.

16. Click the View Manager button in the View tab ➢ Views panel to open the View Manager dialog box, shown at the top of Figure 10.48. You can also start the VIEW command by typing **V↵**.

17. Click New to open the New View / Shot Properties dialog box.

18. In the View Name text box, enter **North_Elev**, as shown at the bottom of Figure 10.48.

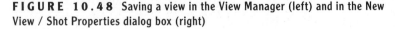

FIGURE 10.47 The UCS dialog box

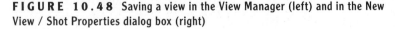

FIGURE 10.48 Saving a view in the View Manager (left) and in the New View / Shot Properties dialog box (right)

19. Click the Current Display radio button and click OK.

Back in the View Manager dialog box, North_Elev appears in the list of views.

 T I P   **You can name and save any view of your drawing and then restore it later.**

20. Click OK again.

Now you can restore the drawing to its original orientation, with the side elevation below the floor plan and right side up. You do this by restoring the preset Top view.

Use the In-Canvas Viewport Control toolbar found in the upper-left corner of the drawing area to restore the preset Top view.

21. Click the View Controls menu (currently displayed as [Top]) from the In-Canvas Viewport Control toolbar, and select Top (see Figure 10.49).

This zooms to Extents view and displays a plan view of the drawing with the X and Y positive directions in their default orientation.

22. Save the current drawing as **I10-12-NorthElevUCS.dwg** (**M10-12-North ElevUCS.dwg**).

[−] [Top] [2D Wireframe]

| Custom Model Views | ▸ |
| √ Top |
| Bottom |
| Left |
| Right |
| Front |
| Back |
| SW Isometric |
| SE Isometric |
| NE Isometric |
| NW Isometric |
| View Manager... |
| √ Parallel |
| Perspective |

FIGURE 10.49 Restoring the preset Top view from the In-Canvas Viewport Control toolbar

You created a new UCS as a tool to flip the drawing upside down without changing its orientation with respect to the WCS. Now you'll use it again to create the front and back elevations.

Making the Front and Back Elevations

You can generate the front and back elevations by using techniques similar to those you have been using for the two side elevations. You need to be able to transfer the heights of building components from one of the side elevations to either of the remaining elevations. To do this, you'll make a copy of the first elevation you drew, rotate it 90°, and then line it up so you can transfer the heights to the front elevation. It's quite easy:

1. Continue using I10-12-NorthElevUCS.dwg (M10-12-NorthElevUCS.dwg), or open it if it's not already open.

2. Zoom out slightly, and then zoom in to a view of the floor plan and the first elevation.

3. Pan the drawing so that the floor plan and elevation are on the left part of the drawing area.

   You need to transfer the height data from the side elevation to the front elevation. To ensure that the front elevation is the same distance from the floor plan as the side elevation, you'll use a 45° line that extends down and to the right from the rightmost and lowermost lines in the floor plan.

4. Turn on Polar Tracking and ensure that Increment Angle is set to 45°. Also make sure that the Object Snap Tracking button on the status bar is toggled on.

5. Set the Endpoint osnap to running and be sure the Midpoint osnap isn't running.

6. Start the LINE command.

7. Move the crosshair cursor to the bottom-right corner of the front stairway handrail in the floor plan. Hold it there for a moment.
   A cross appears at the intersection point. Don't click yet.

8. Move the crosshair cursor to the lower-right corner of the roof pop-out in the floor plan, and hold it there until a cross appears at that point. Don't click yet.

9. Move the crosshair cursor to a point directly to the right of the corner of the roof pop-out and directly under the intersection point of the handrail (see the top of Figure 10.50).
   Vertical and horizontal tracking lines appear and intersect where the crosshair cursor is positioned, and a small X appears at the intersection. A tracking tooltip also appears.

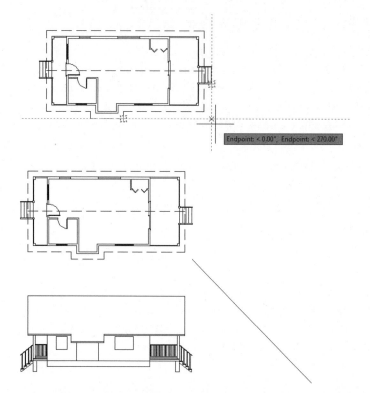

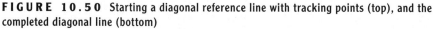

FIGURE 10.50 Starting a diagonal reference line with tracking points (top), and the completed diagonal line (bottom)

10. Click to start a line at this point.

11. Move the crosshair cursor down, away from this point and to the right at a negative 45° angle (or a positive 315° angle).

12. When the 45° Polar Tracking path appears, enter 40'↵ (12200). Press ↵ again.

   This completes the diagonal reference line (see the bottom of Figure 10.50).

13. Start the COPY command, and select the entire south elevation and nothing else. Then press ↵.

14. For the base point, select the left endpoint of the base line of the cabin.

15. For the second point, pick the Intersection osnap, and place the cursor on the diagonal line.

16. When the X symbol with three dots appears at the cursor, click (see Figure 10.51).

17. Then move the cursor to any point on the base line of the south elevation.
     An X appears on the diagonal line where the ground line would intersect it if it were longer (see the top of Figure 10.52). This is called the *implied intersection*: a distinct object snap in itself, and also the osnap that is used when the Intersection osnap is specified but an intersection is not clicked. This is why the three dots appeared after the X symbols.

18. When the X appears, click to locate the copy.

19. Press Esc to end the COPY command.

20. Zoom out to include the copy, and then use Zoom Window to include the floor plan and south elevations (see the bottom of Figure 10.52).

21. Press Esc to terminate the COPY command.

22. Start the ROTATE command, and select the copy of the south elevation; then press ⏎.

23. Activate the Intersection osnap, and click the intersection of the diagonal line with the base line as you did in steps 13 and 14.

24. For the angle of rotation, enter **90**⏎ (see Figure 10.53).

25. Start the MOVE command and, when prompted to select objects, enter **P**⏎⏎ to select the most recently selected objects. The rotated elevation is selected.

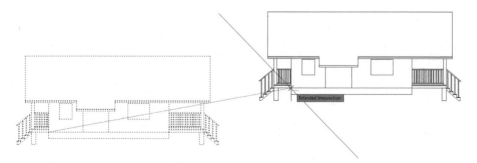

FIGURE 10.51 Using the diagonal line to find the extended intersection

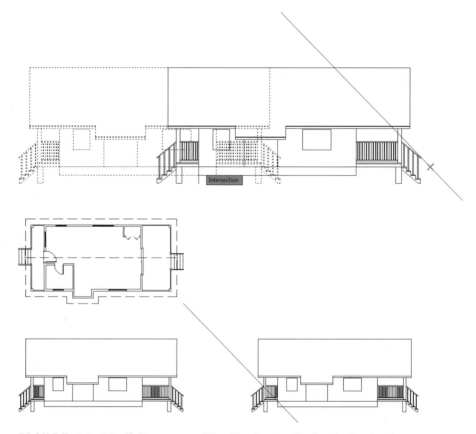

FIGURE 10.52 Making a copy of the side elevation (top) and adjusting the view (bottom)

26. For the base point, click a point in a blank space to the right of the rotated elevation and on the upper part of the drawing area.

27. For the second point, move the cursor down, using Polar Tracking, until the last step on the elevation is lower than the roof pop-out in the plan view. Then click.

28. Zoom out and use Zoom Window to adjust the view (see Figure 10.54).

29. Save the current drawing as **I10-13-FrontElevProjection.dwg** (**I10-13-FrontElevProjection.dwg**).

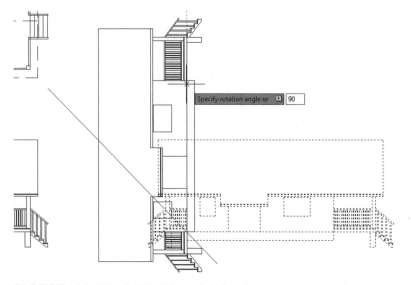

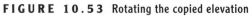

FIGURE 10.53 Rotating the copied elevation

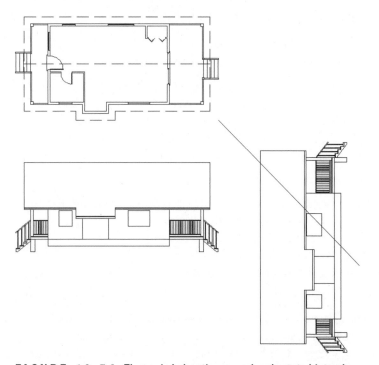

FIGURE 10.54 The copied elevation moved and rotated into place with the view adjusted

The rest of the process for creating the front elevation is straightforward and uses routines you have just learned. Here's a summary of the steps:

1. Continue using I10-13-FrontElevProjection.dwg (I10-13-FrontElev Projection.dwg), or open it if it's not already open.

2. Set up a new UCS for the front elevation showing the east side of the cabin:

   a. From the ViewCube, click the UCS drop-down menu ➤ New UCS.

   b. Rotate the UCS 90° about the z-axis by entering **Z**↵ **90**↵ at the command line.

   c. Use the PLAN command to rotate the drawing to the current UCS.

3. Drop construction lines from the floor plan across the drawing area and height lines, which you'll draw from the copied elevation.

4. Trim or fillet these lines as required, and add any necessary lines:

   a. Draw the roof first and remember that there is a thin layer of roof covering (see the top of Figure 10.55).

   b. Draw the wall, door, and foundation next.
      You won't be able to get the height line for the sliding glass door from the side elevation. It's 7'-3" (2210 mm) from the top of the deck (see the middle of Figure 10.55).

   c. Draw the pop-out, deck, and support posts.
      The support post measures 1'-0" (305 mm) across.
      The railing posts have the same size and spacing on the front of the deck as they do on the sides.

   d. Copy the associative Array object from another elevation, and use the grips to adjust the Item Count.
      This process can create a congested drawing, and you may want to draw the guide lines only as necessary to draw each component and then erase them. (See the bottom of Figure 10.55.)

 T I P Although colors aren't visible in this book's grayscale print, it's a good idea to "layer" your drawing as you go when working with so many extension lines at once. Since each layer has a different color, assigning layers as you go will help you differentiate between objects by color.

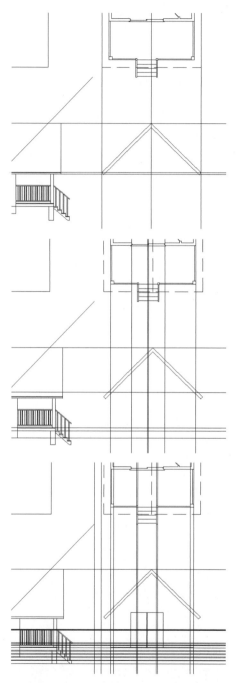

FIGURE 10.55 Incrementally drawing the front elevation starting with the roof (top); the wall, door, and foundation (middle); and finally the deck (bottom)

5. Erase or trim away any lines that represent objects that are visually behind any objects in the foreground.

For instance, do not draw two lines on top of one another in areas where the foundation is behind the steps or support posts, or where the vertical door lines are behind the railings. Only draw the features you would see if you were standing at the front of your cabin.

6. Make sure all the objects reside on the proper A-ELEV-... layer.

When you're finished, the east elevation should look like Figure 10.56.

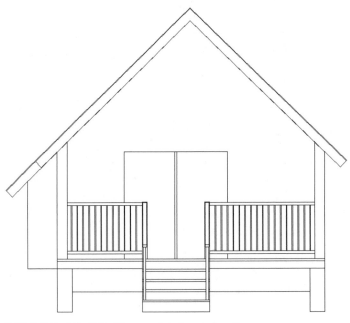

FIGURE 10.56 The completed east elevation

7. Erase the copy of the south elevation and the diagonal transfer line.

8. Name and save the UCS and view (call them both **East_Elev**).

9. Save the current drawing as `I10-14-EastElev.dwg` (`M10-14-East Elev.dwg`).

You can create the rear elevation from a mirrored image of the front elevation. Here are the steps:

1. Continue using `I10-14-EastElev.dwg` (`M10-14-EastElev.dwg`), or open it if it's not already open.

SELECTION CYCLING

When creating elevations, you might accidentally draw a line over an existing line. To catch this error, take the following steps:

1. Turn on Selection Cycling from the status bar.

2. Move your cursor over the suspect line.

   If more than one object exists in a given area, two blue boxes will appear in the upper-right quadrant of the cursor, as shown here:

3. Pick the object, which will open the Selection dialog box.

4. In that dialog box, cycle through each of the overlapping objects.

2. Mirror the front elevation to the opposite side.

3. Set up a UCS for the left elevation:

   a. From the ViewCube, click the UCS drop-down menu ➢ New UCS.

   b. Rotate the UCS 90° about the z-axis by entering **Z↵ 180↵** at the command line.

   c. Use the PLAN command to rotate the drawing to the current UCS. Now you'll revise the elevation to match the left side of the cabin.

4. Temporarily move the railing posts a known distance and angle away from their current locations.

5. Use the STRETCH command and Perpendicular osnap to stretch the stairway and railings to match the stairway location on the back of the cabin as shown on the floor plan.

6. Move the railing posts back to their original locations.

7. Adjust the associative Array objects to add or delete posts as required.

8. Delete the sliding door frame that divides the left and right panels, and then adjust the door to match the extents shown on the plan view.

9. Move the wall lines to the A-ELEV-WALL layer.

10. Add the window with the lower edge at 2'-11" (889 mm) above the base line, and the top edge at 7'-11"(2413 mm) above the base line.
    When you're finished, the elevation should look like Figure 10.57.

11. Name and save the UCS and view (call them both **West_Elev**).

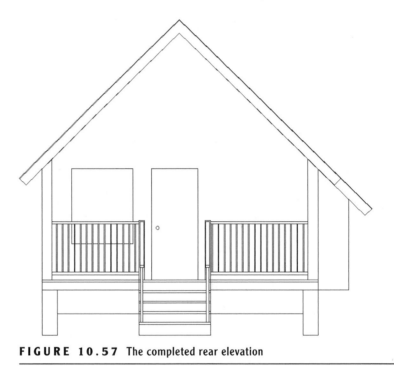

FIGURE 10.57 The completed rear elevation

When you have completed all the elevations, follow these steps to clean up and save the drawing:

1. Return to the WCS: From the ViewCube, click the UCS drop-down menu ➤ WCS.

2. Display the plan view (PLAN command).

3. Erase any remaining construction lines.

4. Thaw the A-ANNO-TEXT layer, and then move the notes down and to the left so they no longer overlap any elevation.

5. Copy and rotate the FLOOR PLAN label under each of the plans, and edit the content appropriately.

6. Zoom out slightly for a full view of all elevations.
The drawing looks like Figure 10.58.

7. Save the drawing as `I10A-FPLAYO.dwg` (`M10A-FPLAYO.dwg`).

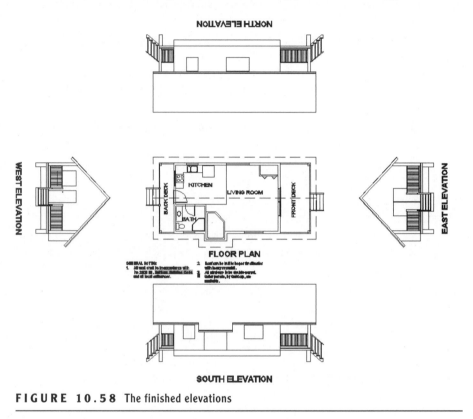

FIGURE 10.58 The finished elevations

Considering Drawing Scale Issues

This last view raises several questions: How will these drawings best fit on a page? How many pages will it take to illustrate these drawings? What size sheet should you use? At what scale will the drawing be printed? In traditional hand drafting, you wouldn't be able to draw the first line without answers to some of these questions. You have completed a great deal of the drawing on the computer without having to make decisions about scale and sheet size because, in AutoCAD, you draw in real-world scale, or full scale. This means that when you tell AutoCAD to draw a 10′ (3048 mm) line, it draws the line 10′ (3048 mm) long. If you inquire how long the line is, AutoCAD will tell you that it's 10′ (3048 mm) long. Your current view of the line might be to a certain scale, but that changes every time you zoom in or out. The line is stored in the computer as 10′ (3048 mm) long.

You need to make decisions about scale when you're choosing the sheet size, putting text and dimensions on the drawing, or using hatch patterns and non-continuous linetypes. (Chapter 11 covers hatch patterns, and Chapter 12 covers dimensioning.) You were able to avoid selecting a scale based on linetypes alone in Chapter 6, "Using Layers to Organize Your Drawing," by setting all three LTSCALE variables to 1. Thanks to the flexibility this method provides, you were able to avoid committing to a scale so early in the project.

Instead you were largely able to postpone the scale decision until you began setting up your title block. At that point, you discovered that the largest scale that would allow you to keep the entire floor plan visible on a single sheet was about ½″ = 1′-0″. That scale has a true ratio of 1:24, or a scale factor of 24. You'll get further into scale factors and true ratios of scales in the next chapter.

If you look at your I10A-FPLAYO.dwg (M10A-FPLAYO.dwg) drawing with all elevations visible on the screen, the dashes in the dashed lines look like they might be too small, so you might need to increase the linetype scale factor. As you may recall, the easiest way to preview how the drawing scale affects linetypes is to change the annotation scale. This is possible because LTSCALE, PSLTSCALE, and MSLTSCALE are each set to 1.

Something else to consider is how the elevations you just drew will fit into your plotted plan set. If you were to thaw the title block's layer now, you would see that your elevations won't all fit. Don't worry about that yet. Beginning with the next chapter, and right on through the end of this book, you'll need to make decisions about scale each step of the way.

Drawing Interior Elevations

Sometimes referred to as *sections*, interior elevations can be constructed using the same techniques you learned for constructing exterior elevations. You drop lines from a floor plan through offset height lines and then trim them away. Interior elevations usually include fixtures, built-in cabinets, and built-in shelves, and they show finishes. Each elevation consists of one wall and can include a side view of items on an adjacent wall if the item extends into the corner.

Not all walls appear in an elevation—usually only those that require special treatment or illustrate special building components. You might use one elevation to show a wall that has a window and to describe how the window is treated or finished, and then assume that all other windows in the building will be treated in the same way unless noted otherwise.

In the next chapter, you'll learn how to use hatch patterns and fills to enhance floor plans and elevations.

If You Would Like More Practice...

Here are three exercises for practicing the techniques you learned in this chapter. The last one will give you practice in basic orthogonal projection.

Exterior Elevations   Open I10A-FPLAYO.dwg (M10A-FPLAYO.dwg) and revise each elevation by adding 1½″ (38 mm) frames around the windows and doors. Add *mullions*, the dividers between window panes, to separate each window into four equal panes and add a rectangular window to the back door. Figure 10.59 shows the revised south elevation with the features added to the windows.

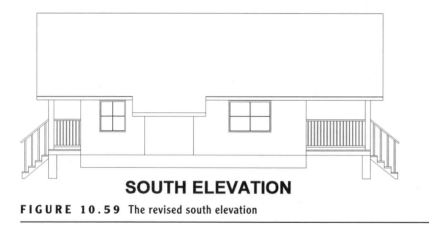

SOUTH ELEVATION

FIGURE 10.59 The revised south elevation

Interior Elevations   For some practice with interior elevations, try drawing one or two elevations. You can measure the heights and sizes of various fixtures in your own home or office as a guide.

Orthogonal Projection   Draw the three views of the block shown in Figure 10.60 following the procedures you used for the cabin elevations, except that in this case, you'll use the procedure that mechanical drafters employ—that is, draw the front view first, and then develop the top and right side views from the front view. The completed drawing, named X10-00-OrthoProject.dwg, can be found on the book's website, **www.sybex.com/go/autocad2012ner**, or by visiting **www.autocadner.com**.

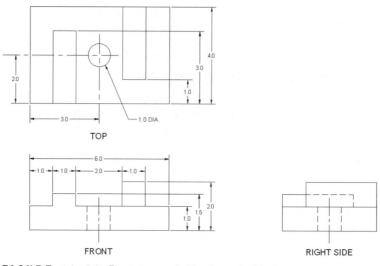

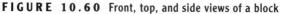

FIGURE 10.60 Front, top, and side views of a block

Are You Experienced?

Now you can...

☑ draw exterior elevations from a floor plan

☑ create associative arrays

☑ use grips to copy objects

☑ add detail to an elevation

☑ set up, name, and save a UCS and a view

☑ transfer height lines from one elevation to another

☑ copy, move, rotate, and mirror elevations

Working with Hatches, Gradients, and Tool Palettes

Hatches *can be abstract* patterns of lines; they can be solid fills; or they can resemble the surfaces of various building materials. With a nearly endless number of combinations, hatches are incredibly versatile, and they provide a way to introduce depth and texture into otherwise flat plans.

Architectural plans frequently use hatches as a way to designate materials, or even varying wall types. Similarly solid and gradient hatches are popular ways to add realism to presentation drawings. This chapter will demonstrate how each of these hatch varying types can be used to compose drawings.

To learn how to hatch and fill areas, you'll start with some of the visible surfaces in the south elevation of the cabin. You'll then move to the floor plan, hatch the floors, and put hatch patterns and fills in the walls and a gradient on the balcony. You'll use the contextual Hatch Creation and Hatch Editor Ribbon tabs for the creation and manipulation of hatches and gradients. Gradient hatches are tool with many options that you can use to create a sense of depth or texture in your drawings.

A key part of a hatch pattern is the boundary, or outermost edge of the pattern. Typically, you'll use the HATCH command to automatically search your drawing for a closed region within the area you select and create this boundary edge for you.

▶ **Selecting a predefined hatch pattern and applying it to a drawing**

▶ **Setting up and applying user-defined hatch patterns**

▶ **Modifying the scale and shape of a hatch pattern**

▶ **Specifying the origin of a hatch pattern**

▶ **Filling an enclosed area with a solid color**

▶ **Filling an enclosed area with a gradient**

▶ **Setting up and using palettes and palette tools**

Hatching the South Elevation

Hatches and fills should be on their own layers so they can be turned off or frozen without also making other objects invisible. You'll begin the exercise by creating new layers for the hatches and assigning colors to them:

1. Open the I10A-FPLAYO.dwg (M10A-FPLAYO.dwg) drawing created in Chapter 10, "Generating Elevations." (See the "If You Would Like More Practice" section.)

    If you did not complete those exercises, the I10A-FPLAYO.dwg (M10A-FPLAYO.dwg) is also included in the Chapter 11 download found on the book's website (**www.sybex.com/go/autocad2012ner**).

 T I P   **To clearly see the visual effect of putting hatch patterns on the south elevation, change the background color for the drawing area to white. Click the Options button at the bottom of the Application menu to open the Options dialog box and then click the Display tab. Click the Colors button and choose 2D Model Space in the Context list, Uniform Background in the Interface Element list, and White in the Color list to make the change.**

---

2. Set up seven new layers as follows:

Layer Name	Color
A-ELEV-DOOR-PATT	21
A-ELEV-FNDN-PATT	91
A-ELEV-GLAZ-PATT	61
A-ELEV-ROOF-PATT	11
A-ELEV-SHAD-BNDY	60
A-ELEV-SHAD-PATT	Black (White) (7)
A-ELEV-WALL-PATT	41

 3. For the A-ELEV-SHAD-BNDY layer only, click the printer icon in the Plot column of the Layer Properties Manager.

The icon changes to a printer with a red circle with a line through it. The objects on that layer will not appear in print regardless of whether they are visible in the drawing area.

4. Make the A-ELEV-ROOF-PATT layer current.
Now any new objects you create will be assigned to this layer.

5. Start the HATCH command by clicking the Hatch button found inside the Home tab ➢ Draw panel.
The contextual Hatch Creation Ribbon tab, shown in Figure 11.1, will load, and the command line will read Pick internal point or [Select objects/seTtings]:. You'll use this same contextual Ribbon tab to create and modify hatch entities in your drawing. Among the choices to make using this Ribbon tab are which pattern to use, the pattern's properties, and also the method for specifying the boundary of the area to be hatched.

6. From the Pattern panel within the contextual Hatch Creation tab, press the down-arrow in the lower-right corner of the Ribbon panel.
A complete list of available hatch patterns appears in the extended panel.

> ◄
>
> **You can also start the HATCH command by typing H↵.**

7. Scroll down within the extended Pattern panel to find and select the AR-RROOF pattern (see the left image in Figure 11.2).
The extended Pattern panel collapses to display the AR-RROOF pattern with a blue background, as shown on the right in Figure 11.2.
Besides the simple ability to select a pattern, hatches provide you many more options to control their display. Many of these options, such as Scale and Angle, are found in the Properties panel on the contextual Hatch Creation tab. The default 0.00° pattern angle is fine, but you need to adjust the Scale setting.
The Hatch Pattern Scale text box defaults to a scale of 1.0000. You can manually enter virtually any number into this text box, or you can use the up- and down-arrows on the right side to increase or decrease the scale.

FIGURE 11.1 The contextual Hatch Creation tab

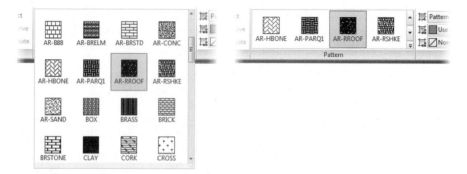

FIGURE 11.2 Selecting the AR-RROOF pattern from the expanded Pattern panel on the contextual Hatch Creation tab (left), and the Pattern panel after selecting the AR-RROOF pattern (right)

8. Enter 6 (150) into the Hatch Pattern Scale text box and press ↵ as shown in Figure 11.3.

9. In the Options section on the right side of the contextual Hatch Creation tab, verify that the Associative option is chosen.

   If the Associative option has been chosen, a blue background appears behind the Ribbon tool. Associative hatches automatically update the areas they cover whenever their boundaries change. If you delete any component of the boundary, however, the hatch becomes nonassociative.

10. Choose the Pick Points button on the far left of the contextual Hatch Creation tab in the Boundaries panel.

11. In the south elevation view, move your cursor somewhere near the middle of the roof area.

    A preview of your hatch appears within the roof area, as shown at the top of Figure 11.4.

12. With this preview correctly displaying the AR-RROOF pattern in the roof area, click and then press ↵ to create the hatch (see the bottom of Figure 11.4).

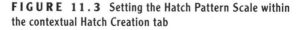

FIGURE 11.3 Setting the Hatch Pattern Scale within the contextual Hatch Creation tab

13. Zoom in to a view of just the south elevation.

Notice how the appearance of the hatch pattern gets more detailed as the roof gets larger on the screen.

14. Save this drawing as `I11-01-RoofHatch.dwg` (`M11-01-RoofHatch.dwg`).

SOUTH ELEVATION

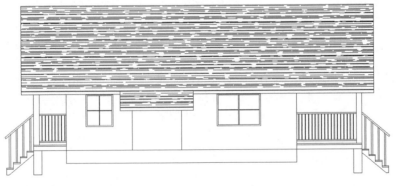

SOUTH ELEVATION

FIGURE 11.4 The Hatch preview displays after the cursor hovers over the roof area (top). The finished hatch pattern displays in the roof area (bottom).

Looking at Hatch Patterns

Let's take a short tour through the available patterns:

1. Continue using `I11-01-RoofHatch.dwg` (`M11-01-RoofHatch.dwg`), or open it if it's not already open.

2. Start the HATCH command.

3. With the contextual Hatch Creation tab open, expand the Pattern panel to browse the library of hatch patterns included with AutoCAD. Start at the top of the Pattern panel; the first group of hatch patterns you will come across contains the ANSI patterns. These are abstract line patterns developed by the American National Standards Institute, and they are widely used by public and private design offices in the United States.

4. Scroll down slightly further to reveal 11 hatch patterns with names that begin with *AR-*. These patterns have been designed to look like architectural and building materials, which is why you see the AR prefix. In addition to the roof pattern you just used, you'll see several masonry wall patterns, a couple of floor patterns, and one pattern each for concrete, wood shakes, and sand.

5. Take a look below the AR- hatch patterns to see a number of non-AR patterns. These are geometrical patterns, some of which use common conventions to represent various materials.

N O T E   As mentioned at the start of this chapter, hatches aren't purely limited to repeating patterns. Gradient hatches are also possible inside AutoCAD. The simplest of these gradient hatches is the linear option, but more-complex gradients are also available from the pattern library.

6. Go almost to the bottom of the Pattern list to find a number of ISO patterns. These are abstract line patterns developed by the International Organization for Standardization.

7. Press the Esc key two times to collapse the Pattern panel, and press it again to cancel the HATCH command.

As you work with hatch patterns, you'll need to adjust the scale factor for each pattern so the patterns will look right when the drawing is printed. The AR patterns are drawn to be used with the scale factor set approximately to the default of one to one—displayed as 1.0000 (1)—and should need only minor adjustment. However, even though the treatment you just chose for the roof is an AR pattern, it is something of an anomaly. Instead of using it as is, you had to change its scale factor to 6.0000 (150) to make it look right in the drawing.

T I P   When you're using one of the AR patterns, begin with a scale factor at 1.0000 until you preview the hatch; then you can make changes. This rule also applies to the 14 ISO patterns displayed on the Pattern panel of the contextual Hatch Creation Ribbon tab.

For the rest of the non-AR patterns, you'll need to assign a scale factor that imitates the true ratio of the scale at which you expect to print the drawing. Table 11.1 gives the true ratios of some of the standard scales used in architecture and construction. When using metric units, the scales are simple ratios (1:50, 1:100, and so on).

TABLE 11.1 Standard scales and their corresponding ratios

Scale	True Scale Factor
1″ = 1′-0″	12
½″ = 1′-0″	24
¼″ = 1′-0″	48
⅛″ = 1′-0″	96
¹⁄₁₆″ = 1′-0″	192

The scale is traditionally written by mixing inches with feet in the expression, which causes some confusion. For example, the third scale in the table, commonly called *quarter-inch scale*, shows that a quarter inch equals 1 foot. A true ratio of this scale must express the relationship by using the same units, as in ¼″ = 1′-0″. Simplifying this expression to have no fractions, you can translate it to, say, 1′ = 48″. This is how you arrive at the true scale factor of 48, or the true ratio of 1:48. The exact method for calculating this ratio can be found in Chapter 8, "Controlling Text in a Drawing."

As you continue through this chapter, take special note of the various scale factors used for different hatch patterns.

Hatching the Rest of the South Elevation

You'll apply hatches to the foundation, support posts, wall, and ground. You'll then work with some special effects.

Using a Concrete Hatch on the Foundation

Follow these steps to hatch the foundation:

1. Continue using I11-01-RoofHatch.dwg (M11-01-RoofHatch.dwg), or open it if it's not already open.

2. From the Home tab ➤ Layers panel, set the current layer to A-ELEV -FNDN-PATT.

3. Start the HATCH command. Then expand the Pattern panel from the contextual Hatch Creation tab to display the library of available hatch patterns.

4. Scroll as necessary to find and select the AR-CONC pattern.

5. Moving to the Properties panel, enter **1 (25)** in the Hatch Pattern Scale text box to set the scale to 1.0000 (25).

6. Expand the Options panel and select the Create Separate Hatches option, as shown in Figure 11.5.

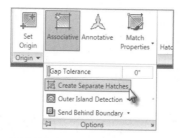

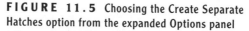

FIGURE 11.5 Choosing the Create Separate Hatches option from the expanded Options panel

When multiple areas are selected for hatching, this option creates a distinct hatch in each area rather than a single hatch consisting of multiple, noncontiguous hatched areas.

7. Move your cursor back to the drawing area, and click once in each rectangle representing the foundation and the deck support posts.

   To visually confirm your hatch area selection, pay attention to the live preview that appears before you pick the internal point for each hatch area. After you've chosen these points, the boundary used to create each hatch insertion ghosts, providing yet another visual cue during the hatch-creation process.

8. Press ↵ or click the Close Hatch Creation button on the contextual Hatch Creation tab to end the HATCH command.

   The Concrete hatch pattern is then applied to the foundation and support areas, as shown in Figure 11.6.

9. Save this drawing as **I11-02-FoundationHatch.dwg** (**M11-02 -FoundationHatch.dwg**).

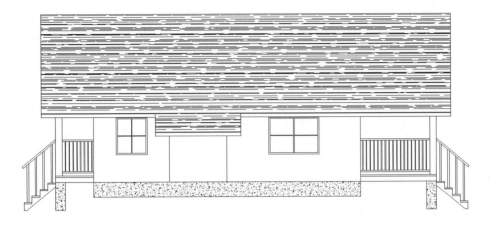

SOUTH ELEVATION

FIGURE 11.6 The south elevation with a Concrete hatch pattern added to the foundation and support posts

Take a moment to pick the hatch insertion for one of the deck support posts. Notice how the hatch insertion is separate from the hatch for the foundation and the other deck support post. By default, all of the areas selected during a single instance of the HATCH command are grouped together as a single hatch entity. Because you chose the option to Create Separate Hatches, each area is a separate hatch entity.

CREATING MULTIPLE FOUNDATION HATCH ENTITIES

When you select the desk support-post hatch entity, you might forget to pick Create Separate Hatches from the Options panel of the contextual Hatch Creation tab. If you do, you can correct the problem without having to erase and then re-create the foundation hatching:

1. Select the foundation hatch to open the contextual Hatch Editor tab.

   This tab is very similar to the Create Hatch tab you have already used.

2. Expand the Options panel and select Separate Hatches.

   What was formerly a single hatch entity will split into three separate hatch entities: the cabin foundation and two deck support posts.

You'll work with the Hatch Editor shortly, in the "Hatching the Pop-Out" section.

Hatching the Wall

For the walls, you'll use the AR-RSHKE pattern, which looks like wood shingles (often called *shakes*). You'll need to account for the openings in the wall for the windows and the pattern change at the pop-out. Here are the steps:

1. Continue using I11-02-FoundationHatch.dwg (M11-02-Foundation Hatch.dwg), or open it if it's not already open.

2. Change the current layer to A-ELEV-WALL-PATT.

3. Start the HATCH command, and go through the same process to apply a hatch to the wall. Here is a summary of the steps:

    a. Expand the Pattern panel on the contextual Hatch Creation tab to choose the AR-RSHKE pattern.

    b. Set the Hatch Pattern Scale to **1 (25)** from the Properties panel.

    c. Verify that Create Separate Hatches is selected from the Options panel.

    d. Using the live preview, pick a point inside the pop-out wall and pick one on each side of the wall.
       When choosing points on either side of the pop-out, make sure you do not to pick a point inside the window.

    Each wall section is hatched using the AR-RSHKE pattern, as shown in Figure 11.7.

4. Save this drawing as **I11-03-WallHatch.dwg** (**M11-03-WallHatch.dwg**).

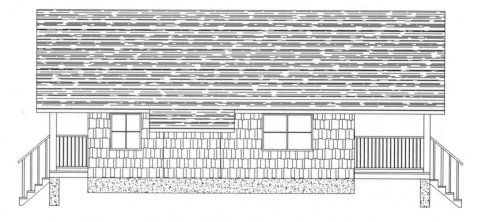

SOUTH ELEVATION

FIGURE 11.7 The completed hatching of the south wall

Even though a hatch entity for each wall section exists, there's not much to distinguish the pop-out from the main wall. The next section demonstrates how to do this by modifying the location where AutoCAD begins the hatch pattern.

Hatching the Pop-Out

The hatch has a *base point*, or *origin* (usually at the drawing's origin of 0,0), which is the starting point for the pattern that is emitted equally in all directions. If you hatch two overlapping areas with separate hatches, the hatches in the overlapping areas will be identical. This is the problem with the pop-out: even though the pop-out wall was a different hatched area than the areas on either side, the pattern appeared to be continuous because all three hatches share the same origin. In this exercise, you'll edit the origin for the pop-out:

1. Continue using I11-03-WallHatch.dwg (M11-03-WallHatch.dwg), or open it if it's not already open.

2. Zoom into and select the AR-RSHKE hatch for the pop-out.
    The contextual Hatch Editor tab opens to display a Ribbon very similar to the contextual Hatch Creation tab you used earlier. Both contextual tabs are nearly identical, with subtle differences such as Create Separate Hatches on the Hatch Creation tab vs. Separate Hatches found on the Hatch Editor tab.

3. Expand the Origin panel on the contextual Hatch Editor tab, and select the Bottom Left button.
    The AR-RSHKE pattern updates and is no longer in line with the AR-RSHKE pattern along the main wall. As you can see from expanding the Origin panel, the software provides a number of predefined origin points out of the box. Another option is to manually define a new origin point.
    Origin points may be defined by graphically picking a location on the screen, or by manually entering a point at the command line.

4. Click the Set Origin button found on the contextual Hatch Editor tab ➤ Origin panel.

5. At the Select point: prompt, choose the lower-left endpoint for the pop-out, as shown in Figure 11.8.

6. Press Esc to deselect the hatch for the pop-out, and exit the HATCH command.

The contextual Hatch Editor tab will also close after you deselect the hatch.

Once complete, the south elevation should resemble Figure 11.9.

7. Save the current drawing as **I11-04-PopOut.dwg** (**M11-04-PopOut.dwg**).

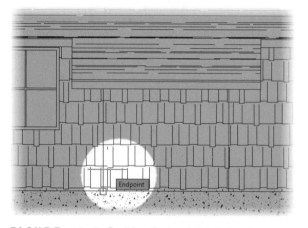

FIGURE 11.8 Revising the hatch origin for the pop-out

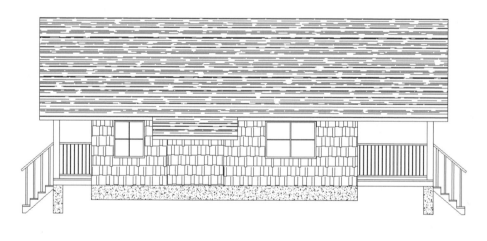

SOUTH ELEVATION

FIGURE 11.9 The pop-out with the revised hatch pattern

Using a Solid-Fill Hatch

The windows will be hatched with a solid fill. You apply this hatch in the same way as the other hatches you've been using, except that you don't have a choice of scale or angle:

1. Continue using I11-04-PopOut.dwg (M11-04-PopOut.dwg), or open it if it's not already open.

2. Make A-ELEV-GLAZ-PATT the current layer.

3. Start the HATCH command to open the contextual Hatch Creation Ribbon tab, and then click the Swatch sample box.

4. Select the first pattern, SOLID, on the Properties panel.

 N O T E   The text boxes for Angle and Scale aren't available because they don't apply to solid fills.

5. Change the value of the Hatch Type pull-down from Pattern to Solid (see Figure 11.10).

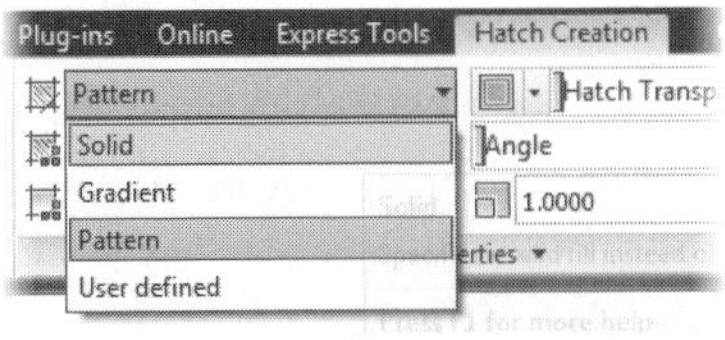

FIGURE 11.10 Changing the Hatch Type from Pattern to Solid

Note that the SOLID pattern is now selected (blue background) in the Pattern panel, and that Background Color, Angle, and Scale are no longer available in the Properties panel and have been grayed out. Because the SOLID hatch pattern is a solid fill, these properties do not apply.

6. Move your cursor back into the drawing area, and select a point in the middle of each glass pane, or the middle of the window if you didn't draw the mullions.

   Like the other hatches you have created, a preview of the final hatch is automatically displayed as you hover over each area.

7. After selecting each glass pane, press ↵ to end the HATCH command. The windows have a solid black (or white) fill (see Figure 11.11).

8. Save the current drawing as **I11-05-SolidFill.dwg** (**M11-05-Solid Fill.dwg**).

T I P   Depending on the quality and resolution of your monitor, solid fills can appear to flow over thin, nonhatched areas. This is only an illusion; the hatch actually stops at the border, as you can see if you zoom in to an area in question.

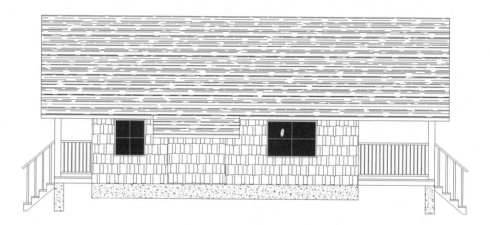

SOUTH ELEVATION

FIGURE 11.11 The windows with a solid fill hatch

Adding Special Effects

To finish this elevation, you need to show shading to give the impression that the roof overhangs the wall.

Implying Shading with a Gradient

When shaded surfaces are illustrated on an exterior elevation, they give a three-dimensional quality to the surface. You'll put some additional hatching at the top portion of the wall to illustrate the shading caused by the roof overhang.

You need to hatch the top 2'-0" (610 mm) of the wall with a gradient. To determine the boundary line of the hatch, you'll turn off the layer that has the shake pattern. You'll then create a guideline to serve as the lower boundary of the hatch:

1. Continue using I11-05-SolidFill.dwg (M11-05-SolidFill.dwg), or open it if it's not already open.

2. Make the A-ELEV-SHAD-BNDY layer current, and then turn off the A-ELEV-WALL-PATT layer.

USING THE LAYER OFF TOOL

Try using the Layer Off tool (LAYOFF command) found on the Home tab ➢ Layers panel to turn off the A-ELEV-WALL-PATT layer.

To use it, simply follow these steps:

1. Start the Layer Off (LAYOFF) command.

2. Select the wall hatching.

Because the wall hatching is on the A-ELEV-WALL-PATT layer, it is turned off by you graphically selecting an object on that layer.

3. Use the Rectangle (RECTANG) command to draw rectangles that extend from the corners, where the roof and vertical lines meet, to 2'-0" (610 mm) below the lowest three roof lines.

   Figure 11.12 shows the rectangles to draw in bold and the windows hidden for clarity.

4. Make the A-ELEV-SHAD-PATT layer current, and then start the HATCH command.

5. From the Properties panel within the Hatch Creation tab, change the Hatch Type property to Gradient (see Figure 11.13).

6. Expand the Gradient Color 1 drop-down (also found on the Properties panel), and pick Select Colors from the bottom of the list.

   This opens the Select Color dialog box, where you can pick the first color for your gradient. Unlike other hatches, gradients do not get their color from the layer they are on; you must explicitly select the color.

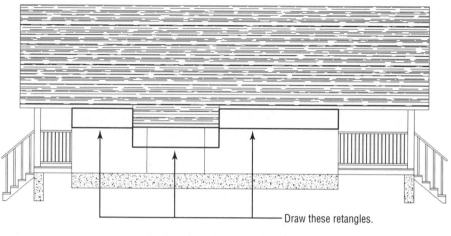

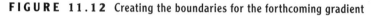

Draw these retangles.

SOUTH ELEVATION

FIGURE 11.12 Creating the boundaries for the forthcoming gradient

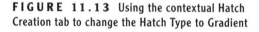

FIGURE 11.13 Using the contextual Hatch
Creation tab to change the Hatch Type to Gradient

 7. Click the Index Color tab in the Select Color dialog box.

8. Select color 250 in the bottom row of swatches (see Figure 11.14), and
then click OK.

   The gradient samples found on the Pattern panel now include gray
in their preview. Because our goal is to simulate shadows being cast
from the roof, it's best to have AutoCAD fade to white.

   Although it's possible to specify 255,255,255, the RGB true color
for white, the better choice is to make this a single-color gradient.

 9. To do this, click the Gradient Colors button just below the drop-down
list you used to select 250 as your first color.

   Doing this disables the Gradient Color 2 drop-down list, and will
force the gradient to fade to white.

10. In the second column of the Properties panel, change the angle to 270.
This will force the gradient to fade from color 250 at the top to white at the bottom.

11. Expand the Pattern panel and choose GR_LINEAR, as shown in Figure 11.15.

12. Click the Select Boundary Objects button on the Boundaries panel of the contextual Hatch Creation tab, and then click the three rectangles that you drew.

Using the Select Objects option, you can select closed polylines, circles, or ellipses as the boundary objects. The hatch inserts immediately after you select the object.

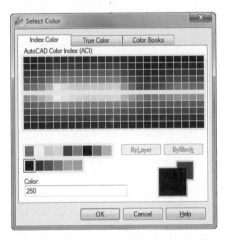

FIGURE 11.14 Selecting the gradient color

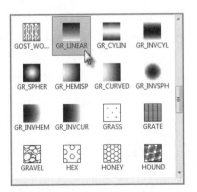

FIGURE 11.15 Selecting the linear gradient type

T I P   An automatic preview is not displayed when you insert hatches by object. Instead, the hatch inserts immediately after selecting the object. If you accidentally choose the wrong object, press and hold the Shift key and select the boundary object you want to remove.

13. With each of the hatches in place, press ↵ to end the HATCH command. When creating hatches, AutoCAD may not always initially display the result properly.

14. Enter **REA**↵ to run the REGENALL command, which forces AutoCAD to reevaluate the drawing and refresh the drawing area.

    Your gradients should look like Figure 11.16. The gradient obscures the windows, but you'll fix that in the next couple of steps.

15. Turn on the A-ELEV-WALL-PATT layer. The shakes return, but the gradient hides a portion of them.

    Although all objects in your drawing so far reside on the same plane, like lines on a piece of paper, visually one object may appear to be on top of another. You can rearrange the order of the objects by selecting them and then changing their location in the stacking order. You need to move the shading behind the hatch pattern.

16. Select all the gradients and then right-click in the drawing area.

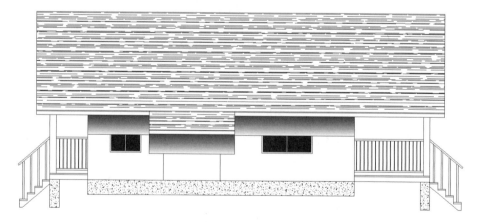

SOUTH ELEVATION

F I G U R E   1 1 . 1 6   The gradient shaded effect

17. From the contextual right-click menu that opens, choose Draw Order ➤ Send To Back, as shown in Figure 11.17.

   The gradient moves behind the shakes (see Figure 11.18). Don't worry about the gradient boundaries; they won't appear when the drawing is plotted.

18. Save this drawing as `I11-06-GradientHatch.dwg` (`M11-06-Gradient Hatch.dwg`).

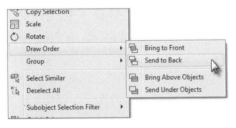

FIGURE 11.17 Sending the gradient objects behind the others in the drawing

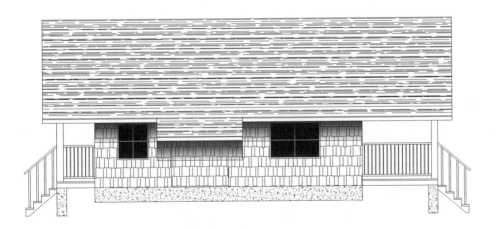

SOUTH ELEVATION

FIGURE 11.18 The gradient shaded effect after moving the gradients to the back

Using Hatches in the Floor Plan

In the floor plan, you can use hatches to fill in the walls or to indicate various kinds of floor surfaces.

So far, you've used only predefined hatch patterns—the 69 patterns that come with AutoCAD. For the floor, you'll use a *user-defined pattern*, which is a series of parallel lines that you can set at any spacing and angle. If you want to illustrate square floor tile, for example, you can select the Double option of the user-defined pattern, which uses two sets of parallel lines—one perpendicular to the other, resulting in a tiled effect. You'll also learn how to control the origin of the pattern and then finish the floor.

Creating the User-Defined Hatch Pattern

You'll use the user-defined pattern for a couple of rooms and then return to the predefined patterns. Follow these steps:

1. With I11-06-GradientHatch.dwg (M11-06-GradientHatch.dwg) open, zoom in to the floor plan and thaw the A-WALL-HEAD and A-FLOR-FIXT layers.

   You can use the header lines to help form a boundary line across an entryway to a room and to keep the hatch pattern from extending to another room.

2. With the floor plan in full view, freeze the A-ROOF and A-ANNO-TEXT layers and then zoom in to the bathroom.

   Even if the rooflines are dashed, they will still form a boundary to a hatch.

3. Create a new layer called **A-FLOR-PATT**.

4. Assign the layer color 141 and make it current.

5. Start the HATCH command to load the contextual Hatch Creation tab.

6. Change the Hatch Type to User Defined from the drop-down on the Properties panel of the contextual Hatch Creation tab.

   After you choose User Defined as the Hatch Type, USER is selected as the current pattern in the Pattern panel, and the Scale text box in the Properties panel is replaced by the Hatch Spacing text box.

7. In the Hatch Spacing text box, change 1″ (1) to 9′ (230).

8. Expand the Properties panel, and click the Double button (see Figure 11.19).

9. Back in the drawing, be sure no osnaps are running, and use the automatic preview to pick two points to match the tiled hatch pattern shown in Figure 11.20.

> **a.** For the first point, pick a location in the bathroom floor area, not touching the fixture lines or the door.
>
> **b.** To finish the bathroom floor hatch, click the floor between the door swing and the door, being careful to not touch the door.

FIGURE 11.19 Defining the hatch pattern

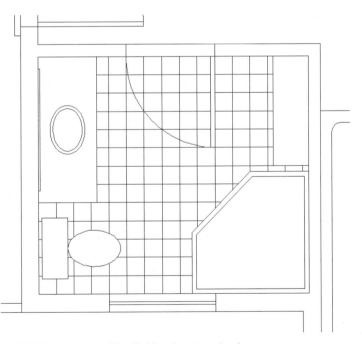

FIGURE 11.20 The tiled hatch pattern in place

10. With the bathroom hatches in place, press ⏎ to end the HATCH command. The tiled hatch pattern should fill the bathroom floor and stop at the header while not encroaching into the door or fixtures (see Figure 11.20).

11. Save this drawing as **I11-07-UserDefinedHatch.dwg** (**M11-07-User DefinedHatch.dwg**).

Note that the user-defined pattern has no scale factor to worry about. You simply set the distance between lines in the Hatch Spacing text box.

W A R N I N G   If you can't get the HATCH command to hatch the desired area, you might have left a gap between some of the lines serving as the hatch boundary. This can prevent AutoCAD from finding the boundary you intend to use. Zoom in to the areas where objects meet, and check to see that there are no gaps, or increase the Gap Tolerance value on the expanded Options panel in the contextual Hatch Creation tab.

Controlling the Origin of the Hatch Pattern

Often, a designer wants to lay out the tile pattern so that the pattern is centered in the room or starts along one particular edge. For this project, the tiles are set to start in the center of the room and move out to the edges, where they're cut to fit. You'll change the hatch pattern's origin to set this up in the kitchen:

1. Continue using I11-07-UserDefinedHatch.dwg (M11-07-UserDefined Hatch.dwg), or open it if it's not already open.

2. Use the Pan and Zoom tools to slide the drawing up until the kitchen occupies the screen. Thaw the A-AREA-NPLT layer.

3. Turn Object Snap Tracking on (on the status bar), and set the Midpoint osnap to be running.

4. Start the HATCH command, and make sure User Defined is still selected as the Hatch Type.

5. From the Properties panel, change the Hatch Spacing to 12" (305 mm) and verify that Double is selected by expanding the Properties panel.

6. Choose the Set Origin tool from the Origin panel of the Hatch Creation tab, and move your cursor back into the drawing area.

7. Use the running Midpoint osnap in conjunction with Object Snap
Tracking to acquire the midpoint of the lower kitchen area line and
the midpoint of the right-side kitchen area line.

When the cursor is positioned properly, two tracking lines and a
tooltip appear (see the top of Figure 11.21).

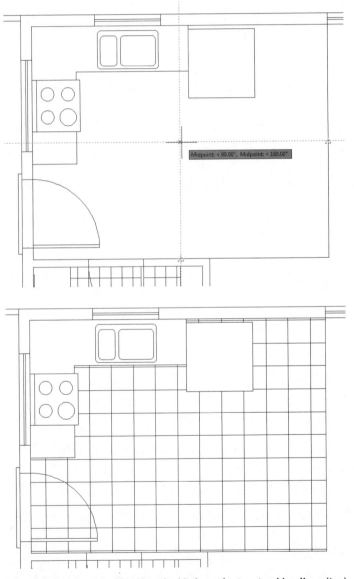

FIGURE 11.21 Hatching the kitchen: the two tracking lines (top)
and the finished, centered hatch (bottom)

This sets the origin of any subsequently created hatch patterns at the center of this room, and you are prompted to `Pick internal point:`.

8. Similar to the way you hatched the bathroom, pick a point anywhere in the main floor area of the kitchen, and then pick a second point between the door swing and the door.

9. After choosing the two points, press ↵ to end the HATCH command.

   This places the hatch of 12″ (305) tiles in the kitchen (see the bottom of Figure 11.21). Notice how the pattern is centered left to right and top to bottom.

10. Save this drawing as **I11-08-HatchOrigin.dwg (M11-08-Hatch Origin.dwg)**.

Each time you change the origin, all subsequent hatch patterns will use the new setting as their origin. For most hatches, the origin isn't important, but if you need to control the location of tiles or specific points of other hatch patterns, you can reset the hatch origin before you create the hatch by clicking Specify New Origin and then entering **0,0**↵.

Finishing the Hatches for the Floors

To finish hatching the floors, you'll use a parquet pattern from the set of predefined patterns in the living room and another user-defined pattern on the two decks:

1. Continue using I11-08-HatchOrigin.dwg (M11-08-HatchOrigin.dwg), or open it if it's not already open.

2. Use Pan and Zoom to adjust the view so it includes the living room.

3. Using the (Layer) Off tool found on the Layers panel of the Home tab, select the wall header for the closet to turn off the A-WALL-HEAD layer.

4. Start the HATCH command, and change the Hatch Type to Pattern from the Properties panel of the contextual Hatch Creation tab.

5. Expand the Pattern panel on the contextual Hatch Creation tab, and select the AR-PARQ1 pattern.

6. Set the scale to 1 (25) from the Properties panel, and verify that the angle is set to 0.

7. Move your cursor back into the drawing area, and use the automatic preview to display what your hatch will look like when inserted into the drawing.

   As you can see in Figure 11.22, the squares look a little small.

8. Return to the contextual Hatch Creation tab, and reset the Hatch Pattern Scale to 1.33 (34).

9. Move your cursor back into the drawing area, pausing inside the living room area to see a preview of the hatch.

10. This looks better; click to insert the parquet pattern, and press ↵ to end the HATCH command.

    The parquet pattern is placed in the living room (see Figure 11.23).

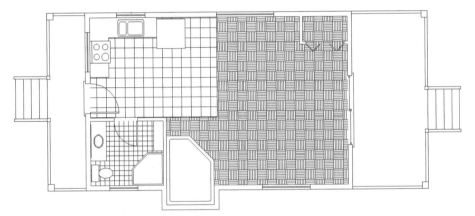

FIGURE 11.22 The parquet hatch with its initial scale of 1 (25)

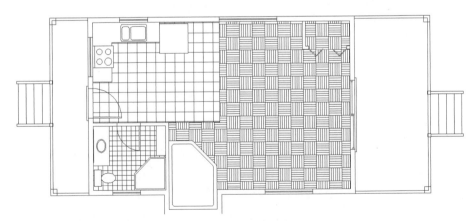

FIGURE 11.23 The parquet hatch in the living room

11. Freeze the A-AREA-NPLT layer.

12. Start the HATCH command, and change the Hatch Type to User Defined from the Properties panel of the contextual Hatch Creation tab.

13. Expand the Properties panel and deselect the Double option.

14. Set the Hatch Angle to 90°, and Hatch Spacing to 6″ (152).

15. Choose the Set Origin tool from the Origin panel, and use the Endpoint osnap to pick the lower-left inside corner of the front deck.

16. Move your cursor anywhere inside the front deck area, pausing for a moment to see the automatic hatch preview display.

17. Assuming the preview looks like Figure 11.24, click to insert the hatch into your drawing, and press ↵ to end the HATCH command.

18. Repeat steps 12 through 17 on the back deck, using the lower-right corner of the deck as the hatch origin.

    The transition between the kitchen and the living room floor coverings isn't as clean and evident as it could be.

19. Draw a polyline with a width of 0 from the corner of the bathroom, perpendicular to the living room window opening, and then directly to that window, as shown in bold in Figure 11.25.

20. Save the drawing as **I11A-FPLAYO.dwg (M11A-FPLAYO.dwg)**.

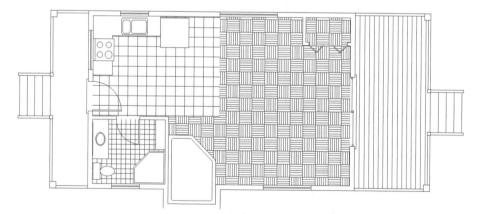

FIGURE 11.24 The user-defined hatch pattern on the front deck

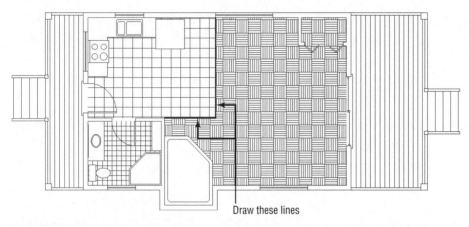

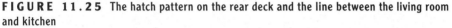
Draw these lines

FIGURE 11.25 The hatch pattern on the rear deck and the line between the living room and kitchen

Modifying the Shape of Hatch Patterns

The next exercise demonstrates how hatches are associative. An *associative hatch pattern* automatically updates when you modify the part of a drawing that is serving as the boundary for the pattern. You'll be changing the current drawing, so before you begin making those changes, save the drawing as it is. Then follow these steps:

1. Continue using I11A-FPLAYO.dwg (M11A-FPLAYO.dwg), or open it if it's not already open.

2. Zoom out and pan to get the floor plan and the north and south elevations in the view.

3. Thaw the A-ANNO-TEXT, A-ROOF, and A-AREA-NPLT layers.
   You'll use the STRETCH command to modify the plan and two side elevations.

4. Turn on Polar Tracking from the status bar.

5. Start the STRETCH command by selecting the Stretch tool on the Home tab ➤ Modify panel.

6. Pick a point above and to the right of the stairway in the north elevation.

7. Drag a window down and to the left until a crossing selection window lands between the two closet doors in the floor plan and ends below the cabin in the south elevation (see the left image of Figure 11.26).

8. Click to complete the window, and then press ↵ to finish the selection process.

9. For the base point, choose a point in the blank area to the right of the selection and click.

10. Move the cursor directly to the right of the point you picked; then enter 5'↵ (1524↵).

    The living room and roof are now longer, and the hatch patterns have expanded to fill the new areas (see the right image of Figure 11.26).

11. Close the current drawing. When prompted, choose to discard the changes.

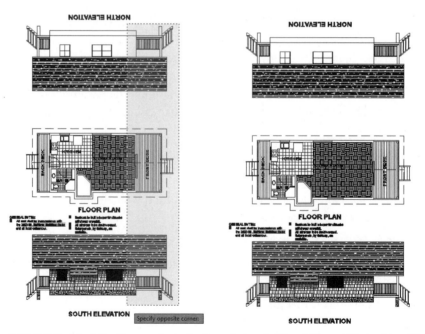
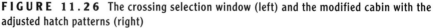

FIGURE 11.26 The crossing selection window (left) and the modified cabin with the adjusted hatch patterns (right)

Hatches are a necessary part of many drawings. You've seen a few of the possibilities AutoCAD offers for using them in plans and elevations.

Creating and Managing Tool Palettes

If you find yourself using particular hatch patterns over and over in various drawings, wouldn't it be advantageous to have them available at a moment's notice instead of setting them up each time? AutoCAD's tool palettes let you do just that and more. Now you'll go through the process of setting up a couple of palettes and customizing them to contain specific hatch patterns, blocks, and commands that are used with the cabin drawings. From these exercises, you'll get the information you need to set up your own custom palettes.

Creating a New Tool Palette

You'll create a new tool palette and then populate it with the blocks you've used so far in the cabin drawing:

1. Open the I11A-FPLAY0.dwg (M11A-FPLAY0.dwg) file and thaw the A-ROOF layer.

2. Click the Tool Palettes tool found on the View tab ➤ Palettes panel to display the Tool Palettes palette set on the screen.

3. Place the cursor on a blank space on the palettes, right-click, and choose New Palette, as shown in Figure 11.27.
   A new, blank palette appears with a small text box on it.

4. Enter **Cabin Blocks**↵ to name the new palette.

5. Open the DesignCenter by clicking its button on the View tab ➤ Palettes panel, by entering **DC**↵, or pressing Ctrl+2 on the keyboard.

6. On the left side of the DesignCenter, click the Open Drawings tab, and then select the current drawing (I11A-FPLAY0.dwg (M11A-FPLAY0.dwg).

7. Navigate to the I11A-FPLAY0.dwg (M11A-FPLAY0.dwg) drawing under the Folders tab or the Open Drawings tab.

8. When you find it, click the plus sign (+) to its left.
   The list of drawing content types in it opens below the drawing.

9. Select Blocks from this list.

Now the right side of the DesignCenter displays the six blocks in
I11A-FPLAY0.dwg (M11A-FPLAY0.dwg), either as small images or by
name only.

 **10.** Click the arrow on the Views button in the DesignCenter toolbar, and
choose Large Icons as the view option to see a display like Figure 11.28.

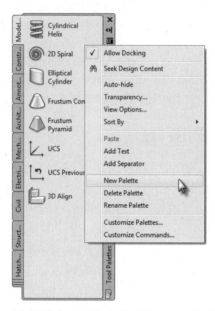

F I G U R E   1 1 . 2 7   Creating a new tool palette

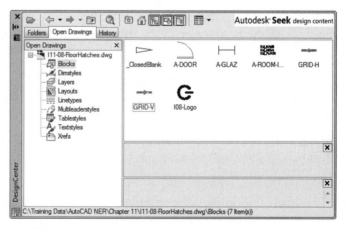

F I G U R E   1 1 . 2 8   The DesignCenter with the Large Icons view enabled

11. Select A-DOOR and then hold down the Shift key and click GRID-V to select the five blocks used in plan view.

12. Click and drag the six blocks over to the Cabin Blocks palette.

    Small images of the blocks appear on the new palette (see Figure 11.29), and they're now available for any drawing. Simply drag a block off the palette and onto the drawing. You can then fine-tune its location, rotate it, and so forth. Any layers used by the block are also brought into the drawing.

FIGURE 11.29 The Cabin Blocks tool palette you've just created

N O T E Tool Palette tools such as blocks are dynamically linked back to the source DWG file. In this example, the five blocks you added to the Cabin Blocks tool palette are now available to any drawing, provided the I11A -FPLAYO.dwg (M11A-FPLAYO.dwg) file still exists in its original location. Moving or deleting the drawing will break the link, consequently breaking the Tool Palette tool as well.

13. Place the cursor on A-DOOR on the new palette, right-click, and then select Properties to open the Tool Properties dialog box.

    It displays information about A-DOOR and provides a means to change many parameters (see Figure 11.30).

14. Change the Description for the A-DOOR tool to "Use for 2′, 2′-6″, 3′, and 3′-6″ doors" so the tooltip will more accurately describe the block's intended application (see Figure 11.30).

15. Close the Tool Properties dialog box, and then move your mouse over the A-DOOR tool to display its description.

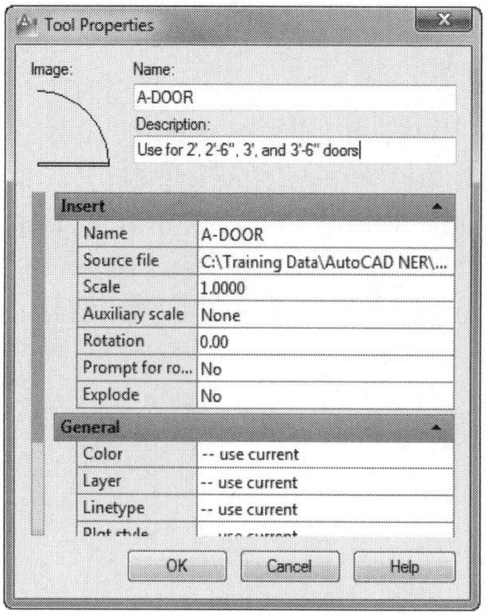

FIGURE 11.30 The Tool Properties
dialog box

Setting Up a Palette for Hatches

To create a palette for hatches, you'll create and name a new palette by using the
same procedure as in the preceding section, but the hatches are assigned to the
palette in a different way:

1. Continue using I11A-FPLAYO.dwg (M11A-FPLAYO.dwg), or open it if
   it's not already open.

2. Right-click a blank space on the Cabin Blocks palette, choose New
   Palette, and then enter **Cabin Hatches**↵ in the text box.

3. Zoom in on the south elevation of the cabin, and click the roof hatch
   to display a grip.

4. Move the cursor to a portion of the roof hatch that isn't close to the
   grip, and then click and drag the hatch pattern over to the new palette (see Figure 11.31).

5. When the cursor is over the palette and a horizontal line appears
   there, release the mouse button.

   The roof hatch is now positioned on the palette and available
   for use in any drawing. Simply drag it off the palette and into the
   enclosed area in the drawing that you want to hatch with the pattern.

6. Place the cursor on the new swatch of AR-RROOF, right-click, and choose Properties.

 The Tool Properties dialog box opens (see Figure 11.32).

7. Change the name from AR-RROOF to **Cabin Roof**, as shown on the left in Figure 11.33.

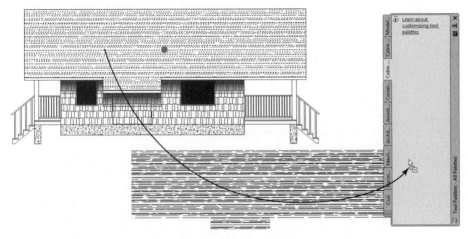

FIGURE 11.31 Copying the roof hatch to the new palette

Tool Properties	
Image:	Name:
	AR-RROOF
	Description:

Pattern	
Tool type	Hatch
Type	Predefined
Pattern name	AR-RROOF
Angle	0.00
Scale	6.0000
Auxiliary scale	None
Spacing	6"
ISO pen width	1.00 mm
Double	No

General	
Color	ByLayer
Layer	A-ELEV-ROOF-PATT

OK   Cancel   Help

FIGURE 11.32 The Tool Properties dialog box for the hatch pattern

8. Enter a description of what the hatch represents, such as **Cabin roof, south elevation** or shakes.

    Notice that the hatch has the angle and scale used on the roof and that the hatch is also on the A-ELEV-ROOF-PATT layer.

9. Use the slider at the left to view all the properties.

10. Click OK to close the dialog box and update the palette (see the right side of Figure 11.33).

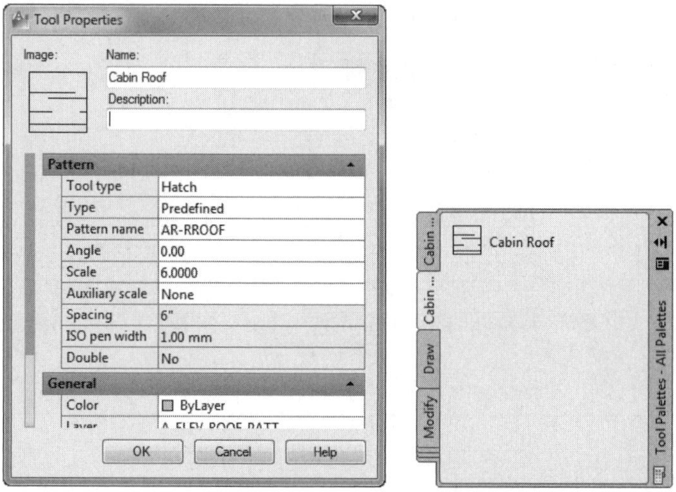

FIGURE 11.33 Renaming the AR-RROOF tool (left), and the Cabin Hatches palette after the first hatch is renamed (right)

By using the Tool Properties dialog box, you can also give hatches color. You can place all the hatches that you've used for the cabin so far on the palette in the same manner. They retain the properties they had in the original drawing, but by using the Tool Properties dialog box, you can change those properties.

Creating a Palette for Commands

Take a moment to look at a few of the sample palettes that come with AutoCAD, and check the properties of some of the items that you see. In addition to blocks and hatches, there are also command icons. These are placed on the palette in a slightly different way from blocks and hatches:

1. Continue using I11A-FPLAYO.dwg (M11A-FPLAYO.dwg), or open it if it's not already open.

2. Right-click the Cabin Hatches palette in a blank area, and choose New Palette from the context menu.

3. Name the new palette **Commands**.

4. Use the Zoom and Pan tools to bring the kitchen floor plan into view.

5. Click to select a single wall line, and then drag it to the palette, just as you dragged the hatches in the previous section.

   This adds the A-WALL line to the Commands tool palette with the rather ambiguous name Line.

6. Right-click the Line tool you just added to the Commands palette and choose Properties.

7. From the Tool Properties dialog box, enter **A-WALL** for the name.

8. Enter **Creates a new wall object** on the A-WALL layer as the description (see Figure 11.34).

9. Repeat the process outlined in steps 5 through 8 to drag several additional objects of various kinds onto the Commands palette (see Figure 11.35).

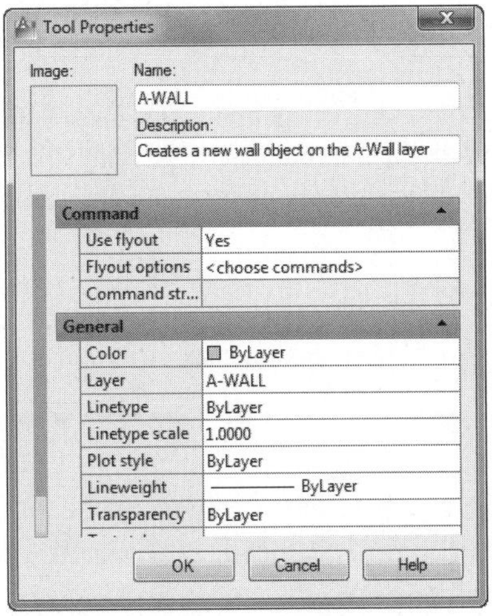

FIGURE 11.34 Changing the name and description for the A-WALL command tool

When you need to use one of these commands, click the icon on the palette.

FIGURE 11.35 The Commands palette with four command icons

USING AUTO-HIDE

If you set the palettes to Auto-Hide, they fold under the palette title bar. When you put your cursor on the bar, the palettes display and then hide a moment after your cursor moves off the palettes. To activate Auto-Hide, follow these steps:

1. Right-click the palette title bar.

2. Choose Auto-Hide from the context menu.

> You can also click the Auto-Hide button under the X at the top of the palette's title bar to activate Auto-Hide.

This has been a brief introduction to the palette feature. To become familiar with palettes so you can use them as you find the need, experiment with the various options. Try right-clicking a blank portion of a palette and investigating the commands available on the resulting context menu. From this menu, you can delete any palette and you can copy and paste tools from one palette to another.

If You Would Like More Practice...

If you would like to practice what you've learned in this chapter, here are a couple of extra exercises.

Creating the Hatch Patterns for the Other Elevations

To create your hatch pattern for the roof, make these changes and additions to I11A-FPLAYO.dwg (M11A-FPLAYO.dwg):

1. Make the A-ELEV-WALL-PATT layer current.

2. Start the HATCH command.

3. Click the Match Properties button on the Options panel of the contextual Hatch Creation tab, and then click the hatch pattern on either side of the pop-out in the south elevation.

   This copies that hatch's properties to the contextual Hatch Creation tab.

4. Change the Hatch Angle in the Properties panel of the Hatch Creation tab to 180.

5. Move your cursor to a point inside the wall in the north elevation to display the automatic preview.

6. Assuming the hatch correctly fills the wall in the north elevation, click and press ⏎ to insert the hatch and end the HATCH command.

7. Repeat the previous process, changing the rotation, pattern, and layer until all the hatches and gradients in the south elevation (except the roof pattern, which appears only in the north and south) appear in the other three elevations.

   ▶ Make sure you're on the correct layer when creating the new hatches.

   ▶ You'll need to draw additional rectangles on the A-ELEV-SHAD -BNDY layer to constrain the new gradients. Use polylines to draw the boundaries in the east and west elevations.

   ▶ Make sure Create Separate Hatches is selected when you create the hatch patterns for the windows.

T I P   As you hatch the east, west, and north elevations, try using the LAYMCUR command (called the Make Object's Layer Current tool on the Home tab ➤ Layers panel). This command will allow you to select an object and set its layer as current.

When you are finished, the remaining elevations should look similar to those in Figure 11.36.

8. Set the UCS back to World, and use the PLAN command to reorient the drawing area.

9. Save this drawing as I11A-FPLAYO.dwg (M11A-FPLAYO.dwg).

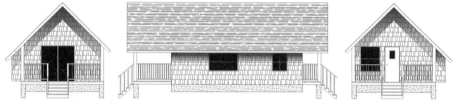

EAST ELEVATION   NORTH ELEVATION   WEST ELEVATION

FIGURE 11.36 The hatch patterns applied to the east elevation (left), the north elevation (middle), and the west elevation (right)

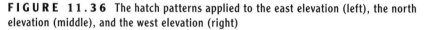 **W A R N I N G**   As layers are added to a drawing after saving a named view, you must select that named view in the View Manager dialog box and then click the Update Layers button to display the layers correctly when you set the view to current.

Creating Your Hatch Palette

It's true that you can use any hatch pattern to represent anything you want, but most professions follow some sort of standard, even if loosely. The ANSI31 pattern of parallel lines is probably the most widely used pattern. Although according to the ANSI standard, it "officially" represents iron, brick, and stone masonry, it's universally accepted as a cross-section view of any material—that is, the part of the object that was sliced through to make the view.

In this exercise, you'll create a new palette of hatches that you might use in your work. Use the same method demonstrated in the previous section of this chapter:

1. Open the DesignCenter.

2. Under the Folders tab, find and select `acad.pat`.

   If you performed a typical installation of AutoCAD, the file should be in the `C:\Program Files\Autodesk\AutoCAD 2012\UserData Cache\Support` folder. LT users should substitute `AutoCAD LT 2012` for `AutoCAD 2012` in the path.

3. Open that file.

4. Use the Large Icons view to view the patterns on the right side of the DesignCenter.

5. On the right side of your screen, create a new tool palette and name it Hatches.

6. Back in the DesignCenter, scroll through and drag any patterns you might use over to the new Hatches palette.

7. Close the DesignCenter.

8. Hold the cursor briefly over the name of each hatch to display a tooltip that describes the name and purpose of the hatch.

9. If you've brought any patterns to the palette that you don't want there, right-click each of them and choose Delete from the context menu.

   Don't worry about changing any of the properties, such as Scale or Rotation. That will come later, as you begin to use these hatches in your own work.

10. Check out the tools on the Hatches And Fills sample palette that comes with AutoCAD.

11. To access a list of all the available sample palettes:

    a. Move the cursor over to the tabs that identify each palette.

    b. Move it down just below the lowest tab, where you see the edges of the tabs that are hidden.

    c. Click the edges of the hidden tabs, and choose a palette from the list to be brought forward and displayed as the top tab.

12. Right-click some of the hatches or fills, and note how the rotation and scale vary for hatches that look the same on the palette.

One hatch, such as ANSI31, might be repeated several times on the same palette, with each occurrence having a different scale or rotation. Notice that the names of the hatches and fills have been removed from the sample hatch palette. Can you figure out how to do this in your own palette or how to store the names?

Are You Experienced?

Now you can...

☑ create a predefined hatch pattern and apply it to a drawing

☑ set up and apply user-defined hatch patterns

☑ modify the scale of a hatch pattern

☑ modify the shape of a hatch pattern

☑ control the origin of a hatch pattern

☑ apply solid fills and gradients

☑ create and populate a tool palette with blocks, hatches, or commands

Dimensioning a Drawing

Dimensions are the final ingredient to include with your cabin drawing. To introduce you to dimensioning, I'll follow a pattern similar to the one I used in Chapter 8, "Controlling Text in a Drawing." You will first create a dimension style that contains the properties for the dimensions, and then you will add the dimensions themselves.

▶ **Setting up a dimension style**

▶ **Dimensioning the floor plan of the cabin**

▶ **Modifying existing dimensions**

▶ **Setting up a multileader style**

▶ **Modifying existing dimension styles**

Introducing Dimension Styles

Dimension styles are similar to text styles but give you more options to control. You set them up in the same way, but many parameters control the various parts of dimensions, including the dimension text. Each dimension has several components:

- ▶ The dimension line
- ▶ Arrows or tick marks
- ▶ Extension lines
- ▶ Dimension text (see Figure 12.1).

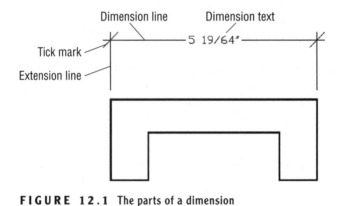

FIGURE 12.1 The parts of a dimension

An extensive set of variables stored with each drawing file controls the appearance and location of these components. You work with these variables through a series of dialog boxes designed to make setting up a dimension style as easy and trouble free as possible. Remember that AutoCAD is designed to be used by drafters from many trades and professions, each of which has its own standards for drafting. To satisfy these users' widely varied needs, AutoCAD dimensioning features have many options and settings for controlling the appearance and placement of dimensions in drawings.

Preparing for Dimensioning

Before you start setting up a dimension style, you need to make a few changes to your drawing to prepare it for dimensioning:

   1. Open I11A-FPLAYO.dwg (M11A-FPLAYO.dwg).

This is the cabin with hatch patterns added to all the views. If you didn't complete the "If You Would Like More Practice" section in Chapter 11, "Working with Hatches, Gradients, and Tool Palettes," you can download the file from the book's website.

2. Create a new layer called **A-ANNO-DIMS**, assign color 2 (Yellow), and make it current.

3. Freeze all the remaining layers except 0, A-ANNO-TEXT, A-DECK, A-DECK-STRS, A-DOOR, A-GLAZ, A-ROOF, A-WALL, and all of the A-ELEV layers without a -PATT or -BNDY suffix.

4. Set the Endpoint and Midpoint object snaps to be running.

5. Set the status bar so that only the Object Snap, Dynamic Input, and Selection Cycling buttons are in their on positions.

6. Click the Annotate tab. Your drawing will look like Figure 12.2.

RESTORING THE STATE OF MULTIPLE LAYERS

The Layer States Manager is an incredibly powerful tool that will allow you to restore the state of a large number of layers. Although it cannot create any layers, it can save, export, and import nearly every layer property found in the Layer Properties Manager palette. By default, these are saved inside the DWG file itself, but they may also be exported to an external file. Assuming you have employed a solid layer standard such as the NCS, you can build a library of layer states to automate tasks such as turning layers on/off, changing the color of layers, and more.

Instead of making the layer visibility changes in step 3 manually, try importing and restoring a layer state found in this chapter's set of download files.

1. Select Manage Layer States from the Layer States drop-down list found on the Home tab ➢ Layers panel.

   The Layer States Manager dialog box opens.

2. Click the Import button in the Layer States Manager dialog box, and browse to the file 12-Start.las, found in the Chapter 12 download.

   To see the file, you may need to change the Files Of Type setting to Layer States in the Import Layer State dialog box.

3. Click Open to load the 12-Start.las file. The Layer State - Successful Import dialog box opens.

(Continues)

RESTORING THE STATE OF MULTIPLE LAYERS *(Continued)*

4. Select the Restore States button from the dialog box, which will automatically apply the imported layer state.

5. You'll look at the restore options in more detail in a moment, so click the Close Dialog button for now.

6. The lower-right corner of the Layer States Manager dialog box has a circular button with an arrow pointing to the right. Click it to expand the dialog box.

   When you are restoring layer states, it's not necessary to restore all properties associated with a layer. Instead, using the expanded Layer States Manager dialog box, you can pick the specific properties to restore by checking or unchecking the associated property.

7. With the 12-Start layer state selected, click the Restore button found at the bottom of the Layer States Manager.

   The Layer States Manager closes, the selected layer properties are restored (all properties in this case), and you are taken back to your drawing.

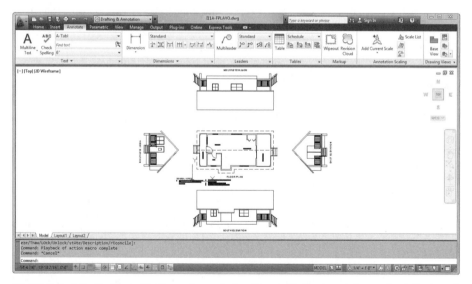

FIGURE 12.2 The cabin floor plan and elevations with the Annotate panels at the top of the drawing area

Making a New Dimension Style

Every dimension variable has a default setting, and these variables as a group constitute the default Standard dimension style. As in defining text styles, the procedure is to copy the Standard dimension style and rename the copy—in effect making a new style that is a copy of the default style. You then make changes to this new style so it has the settings you need to dimension your drawing and save it. Follow these steps:

1. Continue using I11A-FPLAY0.dwg (M11A-FPLAY0.dwg).

2. Click the Dimension, Dimension Style button, the small arrow at the bottom right of the Dimensions panel on the Annotate tab, to open the Dimension Style Manager dialog box (see Figure 12.3).

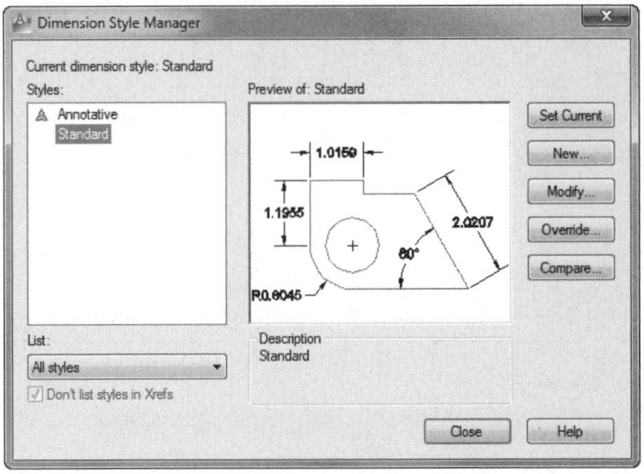

FIGURE 12.3 The Dimension Style Manager dialog box

At the top left in the Styles list box, you'll see Standard highlighted, or ISO-25 if your drawing is in metric.

3. With Standard (ISO-25) highlighted in the Styles window, click the New button on the right side of the Dimension Style Manager dialog box.

   The Create New Dimension Style dialog box shown in Figure 12.4 opens.

4. In the New Style Name field, Copy of Standard (ISO-25) is highlighted. Enter **A-DIMS-PLAN**, but don't press ↵ yet.

   Notice that Standard (ISO-25) is in the Start With drop-down list just below. Because it's the current dimension style in this drawing, the new dimension style you're about to define will begin as a copy of the Standard style. This is similar to the way in which new text styles are defined (as you saw in Chapter 8), taking an existing style that is close to what you need and modifying specific elements. The Use For drop-down list allows you to choose the kinds of dimensions to which the new style will be applied. In this case, it's all dimensions, so you don't need to change this setting.

5. Click the Continue button.

The Create New Dimension Style dialog box is replaced by the New Dimension Style: A-DIMS-PLAN dialog box (see Figure 12.5). It has seven tabs containing parameters that define the dimension style. You have created a new dimension style that is a copy of the Standard style, and now you'll make the changes necessary to set up A-DIMS-PLAN to work as the main dimension style for the floor plan of the cabin.

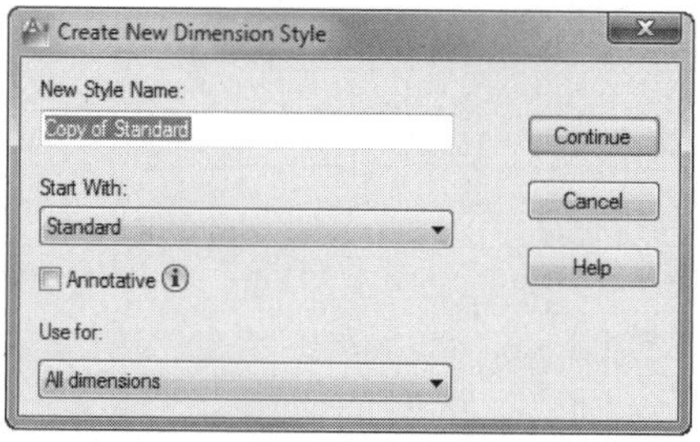

FIGURE 12.4 The Create New Dimension Style dialog box

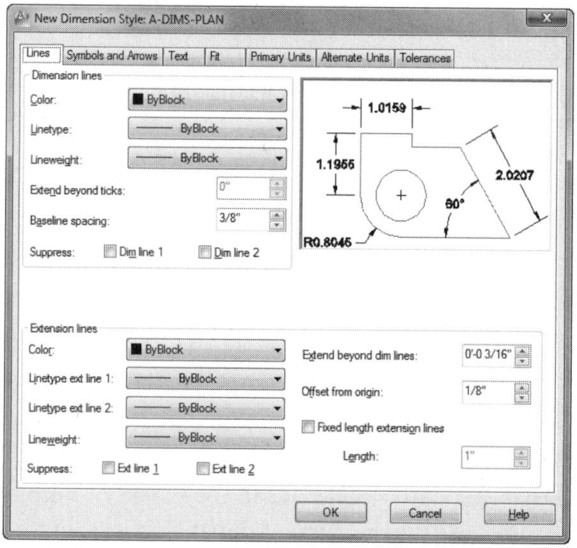

FIGURE 12.5 The New Dimension Style dialog box with A-DIMS-PLAN as the current style and Lines as the active tab

6. Verify that the Lines tab is active (on top). If it's not, click it.

    You'll use the Lines tab to control the appearance of the dimension and extension lines. In most cases, the color, linetype, and lineweight should stay at their default ByBlock value, indicating that an object inherits its color from the block containing it.

7. In the Extension Lines area, change the Offset From Origin setting from 1/16″ (0.63) to 1/8″ (1.25) to increase the gap between the beginning of the extension line and the object being dimensioned.

Setting Up the Symbols And Arrows Tab

The Symbols And Arrows tab has settings that control the appearance of arrowheads and other symbols related to dimensioning.

1. Click the Symbols And Arrows tab and then, in the Arrowheads group, click the down-arrow in the First drop-down list to open the list of arrowheads.

2. Click the Architectural Tick option.

    The drop-down list closes, with Architectural Tick displayed in the First and Second drop-down lists. In the preview window to the right, a graphic displays samples using the new arrowhead type.

3. Verify that Closed Filled is still selected from the Leader drop-down list.

4. Set the Arrow Size parameter to 1/8″ (3.5).

    After the changes, the tab should look like Figure 12.6.

> **Architectural ticks are common for building trades, whereas the Closed Filled option may be used in manufacturing or civil engineering drawings. This list contains options for those and several other arrowheads, dots, and so on.**

Making Changes in the Text Tab

The settings in the Text tab control the appearance of dimension text and how it's located relative to the dimension and extension lines:

1. Click the Text tab in the New Dimension Style dialog box.

    Settings in three groups affect the appearance and location of dimension text.

    Figure 12.7 shows the Text tab. The preview window appears in all tabs and is updated automatically as you modify settings. Look to the Text Appearance group in the upper-left corner of the dialog box, where six settings control how the text looks. You're concerned with only two of them.

2. Click the Browse button that sits at the right end of the Text Style drop-down list to open the Text Style dialog box.

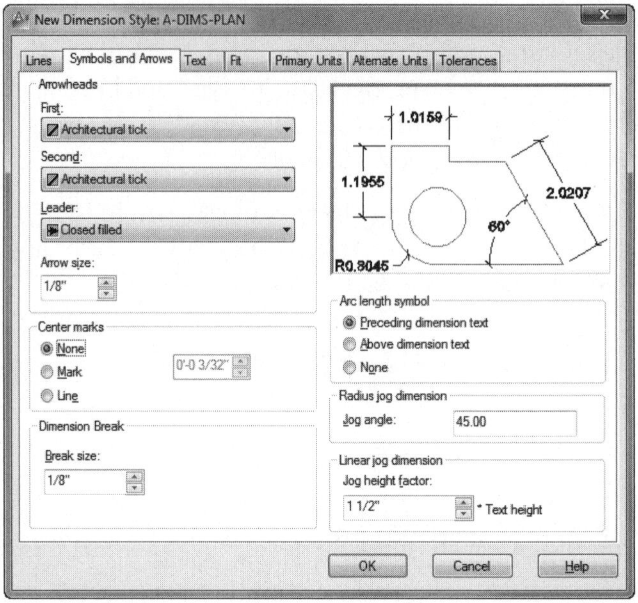

FIGURE 12.6 The Symbols And Arrows tab with the settings for the A-DIMS–PLAN style

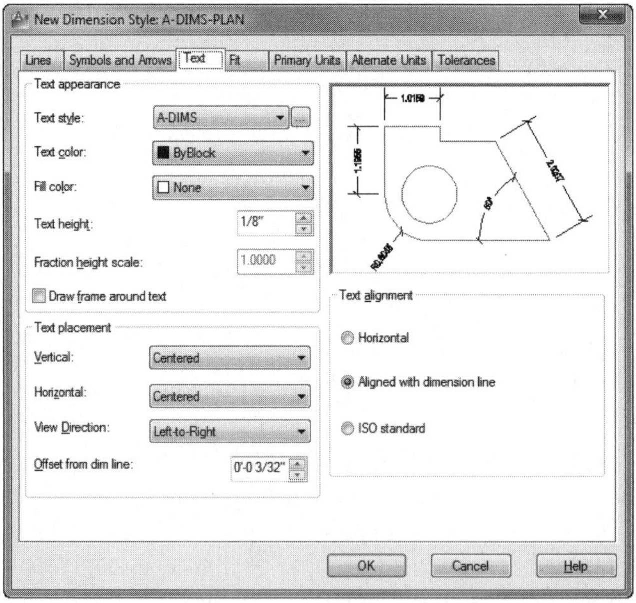

FIGURE 12.7 The Text tab with settings for the A-DIMS–PLAN style

3. Set up a new text style called **A-DIMS** that has the following parameters:

► Arial font

► 0′-0″ (0) height

► 0.8000 width factor

► All other settings at their default

If you need a reminder about creating text styles, refer to Chapter 8. Apply this text style, click the Set Current button, and then close the Text Style dialog box.

4. Back in the Text tab, open the Text Style drop-down list and select the new A-DIMS style from the list.

T I P Setting the text height to 0′-0″ (0) in the Text Style dialog box allows the Text Height parameter of the dimension style to dictate the actual height of the text in the drawing. This allows many different dimension styles to use the same text style, each producing text with different heights. If you give the text a nonzero height in the Text Style dialog box, that height is always used and the Text Height parameter of the dimension style is disregarded. Typically, dimension styles are defined using a text style similar to the A-DIMS one you just created with a 0′-0″ text height.

5. Set the Text Height value to 1/8″ (3.5).

6. Move down to the Text Placement group.

These settings determine where the text is located, vertically and horizontally, relative to the dimension line. You need to change two settings here.

7. Make sure both the Horizontal and Vertical options are set to Centered.

8. Move to the Text Alignment group.

The radio buttons control whether dimension text is aligned horizontally or with the direction of the dimension line. The ISO Standard option aligns text depending on whether the text can fit between the extension lines. Only one of the buttons can be active at a time. Horizontal should already be active.

Some trades and professions use the Centered option for vertical text placement and the Horizontal option for text alignment.

9. Click the Aligned With Dimension Line button.

Notice how the appearance and location of the text changes in the preview window.

This finishes your work in this tab; the settings should look like those in Figure 12.7.

This dialog box has four more tabs with settings, but you'll be making changes in only two of them: Fit and Primary Units.

Working with Settings on the Fit Tab

The settings on the Fit tab control the overall scale factor of the dimension style and how the text and arrowheads are placed when the extension lines are too close together for both text and arrows to fit:

For your own work, you might have to experiment with the settings on this tab.

1. Click the Fit tab in the New Dimension Style dialog box. Figure 12.8 shows the Fit tab as you'll set it.

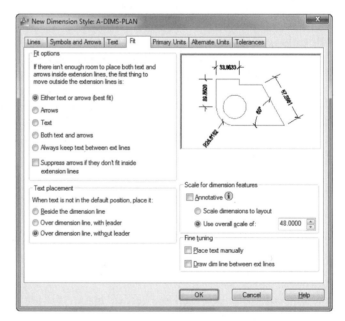

FIGURE 12.8 The new settings in the Fit tab

2. In the upper-left corner, in the Fit Options group, verify that the Either Text Or Arrows (Best Fit) radio button is selected.

I recommend you keep this setting unchanged unless you have a specific need, or the Best Fit option places your dimensions/text incorrectly.

3. In the Text Placement group, click the Over Dimension Line, Without Leader radio button.

4. Move to the Scale For Dimension Features group.
    Be sure the Use Overall Scale Of radio button is active.

5. Set the scale to 48 (50).

6. In the Fine Tuning group, verify that the Draw Dim Line Between Ext Lines option is unchecked.
    The settings on the Fit tab should look like those in Figure 12.8.

Setting Up the Primary Units Tab (Architectural)

If your drawing is set up to use architectural units, continue with this section. If you are using decimal units, skip this section and continue with the next section, "Setting Up the Primary Units Tab (Metric)." In the preview window, you might have noticed that the numbers in the dimension text maintain a decimal format with four decimal places, rather than the feet and inches format of the current architectural units. Dimensions have their own units setting, independent of the basic units for the drawing as a whole. On the Primary Units tab, you'll set the dimension units:

1. Click the Primary Units tab, and take a peek ahead at Figure 12.9 to see how it's organized.
    It has two groups: Linear Dimensions and Angular Dimensions, each of which has several types of settings.

2. In the Linear Dimensions group, make the following changes, starting at the top:

   a. Change the Unit Format setting from Decimal to Architectural.

   b. Change the Precision setting to 0′-0 1/8″.

   c. Change the Fraction Format setting to Diagonal.

   d. In the Zero Suppression group, uncheck 0 inches.

3. In the Angular Dimensions group, leave Decimal Degrees as the Units Format setting. Change Precision to two decimal places, as you did for the basic drawing units in Chapter 3, "Setting Up a Drawing." Leave the Zero Suppression setting as it is.
    After these changes, the Primary Units tab looks like Figure 12.9.

N O T E Zero Suppression controls whether the zero is shown for feet when the dimensioned distance is less than 1 foot and also whether the zero is shown for inches when the distance is a whole number of feet. For the cabin drawing, you'll suppress the zero for feet, but you'll show the zero for inches. As a result, 9″ will appear as 9″, and 3′ will appear as 3′-0″.

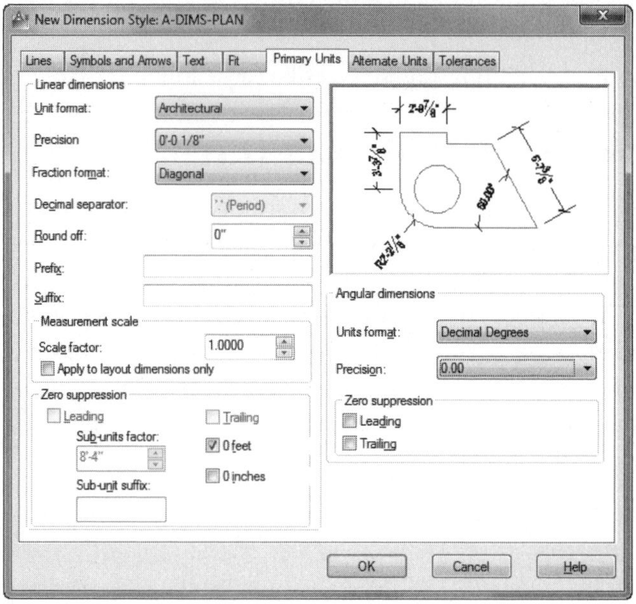

FIGURE 12.9 The Primary Units tab after changes have been made using imperial units

Setting Up the Primary Units Tab (Metric)

If your drawing is set up to use architectural units, and you've completed the previous section, skip this section and continue with the next, "Completing the Dimension Style Setup."

In the preview window, you might have noticed that the numbers in the dimension text maintain a decimal format with four decimal places rather than the feet and inches format of the current architectural units. Dimensions have their own units setting, independent of the basic units for the drawing as a whole. On the Primary Units tab, you'll set the dimension units:

1. Click the Primary Units tab, and take a peek ahead at Figure 12.10 to see how it's organized. It has two groups: Linear Dimensions and Angular Dimensions, each of which has several types of settings.

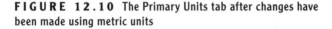

FIGURE 12.10 The Primary Units tab after changes have been made using metric units

2. In the Linear Dimensions group, starting at the top, make the following changes:

   a. Make sure Unit Format is set to Decimal.

   b. Change the Precision setting to 0.

   c. In the Suffix box, enter **mm**⏎, making sure you add a space before the first *m*.

   d. In the Zero Suppression group, make sure Trailing is checked and Leading is not.

N O T E   Zero Suppression controls whether the zero is shown for measurements when the dimensioned distance is less than 1 millimeter and whether the zero is shown when the final digits, to the right of the decimal point in the dimension, are zeros. For the cabin drawing, you'll suppress the trailing zeros but not the leading zeros. As a result, .9500 will appear as 0.95 with Precision set to 0. This won't be a factor during these exercises.

3. In the Angular Dimensions group, leave Decimal Degrees as the Units Format setting and change Precision to two decimal places, as you

did for the basic drawing units in Chapter 3. For now, leave the Zero Suppression group as it is.

After these changes, the Primary Units tab looks like Figure 12.10.

Completing the Dimension Style Setup

Of the last two tabs, any industry involved in global projects may use the Alternate Units tab, and the mechanical engineering trades and professions use the Tolerances tab. You won't need to make any changes to these tabs for this tutorial, but you'll take a brief look at them in the following sections.

It's time to save these setting changes to the new A-DIMS-PLAN dimension style and begin dimensioning the cabin:

1. Click the OK button at the bottom of the New Dimension Style dialog box.

   You're returned to the Dimension Style Manager dialog box (see Figure 12.11).

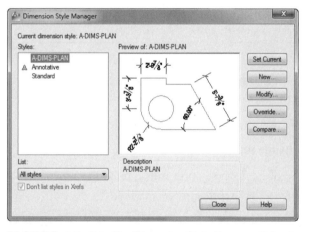

FIGURE 12.11 The Dimension Style Manager dialog box with **A-DIMS-PLAN** listed

A-DIMS-PLAN appears with a gray background in the Styles list box, along with Standard and Annotative. In the lower-right corner of the dialog box, in the Description area, you'll see the name of the new style. See Table 12.1, later in this section, as a reference for the differences between the Standard style that you started with and the A-DIMS-PLAN style.

2. Click A-DIMS-PLAN to highlight it in a dark blue.

3. Click the Set Current button and then click the Close button.

    You're returned to your drawing, and the Dimensions panel displays A-DIMS-PLAN in the Dimension Style drop-down list, as shown in Figure 12.12. This indicates that A-DIMS-PLAN is now the current dimension style.

4. Save your drawing as I12-01-DimensionStyle.dwg (M12-01-Dimension Style.dwg).

FIGURE 12.12 The Dimensions panel showing A-DIMS-PLAN as the current dimension style

You have made changes to 16 settings that control dimensions. This isn't too many, considering that there are more than 50 dimension settings. Table 12.1 summarizes the changes you've made so that the dimensions will work with the cabin drawing.

You'll change a few more settings throughout the rest of this chapter as you begin to dimension the cabin in the next set of exercises. You'll now look briefly at the Alternate Units and Tolerances tabs.

N O T E   The next two sections describe dimensioning features that you won't use in the cabin project. If you would rather begin dimensioning the cabin and look at this material later, skip to the "Placing Dimensions on the Drawing" section.

Exploring the Alternate Units Tab

If your work requires your dimensions to display both metric and architectural units, use the Alternate Units tab in the New Dimension Style dialog box, or in the Modify Dimension Style dialog box when you are changing an existing style. In the example shown in Figure 12.13, the primary units setting is Architectural (Decimal).

T A B L E   1 2 . 1   Changes Made So Far

Tab	Option	Default Setting	A-PLAN-DIMS Setting
Lines	Offset From Origin	0'-0 ¹⁄₁₆″ (0.63)	0'-0 ⅛″ (1.25)
Symbols and Arrows	First	Closed Filled	Architectural Tick
	Second	Closed Filled	Architectural Tick
	Leader	Closed Filled	Closed Filled (Verify)
	Arrow Style	³⁄₁₆″ (2.5)	⅛″ (3.5)
Text	Text Style	Standard	A-DIMS
	Text Alignment	Horizontal	Aligned With Dimension Line
	Text Height	³⁄₁₆″ (2.5)	⅛″ (3.5)
Fit	Fit Options	Either Text or Arrow (Best Fit)	Either Text or Arrow (Best Fit) (Verify)
	Overall Scale	1.000 (1)	48.000 (50)
Primary Units	Unit Format	Decimal	Architectural
	Fraction Format	Horizontal	Diagonal
	Zero Suppression	Feet, Inches (Trailing Only)	Feet Only (Trailing Only)
	Angular Precision	Zero decimal places	Two decimal places

Now you'll set up the alternate units:

1. Continue using I12-01-DimensionStyle.dwg (M12-01-Dimension Style.dwg), or open it if it's not already open.

> **This is identical to the New Dimension Style dialog box that you used in the previous sections.**

2. Click the Dimension Style button on the Annotate Tab ➢ Dimensions panel.

3. Highlight A-DIMS-PLAN in the Dimension Style Manager, if it's not already highlighted.

4. Click the Modify button to open the Modify Dimension Style dialog box.

5. Click the Alternate Units tab.

You'll make only three or four changes on this tab. Look back to Figure 12.13 to see what the style will look like when you're finished here.

6. In the upper-left corner of the tab, select the Display Alternate Units check box.

This makes the rest of the settings on the tab available to you for making changes.

7. If Decimal (Architectural) isn't displayed in the Unit Format drop-down list, select it.

8. If Precision isn't set to 0 (0′-0 1/8″), open that drop-down list and select that level of precision.

9. If the Unit Format under Alternate Units is Decimal, set Multiplier For Alt Units to 25.4.

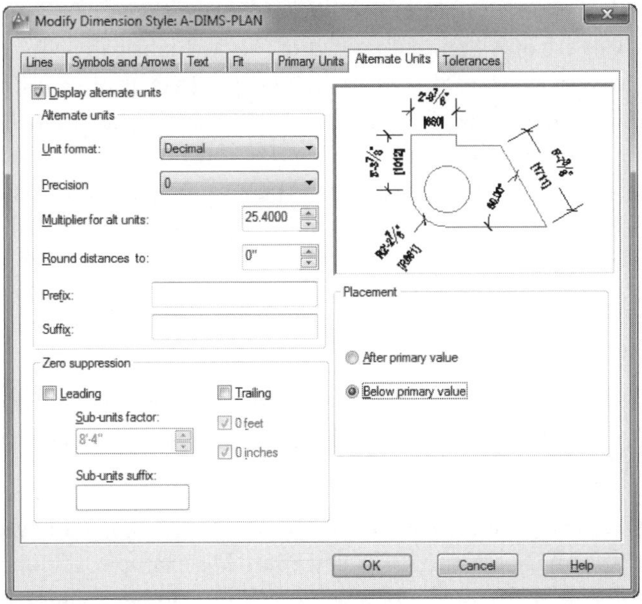

FIGURE 12.13 The Alternate Units tab after being set up for millimeters

If you want centimeters to be the alternate units, change the Multiplier For Alt Units setting to 2.54 and set Precision to 0.00.

This makes millimeters the alternate units. If the alternate units format is Architectural, then set Multiplier For Alt Units to 0.039370. This makes inches the alternate units.

10. In the lower-right quarter of the tab, in the Placement group, select Below Primary Value.

    This has the effect of placing the alternate units below the primary units and on the opposite side of the dimension line. The tab should look like Figure 12.13.

11. Uncheck the Display Alternate Units check box; you don't need to use these settings.

    You won't be using alternate units when you dimension the cabin.

Exploring the Tolerances Tab

AutoCAD offers features with options that help you create several kinds of *tolerances*: allowable variances from the stated dimension. These are very common in the machining and manufacturing industries, where it's understood that the dimensions given are only approximations of the part fabricated. Tolerances are usually measured in thousandths of an inch or hundredths of a millimeter.

The Tolerances tab provides four methods for creating what are called *lateral tolerances*, the traditional kind of tolerance that most draftspeople use. This is the plus or minus kind of tolerance. Open the Modify Dimension Style dialog box, click the Tolerances tab, and look at the choices in the Method drop-down list, shown in Figure 12.14.

Each of these is a method for displaying a plus or minus type of tolerance:

None   No tolerances are displayed.

Symmetrical   This method is for a single plus or minus expression after the base dimension. It's used when the upper allowable limit of deviation is identical to that for the lower limit, as in 1.0625 ± 0.0025.

Deviation   This method is for the instance in which the upper allowable deviation is different from that of the lower deviation. For example, the upper limit of the deviation can be +0.0025, and the lower limit can be −0.0005. The two deviation limits are stacked and follow the base dimension.

Limits   In this method, the tolerances are added to or subtracted from the base dimension, resulting in maximum and minimum total values. The maximum is placed over the minimum. In the example for the Symmetrical method, 1.0650 is the maximum, and 1.0600 the minimum.

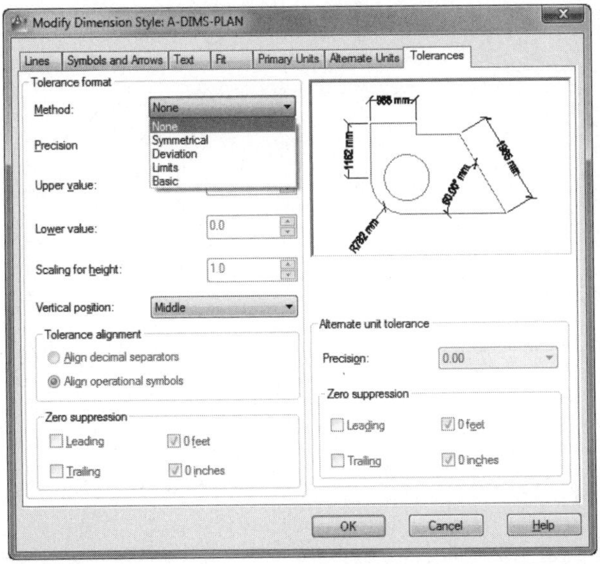

FIGURE 12.14 The Tolerances tab, showing the Method drop-down list options

Basic The base dimension is left by itself, and a box is drawn around it indicating that the tolerances are general, apply to several or all dimensions in boxes, and are noted somewhere else in the drawing. Often, basic dimensions appear when a dimension is theoretical or not exact.

When you select one of these options, one or more of the following settings becomes available. If you select Deviation or Limits, all settings become available:

Precision Controls the overall precision of the tolerances.

Upper Value and Lower Value The actual values of the tolerances.

Scaling For Height The height of the tolerance text. A value of 1 here sets the tolerance text to match that of the base dimension. A value greater than 1 makes the tolerance text greater than the base dimension text, and a value less than 1 makes it smaller than the base dimension text.

Vertical Position Indicates where the base dimension is placed vertically relative to the tolerances. It can be in line with the upper or lower tolerance or in the middle.

At the bottom, the Zero Suppression options (which are not available when Basic is the tolerance format), when checked, suppress extra zeros that occur before or after the decimal point. If you set up the Tolerances tab as shown at the top of Figure 12.15, a dimension looks like the one shown at the bottom of the figure.

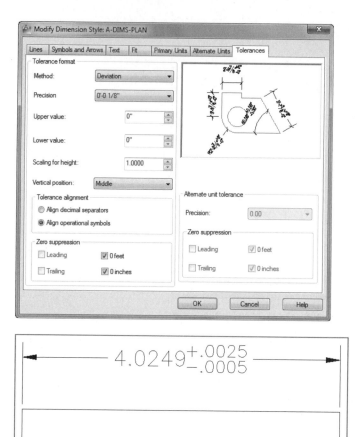

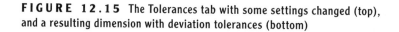

FIGURE 12.15 The Tolerances tab with some settings changed (top), and a resulting dimension with deviation tolerances (bottom)

A more complex family of tolerances is available through the Dimensions panel. It's called *geometric tolerancing* and involves setting up a series of boxes that contain symbols and numbers that describe tolerance parameters for form, position, and other geometric features. Usually two to six boxes appear in a row, with the possibility of multiple rows. These all constitute the *feature control frame*, which eventually is inserted in the drawing and attached in some way to the relevant dimension. Follow these steps:

1. Click the Tolerance button from the expanded Dimensions panel on the Annotate tab to open the Geometric Tolerance dialog box (see Figure 12.16).

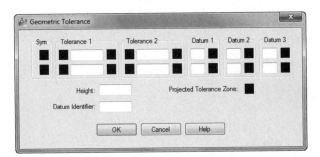

FIGURE 12.16 The Geometric Tolerance dialog box

This is where you will set up the feature control frame. The black squares will contain symbols, and the white rectangles are for tolerance or datum values or for reference numbers.

2. Click in the top Sym box on the left to open the Symbol dialog box.

This contains 14 standard symbols that describe the characteristic form or position for which the tolerance is being used. When you select one of the symbols, the window closes, and the symbol is inserted into the SYM box.

3. Click the icon in the top row that consists of two concentric circles, as shown in Figure 12.17.

FIGURE 12.17 The Symbol dialog box

4. Click the top-left black square in the Tolerance 1 group.

This inserts a diameter symbol.

5. Click the top-right black square in the Tolerance 1 group.

The Material Condition dialog box (see Figure 12.18) opens and displays the three material condition options. When you click one, it's inserted in the top-right square of Tolerance 1. If you need them, you can insert any of these three symbols in Tolerance 2 and Datum 1, 2, or 3.

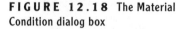

FIGURE 12.18 The Material Condition dialog box

6. Fill in the actual tolerance value(s) and datum references in the text boxes, as shown in Figure 12.19.

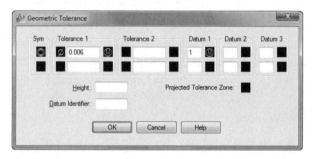

FIGURE 12.19 The Geometric Tolerance dialog box with a few values provided

7. When you're finished, click OK.

You can insert the feature control frame into your drawing like a block and reference it to a part or a dimension, as shown in Figure 12.20.

8. If open, close I12-01-DimensionStyle.dwg (M12-01-Dimension Style.dwg), discarding any changes to the drawing when prompted.

This exercise was intended to show you the tools that AutoCAD provides for setting up the most commonly used lateral and geometric tolerances when you use the Tolerances tab in the Modify Dimension Style dialog box and the Tolerance button on the Dimensions panel. My intention here isn't to explain the methodology of geometric tolerances or the meanings of the various symbols, numbers, and letters used in them. That is a subject beyond the scope of this book.

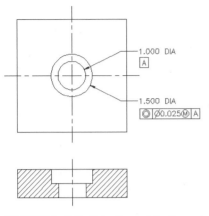

FIGURE 12.20 Geometric dimensioning on a machined part

Placing Dimensions on the Drawing

Upon returning to your drawing, it should still look almost exactly like Figure 12.1 (shown earlier), and it should have the following:

▶ A new layer called A-ANNO-DIMS, which is current

▶ A new dimension style called A-DIMS-PLAN, which is current and is now displayed in the drop-down list on the Dimensions panel

▶ Most of the layers frozen

▶ The Endpoint osnap running (Other osnaps may be running, but only Endpoint is important to this exercise.)

▶ On the status bar: Ortho mode, Polar Tracking, and Object Snap Tracking off

▶ A new text style called A-DIMS, which is current

Placing Horizontal Dimensions

First, you'll dimension across the top of the plan, from the corner of the building to the closet wall, and then to the other features on that wall. Then you'll dimension the decks and roof.

1. Open I12-01-DimensionStyle.dwg (M12-01-DimensionStyle.dwg) and zoom in to the area around the closet.

2. Click the Linear Dimension button at the left side of the Dimensions panel on the Annotate tab to activate the DIMLINEAR command.

If the Linear Dimension button isn't visible, click the down-arrow below the current dimension command and then choose Linear from the drop-down list. The prompt reads Specify first extension line origin or <select object>:.

3. Pick the upper-right corner of the cabin walls.

The prompt changes to Specify second extension line origin:.

4. Activate the Perpendicular osnap, place the cursor over the outside of the closet wall as shown in Figure 12.21, and then click.

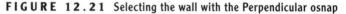

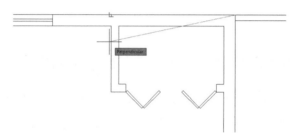

FIGURE 12.21 Selecting the wall with the Perpendicular osnap

5. At the Specify dimension line location or: prompt, click a point above the roof line to place the dimension in the drawing (see the top of Figure 12.22).

Also notice that the left extension line starts perpendicular to the wall you picked.

6. Click anywhere on the new dimension.

The dimension becomes dashed, and five grips appear (see the bottom of Figure 12.22).

N O T E   When you need to adjust a dimension, click and drag the necessary grip. You'll learn more about using grips to modify dimensions in the "Modifying Dimensions" section later in this chapter.

7. Press Esc to deselect the dimension.

8. Save this drawing as `I12-02-HorizDimension.dwg` (`M12-02-Horiz Dimension.dwg`).

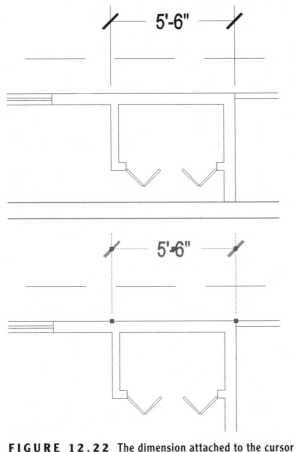
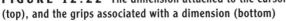

FIGURE 12.22 The dimension attached to the cursor (top), and the grips associated with a dimension (bottom)

Your first dimension is completed.

When dimensioning a drawing, you usually dimension to the outside or center line of the objects and to each significant feature. The next dimension will run from the left side of the first dimension to the right side of the window.

N O T E   Studs are the vertical 2″×4″ (51 mm×102 mm) or 2″×6″ (51 mm×152 mm) members in the framing of a wall. When dimensioning buildings that have stud walls, architects usually dimension to the face of the stud rather than the outside surface of the wall material, but I won't go into that level of detail in this book.

Using the Dimension Continue Command

AutoCAD has an automatic way of placing adjacent dimensions in line with one another—the DIMCONTINUE (Dimension Continue) command. You use it as follows:

1. Continue using I12-02-HorizDimension.dwg (M12-02-HorizDimension.dwg), or open it if it's not already open.

2. Zoom out, and pan until you have a view of the upper wall and roofline, with space above them for dimensions (see Figure 12.23).

3. Start the DIMCONTINUE (Dimension Continue) command by selecting the Continue button on the Annotate tab ➤ Dimensions panel.

   If it's not visible, click the down-arrow next to the Baseline button and choose Continue from the fly-out menu.

   The prompt asks you to Specify a second extension line origin or [Undo/Select] <Select>. All you need to do here is pick a point for the right end of the dimension—in this case, the right corner of the nearest window.

4. Click the right corner of the living room window.

   This draws the second dimension in line with the first (see Figure 12.24). Note that the same prompt has returned to the command window. You can keep picking points to place the next adjacent dimension in line.

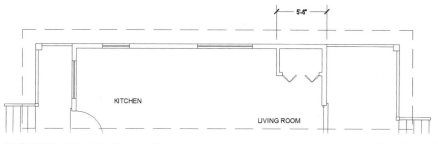

F I G U R E   1 2 . 2 3 The result of zooming and panning for a view of the top of the floor plan

FIGURE 12.24 Using the DIMCONTINUE command

5. Continue adding dimensions with the DIMCONTINUE command by clicking (moving right to left) the endpoints of the window openings, the endpoint of the wall, and the end of the deck.

6. Use the Linear tool to add a dimension for the width of the front deck and the Perpendicular osnap to align the dimension lines.

When you're finished, your dimensions should look like Figure 12.25. Some of the dimensions, particularly on the left end of the cabin, appear cluttered, with some of the arrowheads and text overlapping.

7. Select the dimensions that need adjustment and use the grips near the arrows or at the text to adjust the dimension line or text location (see Figure 12.26).

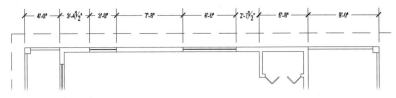

FIGURE 12.25 Dimensions added to each critical point along the top wall

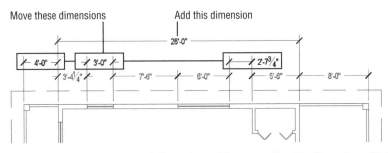
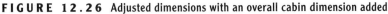

FIGURE 12.26 Adjusted dimensions with an overall cabin dimension added

8. Finally, add a linear dimension from the end of the front deck to the beginning of the cabin, and another overall dimension from one end of the cabin to another, as shown in Figure 12.26.

9. Save this drawing as **I12-03-DimContinue.dwg** (**M12-03-Dim Continue.dwg**).

With the DIMCONTINUE (Dimension Continue) command, you can dimension along a wall of a building quickly just by picking points. AutoCAD assumes that the last extension line specified for the previous dimension will coincide with the first extension line of the next dimension. If the extension line from which you need to continue isn't the last one specified, press ↵ at the prompt, pick the extension line from which you want to continue, and resume the command.

Another automation strategy that you can use with linear dimensions is the Dimension Baseline tool.

Using the Dimension Baseline Command

The DIMBASELINE (Dimension Baseline) command gets its name from a style of dimensioning called *baseline*, in which all dimensions begin at the same point (see Figure 12.27). Each dimension is stacked above the previous one. Because of the automatic stacking, you can use the Dimension Baseline tool for overall dimensions. AutoCAD will stack the overall dimension a set height above the incremental dimensions.

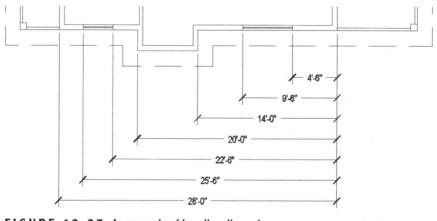

FIGURE 12.27 An example of baseline dimensions

The steps for creating baseline dimensions are listed here:

1. Create a linear dimension.

2. Click the down-arrow next to the Continue button in the Annotate tab ➤ Dimensions panel, and then click the Baseline option.

   The prompt reads Specify a second extension line origin or [Undo/Select] <Select>:, just like the first prompt for the DIMCONTINUE (Dimension Continue) command.

3. Pick the next feature to be dimensioned.

4. Repeat step 3 as necessary to add the required dimensions.

5. Press Esc to end the DIMBASELINE command.

Setting Up Vertical Dimensions

Because you can use the Linear Dimension tool for vertical and horizontal dimensions, you can follow the steps in the previous exercise to do the vertical dimensions on the right side of the floor plan. The only difference from the horizontal dimensioning is that you need two sets of dimensions: one for the wall and another for the deck. The following steps will take you through the process of placing the first vertical dimension. You'll then be able to finish the rest of them by yourself.

1. Continue using I12-03-DimContinue.dwg (M12-03-DimContinue.dwg), or open it if it's not already open.

2. Pan and zoom to get a good view of the right side of the floor plan, including the front deck (see Figure 12.28).

3. Click the Linear button, and then start a vertical dimension from the top of the right exterior wall.

4. Place the second point at the endpoint on the opening of the sliding door.

5. Click to place the dimension between the wall and the FRONT DECK text.

6. Adjust the location of the text if needed (see the left image of Figure 12.29).

T I P   AutoCAD can sometimes be conservative when deciding whether both text and arrows can fit between the extension lines. Try moving the text a bit toward one of the extension lines in one of the 4'-6" dimensions and notice how the arrows move from outside the extension lines to inside.

7. Use the Dimension Continue tool and grips to draw and edit the remaining two dimensions for the front of the cabin (see the right image of Figure 12.29).

8. Using a similar procedure, draw the vertical dimensions for the front deck, placing the dimensions to the right of the deck.

9. Add a horizontal dimension showing the length of the stairway.
    When you're finished, your dimensions should look like those in Figure 12.30.

10. Save this drawing as **I12-04-VerticalDimensions.dwg** (**M12-04 -VerticalDimensions.dwg**).

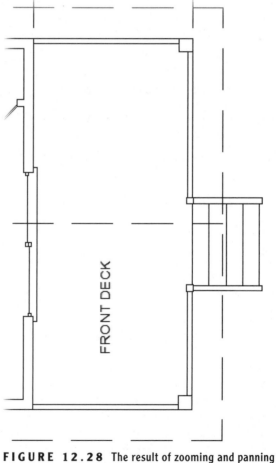

FIGURE 12.28 The result of zooming and panning for a view of the right side of the floor plan

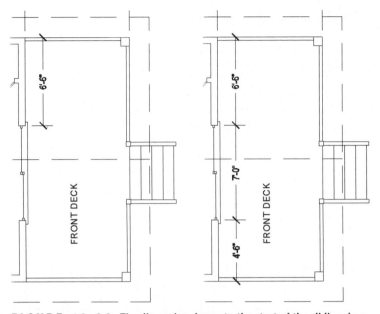

FIGURE 12.29 The dimension drawn to the start of the sliding door opening (left), and the completed first set of vertical dimensions (right)

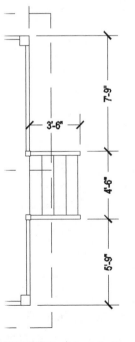

FIGURE 12.30 The dimensions for the front deck

Finishing the Dimensions

You place the rest of the horizontal and vertical dimensions using a procedure similar to the one you used to complete the horizontal dimensions. Here is a summary of the steps:

1. Continue using I12-04-VerticalDimensions.dwg (M12-04-Vertical Dimensions.dwg), or open it if it's not already open.

2. Use the Linear Dimension and Dimension Continue tools to add horizontal dimensions to the bottom side of the building. Move the title and label text as required to display the dimensions clearly.

3. Add dimensions to the rear of the cabin and for the rear deck.

4. Dimension the roof.

5. Dimension the inside of the bathroom:

   a. Start the Linear Dimension (DIMLINEAR) tool.

   b. Press ↵ to allow the selection of an object, rather than a starting point for a dimension.

   c. Click one of the vertical walls, and then click to place the dimension.

   The completed dimensions will be similar to Figure 12.31.

6. Save your drawing as **I12-05-FinishedDimensions.dwg** (**M12-05 -FinishedDimensions.dwg**).

Using Other Types of Dimensions

AutoCAD provides tools for placing radial and angular dimensions on the drawing and for placing linear dimensions that are neither vertical nor horizontal. You'll make some temporary changes to the cabin file that you just saved, so that you can explore these tools and then close the drawing without saving it:

1. Make layer 0 current.

2. Freeze the A-ANNO-TEXT, A-ANNO-DIMS, A-ELEV-DECK, and A-ELEV-DECK-STRS layers.

3. Use the FILLET command to fillet the top-right corner of the roof with a radius of 5'-0" (1525 mm).

4. Start the LINE command, and then pick the lower-right corner of the roof as the start point.

5. Activate the Nearest osnap, and pick a point on the roof's ridgeline. The right end of the cabin should look like Figure 12.32.

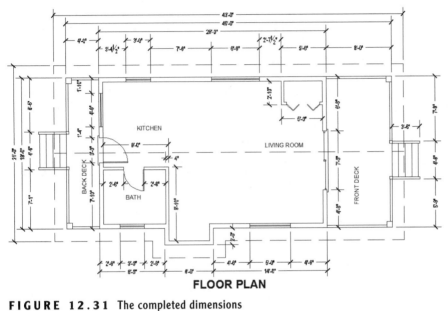

FLOOR PLAN

FIGURE 12.31 The completed dimensions

Using Radial Dimensions

On the drop-down menu on the left side of the Dimensions panel are icons for the Radius, Diameter, and Arc Length dimensions. They all operate the same way and are controlled by the same settings.

Follow these steps to place a *radius dimension* at the filleted corner, measuring the distance from the curve to the center point:

1. Click the Osnap button on the status bar to disable any running osnaps temporarily.

2. Click the arrow below the Linear button on the Annotate tab ➤ Dimensions panel, and then click the Radius button to start the DIMRADIUS command.

3. Click the inside filleted corner well above the midpoint.

The radius dimension appears, and the text is attached to the cursor. Where you pick on the curve determines the angle of the radius dimension (see Figure 12.33).

4. Click to place the radius text in the dimension.

The *R* prefix indicates that this is a radial dimension.

 N O T E   Most of the commands used for dimensioning are prefaced with DIM when you enter them at the command line; that is, DIM is part of the command name. For example, when you click the Radius button on the Annotate tab ➤ Dimensions panel or Dimension toolbar, you see _DIMRADIUS in the command window to let you know that you have started the DIMRADIUS command. You can also start this command by entering DIMRADIUS↵ or DRA↵ (the command alias).

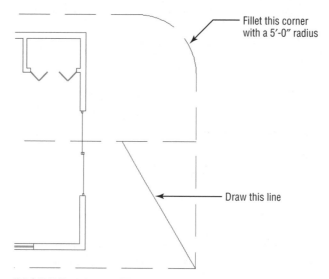

FIGURE 12.32 The right end of the cabin after some temporary changes are implemented

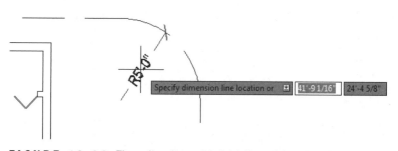

FIGURE 12.33 The radius dimension initially positioned on the curve

The radial dimension you just inserted uses the same architectural tick that the other linear dimensions in your drawing use. Typically, an arrow, not an architectural tick, would be used to illustrate radial dimensions. To fix this, you will need to create a Child Dimension style. You'll learn how to create parent and child dimension styles at the end of this section, under "Setting Up Parent and Child Dimensioning Styles."

Adding a Diameter Dimension

Similar to the radius dimension, a *diameter dimension* measures the distance from one side of a circle or arc, through the center point, to the other end. Follow these steps to place a diameter at the filleted corner:

1. Erase the radius dimension.

2. Click the arrow below the Radius button on the Dimension panel within the Annotate tab, and then click the Diameter button to start the DIMDIAMETER command.

3. Click the inside filleted corner near the location where it meets the vertical wall.

   The diameter dimension appears, and the text is attached to the cursor.

4. Click to place the radius text in the dimension. The Ø prefix indicates that this is a diameter dimension. Where you pick on the curve determines the angle of the radius dimension (see Figure 12.34).

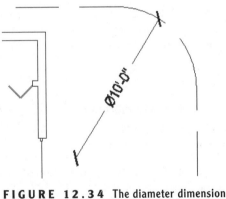

FIGURE 12.34 The diameter dimension positioned on the curve

Like the radial dimension you created a moment ago, the diameter dimension also uses architectural ticks as opposed to the more standard arrows. Completing the process outlined in the "Setting Up Parent and Child Dimensioning Styles" at the end of this section will walk you through how to make this fix.

Add an Arc Length

An arc length dimension measures the length of an arc or polyline arc segment. As shown in Figure 12.35, an arc symbol, or *cap*, precedes the text to identify it as an arc length dimension. Follow these steps to place an arc length dimension at the filleted corner:

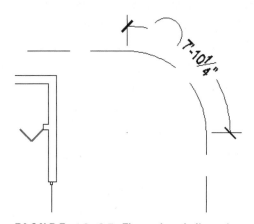

FIGURE 12.35 The arc length dimension positioned on the curve

 T I P   You can change the location of the arc length symbol, from in front of the text to over it, or eliminate it altogether in the Symbols And Arrows tab of the Modify Dimension style dialog box.

1. Erase the diameter dimension.

 2. Click the arrow below the Diameter button on the Dimension panel within the Annotate tab, and then click the Arc Length button to start the DIMARC command.

3. Click anywhere on the arc at the filleted corner, and the arc length dimension appears attached to the cursor.

4. Click to locate the dimension (see Figure 12.35).

Setting Up Parent and Child Dimensioning Styles

The A-DIMS-PLAN dimension style that you set up at the beginning of this chapter applies to all dimensions and is called the parent *dimension style*. You can change settings in this dimension style for particular types of dimensions, such as the radial type. This makes a *child dimension style*.

   The child version is based on the parent version, but it has a few settings that are different. In this way, all your dimensions will be made by using the A-DIMS-PLAN dimension style, but radial dimensions will use a child version of the style. Once you create a child dimension style from the parent style, you refer to both styles by the same name, and you call them a *dimension style family*. Follow these steps to set up a child dimension style for radial dimensions:

1. Click the Dimension Style button at the right end of the Dimensions panel to open the Dimension Style Manager dialog box.

2. With the parent style, A-DIMS-PLAN, highlighted in the Styles list, click the New button to open the Create New Dimension Style dialog box.

3. Open the Use For drop-down list, select Radius Dimensions, and then click the Continue button.

   The New Dimension Style: A-DIMS-PLAN: Radial dialog box opens and has the seven tabs you worked with earlier. Had you selected a different option in the Use For drop-down list, it would replace Radial in the title of the dialog box.

   By default, the values in the Child Dimension Style dialog box will be the same as the values found in its parent. For instance, switching to the Symbols And Arrows tab will reveal that the Arrowhead setting is Architectural Tick, the same as the parent A-DIMS-PLAN style.

4. From the Symbols And Arrows tab, click the Second drop-down list within the Arrowheads group to change from Architectural Tick to Closed Filled, as shown in Figure 12.36.

   The change you just made will not affect the way you actually create dimensions. You'll still use the A-DIMS-PLAN dimension style. The only difference is that when you create a radius dimension, it will use a filled arrow instead of the architectural tick that was used when creating a radius dimension earlier.

5. Click OK to close the New Dimension Style dialog box.

In the Dimension Style Manager dialog box, notice the Styles list; as shown in Figure 12.37, the current dimension style now has a child style for Radial dimensions indented below it.

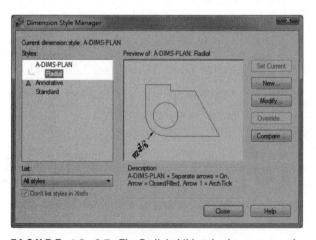

FIGURE 12.36 Changing the Arrowhead style for the Radial A-DIMS-PLAN child style

FIGURE 12.37 The Radial child style shown as a node in the Dimension Style Manager

6. Click Close to close the Dimension Style Manager dialog box.

7. Using the Radius tool found on the Dimensions panel within the Annotate tab, redraw the same radial dimension you created earlier. The result should look like Figure 12.38.

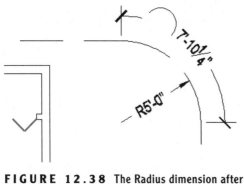

FIGURE 12.38 The Radius dimension after creating a child style

Notice that the arrowhead is no longer an architectural tick, but rather a closed arrow. Despite this override to radial dimensions, linear dimensions will still use the architectural tick.

Using Aligned and Angular Dimensions

To become familiar with the aligned and angular dimension types, you'll experiment with the line you drew from the opposite corner of the roof in the previous exercise.

Using Aligned Dimensions

Aligned dimensions are linear dimensions that aren't horizontal or vertical. You place them in the same way that you place horizontal or vertical dimensions with the Dimension Linear tool. You can also use the Dimension Baseline and Dimension Continue tools with aligned dimensions.

Use the Aligned Dimension tool, which works just like the Linear Dimension tool, to dimension the line you drew at the beginning of this exercise. Follow these steps to add an aligned dimension:

1. Zoom in to the lower-right corner of the cabin roof.

 2. Click the down-arrow on the right side of the Annotate tab ➢ Dimensions panel, and then click the Aligned button.

3. Press ↵ to switch to accept the Select Object option.
The cursor changes to a pickbox.

4. Pick the diagonal line.
The dimension appears attached to the cursor.

5. Click to place the dimension.
Your drawing should look similar to Figure 12.39.

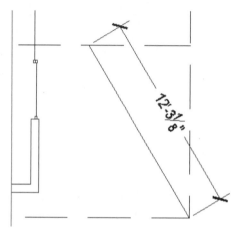

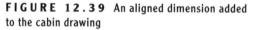

FIGURE 12.39 An aligned dimension added
to the cabin drawing

Using Angular Dimensions

The *angular dimension* is the only basic dimension type that uses angles in the
dimension text instead of linear measurements. Try making an angular dimension
on your own. Because the default arrowhead style for the A-DIMS-PLAN dimension style is Architectural Ticks, you'll want to create another child style for angular
dimensions. Refer to the "Setting Up Parent and Child Dimensioning Styles" exercise
earlier in this chapter for step-by-step instructions on how to do this. To summarize,
you'll need to do the following to create an angular child style:

1. Open the Dimension Style Manager, select the A-DIMS-PLAN dimension style, and click New.

2. Change the Use For drop-down list to Angular, and click Continue.

3. From the Symbols And Arrows tab, change the First and Second
Arrowhead styles to Closed Filled and then click OK.

4. Close out of the Dimension Style Manager to return to your drawing.

With the Angular child style in place, you're ready to add an angular dimension to your drawing. Follow these steps to add an angular dimension to your drawing:

1. Turn off Object Snap mode.

2. Start the DIMANGULAR command by selecting the Angular tool on the Annotate tab ➢ Dimensions panel.

3. Follow the prompts, pick the line you drew, and then pick the horizontal roofline.

4. Pick a point inside your drawing to insert the angular dimension. When you're finished, your drawing will look like Figure 12.40.

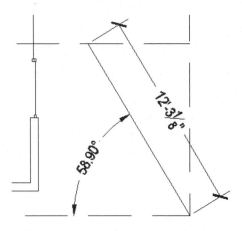

FIGURE 12.40 The roof with the angular dimension added

Using Ordinate Dimensions

Ordinate dimensions are widely used by the mechanical engineering profession and related trades. They differ from the kind of dimensioning you have been doing so far in this chapter in that ordinate dimensioning specifies x- and y-coordinate values for specific points in a drawing based on an absolute or relative Cartesian Coordinate System, rather than on a distance between two points. This method is used to dimension centers of holes in sheet metal or machine parts.

You don't need ordinate dimensions in the cabin project, so you'll now go through a quick exercise in setting them up to dimension the holes in a steel plate. Doing so will give you a glimpse of the tools that AutoCAD provides for this type of work. (If you aren't interested in ordinate dimensioning, move on to the next section, "Using Leader Lines," to modify the dimensions you've already created for the cabin.)

1. Open a new drawing, and leave the units at the default of Decimal with a precision of four decimal places.

2. Turn Polar Tracking on.

3. Set up a new text style, and set 0.125 as the height.

4. Click Apply and then Close to make it the current text style.

5. Draw a rectangle using 0,0 as the first point and 6,–4 as the second.

6. Use Zoom To Extents, and then zoom out to see the area around the object.

7. Use the UCSICON command to move the icon to the Noorigin position.

8. Somewhere in the upper-left quadrant of the rectangle, draw a circle with a radius of 0.35 units.

9. Using Polar Tracking or Ortho mode, copy that circle once directly to the right, once directly below the original, and to two other locations that are not aligned with any other circle, so the configuration looks something like the top of Figure 12.41.

10. Set the Endpoint and Center osnaps to be running, and turn on Ortho mode.

    What you are concerned with in ordinate dimensioning isn't how far the holes are from each other but how far the x- and y-coordinates of the centers of the holes are from a reference point on the plate. You'll use the upper-left corner of the plate as a reference point, or *datum point*, because it's positioned at the origin of the drawing, or at the 0,0 point.

 11. Click the Ordinate button on the drop-down menu on the Dimensions panel.

12. Click the upper-left corner of the rectangular plate, and then move the cursor straight up above the point you picked.

13. When you're about an inch above the plate, click again.

    This sets the first ordinate dimension (see the top of Figure 12.41).

14. Press the spacebar to repeat the DIMORDINATE command.

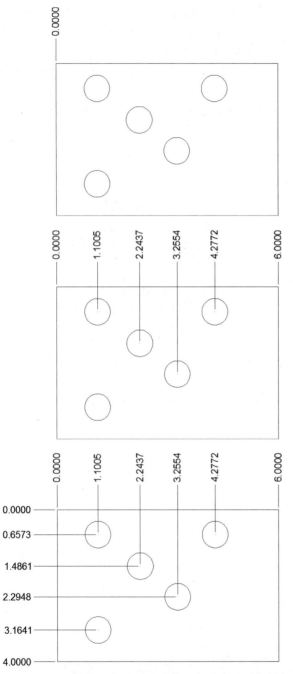

FIGURE 12.41 Placing the first ordinate dimension (top), finishing up the x-coordinate dimensions (middle), and placing the y-coordinate dimensions (bottom)

15. Repeat steps 12 and 13 for the four circles near the middle or upper portions of the plate, using their centers as points to snap to and aligning the ordinate dimensions by eye.

The lower circle is in vertical alignment with the one above it, so it needs no horizontal dimension.

16. Place an ordinate dimension on the upper-right corner of the plate to finish.

Press the F8 key to toggle Ortho mode off if you need to jog an extension line.

The result should look like the middle image of Figure 12.41.

17. Repeat this procedure for the y-ordinate dimensions.

Once again, ignore any circles that are in vertical alignment, but include the upper-left and lower-left corners of the plate (see the bottom of Figure 12.41).

The civil engineering discipline typically uses a different type of ordinate dimensions. A datum reference point is used, but the dimensions are displayed at each point in a format typically referred to as northing and easting. Using this format, the y-coordinate is displayed first as the *northing* location, and separated by a comma, the x-coordinate is displayed as the *easting* location, as shown in Figure 12.42. Because of this special format, most civil engineers choose a product such as AutoCAD Civil 3D that has specialized tools for generating ordinate dimensions in this format.

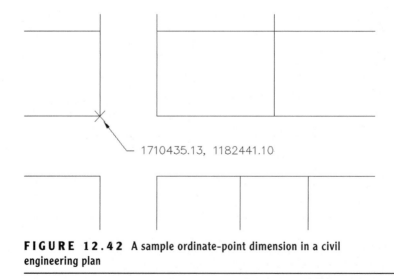

1710435.13, 1182441.10

FIGURE 12.42 A sample ordinate-point dimension in a civil engineering plan

When you change settings for a dimension style, dimensions created when that style was current will automatically update to reflect the changes. You'll modify more dimensions in the next section.

You have been introduced to the basic types of dimensions (linear, radial, leader, and angular) and some auxiliary dimensions (baseline, continue, and aligned) that are special cases of the linear type. You can also use the baseline and continuous dimensions with angular dimensions.

Feel free to save the drawing file you created while working through the last several exercises to refer back to later. For the purposes of this book, you will not use this specific file again, so you can close your drawing without saving the changes.

Using Leader Lines

You will use the MLEADER (Multileader) command to draw an arrow to features in the cabin drawing, in order to add descriptive information. Multileaders are not part of the dimension family, and you can find them on the Multileaders panel.

Creating a Multileader Style

Before you create a leader, you need to create a multileader style, as follows:

1. If it's still open, close the drawing you created during the Ordinate Dimensions exercise, and open the I12-05-FinishedDimensions.dwg (M12-05-FinishedDimensions.dwg).

2. Click the Multileader Style Manager button at the lower right of the Leaders panel's title bar on the Annotate tab.

3. Click the New button in the Multileader Style Manager.

4. In the Create New Multileader Style dialog box that opens, enter **A-DIMS-MLDR** in the New Style Name text box and then click Continue (see Figure 12.43).

    The Modify Multileader Style dialog box opens (see Figure 12.44). This is where you define the leader properties.

5. On the Leader Format tab, verify that the Arrowhead style is set to Closed Filled, and set the Size to 1/8″ (3.5).

6. Click the Leader Structure tab.

    The *landing* is the horizontal line at the end of the leader, just before the text.

7. Make sure the Set Landing Distance option is checked, and then enter 1/8″ (3.5) in the text box (see Figure 12.45).

8. In the Scale group, make sure the Specify Scale radio button is selected and then click in the text box and enter 48↵ (50↵), as shown in Figure 12.45.

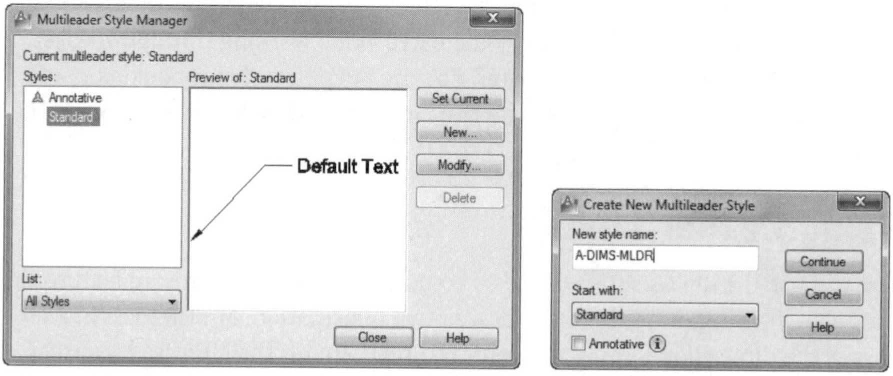

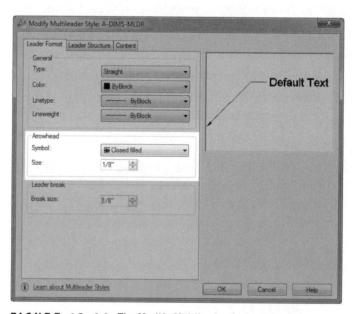

FIGURE 12.43 Creating a new multileader style

FIGURE 12.44 The Modify Multileader Style dialog box

9. Switch to the Content tab shown in Figure 12.46.

10. Expand the Text Style drop-down list, choose A-DIMS, and set the text height to 1/8″ (3.5).

11. In the Leader Connection area, set both the Left Attachment and Right Attachment options to Middle Of Top Line, as shown in Figure 12.46.
    This places the middle of the top line of the leader text even with the landing.

12. Set the Landing Gap value to 1/8″ (3.5), as shown in Figure 12.46.

13. Click the OK button.
    In the Multileader Style Manager, the A-DIMS-MLDR Leader style appears in the Styles list box (see Figure 12.47).

14. Select A-DIMS-MLDR, click Set Current, and then click the Close button.

15. Save this drawing as `I12-06-MLeaderStyle.dwg` (`M12-06-MLeader Style.dwg`).

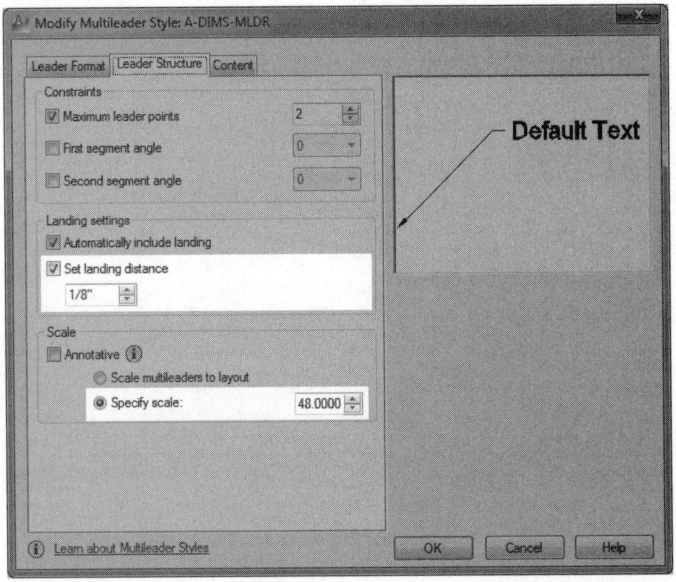

FIGURE 12.45 The Leader Structure tab within the Modify Multileader Style dialog box

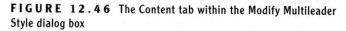

FIGURE 12.46 The Content tab within the Modify Multileader Style dialog box

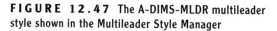

FIGURE 12.47 The A-DIMS-MLDR multileader style shown in the Multileader Style Manager

Adding the Leaders

To add the leaders to the drawing, follow these steps:

    1. Continue using I12-06-MLeaderStyle.dwg (M12-06-MLeaderStyle .dwg), or open it if it's not already open.

2. Zoom in to the front deck.

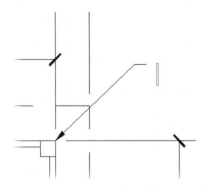

3. Click the Multileader button on the Annotate tab ➤ Leaders panel.

4. Activate the Endpoint osnap, if necessary, and then click the top-right corner of the top-right deck post.

5. At the Specify leader landing location: prompt, click a point above and to the right of the deck.

   The Text Editor tab and panels replace the Annotate tab and panels in the Ribbon, and a flashing vertical cursor appears to the right of the landing, as shown in Figure 12.48.

FIGURE 12.48 The flashing vertical cursor indicates that AutoCAD is waiting for text input.

6. Enter Use only pressure treated lumber for deck and supports.

   Longer notes like this one are typically displayed on several lines.

7. On the contextual Text Editor Ribbon tab ➤ Options panel, click the Ruler tool.

   This displays a ruler with two outward-facing arrows above the multileader text (see the left side of Figure 12.49).

8. Expand the arrows above the multileader text to the right to expand the text box, and distribute the text among several lines (see the right side of Figure 12.49).

9. Click a blank spot in the drawing area to complete the text and return to the Annotate tab.

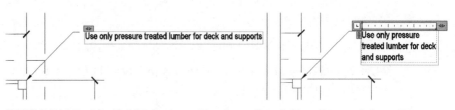

FIGURE 12.49 Multileader text with ruler toolbar (left), and expanded text box distributing text to several lines (right)

T I P   To reposition a leader without moving the arrow, click it and then click the grip at the middle of the landing. Then move the cursor. When you do, the text, landing, and one end of the leader line will all move with the cursor.

10. Pan to the right so that you can see the two windows on the north side of the cabin.

11. Add a leader that starts at the right edge of the 3″ (915 mm) window and then extends below and to the right.

12. Enter **All windows to be double paned** at the text prompt.

13. Adjust the width of the text, and then click a blank spot in the drawing area (see Figure 12.50).

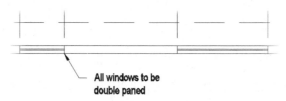

All windows to be
double paned

FIGURE 12.50 The multileader pointing to the first window

Several leader lines can extend from a single landing.

14. Click the Add Leader button on the Leaders panel within the Annotate tab, and then at the Select a multileader: prompt, click the last leader you made.

An arrowhead with a leader appears attached to the cursor and anchored to the landing.

15. Click the left corner of the window to the right and then press ↵.

N O T E   AutoCAD may place the second leader on the right side of the text if it determines that the leader fits better there. If this happens, click the multileader to select it and then move the text to the right. The second leader will reposition itself to the left side of the text.

16. Reposition the text as necessary.

Your drawing should look similar to Figure 12.51.

17. Save this drawing as `I12-07-AddingLeaders.dwg` (`M12-07-Adding Leaders.dwg`).

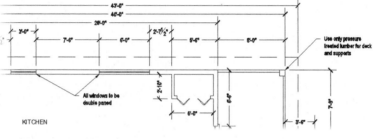

FIGURE 12.51 The cabin drawing with leaders

The final part of this chapter will be devoted to teaching you a few techniques for modifying dimensions.

Modifying Dimensions

You can use several commands and grips to modify dimensions, depending on the desired change. Specifically, you can do the following:

▶ Change the dimension text content

▶ Move the dimension text relative to the dimension line

▶ Move the dimension or extension lines

▶ Change the dimension style settings for a dimension or a group of dimensions

▶ Revise a dimension style

The best way to understand how to modify dimensions is to try a few. You'll look at how to change the content first.

Editing Dimension Text Content

You can modify any aspect of the dimension text. To change the content of text for one dimension, or to add text before or after the dimension, you can use the Properties or Quick Properties palette. You'll change the text in the horizontal dimensions for the cabin and walls by using Quick Properties:

1. Continue using I12-07-AddingLeaders.dwg (M12-07-Adding Leaders.dwg), or open it if it's not already open.

2. Zoom and pan until your view of the floor plan is similar to Figure 12.52.

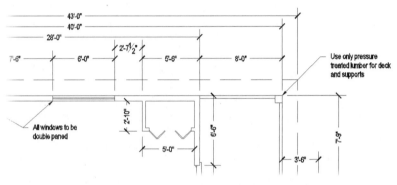

FIGURE 12.52 A modified view of the floor plan

 3. Select the horizontal 40'-0" (8550 mm) cabin dimension near the top of the drawing, and then click the Quick Properties button in the status bar.

> **TIP**   The procedure shown here can also be done in the Text rollout of the Properties palette.

4. Highlight the Text Override field, and enter <> verify in field↵.
   The phrase is appended to the dimension (see Figure 12.53). The <> instructs AutoCAD to add the phrase to the dimension text; if you had not prefixed the override with <>, the phrase would have replaced the dimension text entirely.

5. Press the Esc key, and then click the 5'-6" (1670 mm) dimension, measuring the distance from the end of the cabin to the closet wall.

6. In the Text Override box, enter <> %%P↵.

The ± symbol is now appended to the text (see Figure 12.54).

7. Save this drawing as **I12-08-ModifyDimText.dwg** (**M12-08-ModifyDimText.dwg**).

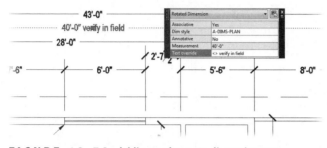

FIGURE 12.53 Adding a phrase to dimension text

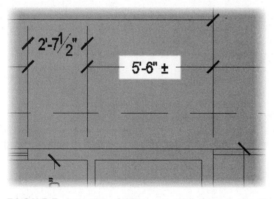

FIGURE 12.54 Adding a special character to dimension text

Unless you have memorized all the ASCII symbol codes, it might be easier to insert symbols into dimension text by using the text-editing tools. To do this, choose Modify ➢ Object ➢ Text ➢ Edit from the menu bar, or enter **TEDIT**↵ and then select the dimension text. The default AutoCAD workspace does not provide access to the DDEDIT command through the Ribbon.

The text is highlighted, and the Text Editor tab is activated. Place the cursor where you want the symbol to appear, and then click the Symbol button in the Insert panel to see a list of available symbols and their related ASCII codes. Click the symbol name to be added (see Figure 12.55).

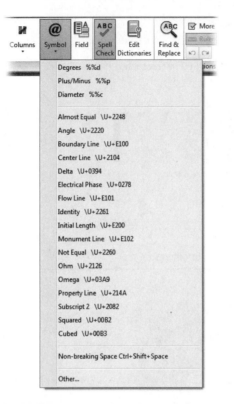

FIGURE 12.55 Inserting symbols
from the Text Editor tab

Next, you'll learn about moving a dimension.

Moving Dimensions

You can use grips to move dimensions. You used grips to move the dimension lines when you were putting in the vertical and horizontal dimensions. This time, you'll move the dimension line and the text:

1. Continue using I12-08-ModifyDimText.dwg (M12-08-ModifyDim Text.dwg), or open it if it's not already open.

2. Zoom in to a view of the upper-left side of the floor plan until you have a view similar to Figure 12.56, which includes the left window and the top of the rear deck and their dimensions.

3. Select the 3'-0" (915 mm) window dimension. Its grips appear.

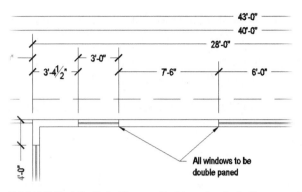

FIGURE 12.56 The result of zooming in to the upper-left side of the floor plan

4. Click the grip on the right arrowhead to activate it.

5. Move the cursor down until the dimension text is just below the roofline.

6. Click again to fix it there.

7. Click the grip that's on the text and, with Polar Tracking on, move the text to the right, outside of the extension line; then click to place it.

8. Press Esc to deselect the dimension (see Figure 12.57).

9. Select either of the leader lines pointing to the two windows.
   The leaders, landing, and leader text ghost, and the grips appear.

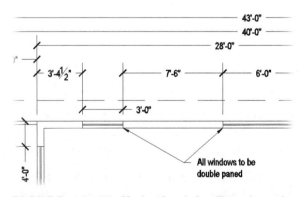

FIGURE 12.57 Moving the window dimension and dimension text with grips

10. Click the grip at the tip of the left leader and then move the grip to the end of the inner pane of the left window (see Figure 12.58).

11. Click the grip at the tip of the right leader, and move the grip to the left end of the inner pane of the right window (also shown in Figure 12.58).

12. Save this drawing as `I12-09-MovingDims.dwg` (`M12-09-MovingDims.dwg`).

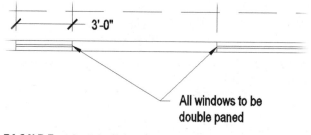

FIGURE 12.58 Using grips to move the position of leader lines

Adjusting Space between Stacked Dimensions

Dimensions for the back deck are stacked in three rows. Since each row of dimensions was placed visually, the spacing between each row is an arbitrary distance. The Adjust Space tool can help fix spacing variations like this one, helping you produce a more polished and professional-looking drawing. To use the Adjust Space tool:

1. Continue using `I12-09-MovingDims.dwg` (`M12-09-MovingDims.dwg`), or open it if it's not already open.

2. Zoom in to the area around the back deck so the deck, stairs, and dimensions are each visible.

 3. Start the `DIMSPACE` command by selecting the Adjust Space tool found on the Dimensions panel on the Annotate tab.

4. From the `Select base dimension:` prompt, pick the 7′ 1″ (2160 mm) dimension.

    The command line prompts you to select the dimensions to space.

5. Select the remaining dimensions for the back deck, as shown in Figure 12.59, and press ↵.

    After selecting the dimensions to space, you are given an option about how you would like them spaced. You can enter a custom value of your choice or let AutoCAD determine the best spacing for you.

6. Press ⏎ to accept the default Auto option.

    The command ends, and all three rows of dimensions are equally spaced, as shown in Figure 12.60.

7. Save this drawing as **I12-10-SpacingDims.dwg** (**M12-10-Spacing Dims.dwg**).

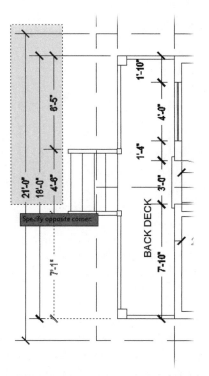

FIGURE 12.59 Selecting the remaining deck dimensions to adjust the spacing

Using Dimension Overrides

You can suppress the left extension line with the Properties palette, which allows you to change a setting in the dimension style for one dimension without altering the style settings. Follow these steps:

1. Continue using I12-10-SpacingDims.dwg (M12-10-SpacingDims.dwg), or open it if it's not already open.

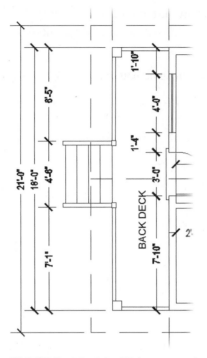

FIGURE 12.60 All three rows of deck dimensions are equally spaced.

2. Thaw the A-WALL-HEAD layer.

   Notice how the white (or black), left extension line for the 8′-0″ (2350 mm) dimension, measuring the width of the bathroom, coincides with the header line for the back door. You could use the Draw Order tools to move the dimension behind the header, but that may still result in a visibly overlapping condition when the drawing is printed. In this case, you'll suppress the extension line, rendering it invisible.

3. Double-click the 8′-0″ (2350 mm) dimension to open the Properties palette.

4. Scroll down to the Lines & Arrows rollout. If this section isn't open, click the arrow to the right.

5. Scroll down the list of settings in this section and click Ext Line 1.

6. Click the down-arrow to the right to open the drop-down list. Click Off.

This suppresses the left extension line of the dimension (see Figure 12.61).

7. Close the Properties palette.

8. Press Esc to deselect the dimension.

9. Save this drawing as `I12-11-DimOverrides.dwg` (`M12-11-Dim Overrides.dwg`).

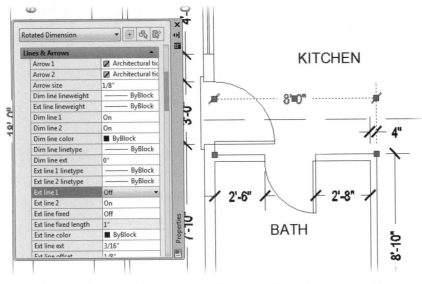

FIGURE 12.61 The 8'-0" (2350 mm) dimension with the left extension line suppressed

To illustrate how dimension overrides work, you suppressed an extension line without having to alter the dimension style. Extension lines are usually the thinnest lines in a drawing. It's usually not critical that they be suppressed if they coincide with other lines, because the other lines will overwrite them in a print.

However, in this example, the left extension line of the 8'-0" (2350 mm) dimension for the bathroom coincides with the line representing the header of the back door. If the Headers layer is turned off or frozen, you will have to unsuppress the extension line of this dimension so that it will be visible spanning the door opening. Also, if you dimension to a noncontinuous line, such as a hidden line, use the dimension style override features to assign special linetypes to extension lines.

N O T E In the practice exercises at the end of this chapter, you'll get a chance to learn how to incorporate centerlines into your dimensions.

Dimensioning Short Distances

When you have to dimension distances so short that the text and the arrows can't fit between the extension lines, a dimension style setting determines where they are placed. To see how this works, you'll add dimensions to the deck for the widths of the handrails and posts as well as the thickness of an interior wall. Then make a change in the Fit tab to alter the A-DIMS-PLAN dimension style to change where it places text that doesn't fit between the extension lines:

1. Continue using I12-11-DimOverrides.dwg (M12-11-DimOverrides.dwg), or open it if it's not already open.

2. Zoom and pan to a view of the upper portion of the front deck so that the horizontal dimensions above the floor plan are visible (see Figure 12.62).

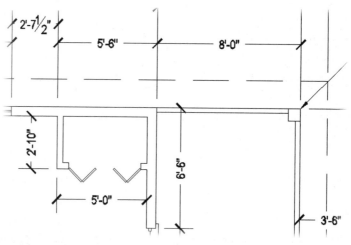

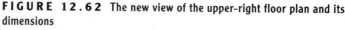

FIGURE 12.62 The new view of the upper-right floor plan and its dimensions

3. Activate the running osnaps if necessary, click the Linear Dimension button, and pick the upper-left corner of the deck post.

4. Pick the lower-left corner of the same deck post.

5. Place the dimension line about 2′ (610 mm) to the left of the deck post. The 8″ (204 mm) dimension is placed even farther to the left of the point you selected (see Figure 12.63).

6. Open the Dimension Style Manager dialog box, click the Modify button, and then, in the Modify Dimension Style dialog box, click the Fit tab.

7. In the Text Placement group, select the Beside The Dimension Line radio button (see Figure 12.64).

Several of the dimensioning commands are also available on the Annotation panel under the Home tab.

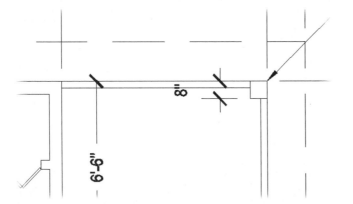

FIGURE 12.63 The text for the short dimension is not placed near the dimension lines.

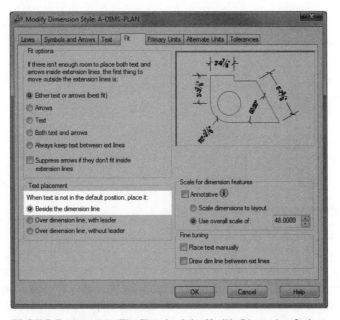

FIGURE 12.64 The Fit tab of the Modify Dimension Style dialog box after making the change

8. Click OK and then Close to shut both dialog boxes.

   The dimension changes to reflect the modification to the style (see Figure 12.65). This is a global change that will affect all future dimensions.

9. Add another dimension measuring the width of the horizontal handrail, and add the text **TYP** after the dimension text, as shown in Figure 12.66.

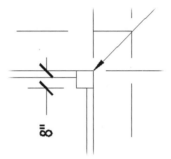

FIGURE 12.65 The short dimension after changing the style

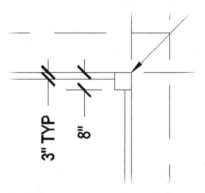

FIGURE 12.66 The handrail dimension after adding the *TYP text*

 N O T E The abbreviation TYP stands for *Typical*; it tells someone reading your plans that all handrails are 3″ in width unless designated otherwise. Refer to the "Editing Dimension Text Content" section if you need a refresher on modifying dimension text.

10. Repeat step 9, and add the TYP abbreviation to the 4″ dimension in the upper-right corner of the bathroom.

This tells someone reading the plans for your cabin that all interior walls are 4″ in width unless designated otherwise.

11. Make any adjustments necessary to make the drawing readable, and then save the drawing as `I12A-FPLAYO.dwg` (`M12A-FPLAYO.dwg`).

This concludes the exercises for dimensions in this chapter. Working successfully with dimensions in your drawing requires an investment of time to become familiar with the commands and settings that control how dimensions appear, how they are placed in the drawing, and how they are modified. The exercises in this chapter have led you through the basics of the dimensioning process. For a more in-depth discussion of dimensions, refer to *Mastering AutoCAD 2012 and AutoCAD LT 2012* by George Omura (Wiley, 2011), or visit this book's website at `www.autocadner.com` for additional resources.

The next chapter will introduce you to external references, which can be used to view a drawing from within another drawing.

If You Would Like More Practice...

In the first practice exercise, you'll get a chance to use the dimensioning tools that you just learned. After that is a short exercise that shows a technique for incorporating centerlines into dimensions.

Dimensioning the Garage Addition

Try dimensioning the garage addition to the cabin (`04A-FPGARG.dwg`) that was shown at the end of Chapter 4, "Developing Drawing Strategies: Part 1." Use the same techniques and standards of dimensioning that you used in this chapter to dimension the cabin; use the DIMS-PLAN dimension style you set up and used in this chapter.

1. Open `04A-FPGARG.dwg`.

2. Use the DesignCenter to bring over the following:

- ▶ A-DIMS-PLAN dimension style
- ▶ A-DIMS text style
- ▶ A-DIMS-MLDR multileader style
- ▶ A-ANNO-DIMS layer.

3. Dimension to the outside edges of exterior walls, the edges of the openings, and the centerlines of interior walls.

4. Drag an A-ROOM-IDEN block and a room label from the cabin drawing into the garage drawing, and then copy and modify them as required.

5. If the leader does not display properly, check the Overall Scale value in the Properties panel and make sure it is set to 64 (70).
   When you're finished, the drawing should look similar to Figure 12.67.

6. When you're finished, save this drawing as **12A-FPGARG.dwg**.

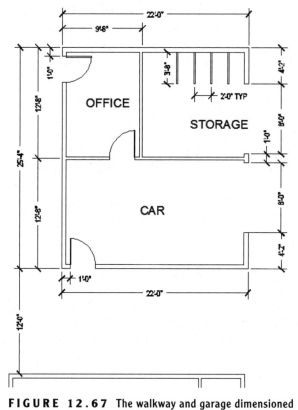

FIGURE 12.67 The walkway and garage dimensioned

Dimensioning to a Centerline

This exercise will show you how to use centerlines as replacements for extension lines in dimensions. I'll use as many of the default settings for text styles, dimension styles, units, and so forth as I can to give you a look at what out-of-the-box, or vanilla, AutoCAD looks like. The drawing you'll make is similar to the one you made in Chapter 2, "Learning Basic Commands to Get Started," but you know so much more now:

1. Choose Application menu ≻ New ≻ Drawing. Then, in the Create New Drawing dialog box, select the acad.dwt template.

2. Start the RECTANG command, and click a point in the lower-left quadrant of the drawing area.

3. For the second point, enter @6,2↵.

4. Use the Zoom Extents tool, and then zoom out a bit.

5. Pan to move the new rectangle down a little (see Figure 12.68).

FIGURE 12.68 The rectangle after panning down

You want to dimension from the upper-left corner of the rectangle to the center of the upper horizontal line and then to the upper-right corner. You'll select the Dimension tool from the menu bar and use the default dimension settings:

1. Create a new layer called **A-ANNO-DIMS**, accept the White color, and make A-ANNO-DIMS current.

2. Set the Endpoint and Midpoint osnaps to be running, and then click the Linear button in the Dimensions panel or in the Annotation panel under the Home tab.

3. Click the upper-left corner of the rectangle, and then click the midpoint of the upper horizontal line of the rectangle.

4. Drag the dimension line up to a point about 1 unit above the upper line of the rectangle, and click.
   This places the first dimension.

5. Click the dimension to make grips appear.

6. Click the grip that is at the midpoint of the upper horizontal line of the rectangle, and with Polar Tracking on, drag it down to a point below the rectangle.

7. Press Esc to deselect the dimension.

8. Click the Continue button, and select the upper-right corner of the rectangle.
   Doing so places the second dimension.

9. Press Esc to end the command.

10. On the Home tab ➤ Properties panel, open the Linetype drop-down list and select Other.

11. In the Linetype Manager dialog box, click the Load button.

12. In the Load Or Reload Linetypes dialog box, scroll down, find and click Center2, and then click OK.
    The Center2 linetype now appears in the Linetype Manager dialog box.

13. Click OK.

14. Double-click the left dimension to open the Properties palette.

15. In the Lines & Arrows rollout, click Ext Line 2 Linetype.

16. Open the drop-down list and select Center2.

17. Press Esc to deselect the dimension.

18. Select the right dimension.

19. On the Properties palette, return to the Lines & Arrows rollout, and click Ext Line 1 Linetype.

20. Open the drop-down list and select Center2.

21. Press Esc to close the Properties palette.

Now there is a centerline through the rectangle that's part of the dimensions. As a final touch, you'll put a centerline symbol at the top of the centerline by using the MTEXT command:

1. Start the MTEXT (Multiline Text) command, and make a small defining window somewhere in a blank portion of the drawing area.

2. Expand the Symbol tool found on the contextual Text Editor Ribbon tab, and select Center Line.

A centerline symbol now appears in the Multiline Text Editor.

3. Highlight it, and change its height from 0.2000 to 0.4000 in the Text Height text box in the Text Style panel, as shown in Figure 12.69.

FIGURE 12.69 Changing the height of the centerline symbol

4. With the text still highlighted, click the Justification button in the Paragraph panel.

5. From the fly-out menu that appears, click Bottom Center (see Figure 12.70).

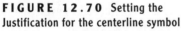

FIGURE 12.70 Setting the Justification for the centerline symbol

6. Click the Close Text Editor button in the Close panel to execute the changes and close the Multiline Text tab.

7. Click the centerline symbol to activate the grips.

8. Click the lower-middle grip, and then click the upper end of the centerline.

This locates the symbol properly.

9. Turn off running osnaps, be sure Polar Tracking is on, and click the same grip you did in the previous step.

10. Move the symbol up slightly to create a space between it and the centerline (see Figure 12.71).

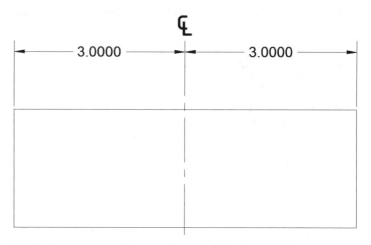

FIGURE 12.71 The centerline symbol and a centerline used as part of two dimensions

This completes the exercise. You can save the drawing if you wish.

Further Exercises

Use the skills you've learned in this chapter to do the following:

▶ Set up a dimension style for your own use.

▶ Dimension a drawing as you would in your own profession or trade.

▶ Dimension any of the other drawings offered in previous chapters, such as the block, the gasket, or the parking lot.

▶ Add dimensions to the cabin elevations.

Are You Experienced?

Now you can...

☑ create a new dimension style

☑ place vertical and horizontal dimensions in a drawing

☑ use radial, aligned, and angular dimensions

☑ create a multileader style

☑ create multileader lines for notes

☑ modify dimension text

☑ override a dimension style

☑ modify a dimension style

Managing External References

The floor plan of a complex building project might actually be a composite of several AutoCAD files that are linked together as external references to the current drawing. This enables parts of a drawing to be worked on at different workstations (or in different offices) while remaining linked to a central host file. In mechanical engineering, a drawing might similarly be a composite of the various subparts that make up an assembly.

External references, or *xrefs*, are DWG files that have been temporarily connected to the current drawing and are used as reference information. The externally referenced drawing is visible in the current drawing. You can manipulate its layers, colors, linetypes, and visibility, and you can modify its objects, but it isn't a permanent part of the current drawing. Changes made to the xref's appearance, such as color or linetype, in the current drawing are not reflected in the xref source drawing.

External references are similar to blocks in that they behave as single objects and are inserted into a drawing in the same way. But blocks are part of the current drawing file, and external references aren't.

Blocks can be exploded back to their component parts, but external references can't. However, external references can be converted into blocks and become permanent parts of the current drawing. In Chapter 7, "Combining Objects into Blocks," you were able to modify the window block and, in so doing, update all instances of the window block in the drawing without having to explode the block. With an external reference, you can apply the same updating mechanism. You can also edit an externally referenced drawing while in the drawing that references it. To manage external references, you need to learn how to set up an xref, manipulate its appearance in the host drawing, and update it.

Before you set up the xref, you'll create a site plan for the cabin. You'll then externally reference the site plan drawing into the cabin drawing. After these exercises, you'll look at a few ways that design offices use external references.

▶ **Understanding external references**

▶ **Creating external references**

▶ **Editing external references**

▶ **Converting external references into blocks**

Drawing a Site Plan

The site plan you'll use has been simplified so that you can draw it with a minimum number of steps and get on with the external referencing. The following are the essential elements:

- ▶ Property lines
- ▶ Access road to the site
- ▶ North arrow
- ▶ Indication of where the building is located on the site

In Figure 13.1, the lines of the site plan constitute the xref, and the rest of the objects are part of the host drawing.

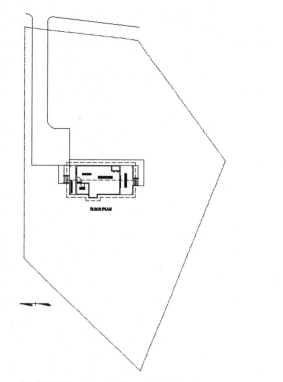

FIGURE 13.1 The cabin with the site plan as an external reference

The first step is to draw the property lines.

Using Surveyor's Units

You draw property lines by using Surveyor's units for angles and decimal feet for linear units. In laying out the property lines, you'll use relative polar coordinates: you'll enter coordinates in the format @*distance<angle*, in which the distance is in feet and hundredths of a foot, and the angle is in Surveyor's units to the nearest minute.

Introducing Surveyor's Units

Surveyor's units, called *bearings* in civil engineering, describe the direction of a line from its beginning point. The direction (bearing), described as a deviation from the north or south (up and down along the y-axis) toward the east or west (right and left along the x-axis), is given as an angular measurement in degrees, minutes, and seconds. The angles used in a bearing can never be greater than 90°, so bearing lines must be headed in one of the four directional quadrants: northeasterly, northwesterly, southeasterly, or southwesterly.

If north is set to be at the top of a plot plan, then south is down, east is to the right, and west is to the left. Therefore, when a line from its beginning goes up and to the right, it's headed in a northeasterly direction; when a line from its beginning goes down and to the left, it's headed in a southwesterly direction; and so on. A line that is headed in a northeasterly direction with a deviation from true north of 30° and 30 minutes is shown as N30d30'E in AutoCAD notation. Figure 13.2 shows examples of a line drawn using Surveyor's units.

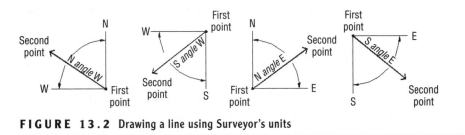

FIGURE 13.2 Drawing a line using Surveyor's units

With the Surveyor's unit system, a sloping line that has an up-and-to-the-left direction has a down-and-to-the-right direction if you start from the opposite end. So, in laying out property lines, it's important to move in the same direction (clockwise or counterclockwise) as you progress from one segment to the next.

The bigger reason to ensure that lines move in the same direction relates to the way property is recorded. In addition to a drawing, or *plat* as surveyors call it, each piece of property has what is known as a *legal description*. This legal description defines one corner as the starting or control point, and then proceeds to textually describe a piece of property by using bearings and distances. Each bearing and distance builds upon the previous and constructs what surveyors call a *traverse*.

N O T E   Constructing, balancing, and closing traverses is a topic unto itself. The point in introducing you to this concept is to help you understand how the geometry behind property lines is in many ways more important than the illustration itself. How you draw a property line has a profound effect on the way that parcel will be deeded and legally defined to a land owner.

Laying Out the Property Lines

Property lines are generally dimensioned using bearing and distance labels. These are different from the dimensions you created in Chapter 12, "Dimensioning a Drawing," as they are typically defined using a couple of pieces of text containing the direction (angle) and distance (length) of a line. Figure 13.3 shows how the piece of property for your cabin may be drawn by a surveyor. You'll set up a new drawing and use the bearings and distances shown in Figure 13.3 to create your cabin's property line in a counterclockwise direction.

1. Click the New button on the Quick Access toolbar, and open a new file using the acad.dwt template.

    All the units in these first few sections are noted as architectural and, in a later section, I'll show you how to bring in a drawing using a different scale.

2. From the Application menu, select Drawing Utilities ➢ Units to open the Drawing Units dialog box.

3. Change the Precision value in the Length group to two decimal places (0.00).

4. In the Angle group, open the Type drop-down list and select Surveyor's Units.

5. Change the Precision value to the nearest minute (N0d00′E).

    The floor plan drawings you have created so far defined each unit as an inch. Because this is a civil/survey drawing, you'll change that by making each drawing unit equal a foot.

6. Change the drawing's Insertion Scale by changing the Units To Scale Inserted Content drop-down list to Feet (Meters).

    Your Drawing Units dialog box should look like Figure 13.4.

You're using decimal linear units in such a way that 1 decimal unit represents 1 foot. In AutoCAD and LT, the foot symbol (′) is used only with architectural and engineering units.

7. Click OK.

You'll need an area of about 250′×150′ for the site plan.

8. Set the Drawing Limits by entering **LIMITS**↵ at the command line.

9. Press ↵ to accept the default of 0.00,0.00 for the lower-left corner. Enter **250,150**↵ (**76.2, 45.72**↵). Don't use the foot sign.

If the menu bar is loaded, you can also set the Drawing Limits from the Format menu.

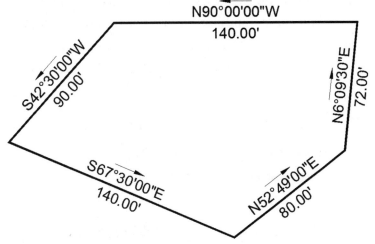

FIGURE 13.3 Property line with bearing and distance labels

FIGURE 13.4 The Drawing Units dialog box set up to use Surveyor's units

10. Enter **Z↵ E↵**, or double-click the middle mouse button to zoom to the drawing's extents.

11. Create a new layer called **C-PROP-LINE**.

12. Assign it the color 4 (Cyan) and make it current.

13. Turn on Dynamic Input in the status bar.

14. Start the LINE command. For the first point, enter **220,130↵ (67,40↵)**. This starts a line near the upper-right corner of the grid.

15. Make sure that Snap is turned off. Then enter the following:

    @140<N90DW↵ (@42<N90DW↵)

    @90<S42D30'W↵ (@27<S42D30'W↵)

    @140<S67D30'E↵ (@42<S67D30'E↵)

    @80<N52D49'E↵ (@24<N52D49'E↵)

    @72<N6D9'30"E↵ (@22<N6D9'30"E↵)

    ↵

The LINE command ends, and all five property lines are drawn (see Figure 13.5).

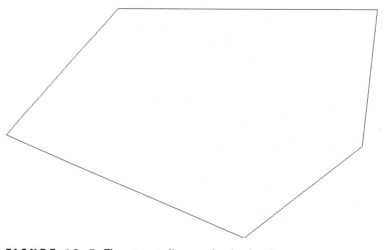

FIGURE 13.5 The property lines on the site drawing

16. Use the ZOOM command to zoom in very tightly on the upper-right corner of your property line.

    Notice how the last property line you drew extends past the starting point (see Figure 13.6). This happens because of the very small amount of rounding that occurs as line segments are drawn with angles to the nearest second. When surveyors use the term *balancing*, or closing a traverse, they are referring to the process of fixing this small margin of error.

17. Clean up the intersection by using the FILLET command with a 0 radius, and perform a Zoom Extents to bring the entire property back into view.

18. Save this drawing as **I13-01-PropertyLine.dwg (M13-01-Property Line.dwg)**.

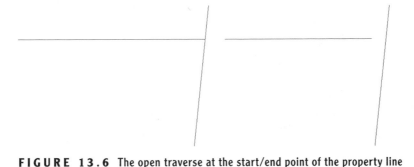

FIGURE 13.6 The open traverse at the start/end point of the property line

Drawing the Driveway

The driveway is 8′ (2.5 m) wide and set in 5′ (1.5 m) from the horizontal property line. The access road is 8′ from the parallel property line. The intersection of the access road line and the driveway lines forms corners; you'll create a *curb return* for each of these intersections with a 3′ radius. The driveway extends 70′ in from the upper-right corner of the property.

You'll continue by laying this out now:

1. Continue using I13-01-PropertyLine.dwg (M13-01-PropertyLine .dwg), or open it if it's not already open.

2. If the entire property line is not in view, perform a Zoom Extents and then zoom out a little more.

3. Offset the topmost horizontal property line 5′ (1.5 m) down. Offset this new line 8′ (2.5 m) down.

WARNING   As you enter distances, be sure to remember that 1 unit is equal to a foot, not an inch as with the floor plan drawings you've created up until this point. Consequently, you will enter *5* and *8* as the offset distances, not 5′ and 8′. Because each unit is equal to a foot, there is no need to include the foot mark after the number.

4. Offset the rightmost property line 8′ (2.5 m) to the right (see the top of Figure 13.7) to show the limits of the access road.

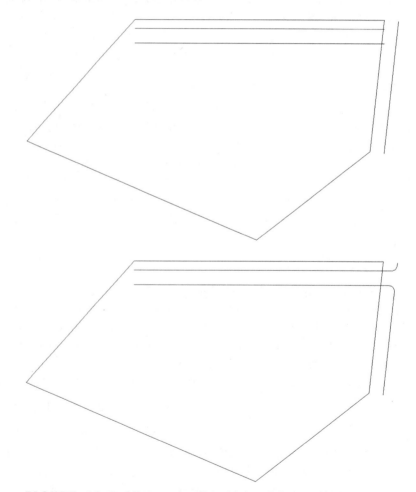

FIGURE 13.7 Offset property lines (top), and the completed intersection of the driveway and access road (bottom)

5. Create a new layer called **C-ROAD**.

6. Assign it the color 3 (Green) and make the C-ROAD layer current.

7. Select the three new lines, and open the Layer drop-down list in the Layers panel of the Home tab.

8. Click the C-ROAD layer to move the selected lines to the C-ROAD layer.

9. Press Esc to deselect the lines.

10. Extend the driveway lines to the access road line.

11. Trim the access road line between the driveway lines.

12. Fillet the two corners where the driveway meets the road by using a 3′ (1 m) radius (see the bottom of Figure 13.7).

13. Save this drawing as `I13-02-DrawingDriveway.dwg` (`M13-02-Drawing Driveway.dwg`).

Finishing the Driveway

A key element of any site plan is information that shows how the building is positioned on the site relative to the property lines. Surveyors stake out property lines. After staking out the property lines, the surveyor will then begin staking building offsets. They are generally placed at critical building corners and used by the contractor to begin constructing the building. In this site, you need only one corner because you're assuming that the front door of the cabin is facing due east.

A close look at Figure 13.1, shown earlier in this chapter, shows that the end of the driveway lines up with the top-rear corner of the cabin. Extending from the driveway are sidewalks that run to the front and rear steps. This locates the cabin on the site (see Figure 13.8).

Imagine the site being on the bluff of a hill overlooking land that falls away to the south and west, providing a spectacular view in that direction. To accommodate this view, you'll want to change the orientation of the site drawing when you externally reference it into the cabin drawing:

1. Continue using `I13-02-DrawingDriveway.dwg` (`M13-02-Drawing Driveway.dwg`), or open it if it's not already open.

2. On the status bar, turn on Object Snap Tracking and make sure the Endpoint osnap is running.

3. Start a line with the first point 83′ (25 m) to the left of the intersection of the upper driveway line and the property line.

4. Draw the line straight down 24′ (7.3 m).

5. Draw another line 22′ (6.7 m) to the right; then end the LINE command.

6. Offset the vertical line 22′ (6.7 m) to the right.
   This will mark the end of the driveway.

7. Fillet the intersection of the upper driveway line and the left vertical line with a radius of 0 and the intersection of the lower driveway line and the right vertical line with a radius of 6′(2 m), as shown in Figure 13.9.

8. To draw the rear sidewalk, use Object Snap Tracking to draw a line that starts 3.333′ [3′-4″ (1.02 m)] up from the lower-left corner of the driveway to a point **10.916′** [10′-11″⌐ (3.26 m)] to the left.

UNDERSTANDING SITE PLAN DIMENSIONING

Civil engineers and surveyors typically use labels instead of dimensions to represent the length of lines and arcs. Because there are no extension lines indicating what's being dimensioned, the placement of the label is key. Unless designated otherwise, a label represents the length of a line or curve until it ends or intersects with another object.

For instance, the 83′ driveway label indicates that the driveway is 83′ long from its intersection with the property line to the point where it ends near your cabin. Because there are no other intersections to consider, it would not matter whether the label were placed above or below the line. Label placement does, however, become important as we take a look at the lower edge of the driveway.

Aside from the start and endpoints, the top side of the lower edge of the driveway does not intersect with any other lines. Therefore the 22′ label indicates the overall length of the line (from endpoint to endpoint). The other side of the line is a slightly different story; the sidewalk intersects with it. Therefore the 18.5′ label indicates the length from the right endpoint to where the line intersects with the sidewalk.

Conventional dimensions like the ones you created in Chapter 12 are used only when representing the distance between two objects, and not for the length of an object. Take, for example, the width of the driveway or sidewalks. Because the measurement was between two objects, not a linear distance along a single object, a conventional dimension is used. As a reminder, the TYP abbreviation means *typical*. This tells you that all of the sidewalks are 3.5′ wide, and both curb returns have a radius of 3′.

9. Continue by drawing a line straight up 3.5′ [3′-6″ (1.06 m)] and then 10.916′ [10′-11″⌐ (3.26 m)] back to the right before you terminate the LINE command.

   See the top of Figure 13.10. You can refer back to Figure 13.8 to see the dimensions if necessary.

10. To draw the side and front sidewalk, start the LINE command again.

11. Pick the lower-left corner of the driveway as the first point.

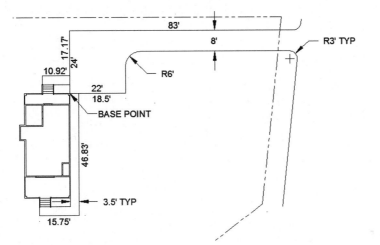

FIGURE 13.8 The driveway and patio lined up with the cabin

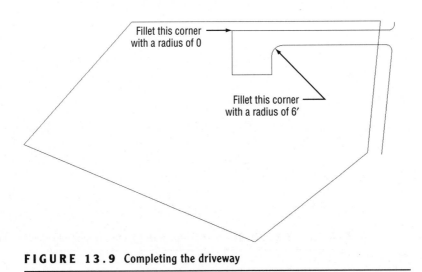

FIGURE 13.9 Completing the driveway

12. Either use the direct-entry method with the following distances to draw the remaining sidewalk lines, or enter the distances and angles as shown:

    43.333<270⏎ (13.22<270⏎)
    12.25<180⏎ (3.67<180⏎)
    3.5<270⏎ (1.06<270⏎)
    15.75<0⏎ (4.73<0⏎)

13. With the LINE command still running, use the Perpendicular osnap to finish the sidewalk, and press ⏎ to end the LINE command.

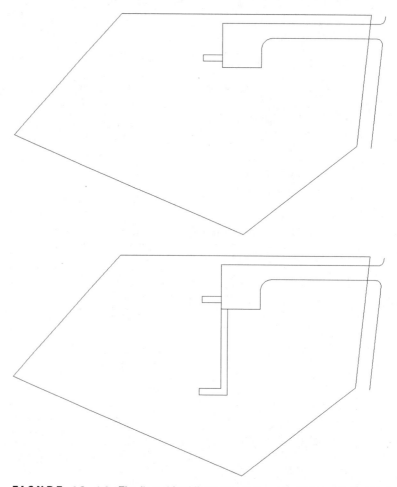

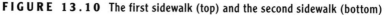

FIGURE 13.10 The first sidewalk (top) and the second sidewalk (bottom)

14. Create a new layer named **C-SWLK** with a color of 2 (Yellow).

N O T E   Because this is a decimal foot drawing, inches are entered as their decimal equivalent. For instance 4″ = 0.333′ because 4″ ÷ 12″ = 0.33. If this drawing were set up using architectural units, the distances in step 7 would be 43′-4″ (43.333), 12′-3″ (12.25), 3′-6″ (3.5), and 15′-9″ (15.75), respectively.

15. Move front and back sidewalks to the newly created layer.

The bottom of Figure 13.10 shows the completed side and front sidewalk.

16. Press ⏎ to end the command.

17. Save this drawing as `I13-03-FinishedDriveway.dwg` (`M13-02-Drawing Driveway.dwg`).

Adding a North Arrow

You've been identifying east to the right of the cabin and north to the top. Now you'll add a North arrow to identify the directions to anybody looking at your drawing. Here's how:

1. Create a new layer named **C-ANNO-NARW** with a color of 2 (Red), and set it as current.

2. Start the INSERT command, and use the Browse button to locate the `I-SITE-MISC-NARW.dwg` (`M-SITE-MISC-NARW.dwg`) file found in the Chapter 13 download.

If you haven't already, you can download the dataset for this chapter from this book's website at **www.sybex.com/go/autocad2012ner** or from **www.autocadner.com**.

3. From the Insert dialog box, make sure Insertion Point is the only property set to Specify On-Screen and click OK.

4. Place the block in the upper-left quadrant of the plan, just outside the property line, as shown in Figure 13.11.

5. Open the Layer Properties Manager dialog box and change the linetype for the C-PROP-LINE layer to PHANTOM2.

You'll have to load this linetype; review Chapter 6, "Using Layers to Organize Your Drawing," if necessary.

6. Verify that LTSCALE, PSLTSCALE, and MSLTSCALE are each set to 1, and change the Annotation Scale to 1:20 (1:2).

You'll see the PHANTOM2 linetype for the property lines.

Finally, you need to set the base point—that is, the location that will be attached to the cursor when this drawing is inserted as a block or external reference.

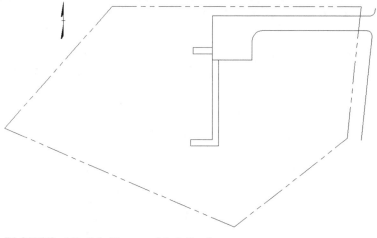

FIGURE 13.11 The completed site plan

7. Type **BASE.↵** and click the lower-left corner of the driveway. Refer to Figure 13.8 if necessary.

   Your drawing should look like Figure 13.11.

8. Save this drawing in your Training Data folder as **I13C-SPLAYO.dwg** (**M13C-SPLAYO.dwg**).

 T I P   **You can begin to see how NCS provides a certain consistency between disciplines. C is the discipline code for *civil plans*, and SP stands for *site plan*. Therefore, this is a civil site plan layout drawing.**

This completes the site plan. The next step is to attach the site plan as an external reference into the cabin drawing.

Setting Up an External Reference

When you set up an external reference, you go through a process similar to that of inserting a block into a drawing, as you did in Chapter 7. You select the drawing to be referenced and specify the location of its insertion point. There are options for the X scale factor, Y scale factor, and rotation angle, as there are for inserting blocks. Here, as with blocks, you can set up the command so that it uses the defaults for these options without prompting you for approval.

Using the External References Palette

You can run all external reference operations through the External References palette, which you can open by clicking the Insert tab and then clicking the External References button (small arrow in the lower-right corner) on the Reference panel, or by entering **XR↵**. The External References palette is capable of referencing a wide assortment of file types in addition to AutoCAD drawing (DWG) files. Popular *raster image* formats such as JPG and TIF can be referenced as images in addition to DWF, DGN, and PDF files. DWF files are *vector image* files produced by several Autodesk products and are similar to Adobe PDF files. Files that have the .dgn extension are drawings created with the MicroStation CAD software from Bentley Systems.

The following two series of steps will guide you through the process of attaching I13C-SPLAY0.dwg (M13C-SPLAY0.dwg) to I12A-FPLAY0.dwg (M12A-FPLAY0.dwg) as an xref:

1. Open I12A-FPLAY0.dwg (M12A-FPLAY0.dwg) from your Training Data folder (or from this chapter's download) and zoom to the drawing's extents.

2. Create a new layer called **A-ANNO-REFR**.

3. Assign color 7 (white) as the layer color, and make the A-ANNO-REFR layer current.

4. Click the Insert tab, and then click the External References button (small arrow in the lower-right corner of the Reference panel) to open the External References palette.

5. Click the Attach DWG button in the palette toolbar, as shown in Figure 13.12.
   The Select Reference File dialog box opens.

6. In the Select Reference File dialog box that opens, locate the Training Data folder (or the folder in which your training files are stored) and select I13C-SPLAY0.dwg (M13C-SPLAY0.dwg).
   A thumbnail image of the drawing appears in the preview window, as shown in Figure 13.13.

7. Click Open to open the Attach External Reference dialog box, and then click the Show Details button in the bottom-left corner to display the reference paths (see Figure 13.14).

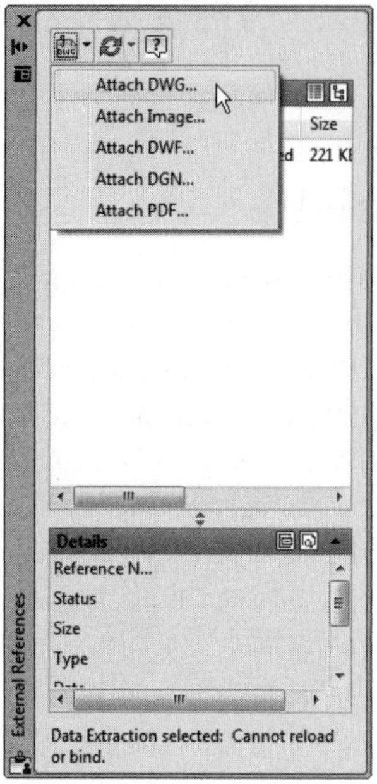

FIGURE 13.12 The Attach DWG
button on the External References palette

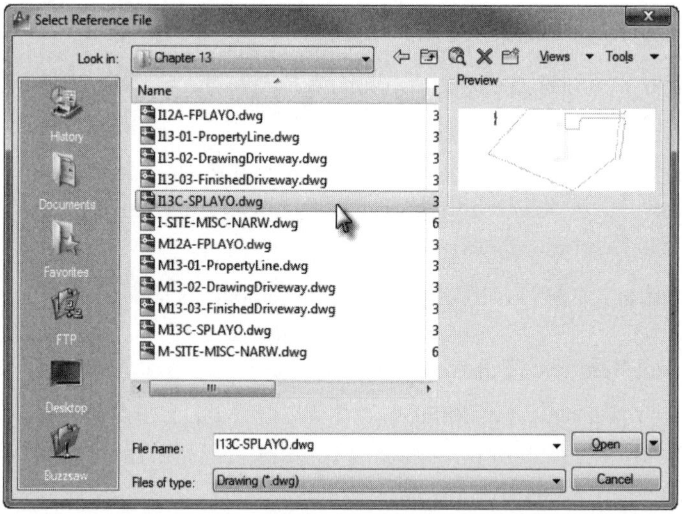

FIGURE 13.13 Select the xref in the Select Reference File dialog box.

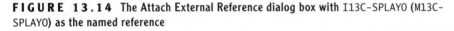

FIGURE 13.14 The Attach External Reference dialog box with I13C-SPLAYO (M13C-SPLAYO) as the named reference

The file being referenced, I13C-SPLAYO.dwg (M13C-SPLAYO.dwg), appears in the Name drop-down list at the top of the dialog box, with the full path of the file's location at the bottom. The middle of the dialog box contains three options for the insertion process, which are like those in the Insert dialog box that you used for inserting blocks in Chapter 7. Note that only the insertion point is set to be specified on the screen. The Scale and Rotation options should be set to use their default settings. If they aren't, click the appropriate check boxes so that this dialog box matches Figure 13.14. Continue as follows:

1. With the Attach External Reference dialog box still open, check Specify On-Screen for the Insertion Point, and leave it unchecked for Scale and Rotation.

2. Make sure Overlay is selected in the Reference Type group, and set the path type to Relative Path.

   The Attach External Reference dialog box should look like Figure 13.14.

3. Click OK.

   You return to your drawing, and the site plan drawing appears and moves with the base point attached to the crosshair cursor.

Note the difference between the Found In and Saved Path options listed at the bottom of the External References palette. The different path types are explained in the "Making Sense of the Different Path Types" sidebar.

MAKING SENSE OF THE DIFFERENT PATH TYPES

The default path type for external references is Full Path. When the Full Path option is selected, the referenced file is located at the absolute path that includes the drive, folder, and subfolder where the file is stored. Using this path type requires other users of the drawing to have the same file structure. This means that moving a referenced drawing from its original location will break the reference, and it will no longer display in your drawing unless you redefine the path.

Your second option is Relative Path. When this option is selected, AutoCAD will store a path relative to the host drawing. A major advantage of this method is seen when both drawings are stored on the same drive letter (C:\). Because both drawings are on the same drive, the relative path would not include the drive letter as the Full Path would. This means you can move your project to another drive or burn it to CD/DVD, and the external references will still work, provided the directory structure remains unchanged.

Since both the host drawing and reference drawing must be located in the same folder, the final option is hardly used. The No Path option does as its name implies, and stores only the drawing name. Consequently, AutoCAD will search only the same directory as the host file to resolve the reference.

Among the three choices available to you, the Relative Path option is the preferred choice. Should you choose to use the Relative Path option, make sure to save your drawing before you create the external reference. Because the reference path is based on where the two files are saved, the Relative Path option requires the drawing be saved prior to choosing it.

4. Click at the top-left corner of the rear deck post to be the insertion point, and then zoom to the drawing's extents.

The xref drawing is attached and appears in the site plan (see Figure 13.15).

 T I P   If the site plan I13C-SPLAYO (M13C-SPLAYO) **is screened back or transparent after attaching it as an xref, expand the Reference tab on the Insert tab and deselect the Xref Fading button.**

5. Save this drawing as **I13-04-ExternalReference.dwg** (M13-04-ExternalReference.dwg).

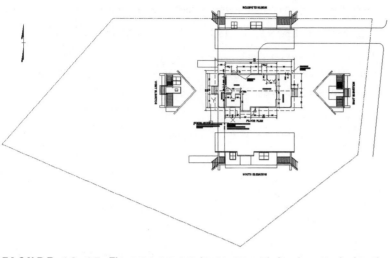

FIGURE 13.15 The I13C-SPLAY0 (M13C-SPLAY0) **drawing attached to the** I12A-FPLAY0 (M12A-FPLAY0) **drawing**

Notice the scale of the site layout drawing. Despite the difference in units (the site drawing was set up with each unit equal to a foot, and this floor plan drawing is set up with each unit equal to an inch), AutoCAD automatically scaled the site plan to the correct size. This conversion was performed based on the Insertion Units setting you made with the UNITS command. As you may recall, your floor plan drawing had this set to inches, whereas your site plan was set to feet. Being diligent as you set up your drawings has allowed you to work smarter by letting AutoCAD handle this small, but incredibly important detail.

ATTACHMENT AND OVERLAY: WHAT'S THE DIFFERENCE?

External references are especially popular in architectural and engineering projects. This is partially because each discipline is typically completed by separate teams. By dividing a project into logical segments with external references, one member of the architectural design team can work on the first-floor plan at the same time another team member is working on the first-floor furniture plan, for example. While the architectural team advances their design, a member of the electrical design team could reference their individual drawings to begin work on the first-floor lighting plan. External references also provide a way for project teams to assemble different plan sheets.

(Continues)

ATTACHMENT AND OVERLAY: WHAT'S THE DIFFERENCE? *(Continued)*

Because xrefs are such an integral part of so many projects, it's especially important to think before you reference. Choosing the wrong reference type can have an ill effect on the entire project.

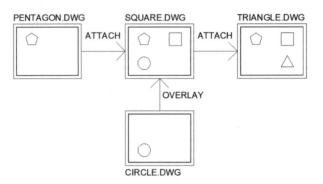

In this image, the SQUARE.DWG has two drawings referenced into it: PENTAGON .DWG and CIRCLE.DWG. The External Reference Type for PENTAGON.DWG is Attachment, whereas the External Reference Type for the CIRCLE.DWG is Overlay. Despite the differing reference types, there is no difference in what's shown in the SQUARE.DWG; you're able to see the pentagon, circle, and square.

The difference between the Attachment and Overlay reference types is not seen until you try referencing the SQUARE.DWG into another drawing—TRIANGLE.DWG in our example. Take note of the objects displayed in the TRIANGLE.DWG. Both the pentagon and square are shown; however, the circle is not.

The Overlay Reference Type

When an xref reference type is set to Overlay, that reference is dropped when referenced into another drawing. In the example, the CIRCLE.DWG was referenced into SQUARE.DWG as an overlay reference. As a result, it displays in SQUARE.DWG, but not when SQUARE.DWG is referenced into another drawing (TRIANGLE.DWG).

The Attachment Reference Type

When an xref Reference Type is set to Attachment, that reference always remains. Although PENTAGON.DWG was never referenced into TRIANGLE .DWG, the objects within it still display. In this scenario, PENTAGON.DWG

(Continues)

ATTACHMENT AND OVERLAY: WHAT'S THE DIFFERENCE? *(Continued)*

is a nested external reference. That is to say PENTAGON.DWG displays in TRIANGLE.DWG because it was attached to SQUARE.DWG, and it will be a nested reference in any drawing into which SQUARE.DWG is referenced.

Beware of Circular References

A danger of using the Attachment reference type is the potential for circular references. In the previous example, PENTAGON.DWG is attached to SQUARE.DWG, and SQUARE.DWG is attached to TRIANGLE.DWG. This means that PENTAGON.DWG is a nested reference inside TRIANGLE.DWG. Because the Attachment reference type was used, you cannot reference TRIANGLE.DWG into SQUARE.DWG or PENTAGON.DWG without creating a circular reference.

A circular reference occurs when a drawing contains a sequence of nested references that refer back to itself. Because everything to the left is a nested reference, the reference sequence PENTAGON.DWG → SQUARE.DWG → TRIANGLE.DWG → PENTAGON.DWG is a circular reference.

For this reason, I recommend that you always default to the Overlay reference type unless you have a very specific reason to use the Attachment reference type. Using the Overlay reference type will allow you to create references between any drawings without worrying about circular references.

Organizing the Drawing Objects

The attached xref appears exactly as it did when it was the current drawing. The drawing is cluttered now, and when you use this file as part of a site plan, or part of the cabin drawing, you don't want all the information to be visible. In fact, you want most of the information to be invisible. You'll ultimately accomplish this by freezing many of the layers in the drawing viewports, as explained in Chapter 14, "Using Layouts to Set Up a Print." For now, you'll just move the elevations and notes out of the site area by using a layer state to return to the current layer configuration. Here's how:

1. Continue using I13-04-ExternalReference.dwg (M13-04-External Reference.dwg), or open it if it's not already open.

2. Expand the Layer State drop-down list from the Layers panel on the Home tab, and select Manage Layer States (see Figure 13.16).

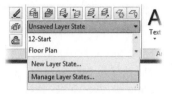

FIGURE 13.16 Accessing the
Layer States Manager from the Ribbon

3. In the Layer States Manager dialog box, click New and then name
   this new state **Plan and Elev No Hatch**.

4. Click OK to close the New Layer State To Save dialog box.

5. Click Close to save the layer state and return to the drawing.

6. Turn on and thaw all the layers.

**Experiment with
the** LAYON **(Turn
All Layers On) and**
LAYTHW **(Thaw All
Layers) commands
found by expanding
the Layers panel on
the Home tab.**

7. Carefully move the elevations and notes outside of the property line.
   Figure 13.17 shows the elevations stacked on the right side of the
   drawing area.

8. Expand the Layer States drop-down list once again and choose the
   Plan And Elev No Hatch state.
   This restores the selected state, and the layers return to the condi-
   tions they had when the layer state was saved.

9. Save this drawing as **I13-04-ExternalReference.dwg** (**M13-04-External
   Reference.dwg**).

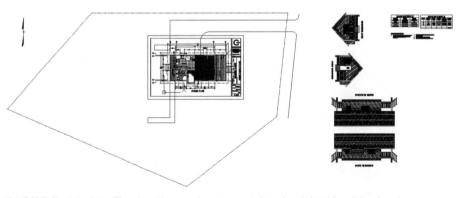

FIGURE 13.17 The elevations and notes moved to the right side of the drawing area

Moving and Rotating an Xref

Now you need to rotate the site plan to match the orientation of the cabin:

1. Continue using I13-04-ExternalReference.dwg (M13-04-External Reference.dwg), or open it if it's not already open.

2. Freeze the A-ANNO-DIMS layer.

3. Start the ROTATE command, click the site plan, and then press ↵.

4. To specify the insertion point of the xref as the rotation point, activate the Insert object snap and then click any object from the site plan.

5. At the Specify rotation angle or: prompt, enter **90**↵.
   The site plan is rotated 90° counterclockwise, matching the orientation of the cabin (see Figure 13.18).

6. Save the current drawing, I13-05-OrganizeObjects.dwg (M13-05 -OrganizeObjects.dwg), as **I13-06-XRefRotate.dwg (M13-06-XRef Rotate.dwg)**.

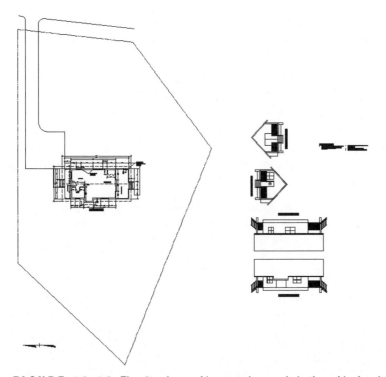

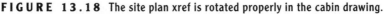

FIGURE 13.18 The site plan xref is rotated properly in the cabin drawing.

You have established I13C-SPLAY0 (M13C-SPLAY0) as an external reference in this drawing. The next step is to make revisions to I13C-SPLAY0 (M13C-SPLAY0) and see how they are reflected in the host drawing.

Modifying an Xref Drawing

You can modify an xref drawing by following this general procedure:

1. Make the xref the current drawing.

2. Make the modification.

3. Save the changes.

4. Make the host drawing current.

5. Reload the xref.

AutoCAD users can also modify an xref by using a special modification command while the host drawing is current. This section demonstrates both methods. You'll start by opening I13C-SPLAY0.dwg (M13C-SPLAY0.dwg) and adjusting the width of the road. Then you'll make I13C-SPLAY0 (M13C-SPLAY0) current again and use AutoCAD to modify the site plan as an xref, changing the property line and moving the North arrow.

Modifying an Xref by Making It the Current Drawing

The longest part of the driveway is 8'-0" wide, and you want to increase that to 10'-0". You'll make the change in the site plan drawing and then reload it into the cabin drawing:

1. With I13C-SPLAY0.dwg (M13C-SPLAY0.dwg) as the current drawing, zoom in to the area that includes the road and the driveway.

2. Offset the lower road line 2' (0.6 m) downward, as shown in the top of Figure 13.19.

3. Fillet the right side with a radius of 3' (1 m) and the left at 6' (2 m).

4. Delete the original line and radii.
   Your driveway is now 10' wide, as shown at the bottom of Figure 13.19.

5. Save the I13C-SPLAY0.dwg (M13C-SPLAY0.dwg) drawing.

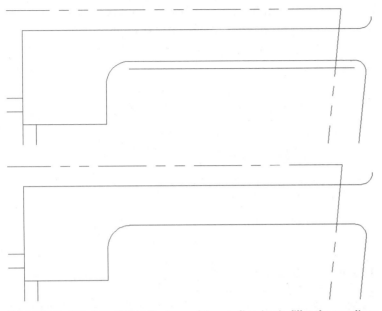

FIGURE 13.19 Offset the lower driveway line (top), fillet the new lines, and delete the existing radii (bottom).

N O T E   Remember that 1 unit in the site plan drawing is equal to a foot, not an inch as in the floor plan drawing. Consequently, the foot mark is not needed as you enter distances. For example, to complete step 2, enter 2↵, not 2′.

Although you'll make more changes later, this concludes the modifications you'll make to the site plan in this exercise. Now you can return to the cabin drawing.

1. Switch to the I13C-SPLAYO.dwg (M13C-SPLAYO.dwg) file.

   A balloon message appears at the bottom of the AutoCAD window (see Figure 13.20), pointing to the Manage Xrefs icon in the tool tray. This indicates that an externally referenced drawing has been saved after it was attached to the current drawing. You could click the blue link text to reload the file, but for this exercise, you will look at the External References palette and reload the file from there.

2. Open the External References palette, as shown in Figure 13.21, and stretch it to make it wider.

   The palette shows most of the pertinent information regarding the externally referenced files in the scene, including the status.

When you pause the cursor over a reference, a cue card displays a thumbnail image and additional information about that file. In this case, the palette indicates that I13C-SPLAY0 (M13C-SPLAY0) needs reloading.

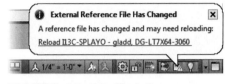

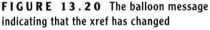

FIGURE 13.20 The balloon message indicating that the xref has changed

FIGURE 13.21 The External References palette showing the status of the xrefs

3. Select the I13C-SPLAY0 (M13C-SPLAY0) xref in the palette, right-click, and choose Reload from the context menu.

This causes AutoCAD to reevaluate the external reference and update the current drawing. The cabin drawing now shows the 10′ wide access road from the site plan drawing (see Figure 13.22).

4. Close the I13C-SPLAY0 (M13C-SPLAY0) file, but leave the I13-06-XRef Rotate.dwg (M13-06-XRefRotate.dwg) file open.

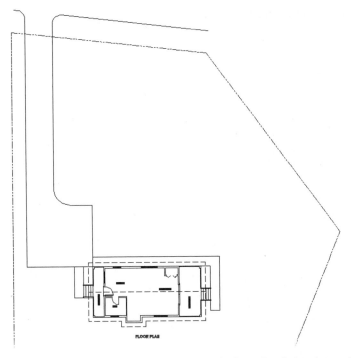

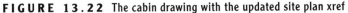

FLOOR PLAN

FIGURE 13.22 The cabin drawing with the updated site plan xref

In this exercise, you saw how a host drawing is updated when the drawing that is externally referenced is made current, modified, saved, and then reloaded as an xref. Layers become an even more important tool when using external references. You can set them up one way in the actual drawing and another way in the xref of that drawing in a host file. In fact, you can externally reference the same drawing into any number of host files; have the layer characteristics of visibility, color, and linetype be different in each host file; and save them as such with each host file. External referencing is a powerful feature of AutoCAD, and you'll learn more about the possible applications of this tool toward the end of this chapter.

Modifying an Xref from within the Host Drawing

Sometimes all you need to do is make a minor edit to a referenced drawing. The Edit Reference In-Place (REFEDIT) command provides an excellent way of doing this without leaving the drawing you're in. You can't do things like create a new layer with this tool, but many of the regular editing commands are available when you use it. You'll make a few modifications to the site plan xref to demonstrate this feature.

1. In the I13-06-XRefRotate.dwg (M13-06-XRefRotate.dwg) file, make layer 0 current.

2. Zoom in to see the cabin and the lower portion of the property line (see Figure 13.23).

3. Select the property line or any other object belonging to the I13C -SPLAY0.dwg (M13C-SPLAY0.dwg) drawing.

   This opens the contextual External Reference Ribbon tab (Figure 13.24), which contains many of the most commonly used External Reference commands.

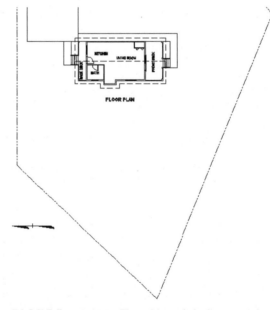

FIGURE 13.23 The cabin and the lower portion of the property line

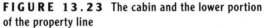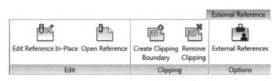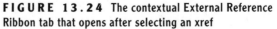

FIGURE 13.24 The contextual External Reference Ribbon tab that opens after selecting an xref

4. On the Edit panel of the contextual External Reference tab, pick the Edit Reference In-Place (REFEDIT) command.

    Alternatively, you could also start the REFEDIT command from the Reference panel on the Insert tab, or by selecting the xref and using the right-click contextual menu to choose the Edit Xref In-Place option. The Reference Edit dialog box opens (see Figure 13.25). On the Identify Reference tab, I13C–SPLAYO (M13C–SPLAYO) is listed as the selected xref with the North Arrow block shown as a nested reference. A preview window illustrates the xref drawing.

The REFEDIT command edits both blocks and xrefs. So, in AutoCAD's technical vocabulary for this command and its prompts, both blocks and xrefs are referred to as *references*.

FIGURE 13.25 The Reference Edit dialog box

5. Click OK. The contextual Edit Reference panel appears at the right end of every Ribbon tab.

WARNING   If you have the AutoSave tool set to periodically save your drawing automatically (Application menu ➢ Options ➢ Open and Save ➢ File Safety Precautions ➢ Automatic Save or SAVETIME↵), this feature is disabled during reference editing.

    You're now free to use many of the drawing and modifying commands on the site plan drawing that you just selected.

6. Open the Layer Properties Manager and notice that several new layers now appear.

    At the top are

    ▶ 0C-PROP-LINE

    ▶ 0C-ROAD

Lower in the list are

▶ 0-REfEdit0

▶ I13C-SPLAYO |C-PROP-LINE (M13C-SPLAYO |C-PROP-LINE)

▶ I13C-SPLAYO |C-ROAD (M13C-SPLAYO |C-ROAD)

The layer names separated by the pipe (|) symbol indicate that these are layers from the externally referenced C-SPLAY1 drawing and are referred to as *xref-dependent*. C-SPLAY1|C-PROP-LINE and C-SPLAY1|C-ROAD appear in the Layer Properties Manager even when you are not editing an xref in-place.

One restriction in the layer tools is that you can't make an xref-dependent layer current in the host drawing. The layers at the top of dialog box, the ones with the dollar sign ($) symbols, are temporary and will hold any objects created on them in the editing session and then shift those objects to the proper xref layer at the conclusion of the editing session.

7. Make the 0C-PROP-LINE layer current, and then offset the lower-right diagonal property line 10'-0" (3048) to the right (see Figure 13.26).

WARNING   When using the REFEDIT command to modify a drawing that has different units than the current drawing, the current drawing always takes precedence. In this example, although the reference you're editing is set up in decimal feet, the current drawing is set up in architectural units. Consequently, you must enter the foot symbol to offset the property line 10'.

8. Fillet the two lines that intersected with the line you just offset to the newly created line by using a radius of 0.

9. Erase the original line (see Figure 13.26).

 10. Select the Save Changes button on the contextual Edit Reference Ribbon panel appended to the end of each Ribbon tab.

11. When the Warning dialog box opens, click OK.
    Your changes to the site plan are now saved back to the I13C-SPLAYO .dwg (M13C-SPLAYO.dwg) file, and the Edit Reference In-Place tool is terminated.

12. Use Zoom To Extents, and then zoom out a little to a view of the whole site (see Figure 13.27).

13. Save this drawing. It's still named I13-06-XRefRotate.dwg (M13-06 -XRefRotate.dwg).

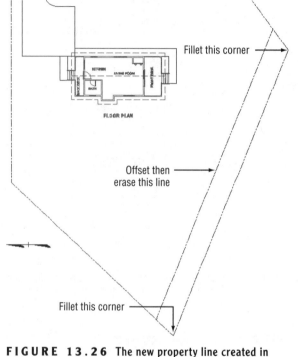

FLOOR PLAN

Fillet this corner

Offset then erase this line

Fillet this corner

FIGURE 13.26 The new property line created in the externally referenced site plan

In this exercise, you saw how a host drawing is updated when its external reference is changed and how you can control the appearance of objects in the xref drawing from the host drawing by working with the xref-dependent layers. You also saw how you can modify objects in the xref from the host drawing by using the in-place xref editing tool. A drawing can serve as an external reference in several host drawings at the same time and have a different appearance in each one, including location, rotation, and scale. The results of in-place xref editing, however, must be saved back to the original drawing in order to be viewed in the xref. In-place xref editing is usually done only when the results are meant to be permanent changes in the original source drawing.

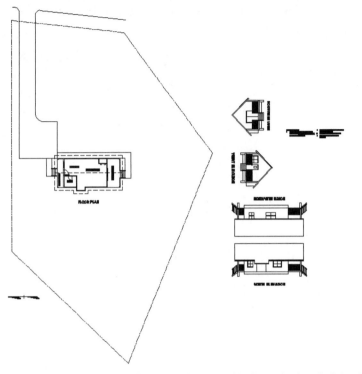

FIGURE 13.27 The floor plan drawing with the revised xref of the site plan

Adding an Image to a Drawing

Not only can you externally reference other drawing files into the current drawing, but you can also reference image files. Using this feature, you can add digital photographs or scanned images, such as artist renderings and construction forms, to a drawing. The procedure is similar to adding an externally referenced drawing; just follow these steps:

1. Continue using I13-06-XRefRotate.dwg (M13-06-XRefRotate.dwg), or open it if it's not already open.

2. Create a new layer named **A-ANNO-REFR-IMAG**, and make it current.

3. Open the External References palette from the View tab ➢ Palettes panel.

4. Right-click a blank area in the File References area below the existing filenames, and choose Attach Image from the context menu shown in Figure 13.28 to open the Select Image File dialog box.

You can also click the down-arrow next to the Attach DWG button and choose Attach Image from the context menu.

5. Navigate to the CabinLand.jpg file included with the download for this chapter, and then click the Open button (see Figure 13.29).

You can download the CabinLand.jpg file from this book's web page, **www.sybex.com/go/autocad2012ner** or **www.autocadner.com**.

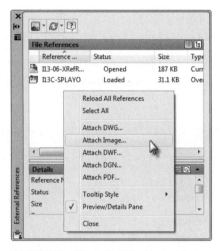

FIGURE 13.28 Attaching an image from the External References palette

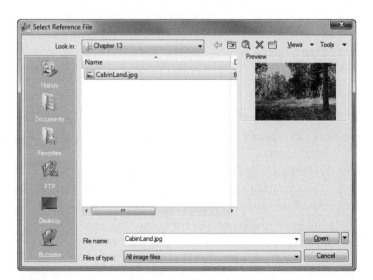

FIGURE 13.29 Selecting the image to be referenced in the Select Reference File dialog box

Most of the common image file formats, such as JPG and TIF, are compatible with AutoCAD 2012.

N O T E   AutoCAD 2012 expands the list of compatible formats to include other popular image file formats, such as USGS Digital Orthophoto Quadrangle (DOQ); Multiresolution Seamless Image Database, or MrSID (SID); and Adobe Photoshop (PSD) documents. Both DOQ and SID files are especially popular in the civil engineering and geographical information systems (GIS) fields, whereas Adobe Photoshop documents are popular in graphic design fields.

The Attach Image dialog box that opens is similar to the External Reference dialog box that you saw earlier in this chapter.

6. Select Relative Path for the path type. Check the Specify On-Screen options for both Scale and Insertion point (see Figure 13.30), and then click OK.

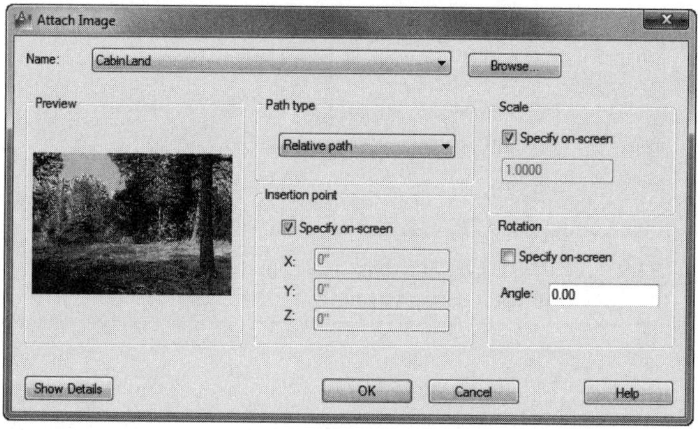

FIGURE 13.30 Select Relative Path for the path type in the Attach Image dialog box.

7. In the drawing area, click once to designate the lower-left corner of the image, move the cursor, and then click again to create the rectangular frame for the image.

The image appears inside the frame (see Figure 13.31). The exact size and location of the frame are unimportant for this exercise, so ignore them for now. In the next chapter, you will decide how to view the image in the context of the rest of the drawing.

When you select an image file, a preview appears in the Select Reference File dialog box. You can use the arrow buttons on the keyboard to quickly change the selection and associated preview image.

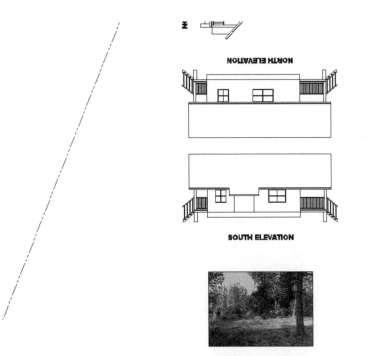

FIGURE 13.31 Placing the referenced image in the drawing

The IMAGEFRAME variable determines the visibility of the image frame:

▶ Setting the variable to 0 (zero) causes the frame to be invisible.

▶ Setting the variable to 1 displays the frame, and also shows the frame when the drawing is plotted (plotting is covered in Chapter 15, "Printing an AutoCAD Drawing").

▶ Setting IMAGEFRAME to 2 displays the frame in the viewport, but it does not display the frame when the drawing is plotted.

This variable affects all the images in the drawing, and prior to AutoCAD 2012, also controlled whether an image could be selected.

8. Enter IMAGEFRAME↵ 0↵ to set the variable to 0.

9. Save the cabin drawing as I13A-FPLAYO.dwg (M13A-FPLAYO.dwg) and then close the file.

That's all there is to adding images to AutoCAD drawings. You can move and rotate the image by using the same tools as with any other object. You can resize the image by selecting the frame and adjusting the grips. You get access to some rudimentary image-editing tools when you double-click the image frame. Feel free to experiment with those tools, but do not be concerned about altering the image file; these adjustments affect only the image's display inside AutoCAD.

Putting Xrefs to Use

External references have many different uses. I'll describe two common applications to illustrate their range.

Suppose you're working on a project as an interior designer and a subcontractor to the lead architect. The architect gives you a drawing of a floor plan that is still undergoing changes. You load this file onto your hard drive in a specially designated folder, and then you externally reference it into your drawing as a background—a drawing to be used as a reference to draw over. You can proceed to lay out furniture, partitions, and so on while the architect is still refining the floor plan.

At an agreed-on time, the architect gives you a revised version of the floor plan. You overwrite the one that you have on your computer with the latest version. You can then reload the xref into your furniture layout drawing, and the newer version of the floor plan will be the background. In this example, the lead architect might also send the same version of the floor plan to the structural and mechanical engineers and the landscape architect, all of whom are working on the project and using the architect's floor plan as an xref in their respective host drawings (see Figure 13.32).

Xrefs are often used when parts of a job are being done in an office where a network is in place. Suppose a project involves work on several buildings that are all on the same site. If the project uses xrefs, each building can be externally referenced to the site plan. This keeps the site plan drawing file from getting too large and allows the project work to be divided among different workstations; in addition, the project manager can open the host site plan and keep track of progress on the whole project (see Figure 13.33).

These two applications for setting up xrefs in relation to a host file are applicable to almost any profession or trade using AutoCAD.

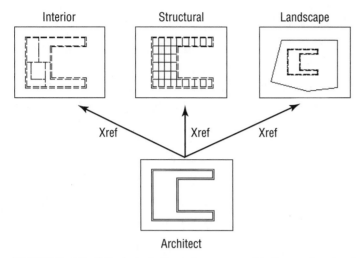

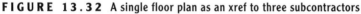

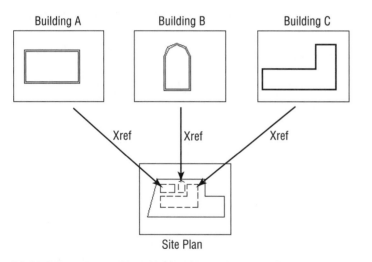

FIGURE 13.32 A single floor plan as an xref to three subcontractors

FIGURE 13.33 Three buildings as xrefs to a single site plan

Exploring Additional Xref Features

You have seen how you can modify an xref in the host or the original drawing and how to bring in images. A few other features of external references deserve mention.

Setting the Xref Path

When you attach an xref to the host drawing, AutoCAD stores the name of the xref and its path.

Each time you open the host drawing, AutoCAD searches for any xrefs saved with the host file and displays them in the host drawing. If the xref drawing is moved to a new folder after the xref has been attached to a host, AutoCAD won't be able to find the xref or display it. To avoid that situation, you must update the host drawing with the new path to the xref file. Let's go through a quick exercise to illustrate how this works:

1. Use Windows Explorer to create a new subfolder called **Xref** within the Training Data folder you previously set up.

2. Move I13C-SPLAYO.dwg (M13C-SPLAYO.dwg) to this folder.

3. Return to AutoCAD and open I13A-FPLAYO.dwg (M13A-FPLAYO.dwg) again.

   The xref doesn't show up, and the References - Unresolved Reference Files dialog box opens (see Figure 13.34).

   AutoCAD is unable to find the xref because the path has changed.

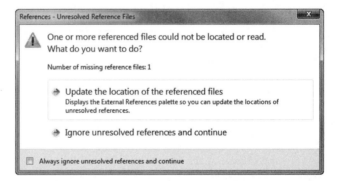

FIGURE 13.34 References - Unresolved Reference Files dialog box

4. Click the Update The Location Of The Referenced Files option to open the External References palette.

   In the Details area where xrefs are listed, the path appears for each xref under the heading Saved Path (see Figure 13.35). The dot back-slash (.\) preceding the filename indicates that the current file path is relative and in the same folder as the current drawing. You can slide the scroll bar to the right—or widen the palette—to see the full path. Notice also that the Status column for this xref reads Not Found.

5. Click the I13C-SPLAYO (M13C-SPLAYO) xref to highlight it.

6. Move down to the Details area, and click the blank space to the right of Found At.

7. A button with three dots appears at the right end of the blank space. Click it.

   This opens the Select New Path dialog box.

8. Find the I13C-SPLAYO.dwg (M13C-SPLAYO.dwg) drawing in the new Xref folder, highlight it, and click Open.

   Back in the External References palette, the path has been updated to reflect the current location for I13C-SPLAYO.dwg (M13C-SPLAYO.dwg).

9. Move or minimize the palette and then perform a Zoom Extents.

   You can see that the xref is restored in your drawing.

 W A R N I N G   When you're working with xrefs, be careful where you store files that are acting as xrefs to other files. All the files' paths must remain valid for the xrefs to be located.

FIGURE 13.35 The missing xref is identified in the External References palette.

Binding Xrefs

On occasion, you'll want to attach an xref to the host drawing permanently. If you send your drawing files to a printing service to be plotted, including a set of xref files can complicate things. Also, for archiving finished work, it might be better to reduce the number of files. On some occasions, the xref might be revised for the last time and no longer need to be a separate file. In all these situations, you'll use the BIND command to convert an external reference into a block that is stored permanently in the host drawing:

1. In the External References palette, right-click I13C-SPLAY0 (M13C -SPLAY0) in the File References list.

2. Choose Bind from the context menu to open the Bind Xrefs/DGN Underlays dialog box (see Figure 13.36).

FIGURE 13.36 The Bind Xrefs/DGN Underlays dialog box

The two options in the Bind Type area have to do with how layers are treated when an xref is bound to the host drawing:

Bind   This is the default. It sets the xref layers to be maintained as unique layers in the host drawing.

Insert   With the Insert option, layers that have the same name in the two drawings are combined into one layer.

None of the layers in I13C-SPLAY0.dwg (M13C-SPLAY0.dwg) has the same name as any layer in I13A-FPLAY0.dwg (M13A-FPLAY0.dwg). Let's use the Insert option.

3. Change the Bind Type to Insert, and click OK.
   The xref disappears from the File References list.

4. Close the External References palette.
   Your drawing looks unchanged.

5. Click the site plan and then open the Properties palette.

The field at the top of the palette identifies the site plan as a block reference, as shown in Figure 13.37.

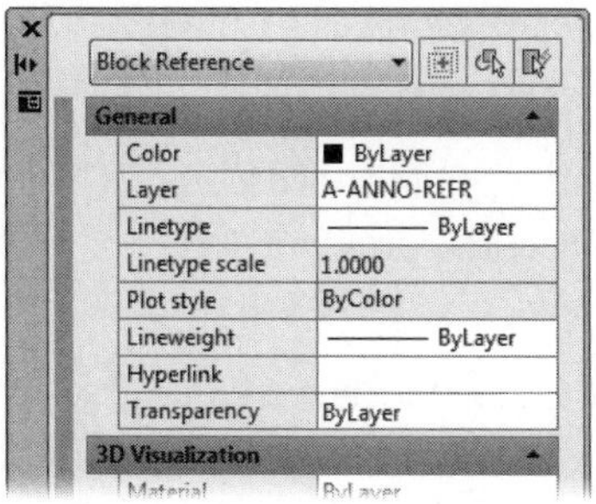

FIGURE 13.37 The top of the Properties palette with the former xref selected

6. Open the Layer Properties Manager.

    Figure 13.38 shows that the site plan's layers have all become layers in the I13A-FPLAYO.dwg (M13A-FPLAYO.dwg) drawing and no longer have the I13C-SPLAYO| (M13C-SPLAYO|) prefix.

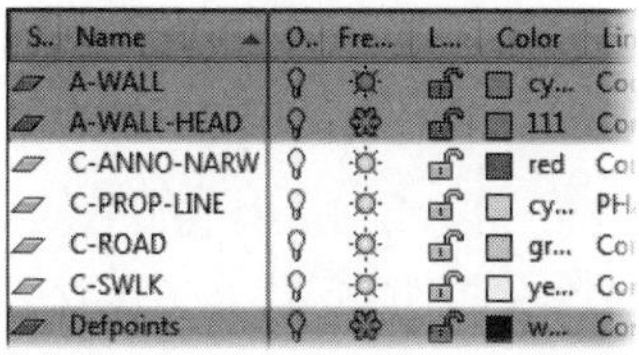

FIGURE 13.38 The Layer Properties Manager showing the new layers

7. Click the Insert button in the Block panel of the Insert tab.

8. In the Insert dialog box, open the Name drop-down list.

    I13C-SPLAYO (M13C-SPLAYO) is listed here as a block, along with the window and door blocks that you created in Chapter 7 and the Grid and North Arrow blocks. A few additional blocks might be on the list. These blocks are used by the dimensions in the drawing.

9. Close the drop-down list by clicking a blank portion of the dialog box, and then click Cancel to return to your drawing.

    The site plan is now a permanent part of the I13A-FPLAYO.dwg (M13A-FPLAYO.dwg) drawing. If you need to make changes to the site plan part of the drawing, you can explode it and use the Modify commands. To edit the site plan while preserving it as a block, you can use the REFEDIT (Edit Reference In-Place) command, and the BEDIT (Block Edit) tool that you used previously in Chapter 7 to modify the window block.

10. You do not want to save the changes in this drawing. Click the Close button in the top-right corner of the drawing area, and then click No in the dialog box that opens.

11. Move the I13C-SPLAYO (M13C-SPLAYO) file back into the Training Data folder where it was prior to starting the exercises in the "Exploring Additional Xref Features" section.

This has been a quick tour of the basic operations used to set up and control external references. There are more features and commands for working with xrefs than I've covered here, but you now know enough to start working with them.

Exploring Further on Your Own

What follows are a few additional operations and features that you might find useful when you delve more deeply into external references. Play around a little and see what you can do:

▶ Externally referenced drawings can also be hosts and have drawings externally referenced to them. These are called *nested xrefs*. There is no practical limit to the number of levels of nested xrefs that a drawing can have.

▶ You can't explode an xref, but you can detach it from the host. The DETACH command is on the context menu that appears when you right-click an xref in the External References palette.

▶ Large, complex drawings that are externally referenced often have their insertion points coordinated in such a way that all xrefs are attached at the 0,0 point of the host drawing. This helps keep drawings aligned properly. By default, any drawing that is externally referenced into a host drawing uses 0,0 as its insertion point. However, you can change the coordinates of the insertion point with the BASE command. With the drawing you want to change current, enter BASE↵ and enter the coordinates for the new insertion point.

▶ You can limit which layers and, to some degree, which objects in a drawing are externally referenced in the host drawing by using indexing and demand loading.

▶ A host drawing can be externally referenced into the drawing that has been externally referenced into the host, causing a circular reference. An option to avoid this scenario is to choose the Overlay option in the Attach External Reference dialog box. Overlays ignore circular xrefs.

▶ If you freeze the layer that was current when an xref was attached, the entire xref is frozen. Turning off this same layer has no effect on the visibility of the xref.

▶ The Unload option—available when you right-click a reference in the External References palette—lets you deactivate xrefs without detaching them from the host file. They stay on the list of xrefs and can be reloaded at any time with the Reload option. This option can be useful when you're working with complex drawings that have many xrefs.

If You Would Like More Practice...

External references provide a versatile way to organize and collaborate on projects. Creating individual files for the various components of a project allows several team members to collaborate in tandem with each other. It is likewise important to consider how you choose to structure this collaborative environment. The following exercises explore both of these concepts, first by creating separate reference files, and then by testing the different reference types:

Building Architectural References

In this chapter, you externally referenced the site plan drawing into the cabin drawing as an architect who was designing the project might have done. If you were the architect, you might want to have several additional drawings. Try doing this:

1. Create several new drawings of furniture and a shed.
   Each object is to have its own layer. Make more than one drawing for some of the objects, such as two beds or tables.

2. Add digital images on their own layers that show real-world examples of the furniture.

3. Externally reference all the furniture and shed drawings into the cabin drawing.

4. Use the Layer States Manager, as covered in Chapter 6, to create layer states for each combination of furniture.

Compare Reference Types

Try using the files found in the `RefTypes` directory of this chapter's download to test out the Attachment and Overlay reference types. See what happens if you try to create a circular reference by doing the following:

1. Open `SQUARE.DWG`, and load `PENTAGON.DWG` as an Attachment reference.

2. Also load `CIRCLE.DWG` as an Overlay reference.
   Use an insertion point of `0,0` and scale of `1` for all xrefs in this exercise.

3. Save `SQUARE.DWG` and open `PENTAGON.DWG`.

4. Use the XREF command to load `SQUARE.DWG`.

5. Save and close the `SQUARE.DWG` and open `TRIANGLE.DWG`.

6. Attach `SQUARE.DWG` to `TRIANGLE.DWG` as either an Attachment or Overlay reference type.

Are You Experienced?

Now you can...

☑ **draw a basic site plan**

☑ **use Surveyor's units to lay out a property line**

☑ **attach an external reference**

☑ **revise a drawing that is externally referenced**

☑ **modify an xref from the host drawing**

☑ **insert image files into an AutoCAD drawing**

☑ **update an xref path**

☑ **bind an xref to a host file**

Using Layouts to Set Up a Print

A design is only as good as your ability to communicate that design with the people building it. Printing, or *plotting* as it's called in AutoCAD, is considered by many to be the final phase of that communication process. Preparing a document set can be just as challenging as plotting it. In this chapter, you will set up sheet files in a way that maximizes the potential of layers and external references. You will learn to further automate the management of your drawing sheets by using Sheet Set Manager.

As you work through this and the next chapter, you'll quickly discover the incredible control you have over nearly every aspect of how a drawing plots. This versatility means you can probably get AutoCAD to plot exactly the way you want it to. However, remembering each of those settings can prove challenging. Consequently, the key to getting consistent plots is to find a way to capture all of those settings in a way that will allow you to reuse them for new drawings in the future.

This chapter strives to employ the most widely accepted practices with a specific focus on capturing settings so they can be reused later. To ensure that you can work through this chapter's exercises exactly as shown in this book, you'll configure your drawings to plot to a DWF file. Plotting to a DWF file is exactly the same as plotting to a real printer. The only difference is the output; instead of a physical print, you'll have a DWF file, which you can view onscreen like a PDF.

To get to a point where you can begin plotting, you will apply the knowledge you've gained from numerous chapters throughout this book, including Chapter 6, "Using Layers to Organize Your Drawing," Chapter 9, "Using Dynamic Blocks and Tables," and Chapter 13, "Managing External References."

▶ **Putting a title block in a layout**

▶ **Setting up viewports in a layout**

▶ **Locking the display of viewports**

▶ **Controlling visibility in viewports**

▶ **Adding text in a layout**

Getting Ready

So far, all of your work has been done in model space. There you drew your cabin by using real-world units, meaning that if a wall was 6′, you drew the wall 6′. It's certainly not possible to print the cabin by using real-world units. Instead, you need to somehow reduce its size. This is where a list of standard scales used by architects and engineers, such as 1/8″ or 1/4″ = 1′-0″ (or 1 = 50), comes into play.

The standard way of accomplishing this is with layout tabs, sometimes referred to by their former name of paper space. Each layout is assigned a printer and paper size, and you adjust the positioning of the drawing and the scale of the print. The part that is difficult to understand is the way two scales are juxtaposed in the same file: the scale of the drawing on the printed paper (usually a standard scale used by architects, such as 1/8″ or ¼″ = 1′-0″ or 1 = 50), and the scale of the layout, which is almost always 1:1, or the actual size of the paper. Other professionals, such as mechanical or civil engineers, set up their drawings the same way. They may use a different set of standard scales such as 1″ = 30′ for the drawing, but the layout almost always remains 1:1.

One way to visualize how layouts—and more specifically, viewports—work is to think about looking through a pair of binoculars. By turning one knob, you can adjust how big or small objects appear, by changing the magnification or scale of the current view. Turning a second knob allows you to adjust how the view is focused—or in the context of AutoCAD, which layers and drawings are viewable, and which ones are not. Finally, moving (panning) to the left or right completely changes everything in the current view.

Another way to visualize how a layout works is to think of it as a second drawing, or a specialized layer, that has been laid over the top of your current drawing. Each layout that you create will have one or more viewports—special windows through which you will view your project at a scale to be printed. The layouts are usually at a scale of 1:1 (actual size) and contain some of the information that you originally included with the building lines, such as the border and title block, notes, scale, North arrow, and so on.

Think for a moment about drawing the floor plan of a building on a traditional drafting table. You draw the building to a scale such as 1/4″ = 1′-0″ (1 = 50). Then, on the same sheet of paper, you print a note using letters that are, say, 1/8″ (3.5 mm) high. If you looked at those letters as being on the same scale as the building, they would measure 6″ (175 mm) high, and that's what we've been doing on the cabin drawing so far. But in traditional drafting, you don't think that way. Instead, you work with two scales in the drawing without thinking about it. So a letter is 1/8″ (3.5 mm) high (actual size), and a part of the building that measures 1/8″ (3.5 mm) on the paper is thought of as being 6″ (175 mm) long, at a scale of 1/4″ = 1′-0″

(1 = 50). Layouts are designed to let you juggle two or more scales in a drawing in the same way in order to set up the drawing to be printed.

Preparing the Title Block

In Chapter 8, "Controlling Text in a Drawing," you created the title block or border for your cabin. As you may recall, you had to draw the title block much larger than the intended plot size of 8½"×11" to fit the entire cabin on the sheet. Since layout tabs always have a standard paper size such as 8½"×11" (A4210 mm×297 mm) assigned, you will need to make a 1:1 version of the title block. Doing this will give you a single reference drawing that will be used as the foundation for each of your plan sheets.

Creating the Title Block Reference

You certainly don't want to waste the time you invested in creating the title block for your cabin in Chapter 8. Therefore, while the primary focus of this section will be to create a usable title block reference, the secondary focus will be to preserve as much of the work you've already done as possible. This will be accomplished by using some commands with which you're already familiar.

To define your title block reference, take the following steps:

1. Open the I13A-FPLAYO.dwg (M13A-FPLAYO.dwg) file you created in the previous chapter, or from this chapter's download found at **www.sybex .com/go/autocad2012ner** or **www.autocadner.com.**

2. Turn on the title block layers A-ANNO-TTLB and A-ANNO-TTLB-TEXT by using the LAYER command.

3. Close or collapse the Layer Properties Manager palette when you're finished.

4. Start the BLOCK command by using the Create tool on the Block panel of the Insert tab.

5. From the Block Definition dialog box, enter **TTLB-1117** (**TTLB-A3**) for the block's name.

6. Click the Pick Insertion Base Point button, and pick the endpoint in the lower-left corner of the outer boundary shown in Figure 14.1.

   You have already used the BLOCK command to select objects manually in your drawing. Another way of selecting objects is to use the Quick Select option to select objects based on a common property.

7. Click the Quick Select button, found in the Objects group of the Block Definition dialog box, to open the Quick Select dialog box shown in Figure 14.2.

The Quick Select dialog box can be used to select any number of objects based on a common property. This property can be anything from the type of object, to all of the circles with a certain linetype. You will use the Quick Select dialog box to find all objects on the A-ANNO -TTLB layers.

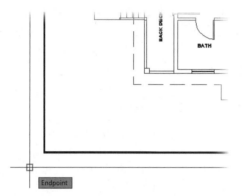

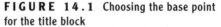

FIGURE 14.1 Choosing the base point for the title block

FIGURE 14.2 Filtering title block layers by using the Quick Select dialog box

8. Using Figure 14.2 as your guide, verify that Apply To is set to Entire Drawing and that Object Type is set to Multiple.

   The Properties combo box updates to list all of the available properties.

9. Select the Layer Property, and then do the following:

   a. Verify that Operator is set to Equals.

   b. Use the Value drop-down list to select the A-ANNO-TTLB layer.

10. Click OK to return to the Block Definition dialog box.

   Upon returning to the Block Definition dialog box, you'll see that the number of objects selected has also updated to reflect the number of objects on the A-ANNO-TTLB layer.

11. Repeat steps 7 to 10, but this time do this:

   a. Select A-ANNO-TTLB-TEXT from the Value drop-down list.

   b. Make sure Append To Current Selection Set is checked in the Quick Select dialog box.

   The number of selected objects is updated once again. This time the value is a combination of the number of objects on both the A-ANNO-TTLB and A-ANNO-TTLB-TEXT layers.

12. Pick the Delete option under the Objects heading, and then check the Open In Block Editor option in the lower-left corner before clicking the OK button.

   The Block Editor opens with the newly created TTLB-1117 (TTLB-A3) block, which you will scale down to its actual 11″×17″ (297 mm×420 mm) size.

13. Start the SCALE command and then do this:

   a. Select the entire title block.

   b. Pick the lower-right corner of the interior boundary as the base point.

14. Instead of entering a scale factor, do this:

   a. Press **R↵** to choose the Reference option.

   b. Pick the lower-left corner of the outer boundary, and then the upper-left corner of the outer boundary (see Figure 14.3).

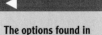

The options found in the Properties combo box will depend on the Object Type you have selected.

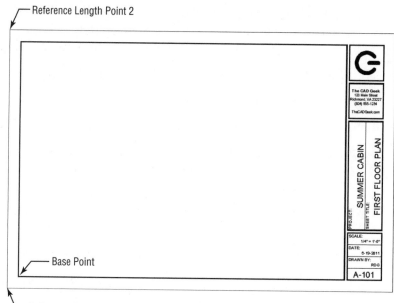

Reference Length Point 2

Base Point

Reference Length Point 1

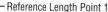

FIGURE 14.3 Specifying a reference length by using the SCALE **command**

15. After choosing the points to define the reference length, enter **11␙** (**297␙**) to scale your title block to the exact height of 11″ (297 mm).

You may need to perform a Zoom Extents to bring the title block back into view.

16. Click the Save Block button on the Open/Save panel of the Block Editor Tab.

17. Exit the Block Editor by clicking the Close Block Editor button on the Close panel.

18. Start the Write Block (WBLOCK) command by expanding the Create Block tool on the Insert tab ➤ Block Definition panel (see the left image in Figure 14.4).

The Write Block dialog box, shown on the right in Figure 14.4, opens.

19. Within the Write Block dialog box, choose Block as the Source and select the TTLB-1117 (TTLB-A3) block from the drop-down list.

20. Finally, click the ellipsis button at the end of the File Name And Path text box to create a file named **I14-01-A-BD1117.dwg** (**M14-01-A-BDA3.dwg**) in your Chapter 14 Training Data directory.

21. Verify that your Write Block dialog box looks like the right side of Figure 14.4 and click OK to finish the command.

22. Save the drawing I13A-FPLAYO.dwg (M13A-FPLAYO.dwg) as **I14A -FPLAYO.dwg** (**M14A-FPLAYO.dwg**), and close it.

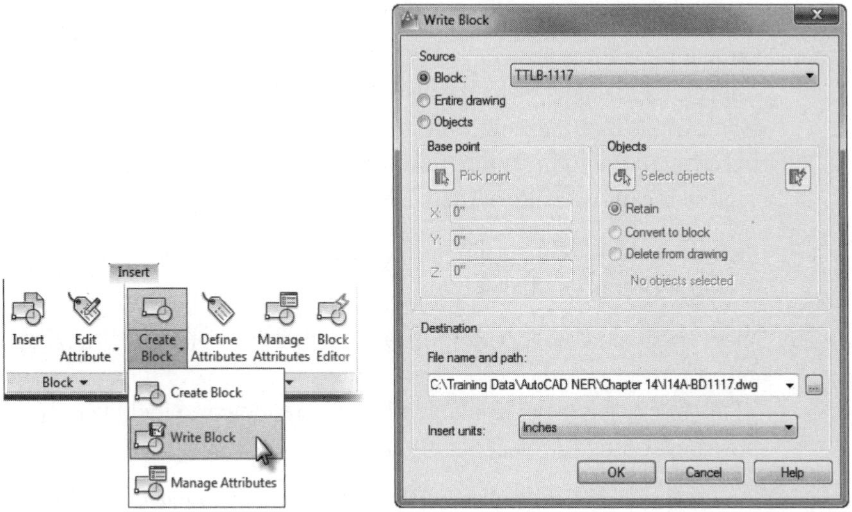

FIGURE 14.4 Starting the Write Block command (left), and the Write Block dialog box (right)

You have now extracted the title block out of your floor plan layout drawing, and created a new drawing with nothing but the title block. The construction document, sometimes called the *CD set*, will use the common 11″×17″ (297 mm×420 mm), or A3, sheet size, corresponding to the title block you drew in Chapter 8. To make your title block usable for any drawing sheet, you'll continue refining your title block reference by adding block attributes in the next exercise.

Defining the Attributes

Instead of starting from scratch, you'll use the title block reference you already have as the foundation for your sheet information block. The following exercise will guide you through the process of creating attributes from the existing text in the title block drawing:

1. Open I14-01-A-BD1117.dwg (M14-01-A-BDA3.dwg) from the Training Data directory if it isn't already open.

2. From the Insert tab ➤ Block Definition panel, select the Define Attributes button to open the Attribute Definition dialog box.

You will create attribute definitions as you did in Chapter 9, except this time you'll focus more on text justification than text style. After all of the attributes are defined, you'll learn how to use the existing text as a template for style by using the MATCHPROP (Match Properties) command.

3. For the first attribute, enter **PROJECT** for the Tag, and **Enter Project Name** for the Prompt.

   Sheet Set Manager is an extensive feature set that helps you manage the drawings that make up your project. It is discussed a little later in this chapter, but for now you'll simply set up your sheet information block so it can use some of these advanced features.

4. Click the Insert Field button found next to the Default text box in the Attribute Definition dialog box.

5. Select the Field Category drop-down list, and then pick the SheetSet option.

   This filters the list of available Field Names down to include only those pertaining to Sheet Set Manager.

6. Choose CurrentSheetSetProjectName from the list of available Field Names, and then pick Uppercase from the Format list on the right.
   The Field dialog box should look like Figure 14.5.

7. Click OK to exit the Field dialog box.

N O T E   Design drawings typically use uppercase letters, especially when prominent items such as titles are designated.

Back in the Attribute Definition dialog box, the Default field now contains #### and has a gray background, as shown in Figure 14.6.

8. Under the Text Settings group, enter the following settings:

   a. Set the Justification to Bottom Center.

   b. Set Text Style to Standard and set Rotation to 90°.

   c. Enter an arbitrary text height, such as 1/8″ (3.5 mm).

   With your settings matching those illustrated in Figure 14.6, click OK.

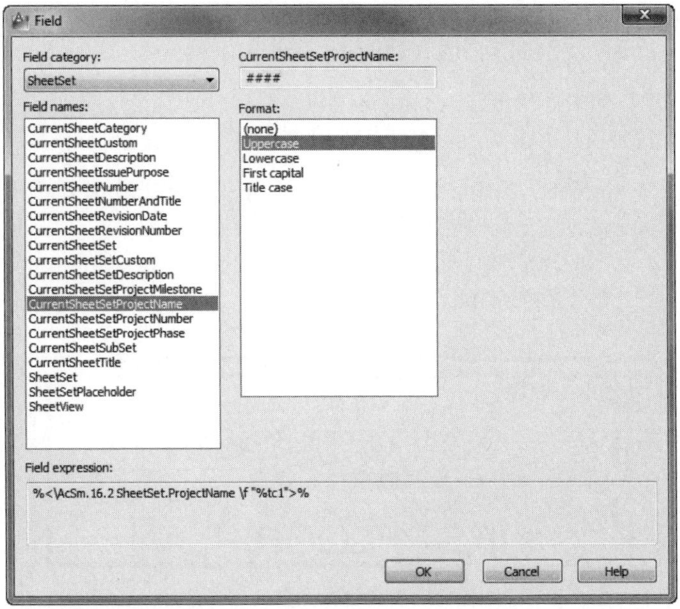

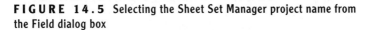

FIGURE 14.5 Selecting the Sheet Set Manager project name from the Field dialog box

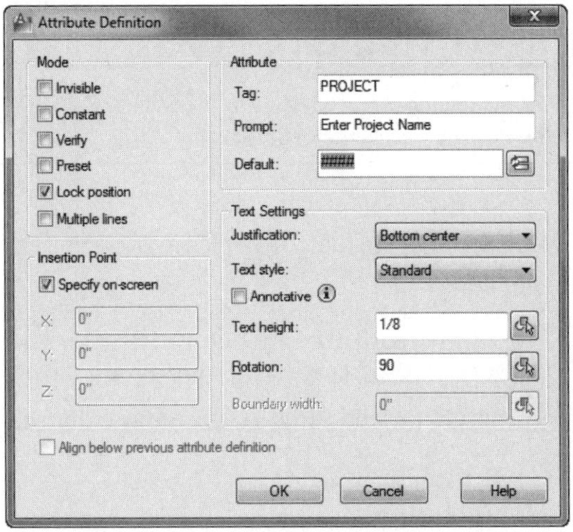

FIGURE 14.6 The Attribute Definition with a field set as the Default value

9. Use the Insertion osnap to place the PROJECT attribute on top of the existing SUMMER CABIN text string.

 10. Select the Match Properties button on the Clipboard panel on the Home tab, or enter **MP↵** to start the MATCHPROP command.

11. With Match Properties running, select the SUMMER CABIN text string as the source object (see the left of Figure 14.7), and then select the PROJECT attribute definition as the destination object (see the right of Figure 14.7).

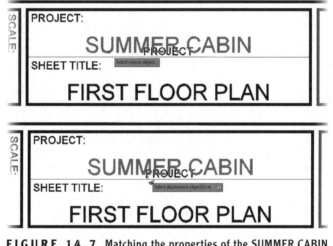

FIGURE 14.7 Matching the properties of the SUMMER CABIN text string with the PROJECT attribute definition

12. Erase the SUMMER CABIN text string to leave the PROJECT attribute definition in its place.

13. Repeat steps 2 to 12 to create attribute definitions for the SHEET_TITLE, SCALE, DATE, DRAWN BY, and SHEET NUMBER blocks. Replace the parameters for the PROJECT attribute definition with the following:

> ▶ SHEET TITLE
>
>> Tag: SHEET_TITLE
>>
>> Prompt: Enter Sheet Title
>>
>> Default: Select the Uppercase CurrentSheetTitle Field under the SheetSet Field Category.

Justification: Bottom Center

Rotation: 90°

▶ SCALE

    Tag: **DRAWING_SCALE**

    Prompt: **Enter Drawing Scale**

    Default: #″ = #′-#″ (# : ##)

    Justification: Bottom Right

▶ DATE

    Tag: **DATE**

    Prompt: **Enter Date Drawn**

    Default: **Select the CurrentSheetRevisionDate under the SheetSet Field Category.**

    Justification: Bottom Right

▶ DRAWN BY

    Tag: **DRAWN_BY**

    Prompt: **Enter Drafter's Initials**

    Default: **Select the Uppercase Author Field under the Document Field Category.**

    Justification: Bottom Right

▶ SHEET NUMBER

    Tag: **SHEET_NO**

    Prompt: **Enter Sheet Number**

    Default: **Select the Uppercase CurrentSheetNumber Field under the SheetSet Field Category.**

    Justification: Middle Center

Adjust the position of the DRAWN_BY and DATE attributes as needed. The title block should look like Figure 14.8.

14. Save your drawing as `I14-02-A-BD1117.dwg` (`M14-02-A-BDA3.dwg`).

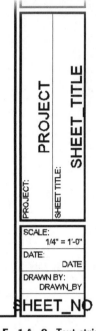

FIGURE 14.8 Text strings replaced with attribute definitions

Instead of static text strings, the title block now has a series of attributes that will make changing—and more important, managing—the variable data within your title block easier. Later in this chapter, you will create plan sheets by using the XREF command to insert the title block into each plan sheet.

Making the Sheet Information Block

Although blocks and xrefs share some properties and behaviors, xrefs cannot be used to manage attributes. Consequently, in addition to the I14-02-A-BD1117.dwg (M14-02-A-BDA3.dwg) file that you have already created, you will also need to create a sheet information block containing your attribute definitions, which will then be inserted into each drawing in your plan set. Use the WBLOCK command to extract the attributes from the title block drawing by doing the following:

1. Open I14-02-A-BD1117.dwg (M14-02-A-BDA3.dwg) from the Training Data directory if it isn't already open.

2. Select each of the attribute definitions, and change the layer to Layer 0 and the Color to ByBlock.

3. Choose Write Block from the Insert tab ➤ Block Definition panel, or enter **WBLOCK**↵ at the command line to open the Write Block dialog box.

4. In the Write Block dialog box, set the following:

   ▶ Source to Objects

   ▶ Base Point to 0,0,0

   ▶ Objects to Delete From Drawing

5. Pick the Select Objects button within the Objects group to return to the drawing.

   When creating attribute blocks, the order in which you select the attributes will dictate the order AutoCAD will use to prompt you when inserting the block. Therefore, it's important to select attributes individually, not using one of the window section methods.

6. Select the attributes in the following order:

   a. SHEET_NO

   b. SHEET_TITLE, PROJECT

   c. DRAWING_SCALE, DRAWN_BY

   d. DATE

7. Press ↵ after you finish selecting the attributes.

8. Back in the Write Block dialog box, click the ellipsis button at the end of the File Name And Path text box to save this block as **TTLB-INFO** in the Chapter 14 Training Data folder.

   When you're finished, the Write Block dialog box should look like Figure 14.9.

9. Click the OK button to create the I-TTLB-INFO.dwg (M-TTLB-INFO.dwg) file.

10. Save your drawing as **I14A-BD1117.dwg** (**M14A-BDA3.dwg**).

When the Write Block dialog box closes, you'll be taken back to the drawing, where you'll see that the block attributes are no longer in the drawing.

N O T E   Notice how the block labels, such as **PROJECT:** and **DRAWN BY:** remain in the drawing. These entities have been kept in the title block reference because they are unlikely to change—and even if they did, they would be the same in every sheet throughout the project. If we hadn't planned to use Sheet Set Manager, you might have chosen to keep the Project Name in the title block reference as well.

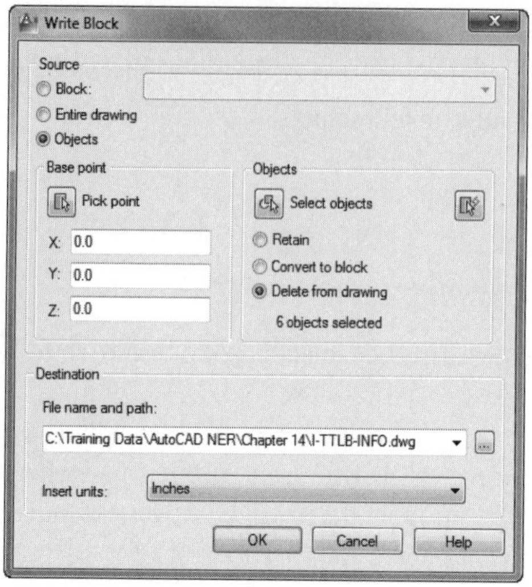

FIGURE 14.9 Defining the TTLB-INFO block unit in the Write Block dialog box

Setting Up a Sheet Template

As mentioned in the introduction to this chapter, you have considerable control over the way your drawings are plotted. The trade-off for this degree of granularity is that you have a large number of settings to manage. Keeping all of these settings set to consistent values throughout a plan set can be rather challenging. One of the best ways to ensure that your entire plan set is configured exactly the same way is to start with a template. By creating a template of a typical plan sheet, you can then create subsequent plan sheets from it, which in turn copies all of the plot settings.

This section focuses on the creation of a sheet template that you'll use later in this chapter to create your plan sheets:

1. Create a directory named **Sheets** in your Chapter 14 directory.
   This directory will be used to store each of the plan sheets.

2. To begin creating your plan sheet template, create a new drawing by choosing Application menu ➤ New ➤ Drawing.

3. Use the down-arrow next to the Open button to select Open With No Template - Imperial (Open With No Template - Metric).
   Before creating a new layout, you should set the AutoCAD interface to display the layouts easily.

4. Right-click an empty area on the status bar, and ensure that Paper/Model, Quick View Layouts, and Quick View Drawings each have a check mark next to them, as shown in Figure 14.10.

FIGURE 14.10 Turn on the Paper/Model and Quick View options in the context menu.

 The Model or Paper Space, Quick View Layouts, and Quick View Drawings buttons appear in the middle of the status bar. By clicking these buttons, you can quickly switch between displaying a layout and looking at model space, which is the way you have been using AutoCAD up to this point.

Each layout has settings that spell out which plotting device is to be used to print the layout and how the print will appear. You specify these settings through a page setup that becomes associated with the layout.

N O T E I use the terms *print* and *plot* interchangeably in this book, as I do *printer* and *plotter*. In the past, *plot* and *plotter* referred to large-format devices and media, but that's not necessarily true today. *Print* and *printer* are more widely used now because of changes in the technology of the large-format devices.

 5. Click the Model button in the status bar to switch from model space to view the drawing through the layout.

The appearance of the drawing area changes to show a view into model space inside a white rectangle, sitting in front of a gray background.

Your drawing has two borders along the perimeter of the white rectangle (one dashed and one solid).

▶ If the UCS icon consists of two arrows inside the solid border (see the left of Figure 14.11), then you are currently working in model space.

▶ If the UCS icon is shaped like a triangle and located in a portion of the drawing area (see the right of Figure 14.11), then you are currently working in paper space.

The solid line is the boundary to the viewport, and the dashed line is the limit of the printable area.

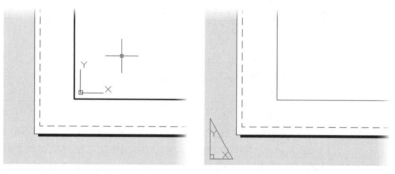

FIGURE 14.11 The layout in model space (left) and in paper space (right)

T I P   You can switch back to paper space when working in model space by moving your cursor outside of the inner, solid rectangle and double-clicking, or by entering PS↵.

Setting the Layout Parameters

The paper shown—that is, the white rectangle—is the default size and orientation for the acad.dwt template. You'll need to set the parameters to utilize the DWFx ePlot plotter (installed with AutoCAD).

1. Click the Quick View Layouts button next to the Layout button in the status bar to turn on the option.

Small thumbnail representations of the existing layouts appear at the bottom of the drawing area, as shown in Figure 14.12.

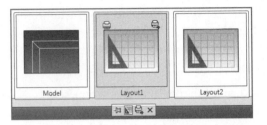

FIGURE 14.12 The drawing's layouts shown by using the Quick View Layouts tool

2. Place the cursor over the Layout1 thumbnail.

It turns blue, and two icons appear within its frame, to indicate that any changes will affect that layout only.

3. Right-click and then select the Page Setup Manager option in the context menu.

After a moment, the Page Setup Manager dialog box opens (see the top of Figure 14.13). This is where you create a new page setup, or assign an existing one, to be associated with a new or selected layout.

4. Click New to open the New Page Setup dialog box.

5. In the New Page Setup Name text box, enter **DWFX-1117 (DWFX-A3)** and click OK.

This opens the Page Setup dialog box, which has DWFX-1117 (DWFX-A3) added to the title bar (see the bottom of Figure 14.13). The DWFX-1117 (DWFX-A3) name also appears toward the top of the dialog box in the Page Setup group. In all, the dialog box has 10 groups containing settings that control how the drawing will fit on the printed page and what part of the drawing is printed.

N O T E This chapter is designed so that you can follow along even if you don't have a printer hooked up to your computer. The plotter used by this book is one that installs with AutoCAD and creates an electronic file with a .dwfx extension. DWF is a format similar to PDF that was defined by Autodesk for the purpose of electronically storing, sharing, and illustrating design drawings.

If you have not created a page setup previously, None will be selected. By default, the Printer/Plotter Name drop-down list also lists all of the plotters (printers) installed on your computer.

6. Select the DWFx ePlot (XPS Compatible).pc3 plotter from the Printer/ Plotter Name drop-down list.

    In the Printer/Plotter group, DWFx ePlot (XPS Compatible).pc3 is the selected plotter.

7. From the drop-down list in the Paper Size group, select ANSI full bleed B (17.00 × 11.00 Inches) or ISO full bleed A3 (420.00 × 297.00 mm).

    Because each printer/plotter will likely have slightly different page sizes, it's best to select the plotter first and the paper size second.

8. With both the plotter and paper size selected, complete your page setup by setting the following parameters:

    ▶ Plot Area

      What to plot: Layout

    ▶ Plot Scale

      Scale: 1:1

      Units: Inches (mm)

T I P   The Scale drop-down list contains several preset scales and a Custom option. To delete unnecessary scales, add new ones, edit existing ones, or rearrange the order of the listing, use the Ribbon to choose Annotate tab ➢ Annotation Scaling panel ➢ Scale List tool, or use the menu bar to choose Format ➢ Scale List, or enter scalelistedit↵ at the command line to open the Edit Drawing Scales dialog box.

    ▶ Plot Style Table (Pen Assignments)

      Plot Style Table: monochrome.ctb

      Display Plot Styles: Checked

    ▶ Drawing Orientation

      Landscape: Selected

    When finished, the Page Setup - DWFX-1117 (Page Setup - DWFX-A3) dialog box should look like Figure 14.14.

9. Click OK. You are returned to the Page Setup Manager dialog box. DWFX-1117 (DWFX-A3) is now on the Page Setups list.

10. Highlight DWFX-1117 (DWFX-A3) and then click Set Current.

    The layout area behind the dialog box changes to match the parameters you set in the Page Setup dialog box.

11. Click Close to close the Page Setup Manager dialog box.

You are returned to your drawing, and Layout1 appears (see Figure 14.15).

You don't want the current viewport, the window that lets you see your drawing from the layout. You will make your own shortly.

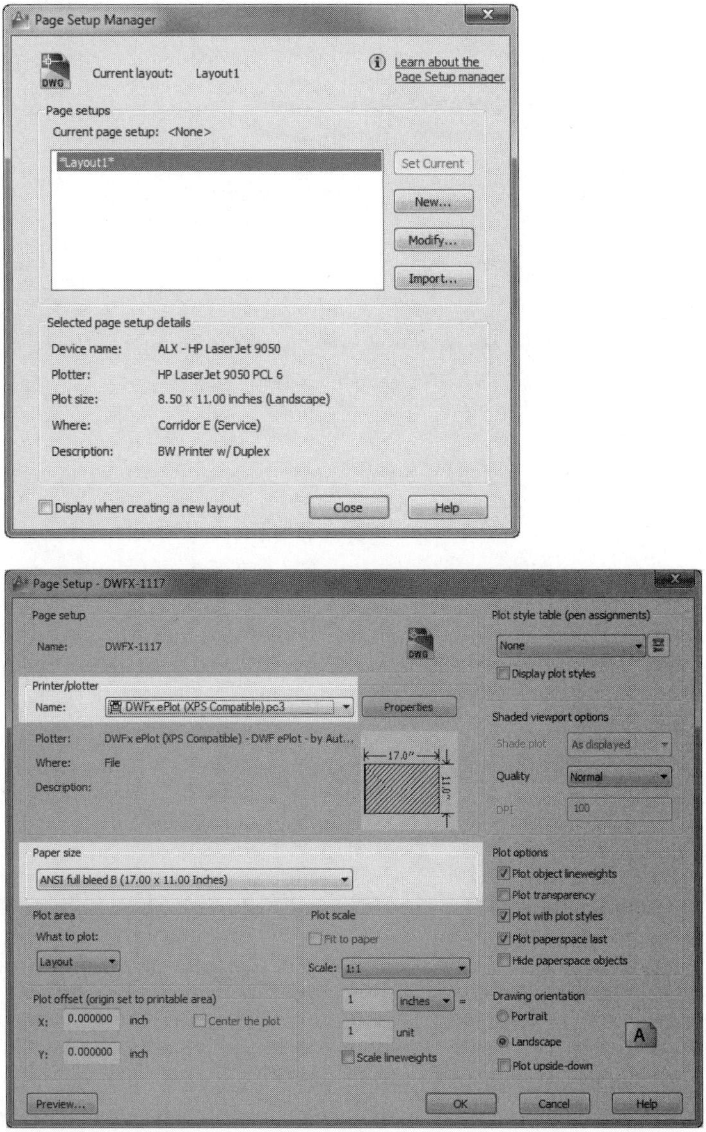

FIGURE 14.13 The Page Setup Manager dialog box (top) and the Page Setup dialog box (bottom)

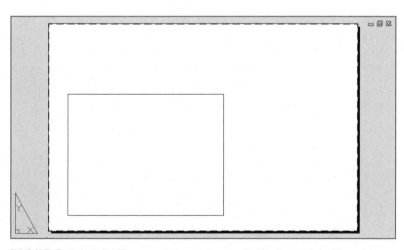

FIGURE 14.14 The completed page setup

FIGURE 14.15 The named page setup applied to Layout1 for the cabin

12. Make sure that you're in paper space, and then enter **E↵ ALL↵** to select all the objects in the layout.

In the command window, you can see that only the viewport is selected.

13. Press ↵ to erase the viewport.

14. Click the Quick View Layouts button once again, this time to right-click Layout2.

15. To remove Layout2 from the current drawing, choose Delete from the contextual menu that appears.

16. Save the current drawing as an AutoCAD drawing template by choosing Application menu ➢ Save As ➢ AutoCAD Drawing Template. Browse to the root of your Chapter 14 directory, and save the drawing as `I14A -BDTPLT.dwt` (`M14A-BDTPLT.dwt`).

17. When the Template Options dialog box opens, enter **Title block layout template**, select English (Imperial) or Metric Measurement, and click OK.

The basic sheet is now set up, but nothing is currently drawn on it. In the next several exercises, you will continue assembling the many pieces that go into a typical title block.

Finishing the Sheet Template

Although nothing is currently drawn in your sheet template, you've taken care of most of the behind-the-scenes settings. All that's left to complete the sheet template is to reference the title block and insert the sheet information block. You created both of these items earlier in the chapter, so this section will mostly be a review of the XREF and INSERT commands.

1. Make sure the `I14A-BDTPLT.dwt` (`M14A-BDTPLT.dwt`) file you created in the preceding exercise is open.
   DWT files open a little differently than normal DWG files.

2. In the Select File dialog box, set the Files Of Type drop-down list to Drawing Template (`*.dwt`) and then browse to the file.

3. Using the Layer Properties Manager, create a new layer named **A-ANNO-NPLT** and assign it the color 1 (Red).

4. Click the printer icon in the Plot column to set A-ANNO-NPLT as a nonplotting layer.
   A red circle with a line through it appears near the icon to indicate that objects on the layer will not plot.

N O T E   The A-ANNO-NPLT layer will be used to create the viewports in this chapter. Viewports will allow you to look through your layout tab and into model space. Each viewport has a boundary that helps you manage it. You'll set the A-ANNO-NPLT layer to No Plot to make this boundary visible on the screen, but invisible when plotted.

5. With the Layer Properties Manager still open, create another new layer named **A-ANNO-REFR**, keep the default White color, and set it current.

You can close, dock, or collapse the Layer Properties Manager palette after creating the A-ANNO-REFR layer.

6. Open the External References palette from the View tab ➤ Palettes panel ➤ External References palette.

7. Right-click anywhere in the File References section of the External References palette and select Attach DWG.

8. In the Select Reference File dialog box, browse to and select the I14A -BD1117.dwg (M14A-BDA3.dwg) file you created earlier in this chapter.

The Attach External Reference dialog box opens; here you will configure how your title block is referenced.

9. Using Figure 14.16 as a guide, set the parameters within the Attach External Reference dialog box as follows:

▶ Reference Type: Overlay

▶ Scale

Specify On-Screen: Unchecked

X, Y, & Z: 1

▶ Insertion Point

Specify On-Screen: Unchecked

X, Y, & Z: 0

▶ Path Type: Relative Path

▶ Rotation

Specify On-Screen: Unchecked

Angle: 0°

10. With these settings in place, click OK.

The title block is referenced in the DWFX-1117 (DWFX-A3) layout tab.

11. Save the current drawing template, keeping its I14A-BDTPLT.dwt (M14A-BDTPLT.dwt) filename. Your sheet template should look like Figure 14.17.

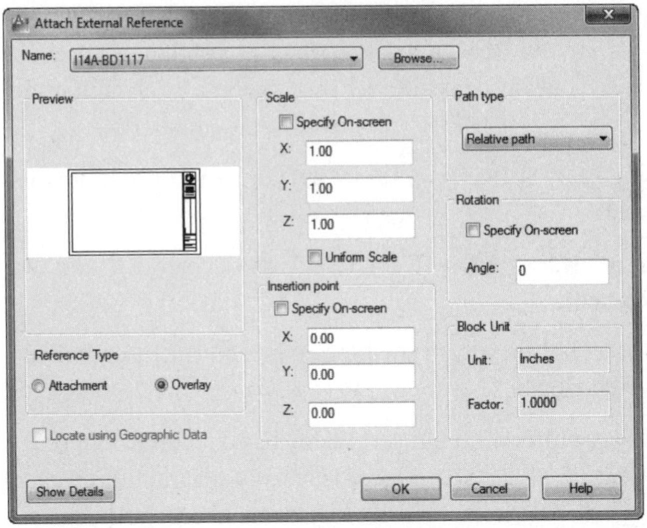

FIGURE 14.16 Attaching the title block as an external reference

FIGURE 14.17 The sheet template with the title block referenced into it

With the title block inserted into your sheet template, all that's left to do is insert the sheet information block. As you may recall, this block was created with several fields embedded as the default value for the block attributes. Many of these tie into

Sheet Set Manager, a feature you'll learn about later in this chapter, but the Drawn By attribute pulls its value from the drawing file properties. In addition to inserting the sheet information block, you'll also learn to set this attribute by changing the drawing file properties.

1. Continue using I14A-BDTPLT.dwt (M14A-BDTPLT.dwt), or open it if it's not already open.

2. Create a layer named **A-ANNO-TTLB-TEXT** with a color of 5, and set the layer as current.

3. Choose the Insert button within the Block panel on the Insert tab to open the Insert dialog box.

4. Select the Browse button in the Insert dialog box, and browse to the I-TTLB-INFO.dwg (M-TTLB-INFO.dwg) you created earlier in this chapter.
   Since the I-TTBL-INFO (M-TTBL-INFO) block, like the title block reference, was created with a common insertion point, you use the default Insertion Point of 0,0,0, Scale of 1, and Rotation of 0.

5. Make sure your Insert dialog box looks like Figure 14.18 and then click OK.

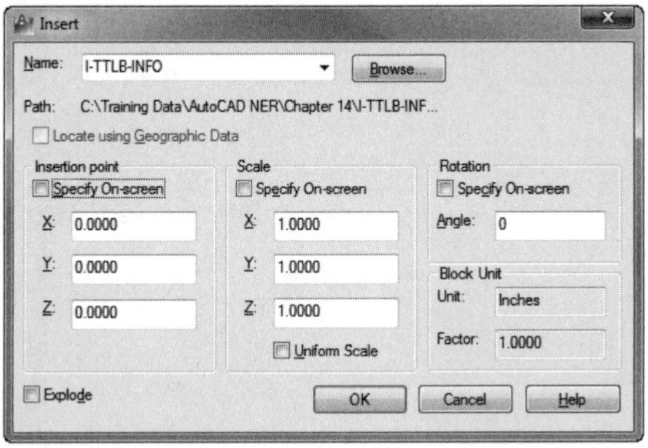

FIGURE 14.18 Inserting the I-TTLB-INFO (M-TTLB-INFO) block

Since the I-TTLB-INFO (M-TTLB-INFO) block contains block attributes, the Edit Attributes dialog box opens upon inserting the block into your drawing.

6. You'll use Sheet Set Manager to populate these attributes, so click OK to accept their default values.

    With the exception of the DRAWN_BY and DRAWING_SCALE attribute, the default value for each of the block attributes contained within the TTLB-INFO block hook into Sheet Set Manager. Instead of hooking into Sheet Set Manager, the DRAWN_BY attribute pulls its value from the drawing's properties. The DRAWING_SCALE attribute will be set separately as you configure viewports later in this chapter.

7. Open the Properties dialog box by choosing Application menu ➢ Drawing Utilities ➢ Drawing Properties.

8. Switch to the Summary tab in the I14A-BDTPLT.dwt (M14A-BDTPLT.dwt) Properties dialog box.

9. From the Summary tab, change the value of the Author field to your initials (see Figure 14.19).

10. Click OK to return to the drawing.

FIGURE 14.19 Changing the Author drawing property

The DRAWN_BY attribute probably won't update as soon as you return to the drawing.

11. Enter **REA**↵ at the command line to force a regeneration of the entire drawing.

As shown in Figure 14.20, the DRAWN_BY attribute displays your initials.

12. Save and close the current I14A-BDTPLT.dwt (M14A-BDTPLT.dwt) file, keeping its name.

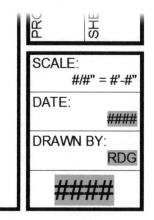

FIGURE 14.20 The Author drawing property displaying as a field in the title block

This concludes the setup of your sheet template drawing. You're now ready to begin creating sheets using this template. The first sheet you'll create, and perhaps one of the simplest, is a cover sheet.

Creating Your First Plan Sheet

The reason you referenced the title block drawing in your plan sheet template was to keep from having to manually reference it in each and every plan sheet. Once you've referenced it in the plan sheet template drawing, AutoCAD will automatically attach the reference, on the correct layer, to each plan sheet you create. Sheet Set Manager provides a slightly more streamlined sheet creation process, but for those times when you may not want to use Sheet Set Manager, this process is one of the more common approaches. Choosing whether to use Sheet Set Manager isn't something you have to do from the start. You'll add the cover sheet you're about to create as an existing drawing to your sheet set.

1. Create a new drawing by using the Application menu or Quick Access toolbar.

2. Use the down-arrow next to the Open button in the Select Template dialog box to choose Open With No Template - Imperial (Open With No Template - Metric).

3. Right-click the Quick View Layouts button in the status bar and choose From Template (see Figure 14.21).

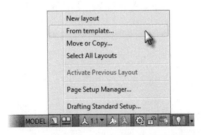

FIGURE 14.21 Selecting the From Template option in the Quick View Layouts context menu

4. Browse to the I14A-BDTPLT.dwt (M14A-BDTPLT.dwt) file you created in the preceding section, and click Open from the Select Template From File dialog box.

5. The Insert Layout(s) dialog box opens, and lists each of the layout tabs in the selected template drawing. Choose the DWFX-1117 (DWFX-A3) option shown in Figure 14.22 and then click OK.

FIGURE 14.22 Selecting the layout to use as a template

A new layout tab named DWFX-1117 (DWFX-A3) is created in the current drawing. This tab is an exact copy of the DWFX-1117 (DWFX-A3) layout tab in the I14A-BDTPLT.dwt (M14A-BDTPLT.dwt) file.

Similar to the layer and file naming standards, the National CAD Standard also has a standard outlining the numbering of drawing sheets. The standard sheet number for an architectural cover sheet is A-000.

6. Select the Quick View Layouts button in the status bar to display thumbnails of the layout tabs in your drawing (see Figure 14.23).

7. Right-click the DWFX-1117 (DWFX-A3) layout tab, and choose Rename from the contextual menu that displays.

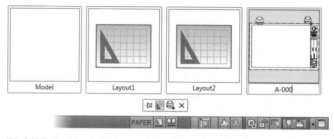

FIGURE 14.23 Renaming a layout tab to match the sheet number

8. Enter A-000 as the new name for the layout tab and then press ↵ (see Figure 14.23).

   You will need only a single layout tab for the cover sheet drawing. Too many layout tabs in a drawing can dramatically affect drawing performance, so you should keep the total number as low as possible. For this reason, you'll delete the unneeded Layout1 and Layout2.

9. Click the Quick View Layouts button on the status bar to display thumbnails of the layouts in your drawing.

10. Right-click Layout1 and choose Delete from the contextual menu that appears. Do the same for Layout2.

   When finished, clicking the Quick View Layouts button will display only two thumbnails: one for Model and another for the A-000 layout.

11. Save your cover sheet as **I-A-000.dwg** (**M-A-000.dwg**) in the Sheets directory you created earlier.

> Because layout tabs are used in many ways, it's important to establish a naming convention for them. One of the most popular conventions is to name the layout tab after the sheet number it represents.

Using Sheet Set Manager

NEW Sheet Set Manager is a robust collection of tools found in AutoCAD that aids in the management and creation of plan sheets. Until the 2012 release, these tools were reserved for the full version of AutoCAD and were not included with AutoCAD LT. New to AutoCAD 2012 is the inclusion of Sheet Set Manager for both the full version of AutoCAD and AutoCAD LT.

To many, Sheet Set Manager is nothing more than a glorified PLOT command. Although it can certainly be used that way, Sheet Set Manager is truly designed to help you manage your plan sheets from the moment you create a sheet to the moment you plot it. This section focuses on using Sheet Set Manager to create and manage your plan sheets. To begin using Sheet Set Manager, you must first create a sheet set.

Creating a New Sheet Set

By using Sheet Set Manager, you can organize each of your drawing sheets (layouts) into what is known as a *sheet set*. A sheet set will store links to each of your drawings, in addition to storing basic information about each drawing and how new drawings should be created. All of this information is stored in a sheet set data (DST) file. This data file is created by completing a wizard enabling you to create a sheet set from scratch or from a template.

To create the sheet set data file for your cabin project, take the following steps:

1. With any drawing open, select the Sheet Set Manager tool found on the Palettes panel of the View tab.

    This opens the Sheet Set Manager palette set.

2. With the Sheet Set Manager palette set open, select the drop-down list on the Sheet List palette and select New Sheet Set, as shown in Figure 14.24.

    The Create Sheet Set dialog box opens.

    The Create Sheet Set dialog box is divided into four segments (pages):

    ▶ Begin

    ▶ Sheet Set Example

    ▶ Sheet Set Details

    ▶ Confirm

The Sheet Set Manager palette set is typically referred to as *Sheet Set Manager*. Sometimes you may see Sheet Set Manager abbreviated as SSM.

FIGURE 14.24 Creating a sheet set by using the Sheet List palette

3. From the Begin step, select An Example Sheet Set, and then click Next.

   This takes you to the second step, Sheet Set Example. Like drawing templates, sheet set templates can be created as well. If you were creating a sheet set from a template, this dialog box is where you would specify that example sheet set.

4. You will build your sheet set from scratch, so select the A Sheet Set To Use As An Example radio button, and then pick Architectural Imperial Sheet Set (Architectural Metric Sheet Set) from the list below.

5. Click Next to advance to the next step.

   Now you'll need to provide a name for your sheet set. Although this name won't be set up to print on any drawings, it's still important to enter a meaningful name that will make sense to you later. In addition to choosing a name for your sheet set, you will also tell AutoCAD where to save your sheet set.

6. In the Name Of New Sheet Set text box, enter **I-Summer Cabin (M-Summer Cabin)**.

   You may enter an optional description in the Description text box.

7. Finally, and perhaps most important, click the ellipsis button at the end of the Store Sheet Set Data File (`.dst`) Here text box to choose the `Sheets` directory you created earlier in this chapter.

   When you're finished, the Create Sheet Set - Sheet Set Details dialog box should look like Figure 14.25.

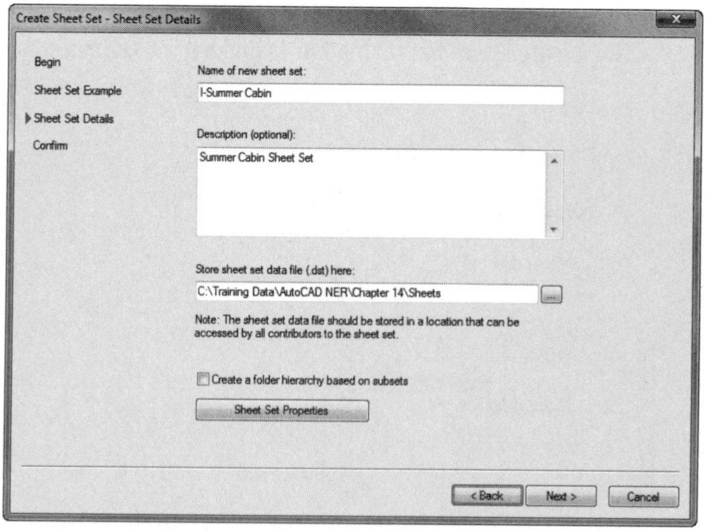

FIGURE 14.25 Choosing a name and location for the sheet set

8. At the bottom of the Create Sheet Set - Sheet Set Details dialog box, pick the Sheet Set Properties button to open the Sheet Set Properties - Summer Cabin dialog box.

Because you selected one of the generic sheet set templates that ship with the product, many of the Sheet Set Properties are set to generic values. You'll change some of these properties to work with your project, and more specifically, the sheet template you created earlier. Look ahead to Figure 14.27 to see the Sheet Set Properties dialog box configured for the Summer Cabin project.

9. Pick the Page Setup Overrides File property under the Sheet Set property group, and then select the ellipsis button.

10. From the Select Template dialog box that opens, browse to and select the I14A-BDTPLT.dwt (M14A-BDTPLT.dwt) file and click Open.

11. Verify that the Sheet Storage Location property under the Sheet Creation group is set to the Sheets directory within your Chapter 14 directory.

12. Choose the Sheet Creation Template property, also under the Sheet Creation group, to browse to and select the same I14A-BDTPLT.dwt (M14A-BDTPLT.dwt) file selected in step 10.

Once you select the template file, the Select Layout As Sheet Template dialog box shown in Figure 14.26 opens.

13. Select the DWFX-1117 (DWFX-A3) layout from the list, and then pick the OK button to exit the dialog box.

14. Verify that the Sheet Set Properties - Summer Cabin dialog box looks like Figure 14.27, and then pick the OK button to save the settings and exit the dialog box.

FIGURE 14.26 Selecting the sheet-creation layout template

15. Back in the Create Sheet Set dialog box, click the Next button to advance to the Confirm portion of the wizard.

16. Click Finish to create the sheet set and exit the wizard.

After the Sheet Set Wizard closes, the Sheet List palette within the Sheet Set Manager palette set will display a number of groups. These were created based on the architectural sheet set template you selected while creating the sheet set (see Figure 14.28).

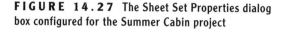

FIGURE 14.27 The Sheet Set Properties dialog box configured for the Summer Cabin project

FIGURE 14.28 The Summer Cabin sheet set

Throughout the life cycle of a project, you may need to make changes that affect the entire sheet set. Sheet Set Manager consists of two parts: the sheet and the sheet set. The difference is that *sheet set properties* affect the entire drawing set (every drawing listed in the Sheet Set Manager sheet list), and *sheet properties* affect only that one individual sheet. The difference between the two will become more apparent the more you work with Sheet Set Manager.

You may recall that the sheet set name does not get plotted on a drawing sheet. Instead, Sheet Set Manager will use a different Project Name property on the individual drawings. This property is a sheet set property, which means it affects the entire drawing set and will be the same for every drawing in the entire set.

17. From the Sheet List palette in Sheet Set Manager, right-click Summer Cabin at the top of the sheet list and select Properties, as shown in Figure 14.29.

FIGURE 14.29 Modifying the properties for the sheet set

The Sheet Set Properties - Summer Cabin dialog box opens to display properties common to the entire sheet set. Notice that the Project Name property under the Project Control group is currently empty.

18. Click the Project Name property to make it active, and enter **Summer Cabin** as the project name, as shown in Figure 14.30.

19. This is the only change you will make for now, so click OK when you're finished.

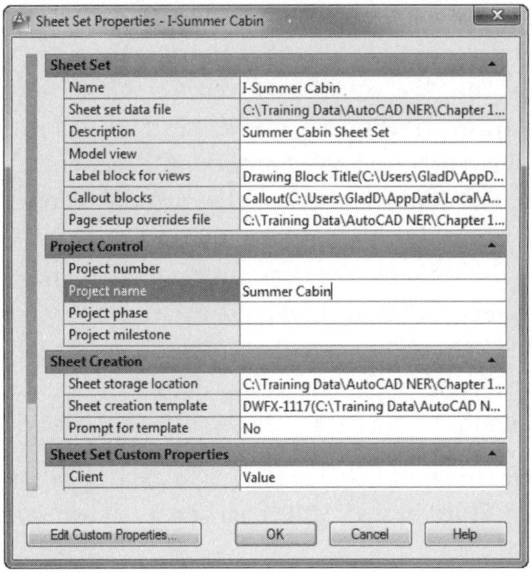

FIGURE 14.30 Changing the Sheet Set Manager
Project Name property

You have now created a sheet set for your cabin project. Currently, the sheet set includes only the collection of settings that tell AutoCAD how you would like to create sheets and where those sheets should be stored. The next several exercises will show you not only how to create new sheets by using Sheet Set Manager, but also how to add existing sheets to a sheet set.

Adding Existing Drawings to a Sheet Set

In the "Creating Your First Plan Sheet" exercise, you created a cover sheet drawing by using the drawing template created in the "Setting Up a Sheet Template" section. Although the drawing was saved alongside the sheet set in the Sheets directory, the A-000.dwg file is not yet part of the Summer Cabin sheet set. Because this drawing was created outside Sheet Set Manager, you'll need to add it manually.

Take these steps to add the cover sheet to your Summer Cabin sheet set:

1. Right-click the Architectural group on the Sheet List panel of Sheet Set Manager and choose Import Layout As Sheet (see Figure 14.31). The Import Layouts As Sheets dialog box opens.

2. From the Import Layouts As Sheets dialog box, click the Browse For Drawings button at the top of the screen. Browse to and select the I-A-000.dwg (M-A-000.dwg) file saved in your Sheets directory.

After you select the I-A-000.dwg (M-A-000.dwg) drawing, the layouts contained within it are listed in the Import Layouts As Sheets dialog box (see Figure 14.32). Because the drawing you selected had only one layout, the A-000 layout is the only one listed.

When you're importing existing layouts, it's important to note the Status column. The status for the A-000 layout should read Available For Import, and the check box should be selected on the left side of the dialog box.

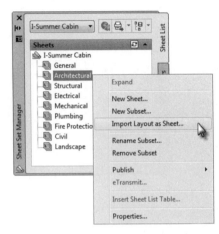

FIGURE 14.31 Importing an existing layout into Sheet Set Manager

FIGURE 14.32 Importing the A-000 layout tab into Sheet Set Manager

3. Click the Import Checked button to import the layout and return to the Sheet Set Manager palette set.

　　The A-000 layout tab imports into the Sheet Set Manager sheet list with the generic name I-A-000 - A-000 (M-A-000 - A-000), as shown on the left in Figure 14.33. For the layout to be useful in Sheet Set Manager, you'll need to provide a more meaningful sheet number and title.

FIGURE 14.33 Accessing the properties for an individual sheet, to replace its default name, in Sheet Set Manager

4. From the Sheet List palette in Sheet Set Manager, right-click the I-A-000 - A-000 (M-A-000 - A-000) sheet and choose Properties, as shown on the right in Figure 14.33.

　　The Sheet Properties dialog box opens to display settings related to the A-000 sheet.

5. Enter the following values, as shown in Figure 14.34:

　　Sheet Title: **Cover Sheet**

　　Sheet Number: **A-000**

　　Revision Date: Today's date

6. Click OK to return to Sheet Set Manager.

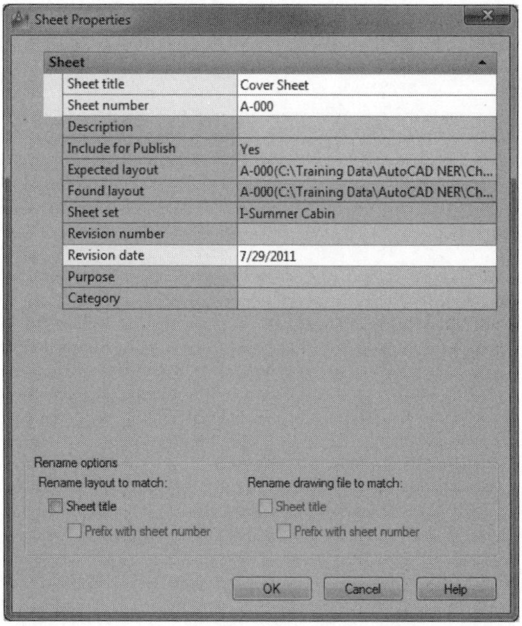

FIGURE 14.34 Changing the properties for sheet A-000

7. Double click the A-000 - Cover Sheet from the Sheet Set Manager sheet list to open it.

You may need to enter **REA.↵** to regenerate the drawing, but notice how the title block is largely completed, as shown in Figure 14.35. All of this information is pulled from the properties you set in Sheet Set Manager.

Notice that the Drawn By blank is empty. Remember, this is not a Sheet Set Manager field; it comes from the DWG file properties.

8. Choose Application menu ➤ Drawing Utilities ➤ Drawing Properties, and then change the Author property on the Summary tab to your initials and click OK.

The Properties dialog box closes, and you return to the drawing. Once again, you may need to enter **REA.↵** to regenerate your drawing, but afterward the sheet information block will reflect this change to the drawing properties.

9. Save and close the current file, I-A-000.dwg (M-A-000.dwg), keeping its name.

FIGURE 14.35 The sheet information block populated with values from Sheet Set Manager

Importing existing layouts into Sheet Set Manager is a great way to build a sheet set out of existing drawings. However, it's also common to use this process when creating new drawings. The next section focuses on the creation of new plan sheets. Later in this chapter, you'll add viewports to the sheets created in the next section. Those sheets will then be copied, creating additional layouts in each of the newly created drawings. You'll then apply the process you learned in this section to import those additional layouts into your sheet set.

Creating Drawings with Sheet Set Manager

Rather than importing existing sheets, you can also create new sheets by using Sheet Set Manager. You may recall setting the Sheet Storage Location and Sheet Creation Template properties as you were creating the sheet set for your Summer Cabin project. These settings will be used to determine the template from which your sheets will be created. Consequently, when creating sheets, Sheet Set Manager will prompt you for only three items: sheet number, sheet name, and drawing filename.

Having too many layouts in a single drawing can dramatically affect drawing performance, so you should keep the total number in a drawing to a minimum. As a point of reference, Autodesk typically recommends storing no more than 10 layout tabs in a single DWG file. (I've said that before—but I've seen far too many users ignore that advice, so it's worth emphasizing.) Sheet Set Manager subscribes to this practice and creates drawings with only a single layout. After configuring your viewports, you'll learn how to copy layouts later in this chapter. Copied layouts can be added to your sheet set by using the same Import Layout As Sheet command used to add the cover sheet to the sheet set.

For now, you'll use Sheet Set Manager to create three drawing files. Each will represent a different portion of your overall sheet set. Specifically, you'll create a drawing for sheets illustrating your floor plan, another for elevations, and yet another for the site plan. You'll copy the initial layout contained in each drawing created in this section later in this chapter. After copying these layouts, you'll import them into your sheet set.

Follow these steps to create drawings for each of the three drawing groups:

1. With any drawing open, right-click Summer Cabin at the top of the Sheet List palette of Sheet Set Manager and select New Sheet, as shown in Figure 14.36.

FIGURE 14.36 Creating a new sheet by using Sheet Set Manager

The New Sheet dialog box shown in Figure 14.37 opens, where you will enter some basic information about the drawing you're about to create. This information will include the sheet number, sheet title, and drawing filename.

N O T E   Take note of the Folder Path and Sheet Template settings. Both are grayed out and cannot be changed. Because you set both of these as properties as you created the sheet set, Sheet Set Manager automatically uses the correct template and saves the drawing in the correct location.

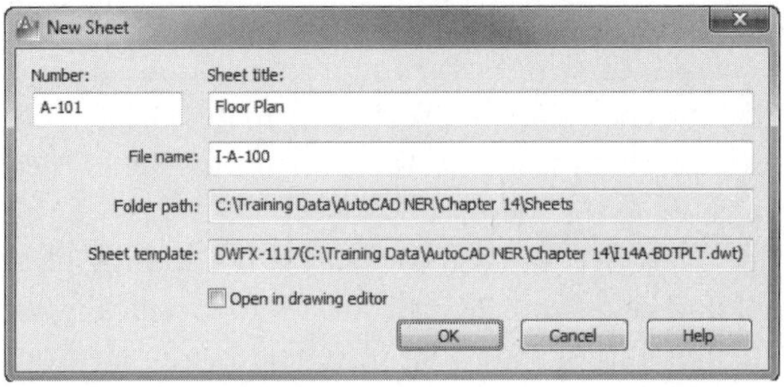

FIGURE 14.37 Entering the sheet number, sheet title, and filename in the New Sheet dialog box

2. Enter A-101 in the Number text box and enter **Floor Plan** for the Sheet Title.

By default, the filename is automatically generated by combining what you enter for the Number and Sheet Title.

3. To change this, click in the File Name text box and enter **I-A-100** (**M-A-100**).

When you're finished, the New Sheet dialog box should look like Figure 14.37.

4. Click OK to create the new drawing.

Take note of where the A-101 sheet is located in the sheet list. Unlike the A-000 drawing you imported earlier, the A-101 sheet doesn't belong to any group. Sheets can be moved and rearranged throughout a sheet set by dragging and dropping them into the desired location. Keep in mind that you're moving only the location where a sheet resides within Sheet Set Manager, and you are not modifying the DWG file nor the directory in which it's stored.

5. Drag and drop the A-101 - Floor Plan drawing from the bottom of the Sheet List palette to the Architectural group, under the A-000 Cover Sheet drawing (see the left of Figure 14.38).

When finished, the A-101 drawing sheet will be listed in the Architectural group after the A-000 drawing sheet (see the right of Figure 14.38).

6. Right-click the Architectural group and select New Sheet.

Notice the layout name and drawing path for the Sheet Template. The Sheet Template path differs from the one you saw in Figure 14.37.

Each group (or *subset*, as they're known in Sheet Set Manager) can have its own settings. You'll need to configure the Architectural subset to use the sheet template and DWFX-1117 (DWFX-A3) layout.

In this case, the sheet A-101 belongs to a group of drawings, each numbered A-100. Instead of naming the file I-A-101.dwg (M-A-101.dwg), name it I-A-100.dwg (M-A-100.dwg) to accurately represent the group of layouts it will contain.

7. Click the Cancel button to exit the New Sheet dialog box.

8. Right-click the Architectural subset and choose Properties.
The Subset Properties dialog box opens.

9. From the Subset Properties dialog box, click in the Sheet Creation
Template property and browse to your I14A-BDTPLT.dwt (M14A-BDTPLT
.dwt) file to select the DWFX-1117 (DWFX-A3) layout, as shown in
Figure 14.39.

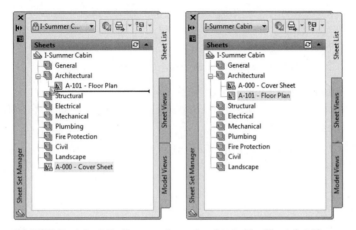

FIGURE 14.38 Rearranging a drawing in the Sheet Set Manager sheet list

FIGURE 14.39 Selecting the DWFX-1117 (DWFX-A3) layout
as the Sheet Creation template for the Architectural subset

10. Return to the Architectural subset and choose New Sheet by right-clicking the subset name.

> The New Sheet dialog box opens once again. This time the Sheet Template path should begin with DWFX-1117 (DWFX-A3) and include the path to your Training Data folder in parentheses.

11. In the New Sheet dialog box, enter the following values:

> Number: A-201
>
> Sheet Title: North Elevation
>
> File Name: I-A-200 (**M-A-200**)

12. Click OK to create the drawing.

13. Change the Sheet Creation Template for the Civil subset to match the Architectural subset, and create a new sheet with the following designations:

> Number: **C-100**
>
> Title: **Site Plan**
>
> Filename: **I-C-100 (M-C-100)**

You should now have a total of four sheets listed in the Sheet Set Manager sheet list—three under the Architectural subset and one under the Civil subset (see Figure 14.40).

FIGURE 14.40 The Sheet List palette after importing the cover sheet and creating three new sheets

Setting Up Layouts

The preceding section guided you through the process of setting up a series of blank drawings and adding each of them to Sheet Set Manager. For now, most of your work with Sheet Set Manager is done. This section focuses on adding content to each of the layouts or plan sheets you have created so far. You'll add content to your plan sheets by cutting a viewport.

Viewports create a hole or window in the layout so that you can see through the layout to the drawing of the building. You can think of the building as residing "underneath" the layout. You'll create these viewports to display your cabin in model space at a precise scale. When you're finished, everything within the dashed border will be printed as if it were a single drawing.

Referencing the Model

Chapter 13 introduced external references (xrefs), which are useful and powerful tools for viewing a second drawing from within the current drawing. In this section, you'll learn to use xrefs to assemble plan sheets, which will allow you to get even more mileage out of them. Xrefs help you combine several drawings into a composite; layouts allow you to set up and print several views of the same file. The layout is a view of your drawing as it will sit on a sheet of paper when printed.

The first step to creating viewports is to make sure there's something in model space to see. You'll do that by referencing the floor plan and site plan layout drawings in your sheet files as necessary. This practice is rather common in the building industry, as a typical building project will include a large number of model files representing the many building trades, and designs within those trades.

For example, the mechanical engineer will likely create several model files, including a duct layout plan, a piping plan if natural gas or chilled water is being used, and an equipment plan. Each of those plans will use the architectural floor plan as a background to the mechanical design, but certain architectural elements, such as the furniture plan, have little relevance to the mechanical engineer. Therefore, to help facilitate the multidisciplinary collaboration required by today's projects, the architect will, like the other disciplines on the project, divide the design across multiple model files.

Although your cabin project consists of only a couple of model files, you'll set up your drawings to use this same collaborative framework by using external references to manage which parts of the project display on a given plan sheet. With the exception of the cover sheet, each of the sheets in your sheet set will reference the I14A-FPLAYO.dwg (M14A-FPLAYO.dwg) file. In addition to the I14A-FPLAYO.dwg (M14A-FPLAYO.dwg), the civil site plan will also reference I13C-SPLAYO.dwg (M13C-SPLAYO.dwg).

Take the following steps to reference the necessary model files into your sheet files:

1. Open the `I-A-100.dwg` (`M-A-100.dwg`) sheet file by double-clicking the A-101 sheet in Sheet Set Manager.

2. With the `I-A-100.dwg` (`M-A-100.dwg`) sheet file open, use the Quick View Layouts button to switch to model space.

3. Set the current layer to A-ANNO-REFR.

4. Use the XREF command to attach `I14A-FPLAYO.dwg` (`M14A-FPLAYO.dwg`) to the current drawing.

5. Configure the Attach External Reference dialog box to match Figure 14.41.

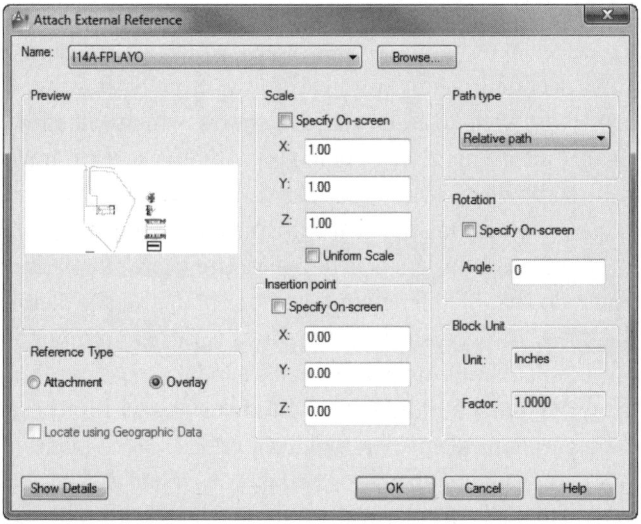

FIGURE 14.41   The Attach External Reference dialog box

6. Save the current drawing, keeping its existing filename.

7. Repeat steps 2 through 6 on the `I-A-200.dwg` (`M-A-200.dwg`) and `I-C-100.dwg` (`M-C-100.dwg`) drawings.

    The Site Plan sheet is the only one that requires two xrefs to compose the entire drawing.

8. Open the `I-C-100.dwg` (`M-C-100.dwg`) if it's not already open.

9. Verify that A-ANNO-REFR is the current layer and I14A-FPLAYO.dwg (M14A-FPLAYO.dwg) is already attached as an xref.

10. Matching the settings shown in Figure 14.42, attach I13C-SPLAYO.dwg (M13C-SPLAYO.dwg).

11. When prompted to specify an insertion point, use the Endpoint osnap to select the upper-left corner of the deck, as shown in Figure 14.43.

12. Keeping their existing filenames, save and close any of the sheet drawings still open: I-A-100.dwg, I-A-200.dwg, I-C-100.dwg (M-A-100.dwg, M-A-200.dwg, M-C-100.dwg).

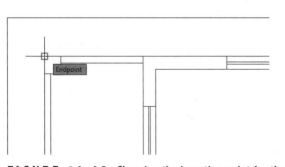

FIGURE 14.42 Attaching the civil site plan drawing

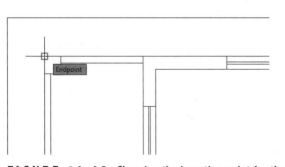

FIGURE 14.43 Choosing the insertion point for the civil site plan xref

You have now attached the necessary external references for each of your plan sheets. Although these references are attached, the actual layouts still contain nothing more than the title block you inserted earlier in this chapter. The next step to constructing your plan sheets will be to cut a hole into your layouts by using viewports. These viewports will allow you to look into model space at an exact scale.

Creating the Paper Space Viewport

Now that the sheet files have been created and the necessary model files referenced, you need to be able to view the model hidden behind the layouts. You will do this by creating a new viewport that won't show up when you plot the drawing. Here's how:

1. Open I-A-100.dwg (M-A-100.dwg), and then use the Layer drop-down list on the Layers panel of the Home tab to change the current layer to A-ANNO-NPLT.

   You'll create your viewports on this layer so the borders for your viewports are not plotted in your final plan sheets.

> **T I P**   Note the color assigned to the A-ANNO-NPLT layer. Because this layer will be used for viewports, it's useful to assign the layer a color that will stand out in your drawing, so you can quickly identify its boundaries as viewport boundaries, and not another AutoCAD object such as a polyline.

   Part of this section focuses on configuring the visibility of layers inside your viewports. When you're creating viewports, it's best to make the objects you'll be displaying in a plan sheet visible from the start.

2. Expand the Layers panel on the Home tab, and then click the Turn All Layers On button to turn on all layers in the current drawing and the drawings referenced in it.

3. Repeat the same process, but this time choose the Thaw All Layers button to thaw all of the layers.

4. Click the View tab and then, in the Viewports panel, click the Rectangular button.

5. At the Specify corner of viewport: prompt, click the endpoint at the upper-right corner of the title block.

6. At the Specify Opposite Corner: prompt, click the endpoint at the lower-left corner of the title block.

Your cabin drawing appears in the new viewport (see Figure 14.44).

7. Open the I-A-200.dwg (M-A-200.dwg) sheet file, and repeat steps 2 to 6, making sure A-ANNO-NPLT is the current layer before creating your viewport.

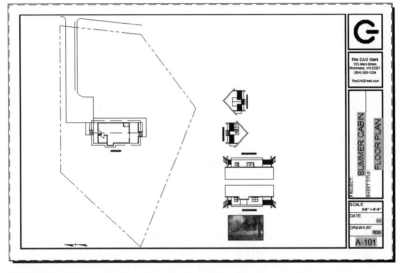

FIGURE 14.44 The cabin displayed through the new viewport

The relationship between paper space and model space is quite interesting. Viewports allow you to peer into model space from your layouts. The end result is a drawing sheet that, when plotted, displays everything drawn in paper space in addition to model space objects drawn inside the viewport boundary. To help you experience how this relationship works, try the following:

1. Place your cursor over an object inside the cabin, click just once, and then move the cursor.

Rather than selecting the object, you began a selection window.

2. Drag the window around some of the objects near the cabin and then click again. Nothing is selected.

3. Move the cursor over both the white and gray areas of the drawing window and notice how the crosshairs appear over both.

This informs you that you are currently working in paper space and can select only paper space objects such as the viewport (after you move the objects into paper space in the next section), the title block, and border. To work on the cabin itself, you need to change to model space. You can do this in two ways:

▶ Click the Model button. This temporarily removes the layout and leaves you with just the drawing, or model.

▶ Switch to model space while a layout is active.

You'll use the latter here.

When you activate model space while a layout is active, it is like opening a window and reaching through the opening to touch the drawing of the building behind the window.

4. Place your cursor within the viewport area and this time double-click. The viewport border becomes bolder and, when you move the cursor beyond the viewport, the cursor changes from a crosshair to an arrow. You are now in model space and are able to select the model space objects, but not any objects that reside in paper space.

5. Double-click the cursor outside the viewport. The crosshair cursor returns, and you are back in paper space.

T I P   You can also click the MODEL button in the middle of the status bar to move from model space to paper space. When you are in paper space, this button changes to PAPER, and it will toggle you back to the current model space viewport.

Setting the Viewport Scale

The layout is set to print to an 11″×17″ (297 mm×420 mm) paper, and you want the contents of the viewport to plot to a specific scale. In this section, you will adjust the viewport scale to display the model space objects at 1/4″ = 1′ (1 = 50) by assigning a viewport scale.

1. Select the viewport. You know that the viewport is selected, and not the border polyline, when the Viewport Scale button appears in the status bar.

T I P   Since the viewport and the title block are drawn atop one another, try using Selection Cycling if you're having a hard time selecting the viewport.

2. Click the Viewport Scale button and, from the drop-down list, choose 1/4″ = 1′-0″, as shown in Figure 14.45.

The viewport scales to 1/4″ = 1′-0″↵↵, and the scale is reflected on the status bar.

3. Double-click in the viewport, if necessary, to switch to model space and then use the Pan tool inside the viewport to adjust the position of the cabin so that the floor plan is centered (see Figure 14.46). The scene is a bit cluttered, but that will be rectified in a later section.

You can also change the viewport scale by selecting the viewport and changing the Standard Scale value in the Properties palette or Quick Properties panel.

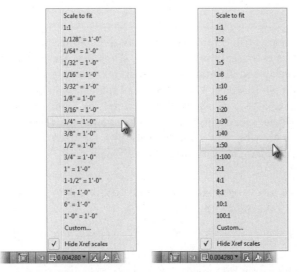

FIGURE 14.45 Selecting the imperial viewport scale (left) and the metric viewport scale (right)

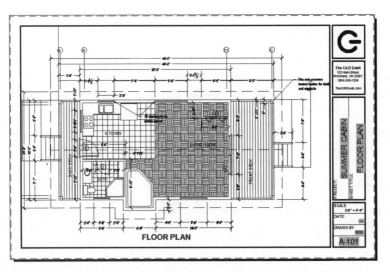

FIGURE 14.46 The cabin drawing zoomed in to the floor plan

T I P   It's recommended you use the actual PAN command instead of the middle mouse button. Because Zoom and Pan are shared by the middle button/wheel on wheel mice, it's easy to accidentally change the drawing scale by zooming. Using the PAN command will avoid this possibility.

---

4. Double-click the gray area outside the title block to switch back to paper space.

T I P   Items such as tables and notes can go either in model space, as shown in this exercise, or in paper space. When they are in paper space, it's easy to develop and maintain a consistent text or table style that appears the same in all drawings. When notes and tables are in model space, you have the flexibility to change their sizes simply by zooming in or out in the viewport. Model space objects can also be shown in any number of layouts in the same drawing. You'll develop your own standard, or adhere to your company's standard, for note and table placement.

---

5. Keeping its current name, save I-A-100.dwg (M-A-100.dwg), and open I-A-200.dwg (M-A-200.dwg).

6. Repeat steps 1 to 4 on the I-A-200.dwg (M-A-200.dwg) file. Instead of using the PAN command to bring the floor plan into view, bring the north elevation into view.

The north elevation currently faces opposite the World UCS. You'll fix the elevation's view in a later exercise.

Copying the Layouts

> You can delete all the paper space layouts, but you can't delete model space.

The layout that you made is an excellent starting point. You will add a few items from the Autodesk Content Explorer, adjust the title block information, and then duplicate the layouts several times to accommodate the different views of your cabin. Each time a layout is copied, all of its contents, including the viewports and their settings, are copied with it. These copies are not interdependent, and any changes made to one are not reflected in the others.

Adding Content from the Autodesk Content Explorer

NEW   Before you copy the layouts, you'll add a block by using the Autodesk Content Explorer and then edit its attributes. The Autodesk Content Explorer is similar to DesignCenter in the way it provides access to blocks, layers, linetypes, styles, and modes. Unlike DesignCenter, Content Explorer is built from an index of user-specified locations spanning from your local hard drive to network paths. The end result is a Google-like index that allows you to quickly access drawing files (and their contents) with a simple search query.

To see how this feature works, you'll use the Autodesk Content Explorer to locate a view title block:

1. Use Sheet Set Manager to open the A-101 layout in the `I-A-100.dwg` (`M-A-100.dwg`) file.

2. Use the Layers drop-down list on the Home tab to make A-ANNO-TTLB -TEXT current.

3. Open the Autodesk Content Explorer on the Plug-Ins tab ➢ Content panel ➢ Explore button.

4. In the Search field atop the Content Explorer palette, enter the search query **Imperial Drawing Title**↵ (**Metric Drawing Title**↵).

    After executing the search query, the Content Explorer returns content from its indexed (Watched Folder) locations (see Figure 14.47).

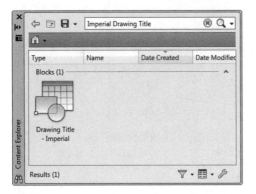

FIGURE 14.47 The Autodesk Content Explorer returning search results

ADDING WATCHED FOLDERS TO CONTENT EXPLORER

The Autodesk Content Explorer will search only indexed content sources. You may add any directory on your local computer to this index by clicking the Add Watched Folder button at the bottom of the Content Explorer palette. Installing the Autodesk Content Service on a file server will allow network directories to be added to the Content Explorer index. To install the Autodesk Content Service on a network server, run the AutoCAD 2012 installer on your server and choose Install Tools & Utilities.

5. Locate the Drawing Title - Imperial (Drawing Title - Metric) block within the search results, and insert it into your drawing by dragging it from the Content Explorer palette into the drawing area (see Figure 14.48).

6. Make the Drawing Name the same as the Sheet Name in Sheet Set Manager by completing the following:

   a. Select the VIEWNAME tag in the Enhanced Attribute Editor.

   b. Right-click in the Value field and select Insert Field.

   c. Change the Field Category to SheetSet, and then select the CurrentSheetTitle Field Name from the Field dialog box.

   d. Click OK.

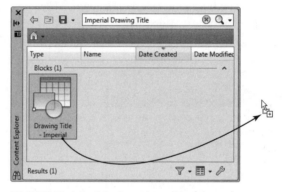
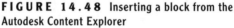

FIGURE 14.48 Inserting a block from the Autodesk Content Explorer

Using Fields to Automatically Acquire Viewport Scale

Instead of manually entering a viewport scale, you'll use a field to dynamically acquire the scale:

1. Erase the contents of the Viewport Scale attribute value.

2. Right-click and select Insert Field.

3. From the Field dialog box that opens, select Objects for Field Category, and Object from the Field Names list box.

   Since the list of AutoCAD objects is quite lengthy, you must first select an object to acquire the properties of an object within a field.

4. Click the Select Objects button, and then select the viewport on sheet A-101.

The Field dialog box updates to display a complete list of available viewport properties (see Figure 14.49).

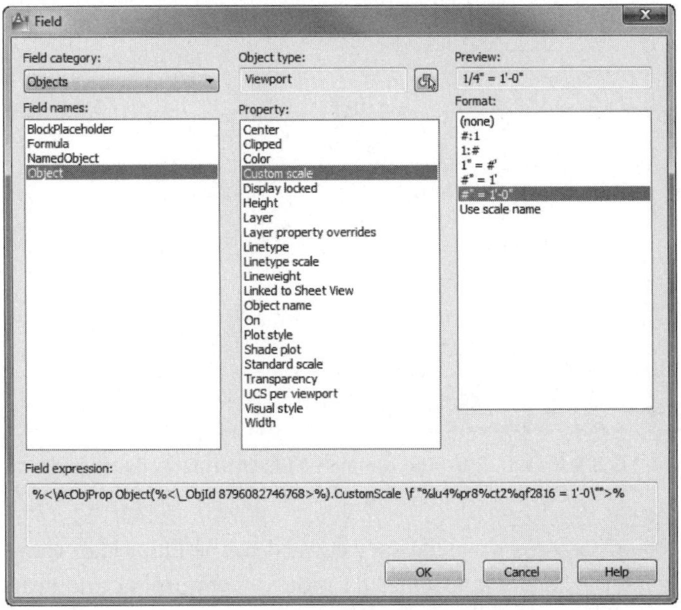

FIGURE 14.49 Acquiring the viewport scale by using fields

5. With the viewport properties displayed within the Field dialog box, choose Custom Scale for Property, and #″ = 1′-0″ (1:#) for Format.

When you are finished, the Field dialog box should look like Figure 14.49.

6. Click OK to return to the Edit Attributes dialog box.

The Viewport Scale attribute is now populated using a field, as shown in Figure 14.50.

7. Click OK to accept the block attribute values.

8. Place the Drawing Title - Imperial (Drawing Title - Metric) block within the layout tab for sheet A-101, and save the I-A-100.dwg (M-A-100.dwg) drawing, keeping the current name.

9. Use the procedure outlined in steps 1–7 to automatically acquire the viewport scale for the SCALE attribute value within the drawing sheet title block.

10. Edit the SCALE attribute by double-clicking the placeholder value.

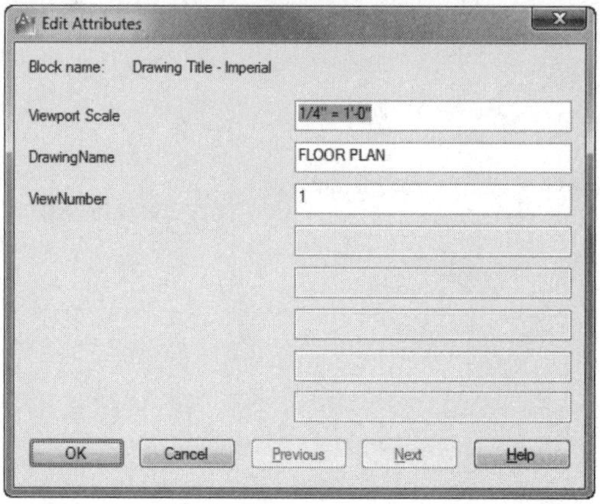

FIGURE 14.50 The completed Edit Attributes dialog box

The new block assigns the necessary context to the Floor Plan view. In addition to the title itself, the block provides a unique view number and drawing scale, two components that are especially helpful as you begin coordinating with contractors and other consultants.

After inserting this block, the static FLOOR PLAN text saved in the I14A -FPLAYO.dwg (M14A-FPLAYO.dwg) is no longer needed. You'll use the Edit Reference In-Place tool to erase this text from the floor plan xref:

1. Make sure I-A-100.dwg (M-A-100.dwg) is open, and switch to Model space by using the Quick View Layouts button in the status bar.

2. Zoom in to the FLOOR PLAN text and then select the I14A-FPLAYO .dwg (M14A-FPLAYO.dwg) xref.

   The contextual External Reference Ribbon tab opens to display common commands related to xrefs.

3. Select the Edit Reference In-Place tool from the Edit panel on the contextual External Reference tab.

   Alternatively, you can double-click the xref, or enter **REFEDIT**⏎ at the command line to start this command.

4. From the Reference Edit dialog box that opens (shown in Figure 14.51), select the I14A-FPLAYO (M14A-FPLAYO) reference and click OK.

The contextual Edit Reference panel is appended to each Ribbon tab.

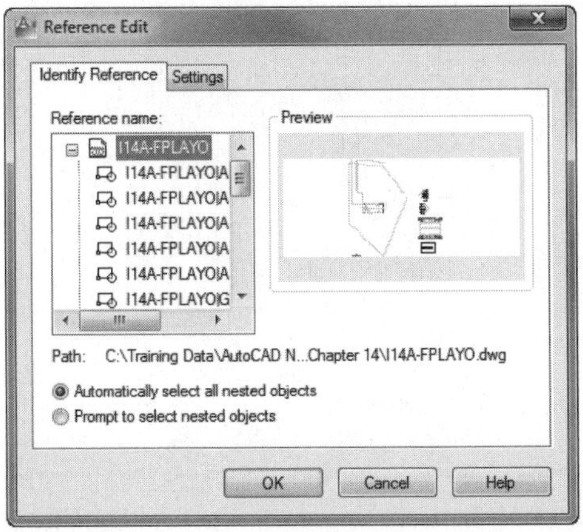

FIGURE 14.51 Opening the I14A-FPLAYO.dwg (M14A-FPLAYO.dwg) reference from the **Reference Edit dialog box**

5. Erase the FLOOR PLAN text.

6. With the floor plan reference open in the Reference Editor, adjust your dimensions as needed so they will fit on your drawing sheet without conflict.

7. After completing these steps, pick the Save Changes (REFCLOSE) button on the contextual Edit References panel.

8. Choose OK from the AutoCAD dialog box alerting you that "All reference edits will be saved."

9. Switch back to the A-101 layout tab, and adjust the location of the Drawing Title block if necessary.

Your A-101 layout should look like Figure 14.52.

10. Save the I-A-100.dwg (M-A-100.dwg) after making these changes.

11. Select the Drawing Title - Imperial (Drawing Title - Metric) block, and right-click to choose the Clipboard ➤ Copy option from the contextual menu that opens.

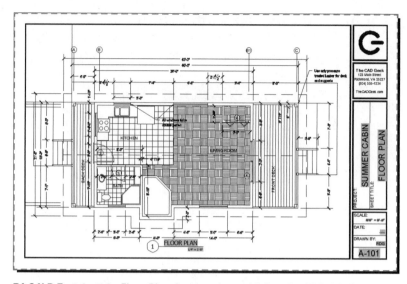

FIGURE 14.52 Floor Plan drawing sheet with Drawing Title block

12. Open the I-A-200.dwg (M-A-200.dwg) file and switch to the A-201 layout if it's not already current.

13. Right-click anywhere in the drawing area and choose Clipboard ➢ Paste To Original Coordinates.

Take note of where the Drawing Title block inserts into the layout tab; its location is exactly the same as the A-101 layout tab. Likewise, the title within the Drawing Title - Imperial (Drawing Title - Metric) block automatically updates to reflect the sheet title from Sheet Set Manager.

14. Double-click the Viewport Scale field within the Drawing Title - Imperial (Drawing Title - Metric) block, and associate it with the viewport for the A-201 sheet.

Refer back to the exercise in the section "Using Fields to Automatically Acquire Viewport Scale" earlier in this chapter for a reminder of the steps required to complete this function.

15. Repeat step 14, and update the SCALE attribute within the drawing sheet title block, along the right edge of the layout tab.

16. Save the current I-A-200.dwg (M-A-200.dwg) drawing, keeping its original name.

Creating Additional Layouts

Your finished document set will include a Floor Plan Materials And Floor Plan Doors plan. The A-101 layout now contains a scaled view of your floor plan. Rather than duplicating all of this work, you'll use the completed A-101 layout as a template for these additional drawings by copying it. Here's how:

1. Open I-A-100.dwg (M-A-100.dwg) by double-clicking the A-101 - Floor Plan sheet from the Sheet List palette in Sheet Set Manager.

   The I-A-100.dwg (M-A-100.dwg) files open, and you are taken to the A-101 layout.

 T I P   Notice the small padlock that displays next to the A-101 sheet in Sheet Set Manager after you open it. This padlock indicates that the drawing is locked, which most likely means someone else has it open. Hover the cursor over the A-101 sheet to display information about the sheet, including who currently has the drawing open. This is especially helpful when multiple people are working on a project at the same time.

2. Right-click the Quick View Layouts button on the status bar, and select Move Or Copy from the contextual menu that opens.

   The Move Or Copy dialog box opens.

3. Select the (Move To End) option in the Before Layout portion of the dialog box, and then check the Create A Copy check box (see Figure 14.53).

4. Click OK to copy the layout and exit the Move Or Copy dialog box.

5. Click the Quick View Layouts button in the status bar to display thumbnails of the layouts in your drawing.

   A second A-101 (2) layout is now listed as one of the layouts.

FIGURE 14.53 Copying a layout by using the Move Or Copy dialog box

6. Right-click the A-101 (2) layout thumbnail and choose Rename.

7. Rename the layout to **A-102** and then press ↵ (see Figure 14.54).

8. Repeat steps 3 and 7 to create another layout named **A-103**.

9. Save the current `I-A-100.dwg` (`M-A-100.dwg`), keeping its existing filename, and then double-click the A-201 sheet from the Sheet Set Manager Sheet List palette to open the `I-A-200.dwg` (`M-A-200.dwg`) file.

10. If you do not already have two tabs (Model and A-201) just under the drawing area shown in Figure 14.55, start the OPTIONS command and go to the Display tab of the Options dialog box.

11. From the Display tab, check the Display Layout And Model Tabs check box found in the Layout Elements group in the lower-left portion of the dialog box.

12. Click OK to exit the Options dialog box and display the layout and Model tabs in the application window (see Figure 14.55).

13. Press and hold the left mouse button, and then press the Ctrl key on your keyboard.

14. Move the mouse to the right, and when a small arrow displays to the right of the A-201 layout tab, release (see the left image of Figure 14.56).

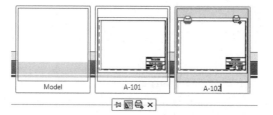

FIGURE 14.54 Renaming the copied A-101 layout

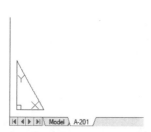

FIGURE 14.55 The Layout and Model tabs displayed in the application window

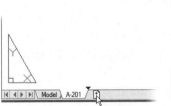

FIGURE 14.56 Using Ctrl+left-click to copy an existing layout (left), and the copied layout (right)

 T I P   If the layout copies to the left of the A-201 layout, use the mouse to drag the A-201 (2) layout to the end, as shown in the right image of Figure 14.56.

15. Repeat steps 13 and 14 until you have a total of four layout tabs.

16. Select and then right-click the A-201 (2) layout tab and select Rename from the contextual menu that opens.

17. Rename the tab to A-202.

18. Repeat this procedure for the other two tabs, renaming them to A-203 and A-204, respectively.

   When finished, the Model and layout tabs should look like Figure 14.57.

19. Save the current I-A-200.dwg (M-A-200.dwg) file (keeping its existing filename).

FIGURE 14.57 Four layout tabs sequentially numbered for each of the elevation drawings

 T I P   To quickly navigate between layout tabs, press Ctrl+Page Up or Ctrl+Page Down. Page Up will cycle to the left, and Page Down will cycle to the right. This also works with worksheets in Microsoft Excel.

You have now created all of the layouts necessary to document your cabin in a construction document set. Although these layouts are saved in the I-A-100.dwg (M-A-100.dwg) and I-A-200.dwg (M-A-200.dwg) drawings, these new layouts are not yet part of your AutoCAD sheet set. Now you need to add these new layouts to the Summer Cabin sheet set.

Adding New Layouts to Sheet Set Manager

Refer to the "Adding Existing Drawings to a Sheet Set" section if you need to refresh your memory on how to do this. To summarize the procedure:

1. Right-click the Architectural subset and choose Import Layout As Sheets.

2. Browse to and select the I-A-100.dwg (M-A-100.dwg) and I-A-200.dwg (M-A-200.dwg) files.

3. Verify that the layouts you added to the I-A-100.dwg (M-A-100.dwg) and I-A-200.dwg (M-A-200.dwg) files are checked (see Figure 14.58).

4. Click the Import Checked button.

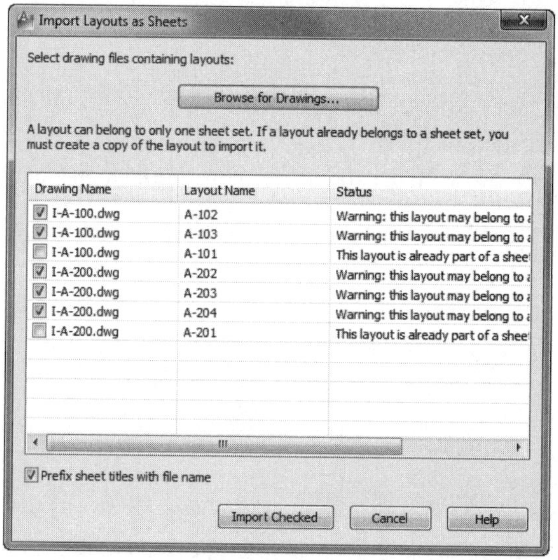

FIGURE 14.58 Importing the new layout tabs into the Summer Cabin sheet set

The A-101 and A-201 layouts should have the status "This layout is already part of a sheet set - not available for import." Because one layout in each drawing is already part of the sheet set, the four new layouts display the status "Warning: this layout may belong to another sheet set."

Renaming and Renumbering Sheets in Sheet Set Manager

Each of the newly created layouts is now part of the Summer Cabin sheet set. Because these layouts were not created using Sheet Set Manager, but rather by copying existing layouts, their name follows a default naming template of *drawing name - layout name*. This exercise will guide you through renaming and renumbering each of these sheets in an efficient manner:

1. With any drawing open, right-click the first sheet representing the newly created layouts in the sheet list, as shown in Figure 14.59, and select Rename & Renumber from the menu that opens.

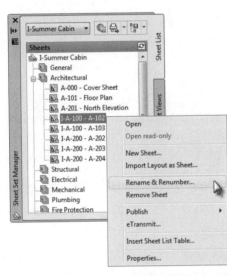

FIGURE 14.59 Choosing the Rename & Renumber option within the Sheet List panel of Sheet Set Manager

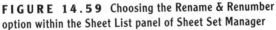

The Rename & Renumber Sheet dialog box shown in Figure 14.60 opens. This dialog box shares many similarities with the New Sheet dialog box but has a number of file management additions. By using the Rename & Renumber Sheet dialog box, you could also rename the layout tabs within each drawing.

The order in which Sheet Set Manager imports the new layouts into your sheet set may vary based on the order they were selected when imported.

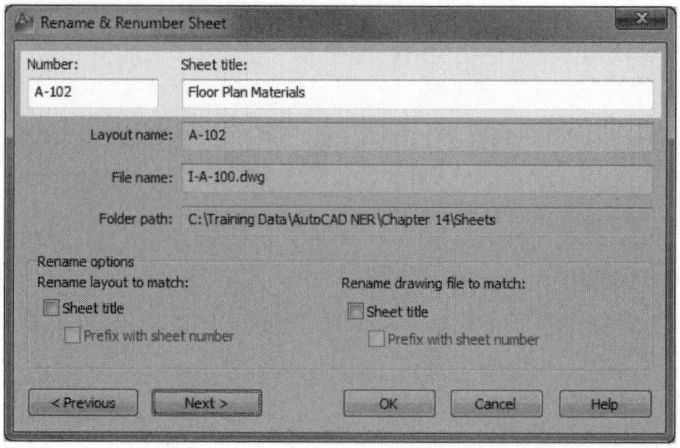

FIGURE 14.60 Renaming and renumbering the new layouts

2. Enter the corresponding values shown in the following table into the Number and Sheet Title fields in the Rename & Renumber Sheet dialog box.

Drawing File	Layout Name	Number	Sheet Title
I-A-100.dwg	A-102	A-102	Floor Plan Materials
(M-A-100.dwg)	A-103	A-103	Floor Plan Doors
I-A-200.dwg	A-202	A-202	East Elevation
(M-A-200.dwg)	A-203	A-203	South Elevation
	A-204	A-204	West Elevation

3. Using this table as your guide, click the Next button and repeat this process for each sheet.

4. After renaming and renumbering each of the newly created layouts, click the OK button to exit the Rename & Renumber Sheets dialog box.

The sheet list in Sheet Set Manager should look like the left image of Figure 14.61.

Note how the sheets are no longer sorted sequentially in the Sheet List palette.

5. Use your mouse to drag each drawing into its proper position.

When you're finished, the Architectural subset should be sorted as shown in the right image of Figure 14.61.

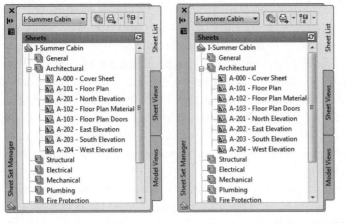

FIGURE 14.61 The renamed sheets (left), sequentially ordered (right)

You have now finished setting up your plan set in Sheet Set Manager. While each of the sheets (layouts) has been created, nothing outside of the title block is drawn on the sheets. In the next several exercises, you'll learn about creating and using viewports to look through paper space (layout), into model space at a specific scale.

Adjusting a Viewport's Contents

When using xrefs to reference only the model files necessary for a given sheet, you can take care of much of the layer management by using the XREF command. But even after you've employed this practice, a quick look at the current A-100 series of plan sheets will reveal a set of sheets that's too cluttered to be useful. A drawing that looks like this would not be acceptable in most production environments, and one of the strengths of AutoCAD is its ability to adjust existing objects in the drawing easily.

External references are typically used in the generation of sheets because, when combined with strong file management standards, they can dramatically reduce clutter in drawings. By grouping similar sheets together into a single file, you can do a large portion of your layer management from model space. Because features such as layer states are much easier to use in model space, you'll generally strive to manage as many layers as possible from model space.

With this in mind, you have a choice to make when any two sheets become dissimilar. Let's use the floor materials layer as an example. It is shown on only one sheet in the entire plan set. Because layers that are frozen or turned off in model space remain that way throughout the entire drawing, you cannot manage that particular layer in the I-A-100.dwg (M-A-100.dwg) model space. There are a couple of ways to address this problem.

First, you may determine that the dissimilarities between it and the other drawings in your set are dramatic enough to justify creating a separate sheet file. Because the layer is used only in a single sheet throughout the entire plan set, you may also choose to further categorize your design by creating a floor finish model file. That way, you wouldn't have to concern yourself with turning that layer off in your other plan sheets, but you could easily reference it in the plan sheet or sheets that needed it.

The other option is to create a viewport override for that layer. Because viewport overrides are hard to track and manage, using them is a less-than-optimal approach, but used sparingly, they can be the right option in some situations. As you create your own plan sets, the method you choose will most often be determined based on the time required for each option. For instance, overriding just one layer in 10 viewports will probably take much longer than simply creating another sheet file for that special case.

This section will allow you to see both approaches employed to manage the contents of your viewports. The A-100 series of drawings will require you to create some viewport layer overrides, whereas the layers for the A-200 series will be managed entirely from model space.

Setting the Linetype Scale

Before you begin configuring the layers in each viewport, let's be sure the layers are displaying correctly. You may have noticed that the rooflines are not dashed, in both model space and paper space. This is because the two variables that control linetype appearance are not set to render lines consistently throughout the entire drawing. To set the linetype scale variables, do the following:

1. Make sure the I-A-100.dwg (M-A-100.dwg) file is open.

2. Set the drawing linetype scale to 1 by entering **LTSCALE**↵ **1**↵ at the command line.

3. To configure AutoCAD so the linetype scale for each viewport is determined by the viewport scale, enter **PSLTSCALE**↵ **1**↵.
   This will ensure a consistent dash length between viewports.

4. Finally, to configure AutoCAD to use the current annotation scale in model space to render dashed lines, enter **MSLTSCALE**↵ **1**↵ at the command line.

When finished, your drawing should look similar to Figure 14.62.

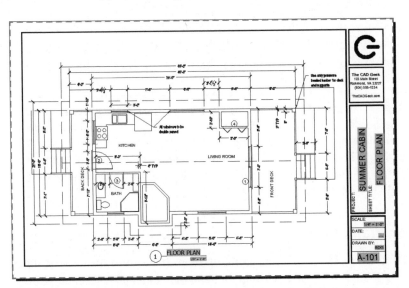

FIGURE 14.62 The Cabin Floor Plan layout after selectively freezing layers in the viewport

Managing the Floor Plan Sheet File

Composed of three differing layouts, the Floor Plan sheet file is rather atypical. Each layout, while similar, has numerous dissimilar elements. Much of the layer management affecting the entire drawing has been taken care of through the use of xrefs. That is, since the civil site plan is not referenced in the I-A-100.dwg (M-A-100.dwg) file, there's no need to worry about turning the layers contained within it off.

Even with the civil site plan layers off the table, there are still plenty of layers whose visibility you need to configure in the Floor Plan sheet file. Since many of these exceptions are for a single sheet, much of the remaining layer management for this sheet file will be done using viewport layer overrides.

1. Make sure the I-A-100.dwg (M-A-100.dwg) file is open, and switch to model space.

    The only layer that's currently visible and that should be frozen in all viewports is the A-AREA-NPLT layer. While it's possible you already changed the Plot layer property, you'll freeze this layer as well.

2. Open the Layer Properties Manager and freeze the I14A-FPLAYO|
A-AREA-NPLT (M14A-FPLAYO|A-AREA-NPLT) layer.

Note how the reference name prefixes the layer name. This allows
you to quickly determine to which xref a layer belongs. Conversely,
layers without such a prefix belong to the current drawing.

T I P   Try selecting the Xref group in the filters section of the Layer
Properties Manager. This will display only layers that are referenced in the
current drawing. To see a list of only the layers in the current drawing, check
the Invert Filter check box in the lower-left corner of the Layer Properties
Manager. If you try this, be sure to select the All group and uncheck the
Invert Filter check box after you're finished.

The Floor Plan Sheet

After adjusting the visibility of layers common to each layout in the current sheet
file, you'll begin addressing layer visibility for the individual plan sheets. First up
is the Floor Plan sheet A-101. In this plan, you do not want the grid, plan materials, or door label layers to display. You will make these changes in this exercise:

1. Make sure the I-A-100.dwg (M-A-100.dwg) file is open, and switch to
the Floor Plan A-101 layout.

2. Double-click anywhere inside the viewport boundary to enter model
space from the viewport.

3. Select the Freeze tool (LAYFRZ) found on the Layers panel of the Home
tab, and then graphically select one of the floor material hatches on
the A-FLOR-PATT layer.

After you select an object on the A-FLOR-PATT layer, that layer is
no longer visible on the screen. Because this change was made from
within a viewport, the change is applied as a viewport override. This
means the A-FLOR-PATT layer will be visible in other viewports in
the same drawing, but will not display in the viewport on sheet A-101.

N O T E   The viewports in layouts are described as *floating* because they can
be moved around. They always reside in the layout portion of the drawing. There
is another kind of viewport in AutoCAD called a *model space, or tiled, viewport*,
which is fixed and exists only in model space. If you want more information on this
subject, search for the phrase *set model space viewports* in the AutoCAD help system. For brevity, in this chapter I refer to floating viewports simply as *viewports*.

4. Using the Freeze tool once again, select one of the door tags (a circle with a number inside it near the doors).

5. Remaining inside the viewport on sheet A-101, open the Layer Properties Manager and locate the 14A-FPLAY1|A-GRID layer.
   If necessary, scroll to the right until you find the VP Freeze column.

6. Click the icon to freeze the grid layer in the current viewport.

7. Close the Layer Properties Manager palette to return to your drawing.

With these layer changes complete, your drawing should look like Figure 14.63.

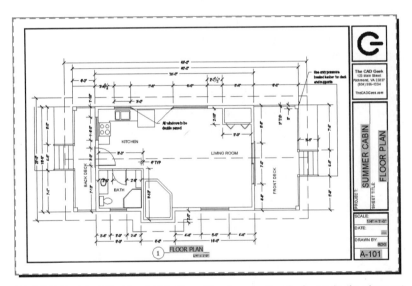

FIGURE 14.63 The A-101 Floor Plan layout after the layers in the viewport are selectively frozen

The Floor Plan Materials Sheet

Similar to the Floor Plan sheet you just finished, you'll apply a series of viewport overrides to the Floor Plan Materials sheet. This time you'll be changing the visibility of the grid, dimension, and door tag layers:

1. Make sure I-A-100.dwg (M-A-100.dwg) is open, and switch to the Floor Plan Materials A-102 layout.

2. Double-click in the viewport, and use the Freeze (LAYFRZ) tool to select any of the dimensions.

The 14A-FPLAY1|A-ANNO-DIMS layer is frozen in the current viewport only.

3. Use the Freeze tool once again to select one of the vertical gridlines above the floor plan.

Selecting one of these lines freezes the 14A-FPLAY1|A-GRID layer.

4. Finally, use the Freeze tool to select one of the door tags to freeze the 14A-FPLAY1|A-ANNO-TABL layer.

5. The Drawing Title block is a dynamic block. Click it and then drag the right end of the horizontal line to the right until it extends underneath the entire title. (See Figure 14.64.)

6. You may choose to use the PAN command to better orient the floor plan on the Plan Materials sheet.

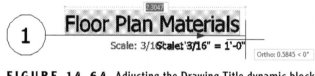

FIGURE 14.64 Adjusting the Drawing Title dynamic block

When finished, your drawing should look like Figure 14.65.

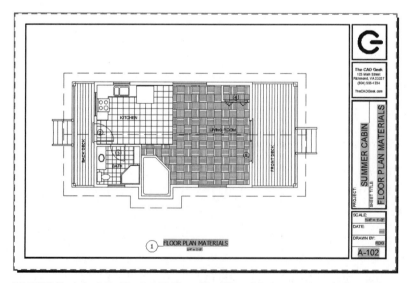

FIGURE 14.65 The A-102 Floor Plan Materials layout after the layers in the viewport are selectively frozen

The Floor Plan Doors Sheet

The Floor Plan Doors sheet is the first layout that requires more than one viewport. Here is a summary of the steps to clean up the drawing:

1. Make the A-103 layout active.

2. Inside the viewport, freeze the A-ANNO-DIMS and A-FLOR-PATT layers.

3. In the status bar, click the Viewport Scale button and choose 3/16″ = 1′-0″ (1:70).

   The viewport zooms out to reflect the smaller scale. To set the metric scale 1:70, it may be necessary to enter **ZOOM**⏎ **1/70**⏎⏎ at the command line.

4. Adjust the length of the horizontal line in the block until it extends underneath the entire title as necessary.

5. Select the viewport and, using the grips, adjust it so that it fits more closely to the floor plan.

   Your drawing should look similar to Figure 14.66.

6. Make the A-ANNO-NPLT layer current.

7. Create a new viewport in the lower-left corner of the layout (see Figure 14.67).

   Refer to the "Creating the Paper Space Viewport" section if you need a refresher.

   The viewport displays all the model space contents. Although the view will be labeled as not having a scale, you should create the viewport with a scale of 1/4″ = 1′-0″ (1:50).

8. Select the I14A-FPLAYO.dwg (M14A-FPLAYO.dwg) xref, right-click, and then choose Open Xref from the contextual menu that opens.

   This opens the I14A-FPLAYO.dwg (M14A-FPLAYO.dwg) file in a new drawing window.

9. Modify the General Notes text box to be a single column, by doing the following:

   a. Place the cursor just after the first note in the left column.

   b. Press the Delete key.

10. To allow more room in the plan sheet, stretch the 1, 2, 3, and 4 grid-lines to be closer to the cabin.

11. Save and close the `I14A-FPLAY0.dwg` (`M14A-FPLAY0.dwg`), and then return to the A-103 layout tab in the `I-A-100.dwg` (`M-A-100.dwg`) file.

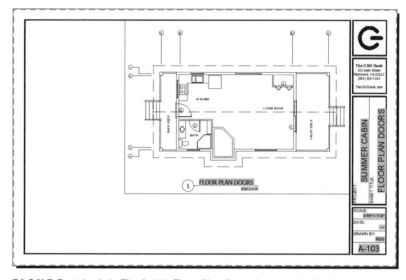

FIGURE 14.66 The A-103 Floor Plan Doors layout after the layers are frozen and the viewport is adjusted

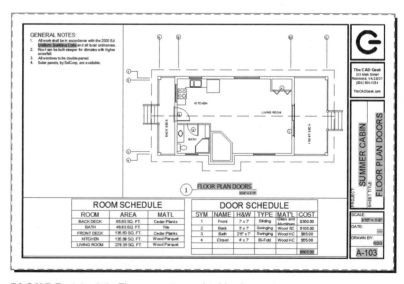

FIGURE 14.67 The new notes and table viewports

12. Copy this viewport, double-click inside the new viewport, and then pan and zoom until the General Notes text fills the viewport.

13. Copy the Drawing Title block under the new viewports, and edit the attributes as shown in Figure 14.67.

N O T E Most plan sheets require some degree of refinement as they are put together. Learning how to switch quickly between different xrefs is imperative in making these edits in an efficient manner. You'll likely determine a preference between editing xrefs in place or opening the reference as you gain more experience with the software.

The floor plan drawings for your plan set are now complete. In this section, you learned how to create viewports at a specific scale, manage the layers in those viewports, and import layouts into Sheet Set Manager. In the next section, you'll apply many of these same concepts to setting up your elevation plan sheets.

Managing the Elevations Sheet File

Much of the preceding section was dedicated to managing layers in viewports. Because a handful of layers were viewable in only one or two viewports, you had to spend a sizeable amount of time creating viewport layer overrides. It's possible that each of the sheets was different enough to justify creating separate DWG files for each sheet.

In contrast, there's no need to create any viewport overrides in your Elevations sheet file. In fact, your elevations are a perfect example of how xrefs can play a role in layer management for plan sheets. There are no conflicting objects or layers in any of the views you'll create. Consequently, you'll simply verify that all of your elevation layers are visible in model space.

You'll start with the south elevation because it is the only one drawn without rotating the UCS. Consequently, it should be the quickest to set up. Here's how:

1. Using Sheet Set Manager, open the A-203 - South Elevation drawing sheet in the I-A-200.dwg (M-A-200.dwg) file.

2. Turn on and thaw all of the layers in the current drawing by using the Turn All Layers On (LAYON) and Thaw All Layers (LAYTHW) tools found on the extended Layers panel on the Home tab.

3. Pan in the viewport so that the south elevation is centered in the viewport.

4. Delete the SOUTH ELEVATION text from the I14A-FPLAYO.dwg (M14A-FPLAYO.dwg) file.

5. Adjust the viewport boundary as necessary so that only the south elevation is viewable on the A-203 drawing sheet.

When you're finished, the South Elevation drawing sheet should look like Figure 14.68.

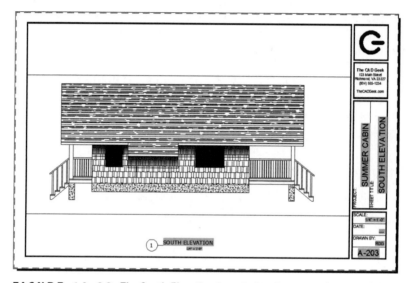

FIGURE 14.68 The South Elevation layout after layers are frozen and the viewport is adjusted

Adjusting the Other Elevation Layouts

The remaining elevations were drawn with a rotated user coordinate system (UCS) so that they appeared in the correct orientation while you were drawing them. However, they are rotated when looking at the drawing in the World Coordinate System (WCS). In a similar fashion, you'll modify the view of each viewport by rotating the UCS:

1. Make the A-202 (East Elevation) layout active, and double-click inside the viewport.

 2. To rotate the UCS, do the following:

   a. Click the View tab and then click the Z button in the Coordinates panel.

   b. Enter **90↵** at the Specify Rotation Angle About Z Axis: prompt.

ENABLE THE COORDINATES PANEL

If the Coordinates panel is not visible from the View tab, do the following:

1. Right-click any panel title to display a contextual right-click menu.

2. From the contextual right-click menu, choose Show Panels ➤ Coordinates.

3. To use the PLAN command to rotate the view to match the UCS, enter **PLAN.↵↵**.

4. Click the Viewport Scale button, and choose 1/4″ = 1′-0″ (1:50) then exit model space.

5. Pan in the viewport so that the east elevation is centered.

6. Adjust the viewport boundary as necessary so that only the east elevation appears on the A-202 layout.

7. Delete the EAST ELEVATION text.

   Your layout should look like Figure 14.69.

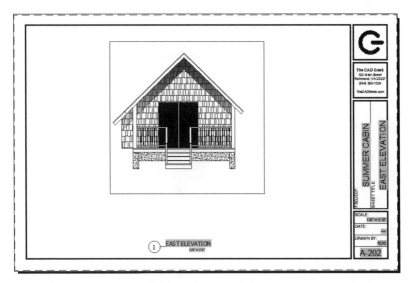

FIGURE 14.69 The East Elevation layout after the layers are frozen and the viewport is adjusted

8. Repeat steps 1 through 7 for the two remaining elevation layouts, substituting the appropriate text and values as required. For example, the
viewport in the A-201 - North Elevation layout must be rotated 180°,
and the A-204 - West Elevation layout must be rotated 270° or −90°.

When the elevations are completed, the A-201 - North Elevation
layout should look like the top of Figure 14.70, and the A-204 - West
Elevation layout should look like the bottom of Figure 14.70.

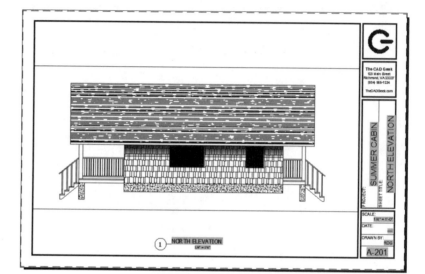

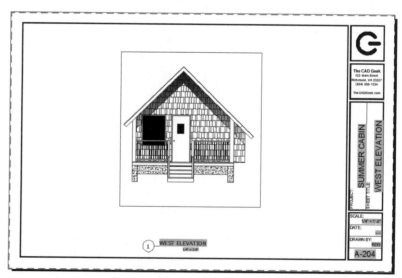

FIGURE 14.70 The North Elevation plan sheet (top) and the West
Elevation plan sheet (bottom)

Setting Up the Site Plan Sheet

The site plan should show the cabin plan, the driveway, the access road, and the image, but not the elevations or much of the information shown on the previous layouts. Because of the odd shape of the property line, you'll delete the current viewport, draw a polyline, and turn that polyline into a viewport. Here's how:

1. Open the I-C-101.dwg (M-C-101.dwg) sheet file and make the C-101 layout current.

2. Switch to the Model thumbnail by using the Quick View Layouts button in the status bar.

3. Make the current layer A-ANNO-REFR, and attach I13C-SPLAYO.dwg (M13C-SPLAYO.dwg) by configuring the Attach External Reference dialog box, as shown in Figure 14.71.

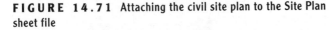

FIGURE 14.71 Attaching the civil site plan to the Site Plan sheet file

4. Use the upper-left corner of the deck as the insertion point for the site plan reference (see Figure 14.72).

5. Make the A-ANNO-NPLT layer current, and create a new viewport extending from the upper-left corner of the title block to the lower-right corner of the title block.

6. Double-click inside the viewport, zoom to the drawing's extents, and then double-click outside of the viewport to switch back to paper space.

7. With the A-ANNO-NPLT layer still current, start the PLINE (Polyline) command and draw a closed polyline that roughly follows the shape of the property, as shown in Figure 14.73.

    The exact shape isn't important because the viewport scale isn't properly set yet.

8. To turn the polyline into a viewport, do the following:

   a. Click the View tab.

   b. Expand the Rectangular tool and click the From Object button in the Viewports panel.

   c. Click the polyline.

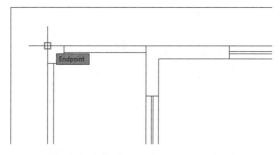

FIGURE 14.72 Specifying the site plan insertion point

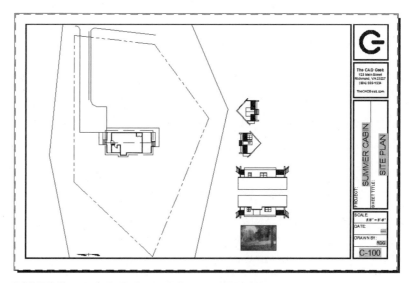

FIGURE 14.73 Draw a polyline around the property.

The new viewport displays the model space contents as well as the original viewport.

9. Delete the rectangular viewport.

T I P The Create Polygonal button can also be used to draw the viewport directly. However, the Polyline tool provides greater control over the shape of the viewport by allowing arc segments, and it allows the viewports to have a width in situations where they are visible when plotted.

Defining a New Viewport Scale

Scales that use the convention *fraction″* = 1′-0″ are said to be using an *architectural scale*. Site plans generally use an *engineering scale*, which uses the convention 1″ = *number′*, where *number* is a multiple of 10. For this site plan, you'll define a new viewport scale and add it to the Viewport Scale drop-down list.

1. Select the viewport, click the Viewport Scale button, and choose Custom to open the Edit Drawing Scales dialog box, as shown in Figure 14.74.

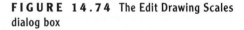

FIGURE 14.74 The Edit Drawing Scales dialog box

---

2. Click the Add button to open the Add Scale dialog box.

The best engineering scale for the site plan, found through experimentation, is 1″ = 20′-0″ (1 = 300). This calculates to a ratio of 1″ = 240″ (1 = 300).

3. In the Name Appearing In Scale List box, enter 1″ = 20′ (1:300) but don't press ↵ yet.

4. In the lower part of the dialog box, set the Paper Units to 1 (1) and the Drawing Units to 240 (300), as shown in Figure 14.75.

FIGURE 14.75 The Add Scale dialog box

5. Click OK in each of the dialog boxes to accept the changes and close them.

6. Select the viewport again, click the Viewport Scale button, and then choose 1′ = 20″ (1:300). The viewport scale changes to match the scale selected.

7. Pan in the viewport or select the viewport in paper space and adjust its endpoints so that only the site information is displayed.

8. Using the Freeze button or the Layer Properties Manager, freeze the following layers in the viewport only:

> A-AREA-NPLT
>
> A-ANNO-DIMS
>
> A-DOOR
>
> A-FLOR-FIXT
>
> A-GRID
>
> A-FLOR-PATT
>
> A-ROOF
>
> A-ANNO-TABL
>
> A-ANNO-TEXT
>
> A-GLAZ

9. Copy the Drawing Title block from another drawing sheet, and change the Viewport Scale to 1″ = 20′ (1:300).

10. Create a new viewport and zoom in to see the referenced image file.

11. Copy and edit the Drawing Title block.
   Your layout should look similar to Figure 14.76.

12. Save the current I-C-101.dwg (M-C-101.dwg), keeping its existing filename.

You've made a set of eight drawings, complete with scaled viewports and designated content. In the next section, you will look at a couple of ways to protect the drawings from accidental errors.

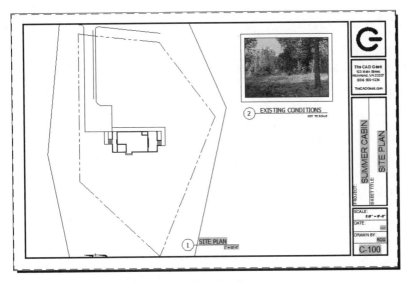

FIGURE 14.76 The completed Site Plan layout

Locking and Turning Off Viewports

One of the common errors that you will make when working with viewports is zooming or panning while in a viewport and then failing to return the viewport to its proper appearance. You can prevent yourself, or anyone else, from editing the viewport view by *locking* the viewport. This feature doesn't prevent you from editing the content of the viewport—just how you access and view it.

When you execute a pan or zoom while inside a locked viewport, AutoCAD temporarily exits the viewport, pans or zooms the equivalent amount in paper space, and then returns to model space. There is a slight lag in time when panning or zooming with this feature on, but it is much less than the time you may spend correcting, replotting, or reissuing a set of drawings that have viewports at the wrong scale factor. Follow this procedure to lock a viewport:

1. Open the I-A-100.dwg (M-A-100.dwg) drawing and make the A-101 layout active if it's not already.

2. Select the viewport, and then click the Lock/Unlock Viewport button next to the Viewport Scale button on the status bar.

   The open lock icon changes to a closed lock. The viewport is now locked.

3. Repeat step 2 for all the viewports that show the cabin in the remaining layouts.

Turning Off Viewports

Beyond controlling the visibility of layers in each viewport, you can also turn off a viewport so that all model space objects within it are invisible:

1. Make the A-103 - Floor Plan Doors layout current, and then select the viewport that shows the table.

2. Right-click and choose Display Viewport Objects; then click No.

   The contents of the viewport disappear (see Figure 14.77). You can accomplish the same result in the Properties palette by opening the drop-down list next to the On option in the Misc rollout and clicking No.

3. Turn the viewport back on.

4. Save this drawing, keeping its existing I-A-100.dwg (M-A-100.dwg) filename.

WHAT YOU DO IN MODEL SPACE AND PAPER SPACE (LAYOUTS)

To summarize, here's a partial list of some of the things you do in each of the two environments.

Model Space   You can perform the following tasks in model space:

▶ Zoom to a scale in a viewport

▶ Work on the building (or the project you are drawing)

▶ Make a viewport current

▶ Control layer visibility globally for the drawing

(Continues)

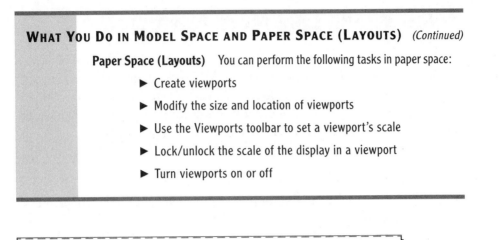

WHAT YOU DO IN MODEL SPACE AND PAPER SPACE (LAYOUTS) *(Continued)*

Paper Space (Layouts)   You can perform the following tasks in paper space:

- ▶ Create viewports
- ▶ Modify the size and location of viewports
- ▶ Use the Viewports toolbar to set a viewport's scale
- ▶ Lock/unlock the scale of the display in a viewport
- ▶ Turn viewports on or off

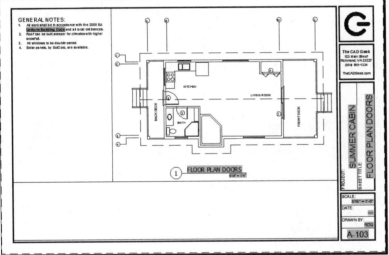

FIGURE 14.77 The Plan Notes layout with the table viewport turned off

Being able to turn off viewports can be an advantage for a complex drawing with many viewports or for one with a lot of information in each viewport. Remember that, even though all the layouts in this drawing are based on one drawing, AutoCAD is drawing at least part of that drawing in each viewport. In a complex drawing, this can slow down the computer, so it's handy to be able to temporarily turn off any viewports on which you aren't working. It's also an easy way to check which objects are in model space and which are on the layout (or in paper space).

You will work with the viewports and layouts again in the next chapter, where you will round out your knowledge of 2D AutoCAD by learning the principles of plotting and printing AutoCAD drawings.

If You Would Like More Practice...

Most plan sets for a building project like this one will include a long list of drawing sheets to document all aspects of its construction. Additional sheets might include an overall site plan, a detailed cross section of your kitchen with cabinets and appliances, or even a series of detail sheets documenting how the foundation should be constructed. To create additional sheets (layouts) like these:

1. Create a new drawing from scratch, attaching the necessary external references.

2. Create another layout for the cabin drawing that has a landscape orientation and is sized to fit a 30″×42″ paper.

3. Create four or more viewports: one for an overall site plan and the others for various views of the drawing.

   Your new layout may look something like Figure 14.78.

4. Save this drawing as I-A-100-extra.dwg (M-A-100-extra.dwg).

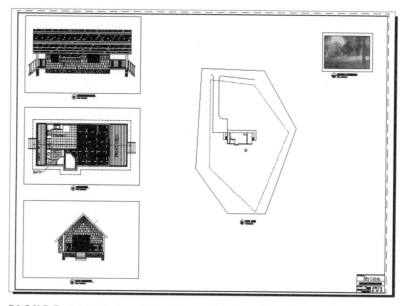

FIGURE 14.78 An additional layout for the cabin project

Are You Experienced?

Now you can...

- ☑ create a layout and associate it with a page setup

- ☑ move between paper space and model space

- ☑ create and manage plan sheets using Sheet Set Manager

- ☑ set up viewports on layouts

- ☑ control layer visibility in individual viewports

- ☑ zoom to a scale in a viewport

- ☑ lock the display of a viewport

- ☑ turn viewports off and on

Printing an AutoCAD Drawing

With today's equipment, there is no difference between printing and plotting. *Printing* used to refer to smaller-format printers, and plotting referred to pen plotters, most of which were for plotting large sheets. But the terms are now used interchangeably. Pen plotters have been virtually replaced by large-format inkjet or laser plotters with a few additional settings not commonly found on other printing devices. Otherwise, as far as AutoCAD is concerned, the differences between plotters and laser, inkjet, and electrostatic printers are minimal. In this book, printing and plotting have the same meaning.

Although you may have a variety of small-format and large-format plotters attached to your computer, this chapter assumes as a standard the DWFx ePlot (XPS Compatible).pc3 plotter. Since each plotter is slightly different, standardizing on this one virtual device will ensure that you're able to follow each of the steps as they are discussed in this chapter.

You will print the layouts inside the A-100.dwg, A-200.dwg, and C-101.dwg drawings from a layout at its default Ledger 11″×17″ (297 mm×420 mm) A3 sheet and at 24″×36″ (594 mm×841 mm) A1 sheet sizes.

In addition to ensuring your ability to plot to each of these formats, plotting to an electronic format similar to DWF or DWFX is not all that uncommon in industry. There is often a need to keep an electronic record of each submittal of a project, and the DWF format is one of the ways this is possible. I'll discuss some other electronic formats later in this chapter, but for now it's more important to note that the purpose of using a DWF plotter is to give you the basic principles for plotting, regardless of whether you have access to a printer or plotter.

▶ **Setting up a drawing to be printed**

▶ **Using the Plot dialog box**

▶ **Looking at plot styles**

▶ **Assigning lineweights to layers in your drawing**

▶ **Selecting the part of your drawing to print**

▶ **Previewing a print**

▶ **Publishing multiple layouts**

▶ **Publishing with Sheet Set Manager**

Using the Plot Dialog Box

The job of getting your AutoCAD file to plot (electronically or as a hard copy) can be broken down into five tasks. You'll need to tell AutoCAD the following:

▶ The printing device you'll use

▶ The lineweight assigned to each object in your drawing

▶ The portion of the drawing you're printing

▶ The sheet size to which you're printing

▶ The scale, orientation, and placement of the print on the sheet

You handle most of these tasks in the Plot dialog box:

1. Open I-A-100.dwg (M-A-100.dwg), shown in Figure 15.1. Click the A-101 layout to make it active, and ensure that you are in paper space.

2. Click the Output tab, and then click the Plot button on the Plot panel to open the Plot dialog box.

   The title bar includes the name of the layout because, in this case, you're printing a drawing from paper space (layout). If you print from model space, the title bar displays the word Model. This dialog box is similar to the Page Setup dialog box you worked with in Chapter 14, "Using Layouts to Set Up a Print," when you were setting up layouts (see Figure 15.2).

> **You can also open the Plot dialog box by pressing Ctrl+P, or by entering PLOT↵ or PRINT↵.**

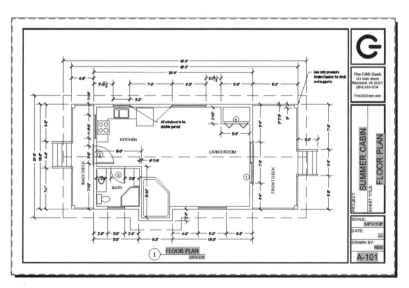

FIGURE 15.1 The A-101 layout showing the floor plan

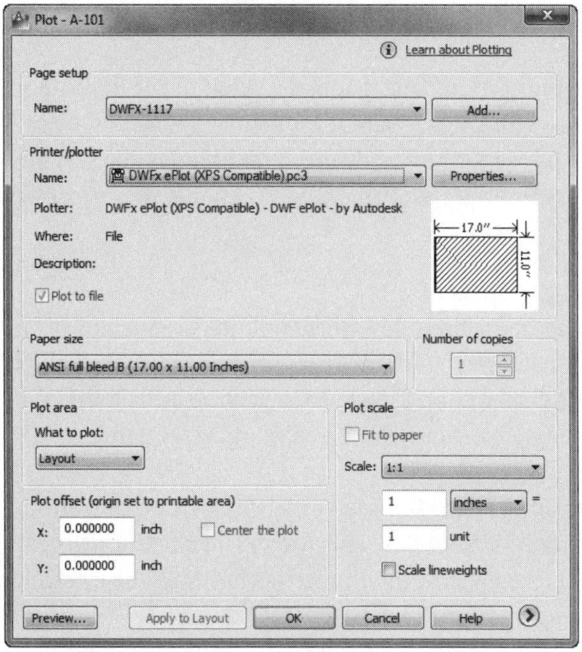

FIGURE 15.2 The Plot dialog box

UNRECONCILED LAYERS

If you receive a Layer Notification Warning dialog box or a notification bubble stating that you have unreconciled layers, you should address the situation before plotting the drawing. *Unreconciled layers* are new layers that have been added since the last time the drawing was saved, the PLOT command was used, or a layer state was saved. The purpose of the warning or notification is to signal you to look at these new layers and determine whether any action is required.

1. Open the Layer Properties Manager, and click Unreconciled New Layers in the left pane to display the list in the right pane.

2. Select all the layers shown, right-click, and choose Reconcile Layer from the context menu.

3. Close the Layer Properties Manager.

All layers are now reconciled, and the warnings should discontinue until you add any new layers.

First, you'll take a quick tour of this dialog box. Then you'll start setting up to print.

You'll see seven areas of settings on this unexpanded version of the dialog box. Some of the buttons and boxes won't be activated. I'll mention others only in passing, because their functions are for more-advanced techniques than those covered in this book. These functions are available when in model space as well.

Printer/Plotter

In the Printer/Plotter group, the Name drop-down list contains the various printing devices to which AutoCAD has been configured. The current one, the DWFx ePlot (XPS Compatible).pc3, is displayed in Figure 15.2. Just below the list, the name of the driver and the assigned port or network path and asset name are displayed for the selected printer.

Clicking the Properties button to the right opens the Plotter Configuration Editor dialog box, which has three tabs of data specific to the current printer. You must have a default printer assigned for the Properties button to be available. Most of this will already be set up by your Windows operating system.

Back in the Plot dialog box, you'll notice that the Plot To File check box is selected and grayed out. This is because the DWF plotter you have selected is a *virtual device*, meaning it cannot create a physical print on a piece of paper and can create only a file. In this case, a DWFX file will be created, which can then be viewed and plotted to an actual piece of paper by using the free Autodesk Design Review program if you want.

When a physical device, such as a printer attached to your computer, is selected in the Plot dialog box, the Plot To File check box will not be grayed out. Selecting it will direct AutoCAD to make and save the print as a PLT file, rather than sending it to the selected printer. Many reproduction service bureaus prefer to receive electronic formats such as PLT, DWF, DWFX, and even PDF files to print, rather than AutoCAD DWG files. Unlike DWG files, the previously mentioned electronic formats do not require you to send all of the support and externally referenced files (fonts, images, external references, and so on) for the drawing to plot correctly.

> Autodesk Design Review is included in the default installation of AutoCAD, and it may also be downloaded from the Autodesk website (`www.autodesk.com/designreview`) for free.

Paper Size and Number of Copies

In the Paper Size group, the drop-down list contains paper sizes that the current plot device can recognize. To the right is the Number Of Copies group, which is grayed out when plotting to a file; this option allows you to specify how many copies of a drawing to plot. When you have a large run of pages to print, it's prudent to print a single copy of each, check for errors or omissions, and then print multiple copies of each page.

Plot Area

In the Plot Area group, a drop-down list contains six options for specifying which portions of your drawing to print: Display, Extents, Limits, View, Window, and Layout. You have already decided which layers will be visible when the print is made by freezing the layers in each viewport whose objects you don't want to print. Now you must decide how to designate the area of the drawing to be printed. As you go through the options, it's useful to think about the choices with regard to two printing possibilities: printing the whole drawing and printing just the floor plan. Using layouts removes much of the guesswork from the plotting process.

To illustrate how these options work, we'll make a couple of assumptions. First, the 1:1 Scale option is selected in the Plot Scale area, so AutoCAD will try to print the drawing at full scale. Second, the drawing will be in landscape orientation.

1. In the Plot Scale group, expand the Scale drop-down list and select 1:1.

2. Verify that the Plot Scale Units drop-down list is set to inches (mm), as shown in Figure 15.2 earlier.

N O T E   You'll learn more about plot scale in the "Plot Scale" section later in this chapter.

3. To expand the dialog box, click the right-pointing arrow in the lower-right corner.

4. Make sure Landscape is selected in the Drawing Orientation group, and then click the left-pointing arrow to collapse the expansion.

The Display Option

The Display option on the What To Plot drop-down list prints whatever is currently on the screen, including the blank area around the drawing.

1. With the sheet in landscape orientation and with the origin in the lower-left corner of the paper space area, choose the Display option.

2. Click the Preview button in the lower-left corner of the Plot dialog box. The plot preview will look like Figure 15.3.

   The drawing doesn't fit well on the sheet with this option. The drawing is oriented and sized correctly, but with the beginning of the plot area in the lower-right corner of the paper space area, it's printed above and to the right of where it should be. A considerable amount of clipping has also occurred, and much of the drawing is not displayed. Printing to Display is a quick method of plotting everything that is shown in the layout but is rarely the best solution when plotting in model space.

3. Right-click and choose Exit, or press the Esc key, to exit the preview mode.

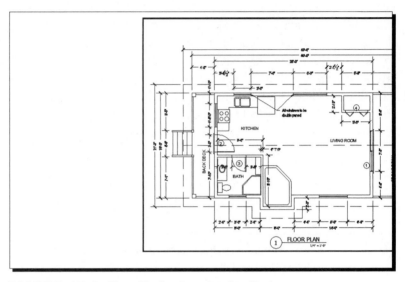

FIGURE 15.3 The cabin drawing printed to Display

The Extents Option

When you select the Extents option, AutoCAD tries to fill the sheet with all visible objects in the drawing.

1. Choose the Extents option.

2. Click the Preview button; the results will look similar to Figure 15.4.
This is closer to acceptable than the Display option, but it's not quite right. The border is off-center because the extents of the drawing begin at the lower-left corner white area in paper space that represents the actual paper. This is a good method to use if the border is not plotted or if there is no border at all. Be aware that if any objects exist in paper space to the left or below the drawing area, they will shift the beginning of the extents and reduce the amount of the actual drawing area that is visible.

3. Press the Esc key to return to the Plot dialog box.

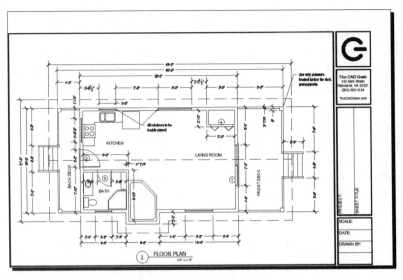

FIGURE 15.4 The drawing printed to Extents

The Limits Option

Do you remember the drawing limits for the cabin drawing that you set in Chapter 3, "Setting Up a Drawing"? As a refresher, perform the following steps:

1. Open the floor plan model file, I14A-FPLAYO.dwg (M14A-FPLAYO.dwg), from the preceding chapter or from the Chapter 15 download.

2. Click the Quick View Layouts button in the status bar to switch to model space.
   Plotting to Limits is not available in a layout.

3. Zoom in to the floor plan, start the PLOT command again, and assign the same DWFx plotter.

4. With the plotter selected, choose Limits from the What To Plot drop-down list.

5. In the Plot Scale section, click the Fit To Paper option.
   Plotting at 1:1 in model space would result in only a miniscule portion of the vast drawing area actually getting plotted.
   When you print to Limits, AutoCAD prints only what lies within the limits, and it pushes what's within the limits to the corner that is the origin of the print.

6. Click the right-facing arrow in the lower-right corner, and make sure Landscape is selected in the Drawing Orientation group.

7. Click the Preview button in the lower-left corner (see Figure 15.5).

This print won't work here because the limits don't cover the entire drawing, and the title block has already been moved into paper space. Printing to Limits can be a good tool for setting up a print, but you'll usually reset the limits from their original defining coordinates to new ones for the actual print.

8. Right-click and choose Exit from the context menu to exit the preview.

 N O T E   If you are in a layout of a DWG file, the Limits option is replaced by Layout in the What To Plot drop-down list in the Plot Area section.

The View Option

When printing to View, you tell AutoCAD to print a previously defined view that was saved with the drawing. When plotting from model space, the View option isn't displayed in the What To Plot drop-down list if you haven't defined and saved any views yet. The View option is never available when plotting from paper space (layouts).

1. Open the I14A-FPLAYO.dwg (M14A-FPLAYO.dwg) from the Chapter 15 download, or update the named views for your elevations, and use the floor plan model file you created in the preceding chapter.

N O T E   Because you moved your elevations in an earlier chapter, you may need to redefine your named views for this exercise to work. The named views stored in the I14A-FPLAYO.dwg (M14A-FPLAYO.dwg) file in the Chapter 15 download have been updated.

2. Start the PLOT command once again, expand the What To Plot drop-down list, and click View.

A new drop-down list appears to the right.

3. Expand the new drop-down list and choose East_elev.

4. Click the Preview button, and the preview should look similar to Figure 15.6.

A view is always taken from the same fixed location. In the preceding chapter, you moved several components of the cabin drawing and might need to update the named views to reflect this. The View option for What To Plot is a valuable tool for setting up partial prints of a drawing.

5. Press Esc to exit the preview, and then click Cancel to close the Plot dialog box.

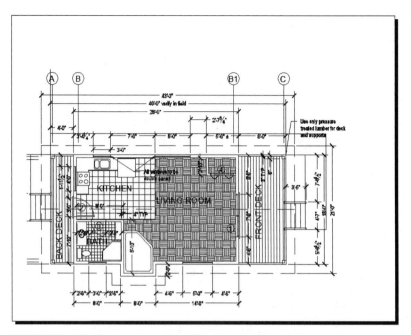

FIGURE 15.5 A preview of the drawing printed to Limits

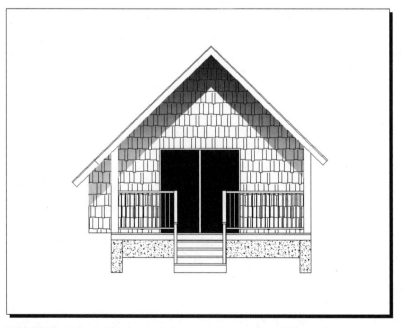

FIGURE 15.6 Plotting model space to a named view (East_elev)

The Window Option

Using a window to define the area of a plot is the most flexible of the methods described so far. It's like using a zoom window in the drawing. When you select this option, you're returned to your drawing, where you'll make a window around the area you want to print. When you return to the Plot dialog box, a Window button appears in the right side of the Plot Area section (see Figure 15.7), in case you need to redefine the window.

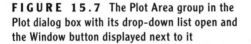

FIGURE 15.7 The Plot Area group in the Plot dialog box with its drop-down list open and the Window button displayed next to it

AutoCAD will print only what is in the window you made, regardless of how it fits on the sheet. This method is similar to the View method just discussed. The difference is that the View method prints a previously defined view (one that was possibly defined by a window, but could also be defined in other ways), and the Window method prints what is included in a window that you define as you're setting up the plot. The window used by the Window method can't be saved and recalled at a later time.

The Layout Option

One of the greatest benefits of layouts is the ability to see on the screen exactly what will be printed. This is the purpose of the Layout option in the Plot dialog box. When printed at a scale of 1:1 and using the paper size designated in the Page Setup dialog box, the printed drawing will look as it does in the layout. The layout option is discussed further in the "Printing a Drawing Using Layouts" section later in this chapter. Whenever you're not simply generating a quick plot of an area inside model space, the layout option is the recommended way to plot drawing sheets.

Plot Scale

On the right side of the Plot dialog box is the Plot Scale group, where you control the scale of the plot. When the Fit To Paper check box is selected, AutoCAD takes whatever area you have chosen to print and automatically scales it so that it will fit on the selected page size. When this option is unchecked, the Scale drop-down list becomes available. This list contains several preset scales to choose from plus a Custom option and any scales that you've added. Some of the scales in the list are displayed as pure ratios, such as 1:50. Others are shown in their standard format, such as 1/4″ = 1′-0″. Below the drop-down list is a pair of text boxes for setting up a custom scale. When you choose a preset scale, these text boxes display the true ratio of that scale.

To set up a custom scale, do the following:

1. Choose the units you're using in your drawing (inches or millimeters).

2. Enter a plotted distance in the text box, just below the Scale drop-down list.

3. In the Units text box below that, enter the number of units in your drawing that will be represented by the distance you entered in the text box above.

   The inches (or millimeters) distance is an actual distance on the plotted drawing, and the units distance is the distance the plotted units represent. For 1/4″ scale (1/4″ = 1′-0″), you can enter several combinations:

= Text Box	Unit Text Box
¼ inch	1 foot
1 inch	4 feet
1 inch	48 inches

AutoCAD can plot to various raster image formats such as JPG. If one of these raster format plotters is selected, the Plot Scale area of the Plot dialog box will use pixels as the unit type.

Layouts are almost always plotted at a scale of 1:1. Half-size sets are common in many design offices; these sets can be made by changing the Plot Scale in the Plot dialog box. I'll come back to these and other scale issues as you prepare a drawing for printing.

Plot Offset and Plot Options

Below Plot Area is the Plot Offset (Origin Set To Printable Area) group, which contains two text boxes and a check box. Select the Center The Plot check box to center the plot on the printed sheet. If this check box isn't selected, by default AutoCAD makes the lower-left corner of your drawing's printable area the origin for that drawing sheet. By changing the settings in the X and Y text boxes, you can move the drawing horizontally or vertically to fit on the page as you want.

When the Center The Plot check box is selected, the X and Y text boxes are disabled for input but display the offset distance from the lower-left corner of the sheet that was necessary to center the drawing.

By using the X and Y settings in the Plot Offset group, you can make one margin wider for a binding (see the top of Figure 15.8). To center your drawing on the page, select the Center The Plot check box (see the bottom of Figure 15.8). If layouts are set up and being used for printing, they determine this setting, and the Center The Plot check box is unavailable.

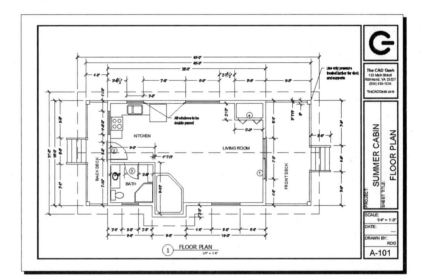

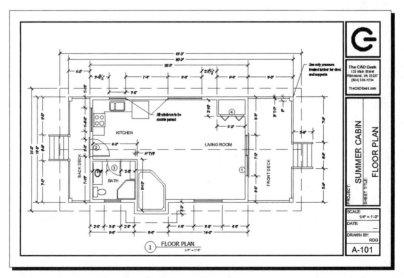

FIGURE 15.8 A print with its X offset set to allow for a binding (top), and with the drawing centered (bottom)

Setting the material to be printed accurately on the page will be a result of trial and error and getting to know your printer. I'll return to this topic shortly when you learn how to get ready to print. If you work in a corporate environment, you should consult your company's CAD standards to see which settings your company uses for plotting.

The Expanded Plot Dialog Box

If the Plot dialog box hasn't already been expanded, click the right-facing arrow in the lower-right corner to expand it to include four additional groups in a stack on the right. For now, you're primarily interested in the group on the bottom, Drawing Orientation (see Figure 15.9).

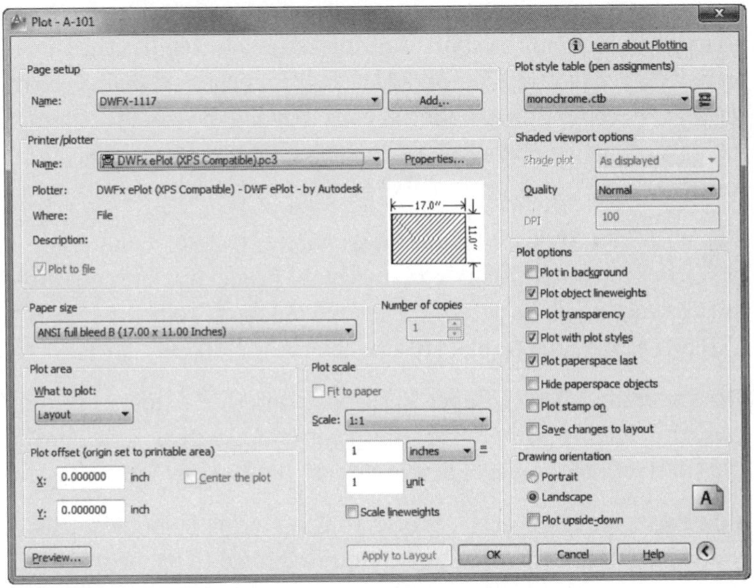

FIGURE 15.9 The expanded Plot dialog box

Drawing Orientation   The settings in this group are self-explanatory. The radio buttons serve as a toggle between the portrait and landscape orientation, and the Plot Upside-Down check box is an on/off toggle. The Plot Upside-Down setting is sometimes used as a way of tricking some plotters to correctly size the binding edge of a drawing. Because items such as OLE (Object Linking and Embedding) objects cannot plot upside-down, using Plot Upside-Down is typically discouraged. The preferred alternative is the X and Y Plot Offset settings in the main part of the Plot dialog box.

Plot Options   This group has eight check boxes that define how the plot is executed. You'll explore many of these settings in more detail throughout this chapter. Here's a brief description of what each setting does:

Plot In Background   When this is checked, plots will process behind the scenes, allowing you to continue working in your drawing. It may be necessary to disable this setting if you're plotting larger, more complicated drawings that take more system memory to process.

Plot Object Lineweights   Instead of using a plot-style table, the Lineweight property assigned to layers and objects throughout the drawing may be used to provide visual separation throughout your drawing with this setting turned on.

Plot Transparency   Similar to enabling or disabling the Transparency drawing mode from the status bar, this check box toggles the same property when plotting. You should keep this unchecked unless you're specifically using transparency in your drawing, because it requires more memory to process even if you don't have transparent objects in your drawing.

Plot With Plot Styles   This setting enables the use of plot-style tables instead of the assigned Lineweight property. Consequently, the lineweight will be determined based on object color when using CTB pen tables, and by plot styles when using STB pen tables.

Plot Paperspace Last   Paper space being another name for layout tabs, this setting will plot anything contained within a viewport, and then will plot objects drawn directly on the Layout tab last.

Hide Paperspace Objects   When working with 3D models, this controls whether the HIDE command is applied to paper space objects.

Plot Stamp On   Plot stamps are used to include information such as plot date, time, and the name of the person who created the plot. Enabling this option will append this information per your specification to your drawings.

Save Changes To Layout   Changes made within the PLOT command will also apply to the page setup for that layout.

Shaded Viewport Options   This group has settings to control the plot for renderings and shaded views and will be covered in later chapters. Onscreen previews may differ from hard-copy plots if your graphics card does not support hardware acceleration.

Plot Style Table (Pen Assignments)   This is where the color and weight of line-types are defined. Plot styles and pen assignments are discussed in the next section of this chapter.

You have taken a quick tour of the Plot dialog box, and you still have the `I-A-100.dwg` (`M-A-100.dwg`), `I-A-200.dwg` (`M-A-200.dwg`), and `I-C-101.dwg` (`M-C-101.dwg`) drawings to print. As you set up the prints a little later in this chapter, refer to this section for an explanation of the tools, if necessary.

Applying Plot-Style Tables

Because of its cost, color plotting is typically reserved for exhibit drawings and other presentation scenarios. Chances are, most of the drawings you'll create will be integrated into a larger construction document set that's prepared in black-and-white. Consider the layers inside your drawing for a moment: each layer has a color assigned to it, which is then used to display the objects drawn on that layer. Without instruction, AutoCAD will screen the lighter colors in your drawing when plotted in black-and-white. Typically, this is not the desired result, and so Plot Style Tables give you control over the way AutoCAD interprets color when plotting.

As you'll learn in this section, plot-style tables do more than determine the color that objects plot when a drawing is plotted. These tables can also control how line-weights are assigned and whether screening is applied. Using plot-style tables to control color, screening, and lineweight is incredibly popular among industry professionals. In this chapter, the `monochrome.stb` table will be used. This table uses the Lineweight layer property to determine the thickness of plotted lines. You'll learn more about the Lineweight layer property later in this chapter.

Introducing Plot-Style Table Files

A *plot style* is a group of settings that is assigned to a layer, a color, or an object. It determines how that layer, color, or object is printed. Plot styles are grouped into *plot-style tables* that are saved as files on your hard drive. Two kinds of plot styles exist:

Color-Dependent   Identified by their .ctb file extension, color-dependent plot-style tables map each of the 255 index colors. Plot styles are determined based on the color of an object.

Named   Identified by their .stb file extension, named plot styles let you specify comprehensible names for your plot styles. You can create as many or as few plot styles as you need. Named plot styles are assigned to layers in the same way colors are.

> **For LT, the plot-style table path is similar but it uses an AutoCAD LT 2012 folder and one called R16.1 instead of R18.2.**

Leave AutoCAD for a moment, and use Windows Explorer to navigate to the following folder: C:\Documents and Settings*your name*\Application Data\ Autodesk\AutoCAD 2012\R18.2\enu\Plotters (in Windows Vista or Windows 7, go to C:\Users*your name*\appdata\roaming\Autodesk\AutoCAD 2012 \r18.2\ enu\plotters). Open the subfolder called Plot Styles; Figure 15.10 shows its contents. Thirteen plot-style table files are already set up. Nine of them are color-dependent plot-style table files, with the extension .ctb; and four are named plot-style table files, with the extension .stb. (If you can't see the .ctb and .stb extensions, choose Tools ➢ Folder Options ➢ View, or in Windows 7 choose Organize ➢ Folder And Search Options ➢ View, and uncheck Hide Extensions For Known File Types.) Finally, you'll see a shortcut to the Add-A-Plot Style Table Wizard, which you use to set up custom plot-style tables. Close Windows Explorer and return to AutoCAD.

Name	Date modified	Type
acad.ctb	3/9/1999 5:17 AM	AutoCAD Color-dependent Plot Style Table File
acad.stb	3/9/1999 5:16 AM	AutoCAD Plot Style Table File
Add-A-Plot Style Table Wizard	2/13/2010 10:18 PM	Shortcut
Autodesk-Color.stb	11/21/2002 10:17 ...	AutoCAD Plot Style Table File
Autodesk-MONO.stb	11/21/2002 11:22 ...	AutoCAD Plot Style Table File
DWF Virtual Pens.ctb	9/11/2001 5:04 PM	AutoCAD Color-dependent Plot Style Table File
Fill Patterns.ctb	3/9/1999 5:16 AM	AutoCAD Color-dependent Plot Style Table File
Grayscale.ctb	3/9/1999 5:16 AM	AutoCAD Color-dependent Plot Style Table File
monochrome.ctb	3/9/1999 5:15 AM	AutoCAD Color-dependent Plot Style Table File
monochrome.stb	3/9/1999 5:15 AM	AutoCAD Plot Style Table File
Screening 25%.ctb	3/9/1999 5:14 AM	AutoCAD Color-dependent Plot Style Table File
Screening 50%.ctb	3/9/1999 5:14 AM	AutoCAD Color-dependent Plot Style Table File
Screening 75%.ctb	3/9/1999 5:13 AM	AutoCAD Color-dependent Plot Style Table File
Screening 100%.ctb	3/9/1999 5:14 AM	AutoCAD Color-dependent Plot Style Table File

FIGURE 15.10 The contents of the Plot Styles folder

Understanding How Plot-Style Table Files Are Organized

Plot-style table files are assigned to a drawing and contain all the plot styles needed to control how that drawing is printed. Color-dependent plot styles control printing parameters through color. There are 255 of them in each color-dependent plot-style table, one for each color. Named plot-style tables, on the other hand, have only as many plot styles as are necessary, possibly only two or three. You'll now look at a plot-style table and see how it's organized:

1. Start the PLOT command to open the Plot dialog box.

2. Expand the dialog box if necessary, and choose acad.ctb from the Plot Style Table drop-down list in the top-right corner (see Figure 15.11).

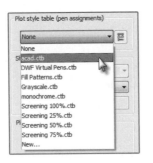

FIGURE 15.11 Assigning a color-dependent plot style to the drawing

3. Click the Edit button next to the drop-down list to open the Plot Style Table Editor dialog box with acad.ctb in its title bar (see Figure 15.12). This dialog box has three tabs. The General tab displays information and a Description text box for input.

4. Click the Table View tab (see Figure 15.13). Now you see the plot styles across the top and the plot-style properties listed down the left side. This tab organizes the information like a spreadsheet. Use the scroll bar to assure yourself that there are 255 plot styles. Notice that each plot style has 12 properties plus a text box for a description. This tab displays the plot-style information in a way that gives you an overview of the table as a whole.

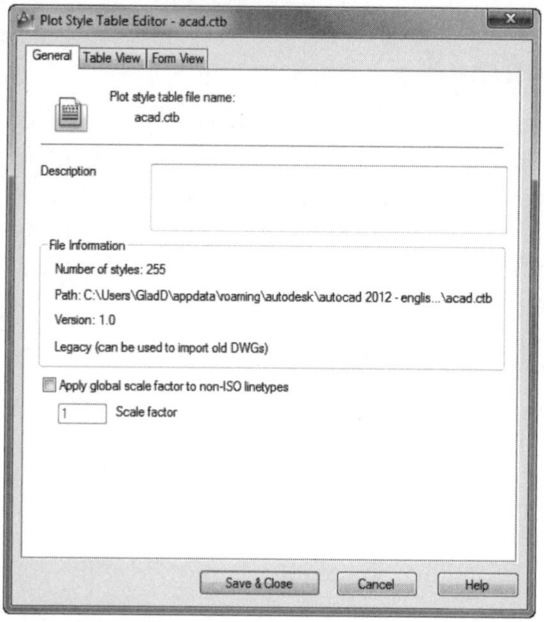

FIGURE 15.12 The General tab of the Plot Style Table Editor dialog box for the acad.ctb file

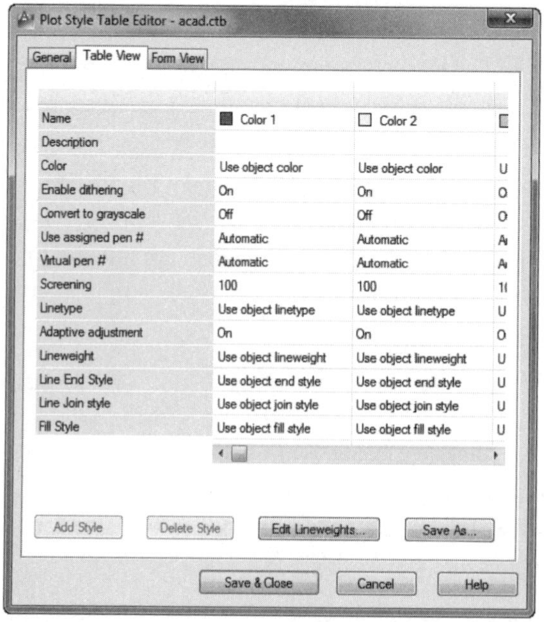

FIGURE 15.13 The Table View tab of the Plot Style Table Editor dialog box for the acad.ctb file

5. Click the Form View tab (see Figure 15.14).

The same information is organized in a slightly different way. Here the plot styles are listed in the box on the left. You can highlight one or more plot styles at a time. The properties of the highlighted styles appear on the right. This view is set up to modify the properties of chosen plot styles. Notice that the first property, Color, has Use Object Color assigned for all plot styles. This means that red objects are plotted in red, blue in blue, and so on. You can override this by expanding the drop-down list and selecting another color.

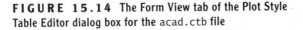

FIGURE 15.14 The Form View tab of the Plot Style Table Editor dialog box for the `acad.ctb` file

6. Click the Cancel button to exit the Plot Style Table Editor, assign the color-dependent `monochrome.ctb` to the drawing, and then open the file for editing.

7. Click the Table View tab. Now look at the Color property.

All plot styles have the color Black assigned (see Figure 15.15).

8. Click Cancel to close the Plot Style Table Editor dialog box and close the Plot Styles dialog box.

Plot Style Table Editor - monochrome.ctb

General | Table View | Form View

Name	■ Color 1	□ Color 2	□
Description			
Color	■ Black	■ Black	■
Enable dithering	On	On	O
Convert to grayscale	Off	Off	O
Use assigned pen #	Automatic	Automatic	A
Virtual pen #	Automatic	Automatic	A
Screening	100	100	1(
Linetype	Use object linetype	Use object linetype	U
Adaptive adjustment	On	On	O
Lineweight	Use object lineweight	Use object lineweight	U
Line End Style	Use object end style	Use object end style	U
Line Join style	Use object join style	Use object join style	U
Fill Style	Use object fill style	Use object fill style	U

Add Style   Delete Style   Edit Lineweights...   Save As...

Save & Close   Cancel   Help

FIGURE 15.15 The Table View tab of the Plot Style Table Editor dialog box for the monochrome.ctb file

The monochrome.ctb file will print all colors in your drawing as black, but won't change the colors in the AutoCAD file. This is the plot-style table you'll use to plot your My Cabin project.

Assigning Plot-Style Tables to Drawings

Each drawing can be assigned only one kind of plot-style table file: color-dependent or named. This is determined when the drawing is first created.

> **NOTE** Even though the type of plot style for a new drawing is fixed in the Plot Style Table Settings dialog box, two utility commands let you switch the type of plot style that a drawing can have and assign a different one. They are the CONVERTPSTYLES and CONVERTCTB commands.

Follow these steps:

1. Open the Application menu, and click the Options button in the lower-right corner.

   This opens the Options dialog box.

2. Click the Plot And Publish tab.

3. Click the Plot Style Table Settings button near the lower-right corner of the dialog box.

Doing so opens the Plot Style Table Settings dialog box. In the uppermost group are the two radio buttons that control which type of plot style a drawing will accept, color-dependent or named (see Figure 15.16). New drawings will accept only the type of plot style that is selected here.

In the Current Plot Style Table Settings group is the Default Plot Style Table drop-down list. Here you can select a plot-style table file (of the type selected by the radio buttons) to be assigned automatically to new drawings. One of the options is None.

4. Close the Plot Style Table Settings dialog box. Then close the Options dialog box.

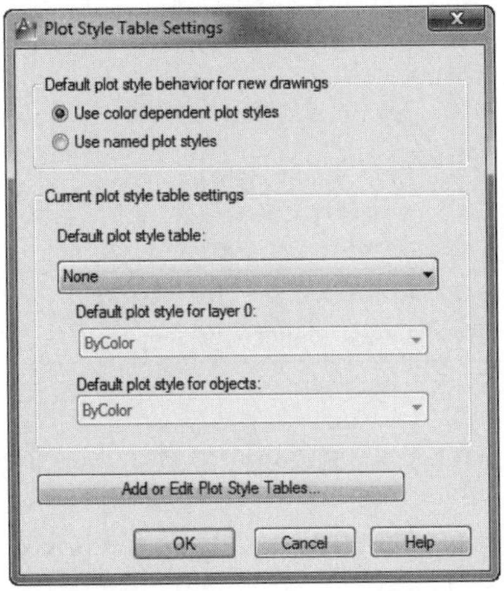

FIGURE 15.16 The Plot Style Table Settings dialog box

Throughout this book, all the drawings that you created (or downloaded) were set up to use color-dependent plot styles, so you can assign this type of plot style to the drawing. Usually, you do this by assigning a particular plot-style table file to a layout or to model space. To finish the tour and this chapter, you'll assign one of the available plot-style table files to the I-A-100.dwg (M-A-100.dwg), I-A-200 (M-A-200), and I-C-101.dwg (M-C-101.dwg) drawings and use the Preview option to see the results:

1. Make I-A-100.dwg (M-A-100.dwg) the current drawing if it isn't already.

2. Click the A-101 layout to make it current.

3. Right-click the Quick View Layouts button in the status bar and select Page Setup Manager.

This opens the Page Setup Manager dialog box, shown in Figure 15.17.

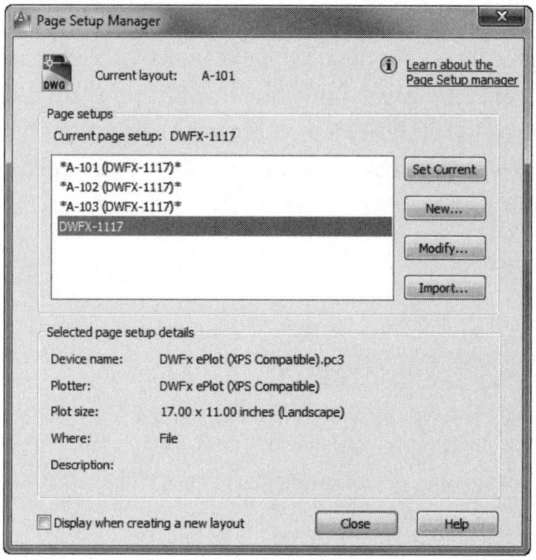

FIGURE 15.17 Accessing the DWFX-1117 (DWFX-A3) page setup from the Page Setup Manager dialog box

4. Select the DWFX-1117 (DWFX-A3) page setup and click the Modify button.

The Page Setup—DWFX-1117 (DWFX-A3) dialog box shown in Figure 15.18 opens after selecting Modify in the Page Setup Manager. This dialog box is nearly identical to the expanded Plot dialog box used by the PLOT command.

5. Change the Plot Style Table to monochrome.ctb, and click OK to exit the Page Setup dialog box (see Figure 15.18).

Because you just modified a page setup that was assigned to a layout, the Question dialog box shown in Figure 15.19 opens, asking you how to apply the changes you just made.

6. Choose Yes to apply the changes to all of the layouts that reference the DWFX-1117 (DWFX-A3) page setup.

7. Start the PLOT command, and expand the dialog box by using the arrow icon in the lower-right corner if it's not expanded already.

8. In the upper-right corner, make sure monochrome.ctb is displayed in the Plot Style Table drop-down list and then click the Preview button.

AutoCAD replaces the colors used in the drawing with black and displays a preview of what the plotted drawing will look like (see Figure 15.20).

9. Cancel out of the PLOT command, and save the I-A-100.dwg (M-A-100.dwg) file (keeping its name).

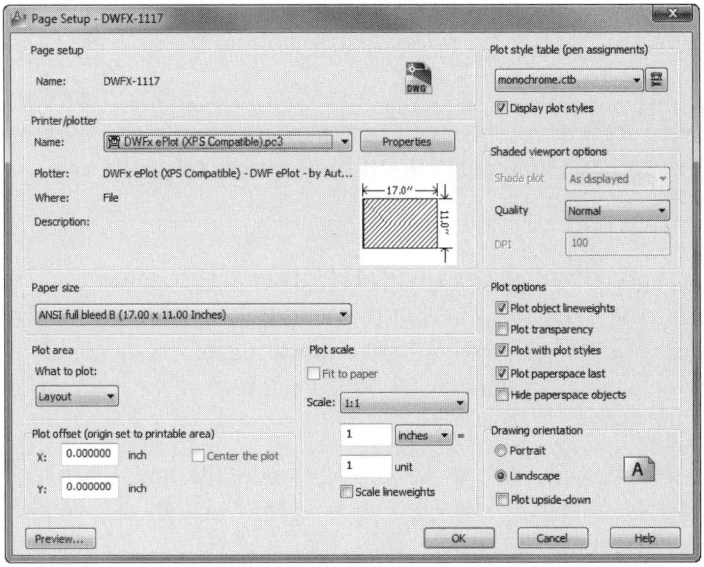

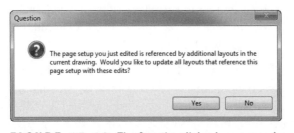

FIGURE 15.18 Modifying the DWFX-1117 (DWFX-A3) page setup to use the monochrome.ctb plot-style table

FIGURE 15.19 The Question dialog box opens when a page setup is applied to multiple layouts.

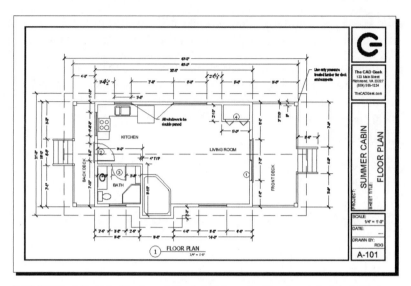

FIGURE 15.20 Preview of the A-101 layout without a plot-style table assigned to it

You've applied the modified DWFX-1117 (DWFX-A3) page setup to all of the layouts inside the A-100.dwg file, but this change hasn't been applied to the other layouts in your plan set. Rather than duplicating efforts by manually changing the plot-style table in each drawing file, you'll import the modified page setup from A-100.dwg.

1. Open the I-A-200.dwg (M-A-200.dwg) file, and then open the Page Setup Manager by right-clicking the Quick View Layouts button on the status bar.

2. From Page Setup Manager, click the Import button and browse to the I-A-100.dwg (M-A-100.dwg) file in your Chapter 15 Training Data folder.

   After selecting the I-A-100.dwg (M-A-100.dwg) file, the Import Page Setups dialog box shown in Figure 15.21 opens to list all the page setups saved inside the selected drawing.

3. Make sure DWFX-1117 (DWFX-A3) is selected and then click OK.

   The Question dialog box opens to ask: "A layout page setup named DWFX-1117 (DWFX-A3) has already been defined. Would you like to redefine it?"

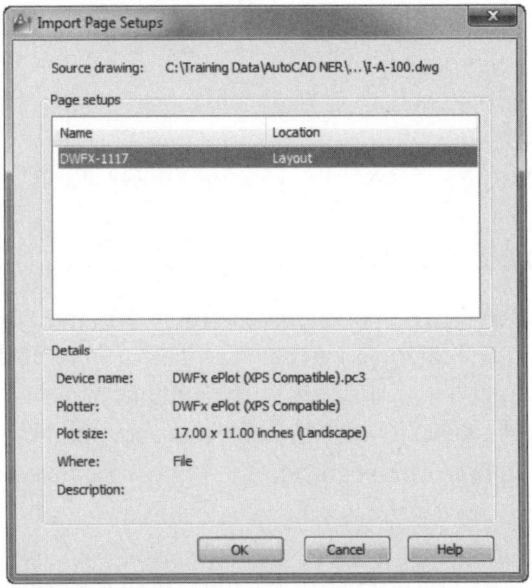

FIGURE 15.21 Selecting the page setups to import from the Import Page Setups dialog box

4. Choose Yes to redefine the existing DWFX-1117 (DWFX-A3) page setup.

   Another version of the Question dialog box opens, this time reading: "The page setup you just edited is referenced by additional layouts in the current drawing. Would you like to update all layouts that reference this page setup?"

5. Choose Yes to apply the changes to the existing layouts in the I-A -200.dwg (M-A-200.dwg) drawing. Close the Page Setup Manager to return to your drawing.

   The DWFX-1117 (DWFX-A3) page setup has been updated inside your elevation drawing to include the monochrome.ctb plot-style table change.

6. Save the I-A-200.dwg (M-A-200.dwg) file (keeping its existing name), and then repeat steps 1 through 5 on the I-C-101.dwg (M-C-101.dwg) file.

Printing a Drawing

You'll learn to plot the individual plan sheets in a moment, but your first task will be to print 14A-FPLAY1.dwg from model space at a scale of 1/4″ = 1′-0″ (1 = 50) on an 11″×17″ (297 mm×420 mm) format printer. In this exercise, you'll use the

DWFx ePlot (XPS Compatible).pc3 printer. Since the DWF plotter will simply plot to a file, you could select any sheet size you wanted. To remain consistent with the layouts you have already created, you will use a standard Letter (A3) sheet size for this exercise.

The first step is to configure your layers by assigning lineweights to them.

Determining Lineweights for a Drawing

Look at the I14A-FPLAY1 (M14A-FPLAY1) drawing as a whole. You need to decide on weights for the various lines. The floor plan is drawn as if a cut were made horizontally through the building, just below the tops of the window and door openings. Everything that was cut will be given a heavy line. Objects above and below the cut will be given progressively lighter lines, depending on how far above or below the cut the objects are located.

In this system, the walls, windows, and doors will be heaviest. The roof, headers, fixtures, deck, and steps will be lighter. For emphasis, you'll make the walls a little heavier than the windows and doors. The hatch pattern will be very light, and the outline of the various components will be heavier for emphasis. Text and the title block information will use a medium lineweight. These are general guidelines; weights will vary with each drawing.

N O T E   Lineweight standards vary for each trade and profession that uses AutoCAD. Details usually follow a system that is independent from the one used by other drawings in the same set. Section lines, hidden lines, centerlines, cutting plane lines, break lines, and so on will all be assigned specific lineweights.

Project Lineweights

You'll use four lineweights for the project, as shown in Table 15.1.

TABLE 15.1 The four lineweights used in the My Cabin project

Weight	Thickness in Inches
Very light	0.005 (0.13 mm)
Light	0.008 (0.20 mm)
Medium	0.010 (0.25 mm)
Heavy	0.014 (0.35 mm)

In I14A-FPLAY1 (M14A-FPLAY1), 30 layers are visible in the floor plan, site plan, and the elevation layouts as they are currently set up. Their lineweights will be assigned as shown in Table 15.2.

TABLE 15.2 Lineweights associated with the layers in the I14A-FPLAY1 (M14A-FPLAY1) drawing

Layer	Lineweight
A-ANNO-DIMS	Very Light
A-ANNO-TABL	Medium
A-ANNO-TEXT	Medium
A-ANNO-TTLB	Medium
A-ANNO-TTLB-TEXT	Medium
A-DECK	Medium
A-DECK-STRS	Light
A-DOOR	Medium
A-ELEV-DECK	Medium
A-ELEV-DECK-STRS	Medium
A-ELEV-DOOR	Medium
A-ELEV-DOOR-PATT	Medium
A-ELEV-FNDN	Light
A-ELEV-FNDN-PATT	Very Light
A-ELEV-GLAZ	Medium
A-ELEV-GLAZ-PATT	Medium
A-ELEV-ROOF	Medium
A-ELEV-ROOF-PATT	Very Light
A-ELEV-SHAD-PATT	Very Light
A-ELEV-TEXT	Medium

(Continues)

TABLE 15.2 *(Continued)*

Layer	Lineweight
A-ELEV-WALL	Medium
A-ELEV-WALL-PATT	Very Light
A-FLOR-FIXT	Light
A-FLOR-PATT	Very Light
A-GLAZ	Medium
A-GRID	Medium
A-ROOF	Very Light
A-TTLB-LABL	Medium
A-WALL	Heavy
A-WALL-HEAD	Light

The site plan model file I13C-SPLAY1.dwg (M13C-SPLAY1.dwg) has five layers of concern. You'll need to open it and assign the lineweights shown in Table 15.3.

TABLE 15.3 Lineweights associated with the layers in the I13C-SPLAY1 (M13C-SPLAY1) drawing

Layer	Lineweight
C-ANNO-NARW	Fine
C-PROP-LINE	Medium
C-ROAD	Medium
C-SITE-REFR	Medium
C-SWLK	Fine

When you look at the lineweights currently assigned to the layers across your two model files, you can generate a third chart that shows what lineweight needs to be assigned to each group of layers, as shown in Table 15.4.

TABLE 15.4 The thickness of each lineweight and the assigned layers

Thickness	Layers
Very Light: 0.005 (0.13)	A-ANNO-DIMS, A-ELEV-FNDN-PATT, A-ELEV-ROOF-PATT, A-ELEV-SHAD-PATT, A-ELEV-WALL-PATT, A-FLOR-PATT, A-ROOF
Light: 0.008 (0.20)	A-DECK-STRS, A-ELEV-FNDN, A-FLOR-FIXT, A-WALL-HEAD, C-ANNO-NARW, C-SWLK
Medium: 0.010 (0.25)	A-ANNO-TABL, A-ANNO-TEXT, A-ANNO-TTLB, A-ANNO-TTLB-TEXT, A-DECK, A-DOOR, A-ELEV-DECK, A-ELEV-DECK-STRS, A-ELEV-DOOR, A-ELEV-DOOR-PATT, A-ELEV-GLAZ, A-ELEV-GLAZ-PATT, A-ELEV-ROOF, A-ELEV-TEXT, A-ELEV-WALL, A-GLAZ, A-GRID, A-TTLB-LABL, C-PROP-LINE, C-ROAD, C-SITE-REFR
Heavy: 0.014 (0.35)	A-WALL

Applying Lineweights to Layers

You'll use Tables 15.1 and 15.2 to apply lineweights to the I14A-FPLAY1 (M14A-FPLAY1) and I13C-SPLAY1 (I13C-SPLAY1) drawings, respectively. The following procedure will guide you through the process:

1. Open I14A-FPLAY1.dwg (M14A-FPLAY1.dwg) from your Chapter 15 directory, and start the LAYER command to display the Layer Properties Manager.

2. Make layer 0 the current layer.
   The A-AREA and Defpoints layers do not plot, so you don't need to be concerned with them at this time, but verify that they are set to not plot. The E-POWR and L-PLNT layers are empty.

3. Click the A-ANNO-DIMS layer to highlight it.

4. Hold down the Ctrl key, and click the A-ELEV-FNDN-PATT, A-ELEV-ROOF-PATT, A-ELEV-SHAD-PATT, A-ELEV-WALL-PATT, A-FLOR-PATT, and A-ROOF layers to select them. Then release the Ctrl key.

5. In the Lineweight column of the Layer Properties Manager dialog box, click one of the highlighted Default words in the Lineweight column to open the Lineweight dialog box (see Figure 15.22).

◄

The I15-FP Lineweight .las (M15-FP Lineweight.las) layer state is also available from the Chapter 15 download, and it will automatically assign the lineweights discussed in this exercise.

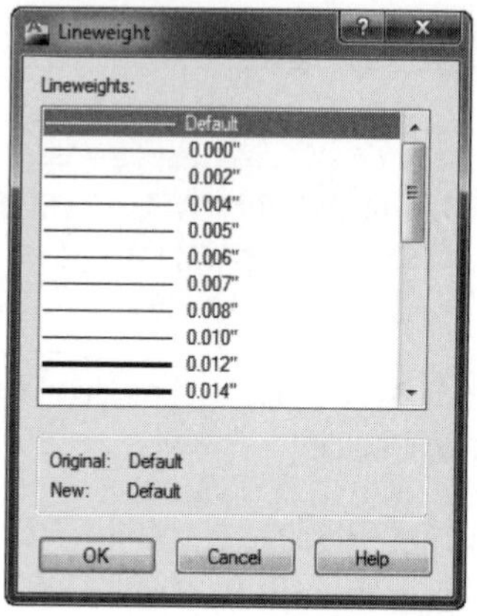

FIGURE 15.22 Assigning a lineweight in the Lineweight dialog box

 NOTE   If your lineweight units are shown in millimeters instead of inches, click Cancel, enter LWUNITS.↵ 0↵, and then reopen the Lineweight dialog box.

6. Click 0.005″ (0.13 mm). Then click OK to assign the lineweight and exit the Lineweight dialog box.

   In the Layer Properties Manager dialog box, the highlighted layers now have a lineweight of 0.005″ (0.13 mm) assigned to them (see Figure 15.23).

7. Repeat steps 3 though 6 three more times to assign the remaining lineweights to the layers within I14A-FPLAY1.dwg (M14A-FPLAY1.dwg):

   a. Assign the 0.008″ (0.20 mm) lineweight to the A-DECK-STRS, A-ELEV-FNDN, A-FLOR-FIXT, and A-WALL-HEAD layers.

   b. Assign the 0.010″ (0.25 mm) lineweight to the A-ANNO-TABL, A-ANNO-TEXT, A-ANNO-TTLB, A-ANNO-TTLB-TEXT, A-DECK, A-DOOR, A-ELEV-DECK, A-ELEV-DECK-STRS, A-ELEV-DOOR, A-ELEV-DOOR-PATT, A-ELEV-GLAZ, A-ELEV-GLAZ-PATT, A-ELEV-ROOF, A-ELEV-TEXT, A-ELEV-WALL, A-GLAZ, and A-GRID layers.

   c. Assign the 0.014″ (0.35 mm) lineweight to the A-WALL layer.

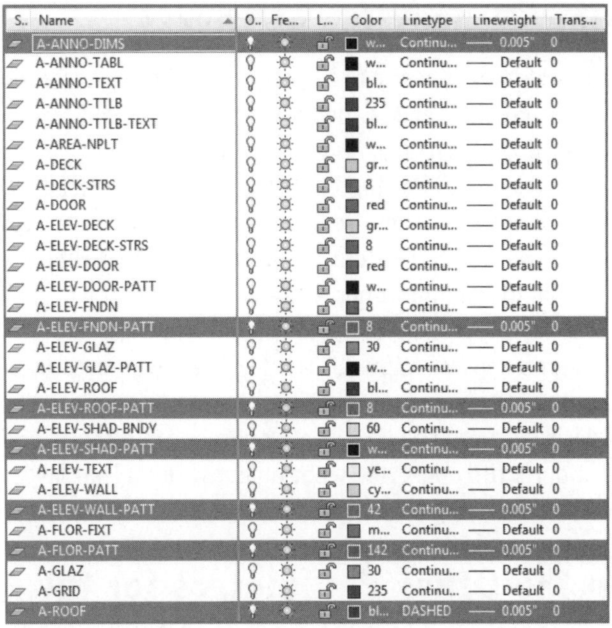

FIGURE 15.23 The new lineweight is shown in the Layer Properties Manager.

8. Save the `I14A-FPLAY1.dwg` (`M14A-FPLAY1.dwg`) file, and open the `13C-SPLAY1.dwg` file.

9. Repeat the previous exercise by applying linetypes to these layers as follows:

a. Assign the 0.008" (0.20 mm) lineweight to the A-ANNO-NARW and C-SWLK layers.

b. Assign the 0.010" (0.25 mm) lineweight to the C-PROP-LINE, C-ROAD, and C-SITE-REFR layers.

10. Save the `I13C-SPLAY1.dwg` (`M13C-SPLAY1.dwg`) file (keeping its existing name).

You have assigned the lineweights. When the print is complete, you can judge whether these lineweight assignments are acceptable or need to be adjusted. In an office, a lot of time is invested in developing a lineweight standard that can be used in most drawings. The development of such a standard is typically led by a CAD manager and decided upon by a CAD committee of key users throughout the company.

The 15-SP `Lineweight.las` layer state is also available from the Chapter 15 download and will automatically assign the lineweights for your civil site plan.

Setting Other Properties of Layers

Two other properties of layers deserve to be mentioned: Plot and Description. Both columns appear at the far-right end of the Layer Properties Manager dialog box.

The Plot feature is a toggle that controls whether the objects on a layer are printed. By default, the control is on. When this feature is turned off for a particular layer, objects on that layer aren't printed but remain visible on the screen. You used this feature to make layers with the NPLT suffix unplottable and, in the future, you might designate a layer set not to print for in-house notes and data that you don't intend to be seen by those who will eventually view your printed drawings.

A Description column appears at the far right of the Layer List window. Clicking in this column on the blue bar of a highlighted layer opens a text box in which you can enter a description of the layer. Layer names are often in code or use abbreviations that don't fully describe what objects are on that layer. Here's a place to remedy that.

Setting Up the Other Parameters for the Print

Now that you have set the lineweights, it's time to move to the Plot dialog box and complete the setting changes you need to make in order to print this drawing. You'll use the Window option to select what you'll print.

1. If it's not already, open the I14A-FPLAY1.dwg (M14A-FPLAY1.dwg) file and switch to model space.

2. In the Layer Properties Manager, select the A-ANNO-TABL, A-FLOR -PATT, A-GRID, and all three Site layers.

3. Click the lightbulb icon to turn off each of the selected layers.

4. Start the PLOT command.

5. In the Plot dialog box, check the Printer/Plotter area to be sure you have DWFx ePlot (XPS Compatible).pc3 displayed in the drop-down list.

6. Check the Paper Size area to verify that ANSI Full Bleed (17.00 × 11.00 Inches) or ISO Full Bleed A3 (420.00 × 297.00 MM) is the selected paper size.

7. Move down to the Plot Area section, open the What To Plot drop-down list, and select Window.

8. In the drawing, turn off Object Snap.

9. To start the window, pick a point just above and to the right of the topmost and rightmost dimensions.

10. To complete the window, click a point below and to the left of the bottom-most and leftmost dimensions.

    Back in the Plot dialog box, Window is displayed in the What To Plot drop-down list, and a new Window button appears on the right side of the Plot Area section.

11. Click this button if you need to redo the window after viewing a preview of the plot.

12. If you have not already done so, click the right-pointing arrow in the lower-right corner of the Plot dialog box to display another column of plotting options.

13. In the Drawing Orientation area in the lower-right corner, be sure Landscape is selected.

14. Assign the `monochrome.ctb` plot-style table by using the Plot Style Table drop-down list in the expanded Plot dialog box.

15. In the Plot Scale area, uncheck Fit To Paper and, if you're using architectural units, open the Scale drop-down list and select 1/4″ = 1'-0″.

    Notice that the text boxes below now read 0.25 and 12, a form of the true ratio for 1/4″ scale. If you're using decimal units, do the following:

    a. Choose Custom from the Scale drop-down list.

    b. Enter 1 in the upper text field and 50 in the lower.

16. In the Plot Offset group, click the Center The Plot check box.

    Your dialog box should look like Figure 15.24.

This completes the setup for your first plot. It's a good idea to preview how it will look as a result of the setup changes before you plot a drawing.

Previewing a Print

The Preview feature gives you the opportunity to view your drawing exactly as it will print.

1. Click the Preview button in the lower-left corner of the Plot dialog box.

    The computer takes a moment to calculate the plot and then displays a full view of your drawing as it will fit on the page (see Figure 15.25). If a Plot Scale Confirm dialog box opens, click Continue.

2. Right-click and choose Zoom Window from the context menu.

3. Make a window that encloses the bathroom, hot tub, and a couple of the dimensions. You have to click and hold down the mouse button, drag open the window, and then release the button.

The new view displays the lineweights you have set up (see Figure 15.26).

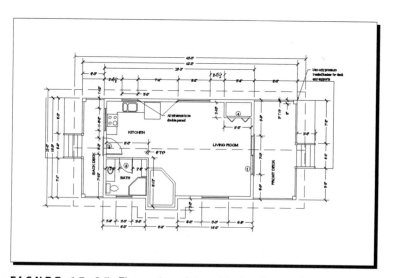

FIGURE 15.24 The Plot dialog box with the current settings

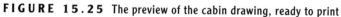

FIGURE 15.25 The preview of the cabin drawing, ready to print

4. Right-click and choose Zoom Original from the context menu to return to the first preview view.

5. Right-click again and choose Exit to return to the Plot dialog box.

   If your print was oriented correctly on the sheet, you're ready to print. If not, recheck the setup steps for errors.

6. At the bottom of the Plot dialog box, click the Apply To Layout button, and then click OK.

7. In the Browse For Plot File dialog box, browse to your Chapter 15 directory, accept the default filename, and click the Save button.

   The computer begins calculating the print and eventually sends it to the printer.

    After the print is done, a notification balloon appears at the lower-right corner of the AutoCAD window (see Figure 15.27). You can turn notifications on and off by right-clicking the Plot/Publish Detail icon in the AutoCAD tray and choosing the appropriate option.

8. Save and close the I14A-FPLAY1.dwg (M14A-FPLAY1.dwg) drawing.

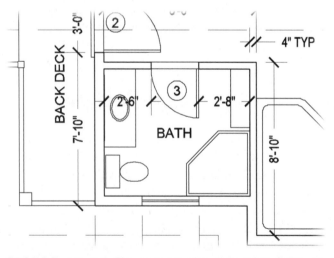

FIGURE 15.26 The zoomed-in view of the cabin showing the lineweights

T I P   On the right side of the Printer/Plotter group of the Plot dialog box, AutoCAD displays a partial preview of the plot in diagram form as you set it up. If there is problem with the setup, AutoCAD displays red lines to warn you, but sometimes this doesn't accurately reflect the actual plot. It's better to use the Preview feature, which provides you with a WYSIWYG view of the plot.

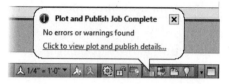

FIGURE 15.27 The notification balloon indicating that the plot is complete

When your print comes out, it should look like Figure 15.25, shown earlier. Check the lineweights of the various components on the print. You might have to make adjustments from what was outlined in this section when plotting to a physical plotter attached to your computer.

Since the DWFx plotter was selected, a DWFX file was created instead of a physical print. The next exercise will introduce you to Autodesk Design Review, a free program from Autodesk that is used to view these electronic plots.

 N O T E   You can change a setting in the Lineweight Settings dialog box to be able to see lineweights in your drawing before you preview a plot, but they aren't very accurate unless you're using layouts. When you print from model space, you have to preview the drawing from the Plot dialog box to see how the lineweights look.

Viewing Plots in Design Review

Autodesk Design Review is a companion product that is included in the default AutoCAD installation and is available as a free download for people without a product such as AutoCAD installed. The public download for Design Review can be found at **http://autodesk.com/designreview**.

With Design Review, you can view, print, and mark up a vast array of file types including DWG, DWFX, PDF, and many common raster image formats. Markups created in Design Review can then be loaded into AutoCAD, allowing for a review cycle that reduces paper consumption and is completely digital. Although Design Review is capable of much more, you'll use it simply to view the DWFX file you plotted to in the previous exercise.

    1. Start Autodesk Design Review by choosing Start ➢ All Programs ➢ Autodesk ➢ Autodesk Design Review 2012.

T I P   **Visit this book's companion site,** www.autocadner.com, **or the author's blog at** www.thecadgeek.com, **for more information about the additional capabilities of Autodesk Design Review.**

2. With Design Review running, use the Quick Access toolbar or choose Application Menu ➤ Open ➤ Open File to open the DWFX file you saved to your Chapter 15 directory in the previous exercise.

   The drawing you plotted displays in the Design Review Canvas (drawing area) shown in Figure 15.28. This is an exact representation of what the drawing would look like had you plotted it to a physical printer or plotter attached to your computer.

3. Close Autodesk Design Review after you've used it to view the electronic plot of your drawing.

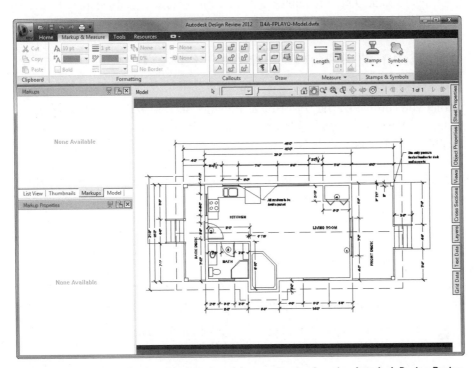

FIGURE 15.28 Viewing the plotted model space drawing by using Autodesk Design Review

The versatility of DWF files extends well beyond the reach of this book. To summarize, the format provides a free way to communicate design information with other project team members whether or not they have AutoCAD installed on their machines. AutoCAD users can further harness the abilities of the DWF and DWFX formats by publishing their designs to a three-dimensional DWF file. Whether you choose to publish in 2D or 3D, the DWF format was specifically designed to interact with Autodesk products and provides an excellent alternative to the PDF format, which often results in a much larger file size.

Printing a Drawing Using Layouts

Plotting drawings using layouts is very similar to plotting from model space. The core difference between the two methods relates to the way your drawing is scaled. When plotting from model space, you must choose a plot scale from the Plot dialog box, whereas that parameter is already taken care of when plotting layouts. Aside from the occasional need to publish a half-size set of drawings, the plot scale inside the Plot dialog box will almost always be set to 1:1.

Updating Model File Layer Properties in Sheet Files

Earlier you completed the "Printing a Drawing" section which, among other things, discussed ways to assign lineweights to layers. Currently, these lineweights are reflected only inside the respective model files such as I14A-FPLAY1 .dwg (M14A-FPLAY1.dwg). By default, changes to the layer properties of an external reference are not reflected in the host drawing, or sheet file in this case. In this section, you'll learn about the VISRETAIN variable and how to use it in conjunction with Layer States to update the lineweights inside your sheet files. Let's get started:

1. Open the I-A-100.dwg (M-A-100.dwg) sheet file and switch to model space.

2. Start the LAYER command to open the Layer States Manager.

3. Click the Layer States Manager button found on the toolbar of the Layer Properties Manager.

4. In the Layer States Manager dialog box, create a new layer state by picking the New button on the right side of the Layer States Manager dialog box.

5. Name your new layer state **15-LayerBackup** and click OK to return to the Layer States Manager.

6. Click the Close button to exit the Layer States Manager.

   Keep the Layer Properties Manager displayed on your screen.

   The VISRETAIN drawing variable controls how layers inside external references are stored inside your drawing. With its default value of 1, layer properties are stored in the host drawing, and changes in the reference drawing are not reflected in the current drawing. Conversely, when this value is set to 0, changes in the xref drawing are reflected in the current drawing.

7. Enter **VISRETAIN**⏎ at the command line, and change its value to **0**.

8. Start the XREF command to open the External References palette.

9. Right-click the I14A-FPLAY1 (M14A-FPLAY1) reference and choose Reload.

   The I14A-FPLAY1.dwg (M14A-FPLAY1.dwg) drawing reloads in the current drawing. Notice the lineweight column in the Layer Properties Manager; the lineweights have updated in the current drawing.

10. Set the VISRETAIN variable back to **1**, and open the Layer States Manager once again.

11. Expand the Layer States Manager by using the arrow icon in the lower-right corner to reveal the Layer Properties To Restore group at the right side of the dialog box.

12. Uncheck the Lineweight check box, as shown in Figure 15.29, and then click the Restore button.

13. Repeat steps 2 through 12 on the I-A-200.dwg (M-A-200.dwg) and I-C-101.dwg (M-C-101.dwg) sheet files.

To avoid overwriting the lineweights just loaded into the A-100 sheet file, you chose not to restore the Lineweight property from your 15-LayerBackup layer state. Had you chosen to restore this property, the lineweights in your drawing would have been set back to Default. A drawback to this method is that any viewport layer overrides you created have been reset to match the properties of that layer in model space.

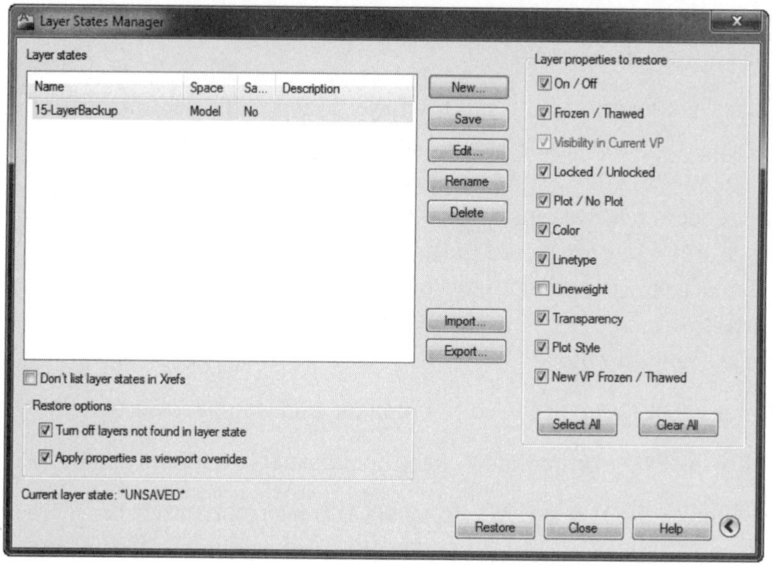

FIGURE 15.29 Restoring all but the Lineweight property from the 15-LayerBackup layer state

This drawback is one of the main reasons that many in industry choose to avoid viewport overrides whenever possible and manage their layers from model space. With the size of your Summer Cabin project, re-creating these viewport overrides shouldn't be too difficult. To summarize, you'll need to re-create the following viewport overrides:

A-101 Layout   VP Freeze: A-FLOR-PATT and A-ANNO-TABL from the 14A-FPLAY1 reference.

A-102 Layout   VP Freeze: A-GRID, A-ANNO-TABL, and A-ANNO-DIMS from the 14A-FPLAY1 reference.

A-103 Layout   VP Freeze: A-FLOR-PATT and A-ANNO-DIMS from the 14A-FPLAY1 reference.

N O T E   Because all the layers are managed from model space in the I-A-200.dwg (M-A-200.dwg) and I-C-101.dwg (M-C-101.dwg) sheet files, there's no need to re-create the viewport overrides in those drawings.

Plotting a Single Layout

With the lineweights properly assigned, you're now ready to begin plotting the layouts that make up your plan set. The rest of this chapter focuses on the multiple ways of plotting layouts from AutoCAD. Each method has its own advantages and disadvantages, and the method you ultimately choose will likely change based on the specific task at hand. To begin our discussion, you'll first look at plotting a single layout.

To summarize, when a layout has been set up properly and is active, you print at a scale of 1:1. The elements of the drawing on the layout are then printed at actual size, and the model space portion of the drawing is printed at the scale to which the viewport has been set. Follow these steps:

1. With I-A-100.dwg (M-A-100.dwg) open, switch to the A-101 layout by using the Quick View Layouts tool.

   For a review of layouts and viewports, see Chapter 14. Your layout should look like Figure 15.30.

2. Make sure you are in paper space to start the PLOT command.

3. You're using the DWFX-1117 (DWFX-A3) page setup. Verify the printer, paper size, and orientation as before.

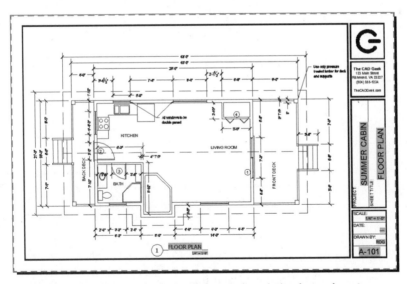

FIGURE 15.30 The cabin drawing ready for printing from a layout

4. Make sure that in the Plot Area group, the current choice displayed in the What To Plot drop-down list is Layout instead of Limits.

5. In the Plot Scale group, the scale has been set to 1:1. This is what you want.

In the Plot Offset group, the Center The Plot check box is grayed out; it isn't needed when using a layout to plot.

6. Expand the Plot dialog box as necessary to verify that the monochrome .ctb Plot Style Table is assigned.

There are no changes to make. Because this layout was set up for printing when it was created, all the settings in the Plot dialog box are automatically set correctly.

7. In the lower-left corner, select Preview.

Your preview should look like Figure 15.31. Notice how the preview looks exactly like the layout, but without the dashed frame.

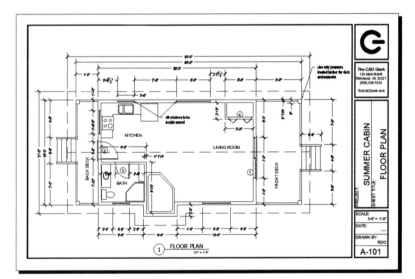

FIGURE 15.31 The preview of the current layout

8. Right-click and choose Exit to close the preview window.

9. Click OK to start the print.

10. Save the resulting electronic plot as I15-A-100.dwfx (M15-A-100.dwfx).

This exercise shows that once a layout has been created, most of the setup work for printing is already done for you. This greatly simplifies the printing process because the parameters of the print are determined before the PLOT command begins.

Printing a Drawing with Multiple Viewports

Multiple viewports in a layout don't require special handling. The print is made with the layout active at a scale of 1:1. For the next print, you'll continue using the DWFx plotter, but with a larger sheet size. *Large-format drawings*, typically defined as anything larger than 11″×17″, are especially common when representing large designs such as buildings.

Printing with a Large-Format Printer

The procedure here varies little from the one you just followed to print the layout at a 1:1 scale. Here you will scale the viewport up to fit on a larger sheet for presentation purposes:

1. Open the I-C-101.dwg (M-C-101.dwg) site plan sheet file, and switch to the C-101 layout (see Figure 15.32).

2. Start the PLOT command to open the Plot dialog box.

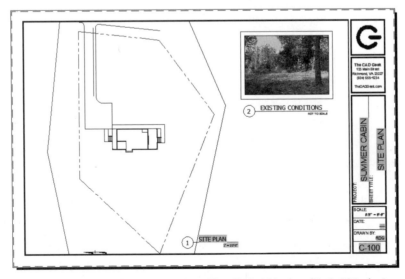

FIGURE 15.32 The site plan sheet file—I-C-101.dwg (M-C-101.dwg)—with the C-101 layout active

In a true production environment, it might be better to create a large-format layout to accommodate large-format plots.

3. Verify that the DWFx plotter is still current, and in the Paper Size area, choose any large-size paper that is recognized by the plotter.

In this example, I'm using a 24″×36″ (594 mm×841 mm) A1 sheet size.

4. In the Plot Area group, choose Extents from the What To Plot drop-down list and then click the Center The Plot option.

5. In the Plot Scale group, check the Fit To Paper option and then check Scale Lineweights.

This option causes AutoCAD to scale the lineweights relative to the amount the layout is scaled to fit to the paper.

6. Click the Preview button.

The white area around the border isn't even (see Figure 15.33). This is because the aspect ratio of the layout is different from that of the 24″×36″ (594 mm×841 mm) A1 paper.

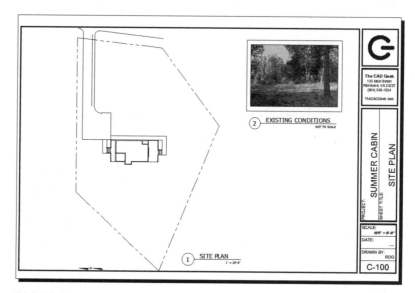

FIGURE 15.33 Preview of the cabin site layout

7. Right-click and choose Exit from the context menu to cancel the preview.

8. Click the OK button to plot this drawing to a new 15-C-101-Enlarged .dwfx file.

9. Close the I-C-101.dwg (M-C-101.dwg) without saving.

Publishing Multiple Layouts

In AutoCAD terminology, you *plot* a single layout or view one or more times. The terms *publishing* and *batch plotting* are interchangeable and refer to assigning several layouts or views to plot in sequence, one or more times. In this exercise, you will publish all your layouts at one time.

1. Open the I-A-100.dwg (M-A-100.dwg) sheet file, select the Output tab, and then click the Batch Plot button in the Plot panel.

   You may also choose the Publish option from the Application menu, or enter **PUBLISH↵**, to open the Publish dialog box (see Figure 15.34). This shows all the layouts, including model space for all open drawings.

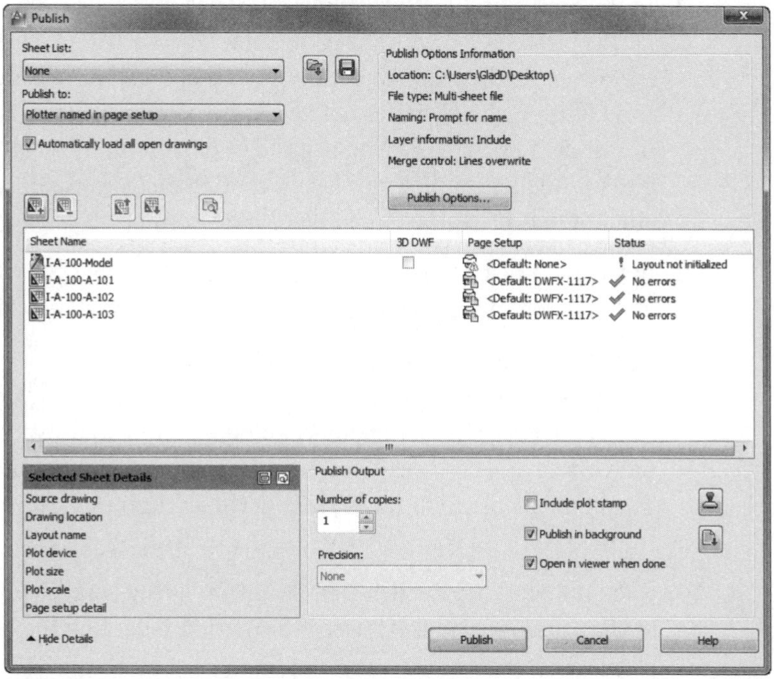

FIGURE 15.34 The Publish dialog box

2. You don't want to plot the objects from model space, so select the Model layout in the Sheet Name list and then click the Remove Sheets button.

3. To prevent the Model sheet from automatically being added in the future, right-click, and then uncheck the Include Model When Adding Sheets option in the context menu.

In the Page Setup column, you can see that all the layouts are set to <Default:DWFX-1117> (<Default:DWFX-A3>). This indicates that all the layouts will use the original page setup designated when the first layout, Cabin Floor Plan, was created. Remember, the other layouts were copied from this original layout.

 4. To add the other sheet files in your plan set, click the Add Sheets button.

5. Select the I-A-000.dwg (M-A-000.dwg), I-A-200.dwg (M-A-200.dwg), and I-C-101.dwg (M-C-101.dwg) sheet files.

   If necessary, drag the sheets into the proper order.

6. Click the Publish button at the bottom of the dialog box.

7. In the Save Sheet List dialog box, click Yes.

   This provides you with the opportunity to save this publishing job as a Drawing Set Description (DSD) file so that it can be reloaded with the Load Sheet List button. It's not always necessary to plot all the layouts in a drawing every time you use the Publish tool. By creating DSD files for frequently published layout combinations, you can reduce the amount of time required to produce hard-copy prints.

8. In the Save List As dialog box that opens, name the DSD file and navigate to your current working directory to place it. Then click Save.

9. The Publish dialog box closes, and the plots begin. If a Processing Background Job dialog box appears, click Close.

   An extensive number of plots can take a while to finish, depending on the size and complexity of the drawings and speed of the printer. The publish operation takes place in the background, so you can continue to work on your drawings as the publishing occurs.

10. Click the Plot And Publish Details button in the bottom-right corner of the AutoCAD window to see information regarding the current and previous plots.

Only one publish operation can occur at one time. If you start one operation before the previous one is completed, you will see the Job Already In Progress dialog box, shown in Figure 15.35, indicating that you must wait before starting the next one.

Without the PUBLISH command, you would have to open each layout tab individually and use the PLOT command to make a print of each layout. In addition to providing out-of-the-box batch plotting capabilities, the option to save a DSD file helps automate the plotting process. These DSD files can be especially helpful for projects for which multiple submittals are expected.

FIGURE 15.35 The Job Already In Progress dialog box

There is one final way of plotting multiple drawings at once, and it is by using Sheet Set Manager. The next section will allow you to harness one of the most popular features of Sheet Set Manager.

Publishing with Sheet Set Manager

 In Chapter 14, you learned how Sheet Set Manager can be used to create and manage drawing sheets (new for AutoCAD LT 2012). Now that it's time to plot your drawings, this section will teach you how to use Sheet Set Manager to plot nearly any combination of sheets.

1. If it's not already displayed on your screen, open the Sheet Set Manager palette set by selecting the Sheet Set Manager tool on the Palettes panel of the View tab on the Ribbon.

2. Expand the drop-down list at the top of the Sheet List palette, and choose Open. Browse to and open the Summer Cabin.dst file in your Chapter 15 directory.

   After you open the sheet set, the Sheet Set Manager palette set should display a list of drawing sheets in your project (see Figure 15.36).

3. Right-click the Summer Cabin sheet set name at the top of the Sheet List palette, and choose Publish ➢ Publish To Plotter from the contextual menu that appears (see Figure 15.37).

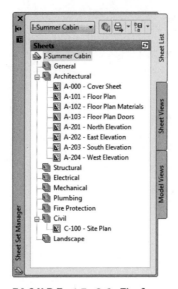

FIGURE 15.36 The Summer
Cabin sheet list displaying a list of
drawing sheets

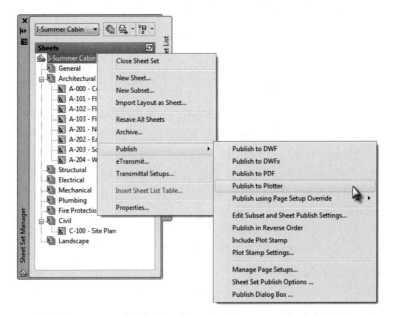

FIGURE 15.37 Publishing the entire sheet set to the default plotter

Choosing the Publish To Plotter option from Sheet Set Manager will use the plotter assigned to each individual layout tab. That is, if half of your layouts had Plotter A assigned to them and the other half had Plotter B, half of your drawing set would plot on each plotter. Therefore, if you plan to use Sheet Set Manager, it's especially important for you to set up each of your drawings in a uniform way. Sheet Set Manager offers you multiple ways of plotting your sheet set:

Publish to DWF/DWFx   Uses the assigned page setup of each layout, and creates a DWF or DWFX file by using the settings such as page size and plot-style table contained within the page setup.

Publish to PDF   Identical to the Publish To DWF or DWFx option with the exception of the output file type. As its name indicates, the Publish To PDF option will create a PDF file, compatible with the popular Adobe Acrobat program.

Publish To Plotter   As previously discussed, this option will use the page setup assigned to each layout and use those settings to publish the sheet set. If different plotters are assigned to the various layouts, your sheet set will plot to separate plotters.

Publish Using Page Setup Override   Among the settings you specified as you created your Summer Cabin sheet set was the location for Page Setup Overrides. This was set to the same template drawing used to create your sheets. Therefore, any additional page setups you create in your sheet template drawing will automatically appear here. Using a Page Setup Override will inherit all of the settings, including the plotter, contained within the page setup.

You don't always need to plot every drawing inside your sheet set. Let's say you want to plot only the Architectural sheets in your plan set. Rather than right-clicking the Summer Cabin sheet set name, you would right-click the Architectural subset to display the contextual menu shown earlier in Figure 15.37. Instead of plotting every drawing in your sheet set, Sheet Set Manager will plot only the sheets under the Architectural subset.

It's also possible to select any combination of sheets and subsets by using the Ctrl key to plot only the sheets you select. Although setting up Sheet Set Manager takes more time than using the PUBLISH command, this versatility, coupled with the sheet management features covered in Chapter 14, makes it a worthwhile investment for a plan set of any notable size.

What's the Difference between DWF and DWFX?

The DWF format was created in 1995, before computing power was what it is today. Creating DWF files will use version 6 of the DWF format. By contrast, the DWFX format is technically version 7 of the DWF format. The major difference between the two versions is interoperability.

The only way to view and open a DWF file is with an Autodesk application such as Design Review. However, DWFX files are built using the Microsoft XML Paper Specification. While you'll still need Design Review to take advantage of the electronic markup features found inside it, DWFX files have the added feature of being compatible with an XPS viewer. An XPS viewer is available for Windows XP and ships with Windows Vista and above. It's also possible to download and install XPS viewing components for Internet Explorer 7 and higher to view DWFX files.

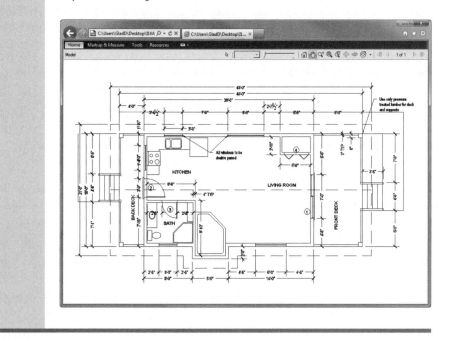

Going Forward

This chapter has been a quick tour and introduction to the plot-style feature, which helps control how your drawing will plot. Getting consistently good output from your AutoCAD drawings requires an investment of time by you, or the office CAD manager/information technologist, to set up the best configuration of your printers and AutoCAD. As you have seen, layouts provide a good tool for setting up plots, once the configuration is right.

The next two chapters cover drawing in 3D (for AutoCAD users only). There you'll learn how to build a comprehensive 3D model and render it to create a photorealistic illustration of how your cabin would look after it was built. You'll also find a glossary of terms related to AutoCAD, AutoCAD LT, building construction, and design that have been discussed in the book. This book's web page (**www.sybex .com/go/autocad2012ner** and **www.autocadner.com**) offers a collection of all the AutoCAD drawings and adjunct files that you'll use or generate throughout the course of this book.

Just because the 3D features found inside AutoCAD aren't included in AutoCAD LT, doesn't mean your journey has to end here. Be sure to visit the companion site at **www.autocadner.com**, where you'll find additional resources to help you continue mastering AutoCAD, and also get answers to any questions that may have arisen as you worked through the book.

If You Would Like More Practice...

This chapter used the virtual DWFx ePlot (XPS Compatible).pc3 device that's included with AutoCAD to create plots of your drawings. Apply the concepts you learned throughout this chapter to plot to a physical printer/plotter installed on your computer. To create a hard-copy plot of a layout tab, follow these steps:

1. Open the PLOT command.

2. Select the physical device you would like to plot to.

3. Choose the best paper size for your device. Remember that many plotters include several versions of the same overall paper size.

4. Set the Plot Area, Plot Offset, and Plot Scale as needed. Use the Preview button to verify each of these settings.

5. Pick a Plot Style Table, and set the Drawing Orientation to Landscape.

6. Validate your plot by clicking the Preview button once again. Make any necessary changes.

7. Click OK to begin plotting your drawing.

Are You Experienced?

Now you can...

☑ set up a drawing to be printed

☑ assign lineweights to layers in your drawing

☑ select the area of your drawing to print

☑ choose a sheet size to use to print your drawing

☑ control the orientation and origin of the print

☑ set the scale of the print

☑ preview a print

☑ print a layout

☑ view electronic plots with Autodesk Design Review

☑ use Sheet Set Manager to publish one or many drawings

☑ publish multiple layouts

☑ navigate through the plot-style features

Creating 3D Geometry

LT has a few 3D viewing tools but none of the 3D solid-modeling tools that AutoCAD supports. Therefore, this chapter doesn't apply to LT.

Nothing in AutoCAD is quite as fascinating as drawing in 3D. While fascinating to create, 3D models are incredibly valuable project assets. Today's architects and engineers are increasingly using AutoCAD's 3D features not only to communicate designs with clients, but also as a design and analysis tool.

Consequently, acquiring some skills in working in 3D is becoming an employment requirement, and it's also a lot of fun. This chapter covers 3D modeling, and the next chapter introduces materials and rendering.

Constructing a 3D model of a building requires many of the tools that you've been using throughout this book and some new ones that you'll be introduced to in this chapter. Your competence in using the basic drawing, editing, and display commands is critical to your successful study of 3D for two reasons. First, drawing in 3D can seem more complex and difficult than drawing in 2D, and it can be frustrating until you get used to it. If you aren't familiar with the basic commands, you'll become that much more frustrated. Second, accuracy is critical in 3D drawing. The effect of errors is compounded, so you must be in the habit of using tools, such as the osnap modes, to maximize your precision.

Don't be discouraged; just be warned. Drawing in 3D is a fascinating and enjoyable process, and the results you get can be astounding. I sincerely encourage you to make the effort to learn some of the basic 3D skills presented here.

Many 3D software packages are on the market today, and some are better for drawing buildings than others. Often, because of the precision that AutoCAD provides, a 3D DWG file is exported to one of these specialized 3D packages for further work, after being laid out in AutoCAD. Two other Autodesk products, 3ds Max and 3ds Max Design, are designed to work with AutoCAD DWG files and maintain a constant link with AutoCAD-produced files. Sometimes drawings are created in 2D, converted to 3D, and then refined into shaded, colored, and textured renderings with specific lights and shadows.

In this chapter, you'll look at the basic techniques of solid modeling and we'll touch on a couple of tools used in mesh and surface modeling. In the process, you'll learn some techniques for viewing a 3D model.

▶ **Setting up a 3D workspace**

▶ **Using the Polysolid tool**

▶ **Using the Boolean functions**

▶ **Extruding 2D objects**

▶ **Creating 3D surfaces**

▶ **Navigating in a 3D environment**

Modeling in 3D

You'll begin by building a 3D model of the cabin, using several techniques for creating 3D solids *and* surfaces. When you use solid-modeling tools, the objects you create are solid, like lumps of clay. They can be added together or subtracted from one another to form more-complex shapes. By contrast, 3D surfaces are composites of two-dimensional planes that stretch over a frame of lines the way a tent surface stretches over the frame inside.

As you construct these 3D objects, you'll become more familiar with the user coordinate system (UCS), learn how it's used with 3D, and begin using the basic methods of viewing a 3D model.

Setting Up the 3D Workspace and Environment

So far, you've been using the Drafting & Annotation workspace to create your drawings. Your first task in transitioning into 3D begins by switching to a new workspace for working in 3D and changing how AutoCAD displays the available tools.

Follow these steps to switch the workspace:

1. Open the I14A-FPLAYO.dwg (M14A-FPLAYO.dwg) file you created previously, or from this chapter's download found at **www.sybex.com/go/ autocad2012ner** or **www.autocadner.com**.

2. Switch to the 3D Modeling workspace by using the Workspace drop-down list on the Quick Access toolbar (see the left image in Figure 16.1).
   Alternatively, the gear icon on the status bar at the bottom of the Application window may also be used to change workspaces (see the right image in Figure 16.1).

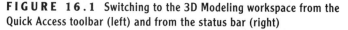

FIGURE 16.1 Switching to the 3D Modeling workspace from the Quick Access toolbar (left) and from the status bar (right)

Switching to the 3D Modeling workspace updates the AutoCAD user interface, deemphasizing the 2D drafting tools used until this point, and placing emphasis on the 3D modeling toolset (see Figure 16.2). While many of the 2D drafting tools have been deemphasized and/or removed from the Ribbon, it's important to note that all AutoCAD commands are still available from the command line. Likewise, it's always possible to restore the complete 2D drafting toolset by switching back to the Drafting & Annotation workspace.

3. Zoom in to the floor plan, make the A-WALL layer current, and freeze all other layers.

   Your drawing and AutoCAD setup will look like Figure 16.3.

FIGURE 16.2 The 3D Modeling workspace

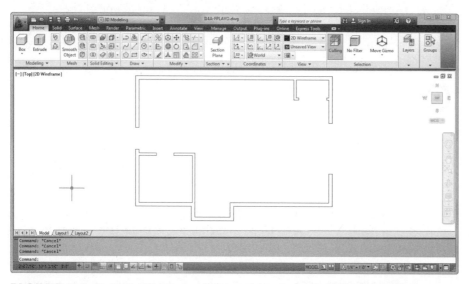

FIGURE 16.3 I14A-FPLAYO.dwg (M14A-FPLAYO.dwg) with all layers turned off except A-WALL

4. If the UCS icon isn't visible on your screen, click the View tab and then click the Show UCS Icon button on the Coordinates panel.

   You'll use the UCS icon in a moment, but for now, keep an eye on it as the drawing changes. Remember that the icon's arrows indicate the positive direction for the x-, y-, and (in 3D) z-axes.

THINKING IN 3D

Try to start thinking of your model in three dimensions. The entire drawing is on a flat plane parallel to the monitor screen. When you add elements in the third dimension, they project straight out of the screen toward you if they have a positive dimension, and straight through the screen if they have a negative dimension. The line of direction is perpendicular to the plane of the screen and is called the *z-axis*. You're already familiar with the x- and y-axes, which run left and right, and up and down, respectively. Think of the z-axis as running into and out of the screen.

Now you'll use the in-canvas viewport controls to change the view from a plan view of the drawing—looking straight down at it—to one in which you're looking down at it from an angle. There are several preselected viewpoints, and here you'll switch to one of them.

 The in-canvas viewport controls are composed of three bracketed menus in the upper-left corner of the drawing window. Starting from the left, these menus are as follows:

▶ Viewport Control

▶ View Controls

▶ View Style Control

You'll use the View Controls menu to change the angle in which the drawing is displayed.

5. Using the in-canvas viewport controls, click the View Controls menu, currently displayed as [Top], and choose SW Isometric, as shown in Figure 16.4.

The view changes to look like Figure 16.5. Notice how the UCS icon has altered with the change of view. The X and Y arrows still run parallel to the side and front of the cabin, but the icon and the floor plan are now at an angle to the screen, and the z-axis is visible. The crosshair cursor is now colored and also displays the z-axis.

Visual styles allow a 3D model to display in several different ways: with nonvisible edges hidden, with materials applied, or even transparently. The most appropriate visual style is often dictated by the task at hand, the context of which will be established in the succeeding exercises.

Currently the most basic of these visual styles, 2D Wireframe, is in use. To get started, you'll change this to one of the 3D visual styles included with the product.

6. Returning to the in-canvas viewport controls, click the Visual Style Controls menu, currently displayed as [2D Wireframe], and select X-Ray (see Figure 16.6).

FIGURE 16.4 Select the Southwest Isometric view from the in-canvas viewport control's View Controls menu.

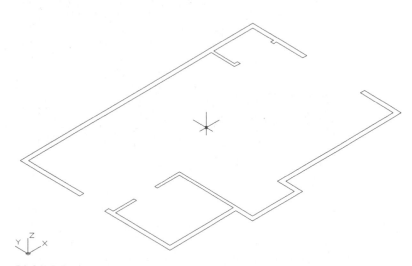

FIGURE 16.5 The walls as displayed from the Southwest Isometric view

The drawing area takes on a dark gray background, and the UCS icon changes to a chunkier, three-color appearance. Also note how the position of the ViewCube in the upper-right corner reflects the current orientation of your drawing (see Figure 16.7). The ViewCube is a navigation tool covered later in this chapter.

7. Save your drawing as `I16-01-ViewSetup.dwg` (`M16-01-ViewSetup.dwg`).

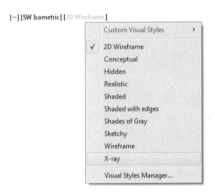

FIGURE 16.6 Selecting the X-Ray visual style

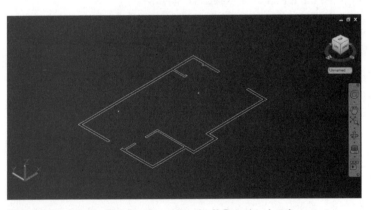

FIGURE 16.7 The drawing using the X-Ray visual style

 NOTE   A common convention in 3D graphics is to color vectors or other axes to indicate elements, so that red indicates the x-axis, green indicates the y-axis, and blue indicates the z-axis. The phrase used to remember this scheme is *RGB = XYZ*. You'll see this convention used several times in this and the next chapter.

Making the Walls

The main task ahead is to create a 3D model of the cabin. You'll use solid elements for the cabin's walls, doors, windows, floor, decks, and steps. You'll learn several ways of viewing your work as you progress. To make the walls, you'll start with the polysolid object and then, like a sculptor, remove from the polysolid everything that isn't an interior or exterior wall. The elements to be removed are the void spaces for the doors and windows.

Creating the Exterior Walls

To make the exterior walls, follow these steps:

1. Continue using I16-01-ViewSetup.dwg (M16-01-ViewSetup.dwg), or open it if it is not already open.

2. Set the Endpoint osnap to be running.

3. Create a new layer called **A-WALL-EXTR-3DOB**, assign it color 22, and make it current.

Polysolid

4. Click the Polysolid tool on the Primitive panel of the Solid tab.
   AutoCAD may pause briefly as it loads the 3D-specific applications.

5. At the _Polysolid 0'-4", Width = 0'-0 1/4", Justification = Center Specify start point or [Object/Height/Width/Justify] <Object>: prompt, enter H⏎ 7'7-1/4"⏎ (2318⏎) to set the object height to 7'-7¼" (2318 mm).
   This is the height where the inside faces of the exterior walls meet the roof.
   The exterior walls are 6" (150 mm) thick, so the polysolid object should be 6" (150 mm) thick as well.

6. Enter W⏎ and then 6⏎ (150⏎) at the Specify width < 0'-0¼"NF prompt.
   The Justification option determines the side of the polysolid on which you will pick the endpoints. You will be picking the outside lines of the cabin in a counterclockwise order, so the justification must be set to Right.

7. Enter J⏎ R⏎.
   You're now ready to begin creating the walls.

8. Use the Endpoint osnap to select the corner for the exterior wall of the cabin nearest to the bottom of the screen, and then move the cursor.
   The first wall appears, and it is tied to the cursor, as shown in Figure 16.8.

9. Moving in the counterclockwise direction, click each of the endpoints along the outside perimeter of the cabin until only one segment separates the last segment from the first.

Your drawing should look like Figure 16.9.

10. Right-click and choose Close from the context menu to close the polysolid.

11. Save your drawing as **I16-02-ExteriorWalls.dwg** (**M16-02-ExteriorWalls.dwg**).

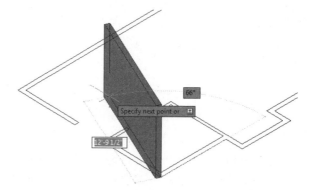

FIGURE 16.8 Starting the first polysolid wall

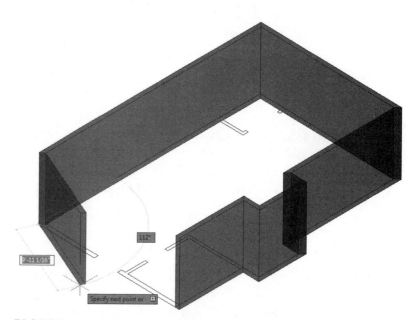

FIGURE 16.9 The exterior walls drawn with polysolids

Adding the Interior Walls

The interior cabin walls are thinner than the exterior walls and will probably have a different material assigned to them. You will make a new layer for these walls and change the polysolid parameters:

1. Continue using I16-02-ExteriorWalls.dwg (M16-02-Exterior Walls.dwg), or open it if it is not already open.

2. Create a new layer called **A-WALL-INTR-3DOB**, assign it color 44, and make it the current layer.

3. Click the upper corner of the ViewCube to change your view to a North East orientation (see Figure 16.10), and zoom in to the lower-left corner of the cabin so you can see the bathroom walls.

4. Start the POLYSOLID command again.

5. Press the down-arrow on the keyboard to expose the context menu at the cursor, and then click the Width option, as shown in Figure 16.11.

6. Enter 4↵ (100↵) to change the width to 4″ (100 mm).

7. Starting with the interior endpoint of the inside wall nearest to the back door, draw the two walls that enclose the bathroom.

> ◀
>
> **You can also start the** POLYSOLID **command by entering PSOLID↵.**

FIGURE 16.10 Using the ViewCube to change the view orientation

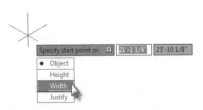

FIGURE 16.11 Choosing the Width option from the context menu

8. Right-click and choose Enter to terminate the command.

   If you have trouble clicking the correct endpoints, temporarily freeze the A-WALL-EXTR-3DOB layer, create the new wall, and then thaw the layer.

9. Press the spacebar to restart the command, and then draw the two walls that surround the closet, starting at the endpoint that is farthest from the sliding glass door.

   Make sure that the walls are justified properly, and then zoom to the drawing's extents. Your drawing should look similar to Figure 16.12.

10. Save your drawing as **I16-03-InteriorWalls.dwg** (**M16-03-Interior Walls.dwg**).

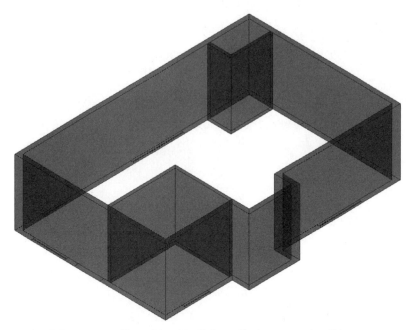

FIGURE 16.12 The cabin with all the walls drawn as polysolids

Creating the Door and Window Block-Outs

Before you add the geometry for the doors and windows, you must make the openings in the walls. You will accomplish this by using the Boolean tools, which can create a single object from the volumes of two overlapping objects called *operands*. There are three Boolean functions:

Union   Union combines the two volumes.

Subtraction   Subtraction deletes one object and the overlapping volume shared with the other.

Intersection   Intersection deletes both objects, leaving only the shared volume behind.

For the doors and windows, you will make solid boxes the size of the openings. You'll then use the Subtract command to create voids by removing the boxes as well as the volume they share with the walls. The boxes act as *block-outs*— volumes that are to be deleted—and their only function is to help delete part of the polysolid wall.

Creating the Door Block-Outs

Follow these steps to make the door block-outs:

1. Continue using I16-03-InteriorWalls.dwg (M16-03-Interior Walls.dwg), or open it if it is not already open.

2. Make a new layer named **A-DOOR-3DOB**, applying color 100 and set it as the current layer.

3. Freeze the two A-WALL 3DOB layers and thaw the A-GLAZ layer.

N O T E   **See Figure 10.1 in Chapter 10, "Generating Elevations," for the window elevations above the floor.**

Boxes (as well as cylinders, cones, and the other 3D objects on the fly-out) are known as *primitives*, and they are often used as the building blocks of more-complex objects.

◄

4. Click the upper corner of the ViewCube to change from the current northeast view to a southwest orientation.

5. Zoom in to the cabin so you can see the back door and the kitchen window.

6. Click the Box button in the Modeling panel of the Home Ribbon tab, or enter **BOX**↵ at the command prompt.
   If the Box tool is not shown, click the down-arrow below the tool on the far-left side of the panel and choose it from the fly-out menu. You will be making a block-out that will act as the operand that is removed from the polysolid.

The box object requires three items of information to be constructed: two points that define the opposing corners of the object's footprint, and a height value.

7. At the prompts, click two opposite corners of the back door opening, as shown in Figure 16.13.

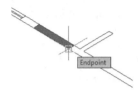

FIGURE 16.13 Defining the footprint of the back door

8. At the Specify height or [2Point]: prompt, enter **7'6.⏎** (**2286.⏎**). The box appears in place (see Figure 16.14).

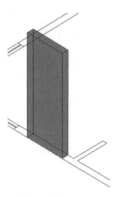

FIGURE 16.14 The first door operand created in place

9. Repeat steps 6 through 8 to create the block-outs for two internal doors and the sliding glass door.

When using the Boolean functions, it's best not to have a situation where the two operands have coplanar faces.

10. Select the box at the back door.

The box's grips appear all around the base and at a single location at the top. Dragging the triangular grips changes the lengths of the

When I instruct you to pick an object when working in 3D, you need to click an edge of the object or a line that helps define the object. If you try to select a surface, the selection may not be recognized.

sides of the box but doesn't change the angles between the sides. The square grips move the corners of the box or the box itself, and the single top grip changes the box's height.

11. Click the triangular grip on the front of the box, and drag it forward to pull the front of the box out from the front of the cabin.

    It doesn't have to be a great distance, just enough so that the box and the frozen polysolid don't share the same plane.

12. Drag the rear triangular grip backward, and position it off the inside of the exterior wall.

    The base of the door should look similar to Figure 16.15.

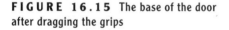

FIGURE 16.15 The base of the door after dragging the grips

13. Repeat the process for the other three door block-outs so that each is thicker than its associated opening.

    Your screen should look similar to Figure 16.16.

14. Save your drawing as **I16-04-DoorBlockOut.dwg** (**M16-04-DoorBlock Out.dwg**).

Creating the Window Block-Outs

As you might expect, making the window block-outs will be just like making the doorway openings. The only difference is that the bottoms of the window openings sit at a different height above the 2D floor plan. Here are the steps:

1. Continue using I16-04-DoorBlockOut.dwg (M16-04-DoorBlockOut .dwg), or open it if it's not already open.

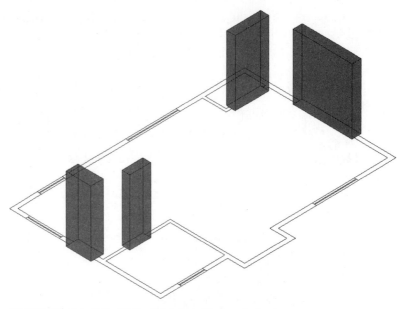

FIGURE 16.16 All the thick door block-outs in place

2. Using the same procedure as in the previous section, create the boxes for all the window block-outs, with each box set to 3′-6″ (1067 mm) tall.

T I P After you make the first window box, the default height for the BOX command is the correct height for the remaining windows. When prompted for the height, just press the spacebar or ↲.

3. Change the thicknesses of the boxes so they overlap the thickness of the outside walls.

Your drawing should look like Figure 16.17.

4. Save your drawing as I16-05-WindowBlockOut.dwg (M16-05-Window BlockOut.dwg).

Moving and Rotating in 3D

When you moved objects in the 2D portion of this book, terms such as *left* and *right* or *up* and *down* were acceptable to use because all movements were associated with the sides of the drawing area. Even when you rotated the views in Chapter 10, it was so you could relate movements to the screen more easily. When working in 3D, however, these terms are no longer easily translated from your intent to proper movement on the screen. Let's take the back door block-out, for example. If I told you to move it *forward*, would that mean into the cabin, away from the cabin, or toward the bottom of the screen? You see what the problem is. When the viewpoint is significantly different from what you may expect, say, from the bottom or the back, then *front* or *back* may be even more confusing.

The First Right-Hand Rule

To help you stay oriented in 3D space, the UCS becomes more important. Each colored axis of the UCS icon points in the positive direction for that particular axis. To understand whether a movement, particularly in the z-axis, is in the positive direction, you should be familiar with the first of two *right-hand rules*.

The *first right-hand rule* relates your hand to the UCS and helps clarify the axis directions. Start by extending the thumb and index finger on your right hand to form an L-shape. Then project your middle finger perpendicular to your palm, as shown in Figure 16.18. The rule states: When your thumb is pointing in the positive X direction, and your index finger is pointing in the positive Y direction, your middle finger must be pointing in the positive Z direction.

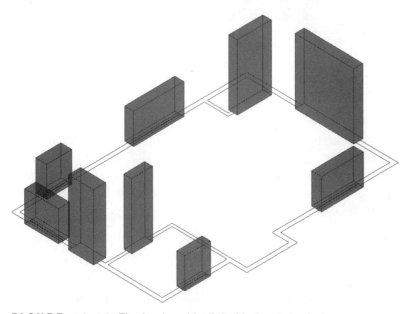

FIGURE 16.17 The drawing with all the block-outs in place

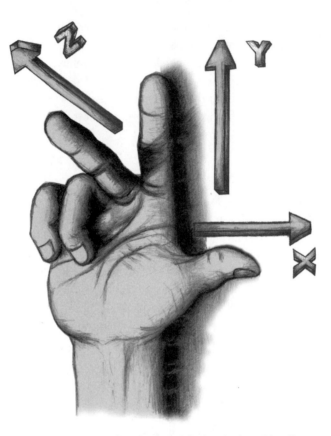

FIGURE 16.18 Use the first right-hand rule to identify x-, y-, and z-axes.

To apply this to the window block-outs in our cabin example, compare your right hand to the UCS icon in the drawing area. With your thumb pointing toward the cabin, and your index finger pointing away from the cabin and to the left, your middle finger then points toward the top of the screen. This indicates that the window block-outs, which are currently resting on the ground plane with the door block-out, need to be moved in the positive Z direction.

1. Continue using I16-05-WindowBlockOut.dwg (M16-05-WindowBlock Out.dwg), or open it if it's not already open.

2. Click the 3D Move tool in the Modify panel on the Home tab.
   With the 3D Move tool, objects are moved using the Move grip tool, which looks similar to the UCS icon.

3. At the `Select objects:` prompt, select the bathroom window block-out and then press ⏎ to end the selection process.

   The Move grip tool appears at the center of the box, as shown in Figure 16.19. Note the different-color arrows that make up the 3D move tool: the color of each arrow matches the RGB = XYZ convention used for the 3D UCS icon.

4. Move the cursor over each of the colored axes of the Move grip tool.

   Notice that the axis turns yellow to indicate that it is current, and a vector appears in line with the axis, as shown in Figure 16.20. When a vector is visible, all movements, whether indicated with the cursor and a mouse click or with input from the keyboard, are constrained to the axis indicated.

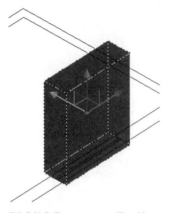

FIGURE 16.19 The Move grip tool at the center of the box

5. Move the cursor over the blue z-axis.

6. When the axis vector appears, click and move the box in the positive Z direction, and enter **2'11**⏎ (**889**⏎).

   The box moves 2'-11" (889 mm) above the wall lines.

 T I P   You can also use the standard Move tool and enter @0,0,2'11 (@0,0,889) to move the box 2'-11" (889 mm) along the z-axis.

---

7. Start the 3D Move tool again, and this time pick the four remaining window block-outs.

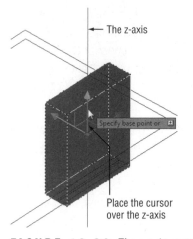

The z-axis

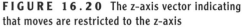

Specify base point or

Place the cursor
over the z-axis

F I G U R E   1 6 . 2 0 The z-axis vector indicating
that moves are restricted to the z-axis

---

8. Move the cursor directly above the Move grip tool and then click and
    drag the z-axis.

    Notice that all four boxes are moving, and each leaves a ghosted
    version of itself at its original location (see Figure 16.21).

9. Enter **2'11↵** (**889↵**) to move the selected block-outs.

10. A move operation in a 3D view can sometimes be deceiving:

     a. Click the Top text located on the ViewCube to switch to the Top
         view, and make sure the block-outs are all located properly.

     b. If they are, use the ViewCube to switch back to the southwest view
         once again. If they're not, undo to the point before the move and
         try it again.

11. Save your drawing as **I16-06-ElevateWindows.dwg** (**M16-06-Elevate**
     Windows.dwg).

Cutting the Openings

You are ready to start the Boolean processes and cut the openings in the walls.
When prompted to select an object, be sure to click on an edge of the 3D objects
and not a face, or the selection may not be successful.

1. Continue using I16-06-ElevateWindows.dwg (M16-06-Elevate
    Windows.dwg), or open it if it's not already open.

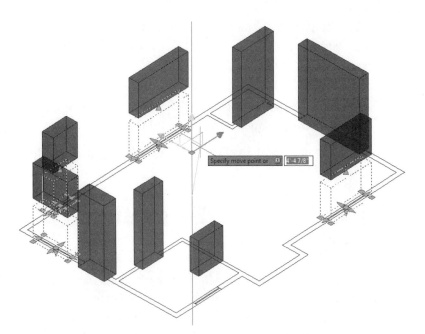

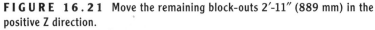

FIGURE 16.21 Move the remaining block-outs 2'-11" (889 mm) in the positive Z direction.

2. Thaw the A-WALL-EXTR-3DOB and A-WALL-INTR-3DOB layers, and freeze the A-GLAZ layer.

3. Click the Subtract button on the Solid Editing panel of the Home tab, or enter **SUBTRACT**↵.

4. At the Select solids and regions to subtract from.. Select objects: prompt, select the exterior wall and then press ↵ to end the selection process.

You can perform the Boolean functions on several objects at one time, but first you will do it to only one.

5. At the Select solids, surfaces and regions to subtract.. Select objects: prompt, select the back door and then press ↵.

The door block-out, and the volume that it shared with the wall, are subtracted from the exterior wall (see Figure 16.22).

6. Start the SUBTRACT command again, and select the exterior wall again.

T I P   If you have trouble seeing the window block-outs, temporarily switch to the 3D Wireframe visual style, execute the Boolean operation, and then switch back to the X-Ray style.

7. When prompted for the objects to subtract, select all the remaining exterior door and window block-outs and then press ↵.

   All the openings appear on the cabin's exterior walls, as shown in Figure 16.23.

8. Repeat the subtraction process on the two interior walls to remove the bathroom and closet door volumes.

9. Save your drawing as **I16-07-ExteriorOpenings.dwg** (**M16-07-Exterior Openings.dwg**).

Creating the Floor, Foundation, and Thresholds

In designing the cabin, you didn't draw a floor, but one was implied. The three exterior doorway openings have thresholds that indicate a small change in level from the cabin floor down to the decks. You'll now create additional objects to make the floor, foundation and supports, and the thresholds. Follow these steps:

1. Continue using I16-07-ExteriorOpenings.dwg (M16-07-Exterior Openings.dwg), or open it if it's not already open.

2. Continuing from the previous set of steps, open the Layer Properties Manager and do the following:

   a. Create the following new layers:

      A-DOOR-THRE-3DOB

      A-FLOR-3DOB

      A-FNDN-3DOB

   b. Make A-DOOR-THRE-3DOB current.

   c. Give each layer a unique color.

   d. Freeze the A-WALL-EXTR-3DOB and A-WALL-INTR-3DOB layers.

   e. Thaw the A-DECK-STRS layer.

   To see where you're going, look ahead to Figure 16.26. You'll use the EXTRUDE command to create a series of solids that represent the thresholds and boxes for the steps and the floor.

> To find your 3D object layers quickly in the Layer Properties Manager, try entering *3DOB in the text box in the upper-right corner.
> ▶

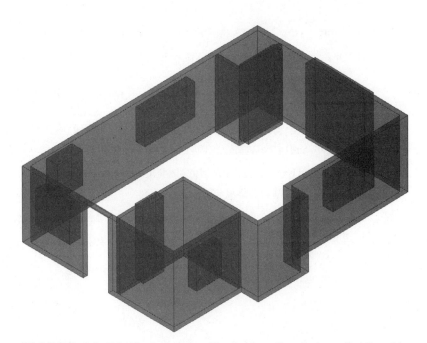

FIGURE 16.22 The back door subtracted from the exterior wall of the cabin

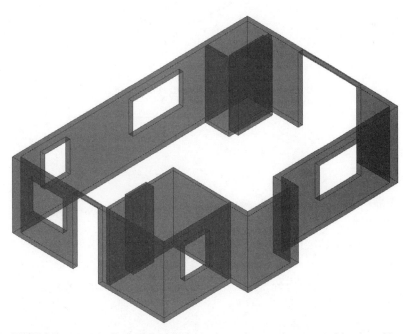

FIGURE 16.23 Each of the interior and exterior openings created for the cabin

3. Zoom in on the back door opening and its threshold.

4. Draw a polyline around the perimeter of the threshold; use the Close option to make the last segment.

For clarity only, the polyline is shown wider than necessary in Figure 16.24.

The Extrude tool extends a 2D object in the Z direction, creating surfaces on the newly formed sides and end caps.

5. Click the Extrude tool in the Modeling panel of the Home tab, select the threshold polyline, and then press ↵.

6. At the `Specify height of extrusion or [Direction/Path/Taper angle] <-1'-0">:` prompt, enter **1.05**↵ (**27**↵).

The first threshold is completed, as shown in Figure 16.25.

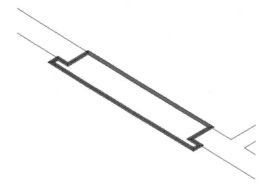

FIGURE 16.24 A polyline drawn around the perimeter of the threshold

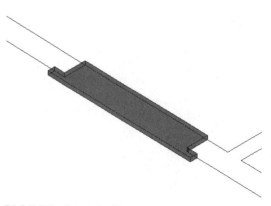

FIGURE 16.25 The extruded polyline

7. Make a similar extruded threshold for the sliding glass door.

8. Make the A-FLOR-3DOB layer current.

9. To create the floor, first draw a polyline around the inside perimeter of the cabin, ignoring the interior walls and thresholds.

10. Start the EXTRUDE command, select the floor polyline, and then extrude it 1″ (25 mm), as shown in Figure 16.26.

11. Save your drawing as **I16-08-Thresholds.dwg (M16-08 -Thresholds.dwg)**.

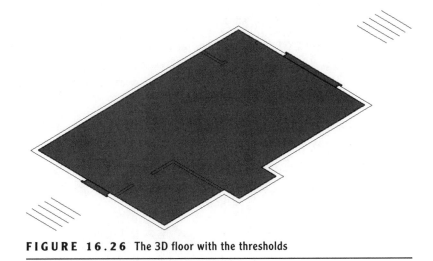

FIGURE 16.26 The 3D floor with the thresholds

Creating the Foundation and Supports

The cabin's foundation is a concrete slab 18″ (457 mm) thick that sits directly on the ground. The foundation supports the structure except where the pop-out projects out from the side wall. At the outside corners of each deck are concrete support posts. All the objects are placed on the 3D-Foundation layer.

1. Continue using I16-08-Thresholds.dwg (M16-08-Thresholds.dwg), or open it if it's not already open.

2. Make the A-FNDN-3DOB layer current, and thaw the A-DECK layer.

3. Freeze the A-FLOR-3DOB and A-DOOR-THRE-3DOB layers.

4. Draw a closed polyline around the outside perimeter of the cabin, making sure you span the pop-out area as if it didn't exist.

Alternatively, you could use the Rectangle (RECTANG) command.

5. Extrude the polyline 18″ (457 mm) in the negative Z direction. You can do this with Dynamic Input active by dragging the extrusion in the negative direction and entering **18.⏎ (457⏎)**, or by dragging it in the positive direction and entering **–18.⏎ (–457⏎)**.

6. Using the Rectangle (RECTANG) command, draw a 12″×12″ (305 mm× 305 mm) rectangle at each of the four outside corners of the decks.

The outside corner of each rectangle should match the outside corner of each deck post corner.

7. Start the EXTRUDE command, select all four rectangles, and then extrude them 2′-10″ (864 mm) in the negative Z direction.

When you're finished, the foundation and supports should look like Figure 16.27.

8. Save your drawing as **I16-09-FoundationSupport.dwg (M16-09-FoundationSupport.dwg)**.

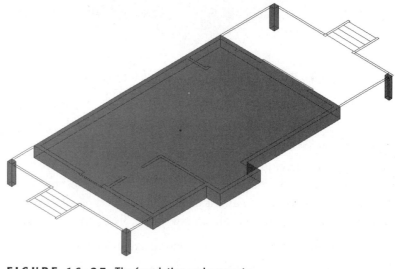

FIGURE 16.27 The foundation and supports

![tip icon] **T I P**   Similar to the way you used Quick Filter to create a Wblock (WBLOCK) earlier in the book, try using the Quick Select button on the Properties palette to select the four foundation posts.

Building the Windows

Now that the openings are in place and the foundation is complete, you just need to build the geometry for the doors and windows. These can be as complete as you like them with sills, drip grooves, tapered panels, kick plates, and so on. For the exercise in this book, however, you'll create fairly simple frames, door panels, and glazing.

1. Continue using I16-09- FoundationSupport.dwg (M16-09- Foundation Support.dwg), or open it if it's not already open.

2. Make a new layer named **A-GLAZ-SILL-3DOB** and set it as the current layer.

3. Freeze the A-FNDN-3DOB layer.

4. Thaw the A-WALL-EXTR-3DOB layer.

5. Zoom in to the kitchen window near the back door.

6. Click the Allow/Disallow Dynamic UCS button in the status bar to turn on Dynamic UCS mode.

   When you are in a command, Dynamic UCS causes the current UCS to adapt to the orientation of whichever face the cursor is over. This is important because, when using creation tools such as the BOX command, the footprint is made in the X and Y plane, and the height is projected along the z-axis. When Dynamic UCS is active, the UCS shown at the cursor overrides the UCS shown by the UCS icon.

7. Start the BOX command and then move your cursor near the UCS icon.

   Notice that the color-coded axes of the crosshairs match the orientation and colors (RGB = XYZ) of the UCS icon axes.

8. Move the cursor over the faces on the back wall of the cabin and see that the blue z-axis now points in the same direction as the UCS icon's y-axis.

   This identifies the orientation of that particular wall's face.

9. With the Endpoint osnap active, click the lower-left outside corner of the kitchen window, and then move the cursor away from that corner.

   The box starts to form with its orientation parallel to the outside wall, and the UCS icon temporarily changes its orientation (see the left of Figure 16.28).

10. Click the opposite outside corner of the window for the base of the new box (see the right of Figure 16.28).

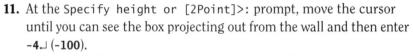

11. At the Specify height or [2Point]>: prompt, move the cursor until you can see the box projecting out from the wall and then enter −4↵ (−100).

    The box's Height parameter projects it 4″ (100 mm) into the window opening. You can switch to a Wireframe visual style to see this more clearly.

12. Turn off Dynamic UCS, select the box, and move it 1″ (25 mm) in the positive X direction to center it in the wall.

    The box you just made will be the frame for the kitchen window. Now you need to make a block-out to subtract from the box to create the opening for the glazing.

For clarity, the illustrations for the kitchen window are shown using the Conceptual visual style.

13. Copy the box you just made, move it in front of the back wall, and then select the copy to expose its grips.

    Use Ortho mode, keyboard input, or the Move grip tool to ensure that the box is moved along the x-axis only.

14. Turn on Polar Tracking.

15. Select each of the four outward-pointing triangular grips along the perimeter, and move them 1″ (25 mm) toward the inside of the box (see the left image of Figure 16.29).

16. Click the triangular grip on the back of the box, and drag it until the box extends all the way through the back wall (see the right image of Figure 16.29).

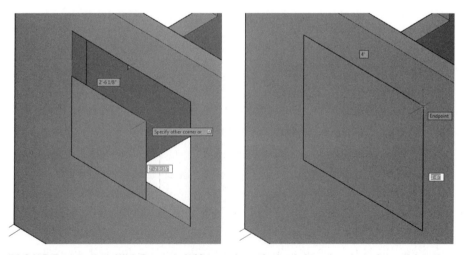

FIGURE 16.28 With Dynamic UCS turned on, the box's base is oriented parallel to the wall (left); the box's base is completed (right).

17. Using the in-canvas viewport controls, switch to the 3D Wireframe visual style and turn on the Selection Cycling tool in the status bar if it's not already.

18. Using the Subtract Boolean function, subtract the block-out from the frame.

19. Switch back to the Conceptual or X-Ray visual style, and your window should look similar to Figure 16.30.

20. Create a new layer named **A-GLAZ-3DOB**, give it a light blue color such as 151, and make it current.

    A polyline can be drawn only in the xy-plane, but a 3D polyline can be drawn along any axis.

21. Click the 3D Polyline button in the Home tab ➤ Draw panel, or enter **3DPOLY**↵ at the command line.

22. Turn on the Midpoint running osnap, and then draw the 3D polyline by using the midpoints of the frame's four, 4″ (100 mm) wide inner corners.

23. Switch to the Wireframe visual style and freeze the A-WALL-EXTR-3DOB layer if you have trouble locating the midpoints.

    Be sure to switch back to the Conceptual or X-Ray visual style and thaw the layer when you are finished.

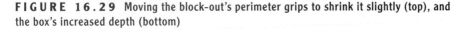

FIGURE 16.29 Moving the block-out's perimeter grips to shrink it slightly (top), and the box's increased depth (bottom)

24. Use the Extrude tool to extrude the glazing 0.25″ (6 mm).

If you have trouble selecting the 3D Polyline, enter **L**↵ to use the Last option at the `Select Objects:` prompt. Your kitchen window should look like Figure 16.31.

25. Save your drawing as **I16-10-KitchenWindow.dwg (M16-10-Kitchen Window.dwg)**.

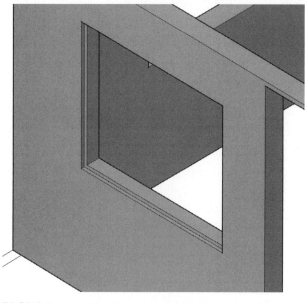

FIGURE 16.30 The completed kitchen window frame

Rotating in 3D (the Second Right-Hand Rule)

When you rotated objects in a 2D environment, all the rotations were perpendicular to the screen, and you never had to consider the axis around which the object was rotating. Because all 2D rotations happened in the xy-plane, the objects were rotated around the z-axis. Positive rotations were in the counterclockwise direction, and negative rotations were clockwise.

In 3D, however, rotation can occur around any axis, and you need to understand whether a rotation should be in the positive or negative direction. Use the *second right-hand rule* to understand how the rotation direction is identified in a 3D environment. It states that if you grasp an axis with your right hand, with your thumb pointing in the positive direction, then your fingers will be curled in the positive rotation direction. Figure 16.32 illustrates this concept.

To rotate an object in 3D, you use the 3D Rotate tool, called a *gripper*, shown in Figure 16.33. It consists of three intersecting circular bands, the center of which is the pivot point of the rotation. Each band is color coded (RGB = XYZ) to identify the axis around which the objects are rotated. When you're prompted for a rotation axis, clicking the green band, for example, restricts the rotation to the y-axis.

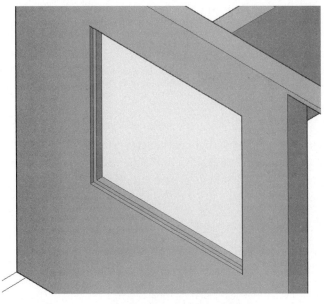

FIGURE 16.31 The completed kitchen window

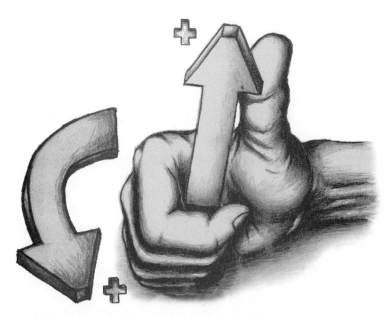

FIGURE 16.32 The right-hand rule as it applies to rotations

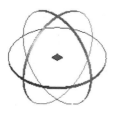

FIGURE 16.33
The 3D Rotate gripper

Completing the Windows

When Boolean operations are used, the component objects, called *operands*, are not replaced with the resulting object; they just become subobjects of it. You always have the ability to edit the operands and alter the object itself. Here's how:

1. Continue using I16-10- KitchenWindow.dwg (M16-10- Kitchen Window.dwg), or open it if it's not already open.

2. Copy the existing window frame and glazing, and move the copy in front of the 5′-0″ (1525 mm) window on the south side of the cabin. Then zoom in to that window.

3. With the two objects selected, click the 3D Rotate tool on the Home tab ➤ Modify panel.

4. At the Specify base point: prompt, click the endpoint of the lower corner of the frame nearest to the cabin.
    The 3D Rotate gripper relocates to the specified corner.

5. At the Pick a rotation axis: prompt, click the blue z-axis ring.
    It turns yellow to indicate that it is the currently selected axis, and a blue line is emitted from the 3D Rotate grip tool to identify the pivot axis.
    Imagine your right hand gripping the blue axis line with your thumb pointing upward, as in the hand shown in Figure 16.32. This shows you that a positive rotation, the direction your fingers are pointing in, is required to rotate the window counterclockwise.

6. Enter **90↵** at the Specify angle start point or type an angle: prompt.
    The window rotates 90° (see Figure 16.34).

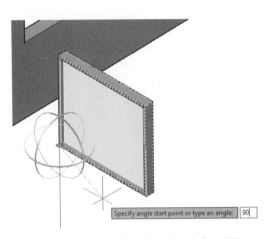

FIGURE 16.34 Rotating the window 90°
counterclockwise

This window is currently 4′-0″ (1220 mm) wide, while the opening is 5′-0″
(1525 mm) wide. You can correct the discrepancy by editing the subobjects of
the window frame. Subobjects are selected by holding the Ctrl key down while
selecting an object. Follow these steps:

1. Turn running object snaps off and turn Polar Tracking on.

2. Select the window frame, right-click, and choose Properties.

3. In the Solid History rollout, choose Yes for the Show History option.
   See Figure 16.35.

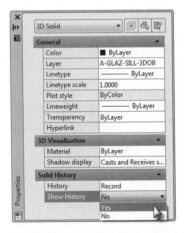

FIGURE 16.35 In the Properties palette,
set the Show History property to Yes.

An outline of the box, used to subtract the volume for the opening, appears as shown in Figure 16.36.

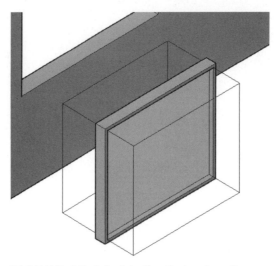

FIGURE 16.36 Selecting the box from the Subtract Boolean operation

4. Hold the Ctrl key down, and click the window frame to select it and expose the grips.

 N O T E   The object that you are editing is the window frame, and the operand is the subobject. You must hold down the Ctrl key when selecting a subobject to expose its grips.

5. Click one of the triangular grips that control the width of the box, and drag it to make the box wider.

6. Enter **12↵** (**305↵**) to stretch the box 12″ (305 mm) in the X direction, as shown in Figure 16.37.
   The side of the window frame is now much wider than the other edges of the frame. You can fix this by adjusting the size of the box operand.

7. Hold the Ctrl key down, and then click to select the box operand and expose its grips.

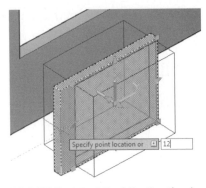

FIGURE 16.37 Adjusting the size
of the window frame

8. Click the triangular grip on the same side that you selected for the
window frame, and drag the grip to make the frame larger.

9. Enter **12↵** (**305↵**), as shown in Figure 16.38.
The operand is extended 12″ (305 mm).

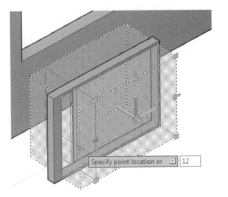

FIGURE 16.38 Adjusting the size of
the box from the Subtract Boolean operation

10. Disable the Show History property by selecting the window and using
the Properties palette.

11. Change the Visual Style to Wireframe.

12. Select the glazing, and then select each of the two exposed endpoints.

13. Use the Midpoint osnap to extend them to the new frame size (see Figure 16.39).

Finally, you need to move the new window into the opening.

14. Turn on the running object snaps. Then select the frame and glazing.

15. Use the Endpoint osnap to pick the lower-left front corner of the frame as the first move point, and the lower-left front corner of the opening as the second point.

The window is moved into place, as shown in Figure 16.40. The frame is flush with the outside wall.

16. Use the 3D Move tool to move the window 1″ (25 mm) in the positive Y direction.

17. Repeat the process in this section to make two of the other three rectangular windows in the cabin. Two of the windows are 3′-0″ (915 mm) wide, and you can simply copy one into the opening of the other.

When you're finished, your drawing should look similar to Figure 16.41.

18. Save your drawing as `I16-11-FinishedWindows.dwg` (`M16-11-Finished Windows.dwg`).

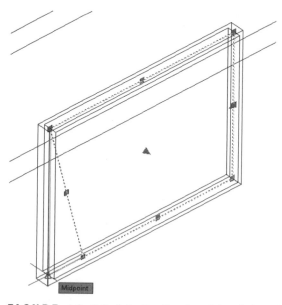

FIGURE 16.39 Adjusting the size of the window glazing

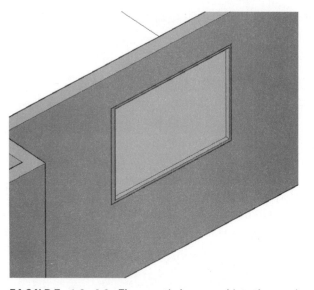

FIGURE 16.40 The new window moved into the opening

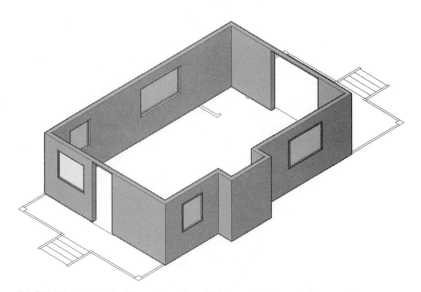
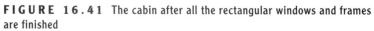

FIGURE 16.41 The cabin after all the rectangular windows and frames are finished

Adding the Pivot and Bifold Doors

For this exercise, you will represent the two pivot doors with simple boxes, and the two bifold doors with extruded polylines. Later, if you choose, you can add knobs and glass panes.

1. Continue using I16-11- FinishedWindows.dwg (M16-11- Finished Windows.dwg), or open it if it's not already open.

2. Set the A-DOOR-3DOB layer as current, and thaw the A-DOOR-THRE -3DOB layer.

3. Zoom in to the back door.
   Rather than moving the primitives as you have been doing, here you'll use Object Tracking to place the start point.

4. Switch to the Wireframe visual style, turn on Object Snap Tracking mode in the status bar, and make sure the Polar Tracking and Intersection running object snaps are on as well.

5. Start the BOX command.

6. At the Specify first corner or [Center]: prompt, place your cursor near the bottom-left outside corner of the front door, where it meets the top of the threshold, until the small cross in the intersection marker appears.

7. Move the cursor in the X direction until the tracking vector appears, and then enter 2↵ (51↵) to set the first corner of the door 2″ (51 mm) from the corner of the opening (see Figure 16.42).

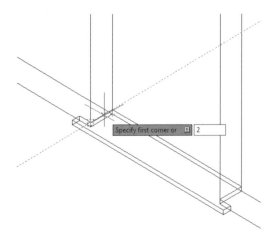

FIGURE 16.42 Locating the first corner of the door box

8. Enter @2,-36↵ (@51,-915) to place the second point of the 3'-0" (915 mm) door.

9. Give the door a height of 7'-6" (2286), the distance from the top of the threshold to the bottom of the door opening.

10. Thaw the A-WALL-INTR-3DOB layer.

11. Use a similar process to add the bathroom door, with these differences:

    ▶ The door is only 2'-6" (762 mm) wide.

    ▶ The door is only 1½" (38 mm) thick.

    ▶ The door is 7'-5" (2261 mm) tall.

    ▶ Offset the door 1¼" (32 mm).

    ▶ Start or move the door 1" (25 mm) above the bottom corner to accommodate the 1" (25 mm) thick floor.

12. Zoom in to the bifold closet doors.

13. Thaw the A-DOOR layer, and change the layer of the bifold doors to A-DOOR-3DOB.

14. Move the four polylines 1" in the Z direction so they rest at the same level as the top of the floor.

15. Start the Extrude tool, and extrude each polyline 7'-5" (2260 mm).

16. Zoom out and switch to the X-Ray visual style.
    Your cabin should look like Figure 16.43.

17. Save your drawing as `I16-12-DoorModel.dwg` (`M16-12-DoorModel.dwg`).

Navigating with the ViewCube

Changing the viewpoint used to view your drawings is especially important in a 3D environment because you are more likely to encounter a situation where foreground objects obscure background objects. The *ViewCube*, the tool in the upper-right corner of the drawing area, is used to access common views quickly, return to a saved view, or navigate freely in the drawing area.

The ViewCube (see Figure 16.44) consists of a center cube with each face labeled to identify the orthographic view that it represents. Clicking any of these labeled faces changes the viewpoint in the drawing area to display the objects from that point of view, based on the world coordinate system (WCS).

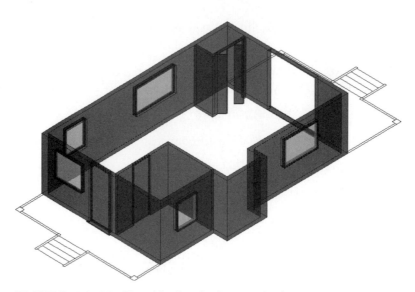

FIGURE 16.43 The cabin after the doors are in place

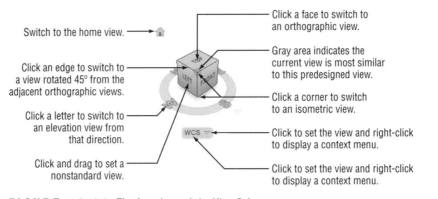

FIGURE 16.44 The functions of the ViewCube

The following examples explain how the ViewCube works:

▶ Clicking the ViewCube face labeled TOP changes the drawing area to display the cabin from the top, with the x-axis pointing to the right and the y-axis pointing to the top of your screen.

▶ Clicking the face labeled FRONT changes the drawing area to display the cabin from the front, the view you designated as the south elevation, with the x-axis pointing to the right and the z-axis pointing to the top.

The orthographic views are not the only viewpoints that you can access from the ViewCube.

▶ Clicking any corner (see the left image in Figure 16.45) changes the drawing area to display the objects from an isometric vantage point that is a combination of the three labeled faces.

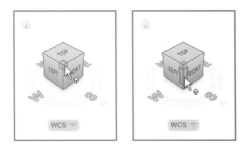

FIGURE 16.45 Clicking a ViewCube corner (left) and clicking a ViewCube edge (right)

▶ Clicking the corner at the intersection of the TOP, FRONT, and LEFT faces produces a view identical to the Southwest Isometric view you selected from the Viewpoint drop-down list.

That corner is currently gray, indicating that it is the viewpoint most similar to the current view.

▶ Clicking any of the edges (see the right image in Figure 16.45) changes the drawing area to display the objects rotated 45° from one of the adjacent orthographic views.

Clicking any of the ViewCube features not only changes the view but also executes a Zoom Extents, displaying all of the visible objects in the drawing area. You'll usually perform a zoom after using the ViewCube. Clicking and dragging the ViewCube changes the viewpoint freely without any constraints.

Surrounding the cube is a ring with the compass directions indicated. Clicking any of the letters switches the view in the drawing area to a view from that direction. For example, clicking the letter E on the ring displays the east elevation of the cabin. This is a view showing the 3D cabin from the east, and not the 2D east elevation that you drew. You can click and drag the ring to rotate the view in a free-form manner.

The ViewCube also provides access to the named UCSs that you created in Chapter 10 and, when a named UCS or the WCS is current, displays the name below the compass ring. Clicking the rectangle shape below the ViewCube opens a context menu (see the left image in Figure 16.46), from which you can select the current view. Right-clicking the rectangle shape opens a context menu where you can, among other things, set the ViewCube settings and designate the current view as the home view (see the right image in Figure 16.46).

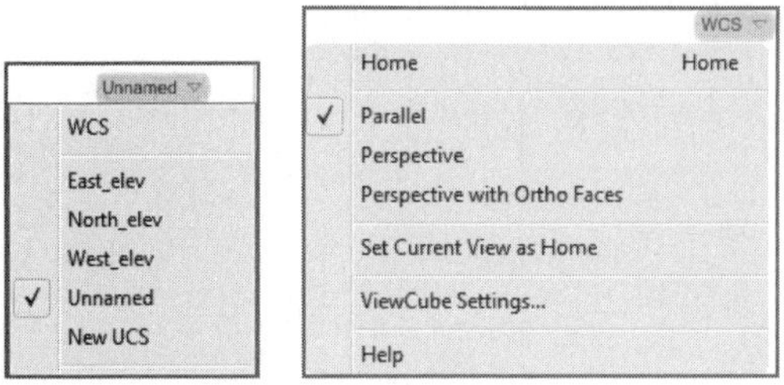

FIGURE 16.46 Selecting the current view from the ViewCube (left), and accessing the right-click context menu (right)

You can quickly switch to the home view by clicking the house icon, which is visible when the cursor is over the ViewCube.

Switching to a predefined view is quick and can often provide the vantage point that you need, but you may need to view your objects from a specific, nonstandard location.

Holding down the Ctrl key while holding down and dragging with the scroll wheel has a function similar to dragging the ViewCube.

Adding the Sliding Door

The remaining door to add is the sliding door on the front of the cabin. Although this is a door, the procedure for creating it will be more like that for the windows you've already made. Here are the steps:

1. Continue using I16-12-DoorModel.dwg (M16-12-DoorModel.dwg), or open it if it's not already open.

2. Click the northeast corner of the ViewCube to display the front of the cabin. Then zoom in to the front door.
   Your view should look similar to Figure 16.47.

3. Make the A-GLAZ-SILL-3DOB layer current.

4. Create a box from the right edge of the patio opening, on top of the threshold that is 3'-7" (1092 mm) wide, 2" (51 mm) thick.

5. Specify the height of the door by using the Perpendicular osnap, as shown in Figure 16.48, to pick one of the upper door frame edges.

6. With the box in place, use the 3D Move tool to position the door 1′ (25 mm) inside the right edge of the patio opening.

7. Create a block-out that is 4′ (102 mm) smaller than the width and height of the frame you just drew, but significantly deeper.

Then center it on the sliding-door frame, as shown in Figure 16.49.

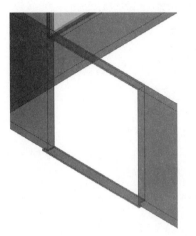

FIGURE 16.47 The view looking at the front of the cabin

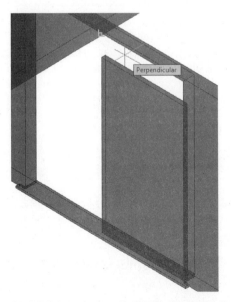

FIGURE 16.48 Using the Perpendicular osnap to choose the door height

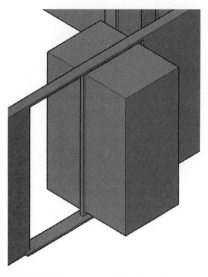

FIGURE 16.49 The first sliding-door
frame and block-out

Some display roughness may occur where the block-out and frame meet, but this is just a function of the current visual style and the thin faces shown.

N O T E   The Conceptual visual style is used in Figure 16.49 as a matter of clarity. Often the opaque nature of the Conceptual style makes objects easier to interpret, whereas at other times the transparent nature of the X-Ray visual style is preferred. Your choice will likely change based on the task at hand.

8. Subtract the block-out from the sliding-door frame.

9. Set the A-GLAZ-3DOB layer as current.

10. Use the 3D Polyline tool to create the boundary to the glazing, extrude it 0.25″ (6 mm), and then center it in the frame.

11. Copy the frame until it butts the opening on the left and then move it 2″ (51 mm) toward the inside of the cabin so that the two door frames are offset (see Figure 16.50).

12. Save your drawing as `I16-13-SlidingDoor.dwg` (`M16-13-Sliding Door.dwg`).

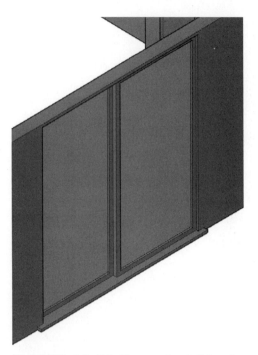

FIGURE 16.50 The completed sliding door with two offset panels

Building the Decks

You're nearly finished modeling the cabin. The next step is to make the two decks by using basic shapes and copying redundant objects. Follow these steps to create the front deck:

1. Continue using I16-13-SlidingDoor.dwg (M16-13-SlidingDoor.dwg), or open it if it's not already open.

2. Make a new layer called **A-DECK-3DOB**, assign it color 240, and make it current.

3. Thaw the A-FNDN-3DOB layer and freeze the other 3DOB layers except A-DOOR-THRE-3DOB and A-WALL-EXTR-3DOB.

4. Click the Box tool and create a box to represent the floor of the deck.

5. Use the Endpoint osnap to locate the two opposite corners of the deck, and then give the box a height of $-1\frac{5}{8}''$ (-41 mm).

Your model should look like Figure 16.51.

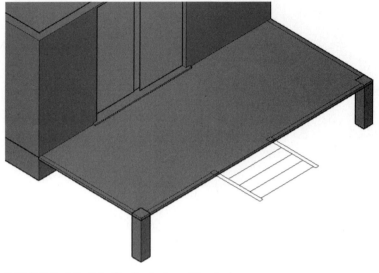

FIGURE 16.51 The beginning of the deck

6. Draw a box that follows the perimeter of the railing on the left side of the deck, and make this box 2″ (51 mm) tall.

7. Move the box 4″ (102 mm) in the Z direction to represent the lower railing.

8. Copy this box, and move the copy 3′-2″ (965 mm) higher to represent the upper railing.

    Your railings should look like those in Figure 16.52.

9. Repeat the process to create the two sets of railings at the front of the deck and on the left side of the stairs. Then copy both sets to the opposite side of the deck.

10. Switch to the right and top views with the ViewCube to check your work and adjust the size of the railings on the right side of the steps.

11. Use the Zoom Previous command (**Z↵ P↵**) to return to the current view (see Figure 16.53).

12. To draw the first railing post, click the down-arrow below the Box button on the Home tab ➤ Modeling panel and choose Cylinder from the fly-out menu.

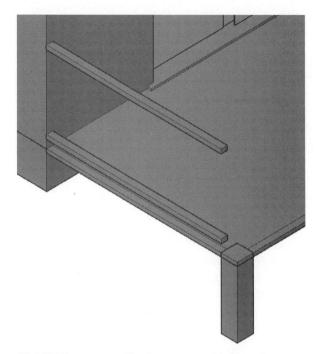

FIGURE 16.52 The first upper and lower railings

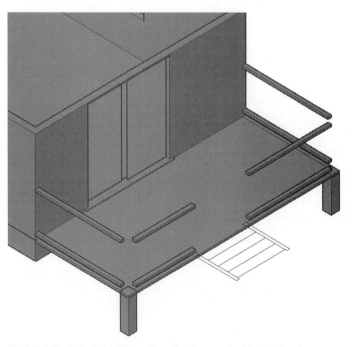

FIGURE 16.53 The railings in place and adjusted for size

13. At the `Specify center point of base or:` prompt, click the midpoint of the first lower railing that you drew, where it meets the exterior wall, and enter **3/8↵** (**9.5↵**) for the radius (see Figure 16.54).

14. At the `Specify height or:` prompt, make sure the cursor is above the cylinder's base, and then enter **3'↵** (**914↵**).

15. To fill in the row of posts, move the first post 3⅝" (92 mm) in the X direction and then copy it 20 times, at 4" (102 mm) increments in the X direction.

The first set of railing posts should look like those shown in Figure 16.55.

T I P   Rather than manually copying the railing post 20 times, try using the Rectangular Array (ARRAYRECT) command. This command includes the source object in the row and column count, so to use it to complete step 9, you'll need to create an array with 1 row and 21 columns.

16. Repeat steps 12 through 15 to draw the posts along the front of the deck, adjusting the count and the direction appropriately. Then copy the posts from the left side of the deck to the right. Add any new post as required.

The completed railing posts should look like those shown in Figure 16.56.

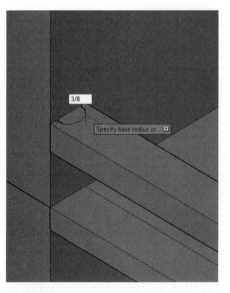

FIGURE 16.54 Creating the first railing post cylinder

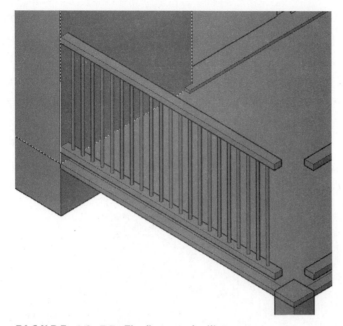

FIGURE 16.55 The first set of railing posts

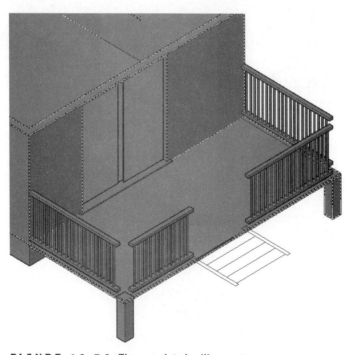

FIGURE 16.56 The completed railing posts

17. Zoom in to the front-left corner of the deck, where the support post sits.

18. Use the Box tool to draw the 8″×8″ (204 mm×204 mm) post and give it a height of 7′-8″ (2337).

    You may need to adjust the height later when the roof is applied.

19. Copy the post to the opposite side of the deck and adjust the placement as necessary.

    Figure 16.57 shows the two support posts in place.

20. Save your drawing as **I16-14-DeckRailing.dwg** (**M16-14-Deck Railing.dwg**).

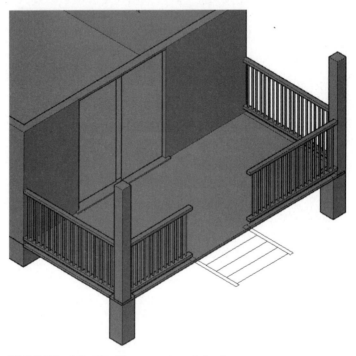

FIGURE 16.57 The support posts in place

Building the Steps

The steps, the step railings, and the posts transition from the ground level to the top of the deck. In this section, you'll build and move the stairs and create and then rotate the handrail:

1. Continue using I16-14-DeckRailing.dwg (M16-14-DeckRailing.dwg), or open it if it's not already open.

2. Create a new layer named **A-DECK-STRS-3DOB** and make it current.

3. Zoom in to see the steps clearly. Then switch to the 3D Wireframe visual style.

   When you drew the steps in the plan view, the lines defining their width were trimmed back to the edge of the handrail. In reality, the steps extend all the way to the outside edges of the handrails.

4. Use the Box tool and Object Snap Tracking or the Apparent Intersection osnap to draw the four steps. Give each box a height of $-1\frac{5}{8}''$ (-41 mm).

5. Switch back to the Conceptual visual style.

   Your steps should look like those in Figure 16.58.

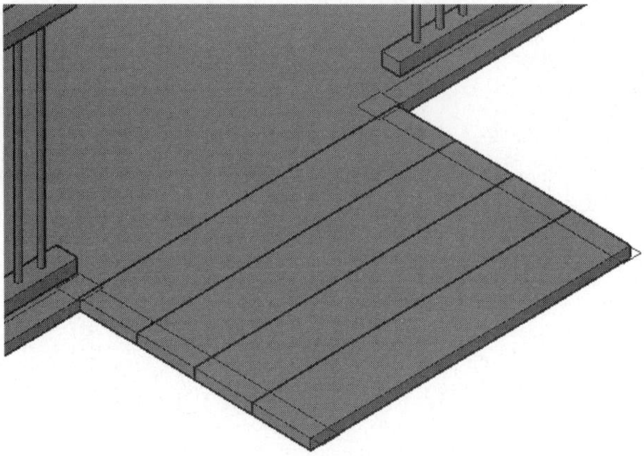

FIGURE 16.58 The front deck steps before setting their elevations

6. Move the step furthest from the deck 24″ (609 mm) in the negative Z direction, the second 16″ (406 mm), and the third one 8″ (203 mm).

   The top step remains flush with the top of the deck.

7. To draw a polyline that you'll extrude to become the *stringer* (the support for the steps), you'll use a 3D Polyline (see Figure 16.59). Follow these steps:

   a. Click the 3D Polyline (3DPOLY) button in the Draw panel.

   b. Using the Object Snap Tracking tool, start the polyline 8″ (203 mm) below the back of the top step.

   c. Use the Endpoint object snap to continue drawing the stringer in a clockwise direction; snap to the corner of the top step.

    d. Follow the bottom and back edges of the steps until you reach the front of the bottom step.

    e. Continue the polyline in the negative Z direction 8″ (203 mm) and then in the negative X direction 8″ (203 mm).

    f. Enter C↵ to close the polyline.

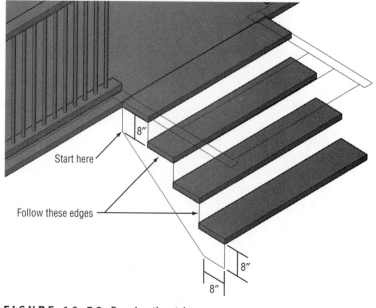

FIGURE 16.59 Drawing the stringer

  8. Extrude the stringer 2″ (51 mm), and move it 2″ (51 mm) in the positive Y direction so that it's tucked under the steps a bit.

  9. Copy or mirror the stringer to the opposite side of the steps.
    The completed steps should look like those shown in Figure 16.60.

 10. Save your drawing as **I16-15-DeckSteps.dwg** (**M16-15-DeckSteps.dwg**).

Creating the Stair Handrails

To create the handrails for the stairs, you'll first draw the vertical posts, create a box at the end of one of one of them, and then rotate it into place. Using the Dynamic UCS tool will ensure that the box is created in the correct orientation.

  1. Continue using I16-15-DeckSteps.dwg (M16-15- DeckSteps.dwg), or open it if it's not already open.

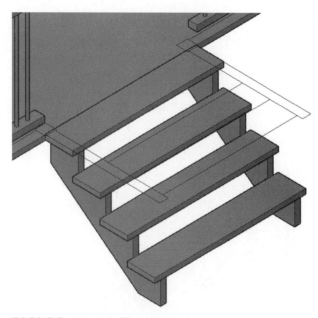

FIGURE 16.60 The completed steps

2. Zoom in to the top of the stairs and draw a box 3'-9" (1143 mm) tall, using the rectangle at the end of the railing to define the footprint.

3. Click the Allow/Disallow Dynamic UCS button in the status bar to turn it on.

4. Start the BOX command.

5. Pick a point on the front surface of the post, and then specify a 2"×2" (51 mm×51 mm) base and a 4'-6" (1372 mm) height for the box.
   The box is created perpendicular to the front surface of the post.

6. Move the handrail so that it is centered on the post and 1" (25 mm) from the top, as shown in Figure 16.61.

7. Start the 3D Rotate tool, on the Modify panel of the Home tab, and select the handrail.

8. At the Specify base point: prompt, pick the midpoint of the handrail where it meets the post.

9. At the Pick rotation axis: prompt, click the green y-axis ring. Then, at the Specify angle start point or type an angle: prompt, enter **-39**⏎ as shown in Figure 16.62.

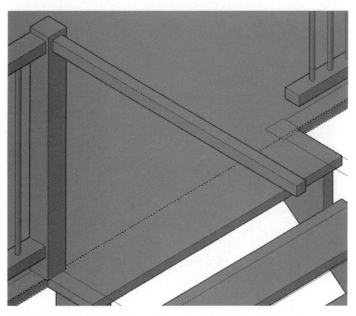

FIGURE 16.61 The box drawn perpendicular to the post

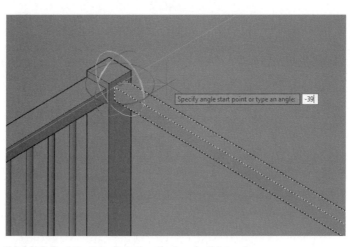

FIGURE 16.62 Rotating the handrail into place

The handrail rotates into place.

The last items to build for this handrail are the 1″ (25 mm) posts that support it.

10. Copy one of the cylindrical railing posts you drew earlier, and space it evenly on the top step, centered under the handrail.

11. Using the grips, adjust the height of each post so that each ends inside the handrail.

T I P **When copying the railing post, try using the Center osnap to acquire the bottom center point. To ensure that the post is properly centered under the top railing post, use the Mid Between 2 Points osnap, and pick the front intersection of the 2D railing post line and the midpoint of the outer edge of the 3D step, as shown here.**

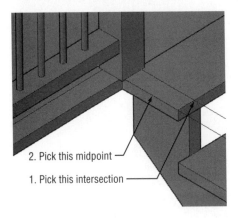

2. Pick this midpoint
1. Pick this intersection

12. Using the endpoints of the steps as a reference, copy the posts to the other steps and then copy the handrail and posts to the opposite side of the steps.

When you are finished, the completed steps should look like Figure 16.63.

13. Save your drawing as **I16-16-Handrails.dwg** (**M16-16-Handrails.dwg**).

Adding the Skirt

The final piece to add to the deck is a *skirt*, a linear member that acts as a connection surface for the structure and a visual shield so the residents can't see under the deck. With the modeling skills and experience that you picked up in the previous chapter, this should be a quick fix; you'll just build a skirt around the three open sides of the decks to obscure the underside. Here's how:

1. Continue using I16-16- Handrails.dwg (M16-16- Handrails.dwg), or open it if it's not already open.

2. Switch to the Wireframe visual style, and make sure that the Endpoint running osnap is active.

3. Make the A-DECK-3DOB layer current.

4. Draw a 2″×6″ (51 mm×153 mm) box on the side and front of the deck, just below the surface, as shown in Figure 16.64.

FIGURE 16.63 The completed steps

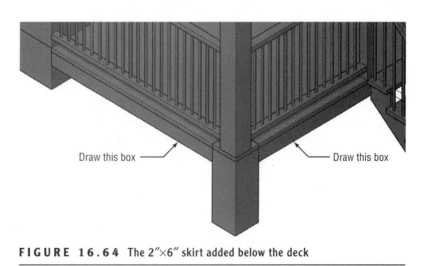

Draw this box ——————

——— Draw this box

FIGURE 16.64 The 2″×6″ skirt added below the deck

Use your preferred visual style to draw the boxes. For clarity, Figure 16.65 uses the Conceptual visual style. The boxes should span the distance from the foundation to the support post and between the support posts, respectively.

5. Copy the shorter box to the opposite side of the deck.

6. Change the visual style back to Conceptual, and your completed deck should look like Figure 16.65.

7. Save your drawing as `I16-17-DeckSkirt.dwg` (`M16-17-DeckSkirt.dwg`).

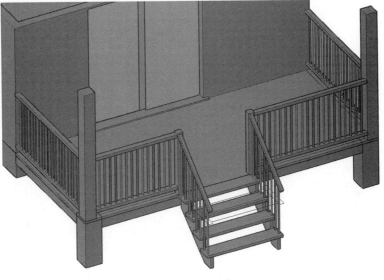

FIGURE 16.65 The completed front deck

Mirroring the Front Deck

Because the front deck is similar to the back deck, you can mirror all the objects that you've already worked hard to create, to the back of the cabin, similar to the way you did in the 2D section of the book. Once the objects are in place, you can edit them to meet the design criteria. Follow these steps to mirror the deck:

1. Continue using `I16-17-DeckSkirt.dwg` (`M16-17-DeckSkirt.dwg`), or open it if it's not already open.

2. Freeze all the layers except A-DECK-3DOB and A-DECK-STRS-3DOB. Then thaw the A-WALL layer.

3. Click the face labeled TOP in the ViewCube to switch to a plan view of the cabin.

4. In the Layer Properties Manager, click the open lock icon in the Lock column next to A-WALL so that objects on the A-WALL layer can't be selected or modified.

5. Select all the deck and step objects.

6. Click the Mirror tool in the expanded Modify panel on the Home tab.

7. For the first point of the mirror line, select the midpoint of the long outside wall on the north side of the cabin, the wall that has the closet attached to the inside of it.

8. For the second point, pick a point directly to the right.

9. Press ↵ to accept the default option not to delete the original objects. (See Figure 16.66.)

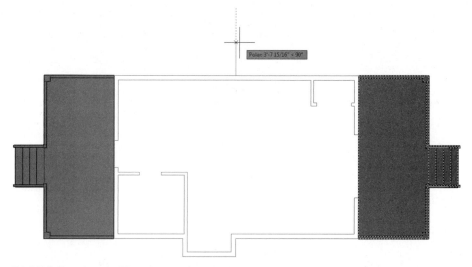

FIGURE 16.66 Mirroring the front deck

TIP   If the length of the cabin is displayed vertically, rather than horizontally, click the counterclockwise-facing arrow (⟲) in the top-right corner of the ViewCube. This will rotate your current view 90° around the z-axis, giving your plan a more familiar orientation.

10. Thaw and lock the A-DECK layer. Then zoom in to the back deck.

11. Change to the Wireframe visual style.

12. Delete any of the handrail posts that exist between the 8″ (204 mm) 3D support posts and the 8″ (204 mm) 2D support posts on both sides of the deck (see Figure 16.67).

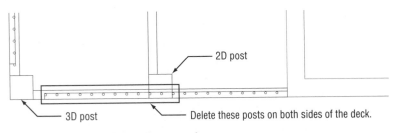

13. Click the Move tool from the Home tab ➢ Modify panel and drag a crossing window, dragging from right to left around the front of the deck and the stairs, as shown in Figure 16.68.

2D post

3D post

Delete these posts on both sides of the deck.

FIGURE 16.67 Delete the posts shown.

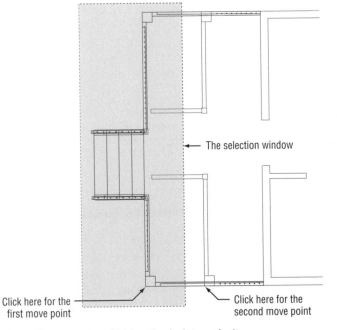

The selection window

Click here for the
first move point

Click here for the
second move point

FIGURE 16.68 Moving the deck to make it narrower

14. Move the deck 4′-0″ (1220 mm) in the X direction to fit the narrower rear deck's size. The floor, railings, and skirt project into the cabin, and will be corrected in the coming steps.

15. Select the deck floor, horizontal railing, and horizontal skirts. Then, using the triangular grips, move their right ends 4′ (1220 mm) to the left, so they extend only to the back wall of the cabin.

Figure 16.69 shows the back of the cabin after adjusting the features.

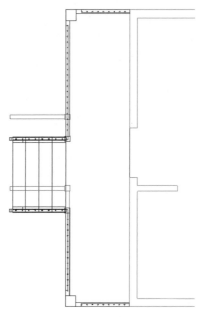

FIGURE 16.69 The rear deck after adjusting the handrails, skirts, and deck floor

16. Delete the 3/4″ (20 mm) handrail posts in the vertical row on the north side of the 3D steps between the 4″ (102 mm) 3D vertical post and the 4″ (102 mm) 2D vertical post (see Figure 16.70).

17. So that you don't accidentally move the deck surface, select the deck, and then click the lightbulb in the lower-right corner of the Application window to choose Hide Objects from the menu that opens.

The lightbulb changes from yellow to red. This indicates that an object isolation is active.

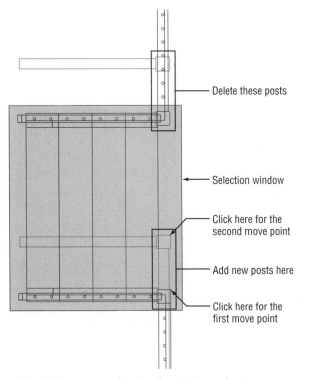

Delete these posts

Selection window

Click here for the
second move point

Add new posts here

Click here for the
first move point

FIGURE 16.70 Moving the deck to make it narrower

18. Using the MOVE command, move the steps into place, as shown in Figure 16.70.

19. Add any new posts that are required on the south side of the steps.

20. Use the triangular grips to adjust the lengths of the railings as required.

21. Click the red lightbulb in the lower-right corner of the Application window and choose End Object Isolation.

22. Change to the Conceptual visual style, and drag the ViewCube to get a good look at the new deck. It should look like Figure 16.71.

23. Save your drawing as **I16-18-BackDeck.dwg** (**M16-18-BackDeck.dwg**).

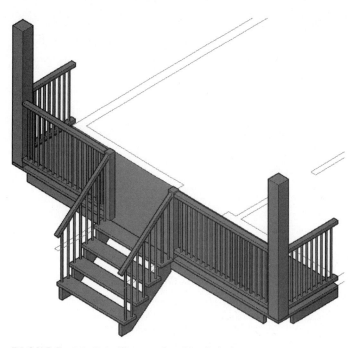

FIGURE 16.71 The completed back deck

Putting a Roof on the Cabin

You'll finish the 3D model of the cabin by constructing a roof. The surface of the roof will be a different color from the roof structure, so you'll make them as two separate objects, each on its own layer. Both objects will be extruded from the east elevation, and you'll use the Boolean Subtract function to cut the roof in the areas where it doesn't project as far as it does over the pop-out. Follow these steps:

1. Continue using I16-18-BackDeck.dwg (M16-18-BackDeck.dwg), or open it if it's not already open.

2. Create two new layers: **A-ROOF-3DOB** with color 32 and **A-ROOF -DECK-3DOB** with color 114. Make A-ROOF-3DOB current.

3. Thaw the A-WALL-EXTR-3DOB and A-ROOF layers.

4. Also thaw all layers beginning with A-ELEV except for those with a -PATT or -BNDY suffix.

5. Click the TOP face of the ViewCube to change the view orientation of your drawing, and then zoom in to your east elevation (see Figure 16.72).

The east elevation is the one that displays the sliding glass door; it is found in the upper-right portion of the drawing file provided in this chapter's download.

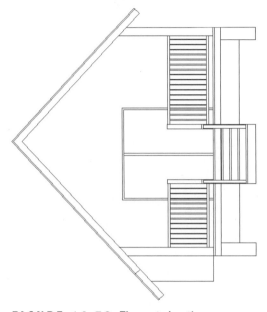

FIGURE 16.72 The east elevation

6. Use the Endpoint osnap and carefully draw a closed polyline around the thin roof surface.

   Make sure that the pline follows both the inner and outer surfaces of the roof covering and extends to the limits of the pop-out. There should be a total of six picks and then the Close option.

7. Make the A-ROOF-DECK-3DOB layer current, and then draw a closed polyline around the perimeter of the roof deck in the east elevation.

8. Pick the southeastern corner of the ViewCube to change to an isometric view of your drawing. Zoom back in to the east elevation.

   The two roof polylines you just created by using the east elevation as a template are still in the 2D drawing plane. You'll use the 3DALIGN command to orient these polylines with the 3D model of your cabin.

9. Choose the 3D Align tool from the Modify panel of the Home tab.

10. At the Select objects: prompt, choose the two polylines you drew in steps 4 and 5.

The 3DALIGN command will change the orientation of the selected objects from one plane to another. To do this, you must select the axis defining the source plane, and finally the destination plane.

To define the source plane, you'll need to select three points: the base point, a second point, and a third point.

11. Select these points, as shown in Figure 16.73.

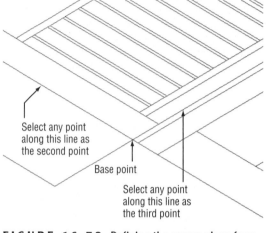

Select any point
along this line as
the second point

Base point

Select any point
along this line as
the third point

FIGURE 16.73 Defining the source plane from the east elevation

12. Without exiting the 3DALIGN command, zoom in to the left deck column on the east side of your cabin, as shown in Figure 16.74.

13. To define the destination plane, select the base, second, and third points, as shown in Figure 16.74.

14. Zoom out so the entire eastern side of your cabin is viewable. Your model should look like Figure 16.75.

15. Use the Extrude tool to extrude the two polylines that you just drew 43′ (13,110 mm).

16. Move the extruded roof 1′-6″ (457 mm) along the positive x-axis. When finished, your cabin should resemble the one shown in Figure 16.76.

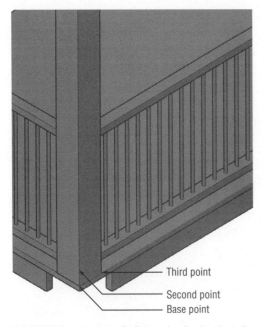

Third point

Second point

Base point

FIGURE 16.74 Defining the destination plane within the 3D model

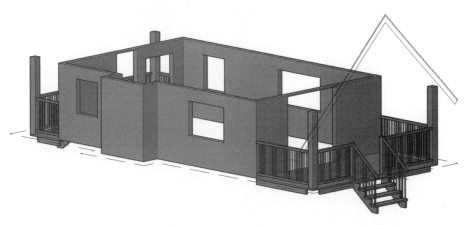

FIGURE 16.75 Eastern edge of the 3D model after aligning the roof polylines to the model

17. The Extrude tool creates the extrusion in the current layer, so select the thinner of the two extrusions and move it to the A-ROOF-SURF -3DOB layer by using the Properties palette.

18. Save your drawing as **I16-19-CabinRoof.dwg** (**M16-19-CabinRoof.dwg**).

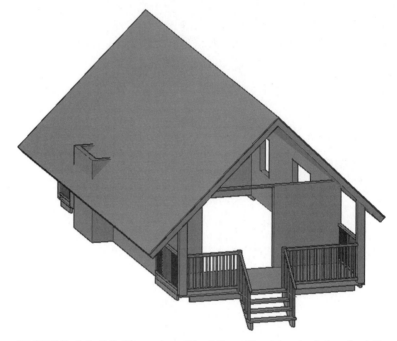

FIGURE 16.76 The eastern side of the cabin with extruded roof polylines correctly aligned

Adjusting the Cabin Walls

The cabin walls were drawn with a constant height. In this section, you'll create the peaks at the front and back of the cabin to accommodate the roof. To accomplish this, you will add segmentation to the top of the walls by using the Slice tool and then move the new edges in the z-axis. Here's how:

1. Continue using I16-19- CabinRoof.dwg (M16-19- CabinRoof.dwg), or open it if it's not already open.

2. Freeze the A-DECK-3DOB, A-DECK-STRS-3DOB, A-ROOF-3DOB, and A-ROOF-DECK-3DOB layers.

3. Click the Slice button on the Solid Editing panel of the Home tab to start the SLICE command.

4. At the Select objects to slice: prompt, pick the exterior walls. The Slice tool uses a plane with an infinite depth to cut the selected objects, so you need two points to define the plane.

5. At the Specify start point of slicing plane or: prompt, use the Midpoint osnap to pick the midpoint of the top of the front wall, as shown in the left image of Figure 16.77.

6. At the Specify second point on plane: prompt, pick the midpoint of the top of the back wall, as shown in the right image of Figure 16.77.

The Slice tool can display both sides of the sliced object or it can delete one of the sides. In this case, you want to keep both sides.

7. At the Specify a point on desired side or [keep Both sides]: prompt, press ↵ or enter **B**↵ to retain both sides.

The new edges appear on the walls (see Figure 16.78), and there are now two sets of exterior walls: one on the south side of the cabin and one on the north. Notice that the slice is centered on the wall, but not centered over the doorway.

Just as you were able to edit the size of a box object by dragging its grips, you can do the same with nonprimitive objects. The grips are available at the edges, faces, and vertices—the points where two or more edges end. You access the subobjects by holding down the Ctrl key and clicking the grip location. The grips won't appear until you click.

FIGURE 16.77 Selecting the first Slice point (left), and selecting the second Slice point (right)

8. Zoom in to the newly sliced area on the front wall. Hold the Ctrl key down and click the middle of the top edge.

   The small, rectangular, red edge grip appears as shown in Figure 16.79.

9. Click the grip, and enter **@0,0,8'2-1/4**↵ (**@0,0,2496**) to move the edge 8'-2¼" (2496 mm) along the z-axis.

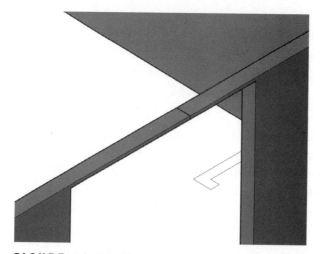

FIGURE 16.78 The new edges created with the Slice tool

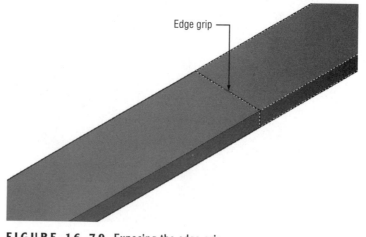

Edge grip

FIGURE 16.79 Exposing the edge grip

The faces bound by the edge are adjusted accordingly and form one-half of the peak, as shown in Figure 16.80.

10. Adjust the edge on the other side of the front wall in the same manner.

11. Zoom out and you'll see that adjusting one end of the sliced object adjusted the other, and the peak is already constructed at the back of the cabin (see Figure 16.81).

12. Thaw all of the A-ROOF layers: A-ROOF, A-ROOF-3DOB, and A-ROOF -DECK-3DOB.

Using the ViewCube to look around the model, you can see that the northern walls and roof are largely OK. However, your walls are protruding out of the roof, along the southern edge of your cabin (see Figure 16.82).

13. Save your drawing as `I16-20-WallPeaks.dwg` (`M16-20-WallPeaks.dwg`).

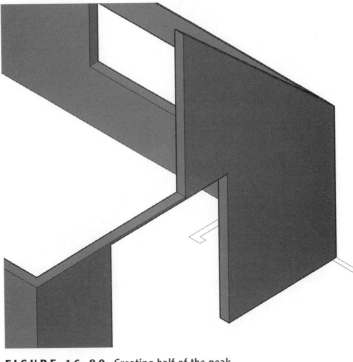

FIGURE 16.80 Creating half of the peak

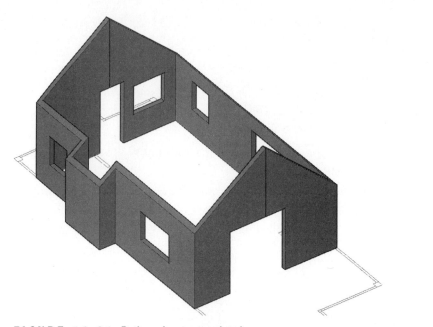

FIGURE 16.81 Both peaks are completed.

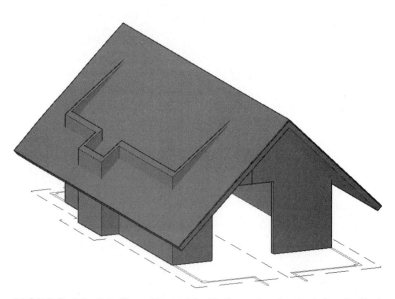

FIGURE 16.82 The cabin model with the roof and extended walls displayed

Tweaking the Roof and Walls

As you can see, the walls poke through the roof on the south side of the cabin, and you still need to modify the roof so that it projects out only over the pop-out. You'll do these tasks by using the subobject grips and Boolean tools.

1. Continue using I16-20- WallPeaks.dwg (M16-20- WallPeaks.dwg), or open it if it's not already open.

2. Use the ViewCube to rotate the view so that you can see the roof that covers the pop-out.

3. Make sure Dynamic UCS is turned on and Endpoint osnaps are running.

4. Start the BOX command.

5. Create a box, starting at the southeast corner of the roof, with a footprint that is 3′-4″ wide and extends to a point 1′-6″ (457 mm) from the pop-out.

6. Give the box some height and then repeat the process on the opposite side of the pop-out, as shown in Figure 16.83.

    The Dynamic UCS tool creates the boxes aligned to the roof.

7. Use the grips to extend the outside edges of the boxes beyond the edges of the roof (see Figure 16.84).

8. Move the boxes so that they protrude through the roof, using the endpoint of one edge as the first point of displacement and the midpoint of the same edge as the second.

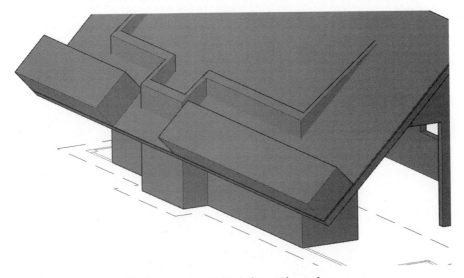

FIGURE 16.83 The boxes to be used to subtract the roof

When you're finished, the model should look similar to the one shown in Figure 16.85.

9. If you subtract both roof objects at the same time, the resultant roof object will be a single entity. Use this procedure to cut the boxes out of the roof:

   a. Copy the boxes in-place by using the same point as the base point and the displacement. This can be done by pressing ↵ at the Specify base point: and Specify displacement: prompts.

   b. Select the roof surface and subtract one set of boxes from it.

   c. Select the roof deck and subtract the second set of boxes from it.

   When you are finished, the roof should look like Figure 16.86.

10. Hold the Ctrl key down and click the middle of the outer wall of the pop-out.

    You may have trouble selecting the proper edge when both of the adjacent faces are visible. If you encounter a problem, try selecting the edge from a northeastern viewpoint.

11. Turn on Ortho mode. Then move the edge downward, below the surface of the roof.

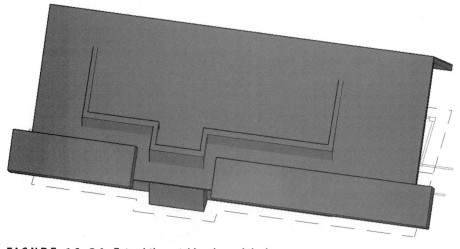

FIGURE 16.84 Extend the outside edges of the boxes.

Figure 16.87 shows the edge being moved from a northeastern viewpoint.

12. Freeze and unlock all the 2D layers (including those with an A-ELEV prefix) and thaw the 3D layers (with a -3DOB suffix).

13. Drag the ViewCube to change to an isometric view, and then adjust the height of the roof support posts so that they extend into the roof deck but not through the roof surface (see Figure 16.88).
    Your completed cabin should look like Figure 16.89.

14. Save your file as **I16-21-RoofWallFinishing.dwg** (**I16-21-RoofWall Finishing.dwg**).

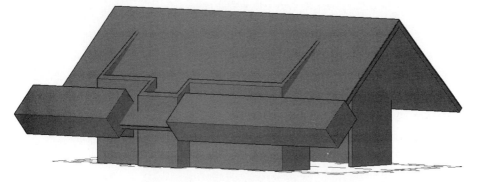

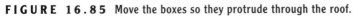

FIGURE 16.85 Move the boxes so they protrude through the roof.

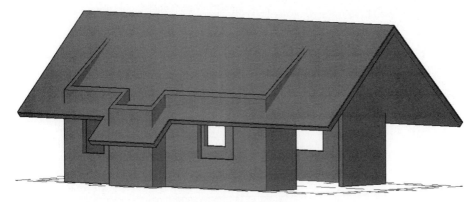

FIGURE 16.86 The roof after subtracting the boxes

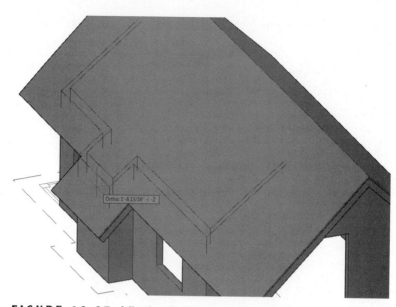

FIGURE 16.87 Adjusting the pop-out walls

FIGURE 16.88 Adjusting the height of the roof support posts

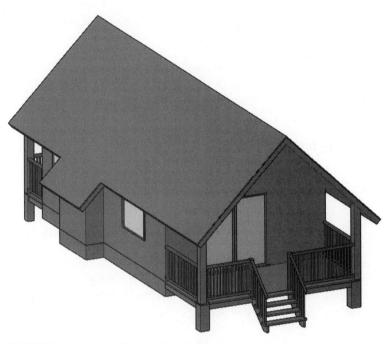

FIGURE 16.89 The completed cabin

Getting Further Directions in 3D

Covering 3D in real depth is beyond the scope of this book, but I can mention a few other tools and features that you might enjoy investigating. Here I'll summarize a few of the solid- and surface-modeling tools that I didn't cover in the tutorial on the cabin. In the next chapter, you'll look at the rendering process as it's approached in AutoCAD.

Using Other Solid-Modeling Tools

You used the box primitive to build the block-outs for the cabin walls, and the cylinder primitive for the railing posts. There are several other primitive shapes, and all of them are found on the fly-out menu on the left edge of the Modeling panel. Six of them are shown and described here. You can also see a description of the creation procedure, as shown in Figure 16.90, by pausing the cursor over any primitive option.

Cone   You specify the center point of the base, the radius of the base, and the height of the pointed tip. The base is parallel to the xy-plane, and the height is perpendicular to it. You can choose for the cone to be elliptical and for the top to be flat instead of pointed.

Sphere   You specify the center point and the radius or diameter.

Pyramid   The pyramid primitive is similar to the cone primitive, but it can have up to 32 flat sides, rather than a curved side.

Wedge   The wedge has a rectangular base and a lid that slopes up from one edge of the base. You specify the base as you do with the box primitive and then enter the height.

Torus   This is a donut shape. You specify a center point for the hole, the radius of the circular path that the donut makes, and the radius of the tube that follows the circular path around the center point.

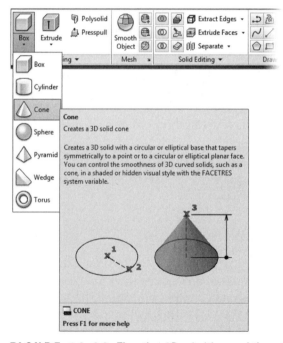

FIGURE 16.90 The other 3D primitives and the extended tooltip for the cone

The other tools on the Modeling panel are for creating additional 3D solids, for manipulating existing 3D shapes, or for using 2D shapes as components for making 3D shapes. You've already used some of these tools, and I'll cover the others here:

Planar Surface   Found exclusively on the Surface tab ➢ Create panel, the Planar Surface tool creates a flat, rectangular surface that is segmented in both directions. The segments are visible only when the object is selected or in a Wireframe visual style (see Figure 16.91).

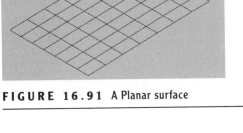

FIGURE 16.91 A Planar surface

Revolve   Select a closed 2D shape, and then define the axis and the angle of rotation. A Revolve object is shown on the left in Figure 16.92.

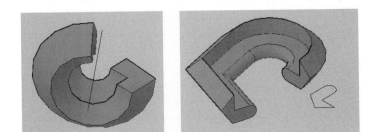

FIGURE 16.92 A Revolve object (left) and a Sweep object (right)

Sweep   Similar to the Extrude tool, the Sweep tool extrudes a 2D shape along a path to create a 3D shape. A Sweep object is shown on the right in Figure 16.92.

Loft   Similar to the Extrude and Sweep tools, the Loft tool extrudes a 2D shape along a path, but it allows you to change cross sections along the path.

Press/Pull   The Press/Pull tool creates a 3D object by extruding the perimeter of an area surrounded by a closed boundary. The left image in Figure 16.93 shows the closed area, and the right image shows the resultant object. The boundary does not have to be a polyline; it can simply be a conglomeration of any objects that combine to define an open area.

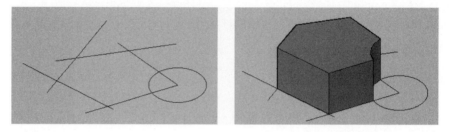

FIGURE 16.93 An enclosed area (left), and the result of using the Press/Pull tool (right)

 Helix   Located on the Home tab ≻ Draw panel, a Helix object is a 2D or 3D spiral (see Figure 16.94). When you use it in conjunction with the Sweep tool, you can create springs, corkscrews, coils, and so forth.

FIGURE 16.94 A helix
extending in the Z direction

There are two other Boolean tools for modifying solids. When you formed the cabin walls, you used the Subtract tool as well as Slice. Two other solids-editing tools, Union and Intersect, create an object based on two overlapping objects:

Union   Joins the two objects and eliminates any internal edges.

Intersect   Finds the volume that two solids have in common and retains that volume while deleting the other portions of the objects.

This is only a brief introduction to the tools for creating and modifying solids, but it should be enough to get you started.

Using Mesh-Modeling Tools

In addition to the solid objects available in AutoCAD, a set of tools is available to create mesh models. Unlike solids, meshes can't be easily manipulated and do not have a true volume, just faces that surround an empty area. For example, imagine this book next to a cellophane wrapper having the same dimensions. The book would be a solid, and the wrapper would be a mesh.

Here is a brief description of a few of the mesh tools found on the Mesh Ribbon tab (see Figure 16.95):

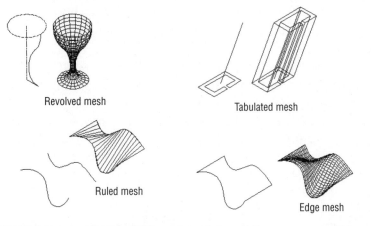

Revolved mesh

Tabulated mesh

Ruled mesh

Edge mesh

FIGURE 16.95 AutoCAD's mesh-modeling tools

Revolved Mesh   Creates a 3D surface mesh by rotating a 2D curved line around an axis of revolution.

Tabulated Mesh   Creates a 3D surface mesh by extruding a 2D object in a direction determined by the endpoints of a line, an arc, or a polyline.

Ruled Mesh   Creates a 3D surface mesh between two selected shapes.

Edge Mesh   Creates a 3D surface mesh among four lines that are connected at their endpoints. Each line can be in 2D or 3D, and the original shape must be a boundary of a shape that doesn't cross or conflict with itself.

Most 3D models today utilize the solid-modeling tools for their basic shapes because the tools for adding, subtracting, slicing, and so forth are easy to use and allow complex shapes to be fabricated quickly. Still, mesh-modeling, legacy tools retained from AutoCAD's initial foray into 3D, have their uses. Any serious 3D modeler will be familiar with both sets of tools.

Using Surface-Modeling Tools

The surface-modeling tools share some similarities with both the solid- and mesh-modeling tools already discussed. Surfaces are like meshes in that they do not have a true volume; the cellophane wrapper analogy also applies to surfaces. On the other hand, you'll notice a number of tools appear on both the Solid and Surface Ribbon tabs.

Tools such as Loft, Sweep, Extrude, and Revolve are found on both tabs, and they are nearly identical in both contexts. The core difference between the two types is the 3D object created. When these tools are used from the Solid tab, they create solid objects, with volume and mass. Using these same tools from the Surface tab will create a skeleton object, a cellophane wrapper, with neither volume nor mass.

Figure 16.96 shows two boxes, each created using the Extrude tool. The box on the left was created using the Extrude tool found on the Solid tab, and is a solid box with a top, bottom, and sides. By comparison, the box on the right was created using the Extrude tool found on the Surface tab. Notice how it lacks both a top and a bottom, but each of its four sides is constructed with smaller rectangles. This grid structure is more easily manipulated into complex shapes, something that's much harder to do using solid objects.

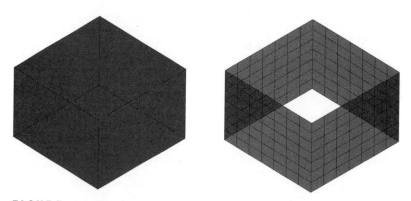

FIGURE 16.96 Rectangles extruded with the Extrude tool on the Solid tab (left), and the Extrude tool on the Surface tab (right)

Surfaces can be created by using any of the tools shown in Figure 16.97.

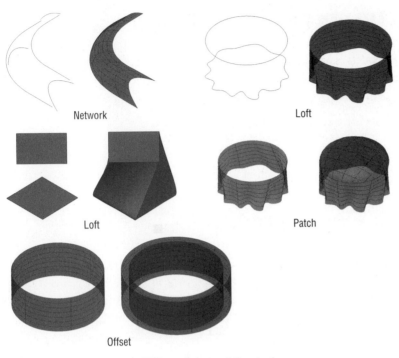

Network

Loft

Loft

Patch

Offset

FIGURE 16.97 AutoCAD's surface-modeling tools

Network   Creates a 3D surface between several curves, other 3D surfaces, or solids in the U and V directions.

Loft   Creates a 3D surface between several 2D cross sections.

Sweep   Creates a 3D surface along a path, similar to the Solid Sweep tool shown in Figure 16.92.

Planar   Creates a flat surface between several coplanar objects.

Extrude   Creates a 3D surface from a 2D or 3D line, curve, or polyline.

Revolve   Creates a 3D surface by rotating a 2D line or curve around an axis.

Blend   Creates a continuous 3D surface between two existing surfaces.

Patch   Creates a 3D surface to close or cap an existing 3D surface.

Offset   Creates a 3D surface parallel to an existing 3D surface.

If You Would Like More Practice...

Creating 3D models is a highly effective way to communicate designs with groups of people who may not otherwise know how to read engineering plans. For more practice modeling in 3D, you can try the following:

▶ Model the kitchen cabinets and appliances.

▶ Add a small window to the back door.

▶ Create mullions for each of your windows.

Are You Experienced?

Now you can...

☑ **change visual styles**

☑ **create linear 3D objects with the Polysolid tool**

☑ **use 3D solid, mesh, and surface tools to generate 3D models**

☑ **extrude 2D shapes into 3D geometry**

☑ **cut holes in objects by using the Subtract Boolean tool**

☑ **resize 3D objects by using grips**

☑ **create 3D surfaces**

☑ **navigate in a 3D scene**

Rendering and Materials

After developing a 3D model, you'll usually want to apply materials and render it to get a better feel for the substance of the project, so that you can produce a clearer presentation for clients.

In this chapter, I'll give you a quick tour of some of these rendering steps as you set up a view of the cabin and render it. Developing a full rendering takes time and patience, but touching on a few of the many steps involved will give you a feel for the process. You've put in a lot of time working your way through this book, and you deserve to have a rendered 3D view of your cabin to complete the process. Be aware, however, that rendering is computationally intensive and can task your computer pretty heavily. It's a good rule to save your file prior to each rendering attempt.

▶ **Using the Loft tool**

▶ **Creating cameras to reproduce views**

▶ **Creating a lighting scheme**

▶ **Enabling and controlling shadow effects**

▶ **Choosing the background**

▶ **Assigning materials to surfaces**

▶ **Adjusting mapping and tiling**

▶ **Saving setup views and lights as restorable scenes**

▶ **Rendering and outputting to a file**

Creating Cameras to Reproduce Views

Similar to saving named views in Chapter 10, "Generating Elevations," using cameras is a method for returning to a saved viewpoint. The most significant advantage of cameras is the ability to select the camera object and change its position or orientation, rather than panning or zooming in the drawing area. Cameras can also be animated to show your model from a variety of locations. Before you place the cameras, however, you'll create some land for your cabin to sit on, so that it no longer appears to be floating in the air.

Using the Loft Tool

The Loft tool builds 3D geometry in one of three ways: by connecting a series of 2D shapes, called *contour lines*, with 3D surfaces; by extruding a cross section along a path; or by controlling the transition between two cross sections with 2D guide curves. You'll use the first method to create a loft object to serve as the land by drawing concentric 3D polylines, converting them to splines, changing their elevations, and then lofting them. Follow these steps:

1. With I16C-SPLAY0.dwg (M16C-SPLAY0.dwg) as the current drawing, change to the Wireframe visual style with the in-canvas viewport controls, and zoom in to the cabin.

2. Make a new layer named **C-TOPO-3DOB**, assign it color 94, and set it as the current layer.

3. Freeze all the other layers except A-DECK-STRS-3DOB and A-FNDN-3DOB.

4. Start the Rectangle (RECTANG) command and draw a closed polyline around the perimeter of the base of the foundation, as shown in Figure 17.1.

5. Use the Endpoint osnap to snap to opposite vertices at the bottom corners of the foundation.

6. Use the Polyline (PLINE) command to draw another closed polyline around the concrete support posts, snapping the outside corner of each, and the outside corners of the stringers (see Figure 17.1).

   You can pick an interim point between each of the long sides of the cabin to break up the perimeter. These are the first two contour lines.

7. Switch to the Insert tab and then choose the Insert tool found on the Block panel to insert the I17-PropBndy.dwg (M17-PropBndy.dwg) file.

> Because each contour you'll draw will have a constant elevation, you'll use a standard polyline instead of a 3D polyline. Standard polylines can have only a single elevation, whereas 3D polylines can have many elevations.

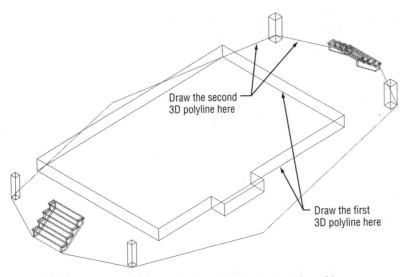

Draw the second
3D polyline here

Draw the first
3D polyline here

FIGURE 17.1 Draw the first two 3D polylines around the cabin.

8. Insert the drawing by using the 0,0,0 insertion point, a uniform scale of 1, and a rotation of 0 degrees.

9. Finally, be sure the Explode check box is selected in the lower-left corner of the Insert dialog box.

   If you haven't already, visit the companion website found at www.sybex.com/go/autocad2012ner or www.autocadner.com to access the Chapter 17 download, which includes the I17-PropBndy.dwg (M17-PropBndy.dwg) file.

10. Turn off Ortho mode or Object Tracking if they are on; then click the TOP face of the ViewCube to switch to a top view.

11. Continue using the PLINE command to draw two more oddly shaped, closed polylines between the cabin and the property line.

12. Change the layer of the inserted property line to the C-TOPO-3DOB layer (see Figure 17.2).

13. Click the Edit Polyline button from the extended Modify panel on the Home tab, or enter PEDIT↵. Enter M↵ to choose the Multiple option.

14. Select the two polylines between the cabin and the property line.

15. Click the Spline option in the context menu, as shown in Figure 17.3, to change the polylines into curved splines and then click ↵.

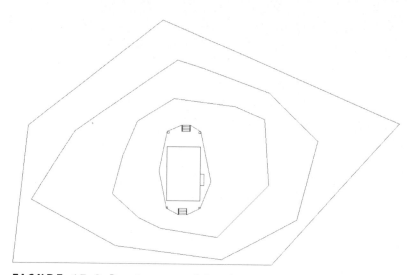
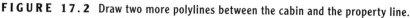

FIGURE 17.2 Draw two more polylines between the cabin and the property line.

FIGURE 17.3 Select Spline
from the context menu.

A *spline* is a curved
line with control
points for adjusting
the curvature.

The last three contour lines you drew are at the same level as the top of the
foundation. You need to move them downward to define the slope of the property away from the cabin:

1. Switch to an isometric view by selecting a corner of the ViewCube.

2. Use the 3D Move (3DMOVE) tool found on the Home tab ➤ Modify panel,
   and then move the spline closest to the cabin foundation down 3′-6″
   (1070 mm) in the negative Z direction.

3. Repeat the 3DMOVE command, moving the spline closest to the property
   line down 4′-4″ (1320 mm), and then moving the polyline that follows
   the property line down 5′-4″ (1625 mm).

   This should provide a gentle slope for the land.

4. Select the Front or Left face of the ViewCube to view your model from the side and verify that each of the contours are lower than the previous (see Figure 17.4).

FIGURE 17.4 The contour lines as viewed from the side

5. Switch back to an isometric view, freezing all layers except C-TOPO-3DOB.

6. Click the Loft button in the Modeling panel on the Home tab.
    It may be hidden under the Extrude button.

7. At the `Select cross sections in lofting order or:` prompt, enter **MO**↵ to set the creation mode.

8. Choose Surface by entering **SU**↵.
    The creation mode is changed to Surface, and the command line once again reads `Select cross sections in lofting order or:`.
    It's important to pick the cross sections for a lofted surface in order; otherwise, the surface may not generate as expected.

9. Press ↵ after you've selected each of the cross sections to advance through the LOFT command.
    Select the outermost polyline and then each subsequent spline or polyline in order, from outside to inside.
    You can adjust how lofted surfaces are created by entering **S**↵ with the LOFT command still running.

10. Verify that the Smooth Fit option is selected in the Loft Settings dialog box that opens, shown in Figure 17.5.
    Smooth Fit creates a soft transition from one contour to the next.

11. At the `Enter an option:` prompt, enter **C**↵ for the Cross Sections Only option.

12. Click OK, and then change to the Conceptual visual style.
    Your cabin land parcel should look similar to Figure 17.6.

13. Thaw all layers with a 3DOB suffix.

14. Save your drawing as **I17-01-LoftedSurface.dwg** (**M17-01-Lofted Surface.dwg**).

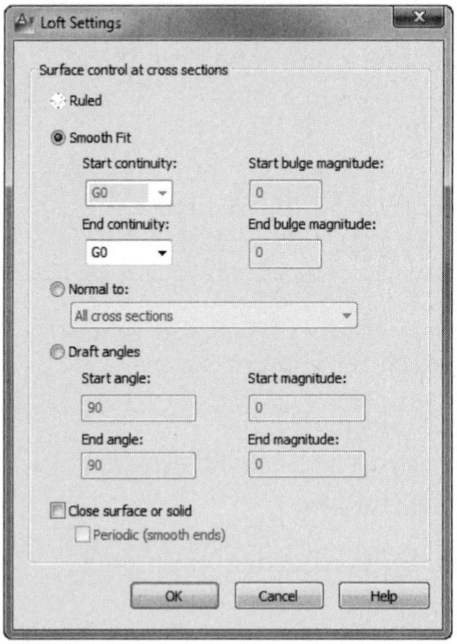

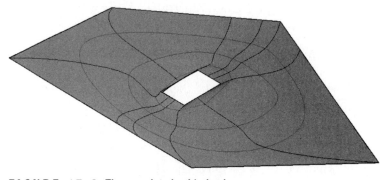

FIGURE 17.5 The Loft Settings dialog box

FIGURE 17.6 The completed cabin land

Creating the Cameras

AutoCAD uses a camera analogy to define reproducible views. The cameras and their respective targets are placed in model space and, using several available grips, are adjusted to capture the desired view.

1. Continue using I17-01-LoftedSurface.dwg (M17-01-Lofted Surface.dwg), or open it if it's not already open.

2. Click the Render tab; then, on the Camera panel, click the Create Camera (CAMERA) button and move the cursor into the drawing area. A camera icon appears at the cursor location.

T I P   If you don't see the Camera panel, right-click the title bar of any panel and choose Show Panels ➢ Camera from the context menu.

3. Click near the edge of the land at a point southeast of the cabin, using the ViewCube as a guide, and then move the cursor again.

Now the camera stays in place, as shown in Figure 17.7, and the target is moved with the cursor. The location of the target determines the orientation of the camera, and the visible cone emitting from the camera shows the camera's *field of view (FOV)*, or the angle visible through the camera's lens.

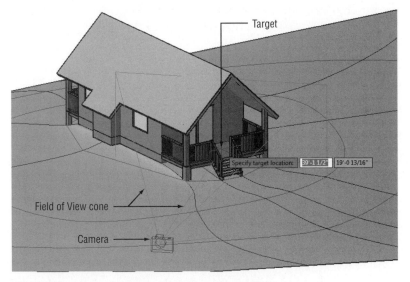

Target

Specify target location: 39'-1 1/2"   19'-0 13/16"

Field of View cone

Camera

FIGURE 17.7 Placing a camera into the drawing

4. Turn off any running osnaps, and then click the middle of the deck to place the target.

The camera disappears temporarily while AutoCAD waits for input at the cursor and the command line.

5. Enter **N↵**, or click Name, to activate the Name option.

6. At the prompt, enter **Cam Southeast**⏎⏎.
   The camera reappears in the drawing area.

7. Create another camera that views the cabin from the northwest corner of the property.

8. Place the target at the middle of the cabin, and name this camera Cam Northwest.

9. Use the ViewCube to change the current view to a viewpoint from the southeast and slightly above the cabin (see Figure 17.8).

10. Select the Cam Southeast camera.
    The Field of View cone and grips are displayed, and the Camera Preview dialog box opens. This dialog box displays the view from the camera in one of the available visual styles (see Figure 17.9). The 3D Wireframe visual style is the default and the one you will use here.

11. Place your cursor over the grip at the center of the camera, and you will see a tooltip that reads Camera Location.

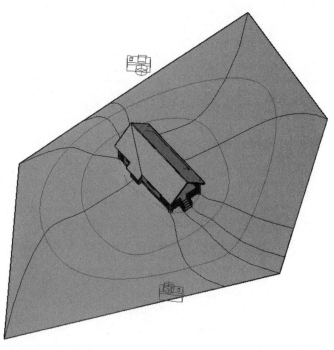

FIGURE 17.8 Viewing the cabin and cameras from above and to the southeast

12. Click the grip, and then move the camera 5′ (1524 mm) up in the Z direction to about eye level.

    You may need to click the grip again for the Camera Preview dialog box to refresh.

 T I P To keep the current X and Y camera location, enter @0,0,5′ to move the camera 5′ in the Z direction.

13. Select the Camera Target grip and move it 7′ (2130 mm) in the Z direction.

    Raising the target brings the cabin more into the preview window.

14. Press Esc to deselect the camera, and then select the Cam Northwest camera.

15. Move it 30′ (9150 mm) in the Z direction to get a higher view of the structure.

16. Next, adjust its view however you like by moving the square Target Location or triangular Lens Length/FOV grips.

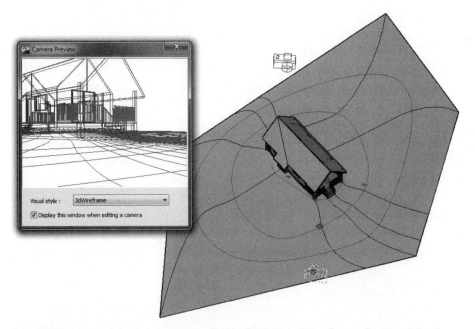

FIGURE 17.9 Selecting the camera displays its grips and the Camera Preview dialog box.

17. Click the View Controls menu from the in-canvas viewport controls, and then Custom Model Views.

Notice that the two cameras now appear in the list, as shown in left image of Figure 17.10.

Alternatively, the list of custom model views is accessible from the View Manager dialog box (see the right side of Figure 17.10). Open this dialog box from the View tab ➤ Views panel.

18. Select Cam Southeast from the list, click the Set Current button, and then click OK.

Your drawing area changes to view the scene from the selected camera, as shown in Figure 17.11.

19. Save your drawing as **I17-02-CreateCameras.dwg** (**M17-02-Create Cameras.dwg**).

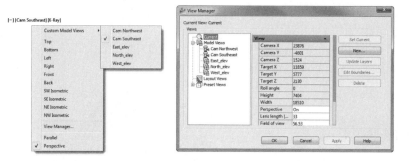

FIGURE 17.10 The View Manager dialog box showing the two new cameras listed

FIGURE 17.11 The cabin as viewed through the Cam Southeast camera

Creating a Lighting Scheme

Without a well-thought-out lighting scheme, the scene can look flat and unappealing. In this section, you will add a light to represent the sun and then an additional light to add ambient illumination to the scene.

Creating a Light Source

AutoCAD has four kinds of lighting, each with a distinct method for distributing light rays into the scene. They are as follows:

Point Light   All light rays are emitted from a single location and diverge as they get farther away. An incandescent lightbulb is a real-world example of a point light, even though the light does not travel in the direction of the light's fixture.

Spotlight   With this type of light, rays are emitted from a single point, but they are restricted to a conical portion of the amount of light that a similar point light would emit. Flashlights and headlights are examples of spotlights.

Distant Light   With this type of light, all light rays are parallel. Although the sun is technically a point light, at the enormous distance the light rays travel to Earth, they are nearly parallel.

Weblight   Photometric light with real-world distributions. These lights can be used in conjunction with light distributions derived by manufacturers of real-world lights. Using manufacturer data to establish lighting distributions helps ensure more-accurate representation of rendered lights than possible using point or spotlights.

Each light type has a unique set of parameters. The sun is a special distant light and has its own settings, including determining the light's position based on the geographic location of the scene and the date and time and the ability to add ambient light to the drawing.

To add this type of light, you'll use tools in the Visualize tab of the Ribbon:

1. Continue using I17-02-CreateCameras.dwg (M17-02-Create Cameras.dwg), or open it if it's not already open.

2. Click the Ribbon's Render tab.

3. In the expanded Lights panel, make sure the Default Lighting option is turned off.
   When it is off, the button will not have a blue background as the cursor pauses over it and there will be no default illumination in the scene.

4. In the Sun & Location panel of the Render tab, check the status of the Sun Status button.

Be sure it's toggled on by verifying that the button has a blue background.

5. Click the Sun Properties button at the right end of the Sun & Location panel to open the Sun Properties palette, as shown in Figure 17.12.

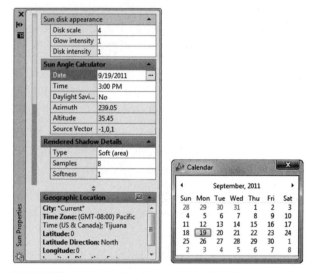

FIGURE 17.12 Set the date in the Sun Properties dialog box.

6. In the Sun Angle Calculator rollout, set Date to 9/19/2011 and Time to 3:00 PM (see Figure 17.12).

The date is set by clicking the button at the right end of the date field and choosing from a calendar.

7. In the Sun & Location panel on the Render tab of the Ribbon, click the Set Location button.

8. When the Geographic Location – Define Geographic Location dialog box appears, select Enter The Location Values as the method to define the location of the cabin drawing (see Figure 17.13).

The palette may be docked on the side of the AutoCAD window.

N O T E If you have Google Earth installed, you could have chosen to import a KML or KMZ file (Google Earth placemark files) or to import the location directly from Google Earth.

The dialog box closes, and the Geographic Location dialog box opens (see Figure 17.14).

You can define nearly any location in the world as the location for the current drawing by entering the latitude and longitude in this dialog box. For your cabin, you'll select the city in which it's located from a map.

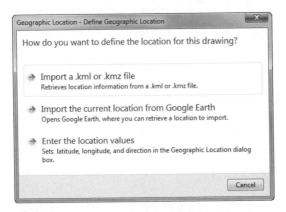

FIGURE 17.13 The Geographic Location – Define Geographic Location dialog box

FIGURE 17.14 The Geographic Location dialog box

9. Click the Use Map button in the top-right corner of the dialog box to open the Location Picker dialog box, as shown in Figure 17.15.

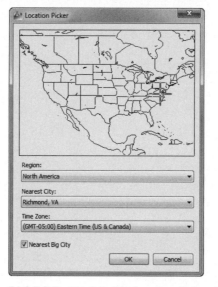

FIGURE 17.15 The Location Picker dialog box

10. In the Region drop-down list below the map, select the region that you prefer.

11. Below that, in the Nearest City drop-down list, select a city within that region.

    The example here uses North America and Richmond, VA. A red cross appears over Richmond (or wherever you've chosen) in the map. The Time Zone drop-down list displays the accurate time zone based on the location you selected (see Figure 17.15).

12. Click OK to close this dialog box. If a dialog box appears asking whether the time zone should be updated, click the Accept Updated Time Zone option.

13. Click OK to close the Geographic Location dialog box.

14. Save your drawing as `I17-03-SetLocation.dwg` (`M17-03-Set Location.dwg`).

T I P   If a particular city is not listed, you can uncheck the Nearest Big City option and then click directly on the map to set the location or enter the longitudinal and latitudinal coordinates in the left side of the Geographic Location dialog box.

Enabling Shadows

Shadows add depth and realism to a scene and tie the objects to the surfaces that they rest on or near. You have significant control over the types of shadows cast by the lights in the drawing and whether those shadows appear in the viewports. You adjust how the shadows appear in the viewport and how they render in the Render tab.

When shadows are turned on, AutoCAD will render them by using one of three methods: simple, sorted, or segment. The simple method is the default used by AutoCAD, and it calculates shadow *shaders* in random order. By contrast, the sorted and segment methods each calculate shadows in the order they are cast, and they produce higher-quality renderings at the cost of machine performance. Segment shadows will produce the highest-quality rendering, but they take the longest time to complete.

To ensure that you'll be able to work through this chapter's exercise in a timely manner, we'll stick to the simple method. Don't be fooled by its name; while it doesn't perform the advanced calculations done by the sorted and segment methods, it still produces a detailed rendering without sacrificing system performance.

1. Continue using I17-03-SetLocation.dwg (M17-03-SetLocation.dwg), or open it if it's not already open.

2. In the Lights panel, click the down-arrow under the No Shadows icon and choose Full Shadows from the fly-out menu, as shown in Figure 17.16.
   This displays an approximation of the shadows in the viewport.

 W A R N I N G   The Full Shadows option requires that your video card utilize hardware acceleration. See the Display Backgrounds and Shadows page of the AutoCAD 2012 help file to determine whether your system is equipped with hardware acceleration.

3. Click the Advanced Render Settings button on the right end of the Render panel's title bar.

4. In the Advanced Render Settings palette that appears, scroll down to the Shadows drop-down list and make sure Mode is set to Simple and Shadow Map is set to On (see Figure 17.17).

5. Close the Advanced Render Settings palette.

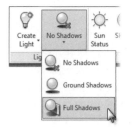

FIGURE 17.16 Choosing the Full Shadows option

*Presentation	
Contrast red	0
Contrast blue	0
Contrast green	0
Contrast alpha	0
Shadows	
Mode	Simple
Shadow map	On
Sampling Multiplier	1
Ray Tracing	
Max depth	9
Max reflections	9
Max refractions	9
Indirect Illumination	
Global Illumination	
Photons/sample	500
Use radius	Off
Radius	1
Max depth	5
Max reflections	5
Max refractions	5
Final Gather	
Mode	Auto
Rays	1000

FIGURE 17.17 The Shadows settings in the Advanced Render Settings palette

Creating the First Render

A *rendering* is the visual result of the program calculating the effects of the lights and materials on the surfaces in the drawing. Let's make a preliminary render now. Later, you'll add materials and a background and then render the drawing again.

1. Click the Render button on the Render panel.

   The Render window opens, and after a few moments, the rendering fills in the graphic area (see Figure 17.18). As you can see, the right side of the cabin is unlit and in total darkness.

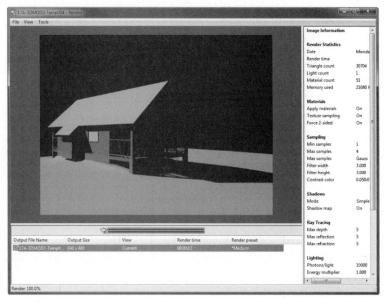

FIGURE 17.18 The first cabin rendering in the Render window

2. Click the Point button in the Lights panel (it may be hidden under another light button), and then click to place the light on the ground about 20′ (6100 mm) northeast of the front deck.

3. Click the Name option in the context menu that appears at the cursor and give the light the name **Northeast Ambient**.

4. Double-click the light to open its Properties palette, and make the following changes:

   Position Z: 30′ (9150)

   Shadows: Off

   Intensity Factor: 60.000

   Lamp Intensity: 15,000 Cd

As with cameras, you should give your lights descriptive names.

5. Click the down-arrow in the Filter Color field and then choose Select Color.

6. In the Select Color dialog box that appears, change the Color Model to RGB, and enter 252, 250, 212 in the Color field, as shown in Figure 17.19.

This gives the light a pale yellow hue.

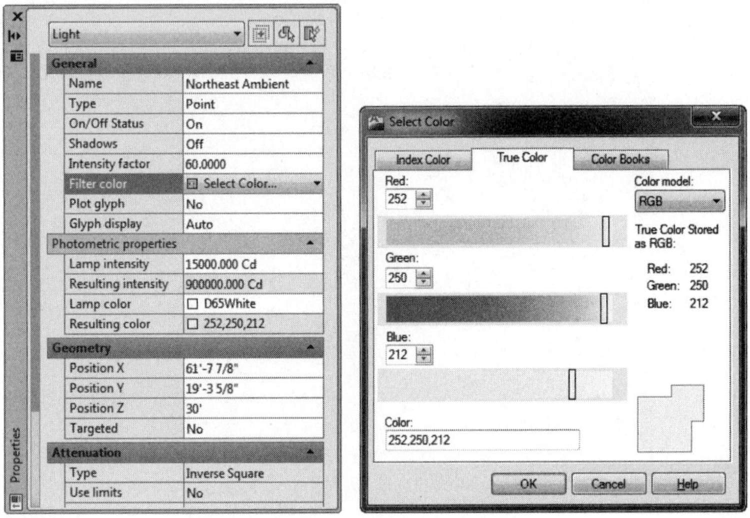

FIGURE 17.19 The properties for the point light

7. Click OK to close the Select Color dialog box and close the Properties palette.

8. Switch back to the Cam Southeast view if necessary and render the scene again.

As you can see in Figure 17.20, this time the shadows on the right side of the cabin are not as stark as they were previously, but the overall appearance is still pretty dark. You need to add some ambient light.

9. Open the Advanced Render Settings palette again, and then click the lightbulb icon next to Global Illumination in the Indirect Illumination drop-down list (see Figure 17.21).

This will add a measure of ambient light into your scene without washing it out.

This rendering looks a bit better than the last. The Render window maintains a history of the recent renderings, and you can compare them by clicking any of the renderings listed in the pane at the bottom of the Render window. To delete a rendering, follow these steps:

a. Select it.

b. Right-click it.

c. Choose Remove From The List.

You can continue to tweak the lighting as you want. For indoor projects that require rendering, a good rule of thumb is to expect to dedicate 15 to 25 percent of the total project time to creating an excellent lighting scheme. For outdoor scenes, dedicating 5 to 10 percent should be sufficient.

10. Save your drawing as **I17-04-FirstRender.dwg** (**M17-04-First Render.dwg**).

The building looks fine, but it would be nice to have something in the background other than the blank screen, and the lights need to be tweaked.

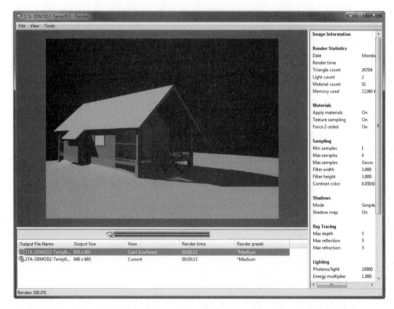

FIGURE 17.20 The cabin rendering after adding the second light

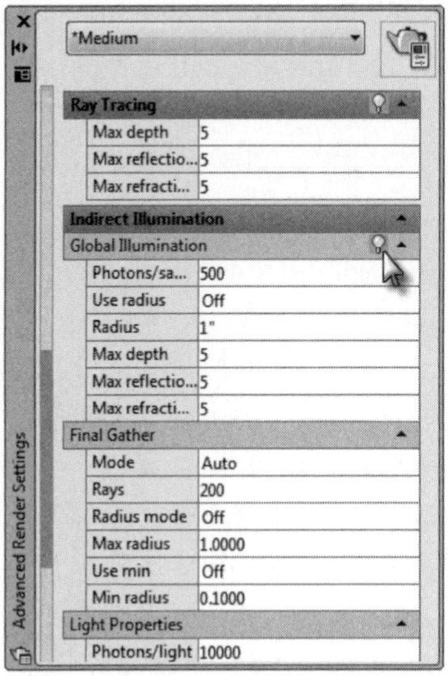

FIGURE 17.21 Turning on Global Illumination

Controlling the Background of the Rendering

The following are some of the options you can set when choosing a background for the rendering:

The AutoCAD Background   This is what you used for the preliminary rendering.

Another Solid Color   Use the slider bars to choose another solid color.

Gradient   You can use varying colors (usually light to dark) blended together.

Image   You can supply or choose a bitmap image.

Sun & Sky Background   You can use a computer-generated sky. This background has the option of introducing additional ambient illumination into the scene.

You'll use the Sun & Sky Background option with the Illumination option here:

1. Continue using I17-04-FirstRender.dwg (M17-04-FirstRender.dwg), or open it if it's not already open.

2. Click the View tab, and then click the Named Views button in the View panel to open the View Manager dialog box.

3. Expand the Model Views entry and then select Cam Southeast.

4. Expand the drop-down list for the Background Override entry in the General rollout, and then choose Sun & Sky, as shown in Figure 17.22. Doing so opens the Adjust Sun & Sky Background dialog box, as shown in Figure 17.23.

N O T E   The sky background options are available only when the lighting units are not set to generic. This is controlled by the LIGHTINGUNITS system variable. Enter LIGHTINGUNITS↵ 2↵ to set the lighting units to International. A setting of 1 sets the lighting units to American, and 0 sets them to generic units.

5. In the Sky Properties rollout, change the Intensity Factor value to 3.

6. Expand the Status drop-down list, and choose Sky Background and Illumination (see Figure 17.23).

7. Click OK to close the Adjust Sun & Sky Background dialog box.

8. Click Set Current in the View Manager dialog box, and then click OK to close it.

9. Open the Advanced Render Settings palette from the Render tab's Render panel.

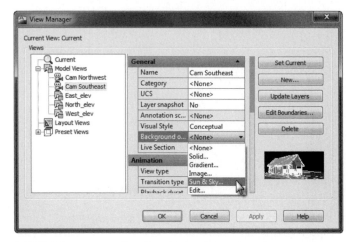

FIGURE 17.22 The Cam Southeast camera selected in the View Manager dialog box

10. Scroll down to the Final Gather rollout, and make sure the Mode is set to Auto or On.

Background Illumination will not work if Final Gather Mode is set to Off.

11. Save your drawing as **I17-05-RenderBackground.dwg** (**M17-05- Render Background.dwg**).

12. Render the scene.

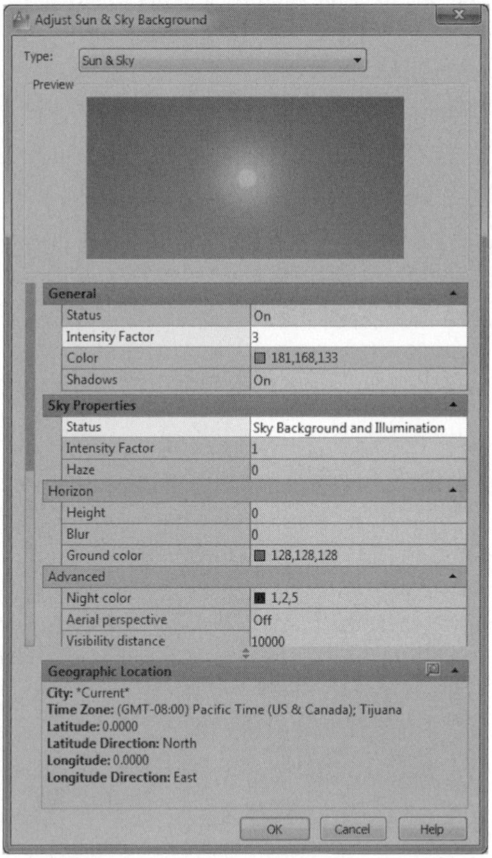

FIGURE 17.23 The Adjust Sun & Sky Background dialog box

It will take a little longer to process this image, and you'll notice that the image in the Render window is replaced twice; the first time with a very rough-looking representation of the cabin and then again with a sharper result. When it is done, the display in your Render dialog box should look similar to Figure 17.24. The background image not only appears behind the cabin and ground, but it also contributes light to the scene.

FIGURE 17.24 The cabin rendered with the Sun & Sky background and additional illumination

N O T E   Rendering is a processor-intensive function. It's not uncommon to experience a lag in computer performance or to hear increased cooling fan activity while a rendering is in progress. To help speed up the rendering time, you're encouraged to leave AutoCAD as the current application and refrain from performing other tasks on your computer if possible.

Adding Materials

Adding the proper materials to a scene can greatly increase the realism of the drawing and convey a better sense of size and texture to the person viewing the image. This chapter assumes that you installed the material library that ships with AutoCAD 2012, along with the rest of the package.

You can assign materials to your drawing objects from several premade libraries, you can create materials from scratch, or you can edit materials that originate from the libraries. In the next exercise, you will apply materials from AutoCAD's libraries:

1. Continue using I17-05-RenderBackground.dwg (M17-05-RenderBackground.dwg), or open it if it's not already open.

2. Click the Render tab, and then click the Materials Browser button in the Materials panel to open the Materials Browser palette, shown in Figure 17.25.

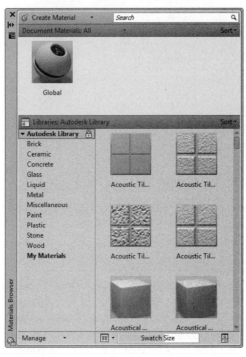

FIGURE 17.25 The Materials Browser palette

The Materials Browser palette is divided into two primary areas:

Document Materials   The upper region of the Materials Browser palette displays the materials that have been loaded into your current drawing. Above the name for each material, a small thumbnail preview of the material displays.

Libraries   AutoCAD materials are filed away into a series of libraries. A list of available libraries along with the material categories within each library display along the left side of the palette. Selecting any library or category on the left will display the materials belonging to that library or category as a series of thumbnails along the right side of the palette. The default installation creates two libraries: the Autodesk Library and the My Materials Library.

Materials may be added to the current drawing from any of the libraries listed in the lower portion of the Materials Browser.

3. If it's not open already, expand Autodesk Library in the Libraries portion of the Materials Browser.

    A list of categories containing an assortment of materials displays.

4. Browsing the Wood category, locate and then select the Red Oak Wild Berries material on the right side of the Materials Browser palette.

    The Red Oak Wild Berries material is added to the Document Materials list at the top of the Materials Browser palette.

5. Repeat steps 3 and 4 to load the materials listed in the following table:

Category	Material Name
Wood	Hardwood
	Pine Yellow Natural No Gloss
Brick	Burgundy 12-inch Running
Glass	Blue Reflective
Metal	Aluminum Satin Brushed
Miscellaneous	Grass Dark Bermuda
	Shakes Weathered
	Shingles - Asphalt 3-Tab Black
Paint	Antique White Flat

All of the materials you'll need for your cabin are now loaded into the current drawing. However, before those materials are used for rendering, they must be assigned to objects in your drawing. Materials can be applied to individual objects, faces, or layers. Whenever possible, it's best to assign materials to an entire layer as opposed to individual objects or faces. Subscribing to this practice will help ensure the manageability of your model.

To assign materials to the layers in your drawing:

1. If you haven't already, switch to the Render tab, and then expand the Materials panel to select the Attach By Layer tool.

   The Material Attachment Options dialog box opens to display a list of materials and layers in the current drawing.

   The Material Attachment Options dialog box, shown in Figure 17.26, is split into two parts:

   ▶ The left side displays a list of materials loaded into the current drawing.

   ▶ The right side displays a list of layers in the current drawing.

   By default, the Global material is assigned to each layer.

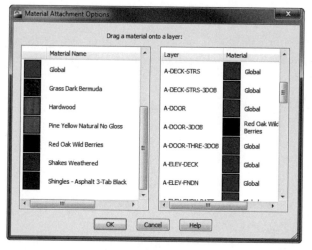

FIGURE 17.26 The Material Attachment Options dialog box

2. Locate the Red Oak Wild Berries material on the left side of the dialog box and the A-DOOR-3DOB layer on the right.

3. Drag the Red Oak Wild Berries material from the left side of the dialog box onto the A-DOOR-3DOB layer on the right.

4. Verify that the material was applied by checking the Material column in the Layer list on the right side of the dialog box.

5. Repeat this procedure by assigning materials to each of your 3DOB layers, as shown in the following table.

Layer	Material
A-DECK-3DOB	Pine Yellow Natural No Gloss
A-DECK-STRS-3DOB	Pine Yellow Natural No Gloss
A-DOOR-THRE-3DOB	Aluminum Satin Brushed
A-FLOR-3DOB	Hardwood
A-FNDN-3DOB	Burgundy 12-inch Running
A-GLAZ-3DOB	Blue Reflective
A-GLAZ-SILL-3DOB	Pine Yellow Natural No Gloss
A-ROOF-3DOB	Shingles - Asphalt 3-Tab Black
A-ROOF-DECK-3DOB	Antique White Flat
A-WALL-EXTR-3DOB	Shakes Weathered
A-WALL-INTR-3DOB	Antique White Flat
C-TOPO-3DOB	Grass Dark Bermuda
Created in earlier exercises:	
A-DOOR-3DOB	Red Oak Wild Berries

6. Save your drawing as I17-06-RenderMaterials.dwg (M17-06-Render Materials.dwg).

7. Render your drawing one more time.

It should look like Figure 17.27. Notice how the roof is reflected in the living room window.

FIGURE 17.27 The cabin rendered with materials applied to the remaining 3D objects

N O T E   During the rendering process, you probably noticed the small, black squares being replaced one at a time by small areas of the rendered drawing. This indicates that AutoCAD is using *bucket rendering*. Before the rendering process begins, AutoCAD determines the sequence to process the squares, called *buckets*, in order to maximize the memory usage and thereby increase the efficiency of the rendering.

Adjusting the Material Mapping

Image maps are the components of a material that consist of image files, such as a JPEG or TIFF. When a material uses an image map, its purpose can be to change the color of an object (diffuse maps), to give the illusion of texture (bump maps), or to define the transparency of a surface (opacity maps).

Adjusting the Map Size

The individual properties of all materials are controlled in the Materials Browser palette. Here you'll find the controls for setting the parameters for the size of the map, which map to use, and several other features for the selected material.

  1. Continue using I17-06-RenderMaterials.dwg (M17-06-Render Materials.dwg), or open it if it's not already open.

2. In the Render tab, click the Materials Browser button in the Materials panel.

3. In the Document Materials portion of the Materials Browser palette, right-click the Shakes Weathered material and select Edit.

    The Materials Editor palette opens to display details about the Shakes Weathered material (see Figure 17.28).

4. From the Materials Editor, click the photographic image found under the Generic group (see Figure 17.28).

    Selecting the image in the Materials Editor palette will open the Texture Editor palette, shown in Figure 17.29.

5. Expand the Transforms group, and then the Scale group to locate the Sample Size setting.

6. Enter 2′-4″ (710 mm) into the Height text box.

    Note how the dimensions shown in the preview at the top of the Texture Editor palette update to reflect this change.

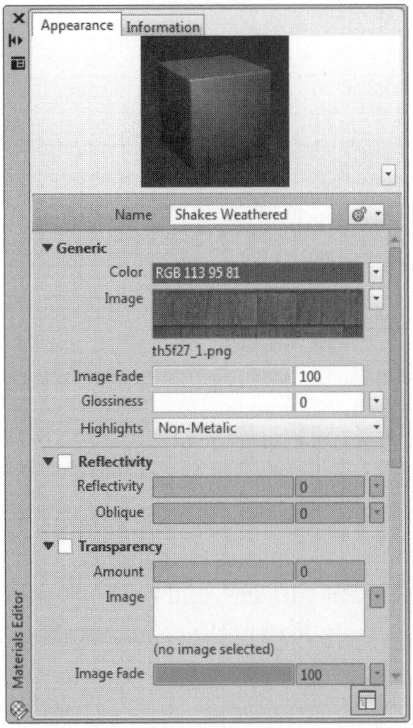

FIGURE 17.28 The Materials palette with the Shakes Weathered material selected

FIGURE 17.29 Modifying the material
scale from the Texture Editor palette

7. Close the Texture Editor, Materials Editor, and Materials Browser palettes, and then change your visual style to Realistic.

   The Realistic style displays the materials and maps, and the changes that you make to them, all at the expense of system performance (see Figure 17.30). You should use this visual style only when necessary.

8. Save your drawing as I17-07-AdjustMaterial.dwg (M17-07-Adjust Material.dwg).

Adding Texture

The exterior walls of the cabin consist of flat surfaces, and there are no features that would cause shadows to be cast. The Bump Map option adds apparent texture by adding shadows where they would appear if the surfaces had texture. In the Maps rollout, you can see that only the Diffuse Map option is checked, meaning that no map is used to define the opacity and bump features of the material. Opacity maps and bump maps don't use any of the color information from an image map, but this doesn't mean that color maps can't be used—only that the grayscale equivalent of the colors will be interpreted by AutoCAD.

1. Continue using I17-07-AdjustMaterial.dwg (M17-07-Adjust Material.dwg), or open it if it's not already open.

2. Open the Materials Editor palette once again by locating the Shakes Weathered material in the Materials Browser palette.

3. Select the check box next to the Bump group heading in the Materials Browser.

4. In the Bump area, click the Select Image button to open the Select Image File dialog box. It should open to the following directory:

   Windows 32-bit **C:\Program Files\Common Files\Autodesk Shared\Materials\Textures\3\Mats**

   Windows 64-bit **C:\Program Files (x86)\Common Files\ Autodesk Shared\Materials\Textures\3\Mats**

   Navigate to one of these directories if the Image File dialog box does not automatically open there.

5. Select the Thermal - Moisture.Shakes.Weathered.jpg file, the same file used as the diffuse map, and then click Open.

> The Thermal - Moisture.Shakes .Weathered.jpg **image is also included in the Chapter 17 download.**
> ◀

FIGURE 17.30 View of the cabin using the Realistic visual style

6. Move the Bump Amount slider to 10 (see Figure 17.31).

Figure 17.32 shows the cabin rendered with the new material parameters.

7. Adjust the mapping and materials for the remaining objects, and then save your file as `I17-08-MaterialTexture.dwg` (`M17-08-Material Texture.dwg`).

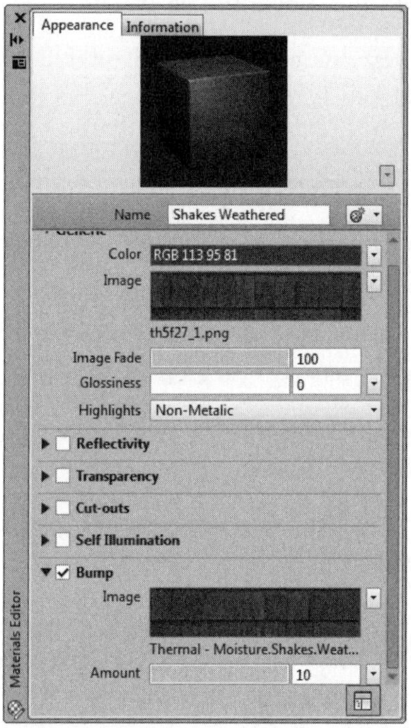

FIGURE 17.31 Changing the amount of bump applied to a material

There are enough tools and features relating to AutoCAD materials to fill several chapters, and this was just an introduction. Some of the features not covered are copying mapping between objects, applying different maps to different surfaces of the same object, and using opacity maps. I strongly encourage you to investigate the full capabilities of the AutoCAD materials.

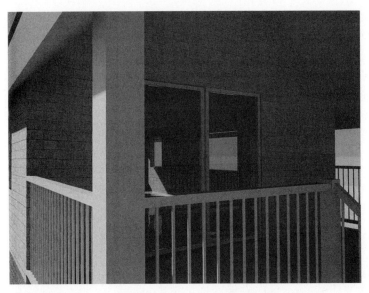

FIGURE 17.32 The cabin with the new material parameters

Rendering to a File

By default, the Render feature creates a rendering in the Render dialog box only. The picture is not saved unless you explicitly tell AutoCAD to save it. You can also instruct the program as to the quality level of the rendering and the size, in pixels, of the image created. Follow these steps:

1. Continue using I17-08-MaterialTexture.dwg (M17-08-Material Texture.dwg), or open it if it's not already open.

2. Switch back to the Conceptual visual style and the Cam Southeast view.

3. From the Render tab's Render panel, click the Render Output File button and then the Browse For File button to open the Render Output File dialog box.

4. Navigate to the folder where you want to place the new image file, and then select a supported image file type in the Files Of Type drop-down list. For this exercise, do the following:

   a. Choose TIF as the file type.

   b. Name the file **Cabin Rendering Small.tif** (see Figure 17.33).

5. Click the Save button.

Depending on the file type you choose in the future, an Options dialog box, similar to the one shown in Figure 17.34, will appear.

6. In the TIFF Image Options dialog box, select 24 Bits (16.7 Million Colors), make sure the Compressed option is checked, and then click OK.

The next time you render the drawing, the rendering will be saved as an image file on your hard drive, and the filename will appear in the Output File Name column of the Render window, with a folder and check mark next to it (see Figure 17.35). The files with clocks and teapots won't be saved, but you can open them in the Render window by clicking the appropriate filename.

FIGURE 17.33 Saving the final cabin rendering

FIGURE 17.34 The TIFF Image Options dialog box

7. In the AutoCAD window, expand the Render Presets drop-down list and select Presentation, as shown in Figure 17.36.

8. Expand the Render panel, expand the Render Output Size drop-down list, and then choose Specify Image Size (see Figure 17.37) to open the Output Size dialog box.

9. In the Output Size dialog box (see Figure 17.38), set Width to 2000 and Height to 1600, and then click OK.

   This is the resolution required to print a 10″×8″ image at 200 dots per inch (dpi).

10. Click the Browse For File button to open the Render Output File dialog box.

11. Name this file **Cabin Rendering Large.tif**, and make it a 24-bit TIF file at 200 dpi. Click OK.

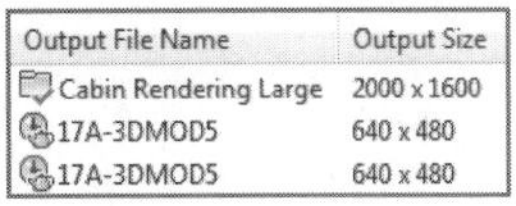

Output File Name	Output Size
Cabin Rendering Large	2000 x 1600
17A-3DMOD5	640 x 480
17A-3DMOD5	640 x 480

FIGURE 17.35 The saved file shown at the bottom of the Render window

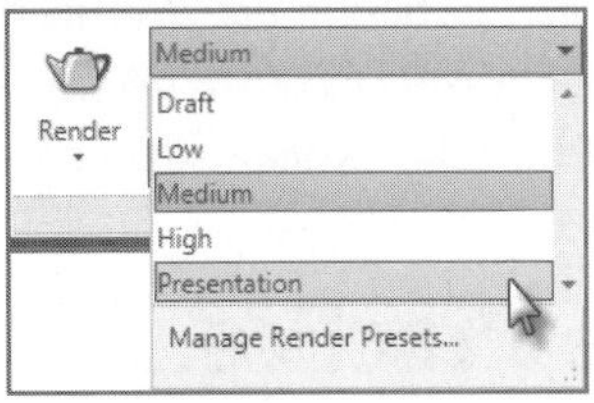

FIGURE 17.36 Choose the Presentation rendering preset.

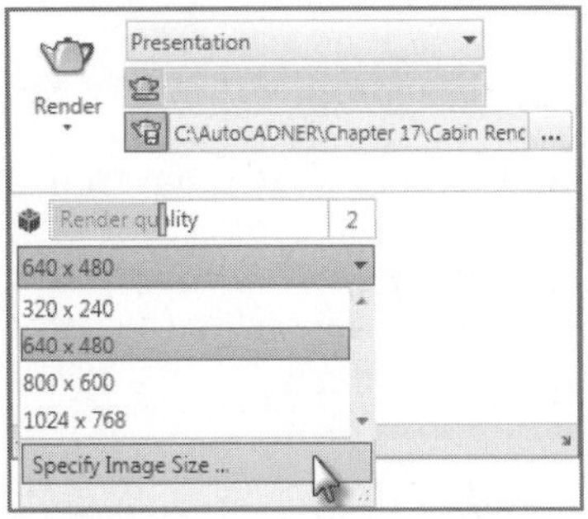

FIGURE 17.37 Set the output size.

12. Save your drawing and then click the Render button again and wait a while as the new image renders.

With the higher quality and larger image size, this may take considerably longer to process.

13. When the rendering is completed, look at the file size in Windows Explorer, and then compare the two images in your image-viewing software. The larger file is much crisper than the smaller image at the expense of increased rendering time.

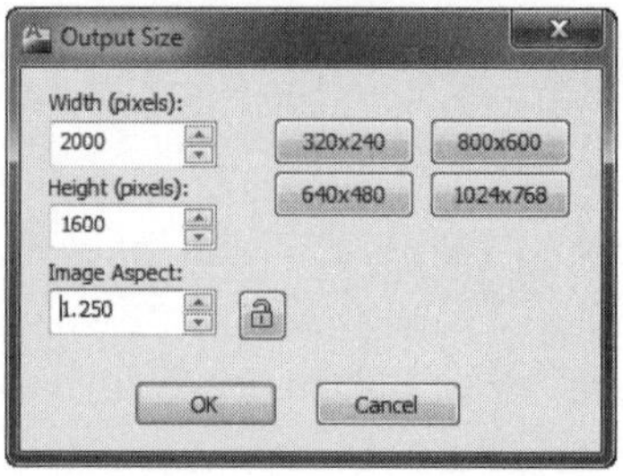

FIGURE 17.38 The Output Size dialog box

This has been a brief introduction to the world of 3D and rendering in AutoCAD, but you should now be oriented to the general way of doing things and have enough tools to experiment further. For a more in-depth discussion of the process, including rendering, see *Mastering AutoCAD 2012 and AutoCAD LT 2012* by George Omura (Wiley, 2011), or visit the companion site for this book at **www.autocadner.com.**

If You Would Like More Practice...

Renderings can be an invaluable way to both explore and validate design alternatives. For more practice working with materials as a way of design validation, you can try the following:

▶ Experiment with different materials for the exterior of your cabin.

▶ Create an additional camera to explore your cabin from another vantage point.

▶ Render your cabin with new materials applied to the scene.

Are You Experienced?

Now you can...

- ☑ create a loft object by using contour lines

- ☑ create and manipulate cameras

- ☑ add sunlight to a scene

- ☑ place a point light

- ☑ specify a scene's real-world location

- ☑ assign materials to the objects in a drawing

- ☑ adjust mapping and tiling

- ☑ render a drawing and save the result as an image file

INDEX

Note to the Reader: Throughout this index **boldfaced** page numbers indicate primary discussions of a topic. *Italicized* page numbers indicate illustrations.

J

M

N

O